FOUNDATIONS OF MICROECONOMICS

delivers a complete, hands-on learning system designed around active learning.

A Learning-by-Doing Approach

The **Checklist** that begins each chapter highlights the key topics covered and the chapter is divided into sections that directly correlate to the Checklist.

The **Checkpoint** that ends each section provides a full page of practice problems to encourage students to review the material while it is fresh in their minds.

Each chapter opens with a question about a central issue that sets the stage for the material.

Why did the price of coffee rise in 2014?

Demand and Supply

4

When you have completed your study of this chapter, you will be able to

CHAPTER CHECKLIST

1 Distinguish between quantity demanded and demand, and explain what determines demand.

2 Distinguish between quantity supplied and supply, and explain what determines supply.

3 Explain how demand and supply determine price and quantity in a market, and explain the effects of changes in demand and supply.

MyEconLab Big Picture Video

 CHECKPOINT 4.1

MyEconLab Study Plan 4.1
Key Terms Quiz
Solutions Video

Distinguish between quantity demanded and demand, and explain what determines demand.

Practice Problems

The following events occur one at a time in the market for smartphones:
- The price of a smartphone falls.
- Producers announce that the price of a smartphone will fall next month.
- The price of a call made from a smartphone falls.
- The price of a call made from a land-line phone increases.
- An increase in memory makes smartphones more popular.

1. Explain the effect of each event on the demand for smartphones.
2. Use a graph to illustrate the effect of each event.
3. Does any event (or events) illustrate the law of demand?

In the News

Airline profits soar yet no relief for passengers

Eye On boxes apply theory to important issues and problems that shape our global society and individual decisions.

Confidence-Building Graphs

use color to show the direction of shifts and detailed, numbered captions guide students step-by-step through the action.

100% of the figures are animated in MyEconLab, with step-by-step audio narration.

EYE on the PRICE OF COFFEE

MyEconLab Critical Thinking Exercise

Why Did the Price of Coffee Rise in 2014?

When a fungus called coffee rust swept through Brazil and other countries of South America in 2014, world coffee production decreased and the price of coffee beans increased.

The table below provides some data on the quantity and price of coffee in 2013 and 2014. What does the data table tell us?

It tells us that the quantity of coffee

You can answer this question from the information provided. You know that an increase in demand brings a rise in the price and an increase in the quantity bought, while a decrease in supply brings a rise in the price and a decrease in the quantity bought.

Because the quantity of coffee decreased and the price increased, there must have been a decrease in the sup-

The figure illustrates the global market for coffee in 2013 and 2014. The demand curve D shows the demand for coffee, which we will assume was the same in both years.

In 2013, the supply curve was S_{2013}, the equilibrium price was \$1.04 per pound and the equilibrium quantity traded was 19.4 billion pounds.

In 2014, decreased coffee produc-

FIGURE 4.4

Change in Quantity Demanded Versus Change in Demand

MyEconLab Animation

❶ A decrease in the quantity demanded
The quantity demanded decreases and there is a movement up along the demand curve D_0 if the price of the good rises and other things remain the same.

❸ A decrease in demand
Demand decreases and the demand curve shifts leftward (from D_0 to D_1) if
- The price of a substitute falls or the price of a complement rises.
- The price of the good is expected to fall.
- Income decreases.*
- Expected future income or credit decreases.
- The number of buyers decreases.

* Bottled water is a normal good.

❷ An increase in the quantity demanded
The quantity demanded increases and there is a movement down along the demand curve D_0 if the price of the good falls and other things remain the same.

❹ An increase in demand
Demand increases and the demand curve shifts rightward (from D_0 to D_2) if
- The price of a substitute rises or the price of a complement falls.
- The price of the good is expected to rise.
- Income increases.
- Expected future income or credit increases.
- The number of buyers increases.

Price (dollars per bottle)

2.50

2.00

1.50

1.00

0.50

D_2
D_0
D_1

0   8   9   10   11   12   13

Quantity (millions of bottles per day)

Practice, Engage, and Assess

- **Enhanced eText**—The Pearson eText gives students access to their textbook anytime, anywhere. In addition to note-taking, highlighting, and bookmarking, the Pearson eText offers interactive and sharing features. Students actively read and learn through auto-graded practice, real-time data-graphs, figure animations, author videos, and more. Instructors can share comments or highlights, and students can add their own, for a tight community of learners in any class.

- **Practice**—Algorithmically generated homework and study plan exercises with instant feedback ensure varied and productive practice, helping students improve their understanding and prepare for quizzes and tests. Draw-graph exercises encourage students to practice the language of economics.

- **Learning Resources**—Personalized learning aids such as Help Me Solve This problem walkthroughs and Figure Animations provide on-demand help when students need it most.

- **Personalized Study Plan**—Assists students in monitoring their own progress by offering them a customized study plan based on Homework, Quiz, and Test results. Includes regenerated exercises with unlimited practice, as well as the opportunity to earn mastery points by completing quizzes on recommended learning objectives.

- **Dynamic Study Modules**—With a focus on key topics, these modules work by continuously assessing student performance and activity in real time and, using data and analytics, provide personalized content to reinforce concepts that target each student's particular strengths and weaknesses.

- **Digital Interactives**—Digital Interactives are engaging assessment activities that promote critical thinking and application of key economic principles. Each Digital Interactive has progressive levels where students can explore, apply, compare, and analyze economic principles. Many Digital Interactives include real time data from FRED® that displays, in graph and table form, up-to-the-minute data on key macro variables. Digital Interactives can be assigned and graded within MyEconLab, or used as a lecture tool to encourage engagement, classroom conversation, and group work.

with MyEconLab®

- **NEW: Math Review Exercises in MyEconLab**—MyEconLab now offers an array of assignable and auto-graded exercises that cover fundamental math concepts. Geared specifically toward principles and intermediate economics students, these exercises aim to increase student confidence and success in these courses. Our new Math Review is accessible from the assignment manager and contains over 150 graphing, algebra, and calculus exercises for homework, quiz, and test use.

$$P = c + dQ_s$$

- **Real-Time Data Analysis Exercises**—Using current macro data to help students understand the impact of changes in economic variables, Real-Time Data Analysis Exercises communicate directly with the Federal Reserve Bank of St. Louis's FRED® site and update as new data are available.

- **Current News Exercises**—Every week, current microeconomic and macroeconomic news articles or videos, with accompanying exercises, are posted to MyEconLab. Assignable and auto-graded, these multi-part exercises ask students to recognize and apply economic concepts to real-world events.

- **Experiments**—Flexible, easy-to-assign, auto-graded, and available in Single Player and Multiplayer versions, Experiments in MyEconLab make learning fun and engaging.

- **Reporting Dashboard**—View, analyze, and report learning outcomes clearly and easily. Available via the Gradebook and fully mobile-ready, the Reporting Dashboard presents student performance data at the class, section, and program levels in an accessible, visual manner.

- **LMS Integration**—Link from any LMS platform to access assignments, rosters, and resources, and synchronize MyLab grades with your LMS gradebook. For students, new direct, single sign-on provides access to all the personalized learning MyLab resources that make studying more efficient and effective.

- **Mobile Ready**—Students and instructors can access multimedia resources and complete assessments right at their fingertips, on any mobile device.

Foundations of
MICROECONOMICS

Robin Bade

Michael Parkin
University of Western Ontario

EIGHTH EDITION

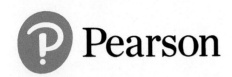

330 Hudson Street, NY NY 10013

Vice President, Business Publishing: Donna Battista
Director of Portfolio Management: Adrienne
    D'Ambrosio
Portfolio Manager: Ashley Bryan
Editorial Assistant: Michelle Zeng
Vice President, Product Marketing: Roxanne McCarley
Director of Strategic Marketing: Brad Parkins
Strategic Marketing Manager: Deborah Strickland
Product Marketer: Tricia Murphy
Field Marketing Manager: Ramona Elmer
Field Marketing Assistant: Kristen Compton
Product Marketing Assistant: Jessica Quazza
Vice President, Production and Digital Studio, Arts
    and Business: Etain O'Dea
Director of Production, Business: Jeff Holcomb
Managing Producer, Business: Alison Kalil
Content Producer: Nancy Freihofer

Operations Specialist: Carol Melville
Creative Director: Blair Brown
Manager, Learning Tools: Brian Surette
Managing Producer, Digital Studio, Arts and
    Business: Diane Lombardo
Digital Studio Producer: Melissa Honig
Digital Studio Producer: Alana Coles
Digital Content Team Lead: Noel Lotz
Digital Content Project Lead: Noel Lotz
Full-Service Project Management and
    Composition: Integra Software Services
Interior Design: Integra Software Services
Cover Design: Jon Boylan
Cover Art: Doug Lemke/www.shutterstock.com
Technical Illustrator: Richard Parkin
Printer/Binder: LSC Communications
Cover Printer: LSC Communications

To Erin, Tessa, Jack, Abby, and Sophie

About the Authors

Robin Bade was an undergraduate at the University of Queensland, Australia, where she earned degrees in mathematics and economics. After a spell teaching high school math and physics, she enrolled in the Ph.D. program at the Australian National University, from which she graduated in 1970. She has held faculty appointments at the University of Edinburgh in Scotland, at Bond University in Australia, and at the Universities of Manitoba, Toronto, and Western Ontario in Canada. Her research on international capital flows appears in the *International Economic Review* and the *Economic Record.*

Robin first taught the principles of economics course in 1970 and has taught it (alongside intermediate macroeconomics and international trade and finance) most years since then. She developed many of the ideas found in this text while conducting tutorials with her students at the University of Western Ontario.

Michael Parkin studied economics in England and began his university teaching career immediately after graduating with a B.A. from the University of Leicester. He learned the subject on the job at the University of Essex, England's most exciting new university of the 1960s, and at the age of 30 became one of the youngest full professors. He is a past president of the Canadian Economics Association and has served on the editorial boards of the *American Economic Review* and the *Journal of Monetary Economics.* His research on macroeconomics, monetary economics, and international economics has resulted in more than 160 publications in journals and edited volumes, including the *American Economic Review*, the *Journal of Political Economy*, the *Review of Economic Studies*, the *Journal of Monetary Economics*, and the *Journal of Money, Credit, and Banking.* He is author of the best-selling textbook, *Economics* (Pearson), now in its Twelfth Edition.

Robin and Michael are a wife-and-husband team. Their most notable joint research created the Bade-Parkin Index of central bank independence and spawned a vast amount of research on that topic. They don't claim credit for the independence of the new European Central Bank, but its constitution and the movement toward greater independence of central banks around the world were aided by their pioneering work. Their joint textbooks include *Macroeconomics* (Prentice-Hall), *Modern Macroeconomics* (Pearson Education Canada), and *Economics: Canada in the Global Environment*, the Canadian adaptation of Parkin, *Economics* (Addison-Wesley). They are dedicated to the challenge of explaining economics ever more clearly to a growing body of students.

Music, the theater, art, walking on the beach, and five grandchildren provides their relaxation and fun.

MICROECONOMICS   Brief Contents

Contents

PART 2   A CLOSER LOOK AT MARKETS

PART 3   HOW GOVERNMENTS INFLUENCE THE ECONOMY

CHAPTER 12
**Private Information and Healthcare
Markets   293**
CHAPTER CHECKLIST   293

PART 5   A CLOSER LOOK AT DECISION MAKERS

CHAPTER 13
**Consumer Choice and
Demand   319**
CHAPTER CHECKLIST   319

PART 6   PRICES, PROFITS, AND INDUSTRY PERFORMANCE

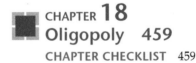

PART 7 INCOMES AND INEQUALITY

Preface

Students know that throughout their lives they will make economic decisions and be influenced by economic forces. They want to understand the economic principles that can help them navigate these forces and guide their decisions. *Foundations of Microeconomics* is our attempt to satisfy this want.

The response to our earlier editions from hundreds of colleagues across the United States and throughout the world tells us that most of you agree with our view that the principles course must do four things well. It must

- Motivate with compelling issues and questions
- Focus on core ideas
- Steer a path between an overload of detail and too much left unsaid
- Encourage and aid learning by doing

The Foundations icon with its four blocks (on the cover and throughout the book) symbolizes this four-point approach that has guided all our choices in writing this text and creating its comprehensive teaching and learning supplements.

WHAT'S NEW IN THE EIGHTH EDITION

New in this Eighth Edition revision are: A further fine-tuning of the content; an enhanced focus on outcome-driven teaching and learning; and a further large investment in enhanced digital features to bring economics to life and provide an exciting interactive experience for the student on all platforms and devices.

■ Fine-Tuning the Content

The content of this revision is driven by the drama of the extraordinary period of economic history in which we are living and its rich display of events and forces through which students can be motivated to discover the economic way of thinking. Persistent slow economic growth; increasing concentration of wealth; headwinds from Europe's stagnant economy and the UK decision to leave the economic union (Brexit); ongoing tensions arising from the loss of American jobs to offshore outsourcing and the political popularity of trade protection; a slowing pace of China's expansion; enhanced concern about carbon emission and climate change; relentless pressure on the federal budget from the demands of an aging population and a sometimes dysfunctional Congress with its associated rising government debt; the dilemma posed by slow, almost decade-long recovery from the global financial crisis and recession and the related question of when and how fast to exit an era of extreme monetary stimulus. These are just a few of these interest-arousing events. All of them feature at the appropriate points in our new edition.

Every chapter contains many small changes, all designed to enhance clarity and currency, and the text and examples are all thoroughly updated to reflect the most recently available data and events.

Because the previous edition's revision was so extensive and well-received, we have limited our interventions and changes in this Eighth Edition to addressing the small number of issues raised by our reviewers and users, ensuring that we are thoroughly up-to-date, and focusing on the new digital tools that we've just described. Nonetheless, some changes that we now summarize are worth noting.

■ Notable Content Changes

In Chapter 1, Getting Started, we have added a new section, *Economics as a Life Skill*, which explains how economics is used as a decision tool, the scientific method the subject employs, and economics as an aid to critical thinking. A new *Eye on Your Life* looks at the BLS data on student time allocation (which contains some surprises).

In Chapter 3, The Economic Problem, we show explicitly how the outward-bowed production possibilities frontier arises from exploiting comparative advantage.

Chapter 7, Government Actions in Markets, has a new section on production quotas, which explains why producers like them and illustrates how a quota expands producer surplus.

Chapter 8, Taxes, explains the Flat Tax and Fair Tax proposals and compares their efficiency and equity properties with those of the existing tax code.

In Chapter 10, Externalities, we have expanded our discussion of carbon emissions and the global challenge of achieving an efficient use of energy resources.

Chapter 11, Public Goods and Common Resources, now uses the efficient provision of transportation infrastructure as its motivating example and discusses the underprovision that results from limited revenue sources.

Chapter 12, retitled Private Information and Healthcare Markets, has a new and expanded coverage of the economics of healthcare insurance and services. It identifies the sources of healthcare market failure and describes and compares alternative solutions including Obamacare and the healthcare systems of Canada and Europe.

In Chapter 20, Economic Inequality, we have broadened our examination of inequality trends with a focus on the income share of the top one percent—the great compression through the mid-1970s and the great divergence of the past 40 years. We have also expanded our coverage of mobility up and down the income quintiles.

■ Outcome-Driven Teaching and Learning

An overarching revision message is that this text, its customized MyEconLab, and classroom resources are built to support an outcome-driven teaching and learning program in which the principles of economics course strengthens

- Problem solving
- Critical thinking
- Decision making
- Citizenship

Problem solving is central to the *Foundations* story. A Checkpoint at the end of each topic, typically three per chapter, provides a pause and opportunity to check understanding with problems, one of which is driven by a recent news clip, and worked solutions. A series of MyEconLab Solutions Videos then give the student an alternative way of reviewing the solutions to these problems.

Critical thinking is encouraged and supported through a series of interactive exercises in MyEconLab. In each chapter, there is one exercise that is based on the question or issue that opens and motivates the chapter, and a second that builds from an *Economics in Your Life* feature.

■ Enhanced eText

The new Enhanced Pearson eText gives students access to their textbook anytime, anywhere. In addition to note-taking, highlighting, and bookmarking, the Pearson eText offers interactive and sharing features. Students actively read and learn through embedded and auto-graded practice, real-time data-graphs, animations, author videos, and more. Instructors can share comments or highlights, and students can add their own, for a tight community of learners in any class.

The new eText includes:

- A Big Picture Video that motivates and summarizes each chapter and provides an outline answer to the chapter's motivating question.
- A series of Concept Videos that illustrate and explain the key ideas in each section of a chapter. These videos also contain animations and explanations of each figure, which can be played separately.
- A series of Solutions Videos that walk the student through the solutions to the Practice Problems and In the News exercises in each Checkpoint.
- Study Plan links that provide opportunities for more practice with problems similar to those in the text, that give targeted feedback to guide the student in answering the exercises.
- Key Terms Quiz links that provide opportunities for students to check their knowledge of the definitions and uses of the key terms.

THE FOUNDATIONS VISION

■ Focus on Core Concepts

Each chapter of *Foundations* concentrates on a manageable number of main ideas (most commonly three or four) and reinforces each idea several times throughout the chapter. This patient, confidence-building approach guides students through unfamiliar terrain and helps them to focus their efforts on the most important tools and concepts of our discipline.

■ Many Learning Tools for Many Learning Styles

Foundations' integrated print and electronic package builds on the basic fact that students have a variety of learning styles. Students have powerful tools at their fingertips: Within the eText, they can get an immediate sense of the content of a chapter by playing the Big Picture video; learn the key ideas by playing the Concept videos; and get a quick walkthrough of the Checkpoint Practice Problems and In the News exercises with the Solutions videos.

In MyEconLab, students can complete all Checkpoint problems and In the News exercises online and get instant feedback; work with interactive graphs and real-time data graphs; assess their skills by taking Practice Tests; receive a personalized Study Plan; and step-by-step help through the learning aid called "Help Me Solve This."

■ Diagrams That Tell the Whole Story

We developed the style of our diagrams with extensive feedback from faculty focus-group participants and student reviewers. All of our figures make consistent use of color to show the direction of shifts and contain detailed, numbered captions designed to direct students' attention step-by-step through the action.

Because beginning students of economics are often apprehensive about working with graphs, we have made a special effort to present material in as many as three ways—with graphs, words, and tables—in the same figure. In an innovation that seems necessary, but is to our knowledge unmatched, nearly all of the information supporting a figure appears on the same page as the figure itself. No more flipping pages back and forth!

■ Real-World Connections That Bring Theory to Life

Students learn best when they can see the purpose of what they are studying, apply it to illuminate the world around them, and use it in their lives.

Eye On boxes offer fresh new examples to help students see that economics is everywhere. Current and recent events appear in *Eye on the U.S. Economy* boxes; we place current U.S. economic events in global and historical perspectives in our *Eye on the Global Economy* and *Eye on the Past* boxes; and we show how students can use economics in day-to-day decisions in *Eye on Your Life* boxes.

Each chapter-opening question is answered in an Eye On box that helps students see the economics behind a key issue facing the world and highlights a major aspect of the chapter's story.

ORGANIZATION

We have organized the sequence of material and chapters in what we think is the most natural order in which to cover the material. But we recognize that there are alternative views on the best order. We have kept this fact and the need for flexibility firmly in mind throughout the text. Many alternative sequences work, and the Flexibility Chart on p. xxxiv explains the alternative pathways through the chapters. In using the flexibility information, keep in mind that the best sequence is the one in which we present the material. And even chapters that the flexibility charts identify as strictly optional are better covered than omitted.

MYECONLAB   MyEconLab

MyEconLab has been designed and refined with a single purpose in mind: to create those moments of understanding that transform the difficult into the clear and obvious. With comprehensive homework, quiz, test, activity, and tutorial options, instructors can manage all their assessment needs in one program.

- All of the Checkpoint and Chapter Checkpoint Problems and Applications can be assigned and automatically graded in MyEconLab.
- Extra problems and applications, including algorithmic, draw-graph, and numerical exercises can be used for student practice or instructor assignment.
- Test Item File questions can be assigned in quiz, test, or homework.
- The Custom Exercise Builder gives instructors the flexibility to create their own problems for assignment.
- The Gradebook records each student's performance and time spent on the Tests and Study Plan and generates reports by student or by chapter.

New for the Eighth Edition is an Enhanced Pearson eText, which includes embedded and auto-graded practice, real-time data graphs, animations, videos, and more. Instructors can share comments or highlights, and students can add their own, for a tight community of learners in any class.

With the Pearson eText 2.0 mobile app students can access the Enhanced eText and all its functionality from their computer, tablet, or cell phone. Because the student's progress is synced across all of their devices, they can stop what they're doing on one device and pick up again later on another one—without breaking their stride.

■ Features of the Enhanced eText

Big Picture Videos   Big Picture videos, tied to the Chapter Checklist, set the stage for the main concept that will be introduced throughout the chapter. Students can use these videos to prepare for today's lecture or to help them focus on main chapter ideas.

DEMAND and SUPPLY: THE BIG PICTURE

Buyers like a low price, and the lower the price, the greater is the quantity they plan to buy—the law of demand.

Sellers like a high price, and the higher the price, the greater is the quantity they plan to sell—the law of supply.

Too high a price brings a surplus, and too low a price brings a shortage.

When there is a surplus, the price falls; and when there is a shortage, the price rises—the law of market forces.

Concept Videos   Concept videos accompany every major section of each chapter and are designed to briefly present the major concepts and graphical tools covered within key sections. Using text, audio, and animation, Concept videos enable students with different learning styles to efficiently study and review key concepts of the chapter.

Animations   Every textbook figure includes a step-by-step animation, with audio, to help students learn the intuition behind reading and interpreting graphs. These animations may be used for review, or as an instructional aid in the classroom.

Embedded MyEconLab Assessment   Every Checkpoint Practice Problem, every In the News problem, and every Study Plan Problem and Application in the enhanced eText can be worked by the student directly from the eText page on which it occurs. These problems are auto-graded and feed into the MyEconLab's Study Plan, where students receive recommendations based upon their performance.

Key Terms Quiz   The Key Terms Quiz, accessible from each Checkpoint, allows students to check their understanding of key chapter concepts before moving onto the next section. The Interactive Glossary that supports the enhanced eText provides the key term definition, an example, and related terms.

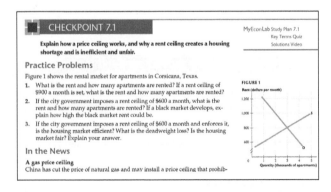

Solutions Videos   Every Checkpoint Practice problem and In the News problem is supported by a Solutions video that provides a step-by-step working of the problem, including graphical analysis. Text, audio, and animation ensure that a student understands how to set-up and solve each of the problems.

■ MyEconLab also includes:

Economics in the News   Economics in the News is a turn-key solution to bringing current news into the classroom. Updated daily during the academic year, we upload two relevant articles (one micro, one macro) and provide questions that may be assigned for homework or for classroom discussion.

Current News   Each week during the academic year, we upload multi-part microeconomic and macroeconomic exercises, with links to relevant articles, into the MyEconLab assignment manager. These enable instructors to bring current issues and events into the course with easy to assign and auto-graded exercises.

Digital Interactives: Economic principles are not static ideas, and learning them shouldn't be either! Digital Interactives are dynamic and engaging assessment activities that promote critical thinking and application of key economic principles.

Each Digital Interactive has 3 to 5 progressive levels and requires approximately 20 minutes to explore, apply, compare, and analyze each topic.

Digital Interactives can be assigned and graded within MyEconLab, or used as a lecture tool to encourage engagement, classroom conversation, and group work.

Topics include:

Comparative Advantage
Opportunity Cost
Demand & Supply
Elasticity

Math Review Exercises in MyEconLab—MyEconLab now offers an array of assignable and auto-graded exercises that cover fundamental math concepts. Geared specifically toward principles economics students, these exercises aim to increase student confidence and success in these courses. Our new Math Review is accessible from the assignment manager and contains more than 150 exercises for homework, quiz, and test use.

Learning Catalytics   Learning Catalytics helps you generate class discussion, customize your lecture, and promote peer-to-peer learning with real-time analytics. As a student response tool, Learning Catalytics uses students' smartphones, tablets, or laptops to engage them in more interactive tasks and thinking.

- NEW! Upload a full PowerPoint® deck for easy creation of slide questions.
- Help your students develop critical thinking skills.
- Monitor responses to find out where your students are struggling.
- Rely on real-time data to adjust your teaching strategy.
- Automatically group students for discussion, teamwork, and peer-to-peer learning.

Experiments in MyEconLab   Experiments are a fun and engaging way to promote active learning and mastery of important economic concepts. Pearson's Experiments program is flexible and easy for instructors to assign and students to use.

- Single-player experiments, available to assign, allow your students to play against virtual players from anywhere at anytime so long as they have an internet connection.
- Multiplayer experiments allow you to assign and manage a real-time experiment with your class.
- Pre and post-questions for each experiment are available for assignment in MyEconLab.
- Experiments are auto-graded using algorithms that objectively evaluate a student's economic gain and performance during the experiment.

AACSB and Learning Outcomes   All end-of-chapter and Test Item File questions are tagged in two ways: to AACSB standards and to discipline-specific Learning Outcomes. These two separate tagging systems allow professors to build assessments around desired departmental and course outcomes and track results in MyEconLab's gradebook.

Personalized Study Plan   The Personalized Study Plan provides recommendations for each of your students based on his or her ability to master the learning objectives in your course. This allows students to focus their study time by pinpointing the precise areas they need to review and allowing them to use customized practice and learning aids—such as videos, eText, tutorials, and more—to get them back on track. The Study Plan also ensures that your students are mastering the concepts, not just guessing the answers.

Using the report available in the Gradebook, you can then tailor course lectures to prioritize the content where students need the most support—offering you better insight into classroom and individual performance.

Dynamic Study Modules   Dynamic Study Modules help students study effectively on their own by continuously assessing their activity and performance in real time. Here's how it works: students complete a set of questions with a unique answer format that also asks them to indicate their confidence level. Questions repeat until the student can answer them all correctly and confidently. Once completed, Dynamic Study Modules explain the concept using materials from the text. These are available as graded assignments prior to class, and accessible on smartphones, tablets, and computers.

NEW! Instructors can now remove questions from Dynamic Study Modules to better fit their course.

SUPPORT MATERIALS FOR INSTRUCTORS AND STUDENTS

Foundations of Microeconomics is accompanied by the most comprehensive set of teaching and learning tools ever assembled. Each component of our package is organized by Checkpoint topic for a tight, seamless integration with both the textbook and the other components. In addition to authoring the MyEconLab Study Plan and Assignment problems, PowerPoint resources, and Video scripts, we have helped in the reviewing and revising of the Solutions Manual, Instructor's Manual, and Test Item Files to ensure that every element of the package achieves the consistency that students and teachers need.

■ PowerPoint Resources

We have created the PowerPoint resources based on our 24 years of experience using this tool in our own classrooms. We have created four sets of PowerPoint presentations for instructors. They are:

- Lecture notes with full-color, animated figures, and tables from the textbook
- Figures and tables from the textbook, animated with step-by-step walk-through for instructors to use in their own personal slides
- *Eye On* features
- Alternative micro lecture notes with full-color, animated figures and tables that use examples different from those in the textbook

A student version of the lecture notes is also available on MyEconLab.

■ Instructor's Manual

The Instructor's Manual, written by Luke Armstrong and reviewed by Mark Rush, contains chapter outlines and road maps, additional exercises with solutions, a comprehensive Chapter Lecture resource, and a virtual encyclopedia of suggestions on how to enrich class presentation and use class time efficiently. The Instructor's Manual has been updated to reflect changes in the main text as well as infused with a fresh and intuitive approach to teaching this course. The Instructor's Manual is available for download in Word and PDF formats.

■ Solutions Manual

The Solutions Manual, written by Mark Rush and checked for accuracy by Jeannie Gillmore, contains the solutions to all Chapter Checkpoint Study Plan Problems and Applications, Instructor Assignable Problems and Applications, and the Multiple Choice Quiz. The Solutions Manual is available for download in Word and PDF formats.

■ Three Test Item Files and TestGen

More than 6,000 multiple-choice, numerical, fill-in-the-blank, short answer, essay, and integrative questions make up the three Test Item Files that support *Foundations of Microeconomics*. Mark Rush reviewed and edited the updated and new questions from three dedicated principles instructors to form one of the most comprehensive testing systems on the market. Our questions were written by Carol Dole (Jackson University). The entire set of questions is available for download in Word, PDF, and TestGen formats.

All three Test Item Files are available in test generator software (TestGen with QuizMaster). TestGen's graphical interface enables instructors to view, edit, and add questions; transfer questions to tests; and print different forms of tests. Instructors also have the option to reformat tests with varying fonts and styles, margins, and headers and footers, as in any word-processing document. Search and sort features let the instructor quickly locate questions and arrange them in a preferred order. QuizMaster, working with your school's computer network, automatically grades the exams, stores the results on disk, and allows the instructor to view and print a variety of reports.

■ Instructor's Resource Center

This page on the Pearson Higher Education website (www.pearsonhighered.com/IRC) contains the Instructor's Manual, Solutions Manual, and Test Item Files in Word and PDF formats. It also contains the Computerized Test Item Files (with a TestGen program installer) and PowerPoint resources. It is compatible with both Windows and Macintosh operating systems.

For access or more information, contact your local Pearson representative or request access online at the Instructor Resource Center.

ACKNOWLEDGMENTS

Working on a project such as this one generates many debts that can never be repaid. But they can be acknowledged, and it is a special pleasure to be able to do so here and to express our heartfelt thanks to each and every one of the following long list, without whose contributions we could not have produced *Foundations*.

Mark Rush again coordinated, managed, and contributed to our Solutions Manual, Instructor's Manual, and Test Item Files. He assembled, polished, wrote, and rewrote these materials to ensure their close consistency with the text. He and we were in constant contact as all the elements of our text and package came together. Mark also made many valuable suggestions for improving the text and the Checkpoint Problems. His contribution went well beyond that of a reviewer, and his effervescent sense of humor kept us all in good spirits along the way.

Working closely with Mark, Luke Armstrong wrote content for the Instructor's Manual. Carol Dole authored new questions for the Test Item Files.

Luke Armstrong and Carol Dole recorded the narrations that accompany the Big Picture, Concept, and Solutions Videos in the eText. The engaging style and clarity of these outstanding teachers makes these videos a powerful learning tool.

Fred Bounds (Georgia Perimeter College), and Carol Dole provided outstanding reviews of the Study Plan and Assessment problems in MyEconLab that helped to make our exercises as effective as possible.

The ideas from which *Foundations* grew began to form over dinner at the Andover Inn in Andover, Massachusetts, with Denise Clinton and Sylvia Mallory. We gratefully acknowledge Sylvia's role not only at the birth of this project but also in managing its initial development team. Denise was an ongoing inspiration for 15 years, and we are privileged to have had the benefit of her enormous experience.

The success of *Foundations* owes much to its outstanding editors: Director of Portfolio Management, Adrienne D'Ambrosio, and Portfolio Manager, Ashley Bryan. Adrienne's acute intelligence and sensitive understanding of the market have helped sharpen our vision of this text and package over several editions, and Ashley has brought a fresh perspective to this Eight edition revision. The value-added of Adrienne and Ashley is huge. It has been, and we hope it will for many future editions remain, a joy to work with them.

Jonathan Boylan created the new impressive cover design and converted the raw ideas of our brainstorms into an outstandingly designed text.

Melissa Honig, Digital Studio Producer, and Noel Lotz, Digital Content Team Lead have set a new standard for online learning and teaching resources. They have been sources of high energy, good sense, and level-headed advice and quickly found creative solutions to all our technology problems.

Nancy Freihofer, our outstanding, ever calm, Content Producer, worked with a talented team at Integra, Project Editor, Heather Johnson, and designer, art coordinator, and typesetter. Our copy editor, Catherine Baum, gave our work a thorough review and helpful polish, and our proofreader ensured the most error-free text we have yet produced.

Our marketing team, comprised of Ramona Elmer, Tricia Murphy, and Brad Parkins, has been an integral part of this revision process. They have provided great knowledge and strategies to help continuously improve our suite of materials and keep them relevant and valuable in these ever-changing times.

Richard Parkin, our technical illustrator, created the figures in the text, the dynamic figures in the eText, the animated figures in the PowerPoint presentations, created the animations for and assembled the enhanced eText videos, and contributed many ideas to improving the clarity of our illustrations in all media.

Jeannie Gillmore, our long-standing personal assistant, worked closely with us to create MyEconLab Study Plan and Assignment problems and to ensure the highest standards for our feedbacks and "help me solve this" question help.

Finally, our reviewers, whose names appear on the following pages, have made an enormous contribution to this text and MyEconLab resources. Once again we find ourselves using superlatives, but they are called for. In the many texts that we've written, we've not seen reviewing of the quality that we enjoyed on this revision. It has been a pleasure (if at times a challenge) to respond constructively to their many excellent suggestions.

Robin Bade
Michael Parkin
London, Ontario, Canada
robin@econ100.com
mparkin@uwo.ca

FOUNDATIONS OF ECONOMICS: FLEXIBILITY CHART

Micro Flexibility

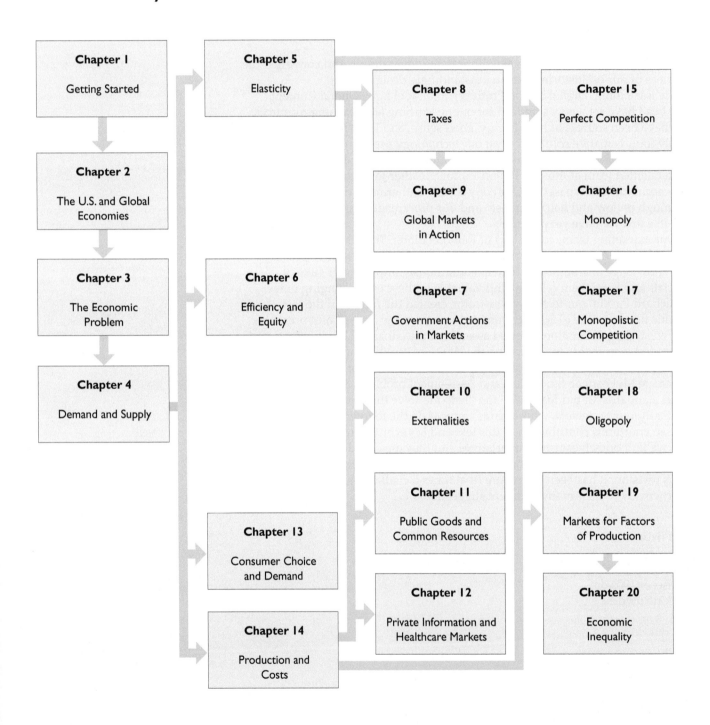

Start here ...

... then jump to any of these ...

... and jump to any of these after doing the prerequisites indicated

Reviewers

Eunice Akoto, Henderson State University

Mehdi Arman, Columbia State Community College

Luke Armstrong, Lee College

Michael Aubry, Cuyamaca College

Bizuayehu Bedane, Southern Illinois University at Carbondale

Victor Claar, Henderson State University

Earl Davis, Nicholls State University

Carol Dole, Jacksonville University

Byron Gangnes, University of Hawaii at Manoa

Leon Hoke, University of Tampa

Christopher Jeffords, Indiana University of Pennsylvania; University of Connecticut

Stephen Jerbic, San Jose State University

Vicki King-Skinner, Coastal Carolina University

David Manifold, Caldwell Community College & Technical Center

Michael Nuwer, State University of New York at Potsdam

Abdulhamid Sukar, Cameron University

Lisa Takeyama, San Francisco State University

Benjamin Zamzow, Campbell University

Ting Zhang, University of Baltimore

Alfredo A. Romero Aguirre, North Carolina A&T State University

Seemi Ahmad, Dutchess Community College

William Aldridge, Shelton State Community College

Rashid B. Al-Hmoud, Texas Tech University

Neil Alper, Northeastern University

Nejat Anbarci, Deakin University

J.J. Arias, Georgia College & State University

Luke A. Armstrong, Lee College

Leland Ash, Skagit Valley College

Ali Ataiifar, Delaware County Community College

John Baffoe-Bonnie, Pennsylvania State University, Delaware County Campus

A. Paul Ballantyne, University of Colorado

Tyra D. Barrett, Pellissippi State Community College

Sue Bartlett, University of South Florida

Gerald Baumgardner, Penn College

Klaus Becker, Texas Tech University

Clive Belfield, Queen's College, City University of New York

William K. Bellinger, Dickinson College

John Bethune, Barton College

Prasun Bhattacharjee, East Tennessee State University

Gautam Bhattacharya, University of Kansas

Gerald W. Bialka, University of North Florida

David Bivin, Indiana University–Purdue University at Indianapolis

Geoffrey Black, Boise State University

Carey Anne Borkoski, Arundel Community College

Jurgen Brauer, Augusta State University

Greg Brock, Georgia Southern University

Barbara Brogan, Northern Virginia Community College

Bruce C. Brown, California State Polytechnic University, Pomona

Christopher Brown, Arkansas State University

James O. Brown, Delta State University

Brian Buckley, Clemson University

Donald Bumpass, Sam Houston State University

Seewoonundun Bunjun, East Stroudsburg University

Nancy Burnett, University of Wisconsin at Oshkosh

James L. Butkiewicz, University of Delaware

Barbara Caldwell, Saint Leo University

Bruce Caldwell, University of North Carolina, Greensboro

Joseph Calhoun, Florida State University

Robert Carlsson, University of South Carolina

Shawn Carter, Jacksonville State University

Regina Cassady, Valencia Community College

Jack Chambless, Valencia Community College

Joni Charles, Southwest Texas State University

Anoshua Chaudhuri, San Francisco State University

Robert Cherry, Brooklyn College

Chi-Young Choi, University of New Hampshire

Paul Cichello, Xavier University

Quentin Ciolfi, Brevard Community College

Victor V. Claar, Henderson State University

Jane L. Cline, Forsyth Technical Community College

Jim Cobbe, Florida State University

John Cochran, University of Chicago

Mike Cohick, Collin County Community College

Ludovic Comeau, De Paul University

Carol Conrad, Cerro Coso Community College

Christopher Cornell, Vassar College

Richard Cornwall, University of California, Davis

Kevin Cotter, Wayne State University

Erik Craft, University of Richmond

Tom Creahan, Morehead State University

Elizabeth Crowell, University of Michigan at Dearborn

Susan Dadres, Southern Methodist University

David Davenport, McLennan Community College

Troy Davig, College of William and Mary

Jeffrey Davis, ITT Technical Institute (Utah)

Lewis Davis, Union College

Dennis Debrecht, Carroll College

Al DeCooke, Broward Community College

Jason J. Delaney, Georgia Gwinnett College

Vince DiMartino, University of Texas at San Antonio

Vernon J. Dobis, Minnesota State University–Moorhead

Carol Dole, Jacksonville University

Kathleen Dorsainvil, American University

John Dorsey, University of Maryland, College Park

Amrik Singh Dua, Mt. San Antonio College

Marie Duggan, Keene State College

Allen Dupont, North Carolina State University
David Eaton, Murray State University
Kevin J. Egan, University of Toledo
Harold W. Elder, University of Alabama
Harry Ellis, University of North Texas
Stephen Ellis, North Central Texas College
Carl Enomoto, New Mexico State University
Chuen-mei Fan, Colorado State University
Chris Fant, Spartanburg Community College
Elena Ermolenko Fein, Oakton Community College
Gary Ferrier, University of Arkansas
Rudy Fichtenbaum, Wright State University
Donna K. Fisher, Georgia Southern University
Kaya Ford, Northern Virginia Community College
Robert Francis, Shoreline Community College
Roger Frantz, San Diego State University
Amanda S. Freeman, Kansas State University
Marc Fusaro, East Carolina University
Arthur Friedberg, Mohawk Valley Community College
Julie Gallaway, Southwest Missouri State University
Byron Gangnes, University of Hawaii
Gay GareschÈ, Glendale Community College
Neil Garston, California State University, Los Angeles
Lisa Geib-Gunderson, University of Maryland
Lisa M. George, City University of New York
Linda Ghent, Eastern Illinois University
Soma Ghosh, Bridgewater State College
Kirk Gifford, Ricks College
Scott Gilbert, Southern Illinois University
Maria Giuili, Diablo Valley Community College
Mark Gius, Quinnipiac College
Gregory E. Givens, University of Alabama
Randall Glover, Brevard Community College
Stephan Gohmann, University of Louisville

Richard Gosselin, Houston Community College
John Graham, Rutgers University
Patricia E. Graham, University of Northern Colorado
Warren Graham, Tulsa Community College
Homer Guevara, Jr., Northwest Vista College
Osman Gulseven, North Carolina State University
Jang-Ting Guo, University of California, Riverside
Dennis Hammett, University of Texas at El Paso
Leo Hardwick, Macomb Community College
Mehdi Haririan, Bloomsburg University
Paul Harris, Camden County Community College
Mark Healy, William Rainey Harper College
Rey Hernandez-Julian, Metropolitan State College of Denver
Gus Herring, Brookhaven College
Michael Heslop, Northern Virginia Community College
Steven Hickerson, Mankato State University
Frederick Steb Hipple, East Tennessee State University
Lee Hoke, University of Tampa
Andy Howard, Rio Hondo College
Yu Hsing, Southeastern Louisiana University
Greg Hunter, California State Polytechnic University, Pomona
Matthew Hyle, Winona State University
Todd Idson, Boston University
Harvey James, University of Hartford
Russell Janis, University of Massachusetts at Amherst
Ricot Jean, Valencia College
Jay A. Johnson, Southeastern Louisiana University
Ted Joyce, City University of New York, Baruch College
Ahmad A. Kader, University of Nevada, Las Vegas
Jonathan D. Kaplan, California State University, Sacramento
Arthur Kartman, San Diego State University
Chris Kauffman, University of Tennessee
Diane Keenan, Cerritos College
Brian Kench, University of Tampa

John Keith, Utah State University
Kristen Keith, University of Toledo
Joe Kerkvliet, Oregon State University
Randall Kesselring, Arkansas State University
Gary Kikuchi, University of Hawaii at Manoa
Douglas Kinnear, Colorado State University
Morris Knapp, Miami Dade Community College
Steven Koch, Georgia Southern University
Kate Krause, University of New Mexico
Stephan Kroll, California State University, Sacramento
Joyce Lapping, University of Southern Maine
Tom Larson, California State University, Los Angeles
Robert Lemke, Florida International University
J. Mark Leonard, University of Nebraska at Omaha
Tony Lima, California State University, Hayward
Joshua Long, Ivy Tech Community College
Kenneth Long, New River Community College
Noel Lotz, Middle Tennessee State University
Marty Ludlum, Oklahoma City Community College
Brian Lynch, Lake Land College
Michael Machiorlatti, Oklahoma City Community College
Roger Mack, De Anza College
Michael Magura, University of Toledo
Mark Maier, Glendale College
Svitlana Maksymenko, University of Pittsburgh
Paula Manns, Atlantic Cape Community College
Dan Marburger, Arkansas State University
Kathryn Marshall, Ohio State University
John V. Martin, Boise State University
Drew E. Mattson, Anoka-Ramsey Community College
Stephen McCafferty, Ohio State University
Thomas S. McCaleb, Florida State University
Katherine S. McCann, University of Delaware

William McLean, Oklahoma State University

Diego Mendez-Carbajo, Illinois Wesleyan University

Evelina Mengova, California State University, Fullerton

Thomas Meyer, Patrick Henry Community College

Meghan Millea, Mississippi State University

Michael Milligan, Front Range Community College

Jenny Minier, University of Miami

David Mitchell, Valdosta State University

Dr. Carl B. Montano, Lamar University

Christine Moser, Western Michigan University

William Mosher, Clark University

Mike Munoz, Northwest Vista College

John R. Mundy, St. Johns River State College

Kevin Murphy, Oakland University

Ronald Nate, Brigham Young University, Idaho

Nasrin Nazemzadeh, Rowan Cabarrus Community College

Michael Nelson, Texas A&M University

Rebecca Neumann, University of Wisconsin—Milwaukee

Charles Newton, Houston Community College Southwest

Melinda Nish, Salt Lake Community College

Lee Nordgren, Indiana University at Bloomington

Norman P. Obst, Michigan State University

Inge O'Connor, Syracuse University

William C. O'Connor, Western Montana College–University of Montana

Fola Odebunmi, Cypress College

Victor I. Oguledo, Florida A&M University

Charles Okeke, College of Southern Nevada

Lydia M. Ortega, St. Philip's College

P. Marcelo Oviedo, Iowa State University

Jennifer Pate, Ph.D., Loyola Marymount University

Sanjay Paul, Elizabethtown College

Ken Peterson, Furman University

Tim Petry, North Dakota State University

Charles Pflanz, Scottsdale Community College

Jonathon Phillips, North Carolina State University

Basharat Pitafi, Southern Illinois University

Anthony Plunkett, Harrison College

Paul Poast, Ohio State University

Greg Pratt, Mesa Community College

Fernando Quijano, Dickinson State University

Andy Radler, Butte Community College

Ratha Ramoo, Diablo Valley College

Karen Reid, University of Wisconsin, Parkside

Mary Rigdon, University of Texas, Austin

Helen Roberts, University of Illinois at Chicago

Greg Rose, Sacramento City College

Barbara Ross, Kapi'olani Community College

Elham Rouhani, Gwinnett Technical College

Jeffrey Rous, University of North Texas

June Roux, Salem Community College

Udayan Roy, Long Island University

Nancy C. Rumore, University of Louisiana–Lafayette

Mark Rush, University of Florida

Rolando Sanchez, Northwest Vista College

Joseph Santos, South Dakota State University

Roland Santos, Lakeland Community College

Mark Scanlan, Stephen F. Austin State University

Ted Scheinman, Mount Hood Community College

Buffie Schmidt, Augusta State University

Jerry Schwartz, Broward Community College

Gautam Sethi, Bard College

Margaret Anne Shannon, Georgia Southern University

Mushtaq Sheikh, Union County College

Michelle Sheran-Andrews, University of North Carolina at Greensboro

Virginia Shingleton, Valparaiso University

Steven S. Shwiff, Texas A & M University—Commerce

Charles Sicotte, Rock Valley College

Issoufou Soumaila, Texas Tech University

Martin Spechler, Indiana University

Leticia Starkov, Elgin Community College

Stela Stefanova, University of Delaware

John Stiver, University of Connecticut

Richard W. Stratton, The University of Akron

Abdulhamid Sukar, Cameron University

Terry Sutton, Southeast Missouri State University

Janet M. Thomas, Bentley College

Donna Thompson, Brookdale Community College

Deborah Thorsen, Palm Beach State College

James Thorson, Southern Connecticut State University

Marc Tomljanovich, Colgate University

Cynthia Royal Tori, Valdosta State University

Ngoc-Bich Tran, San Jacinto College South

Nora Underwood, University of California, Davis

Jogindar S. Uppal, State University of New York

Va Nee L. Van Vleck, California State University, Fresno

Victoria Vernon, Empire State College / SUNY

Christian Weber, Seattle University

Ethel Weeks, Nassau Community College

Jack Wegman, Santa Rosa Junior College

Jason White, Northwest Missouri State University

Benjamin Widner, Colorado State University

Barbara Wiens-Tuers, Pennsylvania State University, Altoona

Katherine Wolfe, University of Pittsburgh

Kristen Wolfe, St. Johns River State College

You're in school!
Did you make the right decision?

Getting Started

**When you have completed your study of this chapter,
you will be able to**

1 Define economics and explain the kinds of questions that
   economists try to answer.

2 Explain the ideas that define the economic way of thinking.

3 Explain how economics is useful as a life skill.

MyEconLab Big Picture Video

1

1.1   DEFINITION AND QUESTIONS

Well, did you make the right decision? Is being in school the best use of your time? You'll soon know how an economist answers this question—for it is an economic question. It arises from the fact that you want more than you can get. You want to be in school. But you also want the time to enjoy your favorite sports and movies, to travel, and to hang out with friends—time that right now you don't have because you've got classes to attend and assignments due. Your time is scarce.

■ Scarcity

Scarcity
The condition that arises because wants exceed the ability of resources to satisfy them.

Our inability to satisfy all our wants is called **scarcity**. The ability of each of us to satisfy our wants is limited by the time we have, the incomes we earn, and the prices we pay for the things we buy. These limits mean that everyone has unsatisfied wants. The ability of all of us as a society to satisfy our wants is limited by the productive resources that exist. These resources include the gifts of nature, our labor and ingenuity, and the tools and equipment that we have made.

Everyone, poor and rich alike, faces scarcity. A student wants Taylor Swift's latest album and a paperback but has only $10.00 in his pocket. He faces scarcity. Gwen Stefani wants to spend a week on the set of *The Voice* in L.A., but she also wants to devote time and energy to her successful clothing line. She faces scarcity. The U.S. government wants to increase spending on homeland security and cut taxes. It faces scarcity. An entire society wants improved healthcare, an Internet connection in every classroom, clean lakes and rivers, and so on. Society faces scarcity. Scarcity is everywhere: Even parrots face scarcity!

Not only do <u>I</u> want a cracker—we <u>all</u> want a cracker!

Faced with scarcity, we must make choices. We must choose among the available alternatives. The student must choose the download or the paperback. Gwen Stefani must choose shooting episodes of *The Voice* or designing her next clothing collection. The government must choose greater security or tax cuts. And society must choose among healthcare, computers, the environment, and so on.

■ Economics Defined

Economics
The social science that studies the choices that individuals, businesses, governments, and entire societies make as they cope with *scarcity*, all the things that influence those choices, and the arrangements that coordinate them.

Economics is the social science that studies the choices that individuals, businesses, governments, and entire societies make as they cope with *scarcity*, all the things that influence those choices, and the arrangements that coordinate them.

The subject has two broad parts:

- Microeconomics, and
- Macroeconomics

Microeconomics

Microeconomics
The study of the choices that individuals and businesses make and the way these choices interact and are influenced by governments.

Microeconomics is the study of the choices that individuals and businesses make and the way these choices interact and are influenced by governments. Some examples of microeconomic questions are: Will you buy a 3-D TV or a standard one? Will Nintendo sell more units of Wii if it cuts the price? Will a cut in the income tax rate encourage people to work longer hours? Will a hike in the gas tax encourage more people to drive hybrid or smaller automobiles? Is music streaming killing song downloads?

Macroeconomics

Macroeconomics is the study of the aggregate (or total) effects on the national economy and the global economy of the choices that individuals, businesses, and governments make. Some examples of macroeconomic questions are: Why did production and jobs expand slowly in the United States during 2014 and 2015? Why are incomes growing much faster in China and India than in the United States? Why is unemployment in Europe so high? Why are Americans borrowing more than $1 billion a day from the rest of the world?

Two big questions define the scope of economics:

- How do choices end up determining *what, how,* and *for whom* goods and services get produced?
- When do choices made in the pursuit of *self-interest* also promote the *social interest*?

◼ What, How, and For Whom?

Goods and services are the objects and actions that people value and produce to satisfy human wants. Goods are *objects* that satisfy wants. Sports shoes and ketchup are examples. Services are *actions* that satisfy wants. Haircuts and rock concerts are examples. We produce a dazzling array of goods and services that range from necessities such as food, houses, and healthcare to leisure items such as Blu-ray players and roller coaster rides.

What?

What determines the quantities of corn we grow, homes we build, and healthcare services we produce? Sixty years ago, farm output was 5 percent of total U.S. production. Today, it is 1 percent. Over the same period, the output of mines, construction, and utilities slipped from 9 percent to 7 percent of total production and manufacturing fell from 28 percent to 12 percent. These decreases in output are matched by increases in the production of a wide range of services, up from 58 percent of total production 60 years ago to 80 percent today. How will these quantities change in the future as ongoing changes in technology make an ever-wider array of goods and services available to us?

How?

How are goods and services produced? In a vineyard in France, a hundred basket-carrying workers pick the annual grape crop by hand. In a vineyard in California, a huge machine and a few workers do the same job. Look around and you will see many examples of this phenomenon—the same job being done in different ways. In some stores, checkout clerks key in prices. In others, they use a laser scanner. One farmer keeps track of his livestock feeding schedules and inventories by using paper-and-pencil records, while another uses a computer. In some plants, GM hires workers to weld auto bodies and in others it uses robots to do the job.

Why do we use machines in some cases and people in others? Do mechanization and technological change destroy more jobs than they create? Do they make us better off or worse off?

Macroeconomics
The study of the aggregate (or total) effects on the national economy and the global economy of the choices that individuals, businesses, and governments make.

Goods and services
The objects (goods) and the actions (services) that people value and produce to satisfy human wants.

In a California vineyard a machine and a few workers do the same job as a hundred grape pickers in France.

A doctor gets more of the goods and services produced than a nurse or a medical assistant gets.

For Whom?

For whom are goods and services produced? The answer depends on the incomes that people earn and the prices they pay for the goods and services they buy. At given prices, a person who has a high income is able to buy more goods and services than a person who has a low income. Doctors earn much higher incomes than do nurses and medical assistants, so doctors get more of the goods and services produced than nurses and medical assistants get.

You probably know about many other persistent differences in incomes. Men, on average, earn more than women. Whites, on average, earn more than minorities. College graduates, on average, earn more than high school graduates. Americans, on average, earn more than Europeans, who in turn earn more, on average, than Asians and Africans. But there are some significant exceptions. The people of Japan and Hong Kong now earn an average income similar to that of Americans. And there is a lot of income inequality throughout the world.

What determines the incomes we earn? Why do doctors earn larger incomes than nurses? Why do men earn more, on average, than women? Why do college graduates earn more, on average, than high school graduates? Why do Americans earn more, on average, than Africans?

Economics explains how the choices that individuals, businesses, and governments make and the interactions of those choices end up determining *what, how,* and *for whom* goods and services are produced. In answering these questions, we have a deeper agenda in mind. We're not interested in just knowing how many Blu-ray players are produced, how they are produced, and who gets to enjoy them. We ultimately want to know the answer to the second big economic question that we'll now explore.

■ Can the Pursuit of Self-Interest Be in the Social Interest?

Every day, you and 321 million other Americans, along with 7.2 billion people in the rest of the world, make economic choices that result in *"what," "how,"* and *"for whom"* goods and services are produced.

Are the goods and services produced, and the quantities in which they are produced, the right ones? Are the scarce resources used in the best possible way? Do the goods and services we produce go to those who benefit most from them?

Self-Interest and the Social Interest

Self-interest
The choices that are best for the individual who makes them.

Social interest
The choices that are best for society as a whole.

Choices that are the best for the individual who makes them are choices made in the pursuit of **self-interest**. Choices that are the best for society as a whole are said to be in the **social interest**. The social interest has two dimensions: *efficiency* and *equity*. We'll explore these concepts in later chapters. For now, think of efficiency as being achieved by baking the biggest possible pie, and think of equity as being achieved by sharing the pie in the fairest possible way.

You know that your own choices are the best ones for you—or at least you *think* they're the best at the time that you make them. You use your time and other resources in the way that you think is best. You might consider how your choices affect other people, but you order a home delivery pizza because you're hungry and want to eat, not because you're concerned that the delivery person or the cook needs an income. You make choices that are in your self-interest—choices that you think are best for you.

When you act on your economic decisions, you come into contact with thousands of other people who produce and deliver the goods and services that you decide to buy or who buy the things that you sell. These people have made their own decisions—what to produce and how to produce it, whom to hire or whom to work for, and so on. Like you, all these people make choices that they think are best for them. When the pizza delivery person shows up at your home, he's not doing you a favor. He's earning his income and hoping for a good tip.

Can it be possible that when each one of us makes choices that are in our own best interest—in our self-interest—it turns out that these choices are also the best choices for society as a whole—in the social interest?

Adam Smith, regarded as the founder of economic science, (see *Eye on the Past* on p. 18) said the answer is *yes*. He believed that when we pursue our self-interest, we are led by an *invisible hand* to promote the social interest.

Is Adam Smith correct? Can it really be possible that the pursuit of self-interest promotes the social interest? Much of the rest of this book helps you to learn what economists know about this question and its answer. To help you start thinking about the question, we're going to illustrate it with four topics that generate heated discussion in today's world. You're already at least a little bit familiar with each one of them. They are

- Globalization
- The information revolution
- Climate change
- Government budget deficit and debt

Globalization

Globalization—the expansion of international trade and the production of components and services by firms in other countries—has been going on for centuries. But in recent years, its pace has accelerated. Microchips, satellites, and fiber-optic cables have lowered the cost of communication and globalized production decisions. When Nike produces more sports shoes, people in Malaysia get more work. When Steven Spielberg makes a new movie, programmers in New Zealand write the code that makes magical animations. And when China Airlines wants a new airplane, Americans who work for Boeing build it.

Workers in Asia make our shoes.

Globalization is bringing rapid income growth, especially in Asia. But globalization is leaving some people behind. Jobs in manufacturing and routine services are shrinking in the United States, and some nations of Africa and South America are not sharing in the prosperity enjoyed in other parts of the world.

The owners of multinational firms benefit from lower production costs and consumers benefit from low-cost imported goods. But don't displaced American workers lose? And doesn't even the worker in Malaysia, who sews your new shoes for a few cents an hour, also lose? Is globalization in the social interest, or does globalization benefit just some at the expense of others?

The Information Revolution

We are living at a time of extraordinary economic change that has been called the *Information Revolution*. This name suggests a parallel with the *Industrial Revolution* of the 1800s and the *Agricultural Revolution* of 12,000 years ago.

The changes that have occurred during the last 35 years are based on one major technology: the microprocessor or computer chip. The spin-offs from faster and cheaper computing have been widespread in telecommunications, music, and the automation of millions of tasks that previously required human decisions. You encounter some of these tasks when you check out at the grocery store or use an ATM. Less visible, but larger in scope, are the robots that assemble cars and move goods around warehouses. Over the next 20 years, more than one third of today's jobs will be done by a new generation of robots.

Robots fill orders at Amazon.

The computing and robot revolution resulted from people pursuing their self-interest. Gordon Moore, the chip maker who set up Intel, and Bill Gates, who quit Harvard to set up Microsoft, weren't thinking how much easier it would be for you to turn in your essay on time if you had a computer. Moore and Gates and thousands of other entrepreneurs were in pursuit of big rewards. Yet their actions made many other people better off. They advanced the social interest.

But are resources used in the best possible way? Or do Intel and Microsoft set their prices too high and put their products out of reach for too many people? And is it in the social interest for robots to take people's jobs?

Climate Change

The Earth is getting hotter and the ice at the two poles is melting. Since the late nineteenth century, the Earth's surface temperature has increased about 1 degree Fahrenheit, and close to a half of that increase occurred over the past 25 years.

Human activity is raising the Earth's surface temperature.

Most climate scientists believe that the current warming has come at least in part from human economic activity—from self-interested choices—and that, if left unchecked, the warming will bring large future economic costs.

Are the individual energy choices that each of us makes damaging the social interest? What needs to be done to make our choices serve the social interest? Would the United States joining with other nations to limit carbon emissions serve the social interest? What other measures might be introduced?

Government Budget Deficit and Debt

Every year since 2000, the U.S. government has run a budget deficit. On average, the government has spent $2.3 billion a day more than it has received in taxes. The government's debt has increased each day by that amount. Over the 15 year period from 2000 to 2015, government debt increased by $12.5 trillion. Your personal share of this debt is $56,000.

A government budget time bomb is ticking as spending grows faster than tax revenues.

This large deficit and debt is just the beginning of an even bigger problem. From about 2020 onwards, the retirement and healthcare benefits to which older Americans are entitled are going to cost increasingly more than current taxes can cover. With no changes in tax or benefit rates, the budget deficit will increase and the debt will swell ever higher.

Deficits and the debts they create cannot persist indefinitely, and debts must somehow be repaid. They will most likely be repaid by you, not by your parents. When we make our voter choices, we pursue our self-interest. Do our choices serve the social interest? Do the choices made by politicians and bureaucrats in Washington and the state capitals promote the social interest, or do they only serve their own self-interests?

The four issues we've just reviewed raise questions that are hard to answer. We'll return to each of them at various points throughout this text and explain when the social interest is served and when there remain problems to be solved.

CHECKPOINT 1.1

Define economics and explain the kinds of questions that economists try to answer.

Practice Problems

1. Economics studies choices that arise from one fact. What is that fact?
2. Provide three examples of wants in the United States today that are especially pressing but not satisfied.
3. In the following three news items, find examples of the *what, how*, and *for whom* questions: "With more research, we will cure cancer"; "A good education is the right of every child"; "Congress raises taxes to curb the deficit."
4. How does a new Starbucks in Beijing, China, influence self-interest and the social interest?
5. How does Facebook influence self-interest and the social interest?

In the News

1. The Bureau of Labor Statistics (BLS) reports that high-paying jobs in healthcare and jobs in leisure, hospitality, and education will expand quickly over the next five years. How does the BLS expect *what* and *for whom* goods and services are produced to change in the next five years?
2. Hewlett-Packard will cut 30,000 jobs and lower its cost by $2.7 billion a year.
   Source: *Fortune*, October 1, 2015

   Explain how Hewlett-Packard's decision made in its self-interest might also be in the social interest.

Solutions to Practice Problems

1. The fact is scarcity—human wants exceed the resources available.
2. Examples would include security from terrorism, cleaner air in our cities, better public schools, and better public infrastructure. (Think of others.)
3. More research is a *how* question, and a cure for cancer is a *what* question. Good education is a *what* question, and every child is a *for whom* question. Raising taxes is a *for whom* question.
4. Decisions made by Starbucks are in Starbucks' self-interest but they also serve the self-interest of its customers and so contribute to the social interest.
5. Facebook serves the self-interest of its investors, users, and advertisers. It also serves the social interest by enabling people to share information.

Solutions to In the News

1. The BLS expects the quantities of goods and services produced by workers in healthcare, leisure, hospitality, and education to increase. For whom they are produced depends on how people's incomes and the prices of goods and services will change in the next five years. The BLS expects workers in these high-paying jobs and expanding industries will get more of them.
2. Hewlett-Packard's product prices might fall and benefit its customers. The laid-off workers will find new jobs, some of which might pay higher wages.

1.2   THE ECONOMIC WAY OF THINKING

The definition of economics and the kinds of questions that economists try to answer give you a flavor of the scope of economics. But they don't tell you how economists *think* about these questions and how they go about seeking answers to them. You're now going to see how economists approach their work.

We'll break this task into two parts. First, we'll explain the ideas that economists use to frame their view of the world. These ideas will soon have you thinking like an economist. Second, we'll look at economics both as a social science and as a policy tool that governments, businesses, and *you* can use.

Six ideas define the *economic way of thinking*:

- A choice is a *tradeoff*
- *Cost* is what you *must give up* to get something.
- *Benefit* is what you gain from something.
- People make *rational choices* by comparing benefits and costs.
- Most choices are *"how much"* choices made at the *margin*.
- Choices respond to *incentives*.

■ A Choice Is a Tradeoff

Tradeoff
An exchange—giving up one thing to get something else.

A **tradeoff** is an exchange—giving up one thing to get something else. Because we face scarcity, we must make choices. And when we make a choice, we select from the available alternatives. You can think about choices as tradeoffs. When you choose one thing, you give up something else that you could have chosen.

Think about what you will do on Saturday night. You can spend the night studying for your next economics test or having fun with your friends, but you can't do both of these activities at the same time. You must choose how much time to devote to each. Whatever choice you make, you could have chosen something else. When you choose how to spend your Saturday night, you face a tradeoff between studying and hanging out with your friends. To get more study time, you must give up some time with your friends.

■ Cost: What You *Must* Give Up

Opportunity cost
The opportunity cost of something is the best thing you must give up to get it.

The **opportunity cost** of something is the best thing you must give up to get it. You most likely think about the cost of something as the money you must spend to get it. But dig a bit deeper. If you spend $10 on a movie ticket, you can't spend it on a sandwich. The movie ticket really costs a sandwich. The *cost* of something is what must be given up to get it, not the money spent on it. Economists use the term *opportunity cost* to emphasize this view of cost.

The biggest opportunity cost you face is that of being in school. This opportunity cost has two components: things you can't afford to buy and things you can't do with your time.

Start with the things you can't afford to buy. You've spent all your income on tuition, residence fees, books, and a laptop. If you weren't in school, you would have spent this money on tickets to ball games and movies and all the other things that you enjoy. But that's only the start of the things you can't afford to buy because you're in school. You've also given up the opportunity to get a job and buy the things that you could afford with your higher income. Suppose that the

The opportunity cost of being in school: things you can't buy and do.

best job you could get if you weren't in school is working as a convenience store manager earning $24,000 a year. Another part of your opportunity cost of being in school is all the things that you would buy with that extra $24,000.

Now think about the time that being a student eats up. You spend many hours each week in class, doing homework assignments, preparing for tests, and so on. To do all these school activities, you must give up what would otherwise be time spent playing your favorite sport, time watching movies, and leisure time spent with your friends.

The opportunity cost of being in school is the best alternative things that you can't afford and that you don't have the time to enjoy. You might put a dollar value on this cost but the cost is the goods and services and time that you give up, not dollars.

The opportunity cost of being in school includes forgone earnings.

Benefit: What You Gain

The **benefit** from something is the gain or pleasure that it brings, measured by what you are *willing to give up* to get it. Benefit is determined by personal *preferences*—by what a person likes and dislikes and the intensity of those feelings. If you get a huge kick out of Madden NFL, that video game brings you a large benefit. And if you have little interest in listening to Yo Yo Ma playing a Vivaldi cello concerto, that activity brings you a small benefit.

Some benefits are large and easy to identify, such as the benefit that you get from being in school. A big piece of that benefit is the goods and services that you will be able to enjoy with the boost to your earning power when you graduate. Some benefits are small, such as the benefit you receive from a slice of pizza.

Economists measure benefit as the most that a person is *willing to give up* to get something. You are willing to give up a lot for something that brings a large benefit. For example, because being in school brings a large benefit, you're *willing to give up* a lot of time and goods and services to get that benefit. But you're willing to give up very little for something that brings a small benefit. For example, you might be willing to give up one iTunes download to get a slice of pizza.

Benefit
The benefit from something is the gain or pleasure that it brings, measured by what you are *willing to give up* to get it.

Rational Choice

A basic idea of economics is that in making choices, people act rationally. A **rational choice** is one that uses the available resources to best achieve the objective of the person making the choice.

But how do people choose rationally? The answer is by comparing the *benefits* and *costs* of the alternative choices and choosing the alternative that makes *net benefit*—benefit minus cost—as large as possible.

You have chosen to be a student. If that choice is rational, as economists assume, your benefit from being in school exceeds the cost, so your net benefit is maximized by being in school. For an outstanding baseball player, a high earning potential makes the opportunity cost of school higher than the benefit from school, so for that person, net benefit is maximized by choosing full-time sport. (*Eye on the Benefit and Cost of School* on p. 12 explores these examples more closely.)

The benefit from a choice is determined by the preferences of the person making the choice, so two people can make different rational choices even if they face the same cost. For example, you might like chocolate ice cream more than vanilla ice cream, but your friend prefers vanilla. So it is rational for you to choose chocolate and for your friend to choose vanilla.

Rational choice
A choice that uses the available resources to best achieve the objective of the person making the choice.

A rational choice might turn out not to have been the best choice after the fact. For example, a farmer might decide to plant wheat rather than soybeans. Then, when the crop comes to market, the price of soybeans might be much higher than the price of wheat. The farmer's choice was rational when it was made, but subsequent events made it less profitable than the alternative choice.

All the rational choices we've just considered (school or not, chocolate or vanilla ice cream, soybeans or wheat) involve choosing between two things. One or the other is chosen. We call such choices *all-or-nothing* choices. Many choices are of this type, but most choices involve *how much* of an activity to do.

◼ How Much? Choosing at the Margin

You can allocate the next hour between studying and video chatting with your friends, but the choice is not all or nothing. You must decide how many minutes to allocate to each activity. To make this decision, you compare the benefit of a little bit more study time with its cost—you make your choice *at the margin*.

Other words for "margin" are "border" or "edge." You can think of a choice at the margin as one that adjusts the border or edge of a plan to determine the best course of action. Making a choice at the **margin** means comparing the relevant alternatives systematically and incrementally.

Marginal Cost

The opportunity cost of a one-unit increase in an activity is called **marginal cost**. The marginal cost of something is what you *must* give up to get *one additional* unit of it. Think about your marginal cost of going to the movies for a third time in a week. Your marginal cost of seeing the movie is what you must give up to see that one additional movie. It is *not* what you give up to see all three movies. The reason is that you've already given up something to see two movies, so you don't count that cost when making a decision to see the third movie.

The marginal cost of any activity increases as you do more of it. You know that going to the movies decreases your study time and lowers your grade. Suppose that seeing a second movie in a week lowers your grade by five percentage points. Seeing a third movie will lower your grade by more than five percentage points. Your marginal cost of moviegoing is increasing as you see more movies.

Marginal Benefit

The benefit of a one-unit increase in an activity is called **marginal benefit**. Marginal benefit is what you gain from having *one more* unit of something. But the marginal benefit from something is *measured* by what you *are willing* to give up to get that *one additional* unit of it.

A fundamental feature of marginal benefit is that it diminishes. Think about your marginal benefit from movies. If you've been studying hard and haven't seen a movie this week, your marginal benefit from seeing your next movie is large. But if you've been on a movie binge this week, you now want a break and your marginal benefit from seeing your next movie is small.

Because the marginal benefit from a movie decreases as you see more movies, you are willing to give up less to see one additional movie. For example, you know that going to the movies decreases your study time and lowers your grade. You pay for seeing a movie with a lower grade. You might be willing to give up ten percentage points to see your first movie in a week, but you won't be willing to take such a big hit on your grade to see a second movie in a week. Your willingness to pay to see a movie decreases as the number of movies increases.

Margin
A choice on the margin is a choice that is made by comparing *all* the relevant alternatives systematically and incrementally.

Marginal cost
The opportunity cost that arises from a one-unit increase in an activity. The marginal cost of something is what you *must* give up to get *one additional* unit of it.

Marginal benefit
The benefit that arises from a one-unit increase in an activity. The marginal benefit of something is *measured* by what you *are willing* to give up to get *one additional* unit of it.

Making a Rational Choice

So, will you go to the movies for that third time in a week? The answer is found by comparing marginal benefit and marginal cost.

If the marginal cost of the movie is less than the marginal benefit from it, seeing the third movie adds more to benefit than to cost. Your net benefit increases, so your rational choice is to see the third movie.

If the marginal cost of the movie exceeds the marginal benefit from it, seeing the third movie adds more to cost than to benefit. Your net benefit decreases, so your rational choice is to spend the evening studying.

When the marginal benefit from something equals its marginal cost, the choice is rational and it is not possible to make a better choice. Scarce resources are being used in the best possible way.

■ Choices Respond to Incentives

The choices we make depend on the incentives we face. An **incentive** is a reward or a penalty—a "carrot" or a "stick"—that encourages or discourages an action. We respond positively to "carrots" and negatively to "sticks." The carrots are marginal benefits; the sticks are marginal costs. A change in marginal benefit or a change in marginal cost changes the incentives that we face and leads us to change our actions.

Most students believe that the payoff from studying just before a test is greater than the payoff from studying a month before a test. In other words, as a test date approaches, the marginal benefit from studying increases and the incentive to study becomes stronger. For this reason, we observe an increase in study time and a decrease in leisure pursuits during the last few days before a test. And the more important the test, the greater is this effect.

A change in marginal cost also changes incentives. For example, suppose that last week, you found your course work easy and you scored 100 percent on your practice quizzes. You figured that the marginal cost of taking an evening off to enjoy a movie was low and that your grade on the next test would not suffer, so you headed to the Cineplex. But this week the going has gotten tough. You're just not getting it, and your practice test scores are low. If you take off even one evening this week, your grade on the next test will suffer. The marginal cost of seeing a movie is now high, so you decide to give the movies a miss.

A central idea of economics is that by observing *changes in incentives*, we can predict how *choices change*.

Incentive
A reward or a penalty—a "carrot" or a "stick"—that encourages or discourages an action.

Changes in marginal benefit and marginal cost change the incentive to study or to enjoy a movie.

EYE on the BENEFIT AND COST OF SCHOOL

Did You Make the Right Decision?

Your decision to be in school is an economic decision. You faced a tradeoff between school, a job, and leisure time. You compared benefits and costs, and you responded to incentives.

Did you make the right decision when you chose school over a full-time job? Or, if you have a full-time job and you're studying in what would be your leisure time, did you make the right choice? Does school provide a big enough benefit to justify its cost?

The Benefits of School

Being in school has many benefits for which people are willing to pay. They fall into two broad categories: present enjoyment and a higher future income.

You can easily make a list of all the fun things you do with your friends in school that would be harder to do if you didn't have these friends and opportunities for social interaction that school provides.

Putting a dollar value on the items in your list would be hard, but it is possible to put a dollar value, or rather an expected dollar value, on the other benefit—a higher future income.

A high-school graduate earns, on average, an annual income of $40,000 a year. A graduate with a bachelor's degree earns, on average, $76,000 a year.

So by being in school, you can expect (on average) to increase your annual earnings by $36,000 a year.

This number is likely to grow as the economy becomes more productive and prices and earnings rise.

The Costs of School

The opportunity cost of being in school is your best forgone alternative. It is all the things you would have been able to enjoy if you were not in school. An opportunity cost is goods and services and time that must be forgone. Putting a dollar value on opportunity cost for a full-time student includes

- Tuition
- Expenditure on books and other study aids
- Forgone earnings

For a student attending a state university in her or his home state, tuition is around $10,000 per year.

Books and other study aids cost around $1,000 per year.

Forgone earnings are the wage of a high-school graduate in a starter job, which is around $24,000 a year.

So the total cost of being in school is about $35,000 per year or $105,000 for a 3-year degree and $140,000 for a 4-year degree.

Net Benefit

The benefit of extra earnings alone brings in $36,000 a year or $360,000 in 10 years and $1,440,000 in a working life of 40 years.

But you are incurring the costs now while you won't enjoy the benefits until some time in the future. We need to lower the benefits to compare them properly with the costs. You'll learn how to do that later in your economics course. But even allowing for the fact that the costs are incurred now while the benefits are received in the future, the net benefit is big!

Is School Always Best?

At the age of 18, Clayton Kershaw was offered a baseball scholarship at Texas A & M. The scholarship wouldn't have covered all the costs of school, but it would have lowered them a long way below those that you face.

But Clayton had an alternative to school. He was considered the top high-schooler available entering the 2006 MLB Draft and he was offered a signing bonus by the Los Angeles Dodgers said to be $2.3 million.

Clayton turned down the baseball scholarship at Texas A & M and signed with the Dodgers.

As the starting pitcher, Clayton's value to the Dodgers is high and earned him a salary of $30 million in 2015.

Clayton Kershaw's opportunity cost of a college education vastly exceeded the benefit he could expect to get from it. So, like you, he made the right decision.

CHECKPOINT 1.2

MyEconLab Study Plan 1.2
Key Terms Quiz
Solutions Video

Explain the ideas that define the economic way of thinking.

Practice Problems

Every week, Kate plays tennis for two hours, and her grade on each math test is 70 percent. Last week, after playing for two hours, Kate considered playing for another hour. She decided to play for another hour and cut her study time by one hour. But last week, her math grade fell to 60 percent. Use this information to work Problems **1** to **4**.

1. What was Kate's opportunity cost of the third hour of tennis?
2. Given that Kate played the third hour, what can you conclude about her marginal benefit and marginal cost of the second hour of tennis?
3. Was Kate's decision to play the third hour of tennis rational?
4. Did Kate make her decision on the margin?

In the News

The *New York Times* reports that cruise lines have been slashing prices and cruise sales are up. It says this surge of interest tells us that despite the uncertain economic climate, people clearly need more fun in their lives and view their vacations as valuable and necessary.

1. In deciding whether to take a cruise, would you face a tradeoff?
2. How would you make a rational choice about taking a cruise?
3. What would be the marginal benefit from a cruise? What would be the marginal cost of a cruise?
4. Why would you expect a lower price to increase the number of people who decide to take a cruise?

Solutions to Practice Problems

1. Kate's opportunity cost of the third hour of tennis was the drop in her grade of ten percentage points.
2. The marginal benefit from the second hour of tennis must have exceeded the marginal cost of the second hour because Kate chose to play the third hour.
3. If marginal benefit exceeded marginal cost, Kate's decision was rational.
4. Kate made her decision on the margin because she compared the benefit and cost of one more hour (marginal benefit and marginal cost).

Solutions to In the News

1. You would face a tradeoff because you would have to forgo something else that you might otherwise do with your resources (time and budget).
2. You would make a rational choice by comparing the marginal benefit from a cruise and the marginal cost of taking one.
3. The marginal benefit from a cruise is the most you are willing to pay for one. The marginal cost is what you would have to pay to take a cruise.
4. With a lower price, more people will have a marginal benefit that exceeds the price and they will choose to take a cruise.

1.3   ECONOMICS AS A LIFE SKILL

Economics is a life skill. It is a decision-making toolkit and, as a social science, it is a platform on which you will build critical thinking skills that prepare you for your career and life.

■ Economics as a Decision Tool

Economics is useful. The economic way of thinking provides you with tools for making decisions in all aspects of your lives:

- Personal
- Business
- Government

Personal Decisions

Should you take a student loan? Should you get a weekend job? Should you rent an apartment or borrow and buy a condo? How should you allocate your time between study, working, volunteering, caring for others, and having fun?

Deciding the answers to these questions involves weighing a marginal benefit and a marginal cost. Although some of the numbers might be hard to pin down, you will make more solid decisions if you approach these questions with the tools of economics.

Business Decisions

Should Sony compete with Apple in the smartphone market? Should Texaco get more oil from the Gulf of Mexico or from Alaska? Should Marvel Studios produce Spider-Man 4, a sequel to Spider-Man 3?

Like personal economic questions, these business questions involve the evaluation of a marginal benefit and a marginal cost. So again, by approaching these questions with the tools of economics and by hiring economists as advisers, businesses can make better decisions.

Government Decisions

Should there be a special tax to penalize corporations that send jobs overseas? Should cheap foreign imports of furniture and textiles be limited? Should the farms that grow beets receive a subsidy?

These government policy questions call for decisions that involve the evaluation of a marginal benefit and a marginal cost and an investigation of the interactions of individuals and businesses. Yet again, by approaching these questions with the tools of economics, governments can make better decisions.

■ Economics as a Social Science

Economists try to understand and predict the effects of economic forces by using the *scientific method* first developed by physicists. The scientific method is a commonsense way of systematically checking what works and what doesn't work. It begins with a question about cause and effect arising from some observed facts. An economist might wonder why computers are getting cheaper and more computers are being used. Are computers getting cheaper because more people are buying them, or are more people buying computers because they are getting cheaper? Or is a third factor causing both the price fall and the quantity increase?

Economic Models

A scientist's second step is to build a model that provides a possible answer to the question of interest. All sciences use models. An **economic model** is a description of the economy or a part of the economy that includes only those features assumed necessary to explain the observed facts.

A model is like a map. If you want to know about valleys and mountains, you use a physical map; if you're studying nations, you use a political map; if you want to drive from *A* to *B* in an unfamiliar city, you use a street map; and if you're a city engineer, you use a map of the cables and conduit under the streets.

In economics, we use mathematical and graph-based models. The questions posed above about the price and quantity of computers bought are answered by a graph-based model called "demand and supply" that you will study in Chapter 4.

Check Predictions of Models Against Facts

A scientist's third step is to check the predictions of a proposed model against the facts. Physicists check whether their models correspond to the facts by doing experiments. For example, with a particle accelerator, a physicist can test a model of the structure of an atom.

Economists have a harder time than physicists, but they still approach the task in a scientific manner. To check predictions of a model against facts, economists use natural experiments, statistical investigations, and laboratory experiments.

A natural experiment is a situation that arises in the ordinary course of economic life in which the one factor of interest is different and other things are equal (or similar). For example, Canada has higher unemployment benefits than the United States, but the people in the two nations are similar. So to study the effect of unemployment benefits on the unemployment rate, economists might compare the United States with Canada.

A statistical investigation looks for a *correlation*—a tendency for the values of two variables to move together (either in the same direction or in opposite directions) in a predictable and related way. For example, cigarette smoking and lung cancer are correlated. Sometimes a correlation shows a causal influence of one variable on the other. Smoking causes lung cancer. But sometimes the direction of causation is hard to determine.

A laboratory experiment puts people (often students) in a decision-making situation and varies the influence of one factor at a time to discover how they respond to changed incentives. Some economists (neuroeconomists) are now studying what happens inside the brain of a decisionmaker.

Disagreement: Normative versus Positive

Economists sometimes disagree. Some disagreements can be settled by checking facts, but others cannot.

Disagreements that can't be settled by facts are *normative*—disagreements about what *should be*. These disagreements turn on subjective values and cannot be tested. The statement "We *should* burn less coal" is normative. You may agree or disagree with it, but you can't test it. It doesn't assert a fact that can be checked. Economists as social scientists try to steer clear of normative statements.

Disagreements that *can* be settled by facts are *positive*—disagreements about *what is*. These disagreements can be settled by careful observation of facts. "Burning coal raises the temperature of the planet" is a positive statement. It can be tested. Sometimes the facts are hard to get and sometimes they are hard to interpret, so disagreement persists. It is an ongoing feature of a healthy science.

Economic model
A description of the economy or a part of the economy that includes only those features assumed necessary to explain the observed facts.

■ Economics as an Aid to Critical Thinking

Throughout your career you will need to engage in *critical thinking*. And throughout your life, if you strive to approach personal and social issues as a critical thinker, you will make better decisions and be a better friend, neighbor, and citizen.

What is Critical Thinking?

Critical thinking is thinking that is logical and fact-based. It is thinking that

- begins with a question
- clarifies the question
- thinks with an open mind about how to answer the question
- identifies potential answers
- seeks the relevant facts to check the potential answers
- ends with a well-reasoned answer

Does this sequence of critical thinking activities seem familiar? It does if you have just read the previous page. You will recognize that critical thinking is just another name for approaching an issue like a scientist. Economic science begins with a question about some economic event or activity; uses the economic way of thinking to clarify the question, think about how to answer it, identify possible answers, and check them against the facts; and arrives at a well-reasoned answer.

As a student, you will have lots of opportunities to practice critical thinking. It will be a feature of almost all your courses, and it will be a major feature of your economics course. What you learn in this course and the critical thinking and economic thinking skills that you develop will enrich your career and your life.

Learning-by-Doing

A central theme of this textbook is that the best way to learn economics is to do it—*learning-by-doing*. The mantra is "work the problem" and "draw the graph." This same message applies to critical thinking. The best way to become skilled at critical thinking is to do it.

To get you started, look at the example of a critical thinking question in *Eye on Your Life* on p. 17. The question is a simple one about facts. It doesn't have a cause-and-effect dimension, but it illustrates the central role that facts play. Facts always trump guesses and beliefs. The question also suggests another valuable activity: cooperating and working with others. Teamwork enables data to be shared and brainstorming a question often triggers better ideas about other possible answers that should be checked.

Throughout this textbook, we present you with a wide variety of critical thinking opportunities. Some arise from your life experiences in *Eye on Your Life* boxes like the one in this chapter. Others arise from economic events and issues in the news. News clips and the critical thinking questions that they raise appear in every chapter.

Also, every chapter starts with a question that is answered with a critical thinking box later in the chapter. The question on the opening page of this chapter and the *Eye on the Benefit and Cost of School* box on p. 12 are examples. Studying these examples and using what you learn to answer the economic questions that arise in your life and in the news will strengthen your critical thinking. You will emerge from your economics course with not only the ability to think like an economist but also more generally to be a critical thinker.

EYE on YOUR LIFE
Your Time Allocation

Your time is a scarce resource and how you allocate it impacts the quality of your life. Your physical fitness depends on how much time you allocate to sports and exercise, and your grade depends on the amount of time you allocate to studying.

Sleeping, personal care, eating and drinking, and traveling take a large chunk of your time, but you have choices about how much time to allocate to each of these activities. You also have choices about how much time to spend working for an income, enjoying sports and other leisure activities, and on educational activities (attending class, doing assignments, and studying).

Do you know the number of hours per day that you allocate to sleeping, personal care, eating and drinking, traveling, working, sports and leisure, and educational activities?

Here is a critical thinking question for you: Who works harder, you or the average student?

This question is one of fact, but answering requires agreement on what we mean by "works harder" and requires some data (the facts).

Let's agree that we will measure how hard a person works as the average number of hours per weekday spent working and on educational activities.

Next, we need the facts about time allocation—data about your time use and the time use of an average student.

The table above has eight activities and two columns for data. Complete the first column based on your current best guess about your time use.

Now keep a calendar for a normal week, and calculate your actual average hours for each activity. At the end of the week, complete the second column of the table.

How do your actual numbers compare with your guesses? Are there any surprises?

Now we need to compare your time use with that of the average student. The Bureau of Labor Statistics has conducted a survey to get the facts and the figure below shows what it found.

So, what is the answer? Are there any more surprises? Who works more hours, you or the average student?

Does the answer make you want to change your time allocation?

Your Time Use		
Activity	**Guess**	**Actual average**
	(hours per day)	
Sleeping		
Personal care		
Eating and drinking		
Traveling		
Working and related activities		
Leisure and sports		
Educational activities		
Other		
Total	**24.0**	**24.0**

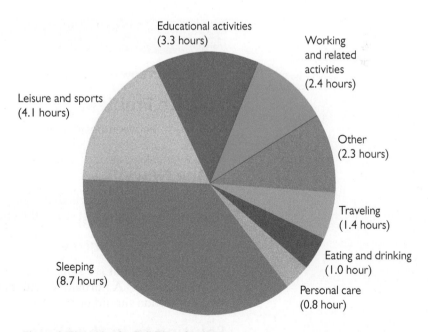

Figure 1 Time Use for Full-Time Students

SOURCE OF DATA: Bureau of Labor Statistics, American Time Use Survey, average on non-holiday weekdays for full-time university and college students 2010–2014.

EYE on the PAST
Adam Smith and the Birth of Economics as a Social Science

Many people had written about economics before Adam Smith did, but he made economics a social science.

Born in 1723 in Scotland, Smith became a full professor at 28 and published his masterpiece, *An Inquiry into the Nature and Causes of the Wealth of Nations,* in 1776.

Adam Smith asked: Why are some nations wealthy while others are poor? His answer: Through the division of labor and free markets, nations become wealthy. To illustrate his argument, he used the example of a pin factory. He guessed that one person, using the hand tools available in the 1770s, might make 20 pins a day. Yet,

he observed, by using the same hand tools but breaking the process into a number of individually small tasks in which people specialize—by the division of labor—ten people could make a staggering 48,000 pins a day.

But a large market is needed to support the division of labor: One factory employing ten workers would need to sell more than 15 million pins a year to stay in business!

Smith saw free competitive markets as a source of wealth. The self-interested pursuit of profit, led by an invisible hand, resulted in resources being used in ways that created the greatest possible value and wealth.

 ## CHECKPOINT 1.3

Explain how economics is useful as a life skill.

Practice Problem

Distinguish between positive and normative statements and provide an example of each.

In the News

The *New York Times* reports that China will end its one-child policy. How would an economist study the effect of this policy change?

Solution to Practice Problem

A positive statement is a statement of fact that can be checked, such as "grocery prices are rising." A normative statement is an opinion that cannot be checked, such as "tuition should be based on family income."

Solution to In the News

As a social scientist, an economist would construct a population model. As a policy adviser, an economist would evaluate the benefits and costs of the change.

CHAPTER SUMMARY

Key Points

1. **Define economics and explain the kinds of questions that economists try to answer.**

   - Economics is the social science that studies the choices that we make as we cope with scarcity and the incentives that influence and reconcile our choices.
   - Microeconomics is the study of individual choices and interactions, and macroeconomics is the study of the national economy and global economy.
   - The first big question of economics is: How do the choices that people make end up determining *what, how,* and *for whom* goods and services are produced?
   - The second big question is: When do choices made in the pursuit of *self-interest* also promote the *social interest*?

2. **Explain the ideas that define the economic way of thinking.**

   - Six ideas define the economic way of thinking:
     1. A choice is a *tradeoff*.
     2. *Cost* is what you *must* give up to get something.
     3. *Benefit* is what you gain when you get something (measured by what you *are willing to* give up to get it).
     4. People make *rational* choices by comparing benefits and costs.
     5. A "how much" choice is made on the *margin* by comparing *marginal benefit* and *marginal cost*.
     6. Choices respond to *incentives*.

3. **Explain how economics is useful as a life skill.**

   - Economics is a tool for personal, business, and government decisions.
   - Economists use the *scientific method* to try to understand how the economic world works. They create economic models and test them using natural experiments, statistical investigations, and laboratory experiments.
   - Economics and the economic way of thinking are foundations on which to build critical thinking skills.

Key Terms

MyEconLab Key Terms Quiz

Benefit, 9	Margin, 10	Scarcity, 2
Economic model, 15	Marginal benefit, 10	Self-interest, 4
Economics, 2	Marginal cost, 10	Social interest, 4
Goods and services, 3	Microeconomics, 2	Tradeoff, 8
Incentive, 11	Opportunity cost, 8	
Macroeconomics, 3	Rational choice, 9	

CHAPTER CHECKPOINT

Study Plan Problems and Applications

1. Provide three examples of scarcity that illustrate why even the 1,826 billion-aires in the world face scarcity.

2. Label each entry in List 1 as dealing with a microeconomic topic or a macroeconomic topic. Explain your answer.

Use the following information to work Problems **3** to **6**.

Jurassic World had world-wide box office receipts of $1.66 billion. The movie's production budget was $150 million with additional marketing costs. A successful movie brings pleasure to millions, creates work for thousands, and makes a few people rich.

3. What contribution does a movie like *Jurassic World* make to coping with scarcity? When you buy a movie ticket, are you buying a good or a service?

4. Who decides whether a movie is going to be a blockbuster? How do you think the creation of a blockbuster movie influences *what, how*, and *for whom* goods and services are produced?

5. What are some of the components of marginal cost and marginal benefit that the producer of a movie faces?

6. Suppose that Chris Pratt had been offered a part in another movie and that to hire him for *Jurassic World*, the producer had to double Chris Pratt's pay. What incentives would have changed? How might the changed incentives have changed the choices that people made?

7. What is the social interest? Distinguish it from self-interest. In your answer give an example of self-interest and an example of social interest.

8. Pam, Pru, and Pat are deciding how they will celebrate the New Year. Pam prefers to take a cruise, is happy to go to Hawaii, but does not want to go skiing. Pru prefers to go skiing, is happy to go to Hawaii, but does not want to take a cruise. Pat prefers to go to Hawaii or to take a cruise but does not want to go skiing. Their decision is to go to Hawaii. Is this decision rational? What is the opportunity cost of the trip to Hawaii for each of them? What is the benefit that each gets?

9. Label each of the entries in List 2 as a positive or a normative statement.

Use the following information to work Problems **10** to **12**.

REI is paying its employees to take Black Friday, Thanksgiving off
REI, the outdoor gear and apparel retailer, is paying employees to celebrate Thanksgiving 2015 by spending Black Friday outdoors with their families.
Source: *Sustainable Brands*, October 28, 2015

10. With Black Friday off with full pay, explain what is free and what is scarce.

11. What is REI's incentive to give its workers Black Friday off? Was REI's decision made in self-interest or in the social interest? Explain your answer.

12. Do you think that REI workers will shop or spend the day with family? Explain your answer.

13. Read *Eye on the Benefit and Cost of School* on p. 12 and explain why both you and Clayton Kershaw made the right decision.

LIST 1

- Motor vehicle production in China is growing by 10 percent a year.
- Coffee prices skyrocket.
- Globalization has reduced African poverty.
- The government must cut its budget deficit.
- Apple sells 20 million iPhone 6 smartphones a month.

LIST 2

- Low-income people pay too much for housing.
- The number of U.S. farms has decreased over the past 50 years.
- Toyota expands parts production in the United States.
- Imports from China are swamping U.S. department stores.
- The rural population in the United States is declining.

Instructor Assignable Problems and Applications

MyEconLab Homework, Quiz, or Test if assigned by instructor

1. Which of the following items are components of the opportunity cost of being a full-time college student who lives at home? The things that the student would have bought with

   - A higher income
   - Expenditure on tuition
   - A subscription to the *Rolling Stone* magazine
   - The income the student will earn after graduating

2. Think about the following news items and label each as involving a *what, how,* or *for whom* question:

   - Today, most stores use computers to keep their inventory records, whereas 20 years ago most stores used paper records.
   - Healthcare professionals and drug companies recommend that Medicaid drug rebates be made available to everyone in need.
   - An increase in the gas tax pays for low-cost public transit.

3. The headlines in List 1 appeared in *The Wall Street Journal*. Classify each headline as a signal that the news article is about a microeconomic topic or a macroeconomic topic. Explain your answers.

4. Your school decides to increase the intake of new students next year. To make its decision, what economic concepts would it have considered? Would the school have used the "economic way of thinking" in reaching its decision? Would the school have made its decision on the margin?

5. Provide examples of (a) a monetary incentive and (b) a non-monetary incentive, a carrot and a stick of each, that governments use to influence behavior.

6. Think about each of the items in List 2 and explain how they affect incentives and might change the choices that people make.

7. Does the decision to make a blockbuster movie mean that some other more desirable activities get fewer resources than they deserve? Is your answer positive or normative? Explain your answer.

8. Provide two examples of economics being used as a tool by (a) a student, (b) a business, and (c) a government. Classify your examples as dealing with microeconomic topics and macroeconomic topics.

LIST 1

- Job Gains Calm Slump Worries
- Washington Post's Profit Falls
- Overcapacity, Fuel Costs Hit Shipping
- U.S. Budget Deficit Expands

LIST 2

- A hurricane hits Central Florida.
- The World Series begins tonight, but a storm warning is in effect for the area around the stadium.
- The price of a personal computer falls to $50.
- Unrest in the Middle East sends the price of gas to $5 a gallon.

Use the following news clip to work Problems **9** to **12**.

Obama unveils major climate change policy
Obama's Clean Power Plan, which will set federal limits on carbon emissions from coal-fired power plants, will cost $8.4 billion and reap benefits of more than $34 billion. Opponents of the plan say it will drive up the cost of electricity for millions of Americans.

Source: CNN, August 3, 2015

9. What are the more than $34 billion of benefits from using less coal to produce electricity? Who receives these benefits: the users of electricity or the owners of power plants, or both the users and the owners?

10. What are the $8.4 billion of costs arising from using less coal to produce electricity? Who bears these costs: the users of electricity or the owners of power plants, or both the users and the owners?

11. Explain why someone might oppose the Clean Power Plan when its benefits exceed its costs.

12. Explain whether the Clean Power Plan has an opportunity cost.

Multiple Choice Quiz

1. Which of the following describes the reason why scarcity exists?

    A. Governments make bad economic decisions.
    B. The gap between the rich and the poor is too wide.
    C. Wants exceed the resources available to satisfy them.
    D. There is too much unemployment.

2. Which of the following defines economics?
Economics is the social science that studies _____.

    A. the best way of eliminating scarcity
    B. the choices made to cope with scarcity, how incentives influence those choices, and how the choices are coordinated
    C. how money is created and used
    D. the inevitable conflict between self-interest and the social interest

3. Of the three big questions, *what, how,* and *for whom,* which of the following is an example of a *how* question?

    A. Why do doctors and lawyers earn high incomes?
    B. Why don't we produce more small cars and fewer gas guzzlers?
    C. Why do we use machines rather than migrant workers to pick grapes?
    D. Why do college football coaches earn more than professors?

4. Which of the following is not a key idea in the economic way of thinking?

    A. People make rational choices by comparing costs and benefits.
    B. Poor people are discriminated against and should be treated more fairly.
    C. A rational choice is made at the margin.
    D. Choices respond to incentives.

5. A rational choice is _____.

    A. the best thing you must forgo to get something
    B. what you are willing to forgo to get something
    C. made by comparing marginal benefit and marginal cost
    D. the best for society

6. Which of the following best illustrates your marginal benefit from studying?

    A. The knowledge you gain from studying two hours a night for a month
    B. The best things forgone by studying two hours a night for a month
    C. What you are willing to give up to study for one additional hour
    D. What you must give up to be able to study for one additional hour

7. The scientific method uses models to _____.

    A. clarify normative disagreements
    B. avoid the need to study real questions
    C. replicate all the features of the real world
    D. focus on those features of reality assumed relevant for understanding a cause-and-effect relationship

8. Which of the following is a positive statement?

    A. We should stop using corn to make ethanol because it is raising the cost of food.
    B. You will get the most out of college life if you play a sport once a week.
    C. Competition among wireless service providers across the borders of Canada, Mexico, and the United States has driven roaming rates down.
    D. Bill Gates ought to spend more helping to eradicate malaria in Africa

APPENDIX: MAKING AND USING GRAPHS

When you have completed your study of this appendix, you will be able to

1 Interpret graphs that display data.

2 Interpret the graphs used in economic models.

3 Define and calculate slope.

4 Graph relationships among more than two variables.

Basic Idea

A graph represents a quantity as a distance and enables us to visualize the relationship between two variables. To make a graph, we set two lines called *axes* perpendicular to each other, like those in Figure A1.1. The vertical line is called the *y*-axis, and the horizontal line is called the *x*-axis. The common zero point is called the *origin*. In Figure A1.1, the *x*-axis measures temperature in degrees Fahrenheit. A movement to the right shows an increase in temperature, and a movement to the left shows a decrease in temperature. The *y*-axis represents ice cream consumption, measured in gallons per day.

To make a graph, we need a value of the variable on the *x*-axis and a corresponding value of the variable on the *y*-axis. For example, if the temperature is 40°F, ice cream consumption is 5 gallons a day at point *A* in Figure A1.1. If the temperature is 80°F, ice cream consumption is 20 gallons a day at point *B* in Figure A1.1. Graphs like that in Figure A1.1 can be used to show any type of quantitative data on two variables.

FIGURE A1.1

Making a Graph   MyEconLab Animation

All graphs have axes that measure quantities as distances.

❶ The horizontal axis (*x*-axis) measures temperature in degrees Fahrenheit. A movement to the right shows an increase in temperature.

❷ The vertical axis (*y*-axis) measures ice cream consumption in gallons per day. A movement upward shows an increase in ice cream consumption.

❸ Point *A* shows that 5 gallons of ice cream are consumed on a day when the temperature is 40°F.

❹ Point *B* shows that 20 gallons of ice cream are consumed on a day when the temperature is 80°F.

■ Interpreting Data Graphs

Scatter diagram
A graph of the value of one variable against the value of another variable.

A **scatter diagram** is a graph of the value of one variable against the value of another variable. It is used to reveal whether a relationship exists between two variables and to describe the relationship. Figure A1.2 shows two examples.

Figure A1.2(a) shows the relationship between expenditure and income. Each point shows expenditure per person and income per person in the United States in a given year from 2000 to 2015. The points are "scattered" within the graph. The label on each point shows its year. The point marked 10 shows that in 2010, income per person was $36,183 and expenditure per person was $32,758. This scatter diagram reveals that as income increases, expenditure also increases.

Figure A1.2(b) shows the relationship during the 1990s between the percentage of Americans who own a cell phone and the average monthly cell-phone bill. This scatter diagram reveals that as the cost of using a cell phone falls, the number of cell-phone subscribers increases.

Time-series graph
A graph that measures time on the *x*-axis and the variable or variables in which we are interested on the *y*-axis.

A **time-series graph** measures time (for example, months or years) on the *x*-axis and the variable or variables in which we are interested on the *y*-axis. Figure A1.2(c) shows an example. In this graph, time (on the *x*-axis) is measured in years, which run from 1980 to 2016. The variable that we are interested in is the price of coffee, and it is measured on the *y*-axis.

A time-series graph conveys an enormous amount of information quickly and easily, as this example illustrates. It shows when the value is

1. High or low. When the line is a long way from the *x*-axis, the price is high, as it was in 1986. When the line is close to the *x*-axis, the price is low, as it was in 2001.

2. Rising or falling. When the line slopes upward, as in 2006, the price is rising. When the line slopes downward, as in 1997, the price is falling.

3. Rising or falling quickly or slowly. If the line is steep, then the price is rising or falling quickly. If the line is not steep, the price is rising or falling slowly. For example, the price rose quickly in 2006 and slowly in 2014. The price fell quickly in 1987 and slowly in 1996.

Trend
A general tendency for the value of a variable to rise or fall over time.

A time-series graph also reveals whether the variable has a trend. A **trend** is a general tendency for the value of a variable to rise or fall over time. You can see that the price of coffee had a general tendency to fall from 1980 to late in 2000. That is, although the price rose and fell, it had a general tendency to fall.

With a time-series graph, we can compare different periods quickly. Figure A1.2(c) shows that the 2000s were different from the 1990s, which in turn were different from the 1980s. The price of coffee started the 1980s high and then fell for a number of years. During the 1990s, the price was on a roller coaster. And during the 2000s, the price rose steadily through 2014. This graph conveys a wealth of information about the price of coffee, and it does so in much less space than we have used to describe only some of its features.

Cross-section graph
A graph that shows the values of an economic variable for different groups in a population at a point in time.

A **cross-section graph** shows the values of an economic variable for different groups in a population at a point in time. Figure A1.2(d) is an example of a cross-section graph. It shows the percentage of people who participate in selected sports activities in the United States. This graph uses bars rather than dots and lines, and the length of each bar indicates the participation rate. Figure A1.2(d) enables you to compare the participation rates in these ten sporting activities, and you can do so much more quickly and clearly than by looking at a list of numbers.

■ **FIGURE A1.2**

Data Graphs

MyEconLab Animation

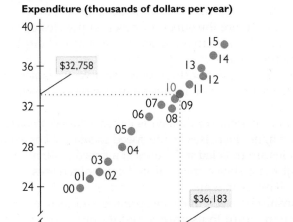

(a) Scatter Diagram: Expenditure and income

(b) Scatter Diagram: Subscribers and cost

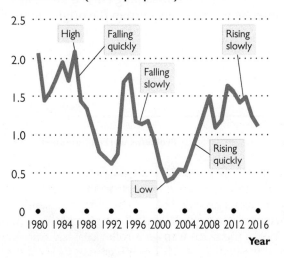

(c) Time Series: The price of coffee

(d) Cross Section: Participation in selected sports activities

A scatter diagram reveals the relationship between two variables. In part (a), as income increases, expenditure almost always increases. In part (b), as the monthly cell-phone bill falls, the percentage of people who own a cell phone increases.

A time-series graph plots the value of a variable on the y-axis against time on the x-axis. Part (c) plots the price of coffee each

year from 1980 to 2016. The graph shows when the price of coffee was high and low, when it increased and decreased, and when it changed quickly and changed slowly.

A cross-section graph shows the value of a variable across the members of a population. Part (d) shows the participation rate in the United States in each of ten sporting activities.

■ Interpreting Graphs Used in Economic Models

We use graphs to show the relationships among the variables in an economic model. An *economic model* is a simplified description of the economy or of a component of the economy such as a business or a household. It consists of statements about economic behavior that can be expressed as equations or as curves in a graph. Economists use models to explore the effects of different policies or other influences on the economy in ways similar to those used to test model airplanes in wind tunnels and models of the climate.

Figure A1.3 shows graphs of the relationships between two variables that move in the same direction. Such a relationship is called a **positive relationship** or **direct relationship**.

Positive relationship or **direct relationship**
A relationship between two variables that move in the same direction.

Linear relationship
A relationship that graphs as a straight line.

Part (a) shows a straight-line relationship, which is called a **linear relationship**. The distance traveled in 5 hours increases as the speed increases. For example, point *A* shows that 200 miles are traveled in 5 hours at a speed of 40 miles an hour. And point *B* shows that the distance traveled in 5 hours increases to 300 miles if the speed increases to 60 miles an hour.

Part (b) shows the relationship between distance sprinted and recovery time (the time it takes the heart rate to return to its normal resting rate). An upward-sloping curved line that starts out quite flat but then becomes steeper as we move along the curve away from the origin describes this relationship. The curve slopes upward and becomes steeper because the extra recovery time needed from sprinting another 100 yards increases. It takes 5 minutes to recover from sprinting 100 yards but 15 minutes to recover from sprinting 200 yards.

Part (c) shows the relationship between the number of problems worked by a student and the amount of study time. An upward-sloping curved line that starts out quite steep and becomes flatter as we move away from the origin shows this

---

FIGURE A1.3

Positive (Direct) Relationships MyEconLab Animation

(a) Positive linear relationship

(b) Positive becoming steeper

(c) Positive becoming less steep

Part (a) shows that as speed increases, the distance traveled in a given number of hours increases along a straight line.

Part (b) shows that as the distance sprinted increases, recovery time increases along a curve that becomes steeper.

Part (c) shows that as study time increases, the number of problems worked increases along a curve that becomes less steep.

relationship. Study time becomes less effective as you increase the hours worked and become more tired.

Figure A1.4 shows relationships between two variables that move in opposite directions. Such a relationship is called a **negative relationship** or **inverse relationship**.

Part (a) shows the relationship between the number of hours spent playing squash and the number of hours spent playing tennis when the total number of hours available is five. One extra hour spent playing tennis means one hour less playing squash and vice versa. This relationship is negative and linear.

Part (b) shows the relationship between the cost per mile traveled and the length of a journey. The longer the journey, the lower is the cost per mile. But as the journey length increases, the fall in the cost per mile becomes smaller. This feature of the relationship is shown by the fact that the curve slopes downward, starting out steep at a short journey length and then becoming flatter as the journey length increases. This relationship arises because some of the costs, such as auto insurance, are fixed, and as the journey length increases, the fixed costs are spread over more miles.

Part (c) shows the relationship between the amount of leisure time and the number of problems worked by a student. Increasing leisure time produces an increasingly large reduction in the number of problems worked. This relationship is a negative one that starts out with a gentle slope at a small number of leisure hours and becomes steeper as the number of leisure hours increases. This relationship is a different view of the idea shown in Figure A1.3(c).

Many relationships in economic models have a maximum or a minimum. For example, firms try to make the largest possible profit and to produce at the lowest possible cost. Figure A1.5 shows relationships that have a maximum or a minimum.

Negative relationship or **inverse relationship**
A relationship between two variables that move in opposite directions.

FIGURE A1.4

Negative (Inverse) Relationships   MyEconLab Animation

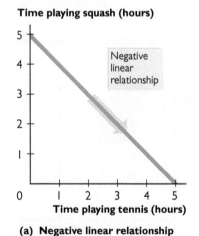

(a) Negative linear relationship

Part (a) shows that as the time playing tennis increases, the time playing squash decreases along a straight line.

(b) Negative becoming less steep

Part (b) shows that as the journey length increases, the cost of the trip falls along a curve that becomes less steep.

(c) Negative becoming steeper

Part (c) shows that as leisure time increases, the number of problems worked decreases along a curve that becomes steeper.

▪ **FIGURE A1.5**

Maximum and Minimum Points

MyEconLab Animation

In part (a), as the rainfall increases, the curve ❶ slopes upward as the yield per acre rises, ❷ is flat at point A, the maximum yield, and then ❸ slopes downward as the yield per acre falls.

In part (b), as the speed increases, the curve ❶ slopes downward as the cost per mile falls, ❷ is flat at the minimum point B, and then ❸ slopes upward as the cost per mile rises.

(a) Relationship with a maximum

(b) Relationship with a minimum

Part (a) shows a relationship that starts out sloping upward, reaches a maximum, and then slopes downward. Part (b) shows a relationship that begins sloping downward, falls to a minimum, and then slopes upward.

Finally, there are many situations in which, no matter what happens to the value of one variable, the other variable remains constant. Sometimes we want to show two variables that are unrelated in a graph. Figure A1.6 shows two graphs in which the variables are unrelated.

▪ **FIGURE A1.6**

Variables That Are Unrelated

MyEconLab Animation

In part (a), as the price of bananas increases, the student's grade in economics remains at 75 percent. These variables are unrelated, and the curve is horizontal.

In part (b), the vineyards of France produce 3 billion gallons of wine no matter what the rainfall is in California. These variables are unrelated, and the curve is vertical.

(a) Unrelated: y constant

(b) Unrelated: x constant

■ The Slope of a Relationship

We can measure the influence of one variable on another by the slope of the relationship. The **slope** of a relationship is the change in the value of the variable measured on the y-axis divided by the change in the value of the variable measured on the x-axis. We use the Greek letter Δ (delta) to represent "change in." So Δy means the change in the value of y, and Δx means the change in the value of x. The slope of the relationship is

$$\Delta y \div \Delta x.$$

If a large change in y is associated with a small change in x, the slope is large and the curve is steep. If a small change in y is associated with a large change in x, the slope is small and the curve is flat.

Figure A1.7 shows you how to calculate slope. The slope of a straight line is the same regardless of where on the line you calculate it—the slope is constant. In part (a), when x increases from 2 to 6, y increases from 3 to 6. The change in x is 4—that is, Δx is 4. The change in y is 3—that is, Δy is 3. The slope of that line is 3/4. In part (b), when x increases from 2 to 6, y *decreases* from 6 to 3. The change in y is *minus* 3—that is, Δy is -3 The change in x is plus 4—that is, Δx is 4. The slope of the curve is $-3/4$.

In part (c), we calculate the slope at a point on a curve. To do so, place a ruler on the graph so that it touches point A and no other point on the curve, then draw a straight line along the edge of the ruler. The slope of this straight line is the slope of the curve at point A. This slope is 3/4.

Slope
The change in the value of the variable measured on the y-axis divided by the change in the value of the variable measured on the x-axis.

FIGURE A1.7

Calculating Slope

MyEconLab Animation

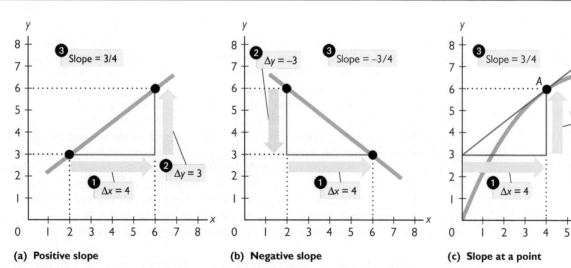

(a) Positive slope

(b) Negative slope

(c) Slope at a point

In part (a), ❶ when Δx is 4, ❷ Δy is 3, so ❸ the slope ($\Delta y \div \Delta x$) is 3/4.

In part (b), ❶ when Δx is 4, ❷ Δy is -3, so ❸ the slope ($\Delta y \div \Delta x$) is $-3/4$.

In part (c), the slope of the curve at point A equals the slope of the red line. ❶ When Δx is 4, ❷ Δy is 3, so ❸ the slope ($\Delta y \div \Delta x$) is 3/4.

■ Relationships Among More Than Two Variables

All the graphs that you have studied so far plot the relationship between two variables as a point formed by the x and y values. But most of the relationships in economics involve relationships among many variables, not just two. For example, the amount of ice cream consumed depends on the price of ice cream and the temperature. If ice cream is expensive and the temperature is low, people eat much less ice cream than when ice cream is inexpensive and the temperature is high. For any given price of ice cream, the quantity consumed varies with the temperature; and for any given temperature, the quantity of ice cream consumed varies with its price.

Figure A1.8 shows a relationship among three variables. The table shows the number of gallons of ice cream consumed per day at various temperatures and ice cream prices. How can we graph these numbers?

To graph a relationship that involves more than two variables, we use the *ceteris paribus* assumption.

Ceteris Paribus

The Latin phrase *ceteris paribus* means "other things remaining the same." Every laboratory experiment is an attempt to create *ceteris paribus* and isolate the relationship of interest. We use the same method to make a graph.

Figure A1.8(a) shows an example. This graph shows what happens to the quantity of ice cream consumed when the price of ice cream varies while the temperature remains constant. The curve labeled 90°F shows the relationship between ice cream consumption and the price of ice cream if the temperature is 90°F. The numbers used to plot that curve are those in the first and fifth columns of the table in Figure A1.8. For example, if the temperature is 90°F, 10 gallons of ice cream are consumed when the price is $3.25 a scoop.

We can also show the relationship between ice cream consumption and temperature while the price of ice cream remains constant, as shown in Figure A1.8(b). The curve labeled $3.25 shows how the consumption of ice cream varies with the temperature when the price of ice cream is $3.25 a scoop. The numbers used to plot that curve are those in the sixth row of the table in Figure A1.8. For example, at $3.25 a scoop, 10 gallons of ice cream are consumed when the temperature is 90°F.

Figure A1.8(c) shows the effect of a change in temperature on the relationship between the quantity of ice cream consumed and the price of ice cream. The blue curve labeled 90°F is the same as the curve in Figure A1.8(a). It is the relationship between the price of ice cream and the quantity consumed on a hot day. The red curve labeled 70°F shows the relationship between the price of ice cream and the quantity consumed on a cooler day when the temperature is 70°F.

On each curve in Figure A1.8(c), "other things remain the same" as the price of ice cream and the quantity consumed change. When other things don't remain the same and the termperature changes, the relationship between the price of ice cream and the quantity consumed changes and the curve shifts. You will encounter this type of shifting relationship at many points in your economics course.

With what you've learned about graphs in this Appendix, you can move forward with your study of economics. There are no graphs in this textbook that are more complicated than the ones you've studied here.

FIGURE A1.8

Graphing a Relationship Among Three Variables

Price	Ice cream consumption (gallons per day)			
(dollars per scoop)	30°F	50°F	70°F	90°F
2.00	12	18	25	50
2.25	10	12	18	37
2.50	7	10	13	27
2.75	5	7	10	20
3.00	3	5	7	14
3.25	2	3	5	**10**
3.50	1	2	3	6

(a) Price and consumption at a given temperature

(b) Temperature and consumption of ice cream at a given price

(c) A change in temperature shifts the curve

The table shows the quantity of ice cream consumed at different prices and different temperatures. For example, if the price is $3.25 a scoop and the temperature is 90°F, 10 gallons of ice cream are consumed. This set of values is highlighted in the table and in parts (a) and (b).

Part (a) shows the relationship between the price and consumption when the temperature is 90°F. The negative slope means that a higher price brings lower consumption.

Part (b) shows the relationship between the temperature and consumption when price is

$3.25 a scoop. The positive slope means that a higher temperature brings greater consumption

Part (c) shows the change in the relationship between price and consumption when the temperature falls from 90°F to 70°F.

MyEconLab Chapter 1 Study Plan

TABLE 1

	A	B	C	D
1	2004	767	33	139
2	2006	620	23	586
3	2008	385	13	1,033
4	2010	226	9	1,162
5	2012	211	11	1,392
6	2014	144	4	1,200

TABLE 2

x	0	1	2	3	4	5
y	32	31	28	23	16	7

TABLE 3

Price (dollars per ride)	Balloon rides (number per day)		
	50°F	70°F	90°F
5	32	50	40
10	27	40	32
15	18	32	27
20	10	27	18

MyEconLab Homework, Quiz, or Test if assigned by instructor

TABLE 4

x	0	1	2	3	4	5
y	0	1	4	9	16	25

TABLE 5

Price (dollars per cup)	Hot chocolate (cups per week)		
	50°F	70°F	90°F
2.00	40	30	20
2.50	30	20	10
3.00	20	10	0
3.50	10	0	0

APPENDIX CHECKPOINT

Study Plan Problems

The spreadsheet in Table 1 provides data on the U.S. economy: Column A is the year; the other columns are quantities sold in millions per year of compact discs (column B), music videos (column C), and singles downloads (column D). Use this spreadsheet to work Problems **1** and **2**.

1. Draw a scatter diagram to show the relationship between the quantities sold of compact discs and music videos. Describe the relationship.

2. Draw a time-series graph of the quantity of compact discs sold. Say in which year or years the quantity sold (a) was highest, (b) was lowest, (c) increased the most, and (d) decreased the most. If the data show a trend, describe it.

3. Is the relationship between x and y in Table 2 positive or negative? Calculate the slope of the relationship when x equals 2 and when x equals 4. How does the slope change as the value of x increases?

4. Table 3 provides data on the price of a balloon ride, the temperature, and the number of rides a day. Draw graphs to show the relationship between
   • The price and the number of rides, when the temperature is 70°F.
   • The number of rides and the temperature, when the price is $15 a ride.

Instructor Assignable Problems

Use the information in Table 1 to work Problems **1** and **2**.

1. Draw a scatter diagram to show the relationship between quantities sold of music videos and singles downloads. Describe the relationship.

2. Draw a time-series graph of the quantity of music videos sold. Say in which year or years the quantity sold (a) was highest, (b) was lowest, (c) decreased the most, and (d) decreased the least. If the data show a trend, describe it.

Use the information in Table 4 on the relationship between two variables x and y to work Problems **3** and **4**.

3. Is the relationship between x and y in Table 4 positive or negative? Explain.

4. Calculate the slope of the relationship when x equals 2 and when x equals 4. How does the slope change as the value of x increases?

5. Table 5 provides data on the price of hot chocolate, the temperature, and the cups of hot chocolate bought. Draw graphs to show the relationship between
   • The price and cups of hot chocolate bought, when the temperature is constant.
   • The temperature and cups of hot chocolate bought, when the price is constant.

Key Terms

MyEconLab Key Terms Quiz

Cross-section graph, 24
Direct relationship, 26
Inverse relationship, 27
Linear relationship, 26
Negative relationship, 27
Positive relationship, 26
Scatter diagram, 24
Slope, 29
Time-series graph, 24
Trend, 24

Who makes the Dreamliner?

The U.S. and Global Economies

2

When you have completed your study of this chapter, you will be able to

1 Describe what, how, and for whom goods and services are produced in the United States.

2 Describe what, how, and for whom goods and services are produced in the global economy.

3 Explain the circular flow model of the U.S. economy and of the global economy.

MyEconLab Big Picture Video

33

2.1 WHAT, HOW, AND FOR WHOM?

Who makes the Dreamliner? Boeing, right? Not exactly right. You'll see in this chapter that 400 firms around the world produce components of this airliner.

Airplanes are one of the many millions of different goods and services produced in the United States today. To see some more, walk around a shopping mall and go inside some of the shops and check the labels to see where things are made. Some are made in the United States but many, perhaps most, are made in other countries. We're going to look at what goods and services get produced and where; how they are produced, and who gets to enjoy them. We begin with *what* we produce in the United States..

■ What Do We Produce?

We place the goods and services produced into two large groups:

- Consumption goods and services
- Capital goods

Consumption Goods and Services

Consumption goods and services
Goods and services that individuals and governments buy and use in the current period.

Consumption goods and services are items that individuals and governments buy and use up in the current period. Consumption goods and services bought by households include items such as housing, automobiles, bottled water, ramen noodles, chocolate bars, Po' boy sandwiches, movies, downhill skiing lessons, and doctor and dental services. Consumption goods and services bought by governments include items such as police and fire services, garbage collection, and education.

Capital Goods

Capital goods
Goods bought by businesses and governments to increase productive resources and to use over future periods to produce other goods and services.

Capital goods are goods that businesses and governments buy to increase productive resources to use during future periods to produce other goods and services. Capital goods bought by businesses include items such as auto assembly lines, shopping malls, airplanes, and oil tankers. Capital goods bought by governments include missiles and weapons systems for national security, public schools and universities, and interstate highways.

Consumption goods and services represent 78.5 percent of U.S. production by value and that percentage doesn't fluctuate much. *Eye on the U.S. Economy* on p. 35 breaks the goods and services down into smaller categories.

Health services is the largest category, with 19.4 percent of the value of total production. Real estate services come next at 14.5 percent. The main components of this item are the services of rental and owner-occupied housing. Professional and business services, which include the services of accountants and lawyers, are 13.2 percent of total production. Other large components of services are education and retail and wholesale trades.

The manufacture of goods represents only 12.1 percent of total production and the largest category of goods produced, chemicals, accounts for less than 2 percent of total production.

Construction accounts for 3.7 percent of production, and utilities, mining, and agriculture together make up only 5.7 percent. The nation's farms produce only a bit more than 1 percent of total production.

EYE on the U.S. ECONOMY
What We Produce

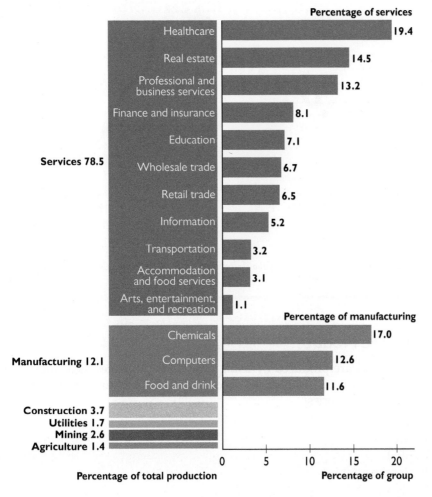

Percentage of services

Service	%
Healthcare	19.4
Real estate	14.5
Professional and business services	13.2
Finance and insurance	8.1
Education	7.1
Wholesale trade	6.7
Retail trade	6.5
Information	5.2
Transportation	3.2
Accommodation and food services	3.1
Arts, entertainment, and recreation	1.1

Services 78.5

Percentage of manufacturing

Manufacturing	%
Chemicals	17.0
Computers	12.6
Food and drink	11.6

Manufacturing 12.1

Construction 3.7
Utilities 1.7
Mining 2.6
Agriculture 1.4

Percentage of total production

Percentage of group

SOURCE OF DATA: Bureau of Economic Analysis.

Healthcare services, ...

education services, ...

and retail trades are among the largest categories of services produced.

Chemicals, ...

computer chips, ...

and food are the largest categories of goods produced in the United States.

EYE on the PAST
Changes in What We Produce

Freeport, Maine, became a shoemaking center in 1881 when the H.E. Davis Shoe Company opened its steam-powered factory in the town. Over the following years, many other shoemakers set up in Freeport and production steadily expanded. The town's shoe production peaked in 1968 after which it shrank rapidly. When the Freeport Shoe Company closed its factory in 1972, it became the fifteenth shoe factory to close in Freeport in four years. Today, the Freeport economy is based on shopping, not shoes.

Freeport's story of shoemaking was repeated across America and the figure tells this broader story. And as manufacturing has shrunk, retail and other services have expanded.

Leather shoe production (millions of pairs per year)

SOURCES OF DATA: *Historical Statistics of the United States Millennial Edition Online* and *Statistical Abstract of the United States*, 2012.

■ How Do We Produce?

Factors of production
The productive resources that are used to produce goods and services—land, labor, capital, and entrepreneurship.

Goods and services are produced by using productive resources. Economists call the productive resources **factors of production**. Factors of production are grouped into four categories:

- Land
- Labor
- Capital
- Entrepreneurship

Land

Land
The "gifts of nature," or *natural resources*, that we use to produce goods and services.

In economics, **land** includes all the "gifts of nature" that we use to produce goods and services. Land is what, in everyday language, we call *natural resources*. It includes land in the everyday sense, minerals, energy, water, air, and wild plants, animals, birds, and fish. Some of these resources are renewable, and some are nonrenewable. The U.S. Geological Survey maintains a national inventory of the quantity and quality of natural resources and monitors changes to that inventory.

The United States covers almost 2 billion acres. About 45 percent of the land is forest, lakes, and national parks. In 2009, almost 50 percent of the land was used for agriculture and 5 percent was urban, but urban land use is growing and agricultural land use is shrinking.

Our land surface and water resources are renewable, and some of our mineral resources can be recycled. But many mineral resources can be used only once. They are nonrenewable resources. Of these, the United States has vast known reserves of coal, oil, and natural gas.

36

Labor

Labor is the work time and work effort that people devote to producing goods and services. Labor includes the physical and mental efforts of all the people who work on farms and construction sites and in factories, shops, and offices. The Census Bureau and Bureau of Labor Statistics measure the quantity of labor at work every month.

In the United States in October 2015, 157 million people had jobs or were available for work. Some worked full time, some worked part time, and some were unemployed but looking for an acceptable vacant job. The total amount of time worked during 2015 was about 282 billion hours.

The quantity of labor increases as the adult population increases. The quantity of labor also increases if a larger percentage of the population takes jobs. During the past 50 years, a larger proportion of women have taken paid work and this trend has increased the quantity of labor. At the same time, a slightly smaller proportion of men have taken paid work and this trend has decreased the quantity of labor.

The *quality* of labor depends on how skilled people are. A laborer who can push a hand cart but can't drive a truck is much less productive than one who can drive. An office worker who can use a computer is much more productive than one who can't. Economists use a special name for human skill: human capital. **Human capital** is the knowledge and skill that people obtain from education, on-the-job training, and work experience.

You are building your own human capital right now as you work on your economics course and other subjects. Your human capital will continue to grow when you get a full-time job and become better at it. Human capital improves the *quality* of labor and increases the quantity of goods and services that labor can produce.

Capital

Capital consists of the tools, instruments, machines, buildings, and other items that have been produced in the past and that businesses now use to produce goods and services. Capital includes hammers and screwdrivers, computers, auto assembly lines, office towers and warehouses, dams and power plants, airplanes, cookie factories, and shopping malls.

Capital also includes inventories of unsold goods or of partly finished goods on a production line. And capital includes what is sometimes called *infrastructure capital*, such as highways and airports.

Capital, like human capital, makes labor more productive. A truck driver can produce vastly more transportation services than someone pushing a hand cart; the Interstate highway system enables us to produce vastly more transportation services than was possible on the old highway system that preceded it.

The Bureau of Economic Analysis in the U.S. Department of Commerce keeps track of the total value of capital in the United States and how it grows over time. Today, the value of capital in the U.S. economy is around $50 trillion.

Financial Capital Is Not Capital   In everyday language, we talk about money, stocks, and bonds as being capital. These items are *financial capital*, and they are not productive resources. Stocks and bonds enable people to provide businesses with financial resources, but they are *not* used to produce goods and services. They are not capital.

EYE on the U.S. ECONOMY
Changes in How We Produce in the Information Economy

The information economy consists of the jobs and businesses that produce and use computers and equipment powered by computer chips. This information economy is highly visible in your daily life.

The pairs of images here illustrate two examples. In each pair, a new technology enables capital to replace labor.

The top pair of pictures illustrate the replacement of bank tellers (labor) with ATMs (capital). Although the ATM was invented almost 50 years ago, when it made its first appearance, it was located only inside banks and was not able to update customers' accounts. It is only in the last decade that ATMs have spread to corner stores and enable us to get cash and check our bank balance from almost anywhere in the world.

The bottom pair of pictures illustrate a more recent replacement of labor with capital: self-check-in. Air passengers today issue their own boarding pass, often at their own computer before leaving home. For international flights, some of these machines now

even check passport details.

The number of bank teller and airport check-in clerk jobs is shrinking, but these new technologies are

creating a whole range of new jobs for people who make, program, install, and repair the vast number of machines.

Entrepreneurship

Entrepreneurship is the human resource that organizes land, labor, and capital to produce goods and services. Entrepreneurs are creative and imaginative. They come up with new ideas about what and how to produce, make business decisions, and bear the risks that arise from these decisions. If their ideas work out, they earn a profit. If their ideas turn out to be wrong, they bear the loss.

The quantity of entrepreneurship is hard to describe or measure. During some periods, there appears to be a great deal of imaginative entrepreneurship around. People such as Sam Walton, who created Wal-Mart, one of the world's largest retailers; Bill Gates, who founded the Microsoft empire; and Mark Zuckerberg, who founded Facebook, are examples of extraordinary entrepreneurial talent. But these highly visible entrepreneurs are just the tip of an iceberg that consists of hundreds of thousands of people who run businesses, large and small.

■ For Whom Do We Produce?

Who gets the goods and services depends on the incomes that people earn. A large income enables a person to buy large quantities of goods and services. A small income leaves a person with a small quantity of goods and services.

People earn their incomes by selling the services of the factors of production they own. **Rent** is paid for the use of land, **wages** are paid for the services of labor, **interest** is paid for the use of capital, and entrepreneurs receive a **profit** (or incur a **loss**) for running their businesses. What are the shares of these four factor incomes in the United States? Which factor receives the largest share?

Figure 2.1(a) answers these questions. It shows that wages were 63 percent of total income in 2014 and rent, interest, and profit were 37 percent of total income. These percentages remain remarkably constant over time. We call the distribution of income among the factors of production the *functional distribution of income.*

Figure 2.1(b) shows the *personal distribution of income*—the distribution of income among households—in 2014. Some households, like that of Clayton Kershaw, earn many millions of dollars a year. These households are in the richest 20 percent who earn 50 percent of total income. Households at the other end of the scale, like those of fast-food servers, are in the poorest 20 percent who earn only 3 percent of total income. The distribution of income has been changing and becoming more unequal. The rich have become richer. But it isn't the case, on the whole, that the poor have become poorer. They just haven't become richer as fast as the rich have.

Rent
Income paid for the use of land.

Wages
Income paid for the services of labor.

Interest
Income paid for the use of capital.

Profit (or loss)
Income earned by an entrepreneur for running a business.

■ **FIGURE 2.1**

For Whom in 2014

MyEconLab Animation

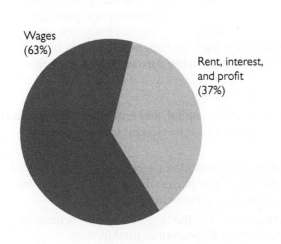

(a) Functional distribution of income

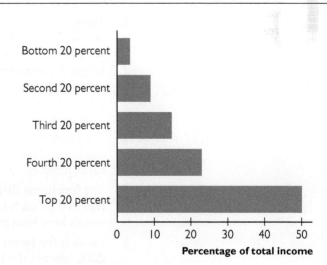

(b) Personal distribution of income

SOURCES OF DATA: Bureau of Economic Analysis, *National Income and Product Accounts*, Table 1.10 and U.S. Census Bureau, *Income and Poverty in the United States*: 2014, Current Population Reports P60-252, 2015.

In 2014, wages (the income from labor) were 63 percent of total income. Rent, interest, and profit (the income from the services of land, capital, and entrepreneurship) totaled the remaining 37 percent.

In 2014, the 20 percent of the population with the highest incomes received 50 percent of total income. The 20 percent with the lowest incomes received only 3 percent of total income.

MyEconLab Study Plan 2.1
Key Terms Quiz
Solutions Video

 CHECKPOINT 2.1

Describe what, how, and for whom goods and services are produced in the United States.

Practice Problems

1. What are the types of goods and services produced? Give an example of each (different from those in the chapter) and distinguish between them.
2. Name the four factors of production and the incomes they earn.
3. Distinguish between the functional distribution of income and the personal distribution of income.
4. In the United States, which factor of production earned the largest share of income in 2014 and what percentage did it earn?

In the News

The frustration that drives people to become entrepreneurs
A study by researchers at Stanford and the University of Chicago discovered that most of the people who quit their jobs and start their own business do so not because they have a billion-dollar idea but because they are frustrated in their jobs.
Source: Chad Brooks, *Business News Daily*, September 16, 2014

Why do people become entrepreneurs? What do we call the income earned by entrepreneurs? Are most people entrepreneurs? What is the factor of production supplied by people who are not entrepreneurs? What is their income called? What percentage of total income does their income represent?

Solutions to Practice Problems

1. The goods and services produced fall into two types: consumption goods and services and capital goods. A hamburger is a consumption good and a haircut is a consumption service. An oil rig and auto assembly line are capital goods. A consumption good or service is an item that is bought by individuals or the government and is used up in the current period. A capital good is bought by businesses or the government and it is used over and over again to produce other goods and services.
2. The factors of production are land, labor, capital, and entrepreneurship. Land earns rent; labor earns wages; capital earns interest; and entrepreneurship earns profit or incurs a loss.
3. The functional distribution of income shows the percentage of total income received by each factor of production. The personal distribution of income shows how total income is shared among households.
4. Labor is the factor of production that earns the largest share of income. In 2014, labor in the United States earned 63 percent of total income.

Solution to In the News

People become entrepreneurs because they are frustrated in their jobs. The income earned by entrepreneurs is called profit. Most people are suppliers of labor, for which they earn a wage. The data in Figure 2.1 show that wage income of labor represents 63 percent of total income.

2.2   THE GLOBAL ECONOMY

We're now going to look at *what, how,* and *for whom* goods and services get produced in the global economy. We'll begin with a brief overview of the people and countries that form the global economy.

■ The People

Visit the Web site of the U.S. Census Bureau and go to the population clocks to find out how many people there are today in both the United States and the entire world. On the day these words were written, November 8, 2015, the U.S. clock recorded a population of 322,115,000. The world clock recorded a global population of 7,284,290,000. The U.S. clock ticks along showing a population increase of one person every 15 seconds. The world clock spins faster, adding 30 people in the same 15 seconds.

■ The Economies

The world's 7.3 billion (and rising) population lives in 176 economies, which the International Monetary Fund classifies into two broad groups:

* Advanced economies
* Emerging market and developing economies

Advanced Economies

Advanced economies are the richest 29 countries (or areas). The United States, Japan, Italy, Germany, France, the United Kingdom, and Canada belong to this group. So do four new industrial Asian economies: Hong Kong, South Korea, Singapore, and Taiwan. The other advanced economies include Australia, New Zealand, and most of the rest of Western Europe. Almost 1 billion people (15 percent of the world's population) live in the advanced economies.

Emerging Market and Developing Economies

Emerging market economies are 28 countries in Central and Eastern Europe and Asia. Almost 500 million people live in these countries—about half of the number in the advanced economies. These countries are important because they are emerging (hence the name) from a system of state-owned production, central economic planning, and heavily regulated markets moving toward a system of free enterprise and unregulated markets.

Developing economies are the 119 countries in Africa, Asia, the Middle East, Europe, and Central and South America. More than 5.5 billion people—almost four out of every five people—live in the developing economies.

Developing economies vary enormously in size, the level of average income, and the rate of growth of production and incomes. But in all the developing economies, average incomes are much lower than those in the advanced economies, and in some cases, they are extremely low.

Five emerging market and developing economies, representing 3 billion people or 42 percent of the world's population and known as BRICS (Brazil, Russia, India, China, and South Africa), hold regular meetings to advance the interests of these nations and draw attention to their development problems.

▪ *What* in the Global Economy

First, let's look at the big picture. Imagine that each year the global economy produces an enormous pie. In 2015, the pie was worth about $113 trillion! To give this number some meaning, if the pie were shared equally among the world's 7.3 billion people, each of us would get a slice worth a bit less than $15,500.

Where Is the Global Pie Baked?

Figure 2.2 shows us where in the world the pie is baked. The advanced economies produce 43 percent—16 percent in the United States, 17 percent in the European Union, and 10 percent in the other advanced economies. This 43 percent of global output (by value) is produced by 15 percent of the world's population.

The BRICS economies, highlighted in the figure, together produce 31 percent of the world's output. China, with 17 percent of world production, dominates this group and South Africa, the group's smallest member, produces barely 1 percent of global output. This 31 percent of the global pie is baked by 42 percent of the world's population.

The remaining 26 percent of the global pie comes from other emerging market and developing economies and is baked by 43 percent of the world's people.

Unlike the slices of an apple pie, those of the global pie have different fillings. Some slices have more oil, some more food, some more clothing, some more housing services, some more autos, and so on. Let's look at some of these different fillings and at some similarities too.

▪ **FIGURE 2.2**

What in the Global Economy in 2015 ⸻⸻⸻⸻⸻ MyEconLab Animation

If we show the value of production in the world economy as a pie, the United States produces a slice that is 16 percent of the total. The European Union produces 17 percent and other advanced economies 10 percent, so together, the advanced economies produce 43 percent of global output.

Another 31 percent of the global pie comes from the BRICS economies. China, which produces 17 percent of world output, dominates this group.

The remaining 26 percent of world output comes from other emerging market and developing economies in Africa, Asia, the Middle East, and the Western Hemisphere.

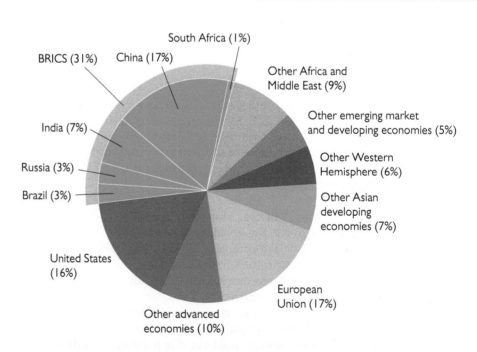

SOURCE OF DATA: International Monetary Fund, World Economic Outlook Database, April 2015.

EYE on the DREAMLINER

MyEconLab Critical Thinking Exercise

Who Makes the Dreamliner?

Boeing designed, assembles, and markets the Dreamliner, but the airplane is made by more than 400 firms on four continents that employ thousands of workers and millions of dollars' worth of specialized capital equipment. The graphic identifies some of the firms and the components they make.

Boeing and these firms make decisions and pay their workers, investors, and raw material suppliers to influence *what*, *how*, and *for whom* goods and services are produced. All these decisions are made in self-interest, and produce an airplane at the lowest possible cost.

Some Differences in What Is Produced

What is produced in the developing economies contrasts sharply with that of the advanced economies. Manufacturing is the big story. Developing economies have large and growing industries, which produce textiles, footwear, sports gear, toys, electronic goods, furniture, steel, and even automobiles and airplanes.

Food production is a small part of the U.S. and other advanced economies and a large part of the developing economies such as Brazil, China, and India. But the advanced economies produce about one third of the world's food. How can this be? *Total* production is much larger in the advanced economies than in the developing economies, but a small percentage of a big number can be a *greater amount* than a large percentage of a small number!

Some Similarities in What Is Produced

If you were to visit a shopping mall in Canada, England, Australia, Japan, or any of the other advanced economies, you would wonder whether you had left the United States. You would see Starbucks, Burger King, Pizza Hut, Domino's Pizza, KFC, Kmart, Wal-Mart, Target, Gap, Tommy Hilfiger, Lululemon, Banana Republic, the upscale Louis Vuitton and Burberry, and a host of other familiar names. And, of course, you would see McDonald's golden arches. You would see them in any of the 119 countries in which one or more of McDonald's 30,000 restaurants are located.

The similarities among the advanced economies go beyond the view from main street and the shopping mall. The structure of *what* is produced is similar in these economies. As percentages of the total economy, agriculture and manufacturing are small and shrinking whereas services are large and expanding.

McDonald's in Shanghai.

◼ *How* in the Global Economy

Goods and services are produced using land, labor, capital, and entrepreneurial resources, and the combinations of these resources used are chosen to produce at the lowest possible cost. Each country or region has its own blend of factors of production, but there are some interesting common patterns and crucial differences between the advanced and developing economies that we'll now examine.

Human Capital Differences

One of the biggest distinguishing features of an advanced economy from an emerging market or developing economy is its quantity of *human capital*. Advanced economies have much higher levels of human capital.

Education levels are the handiest measure of human capital. In an advanced economy such as the United States, almost everyone has completed high school. And 30 percent of the U.S. population has completed 4 years or more of college.

In contrast, in developing economies, the proportion of the population who has completed high school or has a college degree is small. In the poorest of the developing economies, many children even miss out on basic primary education—they just don't go to school at all.

On-the-job training and experience are also much less extensive in the developing economies than in the advanced economies.

Physical Capital Differences

Another major feature of an advanced economy that differentiates it from a developing economy is the amount of capital available for producing goods and services. The differences begin with the basic transportation systems. In the advanced economies, a well-developed highway system connects all the major cities and points of production. Open a map app on your phone. Contrast the U.S. interstate highway system in Texas with the sparse highways of Mexico. You would see a similar contrast if you swiped across the Atlantic Ocean and checked out the highway structures in Western Europe and Africa.

But it isn't the case that the developing economies have no highways and no modern trucks and cars. In fact, some of them have the newest and the best. But the new and best are usually inside and around the major cities—see *Eye on the Global Economy* on p. 45.

The contrasts in the transportation system are matched by those on farms and in factories. In general, the more advanced the economy, the greater are the amount and sophistication of the capital equipment used in production. But again, the contrast is not all or nothing. Some factories in India, China, and other parts of Asia use the very latest technologies. Furniture manufacturing is an example. To make furniture of a quality that Americans are willing to buy, firms in Asia use machines like those in the furniture factories of North Carolina.

The differences in human capital and physical capital between advanced and developing economies have a big effect on *who* gets the goods and services, which we'll now examine.

◼ *For Whom* in the Global Economy

Who gets the world's goods and services depends on the incomes that people earn. We're now going to see how incomes are distributed within economies and across the world.

EYE on the GLOBAL ECONOMY
Differences in How We Produce

Big differences exist in how goods and services are produced and the images here illustrate three examples.

Laundry services (top), transportation services (center), and highway systems (bottom) can use a large amount of capital and almost no labor (left) or use almost no capital and a large amount of labor (right).

Capital-intensive automatic laundry equipment, big trucks, and multi-lane paved freeways are common in advanced economies but rare in poorer developing economies.

Riverside clothes washing, human pedal power, and unsealed dirt tracks are seen only in developing economies.

But we also see huge differences even within a developing economy. The bottom pictures contrast Beijing's capital-intensive highway system with the unpaved and sometimes hazardous roads of rural China.

Personal Distribution of Income

You saw earlier (on p. 39) that in the United States, the lowest-paid 20 percent of the population receives 3 percent of total income and the highest-paid 20 percent receives 50 percent of total income. The personal distribution of income in the world economy is much more unequal. According to World Bank data, the lowest-paid 20 percent of the world's population receives 2 percent of world income and the highest-paid 20 percent receives about 70 percent of world income.

International Distribution

Much of the greater inequality at the global level arises from differences in average incomes among countries. Figure 2.3 shows some of these differences. It shows the dollar value of what people can afford each day on average. You can see that in the United States, that number is $153 a day—an average person in the United States can buy goods and services that cost $153. This amount is around five times the world average. The European Union has an average income of around two thirds that of the United States at $104 per day. Income levels fall off quickly as we move farther down the graph, with Russia at $65 a day, China $39 a day, India $17 a day, and Africa only $11 a day.

As people have lost well-paid manufacturing jobs and found lower-paid service jobs, inequality has increased in the United States and in most other advanced economies. Inequality is also increasing in the developing economies. People with skills enjoy rapidly rising incomes but the incomes of the unskilled are falling.

A Happy Paradox and a Huge Challenge

Despite the increase in inequality inside most countries, inequality across the entire world has decreased during the past 20 years. And most important, according to Xavier Sala-i-Martin, an economics professor at Columbia University, extreme poverty has declined. Professor Sala-i-Martin estimates that between 1976 and 1998, the number of people who earn $1 a day or less fell by 235 million and the number who earn $2 a day or less fell by 450 million. This positive situation arises because in China, the largest nation, incomes have increased rapidly and lifted millions from extreme poverty. Incomes are growing quickly in India too.

Lifting Africa from poverty is today's big challenge. In 1960, 11 percent of the world's poor lived in Africa, but in 1998, 66 percent did. Between 1976 and 1998, the number of people in Africa who earn $1 a day or less rose by 175 million, and the number who earn $2 a day or less rose by 227 million.

FIGURE 2.3

For Whom in the Global Economy in 2015   MyEconLab Animation

In 2015, the average income per person per day in the United States was $153. It was $104 in the European Union and $65 in Russia. The number falls to $39 in China, $17 in India, and $11 in Africa.

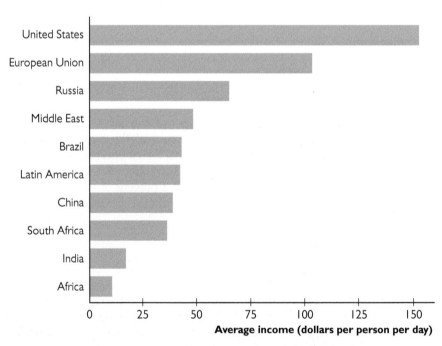

SOURCE OF DATA: International Monetary Fund, World Economic Outlook Database, October 2015.

EYE on YOUR LIFE
The U.S. and Global Economies in Your Life

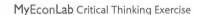

You've encountered a lot of facts and trends about what, how, and for whom goods and services are produced in the U.S. economy and the global economy. How can you use this information? You can use it in two ways:

1. To inform your choice of career
2. To inform your stand on the politics of protecting U.S. jobs

Career Choices

As you think about your future career, you are now better informed about some of the key trends. You know that manufacturing is shrinking.

The U.S. economy is what is sometimes called a *post-industrial economy*. Industries that provided the backbone of the economy in previous generations have fallen to barely a fifth of

the economy today, and the trend continues. It is possible that by the middle of the current century, manufacturing will be as small a source of jobs as agriculture is today.

So, a job in a manufacturing business is likely to lead to some tough situations and possibly the need for several job changes over a working life.

As manufacturing shrinks, so services expand, and this expansion will continue. The provision of health-care, education, communication, wholesale and retail trades, and entertainment are all likely to expand in the future and be sources of increasing employment and rising wages. A job in a service-oriented business is more likely to lead to steady advances in income.

Political Stand on Job Protection

As you think about the stand you will take on the political question of protecting U.S. jobs, you are better informed about the basic facts and trends.

When you hear that manufacturing jobs are disappearing to China, you will be able to place that news in historical perspective. You might reasonably be concerned, especially if you or a member of your family has lost a job. But you know that trying to reverse or even halt this process is flying in the face of stubborn historical trends.

In later chapters, you will learn that there are good economic reasons to be skeptical about any form of protection and placing limits on competition.

CHECKPOINT 2.2

Describe what, how, and for whom goods and services are produced in the global economy.

Practice Problems

1. Describe what, how, and for whom goods and services are produced in developing economies.
2. A Clinton Foundation success story is that it loaned $23,000 to Rwandan coffee growers to support improvements to coffee washing stations and provided technical support. What was the source of the success?

Solutions to Practice Problems

1. In developing countries, agriculture is the largest percentage, manufacturing is an increasing percentage, and services are a small percentage of total production. Most production does not use modern capital-intensive technologies, but some industries do. People who work in factories have rising incomes while those who work in rural industries are left behind.
2. The technical support allowed Rwandan coffee growers to improve their knowledge of coffee farming, which increased their human capital. The improvements to washing stations was a change in physical capital that allowed farmers to increase the quantity of washed coffee.

MyEconLab Concept Video

Circular flow model
A model of the economy that shows the circular flow of expenditures and incomes that result from decision makers' choices and the way those choices interact to determine what, how, and for whom goods and services are produced.

Households
Individuals or groups of people living together.

Firms
The institutions that organize the production of goods and services.

Market
Any arrangement that brings buyers and sellers together and enables them to get information and do business with each other.

Goods markets
Markets in which goods and services are bought and sold.

Factor markets
Markets in which the services of factors of production are bought and sold.

2.3 THE CIRCULAR FLOWS

We can organize the data you've just studied using the **circular flow model**—a model of the economy that shows the circular flow of expenditures and incomes that result from decision makers' choices and the way those choices interact to determine what, how, and for whom goods and services are produced. Figure 2.4 shows the circular flow model.

■ Households and Firms

Households are individuals or groups of people living together. The 124 million households in the United States own the factors of production—land, labor, capital, and entrepreneurship—and choose the quantities of these resources to provide to firms. Households also choose the quantities of goods and services to buy.

   Firms are the institutions that organize the production of goods and services. The 28 million firms in the United States choose the quantities of the factors of production to hire and the quantities of goods and services to produce.

■ Markets

Households choose the quantities of the factors of production to provide to firms, and firms choose the quantities of the services of the factors of production to hire. Firms choose the quantities of goods and services to produce, and households choose the quantities of goods and services to buy. How are these choices coordinated and made compatible? The answer is: by markets.

   A **market** is any arrangement that brings buyers and sellers together and enables them to get information and do business with each other. An example is the market in which oil is bought and sold—the world oil market. The world oil market is not a place. It is the network of oil producers, oil users, wholesalers, and brokers who buy and sell oil. In the world oil market, decision makers do not meet physically. They make deals by telephone, fax, and the Internet.

   Figure 2.4 identifies two types of markets: goods markets and factor markets. Goods and services are bought and sold in **goods markets**; and the services of factors of production are bought and sold in **factor markets**.

■ Real Flows and Money Flows

When households choose the quantities of services of land, labor, capital, and entrepreneurship to offer in factor markets, they respond to the incomes they receive—rent for land, wages for labor, interest for capital, and profit for entrepreneurship. When firms choose the quantities of factor services to hire, they respond to the rent, wages, interest, and profits they must pay to households.

   Similarly, when firms choose the quantities of goods and services to produce and offer for sale in goods markets, they respond to the amounts that they receive from the expenditures that households make. And when households choose the quantities of goods and services to buy, they respond to the amounts they must pay to firms.

   Figure 2.4 shows the flows that result from these choices made by households and firms. The flows shown in orange are *real flows:* the flows of the factors of production that go from households through factor markets to firms and of the goods and services that go from firms through goods markets to households. The flows in the opposite direction are *money flows:* the flows of payments made in exchange for the services of factors of production (shown in blue) and of expenditures on goods and services (shown in red).

Lying behind these real flows and money flows are millions of individual choices about what to consume and what and how to produce. These choices result in buying plans by households and selling plans by firms in goods markets. And the choices result in selling plans by households and buying plans by firms in factor markets that interact to determine the prices that people pay and the incomes they earn, and so determine for whom goods and services are produced. You'll learn in Chapter 4 how markets coordinate the buying plans and selling plans of households and firms and make them compatible.

Firms produce most of the goods and services that we consume, but governments provide some of the services that we enjoy. Governments also play a big role in modifying for whom goods and services are produced by changing the personal distribution of income. We're now going to look at the role of governments in the U.S. economy and add them to the circular flow model.

FIGURE 2.4

The Circular Flow Model   MyEconLab Animation

The orange flows are the services of factors of production that go from households through factor markets to firms and the goods and services that go from firms through goods markets to households. These flows are *real* flows.

The blue flow is the income earned by the factors of production, and the red flow is the expenditures on goods and services. These flows are *money* flows.

The choices that generate these real and money flows determine *what*, *how*, and *for whom* goods and services are produced.

■ Governments

More than 86,000 organizations operate as governments in the United States. Some are tiny like the Yuma, Arizona, school district and some are enormous like the U.S. federal government. We divide governments into two levels:

- Federal government
- State and local government

Federal Government

The federal government's major expenditures provide

1. Goods and services
2. Social Security and welfare payments
3. Transfers to state and local governments

The goods and services provided by the federal government include the legal system, which protects property and enforces contracts, and national defense. Social Security and welfare benefits, which include income for retired people and programs such as Medicare and Medicaid, are transfers from the federal government to households. Federal government transfers to state and local governments are payments designed to provide more equality across the states and regions.

The federal government finances its expenditures by collecting a variety of taxes. The main taxes paid to the federal government are

1. Personal income taxes
2. Corporate (business) income taxes
3. Social Security taxes

In 2015, the federal government spent $4 trillion—about 23 percent of the total value of all the goods and services produced in the United States in that year. The taxes they raised were less than this amount—the government had a deficit.

State and Local Government

The state and local governments' major expenditures are to provide

1. Goods and services
2. Welfare benefits

The goods and services provided by state and local governments include the state courts and police, schools, roads, garbage collection and disposal, water supplies, and sewage management. Welfare benefits provided by state governments include unemployment benefits and other aid to low-income families.

State and local governments finance these expenditures by collecting taxes and receiving transfers from the federal government. The main taxes paid to state and local governments are

1. Sales taxes
2. Property taxes
3. State income taxes

In 2015, state and local governments spent $2.5 trillion or 14 percent of the total value of all the goods and services produced in the United States.

■ Governments in the Circular Flow

Figure 2.5 adds governments to the circular flow model. As you study this figure, first notice that the outer circle is the same as in Figure 2.4. In addition to these flows, governments buy goods and services from firms. The red arrows that run from governments through the goods markets to firms show this expenditure.

Households and firms pay taxes to governments. The green arrows running directly from households and firms to governments show these flows. Also, governments make money payments to households and firms. The green arrows running directly from governments to households and firms show these flows. Taxes and transfers are direct transactions with governments and do not go through the goods markets and factor markets.

Not part of the circular flow and not visible in Figure 2.5, governments provide the legal framework within which all transactions occur. For example, governments operate the courts and legal system that enable contracts to be written and enforced.

■ FIGURE 2.5

Governments in the Circular Flow

MyEconLab Animation

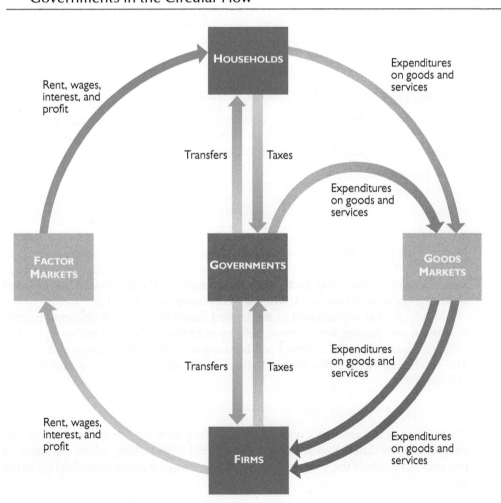

The green flows from households and firms to governments are taxes, and the green flows from governments to households and firms are money transfers.

The red flow from governments through the goods markets to firms is the expenditure on goods and services by governments.

EYE on the PAST
Growing Government

One hundred years ago in 1915, the federal government spent 2 cents out of each dollar earned. Today, the federal government spends 20 cents. Government grew during the two world wars and during the 1960s and 1970s as social programs expanded.

Only during the 1980s and 1990s did big government begin to shrink in a process begun by Ronald Reagan and continued by Bill Clinton. But 9-11 saw the start of a new era of growing government. Fiscal stimulus and bailouts to cope with the global financial crisis sent government spending soaring.

Federal expenditures (percentage of GDP)

SOURCE OF DATA: Budget of the United States Government, Historical Tables, Table 1.1.

■ Circular Flows in the Global Economy

Households and firms in the U.S. economy interact with households and firms in other economies in two main ways: They buy and sell goods and services and they borrow and lend. We call these two activities

- International trade
- International finance

International Trade

Many of the goods that you buy were not made in the United States. Your iPod, Wii games, Nike shoes, smartphone, T-shirt, and bike were made somewhere in Asia or possibly Europe or South or Central America. The goods and services that we buy from firms in other countries are U.S. *imports.*

Much of what is produced in the United States doesn't end up being bought by Americans. Boeing, for example, sells most of the airplanes it makes to foreign airlines. The banks of Wall Street sell banking services to Europeans and Asians. The goods and services that we sell to households and firms in other countries are U.S. *exports.*

International Finance

When firms or governments want to borrow, they look for the lowest interest rate available. Sometimes, that is outside the United States. Also, when the value of our imports exceeds the value of our exports, we must borrow from the rest of the world.

Firms and governments in the rest of the world behave in the same way. They look for the lowest interest rate at which to borrow and the highest at which to lend. They might borrow from or lend to Americans.

Figure 2.6 shows the flows through goods markets and financial markets in the global economy. Households and firms in the U.S. economy interact with those in the rest of the world (other economies) in goods markets and financial markets.

The red flow shows the expenditure by Americans on imports of goods and services, and the blue flow shows the expenditure by the rest of the world on U.S. exports (other countries' imports). The green flow shows U.S. lending to the rest of the world, and the orange flow shows U.S. borrowing from the rest of the world.

It is these international trade and international finance flows that tie nations together in the global economy and through which global booms and slumps are transmitted.

▉ **FIGURE 2.6**

Circular Flows in the Global Economy   MyEconLab Animation

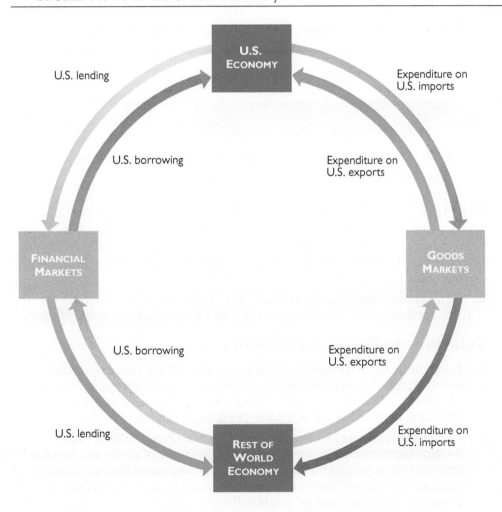

Households and firms in the U.S. economy interact with those in the rest of the world (other economies) in goods markets and financial markets.

The red flow shows the expenditure by Americans on imports of goods and services, and the blue flow shows the expenditure by the rest of the world on U.S. exports (other countries' imports).

The green flow shows U.S. lending to the rest of the world, and the orange flow shows U.S. borrowing from the rest of the world.

EYE on the GLOBAL ECONOMY
The Ups and Downs in International Trade

International trade expanded rapidly after China became a powerful player in the global economy.

At an average growth rate of close to 7 percent a year, world trade has doubled every decade and increased as a percentage of world production.

A mini-recession in 2001 slowed the growth in world trade to a crawl and the 2009 global recession reduced world trade.

After the recession of 2009, world trade bounced back to 27 percent of global production, where it remained in 2015.

Global international trade (percentage of world GDP)

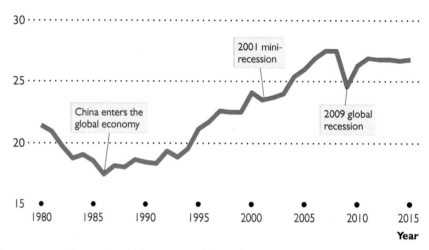

SOURCE OF DATA: International Monetary Fund, World Economic Outlook Database, October 2015.

MyEconLab Study Plan 2.3
Key Terms Quiz
Solutions Video

 ## CHECKPOINT 2.3

Explain the circular flow model of the U.S. economy and of the global economy.

Practice Problems

1. Describe the flows in the circular flow model in which expenditure on consumption goods and services, purchases of new national defense equipment, and payments for labor services appear. Through which market does each flow pass?

2. Of the flows that run between households, firms, and governments in the circular flow model, which ones are real flows and which are money flows?

Solutions to Practice Problems

1. Expenditure on consumption goods and services flows from households to firms through the goods market. Purchases of national defense flow from governments to firms through the goods market. Payments for labor services flow from firms to households through the factor market.

2. The flow of services of factors of production from households to firms through factor markets is a real flow, as are the flows of goods and services from firms to households and from firms to governments through goods markets. The money flows are the flows of factor incomes, household and government expenditures on goods and services, taxes, and transfers.

CHAPTER SUMMARY

Key Points

1. **Describe what, how, and for whom goods and services are produced in the United States.**

   - Consumption goods and services represent 85 percent of total production; capital goods represent 15 percent.
   - Goods and services are produced by using the four factors of production: land, labor, capital, and entrepreneurship.
   - The incomes people earn (rent for land, wages for labor, interest for capital, and profit for entrepreneurship) determine who gets the goods and services produced.

2. **Describe what, how, and for whom goods and services are produced in the global economy.**

   - Forty-three percent of the world's production (by value) comes from the advanced industrial countries and 57 percent comes from the emerging market and developing economies.
   - Production in the advanced economies uses more capital (both machines and human), but some developing economies use the latest capital and technologies.
   - The global distribution of income is more unequal than the U.S. distribution. Poverty has fallen in Asia, but it has increased in Africa.

3. **Explain the circular flow model of the U.S. economy and of the global economy.**

   - The circular flow model of the U.S. economy shows the real flows of factors of production and goods and the corresponding money flows of incomes and expenditures.
   - Governments in the circular flow receive taxes, make transfers, and buy goods and services.
   - The circular flow model of the global economy shows the flows of U.S. exports and imports and the international financial flows that result from lending to and borrowing from other countries.

Key Terms

MyEconLab Key Terms Quiz

Capital, 37
Capital goods, 34
Circular flow model, 48
Consumption goods and services, 34
Entrepreneurship, 38
Factor markets, 48

Factors of production, 36
Firms, 48
Goods markets, 48
Households, 48
Human capital, 37
Interest, 39

Labor, 37
Land, 36
Market, 48
Profit (or loss), 39
Rent, 39
Wages, 39

CHAPTER CHECKPOINT

Study Plan Problems and Applications

1. Which of the following items are *not* consumption goods and services? Explain why not.
   - A chocolate bar   • A ski lift   • A golf ball

2. Which of the following items are *not* capital goods? Explain why not.
   - An auto assembly line   • A shopping mall   • A golf ball

3. Which of the following items are *not* factors of production? Explain why not.
   - Vans used by a baker to deliver bread
   - 1,000 shares of Amazon.com stock
   - Undiscovered oil in the Arctic Ocean

4. Which factor of production earns the highest percentage of total U.S. income? Define that factor of production. What is the income earned by this factor of production called?

5. With more job training and more scholarships to poor American students, which special factor of production is likely to grow faster than in the past?

6. Define the factor of production called capital. Give three examples of capital, different from those in the chapter. Distinguish between the factor of production capital and financial capital.

7. The pace at which new businesses are created in the U.S. economy and the percentage of U.S. jobs in young firms has fallen.

   > Ryan Decker and others, "The Role of Entrepreneurship in U.S. Job Creation and Economic Dynamism."
   > *Journal of Economic Perspectives*, 2014.

   Explain how you would expect these facts to influence *what, how*, and *for whom* goods and services are produced in the United States.

8. In the circular flow model, explain the real flow and/or the money flow in which each item in List 1 belongs. Illustrate your answers on a circular flow diagram.

9. **Why you can get a free college education in Germany but not in California**
   Even American students can get a free college degree in Germany, where high taxes pay for colleges. Despite college being free, fewer students in Germany earn college degrees than in the United States and more enter vocational apprenticeships.

   > Source: *Los Angeles Times*, October 29, 2015

   If California adopted the German model of higher education, how would that change *for whom* goods and services are produced?

10. Read *Eye on the Dreamliner* on p. 43 and then answer the following questions:
    - How many firms are involved in the production of the Dreamliner and how many are identified in the figure on p. 43?
    - Is the Dreamliner a capital good or a consumption good? Explain why.
    - State the factors of production that make the Dreamliner and provide an example of each.
    - Explain how the production of the Dreamliner influences *what, how,* and *for whom* goods and services are produced.
    - Use a diagram to show where in the circular flow model of the global economy the flows of the components listed on p. 43 appear and where the sales of Dreamliners appear.

LIST 1

- You buy a coffee at Starbucks.
- The government buys some Dell computers.
- A student works at a FedEx office.
- Donald Trump rents a building to Marriott hotels.
- You pay your income tax.

Instructor Assignable Problems and Applications

MyEconLab Homework, Quiz, or Test if assigned by instructor

1. Boeing's Dreamliner has had a rocky start.
   - Why doesn't Boeing manufacture all the components of the Dreamliner at its own factory in the United States?
   - Describe some of the changes in *what, how*, and *for whom* that would occur if Boeing manufactured all the components of the Dreamliner at its own factories in the United States.
   - State some of the tradeoffs that Boeing faces in making the Dreamliner.
   - Why might Boeing's decisions in making the Dreamliner be in the social interest?

2. The global economy has seen a fall in the number of landlines and rapid growth in the number of smartphones. In the United States, 41 percent of households have no landline and 90 percent have a smartphone. In Africa, 33 percent have a smartphone. Describe the changes in *what, how*, and *for whom* telecommunication services are produced in the global economy.

3. Which of the entries in List 1 are consumption goods and services? Explain your choice.

4. Which of the entries in List 1 are capital goods? Explain your choice.

5. Which of the entries in List 1 are factors of production? Explain your choice.

6. In the African nation of Senegal, to enroll in school a child needs a birth certificate that costs $25. This price is several weeks' income for many families. Explain how this requirement is likely to affect the growth of human capital in Senegal.

7. **China's income gap widens**
   The income gap has widened in China. In 2014, the pay of workers in the coastal regions increased by 9.7 percent while that of workers in the inland regions grew by 9 percent.

   Source: *South China Morning Post*, May 28, 2015

   Explain how the distribution of personal income in China can be getting more unequal even though the poorest are getting richer.

8. Compare the scale of agricultural production in the advanced and developing economies. In which is the percentage higher? In which is the total amount produced greater?

9. On a diagram of the circular flow model, indicate in which real or money flow each entry in List 2 belongs.

Use the following information to work Problems **10** and **11**.

Poor India makes millionaires at fastest pace
India, with the world's largest population of poor people, also paradoxically created millionaires at the fastest pace in the world. Millionaires increased by 22.7 percent to 123,000. In contrast, the number of Indians living on less than a dollar a day is 350 million and those living on less than $2 a day is 700 million. In other words, there are 7,000 very poor Indians for every millionaire.

Source: *The Times of India*, June 25, 2008

10. How is the personal distribution of income in India changing?

11. Why might incomes of $1 a day and $2 a day underestimate the value of the goods and services that these households actually consume?

LIST 1

- An interstate highway
- An airplane
- A school teacher
- A stealth bomber
- A garbage truck
- A pack of bubble gum
- President of the United States
- A strawberry field
- A movie
- An ATM

LIST 2

- General Motors pays its workers wages.
- IBM pays a dividend to its stockholders.
- You buy your groceries.
- Southwest rents some aircraft.
- Nike pays Serena Williams for promoting its sports shoes.

Multiple Choice Quiz

1. Which of the following classifications is correct?

   A. City streets are consumption goods because they wear out with use.
   B. Stocks are capital goods because when people buy and sell them they make a profit.
   C. The coffee maker in the coffee shop at an airport is a consumption good because people buy the coffee it produces.
   D. White House security is a government service because it is paid for by the government.

2. Which of the following statements about U.S. production is correct?

   A. Construction accounts for a larger percentage of total production than does manufacturing.
   B. Real estate services account for 14.5 percent of the value of total production, larger than any other item of services or goods.
   C. Consumption goods and services represent 78.5 percent of U.S. production by value and that percentage doesn't fluctuate much.
   D. The manufacture of goods represents more than 50 percent of total production.

3. Which of the following items is *not* a factor of production?

   A. An oil rig in the Gulf of Mexico
   B. A ski jump in Utah
   C. A bank loan to a farmer
   D. An orange grove in Florida

4. What is human capital?

   A. A fruit picker
   B. Unskilled labor
   C. Your professor's knowledge of economics
   D. An auto assembly line robot

5. Which of the following statements is correct?

   A. Labor earns wages and entrepreneurship earns bonuses.
   B. Land earns interest and capital earns rent.
   C. Entrepreneurship earns interest and capital earns profit.
   D. Capital earns interest and labor earns wages.

6. How are goods and services produced in the global economy?

   A. Developing countries use less human capital but just as much physical capital as advanced economies.
   B. Emerging economies use more capital-intensive technology than do developing economies.
   C. Human capital in all economies is similar.
   D. Advanced economies use less capital than developing economies.

7. In the circular flow model, which of the following items is a real flow?

   A. The flow of government expenditures to firms for the goods bought
   B. The flow of income from firms to households for the services of the factors of production hired
   C. The flow of U.S. borrowing from the rest of the world
   D. The flow of labor services from households to firms

Is wind power free?

The Economic Problem

3

CHAPTER CHECKLIST

When you have completed your study of this chapter, you will be able to

1 Explain and illustrate the concepts of scarcity, production efficiency, and tradeoff using the production possibilities frontier.

2 Calculate opportunity cost.

3 Explain what makes production possibilities expand.

4 Explain how people gain from specialization and trade.

MyEconLab Big Picture Video

3.1 PRODUCTION POSSIBILITIES

The wind is free, but wind power is not: it must be produced. It is one of the vast array of goods and services produced in the nation's farms, factories, stores, offices, and construction sites. In 2015, 280 billion hours of labor equipped with $55 trillion worth of capital produced $18 trillion worth of goods and services.

Our production capability is enormous, but it is limited by our available resources and by technology. At any given time, we have fixed quantities of the factors of production and a fixed state of technology, so there is a limit to what we can produce. The economic problem is that our wants exceed what it is possible for our resources to produce.

Your task in this chapter is to study a model of the economic problem. We begin with a piece of the model that describes the limits to production, which is called the production possibilities frontier.

■ Production Possibilities Frontier

Production possibilities frontier
The boundary between the combinations of goods and services that can be produced and the combinations that cannot be produced, given the available factors of production and the state of technology.

The **production possibilities frontier** is the boundary between the combinations of goods and services that can be produced and the combinations that cannot be produced, given the available factors of production—land, labor, capital, and entrepreneurship—and the state of technology.

Although we produce millions of different goods and services, we can visualize the limits to production most easily if we look at a model economy that produces just two goods. Imagine an economy that produces only bikes and smartphones. All the land, labor, capital, and entrepreneurship available gets used to produce these two goods.

Land can be used for bike factories or smartphone factories. Labor can be trained to work as bike makers or as smartphone makers. Capital can be used for building bike or smartphone assembly lines. Entrepreneurs can put their talents to making bikes or running smartphone businesses. In every case, the more resources that are used to produce bikes, the fewer are left to produce smartphones.

Suppose that if no factors of production are allocated to producing smartphones, the maximum number of bikes that can be produced is 15 million a year. So one production possibility is no smartphones and 15 million bikes. Another possibility is to allocate sufficient resources to produce 1 million smartphones a year. But these resources must be taken from bike factories. Suppose that the economy can now produce only 14 million bikes a year. As resources are moved from producing bikes to producing smartphones, the economy produces more smartphones but fewer bikes.

The table in Figure 3.1 illustrates these two combinations of smartphones and bikes as possibilities *A* and *B*. Suppose that *C, D, E,* and *F* are other combinations of the quantities of these two goods that the economy can produce. Possibility *F* uses all the resources to produce 5 million smartphones a year and allocates no resources to producing bikes. These six possibilities are alternative combinations of the quantities of the two goods that the economy can produce by *using all of its resources, given the technology.*

The graph in Figure 3.1 illustrates the production possibilities frontier, *PPF*, for smartphones and bikes. Each point on the graph labeled *A* through *F* represents the possibility in the table identified by the same letter. For example, point *B* represents the production of 1 million smartphones and 14 million bikes. These quantities also appear in the table as possibility *B*.

FIGURE 3.1

The Production Possibilities Frontier

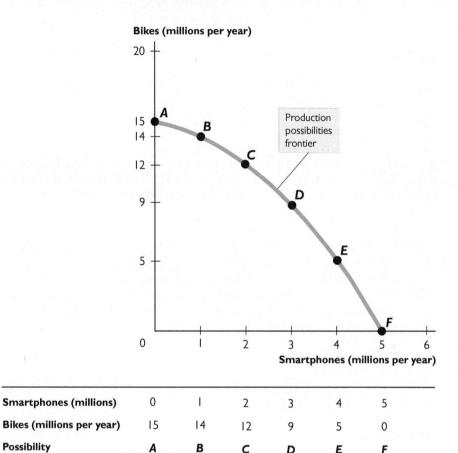

Smartphones (millions)	0	1	2	3	4	5
Bikes (millions per year)	15	14	12	9	5	0
Possibility	**A**	**B**	**C**	**D**	**E**	**F**

The table and the graph show the production possibilities frontier for smartphones and bikes.

Point *A* tells us that if the economy produces no smartphones, the maximum quantity of bikes it can produce is 15 million a year.

Each point *A, B, C, D, E,* and *F* on the graph represents the possibility in the table identified by the same letter.

The line passing through these points is the production possibilities frontier.

The *PPF* shows the limits to production *with the available resources and technology.* If either resources or technology change, the *PPF* shifts. If more resources or better technology become available, the *PPF* shifts outward. If resources are lost, for example in a natural disaster, the *PPF* shifts inward.

The *PPF* is a valuable tool for illustrating the effects of scarcity and its consequences. Let's see how.

How the *PPF* Illustrates Scarcity and Its Consequences

The *PPF* illustrates scarcity and some of its consequences by putting three distinctions in sharp focus. They are the distinctions between

- Attainable and unattainable combinations
- Efficient and inefficient production
- Tradeoffs and free lunches

Attainable and Unattainable Combinations

Because the *PPF* shows the *limits* to production, it separates attainable combinations from unattainable ones. The economy can produce combinations of smartphones and bikes that are smaller than those on the *PPF*, and it can produce any of the combinations *on* the *PPF*. These combinations of smartphones and bikes are attainable. But it is impossible to produce combinations that are larger than those on the *PPF*. These combinations are unattainable.

Figure 3.2 emphasizes the attainable and unattainable combinations. Only the points on the *PPF* and inside it (in the orange area) are attainable. The combinations of smartphones and bikes beyond the *PPF* (in the white area), such as the combination at point *G*, are unattainable. These points illustrate combinations that cannot be produced with the current resources and technology. The *PPF* tells us that the economy can produce 4 million smartphones and 5 million bikes at point *E or* 2 million smartphones and 12 million bikes at point *C*. But the economy cannot produce 4 million smartphones and 12 million bikes at point *G*.

Efficient and Inefficient Production

Production efficiency
A situation in which the economy is getting all that it can from its resources and cannot produce more of one good or service without producing less of something else.

Production efficiency occurs when the economy is getting all that it can from its resources. When production is efficient it is not possible to produce more of one good or service without producing less of something else. For production to be efficient, there must be full employment—not just of labor but of all the available factors of production—and each resource must be assigned to the task that it performs comparatively better than other resources can.

◼ **FIGURE 3.2**

Attainable and Unattainable Combinations

MyEconLab Animation

The production possibilities frontier, *PPF*, separates attainable combinations from unattainable ones. The economy can produce at any point *inside* the *PPF* (the orange area) or at any point *on* the frontier. Any point outside the production possibilities frontier, such as point *G*, is unattainable.

Figure 3.3 illustrates the distinction between efficient and inefficient production. With *inefficient* production, the economy might be producing 3 million smartphones and 5 million bikes at point *H*. With an *efficient* use of the economy's resources, it is possible to produce at a point on the *PPF* such as point *D* or *E*. At point *D*, there are more bikes and the same quantity of smartphones as at point *H*. And at point *E*, there are more smartphones and the same quantity of bikes as at point *H*. At points *D* and *E*, production is efficient.

Tradeoffs and Free Lunches

A **tradeoff** is an exchange—giving up one thing to get something else. You trade off income for a better grade when you decide to cut back on the hours you spend on your weekend job and allocate the time to extra study. The Ford Motor Company faces a tradeoff when it cuts the production of trucks and uses the resources saved to produce more hybrid SUVs. The federal government faces a tradeoff when it cuts NASA's space exploration program and allocates more resources to homeland security. As a society, we face a tradeoff when we decide to cut down a forest and destroy the habitat of the spotted owl.

Tradeoff
An exchange—giving up one thing to get something else.

The production possibilities frontier illustrates the idea of a tradeoff. The *PPF* in Figure 3.3 shows how. If the economy produces at point *E* and people want to produce more bikes, they must forgo some smartphones. In the move from point *E* to point *D*, people trade off smartphones for bikes.

Economists often express the central idea of economics—that choices involve a tradeoff—with the saying "There is no such thing as a free lunch." A *free lunch* is a gift—getting something without giving up something else. What does the

---

◼ **FIGURE 3.3**

Efficient and Inefficient Production, Tradeoffs, and Free Lunches

MyEconLab Animation

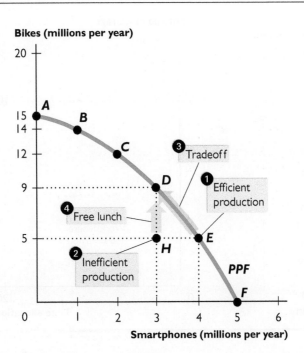

❶ When production occurs at a point on the *PPF*, such as point *E*, resources are used efficiently.

❷ When production occurs at a point inside the *PPF*, such as point *H*, resources are used inefficiently.

❸ When production is efficient— on the *PPF*—the economy faces a tradeoff. To move from point *E* to point *D* requires that some smartphones be given up for more bikes.

❹ When production is inefficient— inside the *PPF*—there is a free lunch. To move from point *H* inside the *PPF* to point *D* on the *PPF* does not involve a tradeoff.

famous saying mean? Suppose some resources are not being used or are not being used efficiently. Isn't it then possible to avoid a tradeoff and get a free lunch?

The answer is yes. You can see why in Figure 3.3. If production is taking place *inside* the PPF at point H, then it is possible to move to point D and increase the production of bikes by using currently unused resources or by using resources in their most productive way. Nothing is forgone to increase production—there is a free lunch.

When production is efficient—at a point on the PPF—choosing to produce more of one good involves a tradeoff. But if production is inefficient—at a point inside the PPF—there is a free lunch. More of some goods and services can be produced without producing less of any others.

So "there is no such thing as a free lunch" means that when resources are used efficiently, every choice involves a tradeoff. Because economists view people as making rational choices, they expect that resources will be used efficiently. That is why they emphasize the tradeoff idea and deny the existence of free lunches. We might *sometimes* get a free lunch, but we *almost always* face a tradeoff.

EYE on YOUR LIFE
Your Production Possibilities Frontier

MyEconLab Critical Thinking Exercise

Two "goods" that concern you a great deal are your grade point average (GPA) and the amount of time you have available for leisure or earning an income. You face a tradeoff. To get a higher GPA you must give up leisure or income. Your forgone leisure or forgone income is the opportunity cost of a higher GPA. Similarly, to get more leisure or more income, you must accept a lower grade. A lower grade is the opportunity cost of increased leisure or increased income.

The figure illustrates a student's PPF. Any point on or inside the PPF is attainable and any point outside the PPF is unattainable. A student who wastes time ends up with a lower GPA than the highest attainable from the time spent studying. But a student who works efficiently achieves a point *on* the PPF and achieves production efficiency.

The student in the figure allocates the scarce 168 hours a week between studying (class and study hours) and other activities (work, leisure, and sleep hours). The student attends class and studies for 48 hours each week and works or has fun (and sleeps) for the other 120 hours. With this allocation of time, and studying efficiently, the student's GPA is 3.

CHECKPOINT 3.1

Explain and illustrate the concepts of scarcity, production efficiency, and tradeoff using the production possibilities frontier.

Practice Problems

1. Table 1 sets out the production possibilities of a small Pacific island economy. Draw the economy's *PPF*.

Figure 1 shows an economy's *PPF* and identifies some production points. Use this figure to work Problems **2** to **4**.

2. Which points are attainable? Explain why.
3. Which points are efficient and which points are inefficient? Explain why.
4. Which points illustrate a tradeoff? Explain why.

In the News

Honeybee decline linked to killer virus
In 2007, the killer virus arrived in Hawaii, where almost all the queen bees used in the United States are bred. Bees are used to pollinate crops that are used in a third of the food we eat.

Source: *The Guardian*, June 8, 2012

Explain how a decline in bee population affects the U.S. *PPF*.

Solutions to Practice Problems

1. The *PPF* is the boundary between attainable and unattainable combinations of goods. Figure 2 shows the economy's *PPF*. The graph plots each row of the table as a point with the corresponding letter.

2. Attainable points: Any point on the *PPF* is attainable and any point inside the *PPF* is attainable. Points outside the *PPF* (F and G) are unattainable. In Figure 1, the attainable points are A, B, C, D, and E.

3. Efficient points: Production is efficient when it is not possible to produce more of one good without producing less of another good. To be efficient, a point must be attainable, so points F and G can't be efficient. Points inside the *PPF* can't be efficient because more goods can be produced, so D and E are not efficient. The only efficient points are those *on* the *PPF*—A, B, and C.

   Inefficient points: Inefficiency occurs when resources are misallocated or unemployed. Such points are *inside* the *PPF*. These points are D and E.

4. Tradeoff: Begin by recalling that a tradeoff is an exchange—giving up something to get something else. A tradeoff occurs when moving along the *PPF* from one point to another point. So moving from any point *on* the *PPF*, point A, B, or C, to another point *on* the *PPF* illustrates a tradeoff.

Solution to In the News

Honeybees are a resource used in the production of many food crops. Before 2007, the United States was at a point on its *PPF*. During the following years, with fewer queen bees, the number of honeybees declined and the quantity of food produced decreased. With no change in other resources and technology, and no change in the quantity of other goods and services produced, the U.S. *PPF* rotated inward.

TABLE 1

Possibility	Fish (pounds)		Berries (pounds)
A	0	and	20
B	1	and	18
C	2	and	15
D	3	and	11
E	4	and	6
F	5	and	0

FIGURE 1

FIGURE 2

3.2 OPPORTUNITY COST

You've seen that moving from one point to another on the *PPF* involves a trade-off. But what are the terms of the tradeoff? *How much* of one item must be forgone to obtain an additional unit of another item—a large amount or a small amount? The answer is given by opportunity cost—the best thing you must give up to get something (see p. 8). We can use the *PPF* to calculate opportunity cost.

■ The Opportunity Cost of a Smartphone

The opportunity cost of producing a smartphone is the number of bikes forgone to get an additional smartphone. It is calculated as the number of bikes forgone divided by the number of smartphones gained.

Figure 3.4 illustrates the calculation. At point *A*, the quantities produced are zero smartphones and 15 million bikes; and at point *B*, the quantities produced are 1 million smartphones and 14 million bikes. To gain 1 million smartphones by moving from point *A* to point *B*, 1 million bikes are forgone, so the opportunity cost of 1 smartphone is 1 bike.

At point *C*, the quantities produced are 2 million smartphones and 12 million bikes. To gain 1 million smartphones by moving from point *B* to point *C*, 2 million bikes are forgone. Now the opportunity cost of 1 smartphone is 2 bikes.

If you repeat these calculations, moving from *C* to *D*, *D* to *E*, and *E* to *F*, you will obtain the opportunity costs shown in the table and the graph.

■ **FIGURE 3.4**

Calculating the Opportunity Cost of a Smartphone   MyEconLab Animation

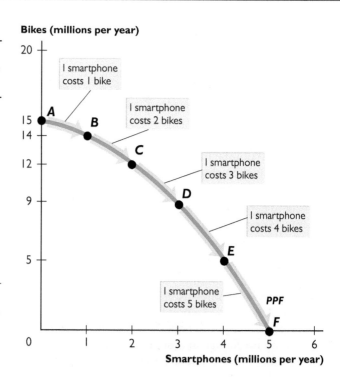

Movement along *PPF*	Decrease in quantity of bikes	Increase in quantity of smartphones	Decrease in bikes divided by increase in smartphones
A to *B*	1 million	1 million	1 bike per phone
B to *C*	2 million	1 million	2 bikes per phone
C to *D*	3 million	1 million	3 bikes per phone
D to *E*	4 million	1 million	4 bikes per phone
E to *F*	5 million	1 million	5 bikes per phone

Along the *PPF* from *A* to *F*, the opportunity cost of a smartphone increases as the quantity of smartphones produced increases.

■ Opportunity Cost and the Slope of the *PPF*

Look at the numbers that we've just calculated for the opportunity cost of a smartphone and notice that they follow a striking pattern. The opportunity cost of a smartphone increases as the quantity of smartphones produced increases.

The magnitude of the *slope* of the *PPF* measures the opportunity cost. Because the *PPF* in Figure 3.4 is bowed outward, its slope changes and gets steeper as the quantity of smartphones produced increases.

When a small quantity of smartphones is produced—between points *A* and *B*—the *PPF* has a gentle slope and the opportunity cost of a smartphone is low. A given increase in the quantity of smartphones costs a small decrease in the quantity of bikes. When a large quantity of smartphones is produced—between points *E* and *F*—the *PPF* is steep and the opportunity cost of a smartphone is high. A given increase in the quantity of smartphones costs a large decrease in the quantity of bikes. Figure 3.5 shows the increasing opportunity cost of a smartphone.

■ Opportunity Cost Is a Ratio

The opportunity cost of a smartphone is the *ratio* of bikes forgone to smartphones gained. Similarly, the opportunity cost of a bike is the *ratio* of smartphones forgone to bikes gained. So the opportunity cost of producing a bike is equal to the inverse of the opportunity cost of producing a smartphone. For example, moving along the *PPF* in Figure 3.4 from *C* to *D* the opportunity cost of a smartphone is 3 bikes. Moving along the *PPF* in the opposite direction, from *D* to *C*, the opportunity cost of a bike is 1/3 of a smartphone.

▓ **FIGURE 3.5**

The Opportunity Cost of a Smartphone   MyEconLab Animation

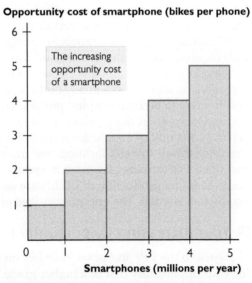

Because the *PPF* in Figure 3.4 is bowed outward, the opportunity cost of a smartphone increases as the quantity of smartphones produced increases.

Smartphones (millions)	0 to 1	1 to 2	2 to 3	3 to 4	4 to 5
Opportunity cost (bikes per phone)	1	2	3	4	5

EYE on the ENVIRONMENT

MyEconLab Critical Thinking Exercise

Is Wind Power Free?

Wind power is not free. To use it, we must give up other goods and services to build wind turbines and transmission lines.

Wind turbines can produce electricity only when the wind is strong enough, but advances in technology are enabling turbines to operate in lower wind conditions.

Some of the best wind farm locations are far from major population centers, so transmission lines can be long and power losses large.

If we produced most of our electricity using wind power, we would be operating inside the *PPF* at a point such as Z.

■ Increasing Opportunity Costs Are Everywhere

Just about every production activity that you can think of has increasing opportunity cost. We allocate the most skillful farmers and the most fertile land to producing food, and we allocate the best doctors and the least fertile land to producing healthcare services. Some resources are equally productive in both activities. If we shift these equally productive resources away from farming to hospitals, we get an increase in healthcare at a low opportunity cost. But if we keep increasing healthcare services, we must eventually build hospitals on the most fertile land and get the best farmers to become hospital porters. The production of food drops drastically and the increase in the production of healthcare services is small. The opportunity cost of a unit of healthcare services rises. Similarly, if we shift resources away from healthcare toward farming, we must eventually use more skilled doctors and nurses as farmers and more hospitals as hydroponic vegetable factories. The decrease in the production of healthcare services is large, but the increase in food production is small. The opportunity cost of producing a unit of food rises.

■ Your Increasing Opportunity Cost

Flip back to the *PPF* in *Eye on Your Life* on p. 64 and think about its implications for your opportunity cost of a higher grade.

What is the opportunity cost of spending time with your friends in terms of the grade you might receive on your exam? What is the opportunity cost of a higher grade in terms of the activities you give up to study? Do you face increasing opportunity costs in these activities?

CHECKPOINT 3.2

Calculate opportunity cost.

Practice Problems

Table 1 shows Robinson Crusoe's production possibilities.

TABLE 1

Possibility	Fish (pounds)		Berries (pounds)
A	0	and	36
B	4.0	and	35
C	7.5	and	33
D	10.5	and	30
E	13.0	and	26
F	15.0	and	21
G	16.5	and	15
H	17.5	and	8
I	18.0	and	0

1. What is his opportunity cost of a pound of berries when Crusoe increases the quantity of berries from 21 pounds to 26 pounds and production is efficient? Does this opportunity cost increase as he produces more berries?
2. If Crusoe is producing 10 pounds of fish and 21 pounds of berries, what is his opportunity cost of an extra pound of berries? And what is his opportunity cost of an extra pound of fish? Explain your answers.

In the News

Cost of meeting 2021 vehicle emission standards
Carbon dioxide emissions from cars must be cut from 130 grams to 95 grams per kilometer. To meet this new standard, the price of a car will rise by $1,350.
Source: *International Business Times*, November 9, 2015

Calculate the opportunity cost of reducing the carbon emission level by 1 gram.

Solutions to Practice Problems

1. If Crusoe's production is efficient, he is producing at a point *on* his *PPF*. His opportunity cost of an extra pound of berries is the quantity of fish he must give up to get the berries. It is calculated as the decrease in the quantity of fish divided by the increase in the quantity of berries as he moves along his *PPF*.

    To increase the quantity of berries from 21 pounds to 26 pounds (from row *F* to row *E* of Table 1), production of fish decreases from 15 pounds to 13 pounds. To gain 5 pounds of berries, Crusoe must forgo 2 pounds of fish. The opportunity cost of 1 pound of berries is the 2 pounds of fish forgone divided by 5 pounds of berries gained—2/5 of a pound of fish.

    Crusoe's opportunity cost of berries increases as he produces more berries. To see why, move Crusoe from row *E* to row *D* in Table 1. His production of berries increases by 4 pounds and his production of fish falls by 2.5 pounds. His opportunity cost of 1 pound of berries increases to 5/8 of a pound of fish.

2. Figure 1 graphs the data in Table 1 and shows Crusoe's *PPF*. If Crusoe is producing 10 pounds of fish and 21 pounds of berries, he is producing at point Z. Point Z is a point *inside* Crusoe's *PPF*. When Crusoe produces 21 pounds of berries, he has enough time available to produce 15 pounds of fish at point *F* on his *PPF*. To produce more fish, Crusoe can move from Z toward *F* on his *PPF* and forgo no berries. His opportunity cost of a pound of fish is zero. Similarly, his opportunity cost of a pound of berries is zero.

FIGURE 1

Solution to In the News

By spending $1,350 extra on a new car, you forgo $1,350 of other goods. With a new car, your emissions fall from 130 grams to 95 grams, a reduction of 35 grams. The opportunity cost of a 1-gram reduction in emissions is $1,350 of other goods divided by 35 grams, or $38.57 of other goods.

3.3 ECONOMIC GROWTH

Economic growth
The sustained expansion of production possibilities.

The *PPF* shows the limits to production with given resources and technology. But over time, resources and technology change and production possibilities expand. A process of sustained expansion of production possibilities is called **economic growth**. Our economy grows when we develop better technologies; improve the quality of labor by education, on-the-job training, and work experience; and acquire more machines (capital) to help us produce.

To study economic growth, we must look at the production possibilities for a consumption good—a smartphone—and a capital good—a smartphone factory. By using resources to produce smartphone factories, the economy can expand its future production possibilities. The greater the production of new capital—of new smartphone factories—the faster is the expansion of production possibilities.

Figure 3.6 shows how the *PPF* can expand. If no new factories are produced (at point *L*), production possibilities do not expand and the *PPF* stays at its original position. By producing fewer smartphones and using resources to produce 2 new smartphone factories (at point *K*), production possibilities expand once the new factories become operational. The *PPF* rotates outward to the new *PPF*.

But economic growth is *not* free. To make it happen, current consumption must decrease. The move from *L* to *K* in Figure 3.6 means forgoing 2 million smartphones now. The opportunity cost of producing new smartphone factories is the decrease in the number of smartphones produced today.

Also, economic growth does not end scarcity. It rotates the *PPF* outward, but on the new *PPF* we continue to face opportunity costs. To keep producing new capital, current consumption must be less than its maximum possible level.

FIGURE 3.6

Expanding Production Possibilities

❶ If firms allocate no resources to producing smartphone factories and produce 5 million smartphones a year at point *L*, the *PPF* doesn't change.

❷ If firms decrease smartphone production to 3 million a year and produce 2 smartphone factories, at point *K*, production possibilities will expand. After a year, the *PPF* rotates outward to the new *PPF* and production can move to point *K'*.

EYE on the U.S. ECONOMY
Expanding Our Production Possibilities

Horizontal drilling and hydraulic fracturing—fracking—combined with recent advances in remote sensing technology have made it possible to extract a large quantity of gas trapped in shale at low cost. The United States has an estimated 750 trillion cubic feet of this gas, enough for more than 90 years at today's extraction rate. The map below shows the locations of these gas deposits.

Figure I shows recent years of shale gas production. During 2010 and 2011, production doubled. The average growth rate since 2010 exceeds 30 percent per year.

Was this increase in gas production achieved by sliding along the PPF and producing less of other goods and servces? No! It was the result of advances in technology and the opening up of additional gas wells.

Figure 2 illustrates how these changes rotated the PPF outward from PPF_{10} in 2010 to PPF_{13} in 2013. Point J is the same on both curves because if we produced at that point (only other goods and services and no gas), we would not get the benefits of the technological advances in gas production. In 2010 we produced at point K, and in 2013 at point K'. Along PPF_{13} the opportunity cost of gas is lower than along PPF_{10}.

Shale gas production (trillions of cubic feet per year)

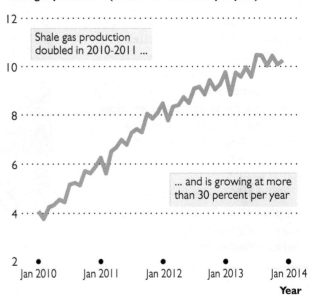

Shale gas production doubled in 2010-2011 ...

... and is growing at more than 30 percent per year

Figure I Shale Gas Production

Other goods and services (units)

Advances in fracking technology and increase in wells expanded production possibilities

Figure 2 Shale Gas Versus Other Goods and Services

SOURCE OF DATA: Energy Information Administration.

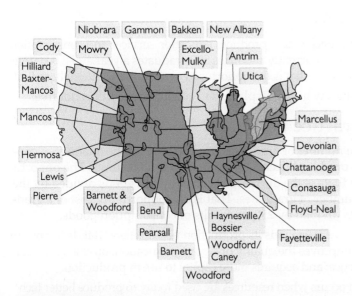

Natural Gas Shale Basins in the United States

EYE on the GLOBAL ECONOMY
Hong Kong's Rapid Economic Growth

Hong Kong's production possibilities per person were 25 percent of those of the United States in 1960. By 2015, they had grown to become equal to U.S. production possibilities per person. Hong Kong grew faster than the United States because it allocated more of its resources to accumulating capital and less to consumption than did the United States.

In 1960, the United States and Hong Kong produced at point *A* on their respective *PPF*s. In 2015, Hong Kong was at point *B* and the United States was at point *C*.

If Hong Kong continues to produce at any point on its *PPF* above *C*, it will grow more rapidly than the United States and its *PPF* will eventually shift out

beyond the *PPF* of the United States. But if Hong Kong produces at a point

below *B*, the pace of expansion of its *PPF* will slow.

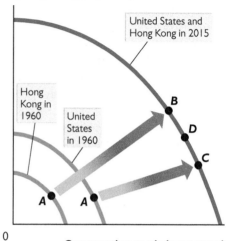

MyEconLab Study Plan 3.3
Key Terms Quiz
Solutions Video

CHECKPOINT 3.3

Explain what makes production possibilities expand.

Practice Problems

1. Table 1 shows an economy that produces education services and consumption goods. If the economy currently produces 500 graduates a year and 2,000 units of consumption goods, what is the opportunity cost of one additional graduate?

2. How does an economy grow? Explain why economic growth is not free.

Solutions to Practice Problems

1. By increasing the number of graduates from 500 to 750, the quantity of consumption goods produced decreases from 2,000 to 1,000 units. The opportunity cost of a graduate is the decrease in consumption goods divided by the increase in the number of graduates. That is, the opportunity cost of a graduate is 1,000 units divided by 250, or 4 units of consumption goods.

2. An economy grows if it expands its production possibilities—if it develops better technologies; improves the quality of labor by education, on-the-job training, and work experience; and acquires more capital to use in production.

Economic growth occurs when resources are used today to produce better technologies, higher-quality labor, or more machines. Those resources cannot be used to produce goods and services today, so the cost of economic growth is the goods and services forgone today. Economic growth is not free.

TABLE 1

Possibility	Education services (graduates)	Consumption goods (units)
A	1,000	0
B	750	1,000
C	500	2,000
D	0	3,000

3.4 SPECIALIZATION AND TRADE

MyEconLab Concept Video

The next time you visit your favorite fast-food restaurant, watch what the workers are doing. You might see one person re-stocking the bread, salad materials, meat, sauces, boxes, and wrappers; another working the grill and another the fry maker; another assembling meals; and yet another taking orders and payments. Imagine how long you would wait for your burger if each worker performed all the tasks needed to fill each customer's not-so-fast-food order.

Specialization makes people more productive in two ways: It brings absolute advantage and comparative advantage.

■ Absolute Advantage and Comparative Advantage

A person has an **absolute advantage** if that person is more productive than another. Being more productive means using fewer inputs or taking less time to produce a good or perform a production task. Being more productive also means being able to produce more with given inputs in a given amount of time.

The specialized workers at McDonald's have an *absolute advantage* over the same number of workers each performing all the tasks needed to make a burger.

A person has a **comparative advantage** in an activity if that person can perform the activity at a lower opportunity cost than anyone else. Recall that the opportunity cost of something is what you must give up to get it.

Notice the contrast between *absolute advantage* and *comparative advantage*. Absolute advantage is about *productivity*—how long does it take to produce a unit of a good. Comparative advantage is about *opportunity cost*—how much of some other good must be forgone to produce a unit of a good.

Specialization boosts productivity in a fast-food kitchen

Absolute advantage
When one person (or nation) is more productive than another—needs fewer inputs or takes less time to produce a good or perform a production task.

Comparative advantage
The ability of a person to perform an activity or produce a good or service at a lower opportunity cost than anyone else.

EYE on the U.S. ECONOMY
No One Knows How to Make a Pencil

Not many products in today's world are as simple as a pencil. Yet the story of how the pencil in your hand got there illustrates the astonishing power of specialization and trade.

When you hold a pencil, you're holding cedar grown in Oregon, graphite mined in Sri Lanka, clay from Mississippi, wax from Mexico, rapeseed oil grown in the Dutch East Indies, pumice from Italy, copper from Arizona, and zinc from Alaska.

These materials were harvested and mined by thousands of workers

equipped with hundreds of specialized tools, all of which were manufactured by thousands of other workers using hundreds more specialized tools. These tools were in turn made of steel, itself made from iron ore, and from other minerals and materials.

Rail, road, and ocean transportation systems moved all these things to custom-built factories that made graphite "leads," erasers, brass to hold the erasers, paint, and glue.

Finally, all these components were bought by a pencil factory which, with

its millions of dollars' worth of custom machinery, put them all together.

Millions of people contributed to making that pencil, many of whom don't even know what a pencil is and *not one of whom knows how to make a pencil.* No one directed all these people. Each worker and business went about its self-interested specialized task trading with each other in markets.

Adapted from *I Pencil*, by Leonard Read, Foundation for Economic Education, 1958.

TABLE 3.1   LIZ'S PRODUCTION POSSIBILITIES

Item	Minutes to produce 1	Quantity per hour
Smoothies	2	30
Salads	2	30

TABLE 3.2   JOE'S PRODUCTION POSSIBILITIES

Item	Minutes to produce 1	Quantity per hour
Smoothies	10	6
Salads	2	30

■ Comparative Advantage: A Model

We're going to explore the idea of comparative advantage and make it concrete by looking at a model economy with two smoothie bars: one operated by Liz and the other operated by Joe. You will see how we identify comparative advantage and how it creates an opportunity for Liz and Joe to gain from specialization and trade.

Liz's Smoothie Bar

Liz operates a high-tech bar. She can turn out *either* a smoothie *or* a salad every 2 minutes. If she spends all her time making smoothies, she produces 30 an hour. If she spends all her time making salads, she also produces 30 an hour (Table 3.1). If she splits her time equally between the two, she can produce 15 smoothies *and* 15 salads an hour. For each additional smoothie Liz produces, she must decrease her production of salads by one, and for each additional salad Liz produces, she must decrease her production of smoothies by one. So

> Liz's opportunity cost of producing 1 smoothie is 1 salad,

and

> Liz's opportunity cost of producing 1 salad is 1 smoothie.

Liz's customers buy smoothies and salads in equal quantities, so Liz splits her time equally between the items and produces 15 smoothies and 15 salads an hour.

Joe's Smoothie Bar

Joe produces smoothies and salads in a smaller bar than Liz's, and he has only one blender—a slow, old machine. Even if Joe uses all his resources to produce smoothies, he can produce only 6 an hour. But Joe is pretty good in the salad department. If he uses all his resources to make salads, he can produce 30 an hour (Table 3.2). Joe's ability to make smoothies and salads is the same regardless of how he splits an hour between the two tasks. He can make a salad in 2 minutes or a smoothie in 10 minutes. For each additional smoothie Joe produces, he must decrease his production of salads by 5. And for each additional salad Joe produces, he must decrease his production of smoothies by 1/5 of a smoothie. So

> Joe's opportunity cost of producing 1 smoothie is 5 salads,

and

> Joe's opportunity cost of producing 1 salad is 1/5 of a smoothie.

Joe's customers, like Liz's, buy smoothies and salads in equal quantities. Joe spends 50 minutes of each hour making smoothies and 10 minutes of each hour making salads. With this division of his time, Joe produces 5 smoothies and 5 salads an hour.

Liz's and Joe's *PPFs*

The *PPF*s in Figure 3.7 illustrate the situation we've just described. In part (a), Liz faces a *PPF* that enables her to produce 15 smoothies and 15 salads. In part (b), Joe faces a *PPF* that enables him to produce 5 smoothies and 5 salads. On Liz's *PPF*, 1 smoothie costs 1 salad. On Joe's *PPF*, 1 smoothie costs 5 salads.

The *PPF*s in Figure 3.7 contrast with the outward-bowed *PPF*s that you've seen earlier in this chapter, which capture the general rule that the opportunity cost of a good increases as we increase its rate of production. It is easier to identify

FIGURE 3.7

Production Possibilities Frontiers

MyEconLab Animation

(a) Liz's *PPF* and production

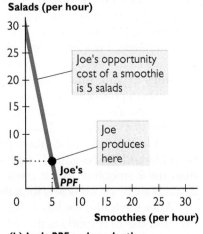

(b) Joe's *PPF* and production

Liz can produce 30 smoothies per hour or 30 salads per hour or any other combination along her *PPF* in part (a). Liz chooses to produce 15 smoothies and 15 salads per hour.

Joe can produce 6 smoothies per hour or 30 salads per hour or any other combination along his *PPF* in part (b). Joe chooses to produce 5 smoothies and 5 salads per hour.

comparative advantage and see the gains from trade when individuals have constant opportunity cost. And as you will soon see, the economy's *PPF* is outward-bowed even when individuals have constant opportunity cost and linear *PPF*s.

Liz's Greater Productivity

You can see from the production numbers that Liz is three times as productive as Joe—her 15 smoothies and 15 salads an hour are three times Joe's 5 smoothies and 5 salads. Liz is more productive than Joe in producing both smoothies and salads, but Liz has a comparative advantage in only one of the activities.

Liz's Comparative Advantage

In which of the two activities does Liz have a *comparative* advantage? Recall that comparative advantage is a situation in which one person's opportunity cost of producing a good is lower than another person's opportunity cost of producing that same good.

You've seen that Liz's opportunity cost of a smoothie is 1 salad, whereas Joe's opportunity cost of a smoothie is 5 salads. To produce 1 smoothie, Liz must forgo 1 salad while Joe must forgo 5 salads. So, because Liz forgoes fewer salads to make a smoothie, she has a comparative advantage in producing smoothies.

What about Joe? Doesn't he have a comparative advantage at anything? He does as you're about to see.

Joe's Comparative Advantage

Look at the opportunity costs of producing salads. For Liz, that opportunity cost is 1 smoothie. But for Joe, a salad costs only 1/5 of a smoothie. Because Joe's opportunity cost of a salad is less than Liz's, Joe has a comparative advantage in producing salads.

It is always true that if one person has a comparative advantage in producing a good, others have a comparative advantage in producing some other good.

**TABLE 3.3   LIZ AND JOE GAIN
FROM TRADE**

(a) Before Trade	Liz	Joe
Smoothies	15	5
Salads	15	5

(b) Specialization	Liz	Joe
Smoothies	30	0
Salads	0	30

(c) Trade		
Smoothies	sell 10	buy 10
Salads	buy 20	sell 20

(d) After Trade		
Smoothies	20	10
Salads	20	10

(e) Gains from Trade		
Smoothies	+5	+5
Salads	+5	+5

■ Achieving Gains from Trade

Liz and Joe run into each other in a bar, where Liz tells Joe about her smoothie business. Her only problem, she says, is that she wants to produce more because customers leave when her lines get too long. Joe describes his own smaller business to Liz. When he explains how he divides his hour between making smoothies and salads, Liz's eyes pop. "Have I got a deal for you!" she exclaims.

Here's Liz's deal. Joe stops making smoothies and produces 30 salads per hour. Liz stops making salads and produces 30 smoothies per hour. That is, they both specialize in producing the good in which they have a comparative advantage—see Table 3.3(b). They then trade: Liz sells Joe 10 smoothies and Joe sells Liz 20 salads—the price of a smoothie is 2 salads—see Table 3.3(c).

Trade at a price of 2 salads per smoothie (1/2 a smoothie per salad) enables both Liz and Joe to gain. Liz gets salads for 1/2 a smoothie each, which is less than the 1 smoothie that it costs her to produce a salad. Joe gets smoothies for 2 salads each, which is less than the 5 salads it costs him to produce a smoothie.

After the trade, Joe has 10 salads (the 30 he produces minus the 20 he sells to Liz) and the 10 smoothies that he buys from Liz. So Joe doubles the quantities of smoothies and salads he can sell. Liz has 20 smoothies (the 30 she produces minus the 10 she sells to Joe) and the 20 salads she buys from Joe. See Table 3.3(d). From specialization and trade, each gains 5 smoothies and 5 salads—see Table 3.3(e).

Liz draws the graphs in Figure 3.8 to illustrate her idea. The blue *PPF* is Liz's and the red *PPF* is Joe's. They are each producing at the points marked *A*. Liz's proposal is that they each produce at the points marked *B*.

After trading, each moves to the point marked *C*. At these points, Liz has 20 smoothies and 20 salads, 5 more of each than she was producing only for herself. Joe has 10 smoothies and 10 salads, also 5 more of each than he was producing only for himself. Because of the gains from specialization and trade, total production increases by 10 smoothies and 10 salads.

Notice that the points *C* are *outside* Liz's and Joe's *PPF*s. Everyone gains and enjoys greater quantities of goods than they can produce on their own.

■ FIGURE 3.8

The Gains from Specialization and Trade   MyEconLab Animation

❶ Before trade, Liz and Joe each produce at point *A* on their respective *PPF*s.

❷ Liz specializes in smoothies and Joe specializes in salads, so they each move to point *B* on their respective *PPF*s.

❸ They exchange smoothies for salads at a price of 2 salads per smoothie. After trade, each goes to point *C*—a point *outside* their individual *PPF*s. They each gain 5 salads and 5 smoothies—the quantities at point *C* minus the quantities at point *A*.

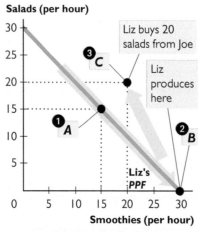

(a) Liz's gains from trade

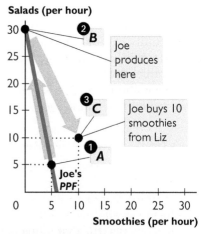

(b) Joe's gains from trade

■ The Economy's Production Possibilities Frontier

With specialization and trade, Liz and Joe get outside their individual *PPF*s, but they produce *on* the economy's *PPF*. Also, despite Liz and Joe having constant opportunity costs, along the economy's *PPF* opportunity cost is increasing—the economy's *PPF* is bowed outward. Figure 3.9 illustrates. The first 30 smoothies produced (by Liz) cost 1 salad each, but the 31st smoothie produced (by Joe) costs 5 salads. Similarly, the first 30 salads produced (by Joe) cost 1/5 smoothie each, but the 31st salad produced (by Liz) costs 1 smoothie. When Liz and Joe specialize, they produce efficiently on the economy's *PPF*. Without specialization and trade, they produce at an inefficient point *inside* the economy's *PPF*.

■ FIGURE 3.9

The Economy's Production Possibilities   MyEconLab Animation

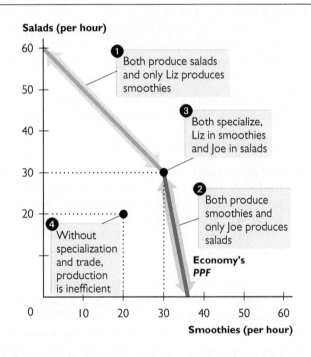

❶ When the economy produces more than 30 salads per hour, both Liz and Joe produce salads but only Liz produces smoothies.

❷ When the economy produces more than 30 smoothies per hour, both Liz and Joe produce smoothies but only Joe produces salads.

❸ When Liz and Joe specialize in their comparative advantage, the economy produces 30 salads and 30 smoothies at an efficient point on the economy's *PPF*.

❹ Without specialization and trade, Liz and Joe produce at an inefficient point inside the economy's *PPF*.

EYE on YOUR LIFE
Your Comparative Advantage

MyEconLab Critical Thinking Exercise

You are expanding your production possibilities by being in school and accumulating human capital.

By discovering your comparative advantage, you will be able to focus on producing the items that make you as well off as possible. Think hard about what you enjoy doing, and what you do comparatively better than others.

In today's world, it is a good idea to try to remain flexible so that you can switch jobs if you discover that your comparative advantage has changed.

Looking beyond your own self-interest, are you going to be a voice that supports or opposes offshore outsourcing?

You've learned in this chapter that

regardless of whether outsourcing remains inside the United States, as it does with Liz and Joe at their smoothie bars, or is global like the outsourcing of jobs by U.S. producers to India, both parties gain from trade.

Americans pay less for goods and services and Indians earn higher incomes.

MyEconLab Study Plan 3.4
Key Terms Quiz
Solutions Video

CHECKPOINT 3.4

Explain how people gain from specialization and trade.

Practice Problems

Tony and Patty produce skis and snowboards. Tables 1 and 2 show their production possibilities. Each week, Tony produces 5 snowboards and 40 skis and Patty produces 10 snowboards and 5 skis.

1. Who has a comparative advantage in producing snowboards? Who has a comparative advantage in producing skis?
2. If Tony and Patty specialize and trade, what are the gains from trade?

In the News

Sweet news after TPP sting

Trans-Pacific Partnership (TPP) trade deal has kept tight restrictions on Australia's sugar exports to the United States. In 2015, U.S. sugar producers received 22¢ per pound while Australian growers received the world price of 12¢ per pound.

Source: *The Land*, October 8, 2015

Which country has a comparative advantage in producing sugar? Explain why both the United States and Australia can gain from free trade in sugar.

Solutions to Practice Problems

1. The person with a comparative advantage in snowboards is the one who has the lower opportunity cost of producing a snowboard. Tony's production possibilities show that to produce 5 more snowboards he must produce 10 fewer skis. So Tony's opportunity cost of a snowboard is 2 skis.

   Patty's production possibilities show that to produce 10 more snowboards, she must produce 5 fewer skis. So Patty's opportunity cost of a snowboard is 1/2 a ski. Patty has a comparative advantage in snowboards because her opportunity cost of a snowboard is less than Tony's. Tony's comparative advantage is in skis. For each ski produced, Tony must forgo making 1/2 a snowboard, whereas Patty must forgo making 2 snowboards for a ski. So Tony's opportunity cost of a ski is lower than Patty's.

2. Patty has a comparative advantage in snowboards, so she specializes in snowboards. Tony has a comparative advantage in skis, so he specializes in skis. Patty makes 20 snowboards and Tony makes 50 skis. Before specializing, they made 15 snowboards and 45 skis. By specializing, total output increases by 5 snowboards and 5 skis. They share this gain by trading.

Solution to In the News

The cost of producing sugar is less in Australia than in the United States, so Australia has a comparative advantage in producing sugar. If Australia specializes in producing sugar and the United States specializes in producing other goods (for example, movies or airplanes) and the two countries engage in free trade, each country can gain and get to a point outside its own *PPF*.

TABLE 1   TONY'S PRODUCTION POSSIBILITIES

Snowboards (per week)		Skis (per week)
25	and	0
20	and	10
15	and	20
10	and	30
5	and	40
0	and	50

TABLE 2   PATTY'S PRODUCTION POSSIBILITIES

Snowboards (per week)		Skis (per week)
20	and	0
10	and	5
0	and	10

CHAPTER SUMMARY

Key Points

1. **Explain and illustrate the concepts of scarcity, production efficiency, and tradeoff using the production possibilities frontier.**

   - The production possibilities frontier, *PPF*, describes the limits to what can be produced by using all the available resources efficiently.
   - Points inside and on the *PPF* are attainable. Points outside the *PPF* are unattainable.
   - Production at any point on the *PPF* achieves production efficiency. Production at a point inside the *PPF* is inefficient.
   - When production is efficient—on the *PPF*—people face a tradeoff. If production is at a point inside the *PPF*, there is a free lunch to be had.

2. **Calculate opportunity cost.**

   - Along the *PPF*, the opportunity cost of *X* (the item measured on the *x*-axis) is the decrease in *Y* (the item measured on the *y*-axis) divided by the increase in *X*.
   - The opportunity cost of *Y* is the inverse of the opportunity cost of *X*.
   - The opportunity cost of producing a good increases as the quantity of the good produced increases.

3. **Explain what makes production possibilities expand.**

   - Technological change and increases in capital and human capital expand production possibilities.
   - The opportunity cost of economic growth is the decrease in current consumption.

4. **Explain how people gain from specialization and trade.**

   - A person has a comparative advantage in an activity if he or she can perform that activity at a lower opportunity cost than someone else.
   - People gain by increasing the production of the item in which they have a comparative advantage and trading.

Key Terms

MyEconLab Key Terms Quiz

Absolute advantage, 73
Comparative advantage, 73
Economic growth, 70

Production efficiency, 62
Production possibilities frontier, 60
Tradeoff, 63

TABLE 1

Corn (bushels)		Beef (pounds)
250	and	0
200	and	300
100	and	500
0	and	600

TABLE 2

Labor (hours)	Entertainment (units)		Good food (units)
0	0	or	0
10	20	or	30
20	40	or	50
30	60	or	60
40	80	or	65
50	100	or	67

FIGURE 1

FIGURE 2

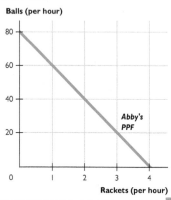

CHAPTER CHECKPOINT

Study Plan Problems and Applications

1. Table 1 shows the quantities of corn and beef that a farm can produce in a year. Draw a graph of the farm's *PPF*. Mark on the graph.
   - An inefficient combination of corn and beef—label this point *A*.
   - An unattainable combination of corn and beef—label this point *B*.
   - An efficient combination of corn and beef—label this point *C*.

Use the following information to work Problems **2** and **3**.

The people of Leisure Island have 50 hours of labor a day that can be used to produce entertainment and good food. Table 2 shows the maximum quantity of *either* entertainment *or* good food that Leisure Island can produce with different quantities of labor.

2. Is an output of 50 units of entertainment and 50 units of good food attainable and efficient? With a production of 50 units of entertainment and 50 units of good food, do the people of Leisure Island face a tradeoff?

3. What is the opportunity cost of producing an additional unit of entertainment? Explain how the opportunity cost of producing a unit of entertainment changes as more entertainment is produced.

Use the following information to work Problems **4** and **5**.

Malaria can be controlled
The World Health Organization's malaria chief says that it is too costly to try to fully eradicate the disease. He says that by using nets, medicine, and DDT it is possible to eliminate 90 percent of malaria cases. But to eliminate 100 percent of cases would be extremely costly.

Source: *The New York Times*, March 4, 2008

4. Make a graph of the production possibilities frontier with malaria control on the *x*-axis and other goods and services on the *y*-axis.

5. Describe how the opportunity cost of controlling malaria changes as more resources are used to reduce the number of malaria cases.

6. Explain how the following events influence U.S. production possibilities:
   - Some retail workers are re-employed building dams and wind farms.
   - More people take early retirement.
   - Drought devastates California's economy.

Use the following information to work Problems **7** and **8**.

Figures 1 and 2 show Tom's and Abby's production possibilities. Tom uses all his resources and produces 2 rackets and 20 balls an hour. Abby uses all her resources and produces 2 rackets and 40 balls an hour.

7. What is Tom's opportunity cost of producing a racket? What is Abby's opportunity cost of a racket? Who has a comparative advantage in producing rackets? Who has a comparative advantage in producing balls?

8. If Tom and Abby specialize and trade balls and rackets at the price of 15 balls per racket, what are Tom's and Abby's gains from trade?

9. Read *Eye on the Environment* on p. 68 and describe a tradeoff faced when deciding how to generate electricity and whether to use wind power.

Instructor Assignable Problems and Applications

MyEconLab Homework, Quiz, or Test if assigned by instructor

Use the following information to work Problems **1** to **4**.

Representatives Waxman of California and Markey of Massachusetts proposed a law to limit greenhouse gas emissions from electricity generation and require electricity producers to generate a minimum percentage of power using renewable fuels, with some emission rights to be auctioned. The Congressional Budget Office estimated that the government would receive $846 billion from auctions and would spend $821 billion on incentive programs and compensation for higher energy prices. Electricity producers would spend $208 million a year to comply with the new rules. (Think of these dollar amounts as dollars' worth of other goods and services.)

1. Would the Waxman-Markey law achieve production efficiency?

2. Is the $846 billion that electricity producers would pay for the right to emit greenhouse gasses part of the opportunity cost of producing electricity?

3. Is the $821 billion that the government would spend on incentive programs and compensation for higher energy prices part of the opportunity cost of producing electricity?

4. Is the $208 million that electricity producers will spend to comply with the new rules part of the opportunity cost of producing electricity?

5. The people of Foodland have 40 hours of labor a day to bake pizza and bread. Table 1 shows the maximum quantity of *either* pizza *or* bread that Foodland can bake with different quantities of labor. Can Foodland produce 30 pizzas and 30 loaves of bread a day? If it can, is this output efficient, do the people of Foodland face a tradeoff, and what is the opportunity cost of producing an additional pizza?

Use Table 2, which shows a farm's production possibilities, to work Problems **6** and **7**.

6. If the farm uses its resources efficiently, what is the opportunity cost of an increase in chicken production from 300 pounds to 500 pounds a year? Explain your answer.

7. If the farm adopted a new technology, which allows it to use fewer resources to fatten chickens, explain how the farm's production possibilities will change. Explain how the opportunity cost of producing a bushel of soybean will be affected.

8. In an hour, Sue can produce 40 caps or 4 jackets and Tessa can produce 80 caps or 4 jackets. Who has a comparative advantage in producing caps? If Sue and Tessa specialize and trade, who will gain?

Use the following opinion to work Problems **9** to **11**.

Free Internet?
Everyone should have free Internet access to education, news, jobs, and more.

9. Explain how Internet access has changed the production possibilities and the opportunity cost of producing education and news.

10. Sketch a *PPF* curve with education and news on the *x*-axis and other goods and services on the *y*-axis before and after the Internet.

11. Explain why it is not possible for everyone to have free Internet access to education, news, jobs, and more.

TABLE 1

Labor (hours)	Pizzas		Bread (loaves)
0	0	or	0
10	30	or	10
20	50	or	20
30	60	or	30
40	65	or	40

TABLE 2

Soybean (bushels per year)		Chicken (pounds per year)
500	and	0
400	and	300
200	and	500
0	and	600

Multiple Choice Quiz

1. Table 1 shows the production possibilities of an island community. Choose the best statement.

A. This community has enough resources to produce 2 pounds of fish and 36 pounds of berries.

B. This community cannot produce 2 pounds of fish and 36 pounds of berries because this combination is inefficient.

C. This community will waste resources if it produces 2 pounds of fish and 22 pounds of berries.

D. This community can produce 2 pounds of fish and 30 pounds of berries but this combination is inefficient.

2. Table 1 shows the production possibilities of an island community. Choose the best statement.

A. Suppose that this community produces 3 pounds of fish and 20 pounds of berries. If it decides to gather more berries, it faces a tradeoff.

B. When this community produces 4 pounds of fish and 12 pounds of berries it faces a tradeoff, but it is inefficient.

C. Suppose that this community produces 5 pounds of fish and 0 pounds of berries. If it decides to gather some berries, it will get a free lunch.

D. If this community produces 3 pounds of fish and 22 pounds of berries, production is efficient but to produce more fish it faces a tradeoff.

3. Table 1 shows the production possibilities of an island community. This community's opportunity cost of producing 1 pound of fish _____.

A. is the increase in the quantity of berries gathered as the quantity of fish increases by 1 pound

B. increases as the quantity of berries gathered increases

C. is 10 pounds of berries if the quantity of fish increases from 2 to 3 pounds

D. increases as the quantity of fish caught increases

4. Table 1 shows the production possibilities of an island community. Choose the best statement.

A. When a drought hits the island, its *PPF* rotates outward.

B. When the islanders discover a better way of catching fish, the island's *PPF* rotates outward.

C. When islanders reduce the time they spend gathering berries, the *PPF* rotates inward.

D. If the islanders decide to spend more time gathering berries but continue to spend the same amount of time fishing, they face a tradeoff.

5. Mary makes 10 pies and 20 cakes a day and her opportunity cost of producing a cake is 2 pies. Tim makes 20 pies and 10 cakes a day and his opportunity cost of producing a cake is 4 pies. If Mary and Tim specialize in producing the good in which each has a comparative advantage, _____.

A. Mary produces only pies

B. Tim produces both pies and cakes

C. Mary produces only cakes while Tim produces only pies

D. Tim produces only cakes while Mary produces only pies

TABLE 1

Possibility	Fish (pounds)		Berries (pounds)
A	0	and	40
B	1	and	36
C	2	and	30
D	3	and	22
E	4	and	12
F	5	and	0

Why did the price of coffee rise in 2014?

Demand and Supply

When you have completed your study of this chapter, you will be able to

1 Distinguish between quantity demanded and demand, and explain what determines demand.

2 Distinguish between quantity supplied and supply, and explain what determines supply.

3 Explain how demand and supply determine price and quantity in a market, and explain the effects of changes in demand and supply.

CHAPTER CHECKLIST

MyEconLab Big Picture Video

COMPETITIVE MARKETS

When you want a latte you go to a coffee shop. When a coffee shop needs to restock with beans and milk, it calls its suppliers of those items. You, your favorite coffee shop, and the shop's suppliers are trading in *markets*.

You learned in Chapter 2 that a market is any arrangement that brings buyers and sellers together. A market has two sides: demand (buyers) and supply (sellers). There are markets for *goods* such as a latte and a bagel, running shoes, apples, and hiking boots; for *services* such as airplane trips, haircuts, and tennis lessons; for *resources* such as coffee beans, computer programmers, and tractors; and for *manufactured components* such as memory chips and auto parts. There are also markets for money such as Japanese yen and for financial securities such as Facebook stock. Only imagination limits what can be traded in markets.

Some markets are physical places where buyers and sellers meet and where an auctioneer or a broker helps to determine the prices. Examples of this type of market are the New York Stock Exchange; wholesale fish, meat, and produce markets; and used car auctions.

Some markets are virtual spaces where buyers and sellers never meet face-to-face but connect over telephone lines or the Internet. Examples include currency markets, e-commerce Web sites such as Amazon.com and iTunes, auction sites such as eBay, and travel Web sites.

But most markets are unorganized collections of buyers and sellers. You do most of your trading in this type of market. An example is the market for coffee and snacks. The buyers in this $75-billion-a-year market are the more than 100 million Americans who regularly drink coffee. The sellers are the 55,000 coffee shops and snack bars. Each buyer can visit several different sellers, and each seller knows that the buyer has a choice of many alternatives.

Markets vary in the intensity of competition that buyers and sellers face. In this chapter, we're going to study a *competitive market* that has so many buyers and so many sellers that no single buyer or seller can influence the price.

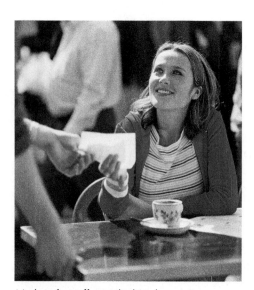
Markets for coffee and a bagel ...

running shoes ...

and airline travel.

4.1   DEMAND

MyEconLab Concept Video

First, we'll study the behavior of buyers in a competitive market. The **quantity demanded** of any good, service, or resource is the amount that people are willing and able to buy during a specified period at a specified price. For example, when spring water costs $1 a bottle, you decide to buy 2 bottles a day. The 2 bottles a day is your quantity demanded of spring water.

The quantity demanded is measured as an amount *per unit of time.* For example, your quantity demanded of water is 2 bottles *per day.* We could express this quantity as 14 bottles per week, or some other number per month or per year. A particular number of bottles without a time dimension has no meaning.

Many things influence buying plans, and one of them is price. We look first at the relationship between quantity demanded and price. To study this relationship, we keep all other influences on buying plans the same and we ask: How, other things remaining the same, does the quantity demanded of a good change as its price varies? The law of demand provides the answer.

Quantity demanded
The amount of any good, service, or resource that people are willing and able to buy during a specified period at a specified price.

■ The Law of Demand

The **law of demand** states

> Other things remaining the same, if the price of a good rises, the quantity demanded of that good decreases; and if the price of a good falls, the quantity demanded of that good increases.

So the law of demand states that when all other things remain the same, if the price of an iPhone falls, people will buy more iPhones; or if the price of a baseball ticket rises, people will buy fewer baseball tickets.

Why does the quantity demanded increase if the price falls, all other things remaining the same?

The answer is that, faced with a limited budget, people always have an incentive to find the best deals available. If the price of one item falls and the prices of all other items remain the same, the item with the lower price is a better deal than it was before, so some people buy more of this item. Suppose, for example, that the price of bottled water fell from $2 a bottle to $1.50 a bottle while the price of Gatorade remained at $2 a bottle. Wouldn't some people switch from Gatorade to water? By doing so, they save 50¢ a bottle, which they can spend on other things they previously couldn't afford.

Think about the things that you buy and ask yourself: Which of these items does *not* obey the law of demand? If the price of a new textbook were lower, other things remaining the same (including the price of a used textbook), would you buy more new textbooks? Then think about all the things that you do not buy but would if you could afford them. How cheap would a computer have to be for you to buy *both* a tablet and a laptop? There is a price that is low enough to entice you!

Law of demand
Other things remaining the same, if the price of a good rises, the quantity demanded of that good decreases; and if the price of a good falls, the quantity demanded of that good increases.

■ Demand Schedule and Demand Curve

Demand is the relationship between the quantity demanded and the price of a good when all other influences on buying plans remain the same. The quantity demanded is *one* quantity at *one* price. *Demand* is a *list of quantities at different prices* illustrated by a demand schedule and a demand curve.

Demand
The relationship between the quantity demanded and the price of a good when all other influences on buying plans remain the same.

Demand schedule
A list of the quantities demanded at each different price when all the other influences on buying plans remain the same.

A **demand schedule** is a list of the quantities demanded at each different price when *all the other influences on buying plans remain the same*. The table in Figure 4.1 is one person's (Tina's) demand schedule for bottled water. This schedule tells us that if the price of water is $2.00 a bottle, Tina buys no water. Her quantity demanded is 0 bottles a day. If the price of water is $1.50 a bottle, her quantity demanded is 1 bottle a day. Tina's quantity demanded increases to 2 bottles a day at a price of $1.00 a bottle and to 3 bottles a day at a price of 50¢ a bottle.

Demand curve
A graph of the relationship between the quantity demanded of a good and its price when all the other influences on buying plans remain the same.

A **demand curve** is a graph of the relationship between the quantity demanded of a good and its price when all the other influences on buying plans remain the same. The points on the demand curve labeled *A* through *D* represent the rows *A* through *D* of the demand schedule. For example, point *B* on the graph represents row *B* of the demand schedule and shows that the quantity demanded is 1 bottle a day when the price is $1.50 a bottle. Point *C* on the demand curve represents row *C* of the demand schedule and shows that the quantity demanded is 2 bottles a day when the price is $1.00 a bottle.

The downward slope of the demand curve illustrates the law of demand. Along the demand curve, when the price of the good *falls*, the quantity demanded *increases*. For example, in Figure 4.1, when the price of a bottle of water falls from $1.00 to 50 cents, the quantity demanded increases from 2 bottles a day to 3 bottles a day. Conversely, when the price *rises*, the quantity demanded *decreases*. For example, when the price rises from $1.00 to $1.50 a bottle, the quantity demanded decreases from 2 bottles a day to 1 bottle a day.

FIGURE 4.1

Demand Schedule and Demand Curve

MyEconLab Animation

The table shows Tina's demand schedule that lists the quantity of water demanded at each price if all other influences on buying plans remain the same. At a price of $1.50 a bottle, the quantity demanded is 1 bottle a day.

The demand curve shows the relationship between the quantity demanded and price, other things remaining the same. The downward-sloping demand curve illustrates the law of demand. When the price falls, the quantity demanded increases; and when the price rises, the quantity demanded decreases.

	Price (dollars per bottle)	Quantity demanded (bottles per day)
A	2.00	0
B	1.50	1
C	1.00	2
D	0.50	3

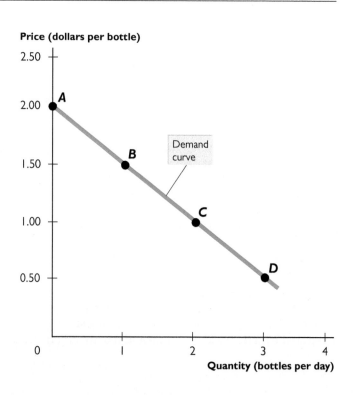

Individual Demand and Market Demand

The demand schedule and the demand curve that you've just studied are for one person. To study a market, we must determine the market demand.

Market demand is the sum of the demands of all the buyers in a market. To find the market demand, imagine a market in which there are only two buyers: Tina and Tim. The table in Figure 4.2 shows three demand schedules: Tina's, Tim's, and the market demand schedule. Tina's demand schedule is the same as before. It shows the quantity of water demanded by Tina at each different price. Tim's demand schedule tells us the quantity of water demanded by Tim at each price. To find the quantity of water demanded in the market, we sum the quantities demanded by Tina and Tim. For example, at a price of $1.00 a bottle, the quantity demanded by Tina is 2 bottles a day, the quantity demanded by Tim is 1 bottle a day, and so the quantity demanded in the market is 3 bottles a day.

Tina's demand curve in part (a) and Tim's demand curve in part (b) are graphs of the two individual demand schedules. The market demand curve in part (c) is a graph of the market demand schedule. At a given price, the quantity demanded on the market demand curve equals the horizontal sum of the quantities demanded on the individual demand curves.

■ FIGURE 4.2

Individual Demand and Market Demand   MyEconLab Animation

Price (dollars per bottle)	Quantity demanded (bottles per day)		
	Tina	Tim	Market
2.00	0	0	0
1.50	1	0	1
1.00	2 +	1 =	3
0.50	3	2	5

The market demand schedule is the sum of the individual demand schedules, and the market demand curve is the horizontal sum of the individual demand curves.

At a price of $1 a bottle, the quantity demanded by Tina is 2 bottles a day and the quantity demanded by Tim is 1 bottle a day, so the total quantity demanded in the market is 3 bottles a day.

(a) Tina's demand   (b) Tim's demand   (c) Market demand

Change in demand
A change in the quantity that people plan to buy when any influence on buying plans other than the price of the good changes.

Substitute
A good that can be consumed in place of another good.

Complement
A good that is consumed with another good.

■ Changes in Demand

The demand curve shows how the quantity demanded changes when the price of the good changes but *all other influences on buying plans remain the same.* When any of these other influences on buying plans change, there is a **change in demand**, which means that there is a new demand schedule and new demand curve. *The demand curve shifts.*

Demand can either increase or decrease and Figure 4.3 illustrates the two cases. Initially, the demand curve is D_0. When demand decreases, the demand curve shifts leftward to D_1. On demand curve D_1, the quantity demanded at each price is smaller. When demand increases, the demand curve shifts rightward to D_2. On demand curve D_2, the quantity demanded at each price is greater.

The main influences on buying plans that change demand are

- Prices of related goods
- Expected future prices
- Income
- Expected future income and credit
- Number of buyers
- Preferences

Prices of Related Goods

Goods have substitutes and complements. A **substitute** for a good is another good that can be consumed in its place. Chocolate cake is a substitute for cheesecake, and bottled water is a substitute for Gatorade. A **complement** of a good is another good that is consumed with it. A helmet is a complement of a bike, and bottled water is a complement of fitness center services.

■ FIGURE 4.3

Changes in Demand

A change in any influence on buying plans, other than a change in the price of the good itself, changes demand and shifts the demand curve.

❶ When demand decreases, the demand curve shifts leftward from D_0 to D_1.

❷ When demand increases, the demand curve shifts rightward from D_0 to D_2.

The demand for a good and the price of one of its substitutes move in the *same direction*. The demand for a good *increases* if the price of one of its substitutes *rises* and *decreases* if the price of one of its substitutes *falls*. For example, the demand for cheesecake increases when the price of chocolate cake rises.

The demand for a good and the price of one of its complements move in *opposite directions*. The demand for a good *decreases* if the price of one of its complements *rises* and *increases* if the price of one of its complements *falls*. For example, the demand for helmets decreases when the price of a bike rises.

Expected Future Prices

A rise in the expected *future* price of a good increases the *current* demand for that good and a fall in the expected *future* price decreases *current* demand. If you expect the price of noodles to rise next week, you buy a big enough stockpile to get you through the next few weeks. Your demand for noodles today has increased. If you expect the price of noodles to fall next week, you buy none now and plan to buy next week. Your demand for noodles today has decreased.

Income

A rise in income brings an increase in demand and a fall in income brings a decrease in demand for a **normal good**. A rise in income brings a *decrease* in demand and a fall in income brings an *increase* in demand for an **inferior good**. For example, if your income increases and you decide to buy more chicken and less pasta, for you, chicken is a normal good and pasta is an inferior good.

Normal good
A good for which demand increases when income increases and demand decreases when income decreases.

Inferior good
A good for which demand decreases when income increases and demand increases when income decreases.

Expected Future Income and Credit

When income is expected to increase in the future, or when credit is easy to get and the cost of borrowing is low, the demand for some goods increases. And when income is expected to decrease in the future, or when credit is hard to get and the cost of borrowing is high, the demand for some goods decreases.

Changes in expected future income and the availability and cost of credit have the greatest effect on the demand for big ticket items such as homes and automobiles. Modest changes in expected future income or credit availability bring large swings in the demand for these items.

Number of Buyers

The greater the number of buyers in a market, the larger is demand. For example, the demand for parking spaces, movies, bottled water, or just about anything is greater in New York City than it is in Boise, Idaho.

Preferences

Tastes or *preferences*, as economists call them, influence demand. When preferences change, the demand for one item increases and the demand for another item (or items) decreases. For example, preferences have changed as people have become better informed about the health hazards of tobacco. This change in preferences has decreased the demand for cigarettes and has increased the demand for nicotine patches. Preferences also change when new goods become available. For example, the development of smartphones has decreased the demand for landlines and has increased the demand for Internet service.

■ Change in Quantity Demanded Versus Change in Demand

The influences on buyers' plans that you've just seen bring a *change in demand*. These are all the influences on buying plans *except for the price of the good*. To avoid confusion, when *the price of the good changes* and all other influences on buying plans remain the same, we say there has been a **change in the quantity demanded**.

The distinction between a change in demand and a change in the quantity demanded is crucial for working out how a market responds to the forces that hit it. Figure 4.4 illustrates and summarizes the distinction:

Change in the quantity demanded
A change in the quantity of a good that people plan to buy that results from a change in the price of the good with all other influences on buying plans remaining the same.

- If the price of bottled water *rises* when other things remain the same, the quantity demanded of bottled water *decreases* and there is a *movement up* along the demand curve D_0. If the price *falls* when other things remain the same, the quantity demanded *increases* and there is a *movement down* along the demand curve D_0.

- If some influence on buyers' plans other than the price of bottled water changes, there is a change in demand. When the demand for bottled water *decreases*, the demand curve *shifts leftward* to D_1. When the demand for bottled water *increases*, the demand curve *shifts rightward* to D_2.

When you are thinking about the influences on demand, try to get into the habit of asking: Does this influence change the quantity demanded or does it change demand? The test is: Did the price of the good change or did some other influence change? If the price changed, then quantity demanded changed. If some other influence changed and the price remained constant, then demand changed.

FIGURE 4.4

Change in Quantity Demanded Versus Change in Demand   MyEconLab Animation

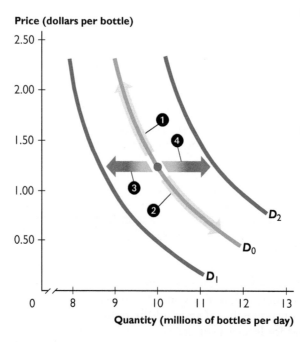

❶ A decrease in the quantity demanded

The quantity demanded decreases and there is a movement up along the demand curve D_0 if the price of the good rises and other things remain the same.

❸ A decrease in demand

Demand decreases and the demand curve shifts leftward (from D_0 to D_1) if

- The price of a substitute falls or the price of a complement rises.
- The price of the good is expected to fall.
- Income decreases.*
- Expected future income or credit decreases.
- The number of buyers decreases.

* Bottled water is a normal good.

❷ An increase in the quantity demanded

The quantity demanded increases and there is a movement down along the demand curve D_0 if the price of the good falls and other things remain the same.

❹ An increase in demand

Demand increases and the demand curve shifts rightward (from D_0 to D_2) if

- The price of a substitute rises or the price of a complement falls.
- The price of the good is expected to rise.
- Income increases.
- Expected future income or credit increases.
- The number of buyers increases.

CHECKPOINT 4.1

Distinguish between quantity demanded and demand, and explain what determines demand.

Practice Problems

The following events occur one at a time in the market for smartphones:
- The price of a smartphone falls.
- Producers announce that the price of a smartphone will fall next month.
- The price of a call made from a smartphone falls.
- The price of a call made from a land-line phone increases.
- An increase in memory makes smartphones more popular.

1. Explain the effect of each event on the demand for smartphones.

2. Use a graph to illustrate the effect of each event.

3. Does any event (or events) illustrate the law of demand?

In the News

Airline profits soar yet no relief for passengers
Airplanes are more crowded than ever and fares are at a five-year high.
                                Source: *USA Today*, January 27, 2015

Does this news clip imply that the law of demand doesn't work in the real world? Explain why or why not.

Solutions to Practice Problems

1. A fall in the price of a smartphone increases the quantity of smartphones demanded but has no effect on the demand for smartphones.
   With the producers' announcement, the expected future price of a smartphone falls, which decreases the demand for smartphones today.
   A fall in the price of a call from a smartphone increases the demand for smartphones because a smartphone call and a smartphone are complements.
   A rise in the price of a call from a land-line phone increases the demand for smartphones because a land-line phone and a smartphone are substitutes.
   With smartphones more popular, the demand for smartphones increases.

2. Figure 1 illustrates the effect of a fall in the price of a smartphone as a movement along the demand curve D.
   Figure 2 illustrates the effect of an increase in the demand for smartphones as the shift of the demand curve from D_0 to D_1 and a decrease in the demand for smartphones as the shift of the demand curve from D_0 to D_2.

3. A fall in the price of a smartphone (other things remaining the same) illustrates the law of demand. Figure 1 illustrates the law of demand. The other events change demand and do not illustrate the law of demand.

Solution to In the News

The law of demand states: If the price of an airline ticket rises, other things remaining the same, the quantity demanded of airline tickets will decrease. The demand curve for airline tickets slopes downward. The law of demand does work in the real world. Airlines can fill planes at high fares because "other things" have not remained the same. The demand for air travel has increased.

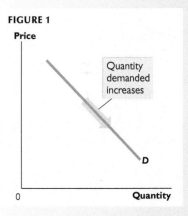

FIGURE 1

Price

Quantity demanded increases

D

0   Quantity

FIGURE 2

Price

Demand increases

D_1

Demand decreases

D_0

D_2

0   Quantity

4.2 SUPPLY

A market has two sides. On one side are the buyers, or demanders, that we've just studied. On the other side of the market are the sellers, or suppliers. We now study the forces that determine suppliers' plans.

Quantity supplied
The amount of any good, service, or resource that people are willing and able to sell during a specified period at a specified price.

The **quantity supplied** of a good, service, or resource is the amount that people are willing and able to sell during a specified period at a specified price. For example, when the price of spring water is $1.50 a bottle, a spring owner decides to sell 2,000 bottles a day. The 2,000 bottles a day is the quantity supplied of spring water by this individual producer. (As in the case of demand, the quantity supplied is measured as an amount *per unit of time.*)

Many things influence selling plans, and one of them is the price. We look first at the relationship between quantity supplied of a good and its price. To study this relationship, we keep all other influences on selling plans the same, and we ask: Other things remaining the same, how does the quantity supplied of a good change as its price varies? The law of supply provides the answer.

■ The Law of Supply

Law of supply
Other things remaining the same, if the price of a good rises, the quantity supplied of that good increases; and if the price of a good falls, the quantity supplied of that good decreases.

The **law of supply** states

> Other things remaining the same, if the price of a good rises, the quantity supplied of that good increases; and if the price of a good falls, the quantity supplied of that good decreases.

So the law of supply states that when all other things remain the same, if the price of bottled water rises, spring owners will offer more water for sale; if the price of a flat-screen TV falls, Sony Corp. will offer fewer flat-screen TVs for sale.

Why, other things remaining the same, does the quantity supplied increase if the price rises and decrease if the price falls? Part of the answer lies in the principle of increasing opportunity cost (see p. 68). Because factors of production are not equally productive in all activities, as more of a good is produced, the opportunity cost of producing it increases. A higher price provides the incentive to bear the higher opportunity cost of increased production. Another part of the answer is that for a given cost, the higher price brings a larger profit, so sellers have greater incentive to increase production.

Think about the resources that you own and can offer for sale to others and ask yourself: Which of these items does *not* obey the law of supply? If the wage rate for summer jobs increased, would you have an incentive to work longer hours and bear the higher opportunity cost of forgone leisure? If the bank offered a higher interest rate on deposits, would you have an incentive to save more and bear the higher opportunity cost of forgone consumption? If the used book dealer offered a higher price for last year's textbooks, would you have an incentive to sell that handy math text and bear the higher opportunity cost of visiting the library (or finding a friend) whenever you needed the book?

■ Supply Schedule and Supply Curve

Supply
The relationship between the quantity supplied and the price of a good when all other influences on selling plans remain the same.

Supply is the relationship between the quantity supplied and the price of a good when all other influences on selling plans remain the same. The quantity supplied is *one* quantity at *one* price. *Supply* is a *list of quantities at different prices* illustrated by a supply schedule and a supply curve.

A **supply schedule** lists the quantities supplied at each different price when all the other influences on selling plans remain the same. The table in Figure 4.5 is one firm's (Agua's) supply schedule for bottled water. It tells us that if the price of water is 50¢ a bottle, Agua plans to sell no water. Its quantity supplied is 0 bottles a day. If the price of water is $1.00 a bottle, Agua's quantity supplied is 1,000 bottles a day. Agua's quantity supplied increases to 2,000 bottles a day at a price of $1.50 a bottle and to 3,000 bottles a day at a price of $2.00 a bottle.

A **supply curve** is a graph of the relationship between the quantity supplied of a good and its price when all the other influences on selling plans remain the same. The points on the supply curve labeled A through D represent the rows A through D of the supply schedule. For example, point C on the supply curve represents row C of the supply schedule and shows that the quantity supplied is 1,000 bottles a day when the price is $1.00 a bottle. Point B on the supply curve represents row B of the supply schedule and shows that the quantity supplied is 2,000 bottles a day when the price is $1.50 a bottle.

The upward slope of the supply curve illustrates the law of supply. Along the supply curve, when the price of the good *rises*, the quantity supplied *increases*. For example, in Figure 4.5, when the price of a bottle of water rises from $1.50 to $2.00, the quantity supplied increases from 2,000 bottles a day to 3,000 bottles a day. And when the price *falls*, the quantity supplied *decreases*. For example, when the price falls from $1.50 to $1.00 a bottle, the quantity supplied decreases from 2,000 bottles a day to 1,000 bottles a day.

Supply schedule
A list of the quantities supplied at each different price when all the other influences on selling plans remain the same.

Supply curve
A graph of the relationship between the quantity supplied of a good and its price when all the other influences on selling plans remain the same.

FIGURE 4.5

Supply Schedule and Supply Curve

MyEconLab Animation

	Price (dollars per bottle)	Quantity supplied (thousands of bottles per day)
A	2.00	3
B	1.50	2
C	1.00	1
D	0.50	0

The table shows a supply schedule that lists the quantity of water supplied at each price if all other influences on selling plans remain the same. At a price of $1.50 a bottle, the quantity supplied is 2,000 bottles a day.

The supply curve shows the relationship between the quantity supplied and price, other things remaining the same. The upward-sloping supply curve illustrates the law of supply. When the price rises, the quantity supplied increases; and when the price falls, the quantity supplied decreases.

■ Individual Supply and Market Supply

The supply schedule and the supply curve that you've just studied are for one seller. To study a market, we must determine the market supply.

Market supply is the sum of the supplies of all the sellers in the market. To find the market supply of water, imagine a market in which there are only two sellers: Agua and Prima. The table in Figure 4.6 shows three supply schedules: Agua's, Prima's, and the market supply schedule. Agua's supply schedule is the same as before. Prima's supply schedule tells us the quantity of water that Prima plans to sell at each price. To find the quantity of water supplied in the market, we sum the quantities supplied by Agua and Prima. For example, at a price of $1.00 a bottle, the quantity supplied by Agua is 1,000 bottles a day, the quantity supplied by Prima is 2,000 bottles a day, and the quantity supplied in the market is 3,000 bottles a day.

Agua's supply curve in part (a) and Prima's supply curve in part (b) are graphs of the two individual supply schedules. The market supply curve in part (c) is a graph of the market supply schedule. At a given price, the quantity supplied on the market supply curve equals the horizontal sum of the quantities supplied on the individual supply curves.

FIGURE 4.6

Individual Supply and Market Supply   MyEconLab Animation

Price (dollars per bottle)	Quantity supplied (thousands of bottles per day)		
	Agua	Prima	Market
2.00	3	4	7
1.50	2	3	5
1.00	1 +	2 =	3
0.50	0	0	0

The market supply schedule is the sum of the individual supply schedules, and the market supply curve is the horizontal sum of the individual supply curves.

At a price of $1 a bottle, the quantity supplied by Agua is 1,000 bottles a day and the quantity supplied by Prima is 2,000 bottles a day, so the total quantity supplied in the market is 3,000 bottles a day.

(a) Agua's supply   (b) Prima's supply   (c) Market supply

■ Changes in Supply

The supply curve shows how the quantity supplied changes when the price of the good changes but *all other influences on selling plans remain the same*. When any of these other influences on selling plans change, there is a **change in supply**, which means that there is a new supply schedule and new supply curve. *The supply curve shifts.*

Supply can either increase or decrease, and Figure 4.7 illustrates the two cases. Initially, the supply curve is S_0. When supply decreases, the supply curve shifts leftward to S_1. On supply curve S_1, the quantity supplied at each price is smaller. When supply increases, the supply curve shifts rightward to S_2. On supply curve S_2, the quantity supplied at each price is greater.

The main influences on selling plans that change supply are

- Prices of related goods
- Prices of resources and other inputs
- Expected future prices
- Number of sellers
- Productivity

Prices of Related Goods

Related goods are either substitutes *in production* or complements *in production*. A **substitute in production** for a good is another good that can be produced in its place. Skinny jeans are substitutes in production for boot cut jeans in a clothing factory.

A **complement in production** of one good is another good that is produced along with it. Cream is a complement in production of skim milk in a dairy.

MyEconLab Concept Video

Change in supply
A change in the quantity that suppliers plan to sell when any influence on selling plans other than the price of the good changes.

Substitute in production
A good that can be produced in place of another good.

Complement in production
A good that is produced along with another good.

▮ **FIGURE 4.7**

Changes in Supply

MyEconLab Animation

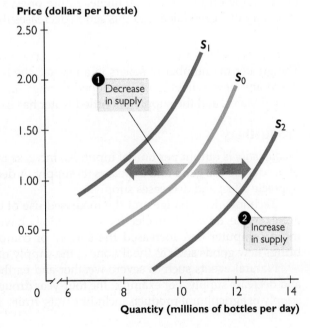

A change in any influence on selling plans other than a change in the price of the good itself changes supply and shifts the supply curve.

❶ When supply decreases, the supply curve shifts leftward from S_0 to S_1.

❷ When supply increases, the supply curve shifts rightward from S_0 to S_2.

A Change in the Price of a Substitute in Production   The supply of a good *decreases* if the price of one of its substitutes in production *rises;* and the supply of a good *increases* if the price of one of its substitutes in production *falls.* That is, the supply of a good and the price of one of its substitutes in production move in *opposite directions.* For example, a clothing factory can produce chinos or button-fly jeans, so these goods are substitutes in production. When the price of button-fly jeans rises, the clothing factory switches production from chinos to button-fly jeans, so the supply of chinos decreases.

A Change in the Price of a Complement in Production   The supply of a good *increases* if the price of one of its complements in production *rises;* and the supply of a good *decreases* if the price of one of its complements in production *falls.* That is, the supply of a good and the price of one of its complements in production move in the *same direction.* For example, when a dairy produces skim milk, it also produces cream, so these goods are complements in production. When the price of skim milk rises, the dairy produces more skim milk, so the supply of cream increases.

Prices of Resources and Other Inputs

Supply changes when the price of a resource or other input used to produce the good changes. The reason is that resource and input prices influence the cost of production. The more it costs to produce a good, the smaller is the quantity supplied of that good at each price (other things remaining the same). For example, if the wage rate of bottling-plant workers rises, it costs more to produce a bottle of water, so the supply of bottled water decreases.

Expected Future Prices

Expectations about future prices influence supply. For example, a severe frost that wipes out Florida's citrus crop doesn't change the production of orange juice today, but it does decrease production later in the year when the current crop would normally have been harvested. Sellers of orange juice will expect the price to rise in the future. To get the higher future price, some sellers will increase their inventory of frozen juice, and this action decreases the supply of juice today.

Number of Sellers

The greater the number of sellers in a market, the larger is the supply. For example, many new sellers have developed springs and water-bottling plants in the United States, and the supply of bottled water has increased.

Productivity

Productivity is output per unit of input. An increase in productivity lowers the cost of producing the good and increases its supply. A decrease in productivity has the opposite effect and decreases supply.

   Technological change and the increased use of capital increase productivity. For example, advances in electronic technology have lowered the cost of producing a computer and increased the supply of computers. Technological change brings new goods such as the iPhone 6, the supply of which was previously zero.

   Natural events such as severe weather and earthquakes decrease productivity and decrease supply. For example, the four-year drought in California decreased the supply of agricultural products including nuts, fruits, and vegetables in 2015.

■ Change in Quantity Supplied Versus Change in Supply

The influences on sellers' plans that you've just considered bring a *change in supply*. These are all the influences on sellers' plans *except the price of the good*. To avoid confusion, when the *price of the good changes* and all other influences on selling plans remain the same, we say there has been a **change in the quantity supplied**.

The distinction between a change in supply and a change in the quantity supplied is crucial for figuring out how a market responds to the forces that hit it. Figure 4.8 illustrates and summarizes the distinction:

- If the price of bottled water *falls* when other things remain the same, the quantity supplied of bottled water *decreases* and there is a *movement down* along the supply curve S_0. If the price *rises* when other things remain the same, the quantity supplied *increases* and there is a *movement up* along the supply curve S_0.
- If any influence on water bottlers' plans other than the price of bottled water changes, there is a change in the supply of bottled water. When the supply of bottled water *decreases*, the supply curve *shifts leftward* to S_1. When the supply of bottled water *increases*, the supply curve *shifts rightward* to S_2.

When you are thinking about the influences on supply, get into the habit of asking: Does this influence change the quantity supplied or does it change supply? The test is: Did the price change or did some other influence change? If the price of the good changed, then quantity supplied changed. If some other influence changed and the price of the good remained constant, then supply changed.

Change in the quantity supplied
A change in the quantity of a good that suppliers plan to sell that results from a change in the price of the good.

FIGURE 4.8

Change in Quantity Supplied Versus Change in Supply

MyEconLab Animation

❶ A decrease in the quantity supplied

The quantity supplied decreases and there is a movement down along the supply curve S_0 if the price of the good falls and other things remain the same.

❸ A decrease in supply

Supply decreases and the supply curve shifts leftward (from S_0 to S_1) if

- The price of a substitute in production rises.
- The price of a complement in production falls.
- A resource price or other input price rises.
- The price of the good is expected to rise.
- The number of sellers decreases.
- Productivity decreases.

❷ An increase in the quantity supplied

The quantity supplied increases and there is a movement up along the supply curve S_0 if the price of the good rises and other things remain the same.

❹ An increase in supply

Supply increases and the supply curve shifts rightward (from S_0 to S_2) if

- The price of a substitute in production falls.
- The price of a complement in production rises.
- A resource price or other input price falls.
- The price of the good is expected to fall.
- The number of sellers increases.
- Productivity increases.

EYE on YOUR LIFE

Understanding and Using Demand and Supply

To truly understand the demand and supply model, it is a good idea to go beyond just memorizing the key terms and definitions and the lists of factors that change demand or change supply. Take ownership of the model by seeing how it explains your buying plans and your selling plans.

Your Buying Plans

Think about the things you buy: the quantities you buy and the prices you pay. These quantities and prices are points on your demand curves.

Now think about how some price changes would change your buying plans. How would your buying plans change if prices at the campus coffee shop increased? For which items would you change your quantity demanded? And for which items would you change your demand?

How would your buying plans change if you started a new job with a higher wage? What would you buy more of? What would you buy less of?

Suppose that you were just about to buy a new smartphone when Apple and Samsung announce plans to launch new phones next month. You figure that the prices of the older models will fall. How will this fall in the expected future price of a smartphone influence your buying plans?

For each thought experiment we've just described, think about whether you are sliding along a demand curve or shifting a demand curve.

Your Selling Plans

Most likely, you don't sell much stuff, but you own one precious resource that you might sell: your time.

If you have a job, think about the number of hours you work and the wage rate you earn. Are you working as many hours as you want to? If you are, you're at a point on the supply curve of your labor services.

How would you respond to a rise in the wage rate? Would you plan to work more hours or fewer hours?

Another thing you own is a pile of textbooks. Think about your selling plan for when your courses are over at the end of the semester. What is the lowest price at which you will sell this textbook? That price is a point on your supply curve of this book to the used book market.

You might also have a few old things that you'd like to sell on eBay. Again, think about your minimum supply-price—the point on your supply curve of these items.

By doing these thought experiments about your selling plans, you can make the idea of supply and the supply curve more concrete.

From Plans to Actions

Your demand and supply curves and the *market* demand and supply curves describe *plans*. They are statements about "what-if." They describe the buying plans and the selling plans at differ-ent possible prices. But when you act on your plan and buy something, someone else must have a plan to sell that item. Your buying plan must match someone else's selling plan.

Neither demand nor supply on its own tells us what actually happens in a market. To find buying plans and selling plans that match, we must look at demand and supply together. That's what you will do in the final section of this chapter. You will see how prices adjust to balance the opposing forces of demand and supply.

The Rest of Your Life

The demand and supply model is going to be a big part of the rest of your life! You will use it again and again during your economics course, so having a firm grasp of it will bring an immediate payoff.

But much more important, by understanding the laws of demand and supply and being aware of how prices adjust to balance these two opposing forces, you will have a much better appreciation of how your economic world works.

Every time you hear someone complaining about a price hike and blaming it on someone's greed, think about the market forces and how demand and supply determine that price.

As you shop for your favorite clothing, music, and food items, try to describe how supply and demand influence the prices of these goods.

CHECKPOINT 4.2

MyEconLab Study Plan 4.2
Key Terms Quiz
Solutions Video

Distinguish between quantity supplied and supply, and explain what determines supply.

Practice Problems

Lumber companies make timber beams from logs. In the process of making beams, the mill produces sawdust, which is made into pressed wood. In the market for timber beams, the following events occur one at a time:

- The wage rate of sawmill workers rises.
- The price of sawdust rises.
- The price of a timber beam rises.
- Next year's expected price of a timber beam rises.
- A new law reduces the amount of forest that can be cut for timber.
- A new technology lowers the cost of producing timber beams.

1. Explain the effect of each event on the supply of timber beams.
2. Use a graph to illustrate the effect of each event.
3. Does any event (or events) illustrate the law of supply?

In the News

Pump prices slide as crude oil falls to six-year low
The average price for regular gasoline at U.S. pumps fell almost 4¢ in March to $2.50 a gallon. The price of crude oil dropped to $43.46 per barrel on March 17, the lowest since March 2009.

Source: *Bloomberg Business*, March 23, 2015

Explain the effect of a lower crude oil price on the supply of gasoline.

Solutions to Practice Problems

1. A rise in workers' wage rates increases the cost of producing a timber beam and decreases the supply of timber beams. A rise in the price of sawdust increases the supply of timber beams because sawdust and timber beams are complements in production. A rise in the price of a timber beam increases the quantity of timber beams supplied but has no effect on the supply of timber beams. A rise in the expected price of a timber beam decreases the supply of timber beams today as producers hold back and wait for the higher price. The new law decreases the supply of timber beams. The new technology increases the supply of timber beams.

2. In Figure 1, an increase in the supply shifts the supply curve from S_0 to S_1, and a decrease in the supply shifts the supply curve from S_0 to S_2. In Figure 2, the rise in the price of a beam creates a movement along the supply curve.

3. A rise in the price of a beam, other things remaining the same, is the only event that illustrates the law of supply—see Figure 2.

Solution to In the News

Crude oil is refined to produce gasoline, so a fall in the price of crude oil lowers the cost of producing gasoline and increases the supply of gasoline.

FIGURE 1

FIGURE 2

Market equilibrium
When the quantity demanded equals the quantity supplied—buyers' and sellers' plans are in balance.

Equilibrium price
The price at which the quantity demanded equals the quantity supplied.

Equilibrium quantity
The quantity bought and sold at the equilibrium price.

Law of market forces
When there is a surplus, the price falls; and when there is a shortage, the price rises.

4.3 MARKET EQUILIBRIUM

In everyday language, "equilibrium" means "opposing forces are in balance." In a market, demand and supply are the opposing forces. **Market equilibrium** occurs when the quantity demanded equals the quantity supplied—when buyers' and sellers' plans are in balance. At the **equilibrium price**, the quantity demanded equals the quantity supplied. The **equilibrium quantity** is the quantity bought and sold at the equilibrium price.

In the market for bottled water in Figure 4.9, equilibrium occurs where the demand curve and the supply curve intersect. The equilibrium price is $1.00 a bottle, and the equilibrium quantity is 10 million bottles a day.

■ Price: A Market's Automatic Regulator

When equilibrium is disturbed, market forces restore it. The **law of market forces** states

> When there is a surplus, the price falls; and when there is a shortage, the price rises.

A *surplus* is the amount by which the quantity supplied exceeds the quantity demanded. If there is a surplus, suppliers must cut the price to sell more. Buyers are pleased to take the lower price, so the price falls. Because a surplus arises when the price is above the equilibrium price, a falling price is exactly what the market needs to restore equilibrium.

A *shortage* is the amount by which the quantity demanded exceeds the quantity supplied. If there is a shortage, buyers must pay a higher price to get more. Sellers are pleased to take the higher price, so the price rises. Because a shortage arises when the price is below the equilibrium price, a rising price is exactly what is needed to restore equilibrium.

FIGURE 4.9

Equilibrium Price and Equilibrium Quantity

MyEconLab Animation

❶ Market equilibrium occurs at the intersection of the demand curve and the supply curve.

❷ The equilibrium price is $1.00 a bottle.

❸ At the equilibrium price, the quantity demanded and the quantity supplied are 10 million bottles a day, which is the equilibrium quantity.

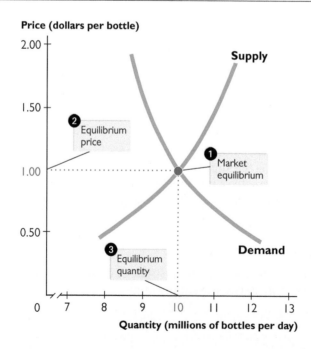

FIGURE 4.10

The Forces That Achieve Equilibrium

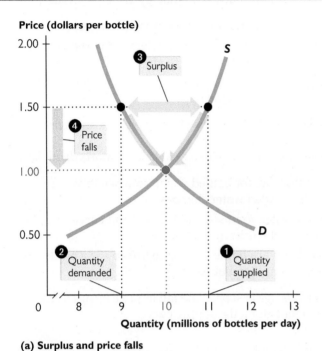

(a) Surplus and price falls

(b) Shortage and price rises

At $1.50 a bottle, ❶ the quantity supplied is 11 million bottles of water, ❷ the quantity demanded is 9 million bottles, ❸ the surplus is 2 million bottles, and ❹ the price falls.

At 75¢ a bottle, ❶ the quantity demanded is 11 million bottles of water, ❷ the quantity supplied is 9 million bottles, ❸ the shortage is 2 million bottles, and ❹ the price rises.

In Figure 4.10(a), at $1.50 a bottle, there is a surplus: The price falls, the quantity demanded increases, the quantity supplied decreases, and the surplus is eliminated at $1.00 a bottle.

In Figure 4.10(b), at 75¢ a bottle, there is a shortage of water: The price rises, the quantity demanded decreases, the quantity supplied increases, and the shortage is eliminated at $1.00 a bottle.

■ **Predicting Price Changes: Three Questions**

Because price adjustments eliminate shortages and surpluses, markets are normally in equilibrium. When an event disturbs an equilibrium, a new equilibrium soon emerges. To explain and predict changes in prices and quantities, we need to consider only changes in the *equilibrium* price and the *equilibrium* quantity. We can work out the effects of an event on a market by answering three questions:

1. Does the event influence demand or supply?
2. Does the event *increase* or *decrease* demand or supply—shift the demand curve or the supply curve *rightward* or *leftward*?
3. What are the new *equilibrium* price and *equilibrium* quantity and how have they changed?

■ Effects of Changes in Demand

Let's practice answering the three questions by working out the effects of an event in the market for bottled water: A new study says that tap water is unsafe.

1. With tap water unsafe, the demand for bottled water changes.
2. The demand for bottled water *increases*, and the demand curve *shifts rightward*. Figure 4.11(a) shows the shift from D_0 to D_1.
3. There is now a *shortage* at $1.00 a bottle. The *price rises* to $1.50 a bottle, and the quantity increases to 11 million bottles.

Note that there is *no change in supply*; the rise in price brings an *increase in the quantity supplied*—a movement along the supply curve.

Let's work out what happens if the price of a zero-calorie sports drink falls.

1. The sports drink is a substitute for bottled water, so when its price changes, the demand for bottled water changes.
2. The demand for bottled water *decreases*, and the demand curve *shifts leftward*. Figure 4.11(b) shows the shift from D_0 to D_2.
3. There is now a *surplus* at $1.00 a bottle. The price *falls* to 75¢ a bottle, and the quantity decreases to 9 million bottles.

Note again that there is *no change in supply*; the fall in price brings a *decrease in the quantity supplied*—a movement along the supply curve.

FIGURE 4.11

The Effects of a Change in Demand

(a) An increase in demand

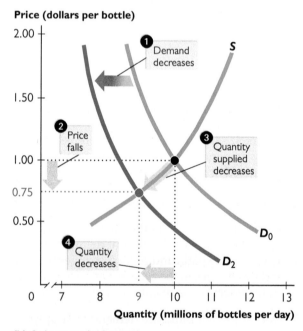

(b) A decrease in demand

❶ An increase in demand shifts the demand curve rightward to D_1 and creates a shortage of water. ❷ The price rises, ❸ the quantity supplied increases, and ❹ the equilibrium quantity increases.

❶ A decrease in demand shifts the demand curve leftward to D_2 and creates a surplus of water. ❷ The price falls, ❸ the quantity supplied decreases, and ❹ the equilibrium quantity decreases.

EYE on the GLOBAL ECONOMY
The Markets for Cocoa and Chocolate

Fast-rising incomes in China and other developing economies and the sweet tooth of millions of newly rich middle classes are sending the consumption of chocolate soaring. With chocolate made from cocoa, the price of cocoa is soaring too.

Look at the data table below. It shows the quantities and prices of cocoa in 2010 and 2014, and it tells us that both the quantity of cocoa produced and the price of cocoa increased.

The quantity produced increased by 25 percent from 4 million tons in 2010 to 5 million tons in 2014.

The price of cocoa doubled from $1,500 to $3,000.

Why did the price of cocoa increase? Was it because demand increased or supply decreased?

You can answer this question with the information in the table. You know that an increase in demand brings a rise in the price and an increase in the quantity bought, while a decrease in supply brings a rise in the price and a decrease in the quantity bought.

Because when the price of cocoa increased, the quantity of cocoa produced and consumed also increased, the demand for cocoa must have increased.

An increase in demand is consistent with the facts about rising incomes in China and other developing economies.

Cocoa is a normal good, so an increase in income brings an increase in the demand for cocoa. The fast-rising incomes in China and other developing economies brought an increase in the demand for cocoa.

The figure illustrates the global market for cocoa in 2010 and 2014. The supply curve S shows the supply of cocoa, which we will assume didn't change between 2010 and 2014.

In 2010, the demand curve for cocoa was D_{2010}, the equilibrium price was $1,500 per ton and the equilibrium quantity of cocoa traded was 4 million tons.

By 2014, the higher incomes in China and other developing economies had increased the demand for cocoa to D_{2014}. The equilibrium price rose to $3,000 per ton and the equilibrium quantity traded increased to 5 million tons.

The higher price of cocoa brought an increase in the quantity of cocoa supplied, which is shown in the figure by the movement up along the supply curve of cocoa.

Year	Quantity of Cocoa (millions of tons per year)	Price of Cocoa (dollars per ton)
2010	4	1,500
2014	5	3,000

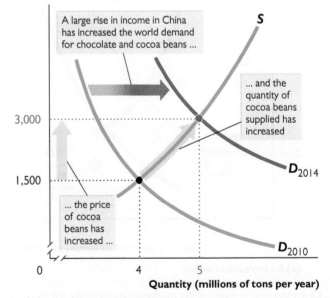

The Market for Cocoa Beans

■ Effects of Changes in Supply

You can get more practice working out the effects of another event in the market for bottled water: European water bottlers buy springs and open new plants in the United States.

1. With more suppliers of bottled water, the supply changes.
2. The supply of bottled water *increases*, and the supply curve *shifts rightward*. Figure 4.12(a) shows the shift from S_0 to S_1.
3. There is now a *surplus* at $1.00 a bottle. The *price falls* to 75¢ a bottle, and the quantity increases to 11 million bottles.

Note that there is *no change in demand*; the fall in price brings an *increase in the quantity demanded*—a movement along the demand curve.

What happens if a drought dries up some springs?

1. The drought is a change in productivity, so the supply of water changes.
2. With fewer springs, the supply of bottled water *decreases*, and the supply curve *shifts leftward*. Figure 4.12(b) shows the shift from S_0 to S_2.
3. There is now a *shortage* at $1.00 a bottle. The *price rises* to $1.50 a bottle, and the quantity decreases to 9 million bottles.

Again, there is *no change in demand*; the rise in price brings a *decrease in the quantity demanded*—a movement along the demand curve.

▨ FIGURE 4.12

The Effects of a Change in Supply

MyEconLab Animation

(a) An increase in supply

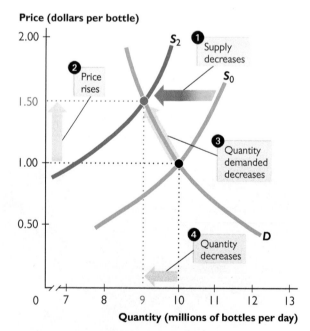

(b) A decrease in supply

❶ An increase in supply shifts the supply curve rightward to S_1 and creates a surplus of water. ❷ The price falls, ❸ the quantity demanded increases, and ❹ the equilibrium quantity increases.

❶ A decrease in supply shifts the supply curve leftward to S_2 and creates a shortage of water. ❷ The price rises, ❸ the quantity demanded decreases, and ❹ the equilibrium quantity decreases.

EYE on the PRICE OF COFFEE

MyEconLab Critical Thinking Exercise

Why Did the Price of Coffee Rise in 2014?

When a fungus called coffee rust swept through Brazil and other countries of South America in 2014, world coffee production decreased and the price of coffee beans increased.

The table below provides some data on the quantity and price of coffee in 2013 and 2014. What does the data table tell us?

It tells us that the quantity of coffee produced decreased by 3.6 percent from 19.4 billion pounds in 2013 to 18.7 billion pounds in 2014, and the price of coffee rose by more than 30 percent from $1.04 per pound to $1.35 per pound.

Did the price of coffee rise because demand increased or because supply decreased?

You can answer this question from the information provided. You know that an increase in demand brings a rise in the price and an increase in the quantity bought, while a decrease in supply brings a rise in the price and a decrease in the quantity bought.

Because the quantity of coffee decreased and the price increased, there must have been a decrease in the supply of coffee.

The supply of coffee decreases if the crop yields decrease or if producers decrease their plantings.

The information that coffee rust swept through Brazil and other countries of South America in 2014 suggests that coffee crop yields decreased, which decreased the supply.

The figure illustrates the global market for coffee in 2013 and 2014. The demand curve D shows the demand for coffee, which we will assume was the same in both years.

In 2013, the supply curve was S_{2013}, the equilibrium price was $1.04 per pound and the equilibrium quantity traded was 19.4 billion pounds.

In 2014, decreased coffee production in Brazil and other countries decreased the supply of coffee to S_{2014}.

The equilibrium price rose to $1.35 per pound and the quantity traded decreased to 18.7 billion pounds.

The higher price brought a decrease in the quantity of coffee demanded, which is shown by the movement up along the demand curve.

	Quantity of Coffee	Price of Coffee
Year	(billions of pounds per year)	(dollars per pound)
2013	19.4	1.04
2014	18.7	1.35

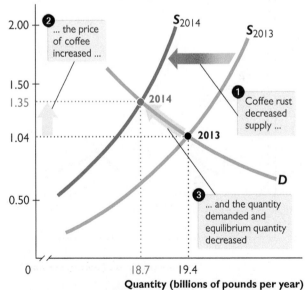

The Market for Coffee in 2013–2014

MyEconLab Concept Video

■ Effects of Changes in Both Demand and Supply

When events occur that change *both* demand and supply, you can find the resulting change in the equilibrium price and equilibrium quantity by combining the cases you've just studied.

Both Demand and Supply Change in the Same Direction

When demand and supply change in the same direction, the equilibrium quantity changes in that same direction, but we need to know the magnitudes of the changes in demand and supply to predict whether the price rises or falls. If demand increases by more than supply increases, the price rises. But if supply increases by more than demand increases, the price falls.

Figure 4.13(a) shows the case when both demand and supply increase and by the same amount. The equilibrium quantity increases. But because the increase in demand equals the increase in supply, neither a shortage nor a surplus arises so the price doesn't change. A bigger increase in demand would have created a shortage and a rise in the price; a bigger increase in supply would have created a surplus and a fall in the price.

Figure 4.13(b) shows the case when both demand and supply decrease by the same amount. Here the equilibrium quantity decreases and again the price might either rise or fall.

FIGURE 4.13

The Effects of Change in *Both* Demand and Supply in the *Same Direction*　　　　MyEconLab Animation

(a) Increase in both demand and supply

(b) Decrease in both demand and supply

❶ An increase in demand shifts the demand curve rightward to D_1 and an increase in supply shifts the supply curve rightward to S_1.
❷ The price might rise or fall, but ❸ the quantity increases.

❶ A decrease in demand shifts the demand curve leftward to D_1 and a decrease in supply shifts the supply curve leftward to S_1.
❷ The price might rise or fall, but ❸ the quantity decreases.

Both Demand and Supply Change in Opposite Directions

When demand and supply change in opposite directions, we can predict how the price changes, but we need to know the magnitudes of the changes in demand and supply to say whether the equilibrium quantity increases or decreases. If demand changes by more than supply, the equilibrium quantity changes in the same direction as the change in demand. But if supply changes by more than demand, the equilibrium quantity changes in the same direction as the change in supply.

Figure 4.14(a) illustrates what happens when demand decreases and supply increases by the same amount. At the initial price, there is a surplus, so the price falls. A decrease in demand decreases the quantity and an increase in supply increases the quantity, so when these changes occur together, we can't say what happens to the quantity unless we know the magnitudes of the changes.

Figure 4.14(b) illustrates what happens when demand increases and supply decreases by the same amount. In this case, at the initial price, there is a shortage, so the price rises. An increase in demand increases the quantity and a decrease in supply decreases the quantity, so again, when these changes occur together, we can't say what happens to the quantity unless we know the magnitudes of the changes in demand and supply.

For all the cases in Figures 4.13 and 4.14 where you "can't say" what happens to price or quantity, draw some examples that go in each direction.

FIGURE 4.14

The Effects of Change in *Both* Demand and Supply in *Opposite Directions*   MyEconLab Animation

(a) Decrease in demand and increase in supply

(b) Increase in demand and decrease in supply

❶ A decrease in demand shifts the demand curve leftward to D_1 and an increase in supply shifts the supply curve rightward to S_1.
❷ The price falls, but ❸ the quantity might increase or decrease.

❶ An increase in demand shifts the demand curve rightward to D_1 and a decrease in supply shifts the supply curve leftward to S_1.
❷ The price rises, but ❸ the quantity might increase or decrease.

MyEconLab Study Plan 4.3
Key Terms Quiz
Solutions Video

CHECKPOINT 4.3

Explain how demand and supply determine price and quantity in a market, and explain the effects of changes in demand and supply.

Practice Problems

TABLE 1

Price (dollars per carton)	Quantity demanded	Quantity supplied
	(cartons per day)	
1.00	200	110
1.25	175	130
1.50	150	150
1.75	125	170
2.00	100	190

Table 1 sets out the demand and supply schedules for milk.

1. What is the equilibrium price and equilibrium quantity of milk?
2. Describe the situation in the milk market if the price were $1.75 a carton and explain how the market reaches equilibrium.
3. A drought decreases the quantity supplied by 45 cartons a day at each price. What is the new equilibrium and how does the market adjust to it?
4. If milk becomes more popular and better feeds increase milk production, describe how the equilibrium price and quantity of milk will change.

In the News

El Niño takes toll on U.S. rice farmers
Dry weather has delayed rice planting and harvests will be low. But wheat is enjoying a bumper crop.

Source: *The Guardian*, September 27, 2015

Using the demand and supply model, explain how the prices of rice and wheat will change and how the markets for rice and wheat will influence each other.

Solutions to Practice Problems

1. Equilibrium price is $1.50 a carton; equilibrium quantity is 150 cartons a day.
2. At $1.75 a carton, the quantity demanded (125 cartons) is less than the quantity supplied (170 cartons), so there is a surplus of 45 cartons a day. The price begins to fall, and as it does, the quantity demanded increases, the quantity supplied decreases, and the surplus decreases. The price will fall until the surplus is eliminated. The price falls to $1.50 a carton.
3. The supply decreases by 45 cartons a day so at $1.50 a carton there is a shortage of milk. The price begins to rise, and as it does, the quantity demanded decreases, the quantity supplied increases, and the shortage decreases. The price will rise until the shortage is eliminated. The new equilibrium occurs at $1.75 a carton and 125 cartons a day (Figure 1).
4. With milk more popular, demand increases. With better feeds, supply increases. If supply increases by more than demand, a surplus arises. The price falls, and the quantity increases (Figure 2). If demand increases by more than supply, a shortage arises. The price rises, and the quantity increases. If demand and supply increase by the same amount, there is no shortage or surplus, so the price does not change, but the quantity increases.

Solution to In the News

A fall in the rice harvest will decrease the supply of rice and raise its price. A bumper wheat harvest will increase the supply of wheat and lower its price. Wheat and rice are substitutes, so a higher price of rice will increase the demand for wheat and a lower price of wheat will decrease the demand for rice.

FIGURE 1

FIGURE 2

CHAPTER SUMMARY

Key Points

1. **Distinguish between quantity demanded and demand, and explain what determines demand.**

   * Other things remaining the same, the quantity demanded increases as the price falls and decreases as the price rises—the law of demand.
   * The demand for a good is influenced by the prices of related goods, expected future prices, income, expected future income and credit, the number of buyers, and preferences. A change in any of these influences changes the demand for the good.

2. **Distinguish between quantity supplied and supply, and explain what determines supply.**

   * Other things remaining the same, the quantity supplied increases as the price rises and decreases as the price falls—the law of supply.
   * The supply of a good is influenced by the prices of related goods, prices of resources and other inputs, expected future prices, the number of sellers, and productivity. A change in any of these influences changes the supply of the good.

3. **Explain how demand and supply determine price and quantity in a market, and explain the effects of changes in demand and supply.**

   * The law of market forces brings market equilibrium—the equilibrium price and equilibrium quantity at which buyers and sellers trade.
   * The price adjusts to maintain market equilibrium—to keep the quantity demanded equal to the quantity supplied. A surplus brings a fall in the price to restore market equilibrium; a shortage brings a rise in the price to restore market equilibrium.
   * Market equilibrium responds to changes in demand and supply. An increase in demand increases both the price and the quantity; a decrease in demand decreases both the price and the quantity. An increase in supply increases the quantity but decreases the price; and a decrease in supply decreases the quantity but increases the price.

Key Terms

MyEconLab Key Terms Quiz

Change in demand, 88

Change in the quantity demanded, 90

Change in the quantity supplied, 97

Change in supply, 95

Complement, 88

Complement in production, 95

Demand, 85

Demand curve, 86

Demand schedule, 86

Equilibrium price, 100

Equilibrium quantity, 100

Inferior good, 89

Law of demand, 85

Law of market forces, 100

Law of supply, 92

Market equilibrium, 100

Normal good, 89

Quantity demanded, 85

Quantity supplied, 92

Substitute, 88

Substitute in production, 95

Supply, 92

Supply curve, 93

Supply schedule, 93

CHAPTER CHECKPOINT

Study Plan Problems and Applications

1. Explain how each of the following events changes the demand for or supply of air travel.
   - Airfares tumble, while long-distance bus fares don't change.
   - The price of jet fuel rises.
   - Airlines reduce the number of flights each day.
   - People expect airfares to increase next summer.
   - The price of train travel falls.
   - The price of a pound of air cargo increases.

Use the laws of demand and supply to explain whether the statements in Problems **2** and **3** are true or false. In your explanation, distinguish between a change in demand and a change in the quantity demanded and between a change in supply and a change in the quantity supplied.

2. The United States does not allow oranges from Brazil (the world's largest producer of oranges) to enter the United States. If Brazilian oranges were sold in the United States, oranges and orange juice would be cheaper.

3. If the price of frozen yogurt falls, the quantity of ice cream consumed will decrease and the price of ice cream will rise.

4. Table 1 shows the demand and supply schedules for running shoes. What is the market equilibrium? If the price is $70 a pair, describe the situation in the market. Explain how market equilibrium is restored. If a rise in income increases the demand for running shoes by 100 pairs a day at each price, explain how the market adjusts to its new equilibrium.

5. "As more people buy fuel-efficient hybrid cars, the demand for gasoline will decrease and the price of gasoline will fall. The fall in the price of gasoline will decrease the supply of gasoline." Is this statement true? Explain.

6. **OPEC deadlocked on oil production hike**

   Oil prices exceeded the $100-a-barrel mark Wednesday after OPEC said it could not reach an agreement about raising crude production.

   Source: CNN Money, June 8, 2011

   Suppose that OPEC members had agreed to increase production. Use a graph of the oil market to show the effect of this decision on the market equilibrium.

Use the following information to work Problems **7** and **8**.

Rain delays to U.S. planting lift corn and soybean prices
Heavy rain has delayed the planting of corn and soybean and soggy conditions have slowed the winter wheat harvest.

   Source: *Financial Times*, June 25, 2015

7. Explain how heavy rain and soggy conditions will change the prices of corn, soybean, and wheat.

8. Use graphs to show how supply and demand will change in the markets for corn, soybean, and wheat.

 9. Read *Eye on the Price of Coffee* on p. 105 and explain how we know that the price increased in 2014 because the supply of coffee decreased and not because the demand for coffee increased.

TABLE 1

Price (dollars per pair)	Quantity demanded	Quantity supplied
	(pairs per day)	
60	1,000	400
70	900	500
80	800	600
90	700	700
100	600	800
110	500	900

Instructor Assignable Problems and Applications

1. Why can we be confident that the market for coffee is competitive and that a decrease in supply rather than the greed of coffee growers is the reason for the 2014 rise in price?

2. What is the effect on the equilibrium price and equilibrium quantity of orange juice if the price of apple juice decreases and the wage rate paid to orange grove workers increases?

3. What is the effect on the equilibrium in the orange juice market if orange juice becomes more popular and a cheaper robot is used to pick oranges?

4. **Concerns over winter wheat may boost price**
   Concerns about the U.S. winter wheat crop and dry conditions in other wheat-producing nations have increased the price of wheat.
   Source: Agweb.com, July 6, 2015

   Explain how an upcoming harvest influences today's price of wheat.

Table 1 shows the demand and supply schedules for boxes of chocolates in an average week. Use this information to work Problems **5** and **6**.

5. If the price of chocolates is $17.00 a box, describe the situation in the market. Explain how market equilibrium is restored.

6. During Valentine's week, more people buy chocolates and chocolatiers offer their chocolates in special red boxes, which cost more to produce than the everyday box. Set out the three-step process of analysis and show on a graph the adjustment process to the new equilibrium. Describe the changes in the equilibrium price and the equilibrium quantity.

7. After a severe bout of foreclosures and defaults on home loans, banks made it harder for people to borrow. How does this change influence
   * The demand for new homes?
   * The supply of new homes?
   * The price of new homes?
   Illustrate your answer with a graphical analysis.

8. **Bacon is 25 percent cheaper**
   Bacon is 25 percent cheaper now than a year ago and bacon sales are up 13 percent on the year. At the same time, the bird flu virus is killing millions of chickens, raising egg prices.
   Source: *CNN Money*, May 20, 2015

   Explain how this news clip illustrates: (a) the law of demand and why the price of bacon fell, and (b) how the markets for bacon and eggs influence each other. Draw a graph to illustrate your explanation.

9. "As more people buy smartphones, the demand for smartphone service increases and the price of smartphone service falls, which decreases the supply of smartphone service." Is this statement true or false? Explain.

10. **China slowdown could bring good news**
    China's economic slowdown could help reduce the cost of steel used by U.S. auto makers.
    Source: *The Wall Street Journal*, September 8, 2015

    Explain how an economic slowdown in China influences the global steel market. What happens to the equilibrium price of steel?

TABLE 1

Price (dollars per box)	Quantity demanded	Quantity supplied
	(boxes per day)	
13.00	1,600	
14.00	1,500	1,300
15.00	1,400	1,400
16.00	1,300	1,500
17.00	1,200	1,600
18.00	1,100	1,700

Multiple Choice Quiz

1. Which of the following events illustrates the law of demand: Other things remaining the same, a rise in the price of a good will _____.
   A. decrease the quantity demanded of that good
   B. increase the demand for a substitute of that good
   C. decrease the demand for the good
   D. increase the demand for a complement of that good

2. In the market for jeans, which of the following events increases the demand for a pair of jeans?
   A. The wage rate paid to garment workers rises.
   B. The price of a denim skirt (a substitute for jeans) rises.
   C. The price of denim cloth falls.
   D. New technology reduces the time it takes to make a pair of jeans.

3. Other things remaining the same, a fall in the price of peanuts will _____.
   A. increase the supply of peanuts
   B. decrease the supply of peanut butter
   C. decrease the quantity supplied of peanuts
   D. decrease the supply of peanuts

4. In the market for smartphones, which of the following events increases the supply of smartphones?
   A. New technology lowers the cost of making a smartphone
   B. A rise in the price of an e-book reader (a substitute in production)
   C. An increase in people's incomes
   D. A rise in the wage rate paid to electronics workers

5. When floods wiped out the banana crop in Central America, the equilibrium price of bananas _____ and the equilibrium quantity of bananas _____.
   A. rose; increased
   B. rose; decreased
   C. fell; increased
   D. fell; decreased

6. A decrease in the demand for chocolate with no change in the supply of chocolate will create a _____ of chocolate at today's price, but gradually the price will _____.
   A. surplus; fall
   B. shortage; fall
   C. surplus; rise
   D. shortage; rise

7. Many Americans are selling their cars and buying new fuel-efficient hybrids. Other things remaining the same, in the market for used cars, _____ and in the market for hybrids _____.
   A. supply increases and the price falls; demand increases and the price rises
   B. demand decreases and the price rises; supply increases and the price falls
   C. both demand and supply decrease and the price might rise, fall, or not change; demand increases and the price rises
   D. demand decreases, supply increases, and the price falls; supply increases and the price falls

What do you do when Starbucks raises the price of a latte?

Elasticities of Demand and Supply

When you have completed your study of this chapter, you will be able to

1 Define and calculate the price elasticity of demand, and explain the factors that influence it.

2 Define and calculate the price elasticity of supply, and explain the factors that influence it.

3 Define the cross elasticity of demand and the income elasticity of demand, and explain the factors that influence them.

 MyEconLab Big Picture Video

5.1 THE PRICE ELASTICITY OF DEMAND

Price elasticity of demand
A measure of the responsiveness of the quantity demanded of a good to a change in its price when all other influences on buyers' plans remain the same.

Starbucks knows that if it raises the price of a latte and everything else remains the same, the quantity of lattes that it sells—the quantity demanded—will decrease. But by how much? To answer this question, Starbucks needs to know how responsive the quantity of latte demanded is to a change in its price. Elasticity provides this information.

The **price elasticity of demand** is a measure of the responsiveness of the quantity demanded of a good to a change in its price when all other influences on buyers' plans remain the same.

To determine the price elasticity of demand, we compare the percentage change in the quantity demanded with the percentage change in price.

■ Percentage Change in Price

If Starbucks changes its price of a latte by $2, the percentage change in price depends on whether the price has gone up or down.

A Rise in Price

Suppose that Starbucks raises the price of a latte from $3 to $5. The percentage change is calculated as the change in price divided by the initial price, all multiplied by 100. The formula for the percentage change is

$$\text{Percentage change in price} = \left(\frac{\text{New price} - \text{Initial price}}{\text{Initial price}}\right) \times 100.$$

In this example, the initial price is $3 and the new price is $5, so

$$\begin{array}{l}\text{Percentage} \\ \text{change in price}\end{array} = \left(\frac{\$5 - \$3}{\$3}\right) \times 100 = \left(\frac{\$2}{\$3}\right) \times 100 = 66.67 \text{ percent.}$$

A Fall in Price

Now suppose that Starbucks cuts the price of a latte from $5 to $3. The initial price is now $5 and the new price is $3, so the percentage change in price is

$$\begin{array}{l}\text{Percentage} \\ \text{change in price}\end{array} = \left(\frac{\$3 - \$5}{\$5}\right) \times 100 = \left(\frac{-\$2}{\$5}\right) \times 100 = -40 \text{ percent.}$$

The same price change, $2, over the same interval, between $3 and $5, is a different absolute percentage change—66.67 percent if the price rises and 40 percent if the price falls.

Because elasticity compares the percentage change in the quantity demanded with the percentage change in price, we need a measure of percentage change that does not depend on the direction of the price change. The measure that economists use is called the *midpoint method*.

The Midpoint Method

To calculate the percentage change in price using the midpoint method, we divide the change in the price by the *average price*—the *average* of the new price and the initial price—and then multiply by 100. The average price is at the midpoint between the initial and the new price, hence the name *midpoint method*.

The formula for the percentage change using the midpoint method is

$$\text{Percentage change in price} = \left(\frac{\text{New price} - \text{Initial price}}{(\text{New price} + \text{Initial price}) \div 2} \right) \times 100.$$

In this formula, the numerator (New price − Initial price) is the same as before. The denominator, (New price + Initial price) ÷ 2, is the average of the new price and the initial price.

To calculate the percentage change in the price of a Starbucks latte using the midpoint method, put $5 for new price and $3 for initial price in the formula:

$$\begin{aligned}\text{Percentage} \atop \text{change in price} &= \left(\frac{\$5 - \$3}{(\$5 + \$3) \div 2} \right) \times 100 = \left(\frac{\$2}{\$8 \div 2} \right) \times 100 \\ &= \left(\frac{\$2}{\$4} \right) \times 100 = 50 \text{ percent.}\end{aligned}$$

Because the average price is the same regardless of whether the price rises or falls, the percentage change in price calculated by the midpoint method is the same (magnitude) for a price rise and a price fall. In this example, it is 50 percent.

■ Percentage Change in Quantity Demanded

Suppose that when the price of a latte rises from $3 to $5, the quantity demanded decreases from 15 cups to 5 cups an hour. The percentage change in the quantity demanded using the midpoint method is

$$\begin{aligned}\text{Percentage change} \atop \text{in quantity} &= \left(\frac{\text{New quantity} - \text{Initial quantity}}{(\text{New quantity} + \text{Initial quantity}) \div 2} \right) \times 100 \\ &= \left(\frac{5 - 15}{(5 + 15) \div 2} \right) \times 100 = \left(\frac{-10}{20 \div 2} \right) \times 100 \\ &= \left(\frac{-10}{10} \right) \times 100 = -100 \text{ percent.}\end{aligned}$$

When the price of a good *rises*, the quantity demanded of it *decreases*—a *positive* change in price brings a *negative* change in the quantity demanded. Similarly, when the price of a good *falls*, the quantity demanded of it *increases*—this time a *negative* change in price brings a *positive* change in the quantity demanded.

To compare the percentage changes in price and quantity demanded, we use the magnitudes of the percentage changes and we ignore the minus sign.

■ Comparing the Percentage Changes in Price and Quantity

To determine the responsiveness of the quantity of Starbucks lattes demanded to its price, we compare the two percentage changes we've just calculated. The percentage change in quantity demanded is 100 percent and the percentage change in price is 50 percent. In this case, the percentage change in the quantity of Starbucks lattes demanded is greater than the percentage change in its price. But it might have been equal or less. Let's see how we classify degrees of responsiveness.

Elastic demand
When the percentage change in the quantity demanded exceeds the percentage change in price.

Unit elastic demand
When the percentage change in the quantity demanded equals the percentage change in price.

Inelastic demand
When the percentage change in the quantity demanded is less than the percentage change in price.

Perfectly elastic demand
When the quantity demanded changes by a very large percentage in response to an almost zero percentage change in price.

Perfectly inelastic demand
When the percentage change in the quantity demanded is zero for any percentage change in the price.

■ Elastic and Inelastic Demand

If we collected data on the prices and quantities of Starbucks lattes and a number of other goods and services and we were careful to check that other things had remained the same, we could calculate lots of percentage changes in prices and quantities demanded. We could then classify the demands by their degree of responsiveness of quantity demanded to price.

Our calculations would fall into three groups: The percentage change in the quantity demanded might exceed the percentage change in price (as in the example of Starbucks lattes), be equal to the percentage change in price, or be less than the percentage change in price. Each of these three possibilities defines three ranges for the price elasticity of demand:

- When the percentage change in the quantity demanded exceeds the percentage change in price, demand is **elastic**.
- When the percentage change in the quantity demanded equals the percentage change in price, demand is **unit elastic**.
- When the percentage change in the quantity demanded is less than the percentage change in price, demand is **inelastic**.

Figure 5.1 shows the different types of demand curves that illustrate the range of possible price elasticities of demand. Part (a) shows an extreme case of an elastic demand called a **perfectly elastic demand**—an almost zero percentage change in the price brings a very large percentage change in the quantity demanded. Consumers are willing to buy any quantity of the good at a given price but none at a higher price. Part (b) shows an elastic demand—the percentage change in the quantity demanded exceeds the percentage change in price. Part (c) shows a unit elastic demand—the percentage change in the quantity demanded equals the percentage change in price. Part (d) shows an inelastic demand—the percentage change in the quantity demanded is less than the percentage change in price. Finally, part (e) shows an extreme case of an inelastic demand called a **perfectly inelastic demand**—the percentage change in the quantity demanded is zero for any percentage change in price.

■ Influences on the Price Elasticity of Demand

What makes the demand for some things elastic and the demand for others inelastic? The influences on the price elasticity of demand fall into two groups:

- Availability of substitutes
- Proportion of income spent

Availability of Substitutes

The demand for a good is elastic if a substitute for it is easy to find. Soft drink containers can be made of either aluminum or plastic and it doesn't matter which, so the demand for aluminum is elastic.

The demand for a good is inelastic if a substitute for it is hard to find. Oil has poor substitutes (imagine a coal-fueled car), so the demand for oil is inelastic.

Three main factors influence the ability to find a substitute for a good: whether the good is a luxury or a necessity, how narrowly the good is defined, and the amount of time available to find a substitute for it.

■ FIGURE 5.1

The Range of Price Elasticities of Demand

MyEconLab Animation

(a) Perfectly elastic demand

(b) Elastic demand

(c) Unit elastic demand

(d) Inelastic demand

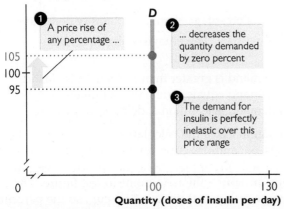

(e) Perfectly inelastic demand

1 A price rise brings **2** a decrease in the quantity demanded. The relationship between the percentage change in the quantity demanded and the percentage change in price determines **3** the price elasticity of demand, which ranges from perfectly elastic (part a) to perfectly inelastic (part e).

Luxury Versus Necessity   We call goods such as food and housing *necessities* and goods such as exotic vacations *luxuries*. A necessity has poor substitutes—you must eat—so the demand for a necessity is inelastic. A luxury has many substitutes—you don't absolutely have to go to the Galapagos Islands this summer—so the demand for a luxury is elastic.

Narrowness of Definition   The demand for a narrowly defined good is elastic. For example, the demand for Starbucks lattes is elastic because a Panera latte is a good substitute for a Starbucks latte. The demand for a broadly defined good is inelastic. For example, the demand for coffee is inelastic because tea is a poor substitute for coffee.

Time Elapsed Since Price Change   The longer the time that has elapsed since the price of a good changed, the more elastic is the demand for the good. For example, when the price of gasoline increased steeply during the 1970s and 1980s, the quantity of gasoline demanded didn't change much because many people owned gas-guzzling automobiles—the demand for gasoline was inelastic. But eventually, fuel-efficient cars replaced gas guzzlers and the quantity of gasoline demanded decreased—the demand for gasoline became more elastic.

Proportion of Income Spent

A price rise, like a decrease in income, means that people cannot afford to buy the same quantities of goods and services as before. The greater the proportion of income spent on a good, the greater is the impact of a rise in its price on the quantity of that good that people can afford to buy and the more elastic is the demand for the good. For example, toothpaste takes a tiny proportion of your budget and housing takes a large proportion. If the price of toothpaste doubles, you buy almost as much toothpaste as before. Your demand for toothpaste is inelastic. If your apartment rent doubles, you shriek and look for more roommates. Your demand for housing is more elastic than is your demand for toothpaste.

MyEconLab Concept Video

■ Computing the Price Elasticity of Demand

To determine whether the demand for a good is elastic, unit elastic, or inelastic, we compute a numerical value for the price elasticity of demand by using the following formula:

$$\text{Price elasticity of demand} = \frac{\text{Percentage change in quantity demanded}}{\text{Percentage change in price}}.$$

- If the price elasticity of demand is greater than 1, demand is elastic.
- If the price elasticity of demand equals 1, demand is unit elastic.
- If the price elasticity of demand is less than 1, demand is inelastic.

Figure 5.2 illustrates and summarizes the calculation for the Starbucks latte example. Initially, the price is $3 and 15 cups an hour are demanded—the initial point in the figure. Then the price rises to $5 and the quantity demanded decreases to 5 cups an hour—the new point in the figure. The price rises by $2 a cup and the average (midpoint) price is $4 a cup, so the percentage change in price is 50. The quantity demanded decreases by 10 cups an hour and the average (midpoint) quantity is 10 cups an hour, so the percentage change in quantity demanded is 100.

FIGURE 5.2

Price Elasticity of Demand Calculation

MyEconLab Animation

❶ At the initial point, the price is $3 and the quantity demanded is 15 cups an hour.

❷ At the new point, the price is $5 and the quantity demanded is 5 cups an hour.

❸ The change in price is $2 and ❹ the average price is $4, so the percentage change in price equals ($2 ÷ $4) × 100, which is 50 percent.

❺ The change in the quantity demanded is 10 cups and ❻ the average quantity demanded is 10 cups, so the percentage change in quantity demanded equals (10 ÷ 10) × 100, which is 100 percent.

❼ The price elasticity of demand equals (100 percent ÷ 50 percent), which is 2.

Using the above formula, you can see that the price elasticity of demand for Starbucks lattes is

$$\text{Price elasticity of demand} = \frac{100 \text{ percent}}{50 \text{ percent}} = 2.$$

The price elasticity of demand is 2 at the midpoint between the initial price and the new price on the demand curve. Over this price range, the demand for Starbucks lattes is elastic.

■ Interpreting the Price Elasticity of Demand Number

The number we've just calculated for Starbucks lattes is only an example. We don't have real data on the price and quantity. But if we did have real data and we discovered that the price elasticity of demand for Starbucks lattes is 2, what does this number tell us?

It tells us three main things:

1. The demand for Starbucks lattes is elastic. Being elastic, the good has plenty of convenient substitutes (such as other brands of latte) and takes only a small proportion of buyers' incomes.

2. Starbucks must be careful not to charge too high a price for its latte. Pushing the price up brings in more revenue per cup but wipes out a lot of potential business.

3. The flip side of the second point: Even a slightly lower price could create a lot of potential business and end up bringing in more revenue.

MyEconLab Concept Video

■ Elasticity Along a Linear Demand Curve

Slope measures responsiveness. But elasticity is *not* the same as *slope*. You can see the distinction most clearly by looking at the price elasticity of demand along a linear (straight-line) demand curve. The slope is constant, but the elasticity varies. Figure 5.3 shows the same demand curve for Starbucks lattes as that in Figure 5.2 but with the axes extended to show lower prices and larger quantities demanded.

Let's calculate the elasticity of demand at point *A*. If the price rises from $3 to $5 a cup, the quantity demanded decreases from 15 to 5 cups an hour. The average price is $4 a cup, and the average quantity is 10 cups—point *A*. The elasticity of demand at point *A* is 2, and demand is elastic.

Let's calculate the elasticity of demand at point *C*. If the price falls from $3 to $1 a cup, the quantity demanded increases from 15 to 25 cups an hour. The average price is $2 a cup, and the average quantity is 20 cups—point *C*. The elasticity of demand at point *C* is 0.5, and demand is inelastic.

Finally, let's calculate the elasticity of demand at point *B*, which is the midpoint of the demand curve. If the price rises from $2 to $4 a cup, the quantity demanded decreases from 20 to 10 cups an hour. The average price is $3 a cup, and the average quantity is 15 cups—point *B*. The elasticity of demand at point *B* is 1, and demand is unit elastic.

Along a linear demand curve,

- Demand is unit elastic at the midpoint of the curve.
- Demand is elastic at all points above the midpoint of the curve.
- Demand is inelastic at all points below the midpoint of the curve.

FIGURE 5.3

Elasticity Along a Linear Demand Curve

MyEconLab Animation

On a linear demand curve, the slope is constant, but the elasticity decreases as the price falls and the quantity demanded increases.

❶ At point A, demand is elastic.

❷ At point B, which is the midpoint of the demand curve, demand is unit elastic.

❸ At point C, demand is inelastic.

Demand is elastic at all points above the midpoint of the demand curve and inelastic at all points below the midpoint of the demand curve.

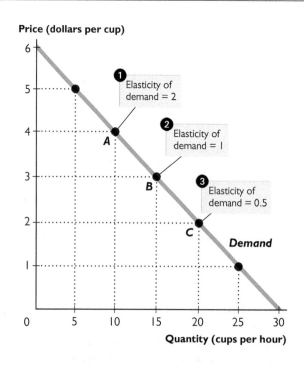

Price (dollars per cup)

❶ Elasticity of demand = 2

❷ Elasticity of demand = 1

❸ Elasticity of demand = 0.5

Demand

Quantity (cups per hour)

EYE on the GLOBAL ECONOMY
Price Elasticities of Demand

A wealthy American student is casual about her food. It costs only a few dollars a day, and she's going to have her burger, even at double the price. But a poor Tanzanian boy takes his food with deadly seriousness. He has a tough time getting, preparing, and even defending his food. A rise in the price of food means that he must cut back and eat even less.

The figure shows the percentage of income spent on food and the price elasticity of demand for food in ten countries. The larger the proportion of income spent on food, the larger is the price elasticity of demand for food.

As the low-income countries become richer, the proportion of income they spend on food will decrease and their demand for food will become more inelastic. Consequently, the world's demand for food will become more inelastic.

Harvests fluctuate and bring fluctuations in the price of food. As the world demand for food becomes more and more inelastic, the fluctuations in the prices of food items will become larger.

The table shows a few real-world price elasticities of demand. The numbers in the table range from 1.52 for metals to 0.12 for food. Metals have good substitutes, such as plastics, while food has virtually no substitutes. As we move down the list of items, they have fewer good substitutes and are more likely to be regarded as necessities.

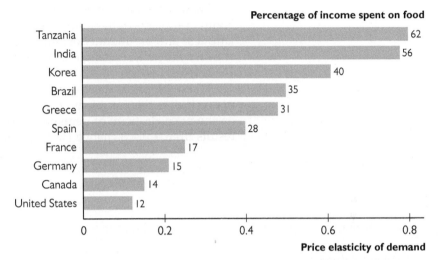

Percentage of income spent on food

Country	
Tanzania	62
India	56
Korea	40
Brazil	35
Greece	31
Spain	28
France	17
Germany	15
Canada	14
United States	12

Price elasticity of demand

Some Price Elasticities of Demand

Good or Service	Elasticity
Elastic Demand	
Metals	1.52
Electrical engineering products	1.39
Mechanical engineering products	1.30
Furniture	1.26
Motor vehicles	1.14
Instrument engineering products	1.10
Professional services	1.09
Transportation services	1.03
Inelastic Demand	
Gas, electricity, and water	0.92
Oil	0.91
Chemicals	0.89
Beverages (all types)	0.78
Clothing	0.64
Tobacco	0.61
Banking and insurance services	0.56
Housing services	0.55
Agricultural and fish products	0.42
Books, magazines, and newspapers	0.34
Food	0.12

SOURCES OF DATA: See p. C1.

■ Total Revenue and the Price Elasticity of Demand

Total revenue
The amount spent on a good and received by its seller and equals the price of the good multiplied by the quantity sold.

Total revenue is the amount spent on a good and received by its seller and equals the price of the good multiplied by the quantity of the good sold. For example, suppose that the price of a Starbucks latte is $3 and that 15 cups an hour are sold. Then total revenue is $3 a cup multiplied by 15 cups an hour, which equals $45 an hour.

We can use the demand curve for Starbucks lattes to illustrate total revenue. Figure 5.4(a) shows the total revenue from the sale of lattes when the price of a latte is $3 and the quantity of lattes demanded is 15 cups an hour. Total revenue is shown by the blue rectangle, the area of which equals $3, its height, multiplied by 15, its length, which equals $45.

When the price changes, total revenue can change in the same direction, the opposite direction, or remain constant. Which of these outcomes occurs depends on the price elasticity of demand. By observing the change in total revenue that results from a price change (with all other influences on the quantity remaining

■ FIGURE 5.4

Total Revenue and the Price Elasticity of Demand

MyEconLab Animation

Part (a) show the demand for Starbucks lattes. Total revenue equals price multiplied by quantity. When the price of a latte is $3, the quantity demanded is 15 cups an hour and total revenue equals $45 an hour. But when the price rises to $5, the quantity demanded decreases to 5 cups an hour and total revenue decreases to $25 an hour.

Starbucks' total revenue decreases when it raises its price because the demand for Starbucks lattes is elastic.

Part (b) shows the demand for textbooks. When the price is $50 a book, the quantity demanded is 5 million books a year and total revenue equals $250 million a year. When the price rises to $75 a book, the quantity demanded decreases to 4 million books a year and total revenue increases to $300 million a year.

When the textbook price rises, total revenue increases because the demand for textbooks is inelastic.

(a) Total revenue and elastic demand: Starbucks lattes

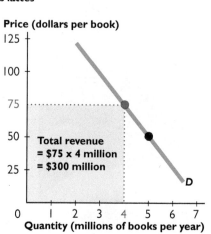

(b) Total revenue and inelastic demand: textbooks

unchanged), we can estimate the price elasticity of demand. This method of estimating the price elasticity of demand is called the **total revenue test**.

If demand is elastic, a given percentage rise in price brings a larger percentage decrease in the quantity demanded, so total revenue—price multiplied by quantity—decreases. Figure 5.4(a) shows this outcome. When the price of a latte is $3, the quantity demanded is 15 cups an hour, so total revenue ($3 × 15) equals $45. If the price of a latte rises to $5, the quantity demanded decreases to 5 cups an hour, so total revenue ($5 × 5) *decreases* to $25.

If demand is inelastic, a given percentage rise in price brings a smaller percentage decrease in the quantity demanded, so total revenue increases. Figure 5.4(b) shows this outcome. When the price of a textbook is $50, the quantity demanded is 5 million textbooks a year and total revenue ($50 × 5 million) is $250 million. If the price of a textbook rises to $75, the quantity demanded decreases to 4 million textbooks a year and total revenue ($75 × 4 million) *increases* to $300 million.

The relationship between the price elasticity of demand and total revenue is

- If price and total revenue change in opposite directions, demand is elastic.
- If a price change leaves total revenue unchanged, demand is unit elastic.
- If price and total revenue change in the same direction, demand is inelastic.

Total revenue test
A method of estimating the price elasticity of demand by observing the change in total revenue that results from a price change (with all other influences on the quantity sold remaining unchanged).

MyEconLab Critical Thinking Exercise

EYE on ELASTICITY AT THE COFFEE SHOP
What Do You Do When Starbucks Raises the Price of a Latte?

When Starbucks raises the price of a latte, the first thing to do is look at the price of lattes in other conveniently located coffee shops. Suppose they have not increased and you can get an acceptable latte for a lower price at Dunkin' Donuts. You decide to switch your allegiance and keep drinking the same quantity of latte.

Soon though, all the coffee shops in your neighborhood have raised their price. Your daily latte is more expensive, no matter how you satisfy your craving for it. You look at the dwindling change in your pocket and decide to return to Starbucks but trim your latte consumption by a cup a week.

Price Elasticity of Demand

We can translate this account of your possible response to a hike in Starbucks' price into some estimates of your price elasticity of demand for Starbucks latte and for latte in general.

Close Substitutes

When Starbucks alone has a higher price, you decrease the quantity of Starbucks latte to zero, so your price elasticity of demand for Starbucks latte is high—it is elastic.

A Starbucks latte and a Dunkin' Donuts latte are different, but for some people they are reasonably close substitutes. So when Starbucks alone

raises its price of a latte, the quantity sold by Starbucks changes a lot—the demand for a Starbucks latte is elastic.

Poor Substitutes

Later, when all the coffee shops have raised the price of a latte, you return to Starbucks but cut back a bit on your consumption of latte. Your price elasticity of demand for latte of all types is low—it is inelastic.

Latte, tea, water, juice, and other drinks are poor substitutes. So when the price of a latte rises, the quantity of latte bought decreases but not by very much—the demand for lattes of all types is inelastic.

EYE on the U.S. ECONOMY
Two Applications of the Price Elasticity of Demand

Orange Prices and Total Revenue

Is a Florida frost that damages the orange crop bad news or good news for orange growers? Does the frost decrease or increase growers' total revenue? Knowledge of the price elasticity of demand for oranges enables us to answer these questions.

If supply changes and demand doesn't change, the percentage change in the equilibrium quantity equals the percentage change in the quantity demanded. And the magnitude of the change in the price and quantity depends on the elasticity of demand.

Economists have estimated that the demand for oranges is inelastic. So if a frost in Florida decreases the orange harvest and decreases the equilibrium quantity of oranges by 1 percent, the price of oranges will rise by more than 1 percent.

Because the price rises by a larger percentage than the percentage decrease in quantity, total revenue increases.

A Florida frost is bad news for buyers of orange juice and for growers who lose their crops, but good news for other orange growers.

So when a Florida frost strikes, the price of oranges rises by a larger percentage than the percentage decrease in the quantity of oranges and the total revenue of the orange growers increases.

A frost is bad news for consumers and growers who lose their crops, but good news for other growers.

Addiction and Elasticity

We can gain insights that might help to design potentially effective policies for dealing with addiction to drugs, whether legal (such as tobacco and alcohol) or illegal (such as meth or heroin).

Nonusers' demand for addictive substances is elastic. A moderately higher price leads to a substantially smaller number of people trying a drug and so exposing themselves to the possibility of becoming addicted. But the existing users' demand for addictive substances is inelastic. Even a substantial price rise brings only a modest decrease in the quantity demanded.

These facts about the price elasticity of demand mean that high taxes on cigarettes and alcohol limit the number of young people who become habitual users of these products, but high taxes have only a modest effect on the quantities consumed by established users.

Similarly, effective policing of imports of an illegal drug that limits its supply leads to a large price rise and a substantial decrease in the number of new users but only a small decrease in the quantity consumed by addicts.

Expenditure on the drug by addicts increases. Further, because many drug addicts finance their purchases with crime, the amount of theft and burglary increases.

Because the price elasticity of demand for drugs is low for addicts, any successful policy to decrease drug use will be one that focuses on the demand for drugs and attempts to change preferences through rehabilitation programs.

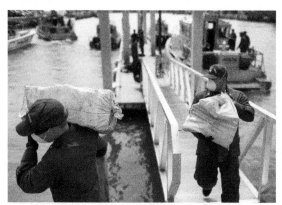

Cracking down on imports of illegal drugs limits supply, which leads to a higher price. But it also increases the expenditure on drugs by addicts and increases the crime that finances addiction.

CHECKPOINT 5.1

MyEconLab Study Plan 5.1
Key Terms Quiz
Solutions Video

Define and calculate the price elasticity of demand, and explain the factors that influence it.

Practice Problems

When the price of a good increased by 10 percent, the quantity demanded of it decreased by 2 percent.

1. Is the demand for this good elastic, unit elastic, or inelastic?

2. Does this good have close substitutes or poor substitutes? Is this good more likely to be a necessity or a luxury and to be narrowly or broadly defined? Why?

3. Calculate the price elasticity of demand for this good; explain how the total revenue from the sale of the good has changed; and explain which of the following goods this good is most likely to be: orange juice, bread, toothpaste, theater tickets, clothing, blue jeans, or Super Bowl tickets.

In the News

Samsung and LG slash prices to take sales from Apple
Apple's new iPhone 6 sold out quickly in the United States and to avoid the same outcome in other national markets, Samsung and LG cut the prices of their Galaxy and V10 smartphones by over 10 percent.
Source: International Business Times, October 27, 2015

Will a price cut by Samsung and LG increase their total revenue? If Apple also cuts its prices, what will happen to the total revenue from all smartphone sales?

Solutions to Practice Problems

1. The demand for a good is *inelastic* if the percentage decrease in the quantity demanded is less than the percentage increase in its price. In this example, a 10 percent price rise brings a 2 percent decrease in the quantity demanded, so demand is inelastic.

2. Because the good has an inelastic demand, it most likely has poor substitutes, is a necessity rather than a luxury, and is broadly defined.

3. Price elasticity of demand equals the percentage change in the quantity demanded divided by the percentage change in price. In this example, the price elasticity of demand is 2 percent divided by 10 percent, or 0.2. An elasticity less than 1 means that demand is inelastic. When demand is inelastic, a price rise increases total revenue. This good is most likely a necessity (bread), or has poor substitutes (toothpaste), or is broadly defined (clothing).

Solution to In the News

The Apple 6s, Galaxy S6, and LG V10 offer similar features and functions, so they are close substitutes and the demand for any one of them alone is elastic. If the prices of only Samsung and LG fall by 10 percent, the quantity sold will increase by more than 10 percent and the two firms' total revenue will increase. But a smartphone has poor substitutes, so if Apple also cuts its prices, the total revenue of all three firms will decrease because the demand for smartphones is inelastic.

5.2 THE PRICE ELASTICITY OF SUPPLY

You know that when demand increases, the equilibrium price rises and the equilibrium quantity increases. But does the price rise by a large amount and the quantity increase by a little? Or does the price barely rise and the quantity increase by a large amount? To answer this question, we need to know the price elasticity of supply.

The **price elasticity of supply** is a measure of the responsiveness of the quantity supplied of a good to a change in its price when all other influences on sellers' plans remain the same. We determine the price elasticity of supply by comparing the percentage change in the quantity supplied with the percentage change in price.

Price elasticity of supply
A measure of the responsiveness of the quantity supplied of a good to a change in its price when all other influences on sellers' plans remain the same.

■ Elastic and Inelastic Supply

The supply of a good might be

- Elastic
- Unit elastic
- Inelastic

Figure 5.5 illustrates the range of supply elasticities. Figure 5.5(a) shows the extreme case of a **perfectly elastic supply**—an almost zero percentage change in price brings a very large percentage change in the quantity supplied. Figure 5.5(b) shows an **elastic supply**—the percentage change in the quantity supplied exceeds the percentage change in price. Figure 5.5(c) shows a **unit elastic supply**—the percentage change in the quantity supplied equals the percentage change in price. Figure 5.5(d) shows an **inelastic supply**—the percentage change in the quantity supplied is less than the percentage change in price. And Figure 5.5(e) shows the extreme case of a **perfectly inelastic supply**—the percentage change in the quantity supplied is zero when the price changes.

Perfectly elastic supply
When the quantity supplied changes by a very large percentage in response to an almost zero percentage change in price.

Elastic supply
When the percentage change in the quantity supplied exceeds the percentage change in price.

Unit elastic supply
When the percentage change in the quantity supplied equals the percentage change in price.

■ Influences on the Price Elasticity of Supply

What makes the supply of some things elastic and the supply of others inelastic? The two main influences on the price elasticity of supply are

- Production possibilities
- Storage possibilities

Inelastic supply
When the percentage change in the quantity supplied is less than the percentage change in price.

Production Possibilities

Some goods can be produced at a constant (or very gently rising) opportunity cost. These goods have an elastic supply. The silicon in your computer chips is an example of such a good. Silicon is extracted from sand at a tiny and almost constant opportunity cost, so the supply of silicon is perfectly elastic.

Some goods can be produced in only a fixed quantity. These goods have a perfectly inelastic supply. A beachfront home in Malibu can be built only on a unique beachfront lot, so the supply of these homes is perfectly inelastic.

Hotel rooms in New York City can't easily be used as office accommodation and office space cannot easily be converted into hotel rooms, so the supply of hotel rooms in New York City is inelastic. Paper and printing presses can be used to produce textbooks or magazines, and the supplies of these goods are elastic.

Perfectly inelastic supply
When the percentage change in the quantity supplied is zero for any percentage change in the price.

FIGURE 5.5

The Range of Price Elasticities of Supply   MyEconLab Animation

(a) Perfectly elastic supply

(b) Elastic supply

(c) Unit elastic supply

(d) Inelastic supply

(e) Perfectly inelastic supply

① A price rise brings ② an increase in the quantity supplied. The relationship between the percentage change in the quantity supplied and the percentage change in price determines ③ the price elasticity of supply, which ranges from perfectly elastic (part a) to perfectly inelastic (part e).

Time Elapsed Since Price Change   As time passes after a price change, it becomes easier to change production plans and supply becomes more elastic. For some items—fruits and vegetables are examples—it is difficult or perhaps impossible to change the quantity supplied immediately after a price change. These goods have a perfectly inelastic supply on the day of a price change. The quantities supplied depend on crop-planting decisions that were made earlier. In the case of oranges, for example, planting decisions have to be made many years in advance of the crop being available.

Many manufactured goods also have an inelastic supply if production plans have had only a short period in which to change. For example, before it launched the Wii in November 2006, Nintendo made a forecast of demand, set a price, and drew up a production plan to supply the United States with the quantity that it believed people would be willing to buy. It turned out that demand outstripped Nintendo's earlier forecast. The price of the Wii increased on eBay, an Internet auction market, to bring market equilibrium. At the high price that emerged, Nintendo would have liked to ship more units of Wii, but it could do nothing to increase the quantity supplied in the near term. The supply of Wii was inelastic.

As time passes, the elasticity of supply increases. After all the technologically possible ways of adjusting production have been exploited, supply is extremely elastic—perhaps perfectly elastic—for most manufactured items. In 2007, Nintendo was able to step up the production rate of Wii units and the price on eBay began to fall. The supply of Wii had become more elastic as production continued to expand.

Storage Possibilities

The elasticity of supply of a good that cannot be stored (for example, a perishable item such as fresh strawberries) depends only on production possibilities. But the elasticity of supply of a good that can be stored depends on the decision to keep the good in storage or to offer it for sale. A small price change can make a big difference to this decision, so the supply of a storable good is highly elastic. The cost of storage is the main influence on the elasticity of supply of a storable good. For example, rose growers in Colombia, anticipating a surge in demand on Valentine's Day in February, hold back supplies in late January and early February and increase their inventories of roses. They then release roses from inventory for Valentine's Day.

Fresh strawberries must be sold before they deteriorate, so their supply is inelastic.

■ Computing the Price Elasticity of Supply

To determine whether the supply of a good is elastic, unit elastic, or inelastic, we compute a numerical value for the price elasticity of supply in a way similar to that used to calculate the price elasticity of demand. We use the formula:

$$\text{Price elasticity of supply} = \frac{\text{Percentage change in quantity supplied}}{\text{Percentage change in price}}.$$

- If the price elasticity of supply is greater than 1, supply is elastic.
- If the price elasticity of supply equals 1, supply is unit elastic.
- If the price elasticity of supply is less than 1, supply is inelastic.

Let's calculate the price elasticity of the supply of roses. Suppose that in a normal month, the price of roses is $40 a bouquet and 6 million bouquets are supplied. And suppose that in February, the price rises to $80 a bouquet and the quantity supplied increases to 24 million bouquets. Figure 5.6 illustrates the supply of roses and summarizes the calculation. The figure shows the initial point at $40 a bouquet and the new point at $80 a bouquet. The price increases by $40 a bouquet and the average, or midpoint, price is $60 a bouquet, so the percentage change in the price is 66.67 percent. The quantity supplied increases by 18 million bouquets. and the average, or midpoint, quantity is 15 million bouquets, so the percentage change in the quantity supplied is 120 percent.

Using the above formula, you can see that the price elasticity of supply of roses is

$$\text{Price elasticity of supply} = \frac{120 \text{ percent}}{66.67 \text{ percent}} = 1.8.$$

The price elasticity of supply is 1.8 at the midpoint between the initial point and the new point on the supply curve. In this example, over this price range, the supply of roses is elastic.

FIGURE 5.6

Price Elasticity of Supply Calculation   MyEconLab Animation

❶ At the initial point, the price is $40 a bouquet and the quantity supplied is 6 million bouquets a month.

❷ At the new point, the price is $80 a bouquet and the quantity supplied is 24 million bouquets a month.

❸ The change in price is $40, and ❹ the average price is $60, so the percentage change in the price equals ($40 ÷ $60) × 100, which is 66.67 percent.

❺ The change in the quantity supplied is 18 million bouquets and ❻ the average quantity supplied is 15 million bouquets, so the percentage change in quantity supplied is (18 million ÷ 15 million) × 100, which is 120 percent.

❼ The price elasticity of supply is 120 percent ÷ 66.67 percent, which equals 1.8.

MyEconLab Study Plan 5.2

Key Terms Quiz

Solutions Video

 CHECKPOINT 5.2

Define and calculate the price elasticity of supply, and explain the factors that influence it.

Practice Problems

A 10 percent increase in the price of a good increased the quantity supplied of the good by 1 percent after one month and by 25 percent after one year.

1. Is the supply of this good elastic, unit elastic, or inelastic? Is this good likely to be produced using factors of production that are easily obtained? What is the price elasticity of supply of this good?

2. What is the price elasticity of supply after one year? Has the supply of this good become more elastic or less elastic? Why?

In the News

Tuition and enrollment data

Enrollment increased from 15,539,000 in 2000 to 20,618,000 in 2013. The net cost of college (average for all types) increased from $12,357 to $14,860.

Source: trends.collegeboard.org, 2015

Calculate the price elasticity of supply of college. Is the supply of college elastic or inelastic?

Solutions to Practice Problems

1. The supply of a good is *inelastic* if the percentage increase in the quantity supplied is less than the percentage increase in price. In this example, a 10 percent price rise brings a 1 percent increase in the quantity supplied, so supply is inelastic. Because the quantity supplied increases by such a small percentage after one month, the factors of production that are used to produce this good are more likely to be difficult to obtain.
The price elasticity of supply equals Percentage change in the quantity supplied divided by Percentage change in the price. In this example, the price elasticity of supply equals 1 percent divided by 10 percent, or 0.1.

2. The price elasticity of supply equals Percentage change in the quantity supplied divided by Percentage change in the price. After one year, the price elasticity of supply is 25 percent divided by 10 percent, or 2.5. The supply of the good has become more elastic over the year since the price rise. Possibly other producers have gradually started producing the good and with the passage of time more factors of production can be reallocated.

Solution to In the News

The demand for college increased, so we can use these data to calculate the price elasticity of supply of college. The price elasticity of supply equals the percentage change in the quantity supplied divided by the percentage change in the price. Using the midpoint method (see the calculations in the margin), the quantity supplied increased by 28.1 percent and the price increased by 18.4 percent. The elasticity of supply is 28.1 percent divided by 18.4 percent, which is 1.53. Because the elasticity of supply is greater than 1, the supply of college is elastic.

Calculations:

The change in price is $2,503, the average price is $13,609, so the percentage change in the price equals ($2,503 ÷ $13,609) × 100, which is 18.4 percent.

The change in the quantity supplied is 5,079,000, the average quantity supplied is 18,078,500, so the percentage change in quantity supplied is (5,079,000 ÷ 18,078,500) × 100, which is 28.1 percent.

5.3   CROSS ELASTICITY AND INCOME ELASTICITY

MyEconLab Concept Video

Domino's Pizza in Chula Vista has a problem. Burger King has just cut its prices. Domino's manager, Pat, knows that pizzas and burgers are substitutes. He also knows that when the price of a substitute for pizza falls, the demand for pizza decreases. But by how much will the quantity of pizza bought decrease if Pat maintains his current price?

Pat also knows that pizza and soda are complements. He knows that if the price of a complement of pizza falls, the demand for pizza increases. So he wonders whether he might keep his customers by cutting the price he charges for soda. But he wants to know by how much he must cut the price of soda to keep selling the same quantity of pizza with cheaper burgers all around him.

To answer these questions, Pat needs to calculate the cross elasticity of demand. Let's examine this elasticity measure.

■ Cross Elasticity of Demand

The **cross elasticity of demand** is a measure of the responsiveness of the demand for a good to a change in the price of a substitute or complement when other things remain the same. It is calculated by using the formula:

Cross elasticity of demand
A measure of the responsiveness of the demand for a good to a change in the price of a substitute or complement when other things remain the same.

$$\text{Cross elasticity of demand} = \frac{\text{Percentage change in quantity demanded of a good}}{\text{Percentage change in price of one of its substitutes or complements}}.$$

Suppose that when the price of a burger falls by 10 percent, the quantity of pizza demanded decreases by 5 percent.* The cross elasticity of demand for pizza with respect to the price of a burger is

$$\text{Cross elasticity of demand} = \frac{-5 \text{ percent}}{-10 \text{ percent}} = 0.5.$$

The cross elasticity of demand for a substitute is positive. A *fall* in the price of a substitute brings a *decrease* in the quantity demanded of the good. The quantity demanded of a good and the price of one of its substitutes change in the *same* direction.

Suppose that when the price of soda falls by 10 percent, the quantity of pizza demanded increases by 2 percent. The cross elasticity of demand for pizza with respect to the price of soda is

$$\text{Cross elasticity of demand} = \frac{+2 \text{ percent}}{-10 \text{ percent}} = -0.2.$$

The cross elasticity of demand for a complement is negative. A *fall* in the price of a complement brings an *increase* in the quantity demanded of the good. The quantity demanded of a good and the price of one of its complements change in *opposite* directions.

---

*As before, these percentage changes are calculated by using the midpoint method.

■ **FIGURE 5.7**

Cross Elasticity of Demand

❶ A burger is a *substitute* for pizza. When the price of a burger falls, the demand curve for pizza shifts leftward from D_0 to D_1. At the price of $10 a pizza, people plan to buy fewer pizzas. The cross elasticity of the demand for pizza with respect to the price of a burger is *positive*.

❷ Soda is a *complement* of pizza. When the price of soda falls, the demand for pizza increases and the demand curve for pizza shifts rightward from D_0 to D_2. At the price of $10 a pizza, people plan to buy more pizzas. The cross elasticity of the demand for pizza with respect to the price of soda is *negative*.

Income elasticity of demand
A measure of the responsiveness of the demand for a good to a change in income when other things remain the same.

Figure 5.7 illustrates these two cross elasticities of demand for pizza. With the price of a pizza constant at $10, when the price of a burger falls, the demand for pizza decreases and the demand curve for pizza shifts leftward from D_0 to D_1. When the price of soda falls, the demand for pizza increases and the demand curve for pizza shifts rightward from D_0 to D_2. The magnitude of the cross elasticity determines how far the demand curve shifts.

■ **Income Elasticity of Demand**

The U.S. and global economies are expanding, and people are enjoying rising incomes. This increasing prosperity brings an increasing demand for most types of goods. But by how much will the demand for different items increase? Will the demand for some items increase so rapidly that we spend an increasing percentage of our incomes on them? And will the demand for some items decrease?

The answer depends on the income elasticity of demand. The **income elasticity of demand** is a measure of the responsiveness of the demand for a good to a change in income when other things remain the same. It is calculated by using the following formula:

$$\text{Income elasticity of demand} = \frac{\text{Percentage change in quantity demanded}}{\text{Percentage change in income}}.$$

The income elasticity of demand falls into three ranges:

• Greater than 1 (normal good, income elastic)
• Between zero and 1 (normal good, income inelastic)
• Less than zero (inferior good)

As our incomes increase: items that have

- An income elastic demand take an increasing share of income
- An income inelastic demand take a decreasing share of income
- A negative income elasticity of demand take an absolutely smaller amount of income.

You can make some strong predictions about how the world will change over the coming years by knowing the income elasticities of demand of different goods and services. Table 5.1 provides a sampling of numbers.

These estimated income elasticities of demand tell us that we can expect air travel—both domestic and international—to become hugely more important; an increasing share of our incomes will be spent on watching movies, eating out in restaurants, using public transportation, and getting haircuts. Two other prominent items not shown in the table, items for which demand is income elastic, are healthcare and education. As our incomes grow, we can expect education and healthcare to take increasing shares of our incomes.

As our incomes grow, we'll spend a decreasing percentage on clothing, phone calls, and food. The income elasticity of demand for food is less than one, even for the poorest people. So we can predict a continuation of the trends of the past—shrinking agriculture and manufacturing, and expanding services.

TABLE 5.1

Some Income Elasticities of Demand

Good or Service	Elasticity
Income Elastic	
Airline travel	5.82
Movies	3.41
Foreign travel	3.08
Electricity	1.94
Restaurant meals	1.61
Local buses and trains	1.38
Haircuts	1.36
Income Inelastic	
Tobacco	0.86
Alcoholic beverages	0.62
Clothing	0.51
Newspapers	0.38
Telephone	0.32
Food	0.14

SOURCES OF DATA: See p. C1.

EYE on YOUR LIFE
Your Price Elasticities of Demand

MyEconLab Critical Thinking Exercise

Pay close attention the next time the price of something that you buy rises. Did you spend more, the same, or less on this item?

Your expenditure on a good is equal to the price of the good multiplied by the quantity that you buy.

But recall that a seller's total revenue is equal to the price of the good multiplied by the quantity sold.

Because your expenditure on a good is equal to the seller's total revenue, the total revenue test that the seller uses to estimate price elasticity of demand can also be used to estimate your price elasticity of demand.

You can determine whether your demand for a good is elastic, unit elastic,

or inelastic by noting how your total expenditure on a good changes when its price changes.

When the price of a good rises, your demand for that good is

- *Elastic* if your expenditure on it decreases.
- *Unit elastic* if your expenditure on it remains constant.
- *Inelastic* if your expenditure on it increases.

Think about why your demand for a good might be elastic, unit elastic, or inelastic by checking back to the list of influences on the price elasticity of demand on p. 116.

Most likely, as we noted in the *Eye on Elasticity at the Coffee Shop* on

p. 123, when the price of a latte rises, you drink almost as many lattes as you did at the lower price. A latte has poor substitutes and your demand for latte is inelastic.

What do you do if the price of smartphone service falls? Do you spend less on smartphone service, as you would if your demand for smartphone service is inelastic? Or do you spend more on smartphone service, which would indicate an elastic demand for smartphone service?

What about your iTunes and Hulu or Netflix? Is your demand for these items elastic or inelastic? Is your demand for textbooks elastic or inelastic? You can estimate all these elasticities.

MyEconLab Study Plan 5.3
Key Terms Quiz
Solutions Video

 ## CHECKPOINT 5.3

Define the cross elasticity of demand and the income elasticity of demand, and explain the factors that influence them.

Practice Problems

1. The quantity demanded of good *A* increases by 5 percent when the price of good *B* rises by 10 percent and other things remain the same. Calculate the cross elasticity of demand. Are goods *A* and *B* complements or substitutes? Describe how the demand for good *A* changes.

2. When income rises by 5 percent and other things remain the same, the quantity demanded of good *C* increases by 1 percent. Calculate the income elasticity of demand for good *C*. Is good *C* a normal good or an inferior good? Describe how the demand for good *C* changes.

In the News

China is the world's fastest-growing market for "vanity" spending
China's market for the consumption of goods aimed at enhancing one's appearance or status grew an average of 15.6 percent a year for the past five years.
Source: qz.com, April 23, 2015

Given the information that incomes grew at about 7 percent a year, is the demand for "vanity" goods in China income elastic or income inelastic? Explain.

Solutions to Practice Problems

1. Cross elasticity of demand = Percentage change in the quantity demanded of good *A* ÷ Percentage increase in the price of good *B*.
    Cross elasticity of demand = 5 ÷ 10, or 0.5.

    Goods *A* and *B* are substitutes because the cross elasticity of demand is positive. When the price of good *B* rises, the quantity demanded of good *A* increases and people switch from good *B* to good *A*. The demand for good *A* increases (Figure 1).

2. Income elasticity of demand = Percentage change in the quantity demanded of good *C* ÷ Percentage increase in income.
    Income elasticity of demand = 1 ÷ 5, or 0.2.

    Income elasticity of demand is positive, so good *C* is a normal good.

    As income rises, the quantity demanded of good *C* increases. The demand for good *C* increases (Figure 2).

Solution to In the News

To know whether the demand for a good is income elastic, we need to calculate the income elasticity of demand. A good with an income elastic demand is one that has an income elasticity of demand greater than 1. If spending on "vanity" goods increased by 15.6 percent per year when incomes grew by 7 percent per year, the income elasticity of demand for "vanity" goods is 15.6 divided by 7, which equals 2.2. The income elasticity of demand for "vanity" goods is greater than 1, so the demand for "vanity" goods is income elastic.

FIGURE 1

Price of good *A*

D_0 D_1

0   Quantity of good *A*

FIGURE 2

Price of good *C*

D_0 D_1

0   Quantity of good *C*

CHAPTER SUMMARY

Key Points

1. Define and calculate the price elasticity of demand, and explain the factors that influence it.

- The demand for a good is elastic if, when its price changes, the percentage change in the quantity demanded exceeds the percentage change in price.
- The demand for a good is inelastic if, when its price changes, the percentage change in the quantity demanded is less than the percentage change in price.
- The price elasticity of demand for a good depends on how easy it is to find substitutes for the good and on the proportion of income spent on it.
- Price elasticity of demand equals the percentage change in the quantity demanded divided by the percentage change in price.
- If demand is elastic, a rise in price leads to a decrease in total revenue. If demand is unit elastic, a rise in price leaves total revenue unchanged. And if demand is inelastic, a rise in price leads to an increase in total revenue.

2. Define and calculate the price elasticity of supply, and explain the factors that influence it.

- The supply of a good is elastic if, when its price changes, the percentage change in the quantity supplied exceeds the percentage change in price.
- The supply of a good is inelastic if, when its price changes, the percentage change in the quantity supplied is less than the percentage change in price.
- The main influences on the price elasticity of supply are the flexibility of production possibilities and storage possibilities.

3. Define the cross elasticity of demand and the income elasticity of demand, and explain the factors that influence them.

- Cross elasticity of demand shows how the demand for a good changes when the price of one of its substitutes or complements changes.
- Cross elasticity is positive for substitutes and negative for complements.
- Income elasticity of demand shows how the demand for a good changes when income changes. For a normal good, the income elasticity of demand is positive. For an inferior good, the income elasticity of demand is negative.

Key Terms

MyEconLab Key Terms Quiz

CHAPTER CHECKPOINT

Study Plan Problems and Applications

When the price of home heating oil increased by 20 percent, the quantity demanded decreased by 2 percent and the quantity of wool sweaters demanded increased by 10 percent. Use this information to work Problems **1** and **2**.

1. Use the total revenue test to determine whether the demand for home heating oil is elastic or inelastic.

2. If the price of a wool sweater did not change, calculate the cross elasticity of demand for wool sweaters with respect to the price of home heating oil. Are home heating oil and wool sweaters substitutes or complements? Why?

3. Figure 1 shows the demand for movie tickets. Is the demand for movie tickets elastic or inelastic over the price range $7 to $9 a ticket? If the price falls from $9 to $7 a ticket, explain how the total revenue from the sale of movie tickets will change. Calculate the price elasticity of demand for movie tickets when the price is $8 a ticket.

4. The price elasticity of demand for Pete's chocolate chip cookies is 1.5. Pete wants to increase his total revenue. Would you recommend that Pete raise or lower his price of cookies? Explain your answer.

Use the following information to work Problems **5** and **6**.

The price of a plane ride rises by 10 percent. The price elasticity of demand for plane rides is 0.5 and the price elasticity of demand for train rides is 0.2. The cross elasticity of demand for train rides with respect to the price of a plane ride is 0.4.

5. Calculate the percentage changes in the quantity demanded of plane rides and train rides.

6. Given the rise in the price of a plane ride, what percentage change in the price of a train ride will leave the quantity demanded of train rides unchanged?

7. A survey found that when incomes increased by 10 percent, the following changes in quantities demanded occurred: spring water up by 5 percent; sports drinks down by 2 percent; cruises up by 15 percent. For which good is demand income elastic? For which good is demand income inelastic? Which goods are normal goods?

8. **Did Starbucks start a pumpkin boom?**
   Ever since Starbucks introduced its famed pumpkin spice latte about a decade ago, pumpkin sales have skyrocketed.
   Source: CNNMoney, October 1, 2014

   The price of pumpkin increased from $286 per ton in 2000 to $732 per ton in 2014 (both prices in 2014 dollars) and the quantity produced increased from 423,000 tons in 2000 to 657,150 in 2014. Calculate the U.S. price elasticity of supply of pumpkin: Is its supply elastic?

9. Read *Eye on Elasticity at the Coffee Shop* on p. 123 and then explain why the demand for latte is inelastic while the demand for a Starbucks latte is elastic. Which demand is likely to be more inelastic: the demand for latte or the demand for coffee?

FIGURE 1

Price (dollars per ticket)

Quantity (tickets per day)

Instructor Assignable Problems and Applications

MyEconLab Homework, Quiz, or Test if assigned by instructor

Use the following data to work Problems **1** and **2**.

When Elle's Espresso Bar increased its prices by 10 percent, the quantity of coffee that Elle sold decreased by 40 percent. When Elle and all her competitors cut their prices by 10 percent, the quantity of coffee sold by Elle increased by only 4 percent.

1. Calculate the price elasticity of demand for Elle's Espresso Bar coffee and the price elasticity of demand for coffee.

2. Explain the difference between the responses to Elle's price hike and price cut. Why did the price increase bring a large response in the quantity sold while the price cut had only a small effect?

3. When rain ruined the banana crop in Central America, the price of bananas rose from $1 to $2 a pound. Growers sold fewer bananas, but their total revenue was unchanged. By what percentage did the quantity demanded of bananas change? Is the demand for bananas elastic, unit elastic, or inelastic?

4. The income elasticity of demand for haircuts is 1.5, and the income elasticity of demand for food is 0.14. You take a weekend job, and the income you have available to spend on food and haircuts doubles. If the prices of food and haircuts remain the same, will you double your expenditure on haircuts and double your expenditure on food? Explain why or why not.

5. Drought cuts the quantity of wheat grown by 2 percent. If the price elasticity of demand for wheat is 0.5, by how much will the price of wheat rise?

   If pasta makers estimate that this change in the price of wheat will increase the price of pasta by 25 percent and decrease the quantity demanded of pasta by 8 percent, what is the pasta makers' estimate of the price elasticity of demand for pasta?

   If pasta sauce makers estimate that, with the change in the price of pasta, the quantity of pasta sauce demanded will decrease by 5 percent, what is the pasta sauce makers' estimate of the cross elasticity of demand for pasta sauce with respect to the price of pasta?

6. "In a market in which demand is price inelastic, producers can gouge consumers and the government should set high standards of conduct for producers to ensure that consumers get a fair deal." Which parts of this statement are positive and which are normative? Explain how you might go about testing the positive part.

Use the following information to work Problems **7** and **8**.

Valentine roses
On Valentine's Day 2015, 257 million roses were sold for about double the normal price. On a normal day, 3 million roses are sold.

Source: aboutflowers.com, 2015

7. Does the information about the market for roses enable us to estimate an elasticity, and if so, which one: the price elasticity of demand, the price elasticity of supply, an income elasticity, or a cross elasticity? Explain your answer.

8. What is the magnitude of the elasticity that you can estimate using the information provided? Explain your answer.

Multiple Choice Quiz

1. When the price of ice cream rises from $3 to $5 a scoop, the quantity of ice cream bought decreases by 10 percent. The price elasticity of demand for ice cream is _____.

   A. 5
   B. 0.2
   C. 50
   D. 2.5

2. In Pioneer Ville, the price elasticity of demand for bus rides is 0.5. When the price of a bus ticket rises by 5 percent, _____.

   A. the demand for bus rides increases by 10 percent
   B. the quantity of bus rides demanded increases by 2.5 percent
   C. the demand for bus rides decreases by 2.5 percent
   D. the quantity of bus rides demanded decreases by 2.5 percent

3. The price elasticity of demand for a good is 0.2. A 10 percent rise in the price will _____ the total revenue from sales of the good.

   A. decrease
   B. increase
   C. decrease the quantity sold with no change in
   D. not change

4. If the price of a good falls and expenditure on the good rises, the demand for the good is _____.

   A. elastic
   B. perfectly elastic
   C. inelastic
   D. unit elastic

5. When the price of a good rises from $5 to $7 a unit, the quantity supplied increases from 110 to 130 units a day. The price elasticity of supply is _____. The supply of the good is _____.

   A. 60; elastic
   B. 10; elastic
   C. 0.5; inelastic
   D. 2; inelastic

6. The cross elasticity of demand for good *A* with respect to good *B* is 0.2. A 10 percent change in the price of good *B* will lead to a _____ percent change in the quantity of good *A* demanded. Goods *A* and *B* are _____.

   A. 2; substitutes
   B. 0.5; complements
   C. −2; complements
   D. −0.5; substitutes

7. A 2 percent increase in income increases the quantity demanded of a good by 1 percent. The income elasticity of demand for this good is _____. The good is a _____ good.

   A. 2; normal
   B. −2; inferior
   C. 1/2; normal
   D. 2; inferior

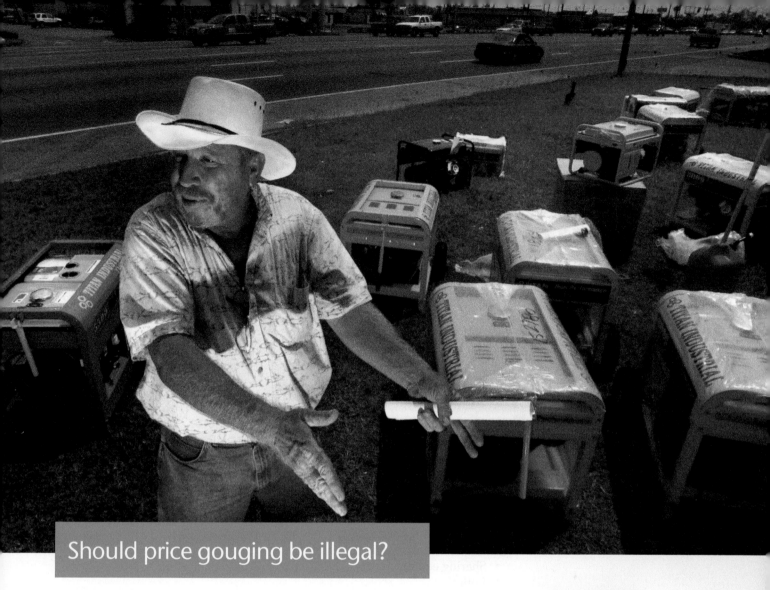

Should price gouging be illegal?

Efficiency and Fairness of Markets

When you have completed your study of this chapter, you will be able to

1 Describe the alternative methods of allocating scarce resources, and define and explain the features of an efficient allocation.

2 Distinguish between value and price, and define consumer surplus.

3 Distinguish between cost and price, and define producer surplus.

4 Evaluate the efficiency of the alternative methods of allocating resources.

5 Explain the main ideas about fairness, and evaluate the fairness of the alternative methods of allocating scarce resources.

MyEconLab Big Picture Video

6.1   ALLOCATION METHODS AND EFFICIENCY

Because resources are scarce, they must be allocated among their competing uses. Doing nothing and leaving resource use to chance is one method of allocation. *Price gouging*—charging an unusually high price for an essential item following a natural disaster—is another. The goal of this chapter is to evaluate the ability of a market price to allocate resources efficiently and fairly.

But market price is only one of several methods of allocating resources. To know whether the market does a good job, we need to compare it with its alternatives. We also need to know what is meant by an efficient and fair allocation.

Economists have much more to say about efficiency than about fairness, so efficiency is the main focus of this chapter. We leave the difficult issue of fairness until the final section. We begin by describing the alternative ways in which resources might be allocated. Then we explain the characteristics of an efficient allocation.

■ Resource Allocation Methods

Resources might be allocated by using any one or some combination of the following methods:

- Market price
- Command
- Majority rule
- Contest
- First-come, first-served
- Sharing equally
- Lottery
- Personal characteristics
- Force

Let's see how each method works and look at an example of each.

Market price allocates resources to those who are willing and able to pay.

Market Price

When a market price allocates a scarce resource, the people who get the resource are those who are willing and able to pay the market price. People who don't value the resource as highly as the market price leave it for others to buy and use.

Most of the scarce resources that you supply get allocated by market price. For example, you sell your labor services in a market. And almost everything that you consume gets bought in a market.

Two kinds of people decide not to buy at the market price: those who can afford to buy but choose not to, and those who are too poor and can't afford to buy.

For many goods and services, distinguishing between those who choose not to buy and those who can't afford to buy doesn't matter. For a few items, that distinction does matter. For example, some poor people can't afford to pay school fees and doctor's fees. The inability of poor people to buy items that most people consider to be essential is not handled well by the market price method and is usually dealt with by one of the other allocation methods.

But for most goods and services, the market turns out to do a good job. We'll examine just how good a job it does later in this chapter.

Command

A **command system** allocates resources by the order (command) of someone in authority. Many resources get allocated by command. In the U.S. economy, the command system is used extensively inside firms and government bureaus. For example, if you have a job, it is most likely that someone tells you what to do. Your labor time is allocated to specific tasks by a command.

Sometimes, a command system allocates the resources of an entire economy. The former Soviet Union is an example. North Korea and Cuba are the only remaining command economies.

A command system works well in organizations in which the lines of authority and responsibility are clear and it is easy to monitor the activities being performed. But a command system works badly when applied to an entire economy. The range of activities to be monitored is just too large, and it is easy for people to fool those in authority. The system works so badly in North Korea that it fails even to deliver an adequate supply of food.

Majority Rule

Majority rule allocates resources in the way that a majority of voters choose. Societies use majority rule for some of their biggest decisions. For example, majority rule decides the tax rates that end up allocating scarce resources between private use and public use. And majority rule decides how tax dollars are allocated among competing uses such as national defense and healthcare for the aged.

Having 200 million people vote on every line in a nation's budget would be extremely costly, so instead of direct majority rule, the United States (and most other countries) use the system of representative government. Majority rule determines who will represent the people, and majority rule among the representatives decides the detailed allocation of scarce resources.

Majority rule works well when the decisions being made affect large numbers of people and self-interest must be suppressed to use resources most effectively.

Contest

A contest allocates resources to a winner (or a group of winners). The most obvious contests are sporting events. Serena Williams and Sloane Stephens do battle on a tennis court, and the winner gets twice as much in prize money as the loser.

But contests are much more general than those in a sports arena, though we don't call them contests in ordinary speech. For example, Bill Gates won a big contest to provide the world's personal computer operating system, and Jennifer Lawrence won a type of contest to rise to the top of the movie-acting business.

Contests do a good job when the efforts of the "players" are hard to monitor and reward directly. By dangling the opportunity to win a big prize, people are motivated to work hard and try to be the "winner." Even though only a few people end up with a big prize, many people work harder in the process of trying to win and so total production is much greater than it would be without the contest.

First-Come, First-Served

A first-come, first-served method allocates resources to those who are first in line. Most national parks allocate campsites in this way. Airlines use first-come, first-served to allocate standby seats at the departure gate. A freeway is an everyday example of first-come, first-served. This scarce transportation resource gets allocated

Command system
A system that allocates resources by the order of someone in authority.

A command allocates resources by the order of someone in authority.

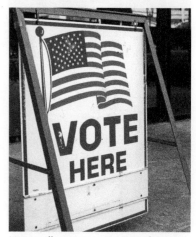

Voting allocates resources in the way that the majority wants.

A contest allocates resources to the winner, in sport and business.

First-come, first-served allocates resources to the first in line.

to the first to arrive at the on-ramp. If too many vehicles enter the freeway, the speed slows and people, in effect, wait in line for a bit of the "freeway" to become free!

First-come, first-served works best when, as in the above examples, a scarce resource can serve just one user at a time in a sequence. By serving the user who arrives first, this method minimizes the time spent waiting in line for the resource to become free.

Sharing Equally

When a resource is shared equally, everyone gets the same amount of it. You perhaps use this method to share dessert at a restaurant. People sometimes jointly own a vacation apartment and share its use equally.

To make equal shares work, people must agree on how to use the resource and must make an arrangement to implement the agreement. Sharing equally can work for small groups who share a set of common goals and ideals.

Sharing allocates resources by mutual agreement.

Lottery

Lotteries allocate resources to those who pick the winning number, draw the lucky cards, or come up lucky on some other gaming system. State lotteries and casinos reallocate millions of dollars' worth of goods and services every year.

But lotteries are far more widespread than state jackpots and roulette wheels in casinos. They are used in a variety of situations to allocate scarce resources. For example, the Lawn Tennis Association operates ballots and draws to allocate Wimbledon tickets and some airports use them to allocate landing slots to airlines.

Lotteries work well when there is no effective way to distinguish among potential users of a scarce resource.

A lottery allocates resources to the one who draws the winning number.

Personal Characteristics

When resources are allocated on the basis of personal characteristics, people with the "right" characteristics get the resources. Some of the resources that matter most to you are allocated in this way. The people you like are the ones you spend the most time with. You try to avoid having to spend time with people you don't like. People choose marriage partners on the basis of personal characteristics. The use of personal characteristics to allocate resources is regarded as completely natural and acceptable.

But this method also gets used in unacceptable ways. Allocating the best jobs to white, Anglo-Saxon males and discriminating against minorities and women is an example.

Personal characteristics allocate resources based on whom we like.

Force

Force plays a crucial role, for both good and ill, in allocating scarce resources. Let's start with the ill.

War, the use of military force by one nation against another, has played an enormous role historically in allocating resources. The economic supremacy of European settlers in the Americas and Australia owes much to the use of this method.

Theft, the taking of the property of others without their consent, also plays a large role. Both large-scale organized crime and small-scale petty crime collectively allocate billions of dollars' worth of resources annually. A large amount of

Force protects the rule of law and facilitates economic activity.

theft today is conducted by using sophisticated electronic methods that move resources from banks and also from thousands of innocent people.

But force plays a crucial positive role in allocating resources. It provides an effective method for the government to transfer wealth from the rich to the poor and is the legal framework in which voluntary exchange in markets takes place.

Most income and wealth redistribution in modern societies occurs through a taxation and benefits system that is enforced by the power of the state. We vote for taxes and benefits—a majority vote allocation—but we use the power of the state to ensure that everyone complies with the rules and pays their allotted share.

A legal system is the foundation on which our market economy functions. Without courts to enforce contracts, it would be difficult to do business. But the courts could not enforce contracts without the ability to apply force if necessary. The state provides the ultimate force that enables the courts to do their work.

More broadly, the force of the state is essential to uphold the principle of the *rule of law*. This principle is the bedrock of civilized economic (and social and political) life. With the rule of law upheld, people can go about their daily economic lives with the assurance that their property will be protected—that they can sue for violations of their property (and be sued if they violate the property of others).

Free from the burden of protecting their property and confident in the knowledge that those with whom they trade will honor their agreements, people can get on with focusing on the activity at which they have a comparative advantage and trading for mutual gain.

In the next sections of this chapter, we're going to see how a market achieves an efficient use of resources, examine obstacles to efficiency, and see how sometimes, an alternative method might improve on the market. But first we need to be clear about the meaning of efficiency. What are the characteristics of an efficient allocation of resources?

■ Using Resources Efficiently

MyEconLab Concept Video

In everyday language, *efficiency* means getting the most out of something. An efficient automobile is one that gets the best possible gas mileage; an efficient furnace is one that uses as little fuel as possible to deliver its heat. In economics, efficiency means getting the most out of the entire economy.

Efficiency and the *PPF*

The *production possibilities frontier* (*PPF*) is the boundary between the combinations of goods and services that can be produced and those that cannot be produced given the available factors of production and state of technology (p. 60). Production is efficient when the economy is *on* its *PPF* (Chapter 3, pp. 62–63). Production at a point *inside* the *PPF* is *inefficient*.

Allocative efficiency is achieved when the quantities of goods and services produced are those that people *value most highly*. To put it another way, resources are allocated efficiently when we cannot produce more of one thing without giving up something else *that people value more highly*. If we can give up some units of one good to get more of something that is *valued more highly*, we haven't achieved the most valued point on the *PPF*.

The *PPF* tells us what it is *possible* to produce but it doesn't tell us about the *value* of what we produce. To find the *highest-valued* point on the *PPF*, we need some information about value. *Marginal benefit* provides that information.

Allocative efficiency
A situation in which the quantities of goods and services produced are those that people *value most highly*—it is not possible to produce more of a good or service without giving up some of another good that people *value more highly*.

Marginal Benefit

Marginal benefit is the benefit that people receive from consuming *one more unit* of a good or service. People's *preferences* determine marginal benefit and we can measure the marginal benefit from a good or service by what people *are willing to* give up to get *one more* unit of it.

The more we have of any good or service, the smaller is our marginal benefit from it—*the principle of decreasing marginal benefit*. Think about your own marginal benefit from pizza. You really enjoy the first slice. A second slice is fine, too, but not quite as satisfying as the first one. But eat three, four, five, six, and more slices, and each additional slice is less enjoyable than the previous one. You get diminishing marginal benefit from pizza. The more pizza you have, the less of some other good or service you are willing to give up to get one more slice.

Figure 6.1 illustrates the economy's marginal benefit schedule and marginal benefit curve for pizza. The schedule and curve show the same information. In the schedule and on the curve, the quantity of other goods that people *are willing to give up* to get one more pizza *decreases* as the quantity of pizza available *increases*.

Marginal Cost

To achieve allocative efficiency, we must compare the marginal benefit from pizza with its marginal cost. *Marginal cost* is the opportunity cost of producing one more unit of a good or service (see p. 10) and is measured by the slope of the production possibilities frontier (see pp. 66–67). The marginal cost of a good increases as the quantity produced of that good increases.

FIGURE 6.1

Marginal Benefit from Pizza

MyEconLab Animation

The table and the graph show the marginal benefit from pizza.

Possibility *A* and point *A* tell us that if 2,000 pizzas a day are produced, people are willing to give up 15 units of other goods for a pizza. Each point *A*, *B*, and *C* on the graph represents the possibility in the table identified by the same letter.

The line passing through these points is the marginal benefit curve. The marginal benefit from pizza decreases as the quantity of pizza available increases.

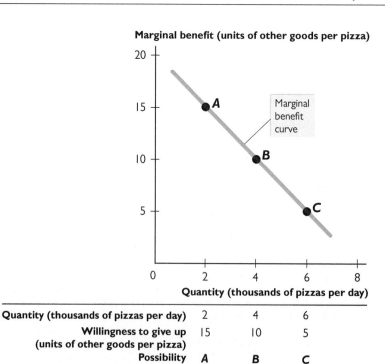

Quantity (thousands of pizzas per day)	2	4	6
Willingness to give up (units of other goods per pizza)	15	10	5
Possibility	*A*	*B*	*C*

Figure 6.2 illustrates the economy's marginal cost schedule and marginal cost curve. In the schedule and along the curve, which show the same information, the quantity of other goods that people *must give up* to get one more pizza *increases* as the quantity of pizza produced *increases*.

We can now use the concepts of marginal benefit and marginal cost to discover the efficient quantity of pizza to produce.

Efficient Allocation

The efficient allocation is the highest-valued allocation. To find this allocation, we compare marginal benefit and marginal cost.

If the marginal benefit from pizza exceeds its marginal cost, we're producing too little pizza (and too many units of other goods). If we increase the quantity of pizza produced, we incur a cost but receive a larger benefit from the additional pizza. Our allocation of resources becomes more efficient.

If the marginal cost of pizza exceeds its marginal benefit, we're producing too much pizza (and too little of other goods). Now if we decrease the quantity of pizza produced, we receive a smaller benefit from pizza but save an even greater cost of pizza. Again, our allocation of resources becomes more efficient.

Only when the marginal benefit and marginal cost of pizza are equal are we allocating resources efficiently. Figure 6.3 on the next page illustrates this efficient allocation and provides a graphical summary of the above description of allocative efficiency.

FIGURE 6.2

Marginal Cost of Pizza

MyEconLab Animation

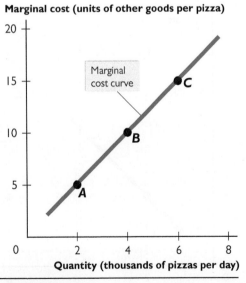

The table and the graph show the marginal cost of a pizza. Marginal cost is the opportunity cost of producing one more unit. It is derived from the *PPF* and is measured by the slope of the *PPF*.

Points A, B, and C on the graph represent the possibilities in the table. The marginal cost curve shows that the marginal cost of a pizza increases as the quantity of pizza produced increases.

Quantity (thousands of pizzas per day)	2	4	6
Must give up (units of other goods per pizza)	5	10	15
Possibility	A	B	C

FIGURE 6.3

The Efficient Quantity of Pizza

MyEconLab Animation

Production efficiency occurs at all points on the *PPF*, but *allocative efficiency* occurs at only one point on the *PPF*.

❶ When 2,000 pizzas are produced in part (a), the marginal benefit from pizza exceeds its marginal cost in part (b). Too few pizzas are being produced. If more pizzas and fewer other goods are produced, the value of production increases and resources are used more efficiently.

❷ When 6,000 pizzas are produced in part (a), the marginal cost of a pizza exceeds its marginal benefit in part (b). Too many pizzas are being produced. If fewer pizzas and more other goods are produced, the value of production increases and resources are used more efficiently.

❸ When 4,000 pizzas a day are produced in part (a), the marginal cost of a pizza equals its marginal benefit in part (b). The efficient quantity of pizzas is being produced. It is not possible to get greater value from the economy's scarce resources. If one less pizza and more other goods are produced, the value of the lost pizza exceeds the value of the additional other goods, so total value falls. And if one more pizza and fewer other goods are produced, the value of the gained pizza is less than the value of the lost other goods, so again total value falls.

(a) On the *PPF*

(b) Marginal benefit equals marginal cost

CHECKPOINT 6.1

MyEconLab Study Plan 6.1
Key Terms Quiz
Solutions Video

Describe the alternative methods of allocating scarce resources, and define and explain the features of an efficient allocation.

Practice Problems

FIGURE 1

1. Which method is used to allocate the following scarce resources?
   - Campus parking space between student areas and faculty areas
   - A spot in a restricted student parking area
   - Textbooks
   - Host city for the Olympic Games

Use Figure 1, which shows a nation's *PPF*, and Table 1, which shows its marginal benefit and marginal cost schedules, to work Problems **2** and **3**.

2. What is the marginal benefit from bananas when 1 pound of bananas is grown? What is the marginal cost of growing 1 pound of bananas?

3. On Figure 1, mark two points: Point *A* at which production is efficient but too much coffee is produced for allocative efficiency; and point *B*, the point of allocative efficiency.

In the News

Jack White announces short run of shows—our best guesses as to where
Fresh off his scorching performance at Coachella Saturday night, rocker Jack White announced he'll do shows unannounced until day-of-show, with tickets priced at $3 and limited to one ticket per person, to be purchased only at the venue on a first-come, first-served basis.
Source: *Billboard Magazine*, April 14, 2015

What method was used to allocate Jack White concert tickets? Was it efficient?

TABLE 1   MARGINAL BENEFIT AND MARGINAL COST

Bananas (pounds)	Willing to give up (pounds of coffee per pound of bananas)	Must give up
1	3	1
2	2	2
3	1	3

Solutions to Practice Problems

FIGURE 2

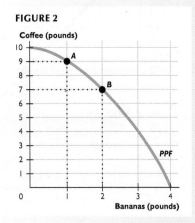

1. Campus parking is allocated by command. The spot in a restricted student parking area is allocated by first-come, first-served. Textbooks are allocated by market price. The Olympic Games' host city is allocated by contest.

2. The marginal benefit from 1 pound of bananas is 3 pounds of coffee. Marginal benefit is the amount of coffee that the nation is *willing to give up* to get *one additional* pound of bananas. The marginal cost of growing 1 pound of bananas is 1 pound of coffee. Marginal cost is the amount of coffee that the nation *must give up* to get *one additional* pound of bananas.

3. Point *A* on Figure 2 shows production efficiency (on the *PPF*) but not allocative efficiency because from Table 1 marginal benefit from bananas exceeds the marginal cost—too few bananas are produced. Point *B* is the point of allocative efficiency: It is on the *PPF* and marginal benefit equals marginal cost.

Solution to In the News

The initial allocation used was first-come, first-served at the venue. But a person who gets a ticket can either use it or sell it at the going market price to someone in the ticket line at the venue. Only if the market price equals the organizer's marginal cost is the allocation of tickets efficient.

6.2 VALUE, PRICE, AND CONSUMER SURPLUS

To investigate whether a market is efficient, we need to understand the connection between demand and marginal benefit and between supply and marginal cost.

■ Demand and Marginal Benefit

In everyday life, when we talk about "getting value for money," we're distinguishing between *value* and *price.* Value is what we get, and price is what we pay. In economics, the everyday idea of value is *marginal benefit*, which we measure as the maximum price that people are willing to pay for another unit of the good or service. The demand curve tells us this price. In Figure 6.4(a), the demand curve shows the quantity demanded at a given price—when the price is $10 a pizza, the quantity demanded is 10,000 pizzas a day. In Figure 6.4(b), the demand curve shows the maximum price that people are willing to pay when there is a given quantity—when 10,000 pizzas a day are available, the most that people are willing to pay for the 10,000th pizza is $10. The marginal benefit from the 10,000th pizza is $10. So:

> A demand curve is a marginal benefit curve. The demand curve for pizza tells us the dollars' worth of other goods and services that people are willing to forgo to consume one more pizza.

■ FIGURE 6.4

Demand, Willingness to Pay, and Marginal Benefit

(a) Price determines quantity demanded

(b) Quantity determines willingness to pay

❶ The demand curve for pizza, *D*, shows the quantity of pizza demanded at each price, other things remaining the same. At $10 a pizza, the quantity demanded is 10,000 pizzas a day.

❷ The demand curve shows the maximum price willingly paid (marginal benefit) for a given quantity. If 10,000 pizzas are available, the maximum price willingly paid for the 10,000th pizza is $10. The demand curve is also the marginal benefit curve *MB*.

■ Consumer Surplus

We don't always have to pay as much as we're willing to pay. When people buy something for less than it is worth to them, they receive a consumer surplus. **Consumer surplus** is the excess of marginal benefit from a good over the price paid for it, summed over the quantity consumed.

Figure 6.5 illustrates consumer surplus. The demand curve for pizza tells us the quantity of pizza that people plan to buy at each price and the marginal benefit from pizza at each quantity. If the price of a pizza is $10, people buy 10,000 pizzas a day. Expenditure on pizza is $100,000, which is shown by the area of the blue rectangle.

To calculate consumer surplus, we must find the consumer surplus on each pizza and add these consumer surpluses together. For the 10,000th pizza, marginal benefit equals $10 and people pay $10, so the consumer surplus on this pizza is zero. For the 5,000th pizza (highlighted in the figure), marginal benefit is $15. So on this pizza, consumer surplus is $15 minus $10, which is $5. For the first pizza, marginal benefit is almost $20, so on this pizza, consumer surplus is almost $10.

Consumer surplus—the sum of the consumer surpluses on the 10,000 pizzas that people buy—is $50,000 a day, which is shown by the area of the green triangle. (The base of the triangle is 10,000 pizzas a day and its height is $10, so its area is ($10 × 10,000) ÷ 2 = $50,000.)

The total benefit is the amount paid, $100,000 (the area of the blue rectangle), plus consumer surplus, $50,000 (the area of the green triangle), and is $150,000. Consumer surplus is the total benefit minus the amount paid, or net benefit to consumers.

Consumer surplus
The marginal benefit from a good or service in excess of the price paid for it, summed over the quantity consumed.

■ FIGURE 6.5

Demand and Consumer Surplus

MyEconLab Animation

❶ The market price of a pizza is $10.

❷ At the market price, people buy 10,000 pizzas a day and spend $100,000 on pizza—the area of the blue rectangle.

❸ The demand curve tells us that people are willing to pay $15 for the 5,000th pizza, so consumer surplus on the 5,000th pizza is $5.

❹ Consumer surplus from the 10,000 pizzas that people buy is $50,000—the area of the green triangle.

The total benefit from pizza is the $100,000 that people pay plus the $50,000 consumer surplus they receive, or $150,000.

MyEconLab Study Plan 6.2
Key Terms Quiz
Solutions Video

CHECKPOINT 6.2

Distinguish between value and price, and define consumer surplus.

Practice Problems

Figure 1 shows the demand curve for DVDs and the market price of a DVD.

1. What is the willingness to pay for the 20th DVD? Calculate the value of the 10th DVD and the consumer surplus on the 10th DVD.

2. What is the quantity of DVDs bought? Calculate the consumer surplus, the amount spent on DVDs, and the total benefit from the DVDs bought.

3. If the price of a DVD rises to $20, what is the change in consumer surplus?

In the News

Airfares stacked against consumers
The airlines change prices from day to day. For example, the fare on one Delta flight from New York to Los Angeles jumped from $755 to $1,143 from a Friday to Saturday in April, then fell to $718 on Sunday.

Source: boston.com, June 22, 2011

Jodi planned a trip from New York to Los Angeles and was equally happy to travel on Friday, Saturday, or Sunday. The Saturday price was the most she was willing to pay. On which day do you predict she travelled and how much consumer surplus did she receive?

Solutions to Practice Problems

1. The willingness to pay for the 20th DVD is the price on the demand curve at 20 DVDs, which is $15 (Figure 2). The value of the 10th DVD is its marginal benefit, which is also the maximum price that someone is willing to pay for it. In Figure 2, the value of the 10th DVD is $20. The consumer surplus on the 10th DVD is its marginal benefit minus the price paid for the DVD, which is $20 − $15 (the length of the green arrow in Figure 2).

2. The quantity of DVDs bought is 20 a day. The consumer surplus from DVDs is ($25 − $15) × 20 ÷ 2 = $100 (the area of the green triangle in Figure 2). The amount spent on DVDs is the price multiplied by the quantity bought, which equals $15 × 20 = $300 (the area of the blue rectangle in Figure 2). The total benefit from DVDs is the amount spent on DVDs plus the consumer surplus from DVDs, which equals $300 + $100 = $400.

3. If the price of a DVD rises to $20, the quantity bought decreases to 10 a day. Consumer surplus decreases to ($25 − $20) × 10 ÷ 2 = $25 (the area of the green triangle in Figure 3). Consumer surplus decreases by $75 (from $100 in Figure 2 to $25 in Figure 3).

Solution to In the News

Being equally happy to travel on any of the three days means that Jodi's marginal benefit from the trip was the same on each day. Because Saturday's price of $1,143 was the most she was willing to pay, that is her marginal benefit. Being rational, Jodi would travel on the day with the lowest price, Sunday, and pay a fare of $718. Her consumer surplus would be her marginal benefit of $1,143 minus the price she paid, $718, which equals $425.

FIGURE 1

FIGURE 2

FIGURE 3

6.3 COST, PRICE, AND PRODUCER SURPLUS

MyEconLab Concept Video

You are now going to learn about cost, price, and producer surplus, which parallels what you've learned about value, price, and consumer surplus.

■ Supply and Marginal Cost

Just as buyers distinguish between *value* and *price,* so sellers distinguish between *cost* and *price.* Cost is what a seller must give up to produce the good, and price is what a seller receives when the good is sold. The cost of producing one more unit of a good or service is its *marginal cost.* It is just worth producing one more unit of a good or service if the price for which it can be sold equals marginal cost. The supply curve tells us this price. In Figure 6.6(a), the supply curve shows the quantity supplied at a given price—when the price of a pizza is $10, the quantity supplied is 10,000 pizzas a day. In Figure 6.6(b), the supply curve shows the minimum price that producers must receive to supply a given quantity—to supply 10,000 pizzas a day, producers must be able to get at least $10 for the 10,000th pizza. The marginal cost of the 10,000th pizza is $10. So:

> A supply curve is a marginal cost curve. The supply curve of pizza tells us the dollars' worth of other goods and services that people must forgo if firms produce one more pizza.

■ FIGURE 6.6

Supply, Minimum Supply Price, and Marginal Cost

MyEconLab Animation

(a) Price determines quantity supplied

(b) Quantity determines minimum supply price

❶ The supply curve of pizza, S, shows the quantity of pizza supplied at each price, other things remaining the same. At $10 a pizza, the quantity supplied is 10,000 pizzas a day.

❷ The supply curve shows the minimum price that firms must be offered to supply a given quantity. The minimum supply price equals marginal cost, which for the 10,000th pizza is $10. The supply curve is also the marginal cost curve MC.

■ Producer Surplus

Producer surplus
The price of a good in excess of the marginal cost of producing it, summed over the quantity produced.

When the price exceeds marginal cost, the firm obtains a producer surplus. **Producer surplus** is the excess of the price of a good over the marginal cost of producing it, summed over the quantity produced.

Figure 6.7 illustrates the producer surplus for pizza producers. The supply curve of pizza tells us the quantity of pizza that producers plan to sell at each price. The supply curve also tells us the marginal cost of pizza at each quantity produced. If the price of a pizza is $10, producers plan to sell 10,000 pizzas a day. The total revenue from pizza is $100,000 per day.

To calculate producer surplus, we must find the producer surplus on each pizza and add these surpluses together. For the 10,000th pizza, marginal cost equals $10 and producers receive $10, so the producer surplus on this pizza is zero. For the 5,000th pizza (highlighted in the figure), marginal cost is $6. So on this pizza, producer surplus is $10 minus $6, which is $4. For the first pizza, marginal cost is $2, so on this pizza, producer surplus is $10 minus $2, which is $8.

Producer surplus—the sum of the producer surpluses on the 10,000 pizzas that firms produce—is $40,000 a day, which is shown by the area of the blue triangle. The base of the triangle is 10,000 pizzas a day and its height is $8, so its area is $(10,000 \times \$8) \div 2 = \$40,000$.

The total cost of producing pizza is the amount received from selling it, $100,000, minus the producer surplus, $40,000 (the area of the blue triangle), and is $60,000 (the red area beneath the *MC* curve). Producer surplus is the total amount received minus the total cost, or net benefit to producers.

FIGURE 6.7

Supply and Producer Surplus

MyEconLab Animation

❶ The market price of a pizza is $10. At this price, producers plan to sell 10,000 pizzas a day and receive a total revenue of $100,000 a day.

❷ The supply curve shows that the marginal cost of the 5,000th pizza a day is $6, so producers receive a producer surplus of $4 on the 5,000th pizza.

❸ Producer surplus from the 10,000 pizzas sold is $40,000 a day—the area of the blue triangle.

❹ The cost of producing 10,000 pizzas a day is the red area beneath the marginal cost curve. It equals total revenue of $100,000 minus producer surplus of $40,000 and is $60,000 a day.

CHECKPOINT 6.3

Distinguish between cost and price, and define producer surplus.

Practice Problems

Figure 1 shows the supply curve of DVDs and the market price of a DVD.

1. What is the minimum supply price of the 20th DVD? Calculate the marginal cost of the 10th DVD and the producer surplus on the 10th DVD.

2. What is the quantity of DVDs sold? Calculate the producer surplus, the total revenue from the DVDs sold, and the cost of producing the DVDs sold.

3. If the price of a DVD falls to $10, what is the change in producer surplus?

In the News

BlackBerry looks for reboot with Android
BlackBerry, the pioneer of smartphones, has almost vanished as Android and Apple phones have dominated the market. BlackBerry is now betting its future on using the Android operating system.
                                                            Source: *Financial Times*, November 6, 2015

As people have switched from BlackBerry to Android and Apple smartphones, how has BlackBerry's producer surplus changed? How has the producer surplus of Apple and the Android smartphone makers such as Samsung and LG changed?

Solutions to Practice Problems

1. The minimum supply price of the 20th DVD is the marginal cost of the 20th DVD, which is $15 (Figure 2). The marginal cost of the 10th DVD is equal to the minimum supply price for the 10th DVD, which is $10. The producer surplus on the 10th DVD is its market price minus the marginal cost of producing it, which is $15 − $10 = $5 (the blue arrow in Figure 2).

2. The quantity sold is 20 a day. Producer surplus equals ($15 − $5) × 20 ÷ 2, which is $100 (the area of the blue triangle in Figure 2). The total revenue is price multiplied by quantity sold, which equals $15 × 20 = $300. The cost of producing DVDs equals total revenue minus producer surplus, which is $300 − $100 = $200 (the red area in Figure 2).

3. If the price falls to $10, the quantity sold decreases to 10 a day. The producer surplus decreases to ($10 − $5) × 10 ÷ 2 = $25 (the area of the blue triangle in Figure 3). The change in producer surplus is a decrease of $75 (from $100 down to $25).

Solution to In the News

Producer surplus is the excess of the price of a good over the marginal cost of producing it, summed over the quantity produced.

For BlackBerry, the demand for its phones decreased, the price fell, and quantity sold decreased. BlackBerry's producer surplus decreased.

For Apple and the Android smartphone makers, demand increased, the quantity sold increased, and their producer surplus increased.

FIGURE 1

FIGURE 2

FIGURE 3

6.4 ARE MARKETS EFFICIENT?

You've seen (pp. 145–146) that an efficient allocation of resources is the highest-valued allocation, and it occurs when marginal benefit equals marginal cost. Continuing with the pizza example, the efficient quantity of pizza is the quantity that people value most highly, the quantity at which the marginal benefit of pizza equals its marginal cost.

The market forces that you studied in Chapter 4 (pp. 100–101) determine the equilibrium quantity and equilibrium price and coordinate the plans of buyers and sellers. Figure 6.8 shows the market for pizza in equilibrium. The demand curve is D, the supply curve is S, the equilibrium price is $10 a pizza, and the equilibrium quantity is 10,000 pizzas a day.

Does this competitive equilibrium deliver the efficient quantity of pizza?

■ Marginal Benefit Equals Marginal Cost

To check whether the equilibrium in Figure 6.8 is efficient, recall the interpretation of the demand curve as a marginal benefit curve and the supply curve as a marginal cost curve. The demand curve tells us the marginal benefit from pizza. The supply curve tells us the marginal cost of pizza. Where the demand curve and the supply curve intersect, marginal benefit equals marginal cost.

■ FIGURE 6.8

An Efficient Market for Pizza

❶ Market equilibrium occurs at a price of $10 a pizza and a quantity of 10,000 pizzas a day.

❷ The supply curve is also the marginal cost curve.

❸ The demand curve is also the marginal benefit curve.

Because at the market equilibrium, marginal benefit equals marginal cost, ❹ the efficient quantity of pizza is produced. The sum of the ❺ consumer surplus and ❻ producer surplus is maximized.

This condition—marginal benefit equals marginal cost—is the condition that delivers an efficient use of resources. Because a competitive equilibrium allocates resources to the activities that create the greatest possible value, it is efficient.

■ Total Surplus Is Maximized

Another way of checking that the equilibrium is efficient is to look at the total surplus that it generates. **Total surplus** is the sum of producer surplus and consumer surplus. A price above the equilibrium might increase producer surplus, but it would decrease consumer surplus by more. And a price below the equilibrium price might increase consumer surplus, but it would decrease producer surplus by more. The competitive equilibrium price maximizes total surplus.

Total surplus
The sum of producer surplus and consumer surplus.

In Figure 6.8, if production is less than 10,000 pizzas a day, someone is willing to buy a pizza for more than it costs to produce. Buyers and sellers will gain if production increases. If production exceeds 10,000 pizzas a day, it costs more to produce a pizza than anyone is willing to pay for it. Buyers and sellers will gain if production decreases. Only when 10,000 pizzas a day are produced is there no unexploited gain from changing the quantity of pizza produced, and total surplus is maximized.

Buyers and sellers each attempt to do the best they can for themselves—they pursue their self-interest. No one plans for an efficient outcome for society as a whole. No one worries about the social interest. Buyers seek the lowest possible price, and sellers seek the highest possible price. But as buyers and sellers pursue their self-interest, this astonishing outcome occurs: The social interest is served.

■ The Invisible Hand

Writing in his *Wealth of Nations* in 1776, Adam Smith was the first to suggest that competitive markets send resources to the uses in which they have the highest value. Smith believed that each participant in a competitive market is "led by an invisible hand to promote an end [the efficient use of resources] which was no part of his intention."

You can see the effects of the invisible hand at work every day. Your campus bookstore is stuffed with texts at the start of each term. It has the quantities that it predicts students will buy. The coffee shop has the variety and quantities of drinks and snacks that people plan to buy. Your local clothing store has the sweatpants and socks and other items that you plan to buy. Truckloads of textbooks, coffee and cookies, and sweatpants and socks roll along our highways and bring these items to where you and your friends want to buy them. Firms that don't know you anticipate your wants and work hard to help you satisfy them.

No government organizes all this production, and no government auditor monitors producers to ensure that they serve the social interest. The allocation of scarce resources is not planned. It happens because prices adjust to make buying plans and selling plans compatible, and it happens in a way that sends resources to the uses in which they have the highest value.

Adam Smith explained why all this amazing activity occurs. "It is not from the benevolence of the butcher, the brewer, or the baker that we expect our dinner," he wrote, "but from their regard to their own interest."

Publishing companies, coffee growers, garment manufacturers, and a host of other producers are led by their regard for *their* own interest to serve *your* interest.

EYE on the U.S. ECONOMY

The Invisible Hand and e-Commerce

You can see Adam Smith's invisible hand idea in the cartoon.

On a hot sunny day, a cold-drinks vendor approaches a man sitting in a park reading a newspaper (the top frame). The vendor has both cold drinks and shade and an opportunity cost and a minimum supply-price of each item. The park bench reader has a marginal benefit from a cold drink and from shade.

A transaction occurs and the invisible hand does its work (the middle frame). The park bench reader buys the vendor's sun shade. This transaction tells us that the reader's marginal benefit from shade exceeds the vendor's marginal cost of shade.

After the transaction (bottom frame), the vendor obtains a producer surplus from selling the shade for more than its opportunity cost, and the reader obtains a consumer surplus from buying the shade for less than its marginal benefit. Both the buyer of shade and the seller are better off.

The umbrella has moved to its highest-valued use and the resource is being used efficiently.

© The New Yorker Collection 1985
Mike Twohy from cartoonbank.com. All Rights Reserved.

The market economy performs activity similar to that illustrated in the cartoon to achieve an efficient allocation of resources. New technologies have cut the cost of using the Internet and during the past few years, hundreds of Web sites have been established that are dedicated to facilitating trade in all types of goods, services, and factors of production.

The electronic auction site eBay (http://www.ebay.com/) has brought a huge increase in consumer surplus and producer surplus, and helps to achieve ever-greater allocative efficiency.

■ Market Failure

You've seen that a competitive market in equilibrium delivers an efficient outcome. But not all markets are competitive and sometimes a competitive market is prevented from achieving an equilibrium. We call a situation in which a market delivers an inefficient outcome a **market failure**. Either too little of an item is produced—*underproduction*—or too much—*overproduction*.

Market failure
An inefficient market outcome.

Underproduction and Overproduction

When underproduction occurs, marginal benefit exceeds marginal cost. Items *not* produced are worth more than they cost. When overproduction occurs, marginal cost exceeds marginal benefit. Items produced cost more than they are worth.

Figure 6.9(a) illustrates underproduction at 5,000 pizzas a day. Every pizza between 5,000 and 9,999 is worth more than it costs to make but it is not produced. Figure 6.9(b) illustrates overproduction at 15,000 pizzas a day. Every pizza produced between 10,001 and 15,000 costs more to make than it is worth.

Deadweight Loss

A **deadweight loss** is the decrease in total surplus that results from inefficient underproduction or overproduction. It is a *social* loss.

The deadweight loss from underproduction equals the area of the gray triangle in Figure 6.9(a). That area is $22,500 [($15 − $6) × 5,000 ÷ 2 = $22,500]. Can you calculate the deadweight loss from overproduction in Figure 6.9(b)?

Deadweight loss
The decrease in total surplus that results from an inefficient underproduction or overproduction.

▨ FIGURE 6.9

Inefficient Outcomes   MyEconLab Animation

(a) Underproduction

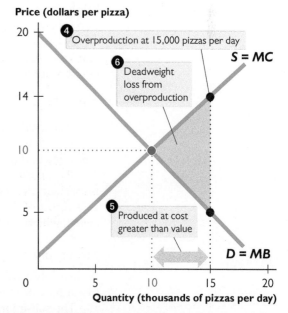

(b) Overproduction

❶ If production is 5,000 pizzas a day, ❷ pizzas not produced are worth more than they cost to make—there is inefficient underproduction. ❸ The gray triangle shows the deadweight loss that arises.

❹ If production is 15,000 pizzas a day, ❺ pizzas produced cost more to make than they are worth—there is inefficient overproduction. ❻ The gray triangle shows the deadweight loss that arises.

■ Sources of Market Failure

Obstacles to efficiency that bring market failure and create deadweight losses are

- Price and quantity regulations
- Taxes and subsidies
- Externalities
- Public goods and common resources
- Monopoly
- High transactions costs

Price and Quantity Regulations

Price regulations that put a cap on the rent a landlord is permitted to charge and laws that require employers to pay a minimum wage sometimes block the price adjustments that balance the quantity demanded and the quantity supplied and lead to underproduction. *Quantity regulations* that limit the amount that a farm is permitted to produce also lead to underproduction.

Taxes and Subsidies

Taxes increase the prices paid by buyers and lower the prices received by sellers. So taxes decrease the quantity produced and lead to underproduction. *Subsidies,* which are payments by the government to producers, decrease the prices paid by buyers and increase the prices received by sellers. So subsidies increase the quantity produced and lead to overproduction.

Externalities

An *externality* is a cost or a benefit that affects someone other than the seller and the buyer of a good. An electric utility creates an *external cost* by burning coal that brings acid rain and crop damage. The utility doesn't consider the cost of pollution when it decides how much power to produce. The result is overproduction.

A condominium owner would provide an *external benefit* if she installed a smoke detector. But she doesn't consider her neighbor's marginal benefit and decides not to install a smoke detector. The result is underproduction.

Public Goods and Common Resources

A *public good* benefits everyone and no one can be excluded from its benefits. National defense is an example. It is in everyone's self-interest to avoid paying for a public good (called the *free-rider problem*), which leads to its underproduction.

A *common resource* is owned by no one but used by everyone. Atlantic salmon is an example. It is in everyone's self-interest to ignore the costs that fall on others as a result of their own use of a common resource (called the *tragedy of the commons*), which leads to overproduction.

Monopoly

A *monopoly* is a firm that is the sole provider of a good or service. Local water supply and cable television are supplied by firms that are monopolies.

The self-interest of a monopoly is to maximize its profit. Because the monopoly has no competitors, it can set the price to achieve its self-interested goal. To achieve its goal, a monopoly produces too little and charges too high a price, which leads to underproduction.

High Transactions Costs

Stroll around a shopping mall and observe the retail markets in which you participate. You'll see that these markets employ enormous quantities of scarce labor and capital resources. It is costly to operate any market. Economists call the opportunity costs of making trades in a market **transactions costs**.

To use market prices as the allocators of scarce resources, it must be worth bearing the opportunity cost of establishing a market. Some markets are just too costly to operate. For example, when you want to play tennis on your local "free" court, you don't pay a market price for your slot on the court. You hang around until the court becomes vacant, and you "pay" with your waiting time.

When transactions costs are high, the market might underproduce.

Transactions costs
The opportunity costs of making trades in a market.

■ Alternatives to the Market

When a market is inefficient, can one of the alternative non-market methods that we described at the beginning of this chapter do a better job? Sometimes it can.

Table 6.1 summarizes the sources of market failure and the possible remedies. Often, majority rule might be used, but majority rule has its own shortcomings. A group that pursues the self-interest of its members can become the majority. For example, price and quantity regulations that create deadweight loss are almost always the result of a self-interested group becoming the majority and imposing costs on the minority. Also, with majority rule, votes must be translated into actions by bureaucrats who have their own agendas.

Managers in firms issue commands and avoid the transactions costs that they would incur if they went to a market every time they needed a job done. First-come, first-served saves a lot of hassle in waiting lines. These lines could have markets in which people trade their place in the line—but someone would have to enforce the agreements. Can you imagine the hassle at a busy Starbucks if you had to buy your spot at the head of the line?

There is no one mechanism for allocating resources efficiently. But markets bypassed by command systems inside firms and supplemented by majority rule and first-come, first-served do an amazingly good job.

■ TABLE 6.1

Market Failure and Some Possible Remedies

Reason for market failure	Possible remedy
1. Price and quantity regulations	Remove regulation by majority rule
2. Taxes and subsidies	Minimize deadweight loss by majority rule
3. Externalities	Minimize deadweight loss by majority rule
4. Public goods	Allocate by majority rule
5. Common resources	Allocate by majority rule
6. Monopoly	Regulate by majority rule
7. High transactions costs	Command or first-come, first-served

CHECKPOINT 6.4

Evaluate the efficiency of the alternative methods of allocating resources.

Practice Problems

Figure 1 shows the market for paper.

1. At the market equilibrium, what are consumer surplus, producer surplus, and total surplus? Is the market for paper efficient? Why or why not?

2. Lobbyists for a group of news magazines persuade the government to pass a law that requires producers to sell 50 tons of paper a day. Is the market for paper efficient? Explain your answer and illustrate it on the figure.

3. An environmental lobbying group persuades the government to pass a law that limits the quantity of paper that producers sell to 20 tons a day. Is the market for paper efficient? If not, what is the deadweight loss?

In the News

Milking taxpayers

American corn and soybean farmers receive subsidies of about $20 billion a year.

Source: *The Economist*, February 14, 2015

Because they receive subsidies, the price they receive for their crops exceeds the market price. Describe the efficiency of the markets for corn and soybean with subsidies in place. If the subsidies (and the taxes that pay them) were decreased, explain how the efficiency of the markets for corn and soybean would change.

Solutions to Practice Problems

1. Market equilibrium is 40 tons a day at a price of $3 a ton (Figure 2). Consumer surplus is ($9 − $3) × 40 ÷ 2, which equals $120 (the area of the green triangle in Figure 2). Producer surplus is ($3 − $1) × 40 ÷ 2, which equals $40 (the area of the blue triangle in Figure 2). Total surplus is the sum of consumer surplus and producer surplus, which is $160.
    The market is efficient because marginal benefit (on the demand curve) equals marginal cost (on the supply curve) and total surplus (consumer surplus plus producer surplus) is maximized.

2. With producers required to sell 50 tons of paper a day, the market is inefficient because marginal cost exceeds marginal benefit. Deadweight loss equals the area of the gray triangle 1 in Figure 3.

3. With production limited to 20 tons a day, the market is inefficient because marginal benefit exceeds marginal cost. The deadweight loss equals the area of the gray triangle 2 in Figure 3.

Solution to In the News

Subsidies to producers induce overproduction and increase the supply of the good. With no change in demand, the market price falls. The price received by producers equals the market price plus the subsidy. Market failure occurs and the market is inefficient. A deadweight loss arises. By decreasing the subsidies (and taxes), overproduction would decrease, the markets for corn and soybean would become more efficient, and the deadweight loss would decrease.

FIGURE 1

FIGURE 2

FIGURE 3

6.5 ARE MARKETS FAIR?

Following a severe winter storm or hurricane, the prices of many essential items jump. Is it fair that disaster victims should be hit with higher prices? Many low-skilled people work for a wage that is below what most would regard as a living wage. Is that fair? How do we decide whether something is fair or unfair?

Economists have a clear definition of efficiency but they do not have a similarly clear definition of fairness. Also, ideas about fairness are not exclusively economic ideas. They involve the study of ethics.

To study ideas about fairness, think of economic life as a game—a serious game—that has *rules* and a *result*. Two broad and generally conflicting approaches to fairness are

- It's not fair if the *rules* aren't fair.
- It's not fair if the *result* isn't fair.

■ It's Not Fair If the *Rules* Aren't Fair

Harvard philosopher Robert Nozick argued for the fair-rules view in a book entitled *Anarchy, State, and Utopia*, published in 1974. Nozick argued that fairness requires two rules:

- The state must establish and protect private property rights.
- Goods and services and the services of factors of production may be transferred from one person to another only by voluntary exchange with everyone free to engage in such exchange.

The first rule says that everything that is valuable—all scarce resources and goods—must be owned by individuals and that the state must protect private property rights. The second rule says that the only way a person can acquire something is to buy it in voluntary trade.

If these rules are followed, says Nozick, the outcome is fair. It doesn't matter how unequally the economic pie is shared provided that the people who bake it supply their services voluntarily in exchange for the share of the pie offered in compensation. Opportunity is equal but the result might be unequal. This fair-rules approach is consistent with allocative efficiency.

■ It's Not Fair If the *Result* Isn't Fair

Most people think that the fair-rules approach leads to too much inequality—to an unfair result: For example, it is unfair for a bank president to earn millions of dollars a year while a bank teller earns only thousands of dollars a year.

But what is "too unequal"? Is it fair for some people to receive twice as much as others but not ten times as much or a hundred times as much? Or is all that matters that the poorest people shouldn't be "too poor"?

There is no easy answer to these questions. Generally, greater equality is regarded as good but there is no measure of the most desirable shares.

The fair-result approach conflicts with allocative efficiency and leads to what is called the **big tradeoff**—a tradeoff between efficiency and fairness that recognizes the cost of making income transfers.

The big tradeoff is based on the fact that income can be transferred to people with low incomes only by taxing people with high incomes. But taxing people's

Big tradeoff
A tradeoff between efficiency and fairness that recognizes the cost of making income transfers.

EYE on PRICE GOUGING

MyEconLab Critical Thinking Exercise

Should Price Gouging Be Illegal?

Price gouging is the practice of selling an essential item for a much higher price than normal, and usually occurs following a natural disaster. In Florida and Texas, where hurricanes happen all too often, price gouging is illegal.

Whether price gouging *should* be illegal depends on the view of fairness employed and on the facts about whether the buyers or the sellers are the poorer group.

The standard view of economists is that price gouging should *not* be illegal and that it is the expected and *efficient* response to a change in demand.

After a hurricane, the demand for items such as generators, pumps, lamps, gasoline, and camp stoves increases and the prices of these items rise in a natural response to the change in demand.

The figure illustrates the market for camp stoves. The supply of stoves is the curve S, and in normal times, the demand for stoves is D_0. The price is $20 per stove and the equilibrium quantity is 5 stoves per day.

Following a hurricane that results in a lengthy power outage, the demand for camp stoves increases to D_1. Provided there is no price-gouging law, the equilibrium price of a stove jumps to $40 and the equilibrium quantity increases to 7 stoves per day.

This outcome is efficient because the marginal cost of a stove (on the supply curve) equals the marginal benefit from a stove (on the demand curve).

If a strict price-gouging law requires the price after the hurricane to be the *same* as the price before the hurricane, the price of a stove is stuck at $20.

At this price, the quantity of stoves supplied remains at 5 per day and a deadweight loss shown by the gray triangle arises. The price-gouging law is inefficient, and the price rise is efficient.

Whether a doubling of the price is *fair* depends on the idea of fairness used. On the *fair-rules* view, the price rise is fair. Trade is voluntary and both the buyer and the seller are better off. On the *fair-result* view, the price rise might be considered unfair if the buyers are poor and the sellers are rich. But if the buyers are rich and the sellers are poor, the price rise would be considered fair even on the fair-result view.

After Hurricane Katrina, John Shepperson bought 19 generators, loaded them into a rented U-Haul vehicle, and drove the 600 miles from his home in Kentucky to a place in Mississippi that had no power. He offered his generators to eager buyers for twice the price he had paid for them. But before he could complete a sale, the Mississippi police swooped in and arrested him. They confiscated his generators and put him in jail for four days. His crime: price gouging.

Was it efficient to stop Mr. Shepperson from selling his generators? Was it fair either to him or his deprived customers?

EYE on YOUR LIFE

Allocation Methods, Efficiency, and Fairness

You live in the national economy, your state economy, your regional economy, and your own household economy. The many decisions you must make affect efficiency and fairness at all these levels. Think about your household economy.

Make a spreadsheet and on it identify all the factors of production that your household owns. Count all the person-hours available and any capital.

Show how these resources are allocated.

By what methods are your household's scarce resources allocated? Identify those allocated by market price; by command; by first-come, first-served; and by equal shares. Are any resources allocated by majority vote?

Now the tough part: Are these resources allocated efficiently—is the

value of your household's resources maximized? Think about how you can check whether marginal benefit equals marginal cost for each of your household's activities.

And now an even tougher question: Are your household's resources allocated fairly? Think about the two ideas of fairness and how they apply in your household.

---

income from employment discourages work. It results in the quantity of labor being less than the efficient quantity. Taxing the income people earn from capital discourages saving and results in the quantity of capital being less than the efficient quantity. With smaller quantities of both labor and capital, the quantity of goods and services produced is less than the efficient quantity. The economic pie shrinks.

Income redistribution creates a tradeoff between the size of the economic pie and the equality with which it is shared. The greater the scale of income redistribution through income taxes, the greater is the inefficiency—the smaller is the pie.

There is a second source of inefficiency: A dollar taken from a rich person does not end up as a dollar in the hands of a poorer person. Some of the dollar is spent on administration of the tax and transfer system, which includes the cost of accountants, auditors, and lawyers. These activities use skilled labor and capital resources that could otherwise be used to produce other goods and services that people value.

You can see that when all these costs are taken into account, transferring a dollar from a rich person does not give a dollar to a poor person. It is even possible that those with low incomes end up being worse off. For example, if a highly taxed entrepreneur decides to work less hard and shut down a business, low-income workers get fired and must seek other, perhaps even lower-paid, work.

■ Compromise

Most people, and probably most economists, have sympathy with the Nozick view but think it too extreme. They see a role for taxes and government income support schemes to transfer some income from the rich to the poor. Such transfers could be considered voluntary in the sense that they are decided by majority voting, and even those who vote against such transfers voluntarily participate in the political process.

Once we agree that using the tax system to make transfers from the rich to the poor is fair, we need to determine just what we mean by a fair tax. We'll look at this big question when we study the tax system in Chapter 8.

MyEconLab Study Plan 6.5
Key Terms Quiz
Solutions Video

 # CHECKPOINT 6.5

Explain the main ideas about fairness, and evaluate the fairness of the alternative methods of allocating scarce resources.

Practice Problems

A winter storm cuts the power supply and isolates a small town in the mountains. The people rush to buy candles from the town store, which is the only source of candles. The store owner decides to ration the candles to one per family but to keep the price of a candle unchanged.

1. Who gets to use the candles? Who receives the consumer surplus and who receives the producer surplus on candles?

2. Is the allocation efficient? Is the allocation fair?

In the News

Water wars are coming
Water use is growing at a faster pace than the rate of population growth. Earth has lots of water, but 97.5 percent of it is in the oceans and is salty. The problem is that a growing number of people have no clean fresh drinking water.
Source: PBS, November 16, 2015

Would a free world market in fresh water achieve a fair use of the world's water resources? Explain why or why not and be clear about the concept of fairness that you are using.

Solutions to Practice Problems

1. The people who buy candles from the town store are not necessarily the people who use the candles. A buyer from the town store can sell a candle and will do so if he or she can get a price that exceeds his or her marginal benefit. The people who value the candles most—who are willing to pay the most—will use the candles.
   Only the people who are willing to pay the most for candles receive the consumer surplus on candles, and the store owner receives the same producer surplus as normal. People who sell the candles they buy from the store receive additional producer surplus.

2. The allocation is efficient because the people who value the candles most use them. Whether the allocation is fair depends on which of the two views of fairness is adopted. In the fair-rules view, if the rule of one candle per family is followed and exchange is voluntary, then the outcome is fair. But in the fair-result view, if the candles are allocated unequally, then the allocation is unfair.

Solution to In the News

If the world market in fresh water were free, the market price would allocate the water. This allocation of water would be fair on the fair-rules view because the exchange of water would be voluntary, but it would not be fair on the fair-result view because poor people who own no water and those living in drought-stricken areas would not be able to afford water.

CHAPTER SUMMARY

Key Points

1. Describe the alternative methods of allocating scarce resources, and define and explain the features of an efficient allocation.

- The methods of allocating scarce resources are market price; command; majority rule; contest; first-come, first-served; sharing equally; lottery; personal characteristics; and force.
- Allocative efficiency occurs when resources are used to create the greatest value, which means that marginal benefit equals marginal cost.

2. Distinguish between value and price, and define consumer surplus.

- Marginal benefit is measured by the maximum price that consumers are willing to pay for another unit of a good or service.
- A demand curve is a marginal benefit curve.
- Value is what people are *willing to* pay; price is what they *must* pay.
- Consumer surplus equals the excess of marginal benefit over price, summed over the quantity consumed.

3. Distinguish between cost and price, and define producer surplus.

- Marginal cost is measured by the minimum price producers must be offered to increase production by one unit.
- A supply curve is a marginal cost curve.
- Opportunity cost is what producers *must* pay; price is what they *receive*.
- Producer surplus equals the excess of price over marginal cost, summed over the quantity produced.

4. Evaluate the efficiency of the alternative methods of allocating resources.

- In a competitive equilibrium, marginal benefit equals marginal cost and resource allocation is efficient.
- Price and quantity regulations, taxes, subsidies, externalities, public goods, common resources, monopoly, and high transactions costs lead to market failure and create deadweight loss.

5. Explain the main ideas about fairness, and evaluate the fairness of the alternative methods of allocating scarce resources.

- Ideas about fairness divide into two groups: fair *rules* and a fair *result*.
- Fair rules require private property rights and voluntary exchange, and a fair result requires income transfers from the rich to the poor.

Key Terms

MyEconLab Key Terms Quiz

Allocative efficiency, 143
Big tradeoff, 161
Command system, 141

Consumer surplus, 149
Deadweight loss, 157
Market failure, 157

Producer surplus, 152
Total surplus, 155
Transactions costs, 159

CHAPTER CHECKPOINT

Study Plan Problems and Applications

At McDonald's, no reservations are accepted; at the St. Louis Art Museum Restaurant, reservations are accepted; at Le Bernardin in New York, reservations are essential. Use this information to answer Problems **1** to **3**.

 1. Describe the method of allocating table resources in these three restaurants.

 2. Why do you think restaurants have different reservation policies, and why might each restaurant be using an efficient allocation method?

 3. Why don't all restaurants use the market price to allocate their tables?

Table 1 shows the demand and supply schedules for sandwiches. Use Table 1 to work Problems **4** to **7**.

 4. Calculate the equilibrium price of a sandwich, the consumer surplus, and the producer surplus. What is the efficient quantity of sandwiches?

 5. If the quantity demanded decreases by 100 sandwiches an hour at each price, what is the equilibrium price and what is the change in total surplus?

 6. If the quantity supplied decreases by 100 sandwiches an hour at each price, what is the equilibrium price and what is the change in total surplus?

 7. If Sandwiches To Go, Inc., buys all the sandwich producers and cuts production to 100 sandwiches an hour, what is the deadweight loss that is created? If Sandwiches To Go, Inc., rations sandwiches to two per person, by what view of fairness would the allocation be unfair?

Use the following information to work Problems **8** and **9**.

Table 2 shows the demand and supply schedules for sandbags before and during a major flood. During the flood, suppose that the government gave all families an equal quantity of sandbags. Resale of sandbags is not permitted.

 8. How would total surplus and the price of a sandbag change?

 9. Would the outcome be more efficient than if the government took no action? Explain.

10. The winner of the men's or women's tennis singles at the U.S. Open is paid twice as much as the runner-up, but it takes two players to have a singles final. Is this compensation arrangement efficient? Is it fair? Explain why it might illustrate the big tradeoff.

11. eBay saves billions for bidders

 On eBay, the bidder who places the highest bid wins the auction and pays only what the second highest bidder offered. Researchers Wolfgang Jank and Galit Shmueli reported that purchasers on eBay in 2003 paid $7 billion less than their winning bids. Because each bid shows the buyer's willingness to pay, the winner receives an estimated consumer surplus of $4 or more.

 Source: *InformationWeek*, January 28, 2008

 What method is used to allocate goods on eBay? How does an eBay auction influence consumer surplus from the good?

12. Read *Eye on Price Gouging* on p. 162 and explain why it was inefficient to stop Mr. Shepperson from selling his generators.

TABLE 1

Price (dollars per sandwich)	Quantity demanded	Quantity supplied
	(sandwiches per hour)	
0	400	0
1	350	50
2	300	100
3	250	150
4	200	200
5	150	250
6	100	300
7	50	350
8	0	400

TABLE 2

Price (dollars per bag)	Quantity demanded before flood	Quantity demanded during flood	Quantity supplied
	(thousands of bags)		
0	40	70	0
1	35	65	5
2	30	60	10
3	25	55	15
4	20	50	20
5	15	45	25
6	10	40	30
7	5	35	35
8	0	30	40

Instructor Assignable Problems and Applications

MyEconLab Homework, Quiz, or
Test if assigned by instructor

1. **Mets World Series ticket prices spike after NLCS win**
   Now that the New York Mets are in baseball's World Series for the first time
   in 15 years, fans who don't have a ticket will pay a hefty $1,667.82 to get one.
   That's the average asking price for a resold ticket, which is the highest since
   World Series price-tracking started in 2010.

   Source: CNBC.com, October 22, 2015

   Why is a $1,667.82 ticket price similar to "price gouging"? Is the high price
   an example of the market price method of allocating scarce resources? Is the
   market for tickets efficient? Is it fair?

Table 1 shows the demand schedule for haircuts and the supply schedule of
haircuts. Use Table 1 to work Problems **2** and **3**.

2. What is the quantity of haircuts bought, the value of a haircut, and the total
   surplus from haircuts?

3. Suppose that all salons agree to charge $40 a haircut. How do consumer sur-
   plus and producer surplus change? What is the deadweight loss created?

In California, farmers pay a lower price for water than do city residents. Use this
information to work Problems **4** to **6**.

4. What is this method of allocation of water resources? Is this allocation of
   water efficient? Is this use of scarce water fair? Why or why not?

5. If farmers were charged the same price as city residents pay, how would the
   price of agricultural produce, the quantity of produce grown, consumer surplus, and producer surplus change?

6. If all water in California is sold for the market equilibrium price, would the
   allocation of water be more efficient? Why or why not?

Use the following information to work Problems **7** and **8**.

The world's largest tulip and flower market
Every day over 19 million tulips and flowers are auctioned at the Dutch market
called "The Bloemenveiling." These Dutch auctions match buyers and sellers.

Source: Tulip-Bulbs.com

In a Dutch auction, the auctioneer announces the highest price. If no one offers
to buy the flowers, the auctioneer lowers the price until a buyer is found.

7. What method is used to allocate flowers at the Bloemenveiling?

8. How does a Dutch flower auction influence consumer surplus and producer
   surplus? Are the flower auctions at the Bloemenveiling efficient?

9. **Take pride in U.S. forests**
   U.S. forestland has been a constant 755 million acres for the past century, but
   the number of trees has increased by 20 percent since 1970, the volume of
   wood has doubled since 1953, and the United States is the world's largest
   supplier of forest products. Decisions by millions of private forest-land owners are responsible for this remarkable performance.

   Source: Frank Beidler letter, *Chicago Tribune*, October 23, 2015

   Is the U.S. timber industry efficient and do forest-land owners operate in the
   social interest or self-interest? What effect does private ownership have on
   the efficiency of the timber industry?

TABLE 1

Price (dollars per haircut)	Quantity demanded	supplied
	(haircuts per day)	
0	100	0
10	80	0
20	60	20
30	40	40
40	20	60
50	0	80

MyEconLab Chapter 6 Study Plan

Multiple Choice Quiz

1. The method of allocation that most stores use during Thanksgiving sales is:
   A. a combination of market price and lottery
   B. first-come, first-served
   C. a combination of contest and command
   D. a combination of market price and first-come, first-served

2. All of the following statements are correct *except* _____.
   A. the value of an additional unit of the good equals the marginal benefit from the good
   B. marginal benefit is the excess of value over the price paid, summed over the quantity consumed
   C. the maximum price willingly paid for a unit of a good is the marginal benefit from it
   D. price is what we pay for a good but value is what we get from it

3. Choose the best statement.
   A. An increase in the demand for a good increases producer surplus.
   B. If producers decrease the supply of the good, their producer surplus will increase.
   C. Producer surplus equals the total revenue from selling the good.
   D. Producer surplus is the excess of the value of the good over the market price, summed over the quantity produced.

4. The market for a good is efficient if _____.
   A. the marginal cost of producing the good is minimized
   B. the marginal benefit from the good is maximized
   C. the consumer surplus is maximized
   D. the total surplus is maximized

5. When the marginal benefit from a good exceeds its marginal cost, _____.
   A. there is overproduction of the good
   B. a deadweight loss, which is the excess of marginal benefit over marginal cost, arises
   C. producer surplus decreases and consumer surplus increases
   D. total production increases and efficiency increases

6. Market failure arises if _____.
   A. there is overproduction of the good but not if there is underproduction
   B. the deadweight loss is zero
   C. producer surplus exceeds consumer surplus
   D. total surplus is not maximized

7. The allocation of resources is fair _____.
   A. in the fair-rules view if everyone has equal opportunity
   B. in the fair-result view if most resources are distributed to the poorest people
   C. in the fair-rules view if owners of the resources are protected by property rights and all transfers of resources are voluntary
   D. in the fair-result view if resources are transferred voluntarily so that everyone has the same quantity

A Fair Shot for Everyone
$10.10
per hour
#RaiseTheWage

A Fair Shot
for Everyone

Can Congress repeal the law
of market forces?

Government Actions
in Markets

**When you have completed your study of this chapter,
you will be able to**

1 Explain how a price ceiling works, and why a rent ceiling creates a
   housing shortage and is inefficient and unfair.

2 Explain how a price floor works, and why the minimum wage creates
   unemployment and is inefficient and unfair.

3 Explain how a production quota works, and why it brings a higher
   price and is inefficient and unfair.

MyEconLab Big Picture Video

7.1   PRICE CEILINGS

Congress might want to set a price or a quantity at a level that it chooses rather than at the level determined by market forces. What are the effects of this type of government action in a market? You'll find the answer in this chapter, starting with a government attempt to place an upper limit on a price.

Price ceiling or price cap
A government regulation that places an *upper* limit on the price at which a particular good, service, or factor of production may be traded.

A government regulation that places an *upper* limit on the price at which a particular good, service, or factor of production may be traded is called a **price ceiling** (or a **price cap**). Trading at a higher price is illegal.

A price ceiling has been used in several markets, but the one that looms largest in everyone's budget is the housing market. The price of housing is the rent that people pay for a house or apartment.

Figure 7.1 illustrates the apartment rental market in Biloxi, Mississippi. The rent is $550 a month, and 4,000 apartments are rented.

■ A Rent Ceiling

Rent ceiling
A regulation that makes it illegal to charge more than a specified rent for housing.

Suppose the mayor of Biloxi gets elected on a promise to impose a **rent ceiling**—a regulation that makes it illegal to charge more than a specified rent for housing.

The effect of a rent ceiling depends on whether it is imposed at a level above or below the equilibrium rent. In Figure 7.1, if the rent ceiling is set *above* $550 a month, nothing would change because people are already paying $550 a month.

But a rent ceiling that is set *below* the equilibrium rent has powerful effects on the market outcome. The reason is that the rent ceiling attempts to prevent the rent from rising high enough to regulate the quantities demanded and supplied. The law and the market are in conflict, and one (or both) of them must yield.

■ FIGURE 7.1

A Housing Market   MyEconLab Animation

The figure shows the demand curve, *D*, and the supply curve, *S*, for rental housing.

❶ The market is in equilibrium when the quantity demanded equals the quantity supplied.

❷ The equilibrium price (rent) is $550 a month.

❸ The equilibrium quantity is 4,000 units of housing.

Figure 7.2 shows a rent ceiling that is set below the equilibrium rent at $400 a month. We've shaded the area *above* the rent ceiling because any rent in this region is illegal. The first effect of a rent ceiling is a housing shortage. At a rent of $400 a month, the quantity of housing supplied is 3,000 units and the quantity demanded is 6,000 units. So at $400 a month, there is a shortage of 3,000 units of housing.

But the story does not end here. The 3,000 units of housing that owners are willing to make available must somehow be allocated among people who are seeking 6,000 units. This allocation might be achieved in two ways:

- A black market
- Increased search activity

A Black Market

A **black market** is an illegal market that operates alongside a government-regulated market. A rent ceiling sometimes creates a black market in housing as frustrated renters and landlords try to find ways of raising the rent above the legally imposed ceiling. Landlords want higher rents because they know that renters are willing to pay more for the existing quantity of housing. Renters are willing to pay more to jump to the front of the line.

Because raising the rent is illegal, landlords and renters use creative tricks to get around the law. One of these tricks is for a new tenant to pay a high price for worthless fittings—perhaps paying $2,000 for threadbare drapes. Another is for the tenant to pay a high price for new locks and keys—called "key money."

Figure 7.3 shows how high the black market rent might go in Biloxi. With strict enforcement of the rent ceiling, the quantity of housing available is 3,000

Black market
An illegal market that operates alongside a government-regulated market.

FIGURE 7.2

A Rent Ceiling Creates a Shortage

 MyEconLab Animation

A rent ceiling is imposed below the equilibrium rent. In this example, the rent ceiling is $400 a month.

❶ The quantity of housing supplied decreases to 3,000 units.

❷ The quantity of housing demanded increases to 6,000 units.

❸ A shortage of 3,000 units arises.

units. But at this quantity, renters are willing to offer as much as $625 a month—the amount determined on the demand curve.

So a small number of landlords illegally offer housing for rents up to $625 a month. The black market rent might be at any level between the rent ceiling of $400 a month and the maximum that a renter is willing to pay of $625 a month.

Increased Search Activity

Search activity
The time spent looking for someone with whom to do business.

The time spent looking for someone with whom to do business is called **search activity**. We spend some time in search activity almost every time we buy something, and especially when we buy a big item such as a car or a home. When a price ceiling creates a shortage of housing, search activity *increases*. In a rent-controlled housing market, frustrated would-be renters do an Internet search or scan the newspapers. Keen apartment seekers race to be first on the scene when news of a possible apartment breaks.

The *opportunity cost* of a good is equal to its price *plus* the value of the search time spent finding the good. So the opportunity cost of housing is equal to the rent plus the value of the search time spent looking for an apartment. Search activity is costly. It uses time and other resources, such as telephones, automobiles, and gasoline that could have been used in other productive ways. In Figure 7.3, to find accommodation at $400 a month, someone who is willing to pay a rent of $625 a month would be willing to spend on search activity an amount that is equivalent to adding $225 a month to the rent ceiling.

A rent ceiling controls the rent portion of the cost of housing but not the search cost. So when the search cost is added to the rent, some people end up paying a higher opportunity cost for housing than they would if there were no rent ceiling.

FIGURE 7.3

A Rent Ceiling Creates a Black Market and Housing Search   MyEconLab Animation

With a rent ceiling of $400 a month,

❶ 3,000 units of housing are available.

❷ Someone is willing to pay $625 a month for the 3,000th unit of housing.

❸ Black market rent might be as high as $625 a month or search activity might be equivalent to adding $225 a month to the rent ceiling.

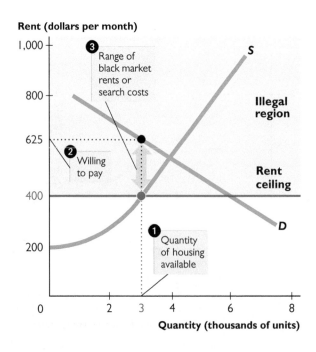

■ Are Rent Ceilings Efficient?

In a housing market with no rent ceiling, market forces determine the equilibrium rent. The quantity of housing demanded equals the quantity of housing supplied. In this situation, scarce housing resources are allocated efficiently because the marginal cost of housing equals the marginal benefit. Figure 7.4(a) shows this efficient outcome in the Biloxi apartment rental market. In this efficient market, total surplus—the sum of *consumer surplus* (the green area) and *producer surplus* (the blue area)—is maximized at the equilibrium rent and quantity of housing (see Chapter 6, pp. 154–155).

Figure 7.4(b) shows that with a rent ceiling, the outcome is inefficient. Marginal benefit from rented housing exceeds its marginal cost. Producer surplus and consumer surplus shrink, and a deadweight loss (the gray area) arises. This loss is borne by the people who can't find housing and by landlords who can't offer housing at the lower rent ceiling.

But the total loss *exceeds* the deadweight loss. Resources get used in costly search activity or in evading the law in the black market. The value of these resources might be as large as the area of the red rectangle. There is yet a further loss: the cost of enforcing the rent ceiling law. This loss, which is borne by taxpayers, is not visible in the figure.

FIGURE 7.4

The Inefficiency of a Rent Ceiling

MyEconLab Animation

(a) Efficient housing market

❶ The market equilibrium is efficient with marginal benefit equal to marginal cost. Total surplus, the sum of ❷ consumer surplus (green area) and ❸ producer surplus (blue area), is maximized.

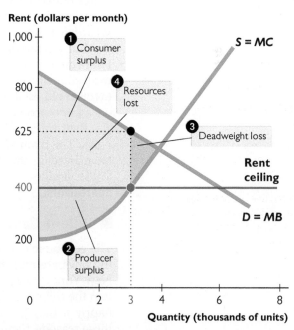

(b) Inefficient housing market

A rent ceiling is inefficient. ❶ Consumer surplus and ❷ producer surplus shrink, a ❸ deadweight loss arises, and ❹ resources are lost in search activity and evading the rent ceiling law.

With rent ceilings, landlords have no incentive to maintain buildings, and both the quality and quantity of housing supplied decrease.

Although a rent ceiling creates inefficiency, not everyone loses. The people who pay the rent ceiling get an increase in consumer surplus, and landlords who charge a black market rent get an increase in producer surplus.

The costs of a rent ceiling that we've just considered are only the initial costs. With the rent below the market equilibrium rent, landlords have no incentive to maintain their buildings. So over time, both the quality and quantity of housing supplied *decrease* and the loss arising from a rent ceiling increases.

The size of the loss from a rent ceiling depends on the elasticities of supply and demand. If supply is inelastic, a rent ceiling brings a small decrease in the quantity of housing supplied. And if demand is inelastic, a rent ceiling brings a small increase in the quantity of housing demanded. So the more inelastic the supply or the demand, the smaller is the shortage of housing and the smaller is the deadweight loss.

■ Are Rent Ceilings Fair?

We've seen that rent ceilings prevent scarce resources from being allocated efficiently—resources do not flow to their highest-valued use. But don't they ensure that scarce housing resources are allocated more fairly?

You learned in Chapter 6 (pp. 161–163) that fairness is a complex idea about which there are two broad views: fair *rules* versus a fair *result*. Rent controls violate the fair-rules view of fairness because they block voluntary exchange. But do they deliver a fair result? Do rent ceilings ensure that scarce housing goes to the poor people whose need is greatest?

Blocking rent adjustments that bring the quantity of housing demanded into equality with the quantity supplied doesn't end scarcity. So when the law prevents the rent from adjusting and blocks the price mechanism from allocating scarce housing, some other allocation mechanism must be used. If that mechanism were one that provided the housing to the poorest, then the allocation might be regarded as fair.

But the mechanisms that get used do not usually achieve such an outcome. First-come, first-served is one allocation mechanism. Discrimination based on race, ethnicity, or sex is another. Discrimination against young newcomers and in favor of old established families is yet another. None of these mechanisms delivers a fair outcome.

Rent ceilings in New York City provide examples of these mechanisms at work. The main beneficiaries of rent ceilings in New York City are families who have lived in the city for a long time—including some rich and famous ones. These families enjoy low rents while newcomers pay high rents for hard-to-find apartments.

■ If Rent Ceilings Are So Bad, Why Do We Have Them?

The economic case against rent ceilings is now widely accepted, so *new* rent ceiling laws are rare. But when governments try to repeal rent control laws, as the New York City government did in 1999, current renters lobby politicians to maintain the ceilings. Also, people who are prevented from finding housing would be happy if they got lucky and managed to find a rent-controlled apartment. For these reasons, there is plenty of political support for rent ceilings.

Apartment owners who oppose rent ceilings are a minority, so their views are not a powerful influence on politicians. Because more people support rent ceilings than oppose them, politicians are sometimes willing to support them too.

CHECKPOINT 7.1

MyEconLab Study Plan 7.1
Key Terms Quiz
Solutions Video

Explain how a price ceiling works, and why a rent ceiling creates a housing shortage and is inefficient and unfair.

Practice Problems

Figure 1 shows the rental market for apartments in Corsicana, Texas.

1. What is the rent and how many apartments are rented? If a rent ceiling of $900 a month is set, what is the rent and how many apartments are rented?

2. If the city government imposes a rent ceiling of $600 a month, what is the rent and how many apartments are rented? If a black market develops, explain how high the black market rent could be.

3. If the city government imposes a rent ceiling of $600 a month and enforces it, is the housing market efficient? What is the deadweight loss? Is the housing market fair? Explain your answer.

In the News

A gas price ceiling
China has cut the price of natural gas and may install a price ceiling that prohibits a price rise of more than 20 percent above a benchmark.
Source: *Bloomberg News*, November 18, 2015

Explain how a cut in the price and a price ceiling will influence consumer surplus, producer surplus, and deadweight loss in China's natural gas market.

Solutions to Practice Problems

1. The equilibrium rent is $800 a month, and 3,000 apartments are rented. A rent ceiling of $900 a month is above the equilibrium rent, so the outcome is the market equilibrium rent of $800 a month with 3,000 apartments rented.

2. A rent ceiling at $600 a month is below the market equilibrium rent, so the number of apartments rented is 1,000 and the rent is $600 a month (Figure 2). In a black market, someone would be willing to rent an apartment for more than the rent ceiling. The highest rent that someone would offer is $1,200 a month. This rent equals someone's willingness to pay for the 1,000th apartment (Figure 2).

3. The housing market is not efficient. With 1,000 apartments rented, marginal benefit exceeds marginal cost and a deadweight loss arises (Figure 2). The deadweight loss is equal to the area of the gray triangle, which equals $(1,200 - 600) \times (3,000 - 1,000) \div 2$. The deadweight loss is $600,000. The housing market is less fair on both views of fairness: It blocks voluntary transactions and does not provide more housing to those most in need.

Solution to In the News

If the price cut and price ceiling keeps the price below the market equilibrium price, then the quantity produced will decrease and a shortage of gas will arise. The marginal benefit from gas will exceed the marginal cost of producing gas, and resources will be used trying to obtain gas. The lower price and reduced quantity will decrease consumer surplus, decrease producer surplus, and create a deadweight loss.

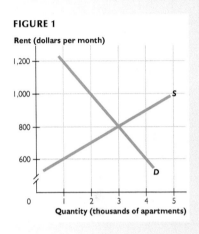

FIGURE 1

Rent (dollars per month)

Quantity (thousands of apartments)

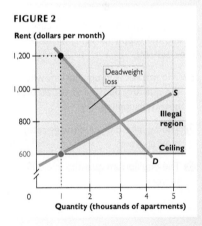

FIGURE 2

Rent (dollars per month)

Quantity (thousands of apartments)

7.2 PRICE FLOORS

Price floor
A government regulation that places a *lower* limit on the price at which a particular good, service, or factor of production may be traded.

You've seen the effects of a price ceiling. Let's now look at the effects of a **price floor**, a government regulation that places a *lower* limit on the price at which a particular good, service, or factor of production may be traded. Trading at a lower price than the price floor is illegal.

Price floors are used in many markets, but the one that looms largest is the labor market. The price of labor is the wage rate that people earn. Demand and supply in the labor market determine the wage rate and the quantity of labor employed.

Figure 7.5 illustrates the market for fast-food servers in Yuma, Arizona. In this market, the demand for labor curve is *D*. On this demand curve, at a wage rate of $13 an hour, the quantity of fast-food servers demanded is zero. If Subway, Burger King, Taco Bell, McDonald's, Wendy's, and the other fast-food places had to pay servers $13 an hour, they wouldn't hire any. They would replace servers with vending machines! But at wage rates below $13 an hour, they would hire servers. At a wage rate of $7 an hour, firms would hire 6,000 servers.

On the supply side of the market, no one is willing to work for $4 an hour. To attract servers, firms must pay more than $4 an hour.

Equilibrium in this market occurs at a wage rate of $7 an hour with 6,000 people employed as servers.

Suppose that the government thinks that no one should have to work for a wage rate as low as $7 an hour and decides that it wants to increase the wage rate. Can the government improve conditions for these workers by passing a minimum wage law? Let's find out.

FIGURE 7.5

A Market for Fast-Food Servers

MyEconLab Animation

The figure shows the demand curve, *D*, and the supply curve, *S*, for fast-food servers.

❶ The market is in equilibrium when the quantity demanded equals the quantity supplied.

❷ The equilibrium price (wage rate) is $7 an hour.

❸ The equilibrium quantity is 6,000 servers.

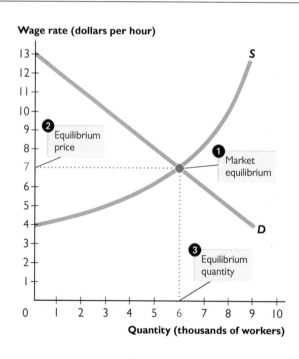

■ The Minimum Wage

A **minimum wage law** is a government regulation that makes hiring labor services for less than a specified wage illegal. Firms are free to pay a wage rate that exceeds the minimum wage but may not pay less than the minimum. A minimum wage is an example of a price floor.

The effect of a price floor depends on whether it is set below or above the equilibrium price. In Figure 7.5, the equilibrium wage rate is $7 an hour, and at this wage rate, firms hire 6,000 workers. If the government introduced a minimum wage below $7 an hour, nothing would change. The reason is that firms are already paying $7 an hour, and because this wage exceeds the minimum wage, the wage rate paid doesn't change. Firms continue to hire 6,000 workers.

But the aim of a minimum wage is to boost the incomes of low-wage earners. So in the markets for the lowest-paid workers, the minimum wage will exceed the equilibrium wage rate.

Suppose that the government introduces a minimum wage of $10 an hour. Figure 7.6 shows the effects of this law. Wage rates below $10 an hour are illegal, so we've shaded the illegal region *below* the minimum wage. Firms and workers are no longer permitted to operate at the equilibrium point in this market because it is in the illegal region. Market forces and political forces are in conflict.

The government can set a minimum wage, but it can't tell employers how many workers to hire. If firms must pay a wage rate of $10 an hour, they will hire only 3,000 workers. At the equilibrium wage rate of $7 an hour, firms hired 6,000 workers, so when the minimum wage is introduced, firms lay off 3,000 workers.

But at a wage rate of $10 an hour, 2,000 people who didn't want to work for $7 an hour will now try to find work as servers. So at $10 an hour, the quantity of

Minimum wage law
A government regulation that makes hiring labor services for less than a specified wage illegal.

FIGURE 7.6

A Minimum Wage Creates Unemployment

MyEconLab Animation

A minimum wage is introduced above the equilibrium wage rate. In this example, the minimum wage rate is $10 an hour.

❶ The quantity of labor demanded decreases to 3,000 workers.

❷ The quantity of labor supplied increases to 8,000 people.

❸ 5,000 people are unemployed.

labor supplied is 8,000 people. With 3,000 workers fired and another 2,000 people looking for work at the higher wage rate, 5,000 people who would like to work as servers are unemployed.

The 3,000 jobs available must somehow be allocated among the 8,000 people who are willing to work as servers. How is this allocation achieved? The answer is by increased job-search activity and illegal hiring.

Increased Job-Search Activity

Finding a good job takes a great deal of time and other resources. With a minimum wage, more people are looking for jobs than the number of jobs available at that wage rate. Frustrated unemployed people spend time and other resources searching for hard-to-find jobs. In Figure 7.7, to find a job at $10 an hour, someone who is willing to work for $5 an hour (on the supply curve) would be willing to spend $5 an hour (the minimum wage rate of $10 an hour minus $5 an hour) on job-search activity. The amount is shown by the red arrow.

Illegal Hiring

With more people looking for work than the number of jobs available, some firms and workers might agree to do business at an illegal wage rate below the minimum wage in a black market. An illegal wage rate might be at any wage rate between the minimum wage of $10 an hour and the lowest wage rate at which someone is willing to work, $5 an hour.

FIGURE 7.7

A Minimum Wage Creates Job Search and Illegal Hiring

MyEconLab Animation

The minimum wage rate is set at $10 an hour:

❶ 3,000 jobs are available.

❷ The lowest wage rate for which someone is willing to work is $5 an hour. In a black market, illegal wage rates might be as low as $5 an hour.

❸ The maximum that might be spent on job search is an amount equivalent to $5 an hour—the $10 an hour they would receive if they found a job *minus* the $5 an hour at which they are willing to work.

EYE on the U.S. ECONOMY
Minimum Wages and Employment

The *Fair Labor Standards Act* sets the federal minimum wage, but most states set their own minimum at a level higher than the federal minimum.

The figure shows the minimum wage since 1993 in terms of what it would buy at 2015 prices.

The minimum wage creates unemployment, but how much? Between 2007 and 2009, when the minimum wage increased by 38 percent (see the figure), the employment of 16- to 19-year-olds fell by 28 percent. How much of that decrease was caused by the rise in the minimum wage.

David Neumark, an economics professor at the University of California, Irvine, has reviewed all the most recent studies on the effects of a minimum wage on employment.

He reports that a 10 percent rise in the minimum wage reduces teen employment by between 1 percent and 3 percent, and 23 states have raised minimum wages to average 11.5 percent higher than the federal minimum.

He says that in 2014, "minimum wages … reduced the number of jobs nationally by about 100,000 to 200,000, relative to the period just before the Great Recession."

Most economists agree with David Neumark. But David Card of the University of California at Berkeley and Alan Krueger of Princeton University have challenged this consensus view. They say that a rise in the minimum wage in California, New Jersey, and Texas *increased* the employment rate of low-income workers.

Most economists are skeptical about their conclusion and see other explanations for the employment increase that Card and Krueger found.

Daniel Hamermesh of the University of Texas at Austin says that Card and Krueger got the timing wrong. Firms anticipated the wage rise and so cut employment before it occurred. Looking at employment changes after the minimum wage increased missed its main effect. Finis Welch of Texas A&M University and Kevin Murphy of the University of Chicago say that the employment effects that Card and Krueger found are caused by regional differences in economic growth, not by changes in the minimum wage.

Pizza delivery people gain from the minimum wage.

Also, looking only at employment misses the supply-side effect of the minimum wage. It brings an increase in the number of people who drop out of high school to look for work.

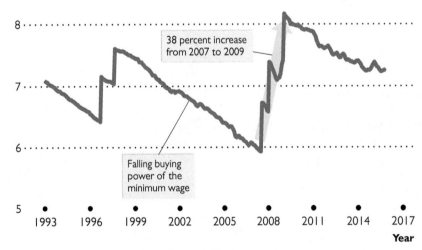

Source of data: Bureau of Labor Statistics.

■ Is the Minimum Wage Efficient?

The efficient allocation of a factor of production is similar to that of a good or service, which you studied in Chapter 6. The demand for labor tells us about the marginal benefit of labor to the firms that hire it. Firms benefit because the labor they hire produces the goods or services that they sell. Firms are willing to pay a wage rate equal to the benefit they receive from an additional hour of labor. In Figure 7.8(a), the demand curve for labor tells us the marginal benefit that the firms in Yuma receive from hiring fast-food servers. The marginal benefit minus the wage rate is a surplus for the firms.

The supply of labor tells us about the marginal cost of working. To work, people must forgo leisure or working in the home, activities that they value. The wage rate received *minus* the marginal cost of working is a surplus for workers.

An efficient allocation of labor occurs when the marginal benefit to firms equals the marginal cost borne by workers. Such an allocation occurs in the labor market in Figure 7.8(a). Firms enjoy a surplus (the blue area), and workers enjoy a surplus (the green area). Total surplus, the sum of these surpluses, is maximized.

Figure 7.8(b) shows the loss from a minimum wage. With a minimum wage of $10 an hour, 3,000 workers are hired. Marginal benefit exceeds marginal cost. The firms' surplus and workers' surplus shrink, and a deadweight loss (the gray area) arises. This loss falls on the firms that cut back employment and the people who can't find jobs at the higher wage rate.

■ FIGURE 7.8

The Inefficiency of the Minimum Wage

MyEconLab Animation

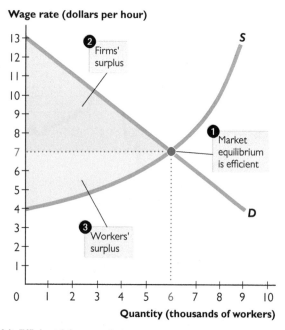

(a) Efficient labor market

❶ The market equilibrium is efficient with marginal benefit equal to marginal cost. Total surplus, the sum of ❷ the firms' surplus (blue area) and ❸ workers' surplus (green area), is maximized.

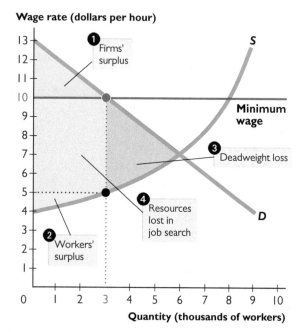

(b) Inefficient labor market

A minimum wage is inefficient. ❶ The firms' surplus and ❷ workers' surplus shrink, a ❸ deadweight loss arises, and ❹ resources are lost in job search.

But the total loss exceeds the deadweight loss. As each unemployed person keeps looking for a job, resources are used in costly job-search activity—writing letters, sending emails, making phone calls, going to interviews, and so on. The value of these resources might be as large as the red rectangle.

■ Is the Minimum Wage Fair?

The minimum wage is unfair on both views of fairness: It delivers an unfair *result* and imposes unfair *rules*. The *result* is unfair because only those people who find jobs benefit. The people unemployed end up worse off than they would be with no minimum wage. And those who get jobs were probably not the least well off. Personal characteristics, which means discrimination, allocates jobs and is another source of unfairness. The minimum wage imposes unfair *rules* because it blocks voluntary exchange. Firms are willing to hire more labor and people are willing to work more, but they are not permitted by the minimum wage law to do so.

■ If the Minimum Wage Is So Bad, Why Do We Have It?

Although the minimum wage is inefficient, not everyone loses from it. The people who find jobs at the minimum wage rate are better off. Other supporters of the minimum wage believe that the elasticities of demand and supply in the labor market are low, so not much unemployment results. Labor unions support the minimum wage because it puts upward pressure on all wage rates, including those of union workers. Nonunion labor is a substitute for union labor, so when the minimum wage rises, the demand for union labor increases.

EYE on PRICE REGULATION

MyEconLab Critical Thinking Exercise

Can Congress Repeal the Law of Market Forces?

When Congress enacts a new law and the President signs it, the outcome is not always exactly what was intended. A mismatch between intention and outcome is almost inevitable when Congress seeks to block the law of market forces.

You've seen the problems created by a minimum wage law, which leaves teenagers without jobs. There would also be problems at the other extreme of the labor market if the law tried to place a cap on executive pay.

In the spring of 2009, the "Cap Executive Officer Pay Act of 2009" was introduced in the Senate. The goal of the Act was to limit the compensation of executives and directors of firms receiving government handouts. The Act defined compensation broadly as all forms of cash receipts, property, and any perks. The cap envisaged was an annual compensation no greater than that of the President of the United States.

This Act never made it into law, but you can see some of the problems that would have arisen if it had.

First, there is the difficult task of determining the President's compensation. Does it include the use of the White House and Air Force One?

Second, assuming the first problem could be solved, placing a cap on executive pay would work like putting a ceiling on home rents which you've studied in this chapter.

The quantity of executive services supplied would decrease and the most talented executives would seek jobs with the unregulated employers. The firms in the most difficulty—those receiving government funding—would face the added challenge of recruiting and keeping competent executives and directors. The deadweight loss from this action would be large. It is fortunate that the idea didn't have legs!

CHECKPOINT 7.2

Explain how a price floor works, and why the minimum wage creates unemployment and is inefficient and unfair.

Practice Problems

FIGURE 1

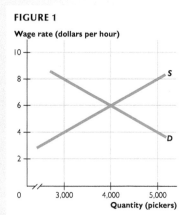

Wage rate (dollars per hour)

Quantity (pickers)

Figure 1 shows the market for tomato pickers in southern California.

1. If California introduces a minimum wage of $4 an hour, how many tomato pickers are employed and how many are unemployed?
2. If California introduces a minimum wage of $8 an hour, how many tomato pickers are employed and how many are unemployed? What is the lowest wage that some workers might be able to earn if a black market develops?
3. If California introduces a minimum wage of $8 an hour, (a) is the minimum wage of $8 an hour efficient? (b) Who gains and who loses from the minimum wage of $8 an hour? Is it fair?

In the News

Will the United States raise the minimum wage to $15?
The labor movement is urging a minimum wage of $15 an hour. Currently, more than 40 percent of employees and 96 percent of fast-food workers earn less than $15 an hour. The U.S. Chamber of Commerce and the National Restaurant Association oppose the increase and say it will hurt small businesses and stifle job creation.

Source: *CBS News*, November 10, 2015

What will be the effects of a $15 an hour minimum wage?

Solutions to Practice Problems

1. The market equilibrium wage rate is $6 an hour, and 4,000 pickers are employed. The minimum wage of $4 an hour is below the equilibrium wage rate, so 4,000 tomato pickers are employed and no worker is unemployed.

FIGURE 2

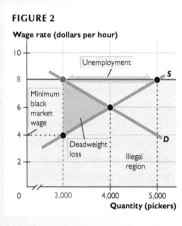

Wage rate (dollars per hour)

Quantity (pickers)

2. The minimum wage of $8 an hour is above the equilibrium wage rate, so 3,000 pickers are employed (determined by the demand) and 5,000 people would like to work as pickers for $8 an hour (determined by the supply), so 2,000 are unemployed (Figure 2). If a black market developed, the lowest wage that someone might be able to earn would be $4 an hour (Figure 2).
3. The minimum wage of $8 an hour is not efficient because it creates a deadweight loss—the marginal benefit to growers exceeds the marginal cost to workers. Tomato pickers who find work at $8 an hour gain. Tomato growers and unemployed pickers lose. The minimum wage is unfair on both the fair-rules and fair-result views of fairness.

Solution to In the News

Given the information about how many workers currently earn less than $15 an hour, we can infer that a minimum wage of $15 an hour exceeds the equilibrium wage rate. Setting the minimum wage at $15 an hour will increase unemployment and create a deadweight loss. Some of this loss will be borne by employers whose profits will fall, but some will be borne by the workers who can't find jobs. Workers who do find jobs will gain.

7.3 PRODUCTION QUOTAS

MyEconLab Concept Video

So far in this chapter, we have examined the effects of government actions that seek to prevent the price from moving toward the equilibrium price. In this final section, we look at a market intervention that aims to block the quantity supplied from moving toward the equilibrium quantity. The tool used for this purpose is a **production quota**, which is a government regulation in a market that places an upper limit on the quantity that may be supplied.

Production quota
A government regulation in a market that places an upper limit on the quantity that may be supplied.

A government can't regulate the quantity supplied without isolating the domestic market from global competition. For this reason, production quotas usually are accompanied by *import quotas*—restrictions on the quantity that can be imported from other countries—that we study in Chapter 9.

To make a production quota effective—to successfully limit the quantity supplied—quotas must be allocated to each producer that sum to the market quota. Also, mechanisms must be used to prevent individual producers from exceeding their quotas.

An effective production quota (accompanied if needed by an import quota) decreases the quantity supplied below the equilibrium quantity. As a result, it raises the price. The higher price clearly damages the consumer, who pays more for a smaller quantity. Whether it benefits the producer depends on the elasticity of demand for the item. If the demand for the item subject to a quota is inelastic, the higher price brings an increase in total revenue and the producer gains. Not surprisingly, quotas are only used when demand is inelastic (see *Eye on the Global Economy*).

To see how consumers lose and producers gain and to see why a production quota is inefficient and unfair, we'll look at an example

■ Production Quota: An Example

To illustrate the effects of a production quota, we'll use the example of the market for dairy products in California. Markets in milk, both liquid and powder, cheese, and other dairy products are regulated by the California Department of Food and Agriculture. A production quota for the market is set and allocations are made to each producer that sum to the market quota.

EYE on the GLOBAL ECONOMY
Production Quotas

What do cranberries, peanuts, sugar, chicken, eggs, milk, cheese, and tobacco have in common?

The answer is that production quotas have been used, either in the past or in the present, to regulate the markets for these items. Each item has an inelastic demand, so if its quantity supplied can be restricted to below the equilibrium quantity, its price rises by a larger percentage than the percentage decrease in the quantity supplied. As a result, producers end up with a greater total revenue and producer surplus.

Consumers lose. The loss incurred by each consumer is too small to complain about, but with millions of consumers, the total loss is large.

Some of what consumers lose is deadweight loss, but most of the consumers' loss is the producers' gain. And because there are many fewer producers than consumers, each producer ends up with a gain that is large enough to be worth paying for in political contributions to legislators who vote to sustain the quotas.

Figure 7.9 illustrates this market. The demand curve, *D*, tells us the quantity demanded at each price and the supply curve, *S*, tells us the quantity supplied at each price.

Free Market Reference Point

In Figure 7.9(a), with no production quota, the equilibrium price is 10 cents per pound and the equilibrium quantity of dairy products is 60 billion pounds per year. The market is efficient because marginal benefit on the demand curve equals marginal cost on the supply curve, and total surplus, the sum of consumer surplus (green triangle) and producer surplus (blue triangle) is maximized.

The Market with an Effective Production Quota

Figure 7.9(b) illustrates the effects of a production quota in this market. The government sets a production quota for the market of 40 billion pounds per year and allocates quotas to each producer that total the same 40 billion pounds. For now, we will assume that no one produces more than the allocated quota so the quantity supplied in the market is the quota quantity of 40 billion pounds.

FIGURE 7.9

The Inefficiency of a Production Quota   MyEconLab Animation

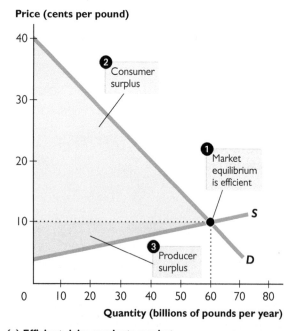

(a) Efficient dairy products market

(b) Inefficient dairy products market with production quota

In the market for dairy products:

❶ With no intervention, the market is competitive and the equilibrium price is 10 cents per pound and the equilibrium quantity of dairy products is 60 billion pounds per year.

❷ Consumer surplus plus ❸ producer surplus is maximized.

❹ The government imposes a production quota of 40 billion pounds per year.

❺ Consumer surplus shrinks, ❻ producer surplus grows, and ❼ a deadweight loss arises.

With no quota, the market is efficient. With a quota, it is inefficient.

At this quantity supplied, if the price remained at 10 cents per pound, there would be a shortage of dairy products. A shortage brings a rise in price and the market would achieve a new equilibrium at a price of 20 cents per pound.

At this smaller quantity and higher price, consumers are worse off. By how much they are worse off is shown by the shrinkage of consumer surplus.

Consumers lose, but dairy farmers gain. They produce a smaller quantity but sell it for a higher price. And the higher price more than counters the smaller quantity because the demand for dairy products is inelastic. Recall that when demand is inelastic, the percentage decrease in quantity is smaller than the percentage rise in price and a rise in price brings an incease in total revenue. You can see that total revenue increases from $6 billion to $8 billion. (Do the math and calculate the elasticity of demand between prices of 10 cents and 20 cents.)

Production Quota is Inefficient

The farmers' gain is smaller than the consumers' loss—the outcome is inefficient and a deadweight loss arises. The decreased quantity is valued on the demand curve more highly than its marginal cost on the supply curve. The area of the gray triangle shows the deadweight loss.

Production Quota is Unfair

A production quota is unfair on both views of fairness: It delivers an unfair *result* and imposes unfair *rules*. The result is unfair because well-off farmers benefit and consumers lose. A production quota imposes an unfair rule because it blocks voluntary exchange. Farmers are willing to produce a larger quantity and consumers are willing to buy the larger quantity, but they are not permitted by the quota to do so.

EYE on YOUR LIFE
Price Ceilings and Price Floors You Encounter

MyEconLab Critical Thinking Exercise

Price ceilings and price floors operate in many of the markets in which you trade, and they require you to take a stand as a citizen and voter.

Unless you live in New York City, you're not likely to live in a rent controlled house or apartment. Because economists have explained the unwanted effects of rent ceilings that you've learned about in this chapter, this type of market intervention is now rare.

But you run into a price ceiling almost every time you use a freeway.

The zero price for using a freeway is a type of price ceiling. The next time you're stuck in traffic and moving at a crawl, think about how a free market in road use would cut the congestion and allow you to zip along.

In Singapore, a transponder on your dashboard keeps track of your road use in dollars and cents as you drive around the city. The price varies with the time of day, the traffic density, and where in the city you are. As a result, you and other drivers are never stuck in slow-moving traffic.

You encounter a price floor in the labor market. Have you wanted a job and been willing and available to work, but unable to get hired? Would you have taken a job for a slightly lower wage if one had been available?

You also encounter price floors in markets for food. You pay more for tomatoes, sugar, oranges, and many other food items than the minimum cost of producing them.

Develop your own policy position on price floors and price ceilings.

MyEconLab Study Plan 7.3
Key Terms Quiz
Solutions Video

CHECKPOINT 7.3

Explain how a production quota works and why it brings a higher price and is inefficient and unfair.

Practice Problems

Figure 1 shows the market for cranberries.

1. What are the equilibrium price and quantity of cranberries? Is the market for cranberries efficient?

2. If the government sets a production quota of 20 billion pounds, what is the quantity of cranberries produced, the quantity demanded, and the price of a pound of cranberries?

3. If the government sets a production quota of 20 billion pounds, is the market for cranberries efficient? What is the deadweight loss created? Who gains and who loses from the production quota? Could the production quota be regarded as being fair?

In the News

Conditions sour for California's dairy farmers
California dairy farmers are being hit by falling prices, drought, and rising feed costs.

Source: *The Wall Street Journal*, October 8, 2015

How would the events in the news clip affect a competitive market in milk? How would a production quota change the effects of these events?

Solutions to Practice Problems

1. The equilibrium price is 10 cents a pound; the equilibrium quantity is 60 billion pounds. The market is efficient—marginal benefit equals marginal cost.

2. The production quota decreases the quantity supplied and the quantity demanded to 20 billion pounds and the price is 30 cents per pound (Figure 2).

3. With the production quota, the market is not efficient because at the quantity produced, the marginal benefit (on the demand curve) exceeds the marginal cost (on the supply curve). The deadweight loss equals $5 billion, of which $4 billion is a decrease in consumer surplus and $1 billion is a decrease in producer surplus. But another $2 billion of consumer surplus is transferred to producers, so consumer surplus decreases by $6 billion. Consumers lose. The change in producer surplus is an increase of $1 billion. Farmers gain. The outcome is unfair on both views of fairness unless farmers are poorer than consumers, in which case it might be fair to boost farmers' incomes.

Solution to In the News

In a competitive milk market, drought and rising feed costs would decrease supply. With no other changes, the price would rise and the equilibrium quantity would decrease. Because the price of milk fell, the demand for California milk must have decreased, most likely from competition with other sources of supply. An effective production quota combined with an import quota would have prevented or lessened the fall in price, but it would not have avoided the decrease in supply caused by drought and rising feed prices.

FIGURE 1

Price (cents per pound)

Quantity (billions of pounds per year)

FIGURE 2

Price (cents per pound)

Quantity (billions of pounds per year)

CHAPTER SUMMARY

Key Points

1. **Explain how a price ceiling works, and why a rent ceiling creates a housing shortage and is inefficient and unfair.**

   - A price ceiling set above the equilibrium price has no effects.
   - A price ceiling set below the equilibrium price creates a shortage and increased search activity or a black market.
   - A price ceiling is inefficient and unfair.
   - A rent ceiling is an example of a price ceiling.

2. **Explain how a price floor works, and why the minimum wage creates unemployment and is inefficient and unfair.**

   - A price floor set below the equilibrium price has no effects.
   - A price floor set above the equilibrium price creates a surplus and increased search activity or illegal trading.
   - A price floor is inefficient and unfair.
   - A minimum wage is an example of a price floor.

3. **Explain how a production quota works, and why it brings a higher price and is inefficient and unfair.**

   - A production quota decreases the quantity produced, decreases the quantity consumed, and raises the price.
   - A production quota is used in the market for an item that has an inelastic demand.
   - A production quota benefits the producer but costs the consumer more than the producer gains—it creates a deadweight loss.
   - A production quota is inefficient and unfair.

Key Terms

MyEconLab Key Terms Quiz

Black market, 171
Minimum wage law, 177
Price cap, 170

Price ceiling, 170
Price floor, 176
Production quota, 183

Rent ceiling, 170
Search activity, 172

CHAPTER CHECKPOINT

Study Plan Problems and Applications

Table 1 shows the demand and supply schedules for on-campus housing. Use Table 1 to work Problems **1** to **3**.

TABLE 1

Rent (dollars per month)	Quantity demanded	Quantity supplied
	(rooms)	
500	2,500	2,000
550	2,250	2,000
600	2,000	2,000
650	1,750	2,000
700	1,500	2,000
750	1,250	2,000

1. If the college puts a rent ceiling on rooms of $650 a month, what is the rent, how many rooms are rented, and is the on-campus housing market efficient?

2. If the college puts a strictly enforced rent ceiling on rooms of $550 a month, what is the rent, how many rooms are rented, and is the on-campus housing market efficient? Explain why or why not.

3. Suppose that with a strictly enforced rent ceiling on rooms of $550 a month, a black market develops. How high could the black market rent be and would the on-campus housing market be fair? Explain your answer.

Table 2 shows the demand and supply schedules for student workers at on-campus venues. Use Table 2 to work Problems **4** to **6**.

TABLE 2

Wage rate (dollars per hour)	Quantity demanded	Quantity supplied
	(student workers)	
10.00	600	300
10.50	500	350
11.00	400	400
11.50	300	450
12.00	200	500
12.50	100	550

4. If the college introduces a minimum wage of $10.50 an hour, how many students are employed at on-campus venues and how many are unemployed?

5. If the college introduces a strictly enforced minimum wage of $11.50 an hour, how many students are employed, how many are unemployed, and what is the lowest wage at which some students would be willing to work?

6. If the college introduces a strictly enforced minimum wage of $11.50 an hour, who gains and who loses from the minimum wage, and is the campus labor market efficient or fair?

Table 3 shows the demand and supply schedules for mushrooms. Use Table 3 to work Problems **7** and **8**.

TABLE 3

Price (dollars per pound)	Quantity demanded	Quantity supplied
	(pounds per week)	
1.00	4,500	0
2.00	4,000	1,000
3.00	3,500	2,000
4.00	3,000	3,000
5.00	2,500	4,000
6.00	2,000	5,000

7. Suppose that the government introduces a production quota for mushrooms and sets it at 3,000 pounds per week. What is the market price of mushrooms? Calculate the producer surplus and the deadweight loss created?

8. Suppose that the government introduces a production quota for mushrooms and sets it at 2,000 pounds a week. What is the market price of mushrooms? Calculate the producer surplus and the deadweight loss? Who gains and who loses?

Use the following news clip to work Problems **9** and **10**.

Venezuelans organize to overcome food shortages

The government of Venezuela controls the price of food and there are shortages of milk, rice, coffee, pasta, sugar, corn flour, and cooking oil. Eggs have disappeared from store shelves. While people stand in line for milk, cheese and yogurt are abundant. People who buy milk at the low price either sell it for a profit or exchange it for food items that other families stand in line to buy.

Source: www.teleSURtv.net/english, November 27, 2015

9. Are Venezuela's price controls price floors or price ceilings? Draw a graph to illustrate the shortages of food created by the price controls.

10. Explain how Venezuela's price controls have changed consumer surplus, producer surplus, total surplus, and the deadweight loss in the markets for milk and cheese. Draw a graph to illustrate your answer.

 11. Read *Eye on Price Regulation* on p. 181 and explain why a mismatch between intention and outcome is inevitable if a price regulation seeks to block the law of market forces.

Instructor Assignable Problems and Applications

MyEconLab Homework, Quiz, or Test if assigned by instructor

1. Suppose that Congress caps executive pay at a level below the equilibrium.

   a. Explain how the quantity of executives demanded, the quantity supplied, and executive pay will change, and explain why the outcome is inefficient.

   b. Draw a graph of the market for corporate executives. On your graph, show the market equilibrium, the pay cap, the quantity of executives supplied and the quantity demanded at the pay cap, and the deadweight loss created. Also show the highest pay that an executive might be offered in a black market.

Use the following information to work Problems 2 to 4.

Concerned about the political fallout from rising gas prices, the U.S. government imposes a price ceiling of $3.00 a gallon on gasoline.

2. Explain how the market for gasoline would react to this price ceiling if the oil-producing nations increased production and drove the equilibrium price of gasoline to $2.50 a gallon. Would the U.S. gasoline market be efficient?

3. Explain how the market for gasoline would react to this price ceiling if a global shortage of oil sent the equilibrium price of gasoline to $3.50 a gallon. Would the U.S. gasoline market be efficient?

4. Under what conditions would the price ceiling create lines at the pumps?

5. Suppose the government introduced a ceiling on lawyers' fees.

   a. How would the amount of work done by lawyers, the consumer surplus of people who hire lawyers, and the producer surplus of law firms change?

   b. Would this fee ceiling result in an efficient and fair use of resources? Why or why not?

Use the following information to work Problems 6 and 7.

New York seals deal on $15 minimum fast-food wage
"Raising the minimum wage to $15 an hour will add fairness to our economy and bring dignity and respect to 2.2 million people, many of whom have been forced to live in poverty for too long," said Governor Andrew Cuomo. Between 135,000 and 200,000 workers will see their hourly wage rise gradually to $15 by the end of 2018 in New York City and by 2021 in the rest of the state.
Source: CNNMoney, September 11, 2015

6. On a graph of the market for fast-food workers, show the effect of the $15 an hour minimum wage on employment of fast-food workers.

7. Explain the effects of the higher minimum wage on the workers' surplus and the firms' surplus. Will the $15 wage bring fairness, dignity, and respect?

Use the following information to work Problems 8 and 9.

Canada's dairy industry is a rich, closed club
If you want to be a dairy farmer, you buy a plot of land and some cows and start to sell your milk. Not in Canada. There, farmers must buy a quota to produce a set amount of milk. The situation is similar in the markets for chicken and eggs.
Source: The Globe and Mail, June 25, 2015

8. Draw a graph to illustrate the Canadian market for milk. With a production quota, show the quantity of milk produced, the price, consumer surplus, producer surplus, and the deadweight loss created.

9. In the Canadian market for milk with a production quota, explain what happens if a drought decreases supply.

Multiple Choice Quiz

1. A rent ceiling creates a _____ of housing if it _____ the equilibrium rent.
   A. surplus; is less than
   B. shortage; is less than
   C. surplus; exceeds
   D. shortage; exceeds

2. A price ceiling imposed below the equilibrium price _____.
   A. creates a black market in which the price might equal or exceed the equilibrium price
   B. creates a black market in which the price equals the price ceiling
   C. leads to increased search activity, which reduces the shortage of the good
   D. increases the demand for the good, which makes the shortage even larger

3. A price ceiling is _____ if it is set _____ the market equilibrium price.
   A. efficient and fair; below
   B. unfair but efficient; equal to
   C. efficient and unfair; above
   D. inefficient and unfair; below

4. A price floor influences the outcome of a market if it is _____.
   A. set below the equilibrium price
   B. set above the equilibrium price
   C. an incentive for buyers to increase demand for the good
   D. an incentive for sellers to decrease supply of the good

5. A minimum wage set above the market equilibrium wage rate _____.
   A. increases both employment and the quantity of labor supplied
   B. decreases unemployment and raises the wage rate of those employed
   C. raises the wage rate of those employed and increases the supply of jobs
   D. increases unemployment and decreases employment

6. A minimum wage is _____.
   A. efficient if the wage paid rises and more people look for jobs
   B. inefficient if workers' surplus decreases and firms' surplus increases
   C. inefficient if job search increases and total surplus decreases
   D. efficient if workers' surplus increases and firms' surplus decreases

7. A production quota set below the market equilibrium quantity _____.
   A. increases the price, increases producer surplus, and is inefficient
   B. creates a shortage and increases farmers' total revenue but is unfair
   C. is inefficient because farmers' marginal cost exceeds consumers' marginal benefit
   D. is efficient because farmers' surplus increases

8. An effective production quota for peanuts with no imports of peanuts will _____.
   A. lower the peanut growers' costs, raise the market price of peanuts, and decrease consumer surplus
   B. raise the price of peanuts, which will decrease the demand for peanuts
   C. make the peanut market more efficient if the demand for peanuts is inelastic
   D. decrease the quantity of peanuts produced, decrease the quantity consumed, and increase the total surplus from peanuts

Does Congress decide who
pays the taxes?

Taxes

**When you have completed your study of this chapter,
you will be able to**

1 Explain how taxes change prices and quantities, are shared by
buyers and sellers, and create inefficiency.

2 Explain how income taxes and Social Security taxes change wage
rates and employment, are shared by employers and workers,
and create inefficiency.

3 Review ideas about the fairness of the tax system and the tradeoff
between efficiency and fairness.

MyEconLab Big Picture Video

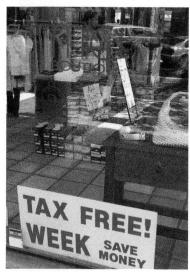

Does "tax free" really mean that the seller pays the tax?

Tax incidence
The division of the tax between the buyer and the seller.

8.1 TAXES ON BUYERS AND SELLERS

Almost every time you buy something—a late-night order of chow mein, a plane ticket, a tank of gasoline—you pay a tax. On some items, you pay a sales tax that is added to the advertised price. On other items, you pay an excise tax—often at a high rate like the tax on gasoline—that is included in the advertised price.

But do you really pay these taxes? When a tax is added to the advertised price, isn't it obvious that *you* pay the tax? Isn't the price higher than it otherwise would be by an amount equal to the tax?

What about a tax that is buried in the price, such as that on gasoline? Who pays that tax? Does the seller just pass on the full amount of the tax to you, the buyer? Or does the seller pay the tax by taking a lower price and leaving the price you pay unchanged?

To answer these questions, let's suppose that TIFS, the Tax Illegal File Sharing lobby, has persuaded the government to collect a $10 tax on every new smartphone and to use the tax revenue to compensate artists. But an argument is raging between those who claim that the buyer benefits from using the smartphone and should pay the tax and those who claim that the seller profits and should pay the tax.

■ Tax Incidence

Tax incidence is the division of the tax between the buyer and the seller. We're going to find the incidence of a $10 tax on smartphones with two different taxes: a tax on the buyer and a tax on the seller.

Figure 8.1 shows the market for smartphones. With no tax, the equilibrium price is $100 and the equilibrium quantity is 5,000 smartphones a week.

When a good is taxed, it has two prices: a price that excludes the tax and a price that includes the tax. Buyers respond only to the price that includes the tax, because that is the price they pay. Sellers respond only to the price that excludes the tax, because that is the price they receive. The tax is like a wedge between these two prices.

Figure 8.1(a) shows what happens if the government taxes the buyer. The tax doesn't change the buyer's willingness and ability to pay. The demand curve, *D*, tells us the *total* amount that buyers are willing and able to pay. Because buyers must pay $10 to the government on each item bought, the curve that tells us what buyers are willing to pay to sellers is the red curve labeled *D − tax*. This curve lies $10 *below* the blue demand curve.

Market equilibrium occurs where the red curve *D − tax* intersects the supply curve, *S*. Buyers pay the equilibrium net-of-tax price $95 plus the $10 tax: $105 per smartphone. Sellers receive the net-of-tax price $95 per smartphone. The government collects a tax revenue of $10 on each of the 2,000 smartphones, or $20,000 (shown by the purple rectangle).

Figure 8.1(b) shows what happens if the government taxes the seller. The tax acts like an increase in the suppliers' cost, so supply decreases and the supply curve shifts to the red curve labeled *S + tax*. This curve tells us what sellers are willing to accept, given that they must pay the government $10 on each item sold. The red curve, *S + tax*, lies $10 *above* the blue supply curve.

Market equilibrium occurs where the red curve *S + tax* intersects the demand curve, *D*. Buyers pay the equilibrium price $105 per smartphone. Sellers receive the net-of-tax price $95, and the government collects a tax revenue of $20,000.

■ **FIGURE 8.1**

A Tax on Smartphones

(a) Government taxes buyer

(b) Government taxes seller

❶ With no tax on smartphones, the price is $100 and 5,000 smartphones a week are bought—in both parts of the figure.

❷ In part (a), a $10 tax on buyers shifts the demand curve down to the red curve *D − tax* and in part (b), a $10 tax on sellers shifts the supply curve up to the red curve *S + tax*.

In both parts of the figure:

❸ The price paid by buyers rises to $105—an increase of $5;

❹ The price received by sellers falls to $95—a decrease of $5;

❺ The quantity bought decreases to 2,000 smartphones a week; and

❻ The government collects tax revenue of $20,000 a week—the purple rectangle.

In both cases, the tax is split equally between the buyer and the seller—each pays $5 per smartphone.

In both cases, the buyer and the seller split the $10 tax and pay $5 each. You can now see that the argument about making the buyer pay or the seller pay is futile. The price the buyer pays, the price the seller receives, and the tax revenue the government receives are the same, regardless of who the government taxes.

In this example, the tax is shared equally between the buyer and the seller. But in most cases, the tax will be shared unequally and might even fall entirely on one side of the market. We'll explore what determines the incidence of a tax, but first let's see how a tax creates inefficiency.

■ Taxes and Efficiency

You've seen that resources are used efficiently when marginal benefit equals marginal cost. You've also seen that a tax places a wedge between the price the buyer pays and the price the seller receives equal to the tax. The buyer's price equals marginal benefit and the seller's price equals marginal cost, so a tax puts a wedge between marginal benefit and marginal cost. The tax decreases the equilibrium quantity to less than the efficient quantity and creates a deadweight loss.

■ Tax Burden

Excess burden
The deadweight loss from a tax.

A tax creates a loss of consumer surplus and producer surplus—a deadweight loss. The amount of tax paid plus the deadweight loss that results from the tax is called the *burden of the tax.* And the deadweight loss is called the **excess burden** of the tax. Because the government uses the tax revenue to provide goods and services that people value, only the excess burden measures the inefficiency of a tax

Figure 8.2 shows the inefficiency of a tax. We'll assume that the government taxes the seller. In part (a), with no tax, marginal benefit equals marginal cost and the market is efficient. In part (b), with a tax, marginal benefit exceeds marginal cost. Consumer surplus and producer surplus shrink. Part of each surplus goes to the government as tax revenue—the purple area—and part becomes a deadweight loss—the gray area.

In this example, the excess burden is large. You can see how large by calculating the area of the deadweight loss triangle. This area equals ($10 × 3,000) ÷ 2, which is $15,000 per week. The tax revenue is $20,000 per week, so the excess burden of the tax is 75 percent of the tax revenue.

■ Incidence, Inefficiency, and Elasticity

In the example of a $10 tax on smartphones, buyers and sellers split the tax equally and the excess burden is large. What determines how the tax is split and the size of its excess burden?

FIGURE 8.2

Taxes and Efficiency

MyEconLab Animation

(a) Efficient outcome

(b) Burden of tax

❶ The market is efficient with marginal benefit equal to marginal cost. Total surplus—the sum of ❷ consumer surplus (green area) and ❸ producer surplus (blue area)—is at its maximum possible level.

A $10 tax drives a wedge between ❶ marginal benefit and ❷ marginal cost. ❸ Consumer surplus and ❹ producer surplus shrink by the amount of the ❺ tax revenue plus the ❻ deadweight loss. The deadweight loss is the excess burden of the tax.

The incidence of a tax and its excess burden depend on the elasticities of demand and supply in the following ways:

- For a given elasticity of supply, the more inelastic the demand for the good, the larger is the share of the tax paid by the buyer.
- For a given elasticity of demand, the more inelastic the supply of the good, the larger is the share of the tax paid by the seller.
- The excess burden is smaller, the more inelastic is demand *or* supply.

■ Incidence, Inefficiency, and the Elasticity of Demand

MyEconLab Concept Video

To see how the division of a tax between the buyer and the seller and the size of the excess burden depend on the elasticity of demand, we'll look at two extremes.

Perfectly Inelastic Demand: Buyer Pays and Efficient

Figure 8.3(a) shows the market for insulin, a vital daily medication of diabetics. Demand is perfectly inelastic at 100,000 doses a week, as shown by the vertical demand curve. With no tax, the price is $2 a dose. A tax of 20¢ a dose raises the price to $2.20, but the equilibrium quantity does not change. The tax leaves the price received by sellers unchanged but raises the price paid by buyers by the entire tax. Marginal benefit equals marginal cost, so the outcome is efficient and no deadweight loss arises.

Perfectly Elastic Demand: Seller Pays and Inefficient

Figure 8.3(b) shows the market for pink marker pens. Demand is perfectly elastic at $1 a pen, as shown by the horizontal demand curve. If pink pens are less expensive than other pens, everyone uses pink. If pink pens are more expensive than other pens, no one uses a pink pen. With no tax, the price of a pink pen is $1 and the quantity is 4,000 pens a week. A tax of 10¢ a pen leaves the price at $1 a pen,

FIGURE 8.3

Incidence, Inefficiency, and the Elasticity of Demand

MyEconLab Animation

(a) Inelastic demand

(b) Elastic demand

In part (a), the demand for insulin is perfectly inelastic. A tax of 20¢ a dose raises the price by 20¢, and the buyer pays all the tax. But marginal benefit still equals marginal cost, so the outcome is efficient.

In part (b), the demand for pink marker pens is perfectly elastic. A tax of 10¢ a pen lowers the price received by the seller by 10¢, and the seller pays all the tax. Marginal benefit exceeds marginal cost, so the outcome is inefficient. The deadweight loss is the excess burden of the tax and measures its inefficiency.

but the equilibrium quantity decreases to 1,000 pens a week. The price paid by the buyer is unchanged, and the seller pays the entire tax. The outcome is inefficient because marginal benefit exceeds marginal cost and a deadweight loss arises.

◼ Incidence, Inefficiency, and the Elasticity of Supply

To see how the division of a tax between the buyer and the seller depends on the elasticity of supply, we'll again look at two extremes.

Perfectly Inelastic Supply: Seller Pays and Efficient

Figure 8.4(a) shows the market for spring water that flows at a constant rate that can't be controlled. Supply is perfectly inelastic at 100,000 bottles a week, as shown by the vertical supply curve. With no tax, the price is 50¢ a bottle and the 100,000 bottles that flow from the spring are bought. A tax of 5¢ a bottle leaves the quantity unchanged at 100,000 bottles a week. Buyers are willing to buy 100,000 bottles a week only if the price is 50¢ a bottle. The price remains at 50¢ a bottle, but the tax lowers the price received by the seller by 5¢ a bottle. The seller pays the entire tax.

Because marginal benefit equals marginal cost, there is no deadweight loss and the outcome is efficient.

Perfectly Elastic Supply: Buyer Pays and Inefficient

Figure 8.4(b) shows the market for sand from which computer-chip makers extract silicon. Supply of this sand is perfectly elastic at a price of 10¢ a pound as shown by the horizontal supply curve. With no tax, the price is 10¢ a pound and 5,000 pounds a week are bought. A tax of 1¢ a pound raises the price to 11¢ a pound and the quantity decreases to 3,000 pounds a week. The buyer pays the entire tax.

Because marginal benefit exceeds marginal cost, a deadweight loss arises and the outcome is inefficient.

◼ **FIGURE 8.4**

Incidence, Inefficiency, and the Elasticity of Supply   MyEconLab Animation

In part (a), the supply of bottled spring water is perfectly inelastic. A tax of 5¢ a bottle lowers the price received by the seller by 5¢ a bottle, and the seller pays all the tax. Marginal benefit equals marginal cost, so the outcome is efficient.

In part (b), the supply of sand is perfectly elastic. A tax of 1¢ a pound increases the price by 1¢ a pound, and the buyer pays all the tax. Marginal benefit exceeds marginal cost, so the outcome is inefficient. The deadweight loss is the excess burden of the tax and measures its inefficiency.

(a) Inelastic supply

(b) Elastic supply

CHECKPOINT 8.1

Explain how taxes change prices and quantities, are shared by buyers and sellers, and create inefficiency.

MyEconLab Study Plan 8.1
Key Terms Quiz
Solutions Video

Practice Problems

Figure 1 shows the market for basketballs, when basketballs are not taxed.

1. If buyers of basketballs are taxed $6 a ball, what price does the buyer pay and how many basketballs do they buy? What is the tax revenue collected?

2. If sellers of basketballs are taxed $6 a ball, what price does the seller receive and how many basketballs do they sell? What is the tax revenue collected?

3. If basketballs are taxed at $6 a ball, what is the excess burden of the tax? Is the demand for basketballs or the supply of basketballs more inelastic? Explain your answer.

In the News

Gas tax increases by 7 cents in Washington State
Washington State gas taxes will rise by 7¢ a gallon now and by a further 4.9¢ a gallon next summer.

Source: *The Seattle Times*, August 1, 2015

If the demand for gasoline is inelastic and the supply of gasoline is elastic, who will pay more of the increase in Washington's gas tax: drivers or the gasoline companies? If there is a big switch to natural gas for big trucks, how will the tax incidence change?

Solutions to Practice Problems

1. With a $6 tax on buyers, the demand curve shifts downward by $6 a ball as shown in Figure 2. The price that the buyer pays is $16 a basketball and 8 million basketballs a week are bought. The tax revenue is $6 × 8 million, which is $48 million a week (the purple rectangle in Figure 2).

2. With a $6 tax on sellers, the supply curve shifts upward by $6 a ball as shown in Figure 3. The price that the seller receives is $10 a basketball and 8 million basketballs a week are sold. The tax revenue is $6 × 8 million, which is $48 million a week (the purple rectangle in Figure 3).

3. The excess burden of the tax is $12 million. Excess burden equals the deadweight loss, the area of the gray triangle, which is (4 million × $6) ÷ 2. The $6 tax increases the price paid by buyers by $1 and lowers the price received by sellers by $5. The seller pays the larger share of the tax because the supply of basketballs is more inelastic than the demand for basketballs.

Solution to In the News

If the demand for gasoline is inelastic and supply is elastic, drivers will pay more of the increase in Washington's gas tax than the gasoline companies will pay. Although the demand for gasoline is inelastic, the availability of natural gas and big trucks switching to natural gas makes the demand for gasoline (and diesel) less inelastic, so the share of the tax paid by drivers will fall and the share paid by the gasoline companies will rise.

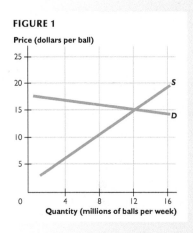

FIGURE 1

Price (dollars per ball)

Quantity (millions of balls per week)

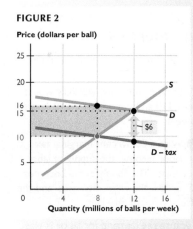

FIGURE 2

Price (dollars per ball)

Quantity (millions of balls per week)

FIGURE 3

Price (dollars per ball)

Quantity (millions of balls per week)

8.2 INCOME TAXES AND SOCIAL SECURITY TAXES

Income taxes and Social Security taxes raise two-thirds of total U.S. government revenue (see *Eye on the U.S. Economy* on p. 199). Who pays these taxes? Are they efficient? Let's find out.

■ The Effects of the Income Tax

An income tax is a tax on the sellers of the services of the factors of production—labor, capital, and land. You've just seen that who pays a tax—the incidence of a tax—depends on the elasticities of demand and supply. These same elasticities also influence the inefficiency created by a tax.

The elasticities of demand and supply are different for each factor of production, so to determine the incidence and inefficiency of an income tax, we must examine its effects on each factor of production separately. Let's look first at the effects of the tax on labor income.

Tax on Labor Income

Figure 8.5 shows the demand curve, *LD*, and the supply curve, *LS*, in a competitive labor market. The equilibrium in this market, with no income tax, occurs when workers earn $19 an hour and work 40 hours a week. This equilibrium is efficient. Firms are willing to pay $19 an hour because that is their marginal gain

FIGURE 8.5

A Tax on Labor Income

With no income tax, workers would earn $19 an hour and work 40 hours a week.

❶ With a 20 percent marginal tax on labor income, the supply of labor decreases. The supply curve becomes *LS + tax*, the wage rate rises, and the after-tax wage rate falls.

Because the demand for labor is elastic and the supply of labor is inelastic, ❷ the tax paid by the employer is less than ❸ the tax paid by the worker.

The quantity of labor employed is less than the efficient quantity, so ❹ a deadweight loss arises.

EYE on the U.S. ECONOMY
Taxes in the United States Today

Federal, state, and local governments in the United States have the six main revenue sources shown in the figure.

Personal income taxes at 39 percent of total tax revenue and Social Security taxes at 25 percent together account for almost two thirds of all tax revenue.

These two taxes fall more on workers than on employers.

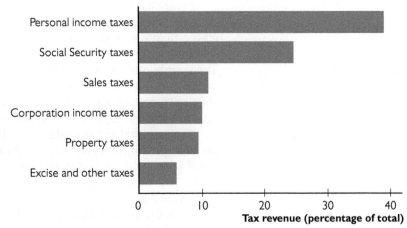

SOURCES OF DATA: Bureau of Economic Analysis, *National Income and Product Accounts*, Tables 1.1.5, 3.2, and 3.3.

from one extra hour of labor. And workers are willing to supply the 40th hour of labor for $19 because that compensates them for the marginal cost of working.

Before working out the effects of the income tax, look closely at the labor demand curve and labor supply curve. One point on the demand curve is the equilibrium 40 hours and $19 an hour. Another point on the demand curve is 35 hours and $20 an hour. The demand for labor is *elastic*. A small percentage rise in the wage rate from $19 to $20 brings a large percentage decrease in hours demanded from 40 to 35 per week. The demand for labor is elastic because firms can easily substitute machines for labor in many tasks. If labor costs too much, it gets replaced by a machine.

Now focus on the supply curve. Two points on that curve are the equilibrium 40 hours and $19 an hour and 35 hours and $16 an hour. The supply of labor is *inelastic*. It takes a large percentage fall in the wage rate from $19 to $16 to bring a large, but smaller percentage, decrease in hours supplied from 40 to 35 per week. The supply of labor is inelastic because most people have few good options other than to work for their income.

Now let's see what happens with a 20 percent marginal tax on labor income. The labor supply curve shifts to LS + tax. If workers are willing to supply the 40th hour a week for $19 with no tax, then with a 20 percent tax, they are willing to supply the 40th hour only if the wage is $23.75 an hour. That is, workers want to get the $19 they received before plus $4.75 (20 percent of $23.75) that they now must pay to the government.

The equilibrium wage rate rises to $20 an hour, but the after-tax wage rate falls to $16 an hour—the tax is $4 an hour. Employment decreases to 35 hours a week. The worker pays most of the tax—$3 compared to the $1 the employer pays—because the demand for labor is elastic and the supply of labor is inelastic. The tax creates a deadweight loss shown by the gray triangle.

Tax on Capital Income

Capital income in the form of interest on bonds and bank deposits is taxed at the normal income tax rate; and capital income in the form of dividends on stocks is taxed as a dividend at 15 percent and as corporate profit at the corporation income tax rate.

Figure 8.6 shows the demand curve, *KD*, and the supply curve, *KS*, in a competitive capital market. Both demand and supply are elastic, but supply is more elastic than demand. A firm's demand for capital is elastic for the same reason that the demand for labor is elastic: Many tasks can be done by machines or labor. The supply of capital is highly elastic, and in Figure 8.6 perfectly elastic, because capital is internationally mobile. In this example, the supply of capital is perfectly elastic at 6 percent a year. Firms can obtain all the capital they wish at this interest rate and with no capital income tax, they use $40 billion of capital.

Suppose that the tax rate on capital income is 40 percent. With a 40 percent tax on capital income, the supply of capital curve shifts to *KS + tax*. With the demand for capital curve *KD*, lenders want to receive an additional 4 percent interest to pay their capital income tax and are not willing to lend for less than 10 percent a year.

With the capital income tax, the quantity of capital decreases to $20 billion and the interest rate rises to 10 percent a year. Firms pay the entire capital income tax, and lenders receive the same after-tax interest rate as they receive in the absence of a capital income tax. The tax creates a deadweight loss shown by the gray triangle.

▨ **FIGURE 8.6**

A Tax on Capital Income   MyEconLab Animation

❶ The supply of capital is highly elastic (here perfectly elastic). With no tax on capital income, the interest rate is 6 percent a year and firms use $40 billion of capital.

❷ With a 40 percent tax on capital income, the supply curve becomes *KS + tax*. The interest rate rises to 10 percent a year, and ❸ firms pay the entire tax.

The quantity of capital used is less than the efficient quantity, so ❹ a deadweight loss arises.

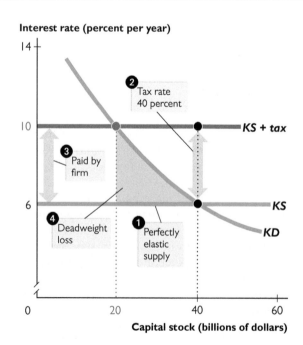

Tax on Income from Land and Other Unique Resources

Each plot of land is unique and its supply is perfectly inelastic. A fixed amount of the resource is supplied regardless of the rent offered for its use.

Figure 8.7(a) illustrates a tax on land income. In this example, a fixed 250 billion acres of land is supplied regardless of the rent. The equilibrium rent is determined by the demand for land. In this example, the equilibrium rent is $1,000 an acre.

When a 40 percent tax is imposed on rent income, landowners pay the entire tax. Their after-tax income falls to $600 an acre. The tax on income from land is efficient and it creates no deadweight loss (excess burden).

Figure 8.7(b) illustrates another example. Suppose that Bradley Cooper is willing to make three movies per year. His supply of services is perfectly inelastic at that quantity. Hollywood studios compete for his services, and the demand curve reflects the studios' willingness to pay for them. The equilibrium price is $20 million per movie. If Bradley pays a 40 percent tax on this income, he receives an after-tax income of $12 million per movie. Bradley pays the entire tax. The price paid by the studios is unaffected by this tax, and Bradley makes the same number of movies with the tax as without it. This tax creates no deadweight loss (excess burden).

▮ **FIGURE 8.7**

A Tax on Land Income and Other Unique Resource Income   MyEconLab Animation

(a) Land income tax

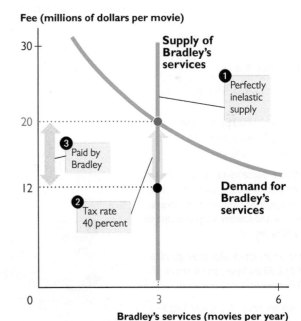

(b) Unique resource income tax

❶ In the markets for land and for the services of Bradley Cooper, supply is highly inelastic (here perfectly inelastic).

❷ With a 40 percent tax on income from these resources, the

equilibrium quantity and the market price remain unchanged,.

❸ Landowners and Bradley pay the entire tax. With no change in the quantity of the resource used, the tax is efficient.

■ The Social Security Tax

The law says that Social Security taxes fall equally on workers and employers. But does this outcome actually occur? You can probably guess that it does not. The Social Security tax is just like the other taxes you've studied in this chapter. Who pays the tax—its incidence—depends on the elasticities of demand and supply in the labor market and not on the wishes of Congress.

Figure 8.8 illustrates the effects of a Social Security tax. In this model labor market, with demand *LD* and supply *LS*, and with no taxes, the wage rate is $12 an hour and 4,000 people are employed. Congress now introduces a Social Security tax of $2.50 per hour and says that employers and workers must pay $1.25 each. Regardless of who sends the money to the government, the tax raises the cost of labor, lowers what workers earn, and lowers employment.

To find the new equilibrium, we find the level of employment at which the gap between what employers are willing to pay and workers are willing to accept equals the $2.50 tax. That employment level is 3,000 people at which employers pay $12.50 an hour and workers receive $10 an hour.

With the $2.50 Social Security tax, employers pay 50¢ an hour and workers pay $2 an hour. This division of the burden of the tax arises because the demand for labor is more elastic than the supply of labor.

The tax law could have required employers or workers to pay the entire tax or split the tax between them in any way, but the amounts of tax paid by workers and employers would remain the same. Congress cannot decide who pays the Social Security tax. When the laws of Congress come into conflict with the laws of economics, economics wins. Congress can't repeal the law of market forces!

FIGURE 8.8

The Social Security Tax   MyEconLab Animation

With no tax, 4,000 people are employed at a wage rate of $12 an hour.

❶ A Social Security tax of $2.50 per hour puts a wedge between what employers pay and what workers receive and lowers employment to 3,000 workers.

❷ Employers pay a higher wage rate of $12.50 an hour, an increase of 50¢ an hour.

❸ Workers receive a lower wage rate of $10 an hour, a decrease of $2 an hour.

❹ The government collects tax revenue shown by the purple rectangle.

Workers pay most of the tax because the demand for labor is more elastic than the supply of labor.

EYE on CONGRESS

MyEconLab Critical Thinking Exercise

Does Congress Decide Who Pays the Taxes?

Congress says that employers and workers pay the same Social Security tax contributions (7.65 percent each in 2015). But because the elasticity of demand for labor is much greater than the elasticity of supply of labor, workers end up paying most of the Social Security tax (see Figure 8.8).

Similarly, because the elasticity of demand for labor is greater than the elasticity of supply, the tax on wage income is paid mainly by workers. In contrast, the tax on capital income falls mainly on borrowers because the supply of capital is highly elastic.

But there is one thing that Congress can do to influence who pays a tax. It can pass a tax law (or tax rebate law) that doesn't impact the margin on which decisions turn.

Congress passed such a law in 2009 as part of the American Recovery and Reinvestment Act, an attempt to kick-start an economy that was struggling to recover from a global financial crisis. The tax rebate, called the "Making Work Pay Tax Credit" gave a single worker a $400 tax break and a couple $800.

A tax credit is a fixed reduction in the amount paid in personal income tax (in the current case, $400). For most people, a tax credit has no effect on their supply of labor. A worker gets the $400 tax credit regardless of how many hours he or she works. The tax credit doesn't influence the work-hours choice.

What influences the work-hours choice is the after-tax hourly wage rate, and that depends on the *marginal* income tax rate.

The figure illustrates the effects of a tax credit. The figure is similar to Figure 8.5 on p. 198. A 20 percent income tax rate shifts the labor supply curve from *LS* to *LS + tax*. With the demand for labor curve *LD*, the 20 percent tax raises the pre-tax wage rate by $1 to $20 per hour, lowers the after-tax wage rate by $3 to $16 per hour, and lowers the average workweek from 40 hours to 35 hours. With no tax credit, the worker pays 75 percent of the tax and the employer pays 25 percent.

Suppose that Congress now passes an Act that gives workers a tax credit of $30 a week. This credit has no effect on the supply of labor because it isn't a credit per hour worked. It is

Shaun Donovan, Director of the Office of Management and Budget

a fixed credit amount independent of the hours worked. Workers now pay only 68 percent of the tax, and employers pay 32 percent of the tax. Congress has worked around the elasticities! Unfortunately for workers, this tax credit is no longer available.

EYE on the PAST
The Origins and History of the U.S. Income Tax

1861 First federal income tax was 3 percent on all incomes above $800 a year.

1872 Income tax was repealed. (Tariffs on imports provided government revenue.)

1895 Income tax reestablished, but the Supreme Court ruled it unconstitutional.

1913 The 16th Amendment to the Constitution made the federal income tax legal.

1913–2015 The top rate increased to 91 percent in World War II, fell to 28 percent during the Reagan era, and today is 39.6 percent.

The bottom rate was below 5 percent until the 1940s when it increased

SOURCE OF DATA: Congressional Joint Committee on Taxation.

to 20 percent. In 1963, the bottom rate decreased and since then, it has fluctuated between 10 percent and

15 percent. Today's bottom rate is 10 percent.

EYE on YOUR LIFE
Tax Freedom Day

MyEconLab Critical Thinking Exercise

The Tax Foundation is an organization that seeks to promote a tax system that is as simple, transparent, and stable as possible, that minimizes excess burden, and that promotes trade and income growth.

Each year, to make the level of taxes as transparent as possible, the Tax Foundation calculates and publicizes "Tax Freedom Day"—the date by when an average U.S. citizen has worked long enough to pay the year's tax bill.

In 2015, "Tax Freedom Day" for Americans was April 10, the 100th day of the year.

The 100 days Americans had to work to pay their taxes in 2015 break

down as follows

Personal income taxes	39 days
Social Security taxes	25 days
Sales and excise taxes	17 days
Corporate income taxes	10 days
Property taxes	9 days

To work out your own "Tax Freedom Day," record all the taxes you pay in a year. Then express this number as a percentage of your annual income. Now find the number of days (as a percentage of 365) that this amount of tax represents and then work out your "Tax Freedom Day".

If you think taxes are high in the United States, think again.

Here are some "Tax Freedom Days" in a few other countries in 2015:

United Kingdom	May 28
Canada	June 6
Norway	July 4
Germany	July 8
Belgium	August 6

Of the advanced countries, only Australia has a similar tax freedom day to the United States. Down Under, they paid their taxes in 2015 by April 10.

The "Tax Freedom Day" is a dramatic way of drawing attention to high *average* taxes, but it is high *marginal* taxes that create inefficiency.

CHECKPOINT 8.2

MyEconLab Study Plan 8.2
Key Terms Quiz
Solutions Video

Explain how income taxes and Social Security taxes change wage rates and employment, are shared by employers and workers, and create inefficiency.

Practice Problems

1. Which income tax is the most efficient and which is the most inefficient, and why: a tax on labor income, a tax on capital income, or a tax on land income?

2. Comparing a tax on labor income, a tax on capital income, and a tax on land income, who pays more of each tax, and why?

3. Explain why Jordan Spieth pays his own Social Security tax and the PGA (the Professional Golfers' Association) pays none of it.

In the News

Want Arizona jobs? Phase out the state income tax
Arizona's state income taxes rank in the middle among U.S. states. The state can promote job creation by abolishing its income taxes.

Source: azcentral, November 30, 2015

Is the news clip correct? Explain the effects of abolishing the state personal income tax and corporation income tax. Will workers or employers benefit most?

Solutions to Practice Problems

1. The income tax that is most efficient is that on the income earned by the factor of production that has the lowest elasticity of demand or supply. The reason is that the deadweight loss from a tax (the excess burden) is smaller if the tax decreases the equilibrium quantity of the factor by a small amount. The supply of land is perfectly inelastic, while the supplies of labor and capital are elastic. So the tax on land income is the most efficient tax.
   For a similar reason, the income tax that is most *inefficient* is that on the income earned by the factor of production that has the *highest* elasticity of demand or supply. The supply of capital is highly elastic, perhaps perfectly elastic, so the tax on capital income is the most inefficient.

2. Who pays more of a tax depends on the relative elasticities of demand and supply. The demand for labor is more elastic than the supply of labor, so workers bear a larger share of the tax on labor income than employers. The supply of capital is more elastic than the demand for capital, so business owners pay more of the tax on capital income than savers and lenders pay. The supply of land is less elastic than the demand for land, so land owners pay more of the tax on land income than renters pay.

3. Jordan Spieth pays his Social Security tax and the PGA pays none of it because the supply of Jordan Spieth's services is (most likely) perfectly inelastic. The elasticities of demand and supply determine who pays the tax.

Solution to In the News

Because the demand for labor is elastic and the supply of labor is inelastic, most of the personal tax cut will benefit workers and it will increase employment. Because the supply of capital is perfectly elastic, most of the corporation tax cut will benefit employers and it, too, will create jobs. So the news clip is correct.

8.3   FAIRNESS AND THE BIG TRADEOFF

We've examined the incidence and the efficiency of different types of taxes. These topics have occupied most of this chapter because they are the issues about taxes that economics can address. But when political leaders debate tax issues, it is fairness, not just incidence and efficiency, that gets the most attention. Democrats complain that Republican tax cuts are unfair because they give the benefits of lower taxes to the rich. Republicans counter that because the rich pay most of the taxes, it is fair that they get most of the tax cuts. No easy answers are available to the questions about the fairness of taxes. Economists have proposed two principles of fairness to apply to a tax system:

- The benefits principle
- The ability-to-pay principle

■ The Benefits Principle

Benefits principle
The proposition that people should pay taxes equal to the benefits they receive from public goods and services.

The **benefits principle** is the proposition that people should pay taxes equal to the benefits they receive from public goods and services. This arrangement is fair because those who benefit most pay the most. The benefits principle makes tax payments and the consumption of government-provided services similar to private consumption expenditures. If taxes are based on the benefits principle, the people who enjoy the largest benefits pay the most for them.

To implement the benefits principle, it would be necessary to have an objective method of measuring each individual's marginal benefit from government-provided goods. In the absence of such a method, the principle can be used to justify a wide range of different taxes.

For example, the benefits principle can justify high gasoline taxes to pay for public highways. Here, the argument would be that those who value the highways most are the people who use them most, and so they should pay most of the cost of providing them. Similarly, the benefits principle can justify high taxes on alcoholic beverages and tobacco products. Here, the argument would be that those who drink and smoke the most place the largest burden on public health-care services and so they should pay the greater part of the cost of those services.

The benefits principle can also be used to justify a higher income tax on those who earn larger incomes. Here, the argument would be that the rich receive a disproportionately large share of the benefit from law and order and security, so they should pay the largest share of providing these services.

■ The Ability-to-Pay Principle

Ability-to-pay principle
The proposition that people should pay taxes according to how easily they can bear the burden.

The **ability-to-pay principle** is the proposition that people should pay taxes according to how easily they can bear the burden. A rich person can more easily bear the burden of providing public goods than a poor person can, so the rich should pay higher taxes than the poor. The ability-to-pay principle involves comparing people along two dimensions: horizontally and vertically.

Horizontal Equity

Horizontal equity
The requirement that taxpayers with the same ability to pay should pay the same taxes.

If taxes are based on ability to pay, taxpayers with the same ability to pay should pay the same taxes, a situation called **horizontal equity**. While horizontal equity is easy to agree with in principle, it is difficult to implement in practice. If two people are identical in every respect, horizontal equity is easy to apply. But how do we compare people who are similar but not identical? The greatest difficulty arises in working out differences in ability to pay that arise from the state of a person's health and from a person's family responsibilities. The U.S. income tax has many special deductions and other rules that aim to achieve horizontal equity.

Vertical Equity

Vertical equity is the requirement that taxpayers with a greater ability to pay bear a greater share of the taxes. This proposition easily translates into the requirement that people with higher incomes should pay higher taxes. But it doesn't tell us how steeply taxes should increase as income increases.

Vertical equity
The requirement that taxpayers with a greater ability to pay bear a greater share of the taxes.

■ Ability to Pay and Tax Progressivity

The relationship between tax rates and income levels—how steeply taxes increase as income increases—is called the degree of *tax progressivity*. To describe tax progressivity, we use two tax rate concepts, the *average* and the *marginal* tax rate.

An **average tax rate** is the percentage of income that is paid in tax. For example, if the tax paid on an income of $50,000 is $10,000, the average tax rate is 20 percent.

A **marginal tax rate** is the percentage of an *additional* dollar of income that is paid in tax. For example, if income increases from $50,000 to $50,001, and the tax paid increases from $10,000.00 to $10,000.30—increases by 30¢—the marginal tax rate is 30 percent.

If the *average* tax rate increases as income increases, the tax is called a **progressive tax**. When a tax is progressive, the marginal tax rate exceeds the average tax rate. To illustrate, think about the above example. At an income of $50,000, the average tax rate is 20 percent. When income rises above $50,000, the marginal tax rate is 30 percent. Suppose that the marginal rate remains at 30 percent for all income levels up to $100,000. Then at $100,000, the average tax rate is 25 percent, an average of 20 percent on the first $50,000 and 30 percent on the second $50,0000.

A progressive tax contrasts with a **proportional tax**, which has the same average tax rate at *all* income levels. When a tax is proportional, the marginal tax rate equals the average tax rate.

A third possibility is a **regressive tax**, which has an average tax rate that decreases as income increases.

Should taxes be progressive, proportional, or regressive? All of these arrangements have higher-income people paying higher taxes, so they all satisfy the basic idea of vertical equity. But most people think that vertical equity can only be achieved with a progressive income tax. And the U.S. federal income tax code reflects this view of fairness as you can see in *Eye on the U.S. Economy* (p. 208).

Average tax rate
The percentage of income that is paid in tax.

Marginal tax rate
The percentage of an additional dollar of income that is paid in tax.

Progressive tax
A tax whose average rate increases as income increases.

Proportional tax
A tax whose average rate is constant at *all* income levels.

Regressive tax
A tax whose average rate decreases as income increases.

■ The Big Tradeoff and Alternative Tax Proposals

Questions about the fairness of taxes conflict with efficiency questions and create the *big tradeoff* that you met in Chapter 6. The taxes that generate the greatest deadweight loss are those on the income from capital. But most capital is owned by a relatively small number of people who have the greatest ability to pay taxes. So a conflict arises between efficiency and fairness. We want a tax system that is efficient, in the sense that it raises the revenue that the government needs to provide public goods and services, but we want a tax system that shares the burden of providing these goods and services fairly.

EYE on the U.S. ECONOMY

The Progressive Income Tax

The U.S. federal income tax is progressive. The average tax rate rises with income and the marginal rate exceeds the average rate. The table and the figure illustrate these facts. The table lists the marginal tax rates and the graph shows the average and marginal tax rates.

Using the numbers in the table, we can calculate the tax paid by a person who earns $50,000 a year. Taxable income is $39,700, which is total income minus deductions. The tax paid is 10 percent of the first $9,225 of taxable income ($923) plus 15 percent of the next $28,225 ($4,234) plus 25 percent of the remaining $2,250 ($563). The total tax equals $5,720, which is 11.4 percent of $50,000. The average tax rate is 11.4 percent.

You can see how the average tax rate rises with income by looking at someone who earns $100,000 a

Taxable income (dollars)	Marginal tax rate (percent)
$0 to $9,225	10.0
$9,226 to $37,450	15.0
$37,451 to $90,750	25.0
$90,751 to $189,300	28.0
$189,301 to $411,500	33.0
$411,501 to $413,200	35.0
$413,201 or more	39.6

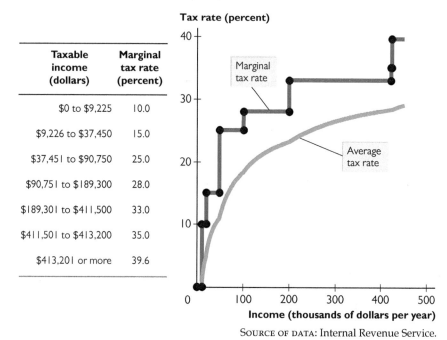

SOURCE OF DATA: Internal Revenue Service.

year. For this person, the tax paid on the first $50,000 is the same as for someone who earns that amount. But the taxes paid on the next $50,000

are $12,500—a 25 percent marginal tax rate. The total tax equals $18,219, which is 18.2 percent of $100,000. The average tax rate is 18.2 percent.

Our tax system is an evolving compromise that juggles these two goals. Part of that evolution is an ongoing conversation about reform proposals. Two of these proposals are

- A flat tax
- The FairTax

A Flat Tax

Flat tax
A tax system with a constant average and marginal tax rate: A proportional tax.

A **flat tax** is a tax system with a constant average and marginal rate. It is a proportional tax.

Eight U.S. states—Colorado, Illinois, Indiana, Massachusetts, Michigan, North Carolina, Pennsylvania, and Utah—tax household incomes at a single rate. Flat tax plans have been proposed for the U.S. federal income tax, but the idea has never had broad support.

The idea has received more support in some Eastern European countries—Albania, Bulgaria, Estonia, Latvia, Lithuania, Macedonia, Romania, Russia,

Slovakia, and Ukraine—where some form of flat tax has been introduced.

You've seen that all taxes are inefficient: They create deadweight loss. A flat tax is less inefficient than a progressive tax because the top tax rate is lower with a flat tax. So compared with a progressive tax, a flat tax strengthens the incentive to work, save, and invest. These productive activities increase income and boost the pace at which incomes grow.

The efficiency gain from a flat tax comes at the cost of placing a larger tax burden on people with low and average incomes and lessening the burden on those with the highest incomes. So the flat tax chooses a point on the big tradeoff that is more efficient but less fair than our current progressive tax system.

The second tax proposal that we examine seeks to replicate the efficiency of a flat tax while remaining a progressive tax and being as fair as our current taxes.

The FairTax

The **FairTax** is a proposal considered by the United States Congress in 1999 to tax the purchase of all consumption goods and services above the poverty level. It is a proposal for a radical reform of the entire U.S. federal tax system. All current federal taxes—personal and corporate income taxes, capital gains taxes, payroll taxes (including Social Security and Medicare taxes), gift taxes, and estate taxes—would be abolished. These taxes would be replaced by a single tax, initially at a 23 percent rate, on the purchase of all new goods and services for personal consumption.

The current federal tax is mainly a tax on income. Income is the *tax base*. The tax base of the FairTax is consumption expenditure, not income. People choose how to allocate their income between consumption and saving. Because the FairTax hits only consumption expenditure, it strengthens the incentive to save. And increased saving finances increased investment in productive business activities, which brings increased job opportunities and incomes. So the FairTax has the efficiency properties of the flat tax.

The "fair" component of the FairTax is that every household receives a monthly payment from the federal government equal to the tax on purchases up to the poverty level. In 2015, the poverty level for a family of two adults and two children was $24,250 per year, so a 23 percent tax on consumption at this level is $5,578 a year or $465 per month.

This monthly payment means that at low incomes, the FairTax is a progressive tax—the average tax rate increases with income. Families with incomes up to the poverty level pay no tax. And families with incomes of double the poverty level who spend all their income on consumption and have no saving pay an average tax equal to 11.5 percent of their income—the average of zero percent on the first $24,250 and 23 percent on the second $24,250.

The FairTax takes an increasing percentage of consumption expenditure, but it doesn't take an increasing percentage of income—it is a regressive tax. The reason is that although a higher income brings higher consumption, the percentage of income spent on consumption decreases with income. So the percentage of income paid in taxes decreases as income increases. This regressive feature of the FairTax makes it appear to be unfair.

So despite its name, the FairTax might be less inefficient than our current progressive taxes, but it could not be considered fairer.

We are left with the current progressive taxes as the best available compromise between efficiency and fairness. The conversation and the search for a better solution to the big tradeoff continues.

FairTax
A proposal to tax the purchase of consumption goods and services above the poverty level, considered by the United States Congress in 1999.

MyEconLab Study Plan 8.3
    Key Terms Quiz
    Solutions Video

 ## CHECKPOINT 8.3

Review ideas about the fairness of the tax system and the tradeoff between efficiency and fairness.

Practice Problems

1. "Retired seniors should pay higher taxes than college students because government-funded healthcare for seniors costs more than government-funded tuition." Is this statement consistent with a principle of tax-system fairness?

2. Florida levies the following taxes: a 5.5 percent corporate income tax; a 6 percent sales tax; taxes of $0.34 a gallon on gasoline, $1.34 a pack on cigarettes, $0.48 a gallon on beer, and $2.25 a gallon on wine; and property taxes that vary across the counties and range from 1.4 percent to 2.0 percent of property values. Classify Florida's taxes into progressive, proportional, and regressive taxes.

3. What are the main differences between a flat tax and the FairTax? Which of the two taxes places a greater weight on efficiency and a smaller weight on fairness in the big tradeoff?

In the News

California voters overwhelmingly back $2-a-pack increase in the cigarette tax with the revenue being used to fund healthcare for the poor.
                                Source: *Los Angeles Times*, September 3, 2015
Which principle of fairness would California use to justify this big tax hike?

Solutions to Practice Problems

1. The statement "Retired seniors should pay higher taxes than college students because government-funded healthcare for seniors costs more than government-funded tuition." is consistent with the benefits principle of tax-system fairness, which is the proposition that people should pay taxes equal to the benefits they receive.

2. If counties with the higher rates are those with high property values, then Florida's property taxes are progressive. The corporate income tax does not vary with income, so this tax is a proportional tax. Because saving increases with income, expenditure as a fraction of income decreases as income increases. The taxes on expenditure (sales tax, gasoline tax, cigarette tax, beer tax, and wine tax) are regressive taxes.

3. The tax base for the flat tax is income and the tax base for the FairTax is expenditure on consumption goods and services. The flat tax is proportional while the FairTax is progressive at low income levels but regressive at high income levels because consumption expenditure decreases as a percentage of income as income increases. The FairTax places a greater weight on efficiency and a smaller weight on fairness.

Solution to In the News

The two principles of fairness are the benefits principle and the ability-to-pay principle. California will justify the tax on the benefits principle because the funds raised will pay for healthcare of the poor, who are most of the smokers.

CHAPTER SUMMARY

Key Points

1. **Explain how taxes change prices and quantities, are shared by buyers and sellers, and create inefficiency.**

   * Regardless of whether a tax is imposed on buyers or sellers, it has the same effects: The price paid by the buyer rises and the price received by the seller falls.
   * A tax creates inefficiency by driving a wedge between marginal benefit and marginal cost and creating a deadweight loss.
   * The less elastic the demand or the more elastic the supply, the greater is the price increase and the larger is the share of the tax paid by the buyer.
   * If demand is perfectly elastic or supply is perfectly inelastic, the seller pays all the tax; if demand is perfectly inelastic or supply is perfectly elastic, the buyer pays all the tax.
   * If demand or supply is perfectly inelastic, the tax creates no deadweight loss and is efficient.

2. **Explain how income taxes and Social Security taxes change wage rates and employment, are shared by employers and workers, and create inefficiency.**

   * The shares of the income tax paid by firms and households depend on the elasticity of demand and the elasticity of supply of the factors of production.
   * The elasticities of demand and supply, not Congress, determine who pays the income tax and who pays the Social Security tax.
   * The more elastic is either the demand or supply of a factor of production, the greater is the excess burden of an income tax.

3. **Review ideas about the fairness of the tax system and the tradeoff between efficiency and fairness.**

   * The two main principles of fairness of taxes—the benefits principle and the ability-to-pay principle—do not deliver universally accepted ideas of fairness.
   * Taxes can be progressive (the average tax rate rises with income), proportional (the average tax rate is constant), or regressive (the average tax rate falls with income). The U.S. income tax is progressive.
   * A flat tax and the FairTax have been proposed as alternative solutions to the "big tradeoff" that are more efficient, but they are generally regarded as less fair than the current tax arrangements.

Key Terms

MyEconLab Key Terms Quiz

CHAPTER CHECKPOINT

Study Plan Problems and Applications

1. In Florida, sunscreen and sunglasses are vital items. If the tax on sellers of these items is doubled from 5.5 percent to 11 percent, who will pay most of the tax increase: the buyer or the seller? Will the tax increase halve the quantity of sunscreen and sunglasses bought?

2. Suppose that the government imposes a $2-a-cup tax on coffee. What determines by how much Starbucks will raise its price? How will the quantity of coffee bought in coffee shops change? Will this tax raise much revenue?

Concerned about the political fallout from rising gas prices, the government cuts the tax on gasoline. Use this information to work Problems **3** and **4**.

3. Explain the effect of this tax cut on the price of gasoline and the quantity bought if, at the same time, the oil-producing nations increase production.

4. Explain the effect of this tax cut on the price of gasoline and the quantity bought if, at the same time, a global shortage of oil sends the price up.

Table 1 illustrates the market for Internet service. Use the information in Table 1 and a demand-supply graph to work Problems **5** and **6**.

5. What is the market price of Internet service? If the government taxes Internet service $15 a month, what price would the buyer of Internet service pay? What price would the seller of Internet service receive?

6. If the government taxes Internet service $15 a month, does the buyer or the seller pay more of the tax? What is the tax revenue? What is the excess burden of the tax? Is the tax proportional, progressive, or regressive?

Figure 1 illustrates the labor market in a country that does not tax labor income. Suppose that the government introduces a Social Security tax on workers of $2 per hour. Use this information to work Problems **7** and **8**.

7. How many workers are employed? What is the wage rate paid by employers and what is the workers' after-tax wage rate? How many workers are no longer employed?

8. If the government splits the Social Security tax equally between workers and employers, how many workers are employed? What is the wage rate paid by employers and what is the workers' after-tax wage rate?

9. What a big tax on soft drinks can do
A big tax on sugary drinks in Mexico has cut consumption. Sellers passed on the entire tax in higher prices. The largest consumers of sugary drinks are the poor who suffer from diabetes and obesity.
Source: *The New York Times*, October 19, 2015

What can we say about the incidence of Mexico's tax on sugary drinks and what can we infer about the elasticities of supply and demand for these drinks? Would this tax be a progressive tax or a regressive tax? On the basis of what principle would this tax be fair?

10. Read *Eye on Congress* on p. 203 and then explain how Congress *can* decide who pays the taxes, regardless of the elasticties of supply and demand. In your explanation, distinguish between taxes that do and taxes that do not impact the margin on which a decision is made.

TABLE 1

Price (dollars per month)	Quantity demanded	Quantity supplied
	(units per month)	
0	30	0
10	25	10
20	20	20
30	15	30
40	10	40
50	5	50
60	0	60

FIGURE 1

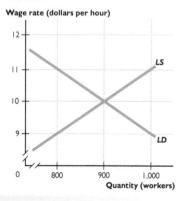

Instructor Assignable Problems and Applications

MyEconLab Homework, Quiz, or
Test if assigned by instructor

Use the following information to work Problems **1** to **3**.

New York has the highest cigarette taxes in the country. The price of an average pack of cigarettes in New York City is $10.60. The combined state and city taxes are $5.95 a pack. The average income of smokers is less than that of non-smokers.

1. Draw a graph to show the effects of the $5.95 tax on the buyer's price, the seller's price, the quantity of cigarettes bought, and the tax revenue. Does the buyer or seller pay more of the tax? Why?

2. What is the effect of the tax on consumer surplus and producer surplus, and what is the excess burden of the tax?

3. Is this tax on cigarettes a progressive, regressive, or proportional tax?

4. The supply of luxury boats is perfectly elastic, the demand for luxury boats is unit elastic, and with no tax on luxury boats the price is $1 million and 240 luxury boats a week are bought.

   Now luxury boats are taxed at 20 percent. What is the price that buyers pay? How is the tax split between buyers and sellers? What is the government's tax revenue? On a graph, show the excess burden of this tax. Is this tax efficient?

5. Figure 1 illustrates the market for chocolate bars. If a new tax of $1.50 a chocolate bar is imposed, what is the change in the quantity of chocolate bars bought, who pays most of the tax, and what is the deadweight loss?

6. In an hour, a baker earns $10, a gas pump attendant earns $6, and a copy shop worker earns $7. Suppose that the government introduces an income tax of $1 an hour. Calculate the marginal tax rates for bakers, gas pump attendants, and copy shop workers. Is this tax progressive or regressive?

7. Larry earns $25,000 and pays $2,500 in tax, while Suzy earns $50,000 and pays $15,000 in tax. If Larry's income increases by $100, his tax increases by $12, but if Suzy's income increases by $100, her tax increases by $35. Calculate the average tax rate and marginal tax rate that Larry pays and that Suzy pays. Is this income tax fair? Explain.

8. A study of the Bush tax cuts of 2001 noted that the top 1 percent of income earners reaped the biggest benefits. What assumptions about the elasticities of demand and supply for high-wage labor and capital might be consistent with this assessment? What other facts about demand and supply and market outcomes would you need to know to verify this claim?

Use the following news clip to work Problems **9** and **10**.

The gas tax is running on empty

The federal gas tax has been stuck at 18.4¢ a gallon since 1993. Today, Americans are driving fewer miles and vehicles have become more fuel-efficient. Less gas consumption means less gas-tax revenue to repair the nation's roads.

Source: *Bloomberg News,* July 17, 2014

9. Would a tax per mile driven be more efficient or less efficient than a tax per gallon of gasoline? Which tax would be more regressive? Explain your answers.

10. Would a tax per mile driven be fairer than a tax per gallon of gasoline? Explain your answer.

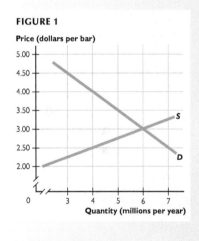

FIGURE 1

Price (dollars per bar)

Multiple Choice Quiz

1. If a tax of $1 a can is imposed on the buyers of sugary drinks, the demand for sugary drinks _____ and the price that buyers pay _____.
   A. doesn't change; doesn't change
   B. doesn't change; rises by $1 a can
   C. decreases; rises by more than $1 a can
   D. decreases; rises by less than $1 a can

2. A tax on sugar will be paid by only _____.
   A. buyers if the supply of sugar is perfectly elastic
   B. sellers if the demand for sugar is perfectly inelastic
   C. buyers if the demand for sugar is perfectly elastic
   D. sellers if the supply of sugar is perfectly elastic

3. If the government imposes a new tax on plastic bags, _____.
   A. total surplus from bags shrinks by more than the amount of tax collected
   B. total surplus from bags shrinks by the amount of the tax revenue collected
   C. a deadweight loss arises equal to the amount of tax revenue collected
   D. the market for plastic bags remains efficient if the tax is fair

4. The demand for labor is more elastic than the supply of labor. An income tax _____ the wage rate paid by employers and _____.
   A. lowers; workers pay all the tax
   B. raises; workers pay most of the tax
   C. does not change; employers pay all the tax
   D. raises; employers pay most of the tax

5. The supply of low-skilled workers in China is perfectly elastic. In 2011, when China cut the tax on these workers' incomes from 5 percent to zero, _____.
   A. employers cut the wage rate but hired the same number of workers
   B. employers cut the wage rate and hired more workers
   C. employers didn't change the wage rate but hired more workers
   D. employers didn't change the wage rate and hired the same number of workers

6. The supply of land is perfectly inelastic, so a tax on land rent is _____.
   A. efficient and the landowner pays all the tax
   B. inefficient because the renter pays all the tax
   C. inefficient if the tax is too high
   D. efficient and the renter pays all the tax

7. The demand for labor is more elastic than the supply of labor. A Social Security tax imposed equally on workers and employers _____.
   A. raises the wage rate by more than the Social Security tax
   B. decreases employment and workers pay most of the tax
   C. increases the wage rate paid by employers by the amount of the tax
   D. is fair because workers and employers pay the same amount of tax

8. The _____ principle of fairness is the proposition that _____.
   A. benefits; people should pay taxes equal to the benefits they receive from the public goods bought with the tax revenue
   B. benefits; people should receive benefits equal to their ability to pay
   C. ability-to-pay; people should pay taxes equal to the benefits they receive
   D. ability-to-pay; people should receive benefits equal to their ability to pay

Who wins and who loses from globalization?

Global Markets in Action

When you have completed your study of this chapter, you will be able to

1 Explain how markets work with international trade.

2 Identify the gains from international trade and its winners and losers.

3 Explain the effects of international trade barriers.

4 Explain and evaluate arguments used to justify restricting international trade.

CHAPTER CHECKLIST

MyEconLab Big Picture Video

Imports
The goods and services that people and firms in one country buy from firms in other countries.

Exports
The goods and services that firms in one country sell to people and firms in other countries.

9.1 HOW GLOBAL MARKETS WORK

Because we trade with people in other countries, the goods and services that we buy and consume are not limited by what we produce. The goods and services that we buy from people and firms in other countries are our **imports**; the goods and services that we sell to people and firms in other countries are our **exports**.

■ International Trade Today

Global trade today is enormous. In 2015, global exports and imports (the two numbers are the same because what one country exports another imports) were about $23 trillion, which is 31 percent of the value of global production. The United States is the world's largest international trader and accounts for 10 percent of world exports and 12 percent of world imports. Germany and China, which rank 2 and 3 behind the United States, lag by a large margin.

In 2015, total U.S. exports were $2.3 trillion, which is about 13 percent of the value of U.S. production. Total U.S. imports were $2.8 trillion, which is about 16 percent of the value of total expenditure in the United States.

The United States trades both goods and services. In 2015, exports of services were $0.75 trillion (33 percent of total exports) and imports of services were $0.5 trillion (16 percent of total imports).

Our largest exports are private services such as banking, insurance, and business consulting. Our largest exports of goods are automobile parts. Our largest import used to be crude oil, and it remains a large item. But in 2015, computers were our largest import. *Eye on the U.S. Economy* (p. 217) provides a bit more detail on ten large exports and imports.

■ What Drives International Trade?

The fundamental force that drives international trade is *comparative advantage*. We defined comparative advantage in Chapter 3 (p. 73) as the ability of a person to perform an activity or produce a good or service at a lower opportunity cost than anyone else. This same idea applies to nations. We can define *national comparative advantage* as the ability of a *nation* to perform an activity or produce a good or service at a lower opportunity cost than *any other nation*.

The opportunity cost of producing a T-shirt is lower in China than in the United States, so China has a comparative advantage in producing T-shirts. The opportunity cost of producing an airplane is lower in the United States than in China, so the United States has a comparative advantage in producing airplanes.

You saw in Chapter 3 how Liz and Joe reaped gains from trade by specializing in the production of the good at which they have a comparative advantage and then trading. Both were better off. This same principle applies to trade among nations.

China has a comparative advantage at producing T-shirts and the United States has a comparative advantage at producing airplanes, so the people of both countries can gain from specialization and trade. China can buy airplanes from the United States at a lower opportunity cost than that at which it can produce them. Americans can buy T-shirts from China for a lower opportunity cost than that at which U.S. firms can produce them. Also, through international trade, Chinese producers can get higher prices for their T-shirts and Boeing can sell airplanes for a higher price. Both countries gain from international trade.

We're going to illustrate the gains from trade that we've just described by studying demand and supply in the global markets for T-shirts and airplanes.

EYE on the U.S. ECONOMY
U.S. Exports and Imports

The blue bars in part (a) of the figure show ten large U.S. exports and the red bars in part (b) show ten large U.S. imports. Some items appear in both parts (a) and (b) because the United States exports and imports items in many of the broad categories.

Three of the leading U.S. exports are services—private services, which include financial, business, professional and technical services (such as the sale of advertising by Google to Adidas, a European sportswear maker), and education (foreign students in our colleges and universities); travel (such as the expenditure on a Florida vacation by a visitor from England); and royalties and license fees (such as fees received by Hollywood movie producers on films shown abroad).

Computers such as laptops and tablets are the largest import. We also import large quantities of industrial ands service machinery, automobiles and parts, clothing, crude oil, and travel. Private services also feature as a large imports category.

Although we import a large quantity of computers, we export some too. We also export the semiconductors (computer chips) inside those imported computers. The Intel chip in a Lenovo laptop built in China and imported into the United States is an example. This chip is made in the United States and exported to China.

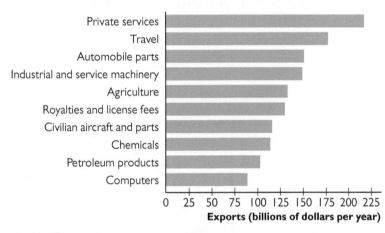

(a) Ten large U.S. exports

The United States exports airplanes ...

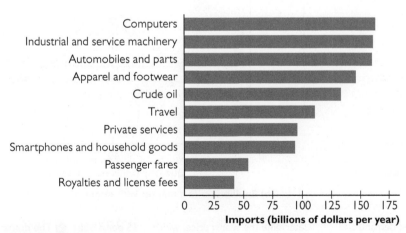

(b) Ten large U.S. imports

SOURCE OF DATA: Bureau of Economic Analysis.

and imports computers.

■ Why the United States Imports T-Shirts

Figure 9.1 illustrates the effects of international trade in T-shirts. The demand curve D_{US} and the supply curve S_{US} show the demand and supply in the U.S. domestic market only. The demand curve tells us the quantity of T-shirts that Americans are willing to buy at various prices. The supply curve tells us the quantity of T-shirts that U.S. garment makers are willing to sell at various prices.

Figure 9.1(a) shows what the U.S. T-shirt market would be like with no international trade. The price of a T-shirt would be $8 and 40 million T-shirts a year would be produced by U.S. garment makers and bought by U.S. consumers.

Figure 9.1(b) shows the market for T-shirts *with* international trade. Now the price of a T-shirt is determined in the world market, not the U.S. domestic market. The world price is *less than* $8 a T-shirt, which means that the rest of the world has a comparative advantage in producing T-shirts. The world price line shows the world price as $5 a T-shirt.

The U.S. demand curve, D_{US}, tells us that at $5 a T-shirt, Americans buy 60 million T-shirts a year. The U.S. supply curve, S_{US}, tells us that at $5 a T-shirt, U.S. garment makers produce 20 million T-shirts. To buy 60 million T-shirts when only 20 million are produced in the United States, we must import T-shirts from the rest of the world. The quantity of T-shirts imported is 40 million a year.

■ **FIGURE 9.1**

A Market with Imports   MyEconLab Animation

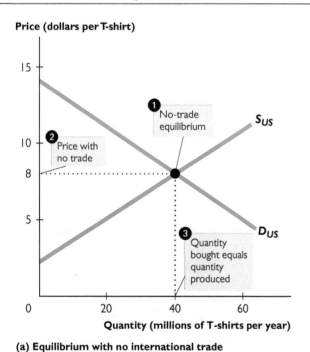

(a) Equilibrium with no international trade

(b) Equilibrium in a market with imports

With no international trade, in part (a), ❶ domestic demand and domestic supply determine ❷ the equilibrium price at $8 a T-shirt and ❸ the quantity at 40 million T-shirts a year.
With international trade, in part (b), world demand and world supply determine the world price, which is $5 per T-shirt. ❹ The domestic price falls to $5 a T-shirt. ❺ Domestic purchases increase to 60 million T-shirts a year, and ❻ domestic production decreases to 20 million T-shirts a year. ❼ 40 million T-shirts a year are imported.

Why the United States Exports Airplanes

Figure 9.2 illustrates the effects of international trade in airplanes. The demand curve D_{US} and the supply curve S_{US} show the demand and supply in the U.S. domestic market only. The demand curve tells us the quantity of airplanes that U.S. airlines are willing to buy at various prices. The supply curve tells us the quantity of airplanes that U.S. aircraft makers are willing to sell at various prices.

Figure 9.2(a) shows what the U.S. airplane market would be like with no international trade. The price of an airplane would be $100 million and 400 airplanes a year would be produced by U.S. aircraft makers and bought by U.S. airlines.

Figure 9.2(b) shows the U.S. airplane market *with* international trade. Now the price of an airplane is determined in the world market, not the U.S. domestic market. The world price is *higher than* $100 million, which means that the United States has a comparative advantage in producing airplanes. The world price line shows the world price as $150 million.

At $150 million per airplane, the U.S. demand curve, D_{US}, tells us that airlines in the United States buy 200 airplanes a year and the U.S. supply curve, S_{US}, tells us that U.S. aircraft makers produce 700 airplanes a year. The quantity produced in the United States (700 a year) minus the quantity purchased by U.S. airlines (200 a year) is the quantity of U.S. exports, which is 500 airplanes a year.

FIGURE 9.2

A Market with Exports

MyEconLab Animation

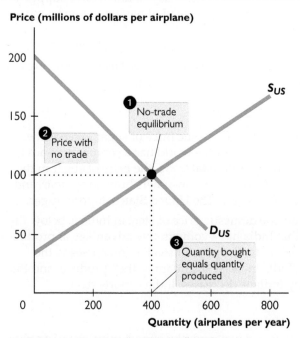

(a) Equilibrium with no international trade

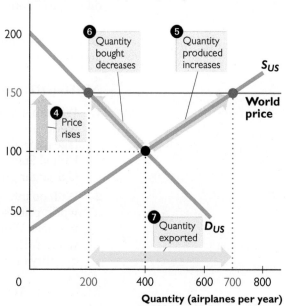

(b) Equilibrium in a market with exports

With no international trade, in part (a), ❶ domestic demand and domestic supply determine ❷ the equilibrium price at $100 million an airplane and ❸ the equilibrium quantity at 400 airplanes a year. With international trade, in part (b), world demand and world supply determine the world price, which is $150 million an airplane. ❹ The domestic price rises. ❺ Domestic production increases to 700 airplanes a year, ❻ domestic purchases decrease to 200 airplanes a year, and ❼ 500 airplanes a year are exported.

MyEconLab Study Plan 9.1
        Key Terms Quiz
        Solutions Video

 CHECKPOINT 9.1

Explain how markets work with international trade.

Practice Problems

1. Suppose that the world price of sugar is 10¢ a pound, the United States does *not* trade internationally, and the U.S. equilibrium price of sugar is 20¢ a pound. The United States then begins to trade internationally.
   • How does the price of sugar in the United States change?
   • Do U.S. consumers buy more or less sugar?
   • Do U.S. sugar growers produce more or less sugar?
   • Does the United States export or import sugar?

2. Suppose that the world price of steel is $100 a ton, India does *not* trade internationally, and the equilibrium price of steel in India is $60 a ton. India then begins to trade internationally.
   • How does the price of steel in India change?
   • How does the quantity of steel produced in India change?
   • How does the quantity of steel bought by India change?
   • Does India export or import steel?

In the News

The great American shale boom
In the past five years, U.S. oil output has doubled. In 2014, the United States and a few smaller countries added 2.4 million barrels a day to total world supply. Thanks to incredible advances in technology, instead of having to import more oil we've cut our reliance on foreign oil.

Source: *Forbes*, November 20, 2015

Describe the comparative advantage that the United States has in producing oil, and explain why its comparative advantage has changed.

Solutions to Practice Problems

1. With no international trade, the U.S. domestic price of sugar exceeds the world price so we know that the rest of the world has a comparative advantage at producing sugar. With international trade, the price of sugar in the United States falls to the world price, U.S. consumers buy more sugar, and U.S. sugar growers produce less sugar. The United States imports sugar.

2. With no international trade, the domestic price of steel in India is below the world price so we know that India has a comparative advantage at producing steel. With international trade, the price of steel in India rises to the world price, steel mills in India increase the quantity they produce, and the quantity of steel bought by Indians decreases. India exports steel.

Solution to In the News

Before new fracking technology was developed, the opportunity cost of producing oil in the United States was higher than the world market price, so the United States imported most of its oil. With the development of fracking, the cost of producing a barrel of oil in the United States is below the world price. Now the United States has a comparative advantage in the production of oil.

9.2   WINNERS, LOSERS, AND NET GAINS FROM TRADE

MyEconLab Concept Video

You've seen how international trade lowers the price of an imported good and raises the price of an exported good. Buyers of imported goods benefit from lower prices, and sellers of exported goods benefit from higher prices. But some people complain about international competition: Not everyone gains. We're now going to see who wins and who loses from free international trade. You will then be able to understand who complains about international competition and why.

We'll also see why we never hear the consumers of imported goods complaining and why we never hear exporters complaining, except when they want greater access to foreign markets. And we'll see why we *do* hear complaints from producers about cheap foreign imports.

EYE on GLOBALIZATION

MyEconLab Critical Thinking Exercise

Who Wins and Who Loses from Globalization?

Economists generally agree that the gains from globalization vastly outweigh the losses, but there are both winners and losers.

The U.S. consumer is a big winner. Globalization has brought iPads, Wii games, Nike shoes, and a wide range of other products to our shops at ever lower prices.

The Indian (and Chinese and other Asian) worker is another big winner. Globalization has brought a wider range of more interesting jobs and higher wages.

The U.S. (and European) textile workers and furniture makers are big losers. Their jobs have disappeared and many of them have struggled to find new jobs, even when they've been willing to take a pay cut.

But one of the biggest losers is the African farmer. Blocked from global agricultural markets by trade restrictions and subsidies in the United States and Europe, globalization is leaving much of Africa on the sidelines.

The U.S. consumer ...

and Indian workers gain from globalization.

But some U.S. workers and ...

African farmers lose.

■ Gains and Losses from Imports

We measure the gains and losses from imports by examining their effect on consumer surplus, producer surplus, and total surplus. The winners are those whose surplus increases and the losers are those whose surplus decreases.

Figure 9.3(a) shows what consumer surplus and producer surplus would be with no international trade. Domestic demand, D_{US}, and domestic supply, S_{US}, determine the price and quantity. The green area shows consumer surplus and the blue area shows producer surplus. Total surplus is the sum of consumer surplus and producer surplus.

Figure 9.3(b) shows how these surpluses change when the market opens to imports. The price falls to the world price. The quantity purchased increases to the quantity demanded at the world price, and consumer surplus expands to the larger green area $A + B + D$. The quantity produced decreases to the quantity supplied at the world price, and producer surplus shrinks to the smaller blue area C.

Part of the gain in consumer surplus, the area B, is a loss of producer surplus—a redistribution of total surplus. But the other part of the increase in consumer surplus, the area D, is a net gain. This increase in total surplus is the gain from imports and results from the lower price and increased purchases.

FIGURE 9.3

Gains and Losses in a Market with Imports

MyEconLab Animation

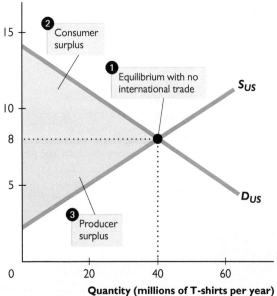

(a) Consumer surplus and producer surplus with no international trade

(b) Gains and losses from imports

With no international trade, ❶ equilibrium at the intersection of the domestic demand and domestic supply curves determines the price and quantity. ❷ The green area shows the consumer surplus and ❸ the blue area shows the producer surplus.

With international trade, the domestic price falls to the world price. ❹ Consumer surplus expands to the area $A + B + D$. Area B is a transfer of surplus from producers to consumers, and ❺ producer surplus shrinks to area C. ❻ Area D is an increase in total surplus.

■ Gains and Losses from Exports

We measure the gains and losses from exports just like we measured those from imports, by examining their effect on consumer surplus, producer surplus, and total surplus.

Figure 9.4(a) shows what the consumer surplus and producer surplus would be with no international trade. Domestic demand, D_{US}, and domestic supply, S_{US}, determine the price and quantity. The green area shows consumer surplus and the blue area shows producer surplus. The two surpluses sum to total surplus.

Figure 9.4(b) shows how the consumer surplus and producer surplus change when the good is exported. The price rises to the world price. The quantity bought decreases to the quantity demanded at the world price, and the consumer surplus shrinks to the green area A. The quantity produced increases to the quantity supplied at the world price, and the producer surplus expands from the blue area C to the larger blue area

Part of the gain in producer surplus, the area B, is a loss in consumer surplus—a redistribution of the total surplus. But the other part of the increase in producer surplus, the area D, is a net gain. This increase in total surplus is the gain from exports and results from the higher price and increased production.

FIGURE 9.4

Gains and Losses in a Market with Exports

MyEconLab Animation

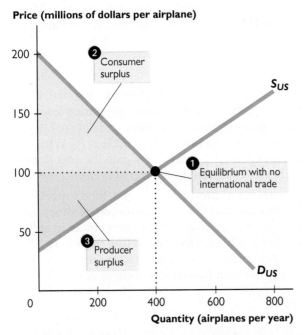

(a) Consumer surplus and producer surplus with no international trade

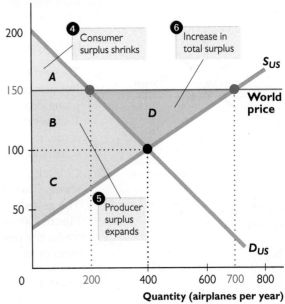

(b) Gains and losses from exports

With no international trade, ❶ equilibrium at the intersection of the domestic demand and domestic supply curves determines the price and quantity. ❷ The green area shows the consumer surplus and ❸ the blue area shows the producer surplus.

With international trade, the domestic price rises to the world price. ❹ Consumer surplus shrinks to the area A. ❺ Producer surplus expands to the area $B + C + D$. Area B is transferred from consumers to producers. ❻ Area D is an increase in total surplus.

CHECKPOINT 9.2

Identify the gains from international trade and its winners and losers.

Practice Problems

Before the 1980s, China did not trade internationally: It was self-sufficient. Then China began to trade internationally in, among other items, coal and shoes. The world price of coal was less than China's domestic price and the world price of shoes was higher than its domestic price.

1. Does China import or export coal? Who in China gains and who loses from international trade in coal? Does China gain from this trade in coal? On a graph of the market for coal in China show the gains, losses, and net gain or loss from international trade in coal.

2. Does China import or export shoes? Who in China gains and who loses from international trade in shoes? Does China gain from this trade in shoes? On a graph of the market for shoes in China, show the gains, losses, and net gain or loss from international trade in shoes.

In the News

The commodity prices nightmare of 2015
Commodity prices have been decimated in 2015: natural gas down 38.5% and nickel down nearly 43%.

Source: *Money Morning*, December 3, 2015

The United States imports nickel from Canada and exports natural gas to Mexico. How do these price falls change the U.S. gains from trade in each good and the distribution of the gains?

Solutions to Practice Problems

1. The rest of the world has a comparative advantage in producing coal. China imports coal, Chinese coal users gain, and Chinese coal producers lose. The gains exceed the losses: China gains from international trade in coal. Figure 1 shows the market for coal in China. The price before trade is P_0. With trade, the price falls to the world price, P_1. Consumers gain the area B, producers lose the area B, and the net gain from trade in coal is D.

2. China has a comparative advantage in producing shoes. China exports shoes, Chinese shoe producers gain, and Chinese consumers of shoes lose. The gains exceed the losses: China gains from international trade in shoes. Figure 2 shows the shoe market in China. The price before trade is P_0. With trade, the price rises to the world price, P_1. Producers gain the area B, consumers lose the area B, and the net gain from trade in shoes is area D.

Solution to In the News

Canada has a comparative advantage in producing nickel, which the United States imports. A fall in the world price increases U.S. imports and increases U.S. consumer surplus and total surplus. The United States has a comparative advantage in producing natural gas, so the fall in the world price decreases U.S. production and exports. U.S. producer surplus decreases, consumer surplus increases, but producers lose more than consumers gain. Total surplus decreases.

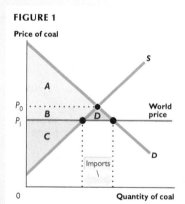

FIGURE 1

Price of coal

FIGURE 2

Price of shoes

9.3 INTERNATIONAL TRADE RESTRICTIONS

MyEconLab Concept Video

Governments use four sets of tools to influence international trade and protect domestic industries from foreign competition. They are

- Tariffs
- Import quotas
- Other import barriers
- Export subsidies

■ Tariffs

A **tariff** is a tax that is imposed on a good when it is imported. For example, the government of India imposes a 100 percent tariff on wine imported from California. When an Indian firm imports a $10 bottle of Californian wine, it pays the Indian government a $10 import duty.

Tariff
A tax imposed on a good when it is imported.

The incentive for governments to impose tariffs is strong. First, they provide revenue to the government. Second, they enable the government to satisfy the self-interest of people who earn their incomes in import-competing industries. As you will see, tariffs and other restrictions on free international trade decrease the gains from trade and are not in the social interest. Let's see how.

EYE on the PAST
The History of U.S. Tariffs

The figure shows the average tariff rate on U.S. imports since 1930. Tariffs peaked during the 1930s when Congress passed the Smoot-Hawley Act. With other nations, the United States signed the General Agreement on Tariffs and Trade (GATT) in 1947. In a series of rounds of negotiations, GATT achieved widespread tariff cuts for the United States and many other nations. Today, the World Trade Organization (WTO) continues the work of GATT and seeks to promote unrestricted trade among all nations.

The United States is a party to many trade agreements with individual countries or regions. These agreements include the North American Free Trade Agreement (NAFTA) and

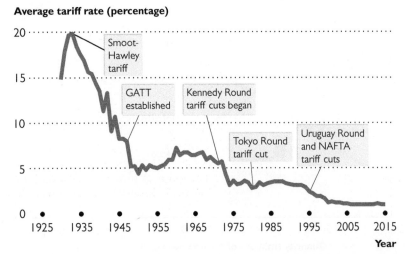

SOURCES OF DATA: The Budget for Fiscal Year 2015, Historical Tables, Table 2.5 and Bureau of Economic Analysis.

the Central American Free Trade Agreement (CAFTA). These agreements have eliminated tariffs on most

goods traded between the United States and the countries of North and Central America.

The Effects of a Tariff

To see the effects of a tariff, let's return to the example in which, with free international trade, the United States imports T-shirts. The T-shirts are imported and sold at the world price. Then, under pressure from U.S. garment makers, the U.S. government imposes a tariff on imported T-shirts. Buyers of T-shirts must now pay the world price plus the tariff. Several consequences follow in the market for T-shirts. Figure 9.5 illustrates these consequences.

Figure 9.5(a) is the same as Figure 9.1(b) and shows the situation with free international trade. The United States produces 20 million T-shirts and imports 40 million T-shirts a year at the world price of $5 a T-shirt.

Figure 9.5(b) shows what happens with a tariff, which is set at $2 per T-shirt. The following changes occur in the U.S. market for T-shirts:

- The price of a T-shirt in the United States rises by $2.
- The quantity of T-shirts bought in the United States decreases.
- The quantity of T-shirts produced in the United States increases.
- The quantity of T-shirts imported into the United States decreases.
- The U.S. government collects a tariff revenue.

FIGURE 9.5

The Effects of a Tariff

MyEconLab Animation

(a) Free trade

(b) Market with tariff

The world price of a T-shirt is $5. With free trade, in part (a), Americans buy 60 million T-shirts. The United States produces 20 million T-shirts and ❶ imports 40 million T-shirts.
In part (b), ❷ with a tariff of $2 per T-shirt, the domestic price rises

to $7 a T-shirt (the world price plus the tariff). Domestic production increases, purchases decrease, and ❸ the quantity imported decreases. ❹ The U.S. government collects tariff revenue of $2 on each T-shirt imported and shown by the purple rectangle.

Rise in Price of a T-Shirt   To buy a T-shirt, Americans must pay the world price plus the tariff, so the price of a T-shirt rises by $2 to $7. Figure 9.5(b) shows the new domestic price line, which lies $2 above the world price line.

Decrease in Purchases   The higher price of a T-shirt brings a decrease in the quantity demanded, which Figure 9.5(b) shows as a movement along the demand curve from 60 million T-shirts at $5 a T-shirt to 45 million T-shirts at $7 a T-shirt.

Increase in Domestic Production   The higher price of a T-shirt stimulates domestic production, which Figure 9.5(b) shows as a movement along the supply curve from 20 million T-shirts at $5 a T-shirt to 35 million T-shirts at $7 a T-shirt.

Decrease in Imports   T-shirt imports decrease by 30 million from 40 million to 10 million a year. Both the decrease in purchases and the increase in domestic production contribute to this decrease in imports.

Tariff Revenue   The government's tariff revenue is $20 million—$2 per T-shirt on 10 million imported T-shirts—shown by the purple rectangle.

Winners, Losers, and the Social Loss from a Tariff

A tariff on an imported good creates winners and losers. When the U.S. government imposes a tariff on an imported good,

- U.S. producers of the good gain.
- U.S. consumers of the good lose.
- U.S. consumers lose more than U.S. producers gain.

U.S. Producers of the Good Gain   Because the price of an imported T-shirt rises by the tariff, U.S. T-shirt producers are now able to sell their T-shirts for a higher price—the world price plus the tariff. As the price of a T-shirt rises, U.S. producers increase the quantity supplied. Because the marginal cost of producing a T-shirt in the United States is less than the higher price of all the T-shirts sold, except for the marginal T-shirt, producer surplus increases. This increase in producer surplus is the gain to U.S. producers.

U.S. Consumers of the Good Lose   Because the price of a T-shirt in the United States rises, the quantity of T-shirts demanded decreases. The combination of a higher price and smaller quantity bought decreases consumer surplus. This loss of consumer surplus represents the loss to U.S. consumers that arises from a tariff.

U.S. Consumers Lose More Than U.S. Producers Gain   You've just seen that consumer surplus decreases and producer surplus increases, but which changes by more? Do consumers lose more than producers gain, or do producers gain more than consumers lose? Or is there just a straight transfer from consumers to producers? To answer these questions, we need to return to the demand and supply analysis of the market for T-shirts and compare the changes in consumer surplus and producer surplus.

Figure 9.6(a) is the same as Figure 9.3(b) and shows the consumer surplus and producer surplus with free international trade in T-shirts. The dark green area is the increase in total surplus that comes from free international trade. By comparing

FIGURE 9.6

The Winners and Losers from a Tariff

MyEconLab Animation

(a) Free trade

(b) Market with tariff

The world price of a T-shirt is $5. With free trade, ❶ the United States imports 40 million T-shirts. ❷ Consumer surplus, ❸ producer surplus, and ❹ the gains from free international trade are as large as possible. ❺ A tariff of $2 per T-shirt raises the price of a

T-shirt to $7. ❻ The quantity imported decreases. ❼ Consumer surplus shrinks by the areas B, C, and D. ❽ Producer surplus expands by area B. ❾ The government's tariff revenue is area C, and ❿ a deadweight loss equal to the two areas D is created.

Figure 9.6(b) with Figure 9.6(a), you can see how a $2 tariff on imported T-shirts changes the surpluses. Producer surplus—the blue area—increases by the area labeled B. The increase in producer surplus is the gain to U.S. producers from the tariff on T-shirts. Consumer surplus—the green area—shrinks.

The decrease in consumer surplus divides into three parts. First, some of the consumer surplus is transferred to producers. The blue area B represents this loss of consumer surplus (and gain of producer surplus). Second, part of the consumer surplus is transferred to the government. The purple area C represents this loss of consumer surplus (and gain of government revenue). When the tariff revenue is spent, both consumers and producers receive some benefit, but there is no expectation that the buyers of T-shirts will receive the benefits of the expenditure of this tariff revenue from T-shirts. The tariff revenue is a loss to buyers of T-shirts.

The third part of the loss of consumer surplus is a transfer to no one: it is a *deadweight loss*. Consumers buy a smaller quantity at a higher price. The two gray areas labeled D represent this loss of consumer surplus. Total surplus decreases by this amount, which is the social loss from the tariff.

Let's now look at the second tool for restricting trade: quotas.

■ Import Quotas

An **import quota** is a quantitative restriction on the import of a good that limits the maximum quantity of a good that may be imported in a given period. The United States imposes import quotas on many items, including sugar, bananas, beef, and textiles.

Quotas enable the government to satisfy the self-interest of people who earn their incomes in import-competing industries. You will see that like a tariff, a quota on imports decreases the gains from trade and is not in the social interest.

The Effects of an Import Quota

The effects of an import quota are similar to those of a tariff. The price rises, the quantity bought decreases, and the quantity produced in the United States increases. Figure 9.7 illustrates the effects.

Figure 9.7(a) shows the situation with free international trade. Figure 9.7(b) shows what happens with a quota that limits imports to 10 million T-shirts a year. The U.S. supply curve of T-shirts becomes the domestic supply curve, S_{US}, plus the quantity that the quota permits to be imported. So the U.S. supply curve becomes the curve labeled $S_{US} + quota$. The price of a T-shirt rises to $7, the

MyEconLab Concept Video

Import quota
A quantitative restriction on the import of a good that limits the maximum quantity of a good that may be imported in a given period.

FIGURE 9.7

The Effects of an Import Quota

MyEconLab Animation

(a) Free trade

(b) Market with quota

With free trade, in part (a), Americans buy 60 million T-shirts at the world price. The United States produces 20 million T-shirts and ❶ imports 40 million T-shirts. In part (b), ❷ with an import quota

of 10 million T-shirts, the U.S. supply curve becomes $S_{US} + quota$. ❸ The price rises to $7 a T-shirt. Domestic production increases, purchases decrease, and ❹ the quantity imported decreases.

quantity of T-shirts bought in the United States decreases to 45 million a year, the quantity of T-shirts produced in the United States increases to 35 million a year, and the quantity of T-shirts imported into the United States decreases to the quota quantity of 10 million a year. All these effects of a quota are identical to the effects of a tariff set at $2 per T-shirt, as you can check in Figure 9.6(b).

Winners, Losers, and the Social Loss from an Import Quota

An import quota creates winners and losers that are similar to those of a tariff but with an interesting difference. When the government imposes an import quota,

- U.S. producers of the good gain.
- U.S. consumers of the good lose.
- Importers of the good gain.
- U.S. consumers lose more than U.S. producers and importers gain.

Figure 9.8 compares the gains from trade under free trade with those under a quota. Figure 9.8(a) shows the consumer surplus and producer surplus with free international trade in T-shirts. By comparing Figure 9.8(b) with Figure 9.8(a), you can see how an import quota of 10 million T-shirts changes the surpluses. Producer surplus—the blue area—increases by the area labeled B. The increase in

FIGURE 9.8

The Winners and Losers from an Import Quota   MyEconLab Animation

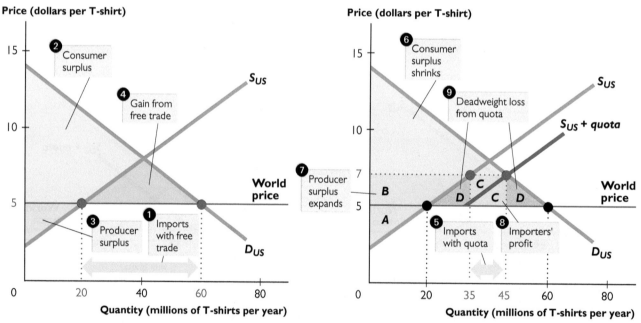

(a) Free trade

The world price of a T-shirt is $5. With free trade, ❶ the United States imports 40 million T-shirts. ❷ Consumer surplus, ❸ producer surplus, and ❹ the gains from free trade are as large as possible. In part (b), an import quota raises the domestic price to $7 a

(b) Market with quota

T-shirt. ❺ The quantity imported decreases. ❻ Consumer surplus shrinks by the areas B, C, and D. ❼ Producer surplus expands by area B. ❽ Importers' profit equals the two areas C, and the quota creates ❾ a deadweight loss equal to the two areas D.

producer surplus is the gain by U.S. producers from the import quota. Consumer surplus—the green area—shrinks. This decrease is the loss to consumers from the import quota.

The decrease in consumer surplus divides into three parts. First, some of the consumer surplus is transferred to producers. The blue area *B* represents this loss of consumer surplus (and gain of producer surplus). Second, part of the consumer surplus is transferred to importers who buy T-shirts for $5 (the world price) and sell them for $7 (the domestic price). The blue areas *C* represent this loss of consumer surplus and the importers' profit.

The third part of the loss of consumer surplus is a transfer to no one: it is a *deadweight loss*. Consumers buy a smaller quantity at a higher price. The two gray areas labeled *D* represent this loss of consumer surplus. Total surplus decreases by this amount, which is the social loss from the import quota.

You can now see the one difference between an import quota and a tariff. A tariff brings in revenue for the government while an import quota brings a profit for the importer. All the other effects are the same, provided the quota is set at the same level of imports that results from the tariff.

■ Other Import Barriers

Two sets of policies that influence imports are

- Health, safety, and regulation barriers
- Voluntary export restraints

Health, Safety, and Regulation Barriers

Thousands of detailed health, safety, and other regulations restrict international trade. For example, U.S. food imports are examined by the Food and Drug Administration to determine whether the food is "pure, wholesome, safe to eat, and produced under sanitary conditions." The discovery of BSE (mad cow disease) in just one U.S. cow in 2003 was enough to close down international trade in U.S. beef. The European Union bans imports of most genetically modified foods, such as U.S.-produced soybeans. Although regulations of the type we've just described are not designed to limit international trade, they have that effect.

Voluntary Export Restraints

A *voluntary export restraint* is like a quota allocated to a foreign exporter of the good. A voluntary export restraint decreases imports just like an import quota does, but the foreign exporter gets the profit from the gap between the domestic price and the world price.

■ Export Subsidies

An **export subsidy** is a payment by the government to the producer to cover part of the cost of production that is exported. The U.S. and European Union governments subsidize farm products. These subsidies stimulate the production and export of farm products, but they make it harder for producers in other countries, notably in Africa and Central and South America, to compete in global markets. Export subsidies bring gains to domestic producers, but they result in overproduction in the domestic economy and underproduction in the rest of the world and so create a deadweight loss (see Chapter 6, p. 157).

Export subsidy
A payment by the government to a producer to cover part of the cost of production that is exported.

MyEconLab Study Plan 9.3
Key Terms Quiz
Solutions Video

 CHECKPOINT 9.3

Explain the effects of international trade barriers.

Practice Problems

Before 1995, the United States imposed tariffs on goods imported from Mexico and Mexico imposed tariffs on goods imported from the United States. In 1995, Mexico joined NAFTA. U.S. tariffs on imports from Mexico and Mexican tariffs on imports from the United States are gradually being removed.

1. Explain how the price that U.S. consumers pay for goods imported from Mexico and the quantity of U.S. imports from Mexico have changed. Who, in the United States, are the winners and losers from this free trade?

2. Explain how the quantity of U.S. exports to Mexico and the U.S. government's tariff revenue from trade with Mexico have changed.

3. Suppose that this year, tomato growers in Florida lobby the U.S. government to impose an import quota on Mexican tomatoes. Explain who, in the United States, would gain and who would lose from such a quota.

In the News

The Trans-Pacific Partnership (TPP)
If the TPP comes into effect, Canada will remove import quotas on American milk, Japan will free imports of American beef, and the United States will remove import tariffs on items such as steel, auto-parts, garments, and solar panels.
Source: *The New York Times*, October 6, 2015

Explain how the changes described in the news clip will change U.S. exports and imports and who in the United States will gain and lose from the TPP.

Solutions to Practice Problems

1. The price that U.S. consumers pay for goods imported from Mexico has fallen and the quantity of U.S. imports from Mexico has increased. The winners are U.S. consumers of goods imported from Mexico and the losers are U.S. producers of goods imported from Mexico.

2. The quantity of U.S. exports to Mexico has increased and the U.S. government's tariff revenue from trade with Mexico has fallen.

3. With an import quota, the price of tomatoes in the United States would rise and the quantity bought would decrease. Consumer surplus would decrease. Growers would receive a higher price, produce a larger quantity, and producer surplus would increase. The U.S. total surplus in the tomato market would be redistributed from consumers to producers, but it would decrease.

Solution to In the News

Removing trade barriers on milk and beef will raise the price at which U.S. farmers can sell each item and exports will increase. U.S. farmers will gain and U.S. consumers will lose. Removing U.S. tariffs on steel and other manufactures will lower their prices in the United States and increase U.S. imports. With the lower prices, U.S. consumer surplus increases—consumers gain. U.S. producer surplus decreases—producers lose. For both exports and imports, total surplus increases.

9.4   THE CASE AGAINST PROTECTION

MyEconLab Concept Video

For as long as nations and international trade have existed, people have debated whether free international trade or protection from foreign competition is better for a country. The debate continues, but most economists believe that free trade promotes prosperity for all countries while protection reduces the potential gains from trade. We've seen the most powerful case for free trade: All countries benefit from their comparative advantage. But there is a broader range of issues in the free trade versus protection debate. Let's review these issues.

■ Three Traditional Arguments for Protection

Three traditional arguments for protection and restricting international trade are

- The national security argument
- The infant-industry argument
- The dumping argument

Let's look at each in turn.

The National Security Argument

The national security argument is that a country must protect industries that produce defense equipment and armaments and those on which the defense industries rely for their raw materials and other intermediate inputs. This argument for protection can be taken too far.

First, it is an argument for international isolation, for in a time of war, there is no industry that does not contribute to national defense. Second, if the case is made for boosting the output of a strategic industry—say aerospace—it is more efficient to achieve this outcome with a subsidy financed out of taxes than with a tariff or import quota. A subsidy would keep the industry operating at the scale that is judged appropriate, and free international trade would keep the prices faced by consumers at their world market levels.

Should producers of national security equipment be protected from international competition?

The Infant-Industry Argument

The **infant-industry argument** is that it is necessary to protect a new industry to enable it to grow into a mature industry that can compete in world markets. The argument is based on an idea called *learning-by-doing*. By working repeatedly at a task, workers become better at that task and can increase the amount they produce in a given period.

There is nothing wrong with the idea of learning-by-doing. It is a powerful engine of human capital accumulation and economic growth. Learning-by-doing can change comparative advantage. If on-the-job experience lowers the opportunity cost of producing a good, a country might develop a comparative advantage in producing that good.

But learning-by-doing does not justify protection. It is in the self-interest of firms and workers who benefit from learning-by-doing to produce the efficient quantities. If the government protected these firms to boost their production, there would be an inefficient overproduction (just like the overproduction in Chapter 6, p. 157).

Historical evidence is against the protection of infant industries. Countries in East Asia that have not given such protection have performed well. Countries that have protected infant industries, as India once did, have performed poorly.

Infant-industry argument
The argument that it is necessary to protect a new industry to enable it to grow into a mature industry that can compete in world markets.

India's protection of manufacturing industries from international competition is generally regarded as a failure.

The Dumping Argument

Dumping
When a foreign firm sells its exports at a lower price than its cost of production.

Dumping occurs when a foreign firm sells its exports at a lower price than its cost of production. You might be wondering why a firm would ever want to sell any of its output at a price below the cost of production. Wouldn't such a firm be better off either selling nothing or, if it could do so, raising its price to at least cover its costs? Two possible reasons why a firm might sell at a price below cost and therefore engage in dumping are

- Predatory pricing
- Subsidy

China, a major producer of solar panels, is accused of dumping them on the U.S. and European markets.

Predatory Pricing   A firm that engages in *predatory pricing* sets its price below cost in the hope that it can drive its competitors out of the market. If a firm in one country tries to drive out competitors in another country, it will be *dumping* its product in the foreign market. The foreign firm sells its output at a price below its cost to drive domestic firms out of business. When the domestic firms have gone, the foreign firm takes advantage of its monopoly position and charges a higher price for its product. The higher price will attract new competitors, which makes it unlikely that this strategy will be profitable. For this reason, economists are skeptical that this type of dumping occurs.

Subsidy   A *subsidy* is a payment by the government to a producer. A firm that receives a subsidy is able to sell profitably for a price below cost. Subsidies are very common in almost all countries. The United States and the European Union subsidize the production of many agricultural products and dump their surpluses on the world market. This action lowers the prices that farmers in developing nations receive and weakens the incentive to expand farming in poor countries. India and Europe have been suspected of dumping steel in the United States.

Whatever its source, dumping is illegal under the rules of the WTO, NAFTA, and CAFTA and is regarded as a justification for temporary tariffs. Consequently, anti-dumping tariffs have become important in today's world.

But there are powerful reasons to resist the dumping argument for protection. First, it is virtually impossible to detect dumping because it is hard to determine a firm's costs. As a result, the test for dumping is whether a firm's export price is below its domestic price. This test is a weak one because it can be rational for a firm to charge a lower price in markets in which the quantity demanded is highly sensitive to price and a higher price in a market in which demand is less price-sensitive.

Second, it is hard to think of a good that is produced by a single firm. Even if all the domestic firms were driven out of business in some industry, it would always be possible to find several and usually many alternative foreign sources of supply and to buy at prices determined in competitive markets.

Third, if a good or service were a truly global natural monopoly, the best way to deal with it would be by regulation—just as in the case of domestic monopolies. Such regulation would require international cooperation.

The three arguments for protection that we've just examined have an element of credibility. The counterarguments are in general stronger, so these arguments do not make the case for protection. They are not the only arguments that you might encounter. There are many others, four of which we'll now examine.

■ Four Newer Arguments for Protection

Four newer and commonly made arguments for restricting international trade are that protection

- Saves jobs
- Allows us to compete with cheap foreign labor
- Brings diversity and stability
- Penalizes lax environmental standards

Saves Jobs

When Americans buy imported goods such as shoes from Brazil, U.S. workers who produce shoes lose their jobs. With no earnings and poor prospects, these workers become a drain on welfare and spend less, which creates a ripple effect of further job losses. The proposed solution is to protect U.S. jobs by banning imports of cheap foreign goods. The proposal is flawed for the following reasons.

First, free trade does cost some jobs, but it also creates other jobs. It brings about a global rationalization of labor and allocates labor resources to their highest-valued activities. Because of international trade in textiles, tens of thousands of workers in the United States have lost jobs because shoe factories and textile mills have closed. Tens of thousands of workers in other countries now have jobs because shoe factories and textile mills have opened there. And tens of thousands of U.S. workers now have better-paying jobs than as shoe makers or textile workers because other export industries have expanded and created more jobs than have been destroyed.

Second, imports create jobs. They create jobs for retailers that sell imported goods and for firms that service those goods. They also create jobs by creating incomes in the rest of the world, some of which are spent on imports of U.S.-made goods and services.

Protection saves some particular jobs, but it does so at a high cost. For example, until 2005, textile jobs in the United States were protected by import quotas imposed under an international agreement called the Multifiber Arrangement (or MFA). The U.S. International Trade Commission (ITC) estimated that because of import quotas, 72,000 jobs existed in textiles that would otherwise have disappeared and that the annual clothing expenditure in the United States was $15.9 billion ($160 per family) higher than it would be with free trade. An implication of the ITC estimate is that each textile job saved cost consumers $221,000 a year. The end of the MFA led to the destruction of a large number of textile jobs in the United States and Europe in 2005.

Few shoe factories remain in the United States and manufacturing jobs have been lost …

… but well-paid professional and service jobs have been created to replace the lost manufacturing jobs.

Allows Us to Compete with Cheap Foreign Labor

With the removal of protective tariffs in U.S. trade with Mexico, some people said that jobs would be sucked into Mexico and that the United States would not be able to compete with its southern neighbor. Let's see what's wrong with this view.

Labor costs depend on the wage rate and the quantity a worker produces. For example, if a U.S. auto worker earns $30 an hour and produces 15 units of output an hour, the average labor cost of a unit of output is $2. If a Mexican auto worker earns $3 an hour and produces 1 unit of output an hour, the average labor cost of a unit of output is $3. Other things remaining the same, the greater the output a worker produces, the higher is the worker's wage rate. High-wage workers produce a large output. Low-wage workers produce a small output.

Although high-wage U.S. workers are more productive, on the average, than lower-wage Mexican workers, there are differences across industries. U.S. labor is relatively more productive in some activities than in others. For example, the productivity of U.S. workers in producing movies, financial services, and customized computer chips is relatively higher than their productivity in the production of metals and some standardized machine parts. The activities in which U.S. workers are relatively more productive than their Mexican counterparts are those in which the United States has a comparative advantage. By engaging in free trade, increasing our production and exports of the goods and services in which we have a comparative advantage, and decreasing our production and increasing our imports of the goods and services in which our trading partners have a comparative advantage, we can make ourselves and the citizens of other countries better off.

Brings Diversity and Stability

A diversified investment portfolio is less risky than one that has "all of its eggs in one basket." The same is true for an economy's production. A diversified economy fluctuates less than an economy that produces only one or two goods.

Most economies—the rich advanced economies of the United States, Japan, and Europe and the developing economies of China and Brazil—have diversified production and do not have this type of stability problem. A few economies, such as Saudi Arabia, have a comparative advantage that leads to the specialized production of only one good. But even these economies can stabilize their income and consumption by investing in a wide range of production activities in other countries.

Penalizes Lax Environmental Standards

A new argument for protection is that many poorer countries, such as Mexico, do not have the same environmental standards that we have, and because they are willing to pollute and we are not, we cannot compete with them without tariffs. If these countries want free trade with the richer and "greener" countries, then they must raise their environmental standards.

This argument for trade restrictions is not entirely convincing. A poor country is less able than a rich one to devote resources to achieving high environmental standards. If free trade helps a poor country to become richer, then it will also help that country to develop the means to improve its environment. But there probably is a case for using the negotiation of free trade agreements such as NAFTA and CAFTA to hold member countries to higher environmental standards. There is an especially large payoff from using such bargaining to try to avoid irreversible damage to resources such as tropical rainforests.

So the four common arguments that we've just considered do not provide overwhelming support for protection. They all have flaws and leave the case for free international trade a strong one.

■ Why Is International Trade Restricted?

Why, despite all the arguments against protection, is international trade restricted? One reason that applies to developing nations is that the tariff is a convenient source of government revenue, but this reason does not apply to the United States where the government has access to income taxes and sales taxes.

Political support for international trade restrictions in the United States and most other developed countries arises from rent seeking. **Rent seeking** is lobbying and other political activity that seeks to capture the gains from trade. You've seen that free trade benefits consumers but shrinks the producer surplus of firms that compete in markets with imports.

The winners from free trade are the millions of consumers of low-cost imports, but the benefit per individual consumer is small. The losers from free trade are the producers of import-competing items. Compared to the millions of consumers, there are only a few thousand producers.

Now think about imposing a tariff on clothing. Millions of consumers will bear the cost in the form of a smaller consumer surplus and a few thousand garment makers and their employees will share the gain in producer surplus.

Because the gain from a tariff is large, producers have a strong incentive to incur the expense of lobbying *for* a tariff and *against* free trade. On the other hand, because each consumer's loss is small, consumers have little incentive to organize and incur the expense of lobbying *for* free trade. The gain from free trade for any one person is too small for that person to spend much time or money on a political organization to lobby for free trade. The loss from free trade will be seen as being so great by those bearing that loss that they will find it profitable to join a political organization to prevent free trade. Each group weighs benefits against costs and chooses the best action for themselves, but the anti-free-trade group will undertake more political lobbying than will the pro-free-trade group.

Rent seeking
Lobbying and other political activity that aims to capture the gains from trade.

EYE on YOUR LIFE
International Trade

MyEconLab Critical Thinking Exercise

International trade plays an extraordinarily large role in your life in three broad ways. It affects you as a

- Consumer
- Producer
- Voter

As a *consumer*, you benefit from the availability of a wide range of low-cost, high-quality goods and services that are produced in other countries.

Look closely at the labels on the goods that you buy. Where was your computer made? Where were your shirt and your shoes made? Where are the fruits and vegetables that you buy, especially in winter, grown?

The answers to all these questions are most likely Asia, Mexico, or South America. A few goods were produced in Europe, Canada, and the United States.

As a *producer* (or as a potential producer if you don't yet have a job), you benefit from huge global markets for U.S. products. Your job prospects would be much dimmer if the firm for which you work didn't have global markets in which to sell its products.

People who work in the aircraft industry, for example, benefit from the huge global market for large passenger jets. Airlines from Canada to China are buying Boeing 737 and 787 aircraft as fast as they can be pushed out of the production line.

Even if you were to become a college professor, you would benefit from international trade in education services when your school admits foreign students.

As a *voter*, you have a big stake in the politics of free trade versus protection. As a buyer, your self-interest is hurt by tariffs and quotas on imported goods. Each time you buy a $20 sweater, you contribute $5 to the government in tariff revenue. But as a worker, your self-interest might be hurt by freer access to U.S. markets for foreign producers.

So as you decide how to vote, you must figure out what trade policy serves your self-interest and what best serves the social interest.

MyEconLab Study Plan 9.4
          Key Terms Quiz
          Solutions Video

CHECKPOINT 9.4

Explain and evaluate arguments used to justify restricting international trade.

Practice Problems

1. Japan sets an import quota on rice. California rice growers would like to export more rice to Japan. What are Japan's arguments for restricting imports of Californian rice? Are these arguments correct? Who loses from this restriction in trade?

2. The United States has, from time to time, limited imports of steel from Europe. What argument has the United States used to justify this quota? Who wins from this restriction? Who loses?

3. The United States maintains an import quota on sugar. What is the argument for this import quota? Is this argument flawed? If so, explain why.

In the News

India looks at raising duty on steel imports to 20%
India's steel imports are 58 percent higher than a year ago and the country's steel producers have complained that cheap imports have driven market prices below their production costs.

Source: The Financial Times, September 10, 2015

What is the argument that Indian steel producers are using to support an increase in the tariff on steel imports? What is wrong with their argument?

Solutions to Practice Problems

1. The main arguments are that Japanese rice is a better quality rice and that the quota limits competition faced by Japanese farmers. The arguments are not correct. If Japanese consumers do not like the quality of Californian rice, they will not buy it. The quota does limit competition and the quota allows Japanese farmers to use their land less efficiently. The big losers are the Japanese consumers who pay about three times the U.S. price for rice.

2. The U.S. argument is that European producers dump steel on the U.S. market. With an import quota, U.S. steel producers will face less competition and U.S. jobs will be saved. Workers in the steel industry and owners of steel companies will win at the expense of U.S. buyers of steel.

3. The argument is that the import quota protects the jobs of U.S. workers. The argument is flawed because the United States does not have a comparative advantage in producing sugar and so an import quota allows the U.S. sugar industry to be inefficient. With free international trade in sugar, the U.S. sugar industry would exist but it would be much smaller and more efficient.

Solution to In the News

Indian steel producers are using the dumping argument: Protection is needed because foreign producers are selling steel in India at prices below the cost of production. What's wrong with this argument is that it is difficult to determine whether foreign producers are selling at prices below their costs and unlikely that they would want to do so. So foreign producers might have a comparative advantage in producing steel.

CHAPTER SUMMARY

Key Points

1. **Explain how markets work with international trade.**

   - Comparative advantage drives international trade.
   - When the world price of a good is lower than the price that balances domestic demand and supply, a country gains by decreasing production and importing the good.
   - When the world price of a good is higher than the price that balances domestic demand and supply, a country gains by increasing production and exporting the good.

2. **Identify the gains from international trade and its winners and losers.**

   - Compared to a no-trade situation, in a market with imports, consumer surplus is larger, producer surplus is smaller, and total surplus is larger with free international trade.
   - Compared to a no-trade situation, in a market with exports, consumer surplus is smaller, producer surplus is larger, and total surplus is larger with free international trade.

3. **Explain the effects of international trade barriers.**

   - Countries restrict international trade by imposing tariffs, import quotas, other import barriers, and export subsidies.
   - Trade restrictions raise the domestic price of imported goods, lower the quantity imported, decrease consumer surplus, increase producer surplus, and create a deadweight loss.

4. **Explain and evaluate arguments used to justify restricting international trade.**

   - The arguments that protection is necessary for national security, for infant industries, and to prevent dumping are weak.
   - Arguments that protection saves jobs, allows us to compete with cheap foreign labor, makes the economy diversified and stable, and is needed to penalize lax environmental standards are flawed.
   - Trade is restricted because protection brings small losses to a large number of people and large gains to a small number of people.

Key Terms

MyEconLab Key Terms Quiz

Dumping, 234	Import quota, 229	Rent seeking, 237
Export subsidy, 231	Imports, 216	Tariff, 225
Exports, 216	Infant-industry argument, 233	

■ ■ CHAPTER CHECKPOINT

Study Plan Problems and Applications

Use Figures 1 and 2 to work Problems **1** to **4**. Figure 1 and Figure 2 show the markets for shoes if there is no trade between the United States and Brazil.

FIGURE 1   U.S. SHOE MARKET

1. Which country has a comparative advantage in producing shoes? With international trade, explain which country would export shoes and how the price of shoes in the importing country and the quantity produced by the importing country would change. Explain which country gains from this trade.

2. The world price of a pair of shoes is $20. Explain how consumer surplus and producer surplus in the United States change as a result of international trade. On the graph, show the change in U.S. consumer surplus (label it *A*) and the change in U.S. producer surplus (label it *B*).

3. The world price of a pair of shoes is $20. Explain how consumer surplus and producer surplus in Brazil change as a result of international trade. Show the change in Brazil's consumer surplus (label it *C*) and the change in Brazil's producer surplus (label it *D*).

4. Who in the United States loses from free trade in shoes with Brazil? Explain.

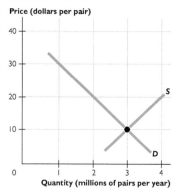

FIGURE 2   BRAZIL'S SHOE MARKET

Use the following information to work Problems **5** to **7**.

5. The supply of roses in the United States is made up of U.S.-grown roses and imported roses. Draw a graph to illustrate the U.S. rose market with free international trade. On your graph, mark the price of roses and the quantities of roses bought, produced, and imported into the United States.

6. Who in the United States loses from this trade in roses and would lobby for a restriction on the quantity of imported roses? If the U.S. government put a tariff on rose imports, show on your graph the U.S. consumer surplus that is redistributed to U.S. producers and also the government's tariff revenue.

7. Suppose that the U.S. government puts an import quota on roses. Show on your graph the consumer surplus that is redistributed to producers and importers and also the deadweight loss created by the import quota.

Use the following information to work Problems **8** to **10**.

U.S. steelmakers seek antidumping action
Steelmakers want the United States to put restrictions on imports from five nations, alleging unfair pricing of steel for the automobile and construction industries.

Source: *Wall Street Journal*, June 3, 2015

8. Explain who in the United States gains and who loses from restrictions on steel imports. How do you expect the prices of automobiles and office towers to be affected?

9. What is dumping? Who in the United States loses from foreign firms' dumping of steel?

10. Explain what an antidumping tariff is. What argument might U.S. steelmakers use to get the government to raise the tariff on steel imports?

11. Read *Eye on Globalization* on p. 221 and draw two graphs to show how U.S. consumers gain from iPads manufactured in China and why Chinese workers also gain.

Instructor Assignable Problems and Applications

MyEconLab Homework, Quiz, or Test if assigned by instructor

Use the following information to work Problems **1** and **2**.

The future of U.S.–India relations
When she was Secretary of State, Hillary Clinton gave a major speech covering all the issues in U.S.–India relations. On economic and trade relations she noted that India maintains significant barriers to U.S. trade. The United States also maintains barriers against Indian imports such as textiles. Mrs. Clinton, President Obama, and Anand Sharma, the Indian Minister of Commerce and Industry, say they want to dismantle these trade barriers.

Source: www.state.gov

1. Explain who in the United States would gain and who might lose from dismantling trade barriers between the United States and India.

2. Draw a graph of the U.S. market for textiles and show how removing a tariff would change producer surplus, consumer surplus, and the deadweight loss from the tariff.

3. The United States exports wheat. Draw a graph to illustrate the U.S. wheat market if there is free international trade in wheat. On your graph, mark the price of wheat and the quantities bought, produced, and exported by the United States.

4. Suppose that the world price of sugar is 20¢ a pound, Brazil does not trade internationally, and the equilibrium price of sugar in Brazil is 10¢ a pound. Brazil then begins to trade internationally.
   • How does the price of sugar in Brazil change? Do Brazilians buy more or less sugar? Do Brazilian sugar growers produce more or less sugar?
   • Does Brazil export or import sugar and why?

5. The United States exports services and imports coffee. Why does the United States gain from exporting services and importing coffee? How do economists measure the net gain from this international trade?

6. In the 1950s, Ford and General Motors established a small car-producing industry in Australia and argued for a high tariff on car imports. The tariff has remained through the years. Until 2000, the tariff was 22.5 percent. What might have been Ford's and General Motors' argument for the high tariff? Is the tariff the best way to achieve the goals of the argument?

Use Figure 1 and the following information to work Problems **7** to **9**.

Figure 1 shows the car market in Mexico when Mexico places no restriction on the quantity of cars imported. The world price of a car is $10,000.

7. If the government of Mexico introduces a $2,000 tariff on car imports, what will be the price of a car in Mexico, the quantity of cars produced in Mexico, the quantity imported into Mexico, and the government's tariff revenue?

8. If the government of Mexico introduces an import quota of 4 million cars a year, what will be the price of a car in Mexico, the quantity of cars produced in Mexico, and the quantity imported?

9. What argument might be used to encourage the government of Mexico to introduce a $2,000 tariff on car imports from the United States? Who will gain and who will lose as a result of Mexico's tariff?

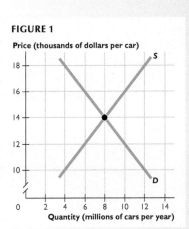

FIGURE 1

Multiple Choice Quiz

1. The fundamental force driving international trade is comparative _____.

  A. advantage: a country exports those goods that have high prices

  B. abundance: the country that produces more than it needs exports the good

  C. advantage: the country with the lower opportunity cost of production exports the good

  D. cost: a country trades with other countries that produce cheaper goods

2. A country will export wheat if, with no international trade, _____.

  A. it produces a surplus of wheat

  B. its opportunity cost of producing wheat is below the world price

  C. its domestic price of wheat exceeds the world price

  D. other countries have a shortage of wheat

3. With free trade between the United States and Canada, the United States exports tomatoes and Canada exports maple syrup. U.S. consumers _____.

  A. of tomatoes gain and Canadian consumers of maple syrup lose

  B. of both tomatoes and maple syrup gain more than either producer

  C. of maple syrup gain more than U.S. producers of maple syrup lose

  D. of tomatoes gain more than U.S. producers of tomatoes lose

4. With free trade between China and the United States, the winners are _____ and the losers are _____.

  A. U.S. consumers of U.S. imports; U.S. producers of the U.S. import good

  B. China's consumers of China's imports; China's producers of its export good

  C. U.S. producers of the U.S. export good; U.S. consumers of U.S. imports

  D. China's consumers of China's export good; China's producers of its imported good

5. The U.S. tariff on paper _____ the U.S. price of paper, _____ U.S. production of paper and _____ the U.S. gains from trade.

  A. raises; increases; increases

  B. doesn't change; increases; increases

  C. doesn't change; doesn't change; decreases

  D. raises; increases; decreases

6. If Korea imposes an import quota on U.S. oranges, losers include Korean _____ of oranges and U.S. _____ of oranges.

  A. consumers; consumers

  B. consumers; producers

  C. producers; consumers

  D. producers; producers

7. The people who support restricted international trade say that _____.

  A. protection saves jobs, in both the United States and foreign economies

  B. U.S. firms won't be able to compete with low-wage foreign labor if trade is free

  C. outsourcing sends jobs abroad, which brings diversification and makes our economy more stable

  D. protection is needed to enable U.S. firms to produce the things at which they have a comparative advantage

How can we limit carbon
emissions?

Externalities

**When you have completed your study of this chapter,
you will be able to**

1 Explain why negative externalities lead to inefficient overproduction and how property rights and pollution taxes can
achieve a more efficient outcome.

2 Explain why positive externalities lead to inefficient underproduction and how public provision, subsidies, and vouchers
can achieve a more efficient outcome.

10

MyEconLab Big Picture Video

MyEconLab Concept Video

Externality
A cost or a benefit that arises from production and that falls on someone other than the producer; or a cost or benefit that arises from consumption and that falls on someone other than the consumer.

Negative externality
A production or consumption activity that creates an external cost.

Positive externality
A production or consumption activity that creates an external benefit.

Negative production externality.

Positive production externality.

EXTERNALITIES IN OUR DAILY LIVES

Climate change is an externality, and a huge one. You will learn what economists say about limiting it in this chapter. But first we need to build a foundation. We begin by classifying and illustrating the range of externalities in our daily lives.

An **externality** is a cost or a benefit that arises from production and that falls on someone other than the producer; or a cost or a benefit that arises from consumption and that falls on someone other than the consumer. An externality can arise from either a production activity or a consumption activity. It can be either a **negative externality**, which imposes an external cost, or a **positive externality**, which provides an external benefit. So there are four types of externalities:

- Negative production externalities
- Positive production externalities
- Negative consumption externalities
- Positive consumption externalities

■ Negative Production Externalities

Negative production externalities are among the most serious challenges faced by the world today. Starting in the Industrial Revolution of the eighteenth century, humans have poured billions of tons of pollutants in the air, oceans, lakes, and rivers.

Power generators, airplanes, and road vehicles are the biggest polluters. Burning coal to generate electricity emits carbon dioxide that warms the planet and it emits other chemicals that pollute the atmosphere. The coal-burning Navajo Generating Station near Page, Arizona, emits about 16 million tons of carbon into the atmosphere every year, an amount similar to that of 3.3 million passenger car miles each year.

Logging and the clearing of forests in California, Oregon, and Washington destroy the habitat of wildlife and also influence the amount of carbon dioxide in the atmosphere.

Noise is another negative production externality. When planes take off and land at LaGuardia airport in New York City, the noise they make imposes a large cost on the people who live under the flight paths. This noise is replicated at airports in every major city around the world.

All these activities are examples of production that brings negative externalities. The costs of these production activities are borne by everyone, and even by future generations.

■ Positive Production Externalities

Positive production externalities are a smaller problem than negative ones. But they pose interesting problems. A notable one arises in the production of fruit and vegetables and honey. To produce honey, bee-keepers locate their hives next to fruit orchards and vegetable farms. The honeybees collect pollen and nectar from the fruit and vegetable blossoms to make the honey. At the same time, they transfer pollen between the blossoms, which helps to fertilize the blossoms. Two positive production externalities are present in this example. Honey producers get a positive production externality from the owners of the orchards and farms; and the fruit growers and vegetable farmers get a positive production externality from the honey producer.

■ Negative Consumption Externalities

Negative consumption externalities are a source of irritation for most of us. Smoking tobacco in a confined space creates fumes that many people find unpleasant and that pose a health risk. So smoking in restaurants and on airplanes generates a negative externality. To avoid this negative externality, many restaurants and all airlines ban smoking. But while a smoking ban avoids a negative consumption externality for most people, it imposes a negative external cost on smokers who would prefer to enjoy the consumption of tobacco while dining or traveling by air.

Negative consumption externality.

Noisy parties and outdoor rock concerts are other examples of negative consumption externalities. They are also examples of the fact that a simple ban on an activity is not a solution. Banning noisy parties avoids the external cost on sleep-seeking neighbors, but it results in the sleepers imposing an external cost on the fun-seeking partygoers.

Leaving beer bottles on the beach, allowing a dog to bark loudly or to foul a neighbor's lawn, and letting a smartphone ring during a lecture are other examples of negative consumption externalities.

■ Positive Consumption Externalities

When you get a flu vaccination, you lower your risk of being infected. If you avoid the flu, your neighbor, who didn't get vaccinated, has a better chance of remaining healthy too. Flu vaccinations generate positive consumption externalities.

When the owner of a historic building restores it, everyone who sees the building gets pleasure. Similarly, when someone erects a spectacular home or other exciting construction or building such as the Walt Disney Concert Hall in Los Angeles, an external consumption benefit flows to everyone who has an opportunity to view it.

Positive consumption externality.

Education, which we examine in more detail in this chapter, is a major example of a positive consumption and production externality.

EYE on YOUR LIFE
Externalities in Your Life

MyEconLab Critical Thinking Exercise

Think about the externalities, both negative and positive, that play a huge part in *your* life; and think about the incentives that attempt to align your self-interest with the social interest.

You respond to the gasoline tax by buying a little less gas than you otherwise would. As you will see in *Eye on Climate Change* (p. 254), this incentive is small compared to that in some other countries. With a bigger gas tax, such

as that in the United Kingdom for example, you would find ways of getting by with a smaller quantity of gasoline and your actions and those of millions of others would make the traffic on our highways much lighter.

You are responding to the huge incentive of subsidized tuition by being in school. Without subsidized college education, fewer people would attend college and university and with fewer

college graduates, the benefits we all receive from living in a well-educated society would be smaller.

Think about your attitude as a citizen–voter to these two externalities. Should the gas tax be higher to discourage the use of the automobile? Should tuition be even lower to encourage even more people to enroll in school? Or have we got these incentives just right in the social interest?

10.1 NEGATIVE EXTERNALITIES: POLLUTION

Climate change is a *negative externality*. It is the unintended consequence of production and consumption activities that create carbon emissions and global warming. We'll address the challenge of limiting climate change in this chapter.

Although climate change from human actions is new, pollution and other environmental problems are not. Preindustrial towns in Europe had sewage disposal problems that brought cholera and plagues that killed millions. Nor is the desire to find solutions to environmental problems new. The fourteenth century development of a pure water supply and the hygienic disposal of garbage and sewage are examples of early efforts to improve the quality of the environment.

Popular discussions about climate change and pollution focus on physical aspects of the problem and not on costs and benefits. A common assumption is that activities that damage the environment are wrong and must cease. An economic study of the same problems emphasizes costs and benefits, and economists talk about the efficient amount of pollution. This emphasis on costs and benefits does not mean that economists have the right answers. Rather, economics provides a set of tools and principles that help to clarify the issues.

We illustrate the economics of a negative externality with the example of a paint factory that dumps waste into a river. The people who live by the river use it for fishing and boating and bear the cost of the pollution. The paint factory does not consider these costs when it decides the quantity of paint to produce. The factory's production decision is based on its own costs of production, not on the costs that it inflicts on others. You're going to see that when external costs are present, output exceeds the efficient quantity and we get more than the efficient quantity of pollution.

The starting point for an economic analysis of a negative externality is the distinction between private costs and social costs.

■ Private Costs and Social Costs

Marginal private cost
The cost of producing an additional unit of a good or service that is borne by the producer of that good or service.

Marginal external cost
The cost of producing an additional unit of a good or service that falls on people other than the producer.

Marginal social cost
The marginal cost incurred by the entire society—by the producer and by everyone else on whom the cost falls. It is the sum of marginal private cost and marginal external cost.

A *private cost* of production is a cost that is borne by the producer of a good or service. *Marginal cost* is the cost of producing an *additional unit* of a good or service. So **marginal private cost** (*MC*) is the cost of producing an additional unit of a good or service that is borne by the producer of that good or service.

You've seen that an *external cost* is a cost of producing a good or service that is *not* borne by the producer but borne by other people. A **marginal external cost** is the cost of producing an additional unit of a good or service that falls on people other than the producer.

Marginal social cost (*MSC*) is the marginal cost incurred by the entire society—by the producer and by everyone else on whom the cost falls—and is the sum of marginal private cost and marginal external cost. That is,

$$MSC = MC + \text{Marginal external cost}$$

We express costs in dollars, but we must always remember that a cost is an opportunity cost—the best thing we give up to get something. A marginal external cost is what someone other than the producer of a good or service must give up when the producer makes one more unit of the item. Something real that people value, such as a clean river or clean air, is given up.

Valuing an External Cost

Economists use market prices to put a dollar value on the cost of pollution. For example, suppose that there are two similar rivers, one polluted and the other clean, with identical homes along the side of each river. The homes on the clean river rent for $1,000 a month more than those on the polluted river. If pollution is the only detectable difference between the two locations, the $1,000 a month rent difference is the social cost per home of the pollution. The $1,000 multiplied by the number of homes on the polluted river is the total external cost of this pollution.

External Cost and Output

Figure 10.1 shows an example of the relationship between output and cost in a polluting paint industry. The marginal cost curve, *MC*, describes the private marginal cost borne by the firms that produce the paint. Marginal cost increases as the quantity of the paint produced increases. If the firms dump waste into a river, they impose an external cost that increases with the amount of the paint produced. The marginal social cost curve, *MSC*, is the sum of the marginal private cost and the marginal external cost. For example, when firms produce 4 million gallons of paint a month, marginal private cost is $1.00 a gallon, marginal external cost is $1.25 a gallon, and marginal social cost is $2.25 a gallon.

In Figure 10.1, as the quantity of the paint produced increases, the amount of pollution increases and the external cost of pollution increases. The quantity of the paint produced and the pollution created depend on how the market for the paint operates. First, we'll see what happens when the industry is free to pollute.

FIGURE 10.1

An External Cost

MyEconLab Animation

The *MC* curve shows the marginal private cost borne by the factories that produce paint. The *MSC* curve shows the sum of marginal private cost and marginal external cost.

When firms produce 4 million gallons of paint a month
❶ Marginal private cost is $1.00 per gallon.

❷ Marginal external cost is $1.25 per gallon.

❸ Marginal social cost is $2.25 per gallon.

■ Production and Pollution: How Much?

When a polluting industry is unregulated, the market outcome is one of inefficient *overproduction.* In the pursuit of their self-interest, firms produce too much, and they pollute too much. Figure 10.2, which illustrates a market for paint in which the producers pollute, explains why.

The demand curve and marginal benefit curve for paint is $D = MB$ (see Chapter 6, p. 148). The supply curve and marginal private cost curve of producers of the paint is $S = MC$ (see Chapter 6, p. 151). The supply curve is the marginal *private* cost curve because when firms make their supply decisions, they pursue their self-interest and consider only the costs that they will bear. The market *equilibrium* occurs where marginal benefit equals marginal *private* cost. The price is $1.00 a gallon and the quantity is 4 million gallons of paint a month. This outcome is inefficient because marginal *social* cost exceeds marginal benefit.

The efficient outcome is when marginal benefit *equals* marginal *social* cost. In Figure 10.2, the efficient quantity is 2 million gallons of the paint a month, where marginal social cost and marginal benefit each equal $1.50 per gallon.

The equilibrium outcome is one of inefficient *overproduction* and the gray triangle shows the deadweight loss that arises in this situation.

If some method can be found to get paint factories to create less pollution and eliminate the deadweight loss, everyone—the owners of the factories and the residents of the riverside homes—can gain. So what can be done to fix the inefficiency? Three methods are available and we'll examine each of them. They are

- Establish property rights
- Mandate clean technology
- Tax or cap and price pollution

FIGURE 10.2

Inefficiency with an External Cost   MyEconLab Animation

The market supply curve is the marginal private cost curve, $S = MC$. The demand curve is the marginal benefit curve, $D = MB$. The marginal social cost curve is *MSC*.

❶ Market equilibrium at a price of $1.00 a gallon and 4 million gallons of paint a month is inefficient because ❷ marginal social cost exceeds ❸ marginal benefit.

❹ The efficient quantity of paint is 2 million gallons a month where marginal benefit equals marginal social cost.

❺ The area of the gray triangle shows the deadweight loss created by the pollution externality.

■ Establish Property Rights

Property rights are legally established titles to the ownership, use, and disposal of factors of production and goods and services that are enforceable in the courts. Establishing property rights where they do not currently exist can confront producers with the costs of their actions and provide them with an incentive to allocate resources efficiently.

To see how property rights work, suppose that the paint producers have property rights on a river and the homes alongside it—they own the river and the homes. The rental income that the paint producers earn on the homes depends on the amount of pollution they create. If people are willing to pay $1,000 a month more to live alongside a pollution-free river, the paint producers can earn that amount for each of the homes they own by not polluting the river.

The forgone rental income from homes alongside a polluted river is an opportunity cost of producing paint. It is part of the paint producers' marginal *private* cost and the paint producers must now decide how to respond to this cost. There are two things they might do:

- Use an abatement technology
- Produce less and pollute less

Use an Abatement Technology

An **abatement technology** is a production technology that reduces or prevents pollution. The catalytic converter in every U.S. car is an example of an abatement technology. Its widespread adoption, along with lead-free gasoline, has dramatically reduced pollution from highway vehicles and helped to achieve the trends in U.S. air quality shown on p. 253.

Abatement technologies are available to reduce carbon emissions from electricity generation and pollution from industrial processes and paint manufacture.

Produce Less and Pollute Less

An alternative to incurring the cost of using an abatement technology is to use the polluting technology but cut production, which will reduce pollution and result in higher income from renting homes by the river. Firms will choose the least-cost alternative method of lowering pollution.

The Coase Theorem

Does it matter whether the polluter or the victim of the pollution owns the resource that might be polluted? The Coase theorem (named for British economist Ronald Coase who was the first to have this remarkable insight) says it doesn't matter.

The **Coase theorem** is the proposition that if property rights exist and the costs of enforcing them are low, then the market outcome is efficient and it doesn't matter who has the property rights.

Application of the Coase Theorem

Suppose that the residents own their homes and the river. Now the factories must pay a fee to the homeowners for the right to dump waste into the river. The greater the quantity of waste dumped, the more the factories must pay. So again, the factories face the opportunity cost of the pollution they create as part of their marginal *private* cost. The quantity of paint produced and the amount of waste

Property rights
Legally established titles to the ownership, use, and disposal of factors of production and goods and services that are enforceable in the courts.

Abatement technology
A production technology that reduces or prevents pollution.

Coase theorem
The proposition that if property rights exist and the costs of enforcing them are low, then the market outcome is efficient and it doesn't matter who has the property rights.

dumped are the same whoever owns the homes and the river. If the factories own them, they bear the cost of pollution because they receive a lower income from home rents. If the residents own the homes and the river, the factories bear the cost of pollution because they must pay a fee to the homeowners. In both cases, the factories bear the cost of their pollution and dump the efficient amount of waste into the river.

Efficient Market Equilibrium With Property Rights

Figure 10.3 illustrates the efficient market outcome with property rights in place. The paint producers face the pollution costs or the abatement costs, whichever is lower. The *MSC* curve includes the cost of producing paint plus either the cost of abatement or the cost of pollution (forgone rent), whichever is lower. This curve, labeled $S = MC = MSC$, is now the market supply curve.

Market equilibrium occurs at a price of $1.50 per gallon and 2 million gallons of paint per month. This outcome is efficient.

If the forgone rent is less than the abatement cost, the factories will still create some pollution, but it will be the efficient quantity. If the abatement cost is lower than the forgone rent, the factories will stop polluting, but they will produce less paint because marginal cost includes the abatement cost.

The Coase property rights solution works only when the cost of reaching an agreement between property owners is low. In many situations, these negotiation costs are high, so this solution is not available and government action is needed. One such action is to mandate the use of a clean abatement technology.

FIGURE 10.3

Property Rights Achieve an Efficient Outcome   MyEconLab Animation

❶ With property rights, the marginal cost curve that excludes the cost of pollution shows only part of the producers' marginal cost.

The marginal private cost curve includes ❷ the cost of pollution, so the supply curve of paint is $S = MC = MSC$.

❸ Market equilibrium is at a price of $1.50 a gallon and a quantity of 2 million gallons of paint a month. The market outcome is efficient because ❹ marginal social cost equals marginal benefit.

■ Mandate Clean Technology

The governments of most countries regulate what may be emitted into the atmosphere and dumped in rivers and lakes. The direct regulation of what is and is not legally permitted is called **command-and-control regulation**.

Command-and-control environmental regulation in the United States is conducted under the provisions of the Clean Air Act of 1970 and the Clean Water Act of 1972. These Acts give the Environmental Protection Agency (EPA) the authority to issue regulations that limit emissions and achieve defined air and water quality standards.

The EPA has issued thousands of regulations that require chemical plants, utilities, and steel mills to adopt best-practice pollution-abatement technologies and to either eliminate or limit their emissions of specified pollutants. Other regulations have been issued that govern road vehicle emission limits, which must be met by vehicle manufacturers.

Command-and-control regulation works particularly well for keeping water resources clean because even a small breach of safety standards can bring a large catastrophic consequence. An example is what happened in Michigan when the state switched Flint's water supply from Lake Huron (clean) to the Flint River (polluted). Tap water became discolored and its lead level tripled, prompting residents to bring a class action against the state. But Flint's problem is rare because command-and-control water regulation is usually effective.

Although command-and-control regulation provides clean water and has improved air quality, economists see three problems with this approach. It doesn't confront individual producers with incentives to limit pollution. A one-size-fits-all solution is generally not the lowest-cost solution to a pollution problem. And lawmakers are subject to lobbying by the polluters whose actions they seek to control. The third approach for dealing with pollution directly addresses these three concerns.

Command-and-control regulation
The direct regulation of what is and is not permitted.

A Supreme Court decision says greenhouse gas emissions are pollution—the EPA must regulate them.

■ Tax or Cap and Price Pollution

Governments use two main methods of confronting polluters with the costs of their decisions:

* Taxes
* Cap-and-trade

Taxes

Governments can use taxes as an incentive for producers to reduce the pollution they create. Taxes used in this way are called Pigovian taxes, (named for Arthur Cecil Pigou, the British economist who first worked out this method of dealing with external costs during the 1920s).

By setting the tax equal to the marginal external cost (or marginal abatement cost if it is lower), firms can be made to behave in the same way as they would if they bore the cost of the externality directly.

To see how government actions can change the outcome in a market with external costs, let's return to the example of paint factories and the river. Assume that the government has assessed the marginal external cost of pollution accurately and imposes a tax on the factories that exactly equals this cost. The producers are now confronted with the social cost of their actions. The market equilibrium is one in which price equals marginal social cost—an efficient outcome.

Figure 10.4 illustrates the effects of a Pigovian tax on pollution from paint factories. The curve $D = MB$ is the market demand for paint and the marginal benefit curve. The curve MC is the marginal private cost of producing paint. The tax equals the marginal external cost of the pollution. We add this tax to the marginal private cost to find the market supply curve, the curve labeled $S = MC + tax$. This curve is the market supply curve because it tells us the quantity of paint supplied at each price, given the factories' marginal cost and the tax they must pay. This curve is also the marginal social cost curve MSC because the pollution tax has been set equal to the marginal external cost at the quantity produced.

Demand and supply now determine the market equilibrium price at $1.50 per gallon and a quantity of 2 million gallons of paint a month. At this quantity of paint produced, the marginal social cost is $1.50 per gallon and the marginal benefit is $1.50 per gallon, so the market outcome is efficient. The factories incur a marginal private cost of 90¢ per gallon and pay a pollution tax of 60¢ per gallon. The government collects tax revenue of $1.2 million per month.

Cap-and-Trade

Cap-and-trade places a cap or ceiling on emissions and assigns or sells emission rights to individual producers who are then free to trade permits with each other. It is a tool that seeks to combine the power of government to limit total emissions with the power of the market to minimize cost and maximize benefit.

A government that uses this method must first estimate the efficient quantity of pollution and set the overall emissions cap to achieve the efficient outcome. Then the government must somehow allocate shares of the cap to individual

---

■ **FIGURE 10.4**

A Pollution Tax   MyEconLab Animation

❶ A pollution tax is imposed that is equal to the marginal external cost of pollution.

Because the pollution tax equals the marginal external cost, the supply curve is the marginal social cost curve:
$S = MC + tax = MSC$.

❷ Market equilibrium is efficient because ❸ marginal social cost equals marginal benefit.

❹ The government collects tax revenue equal to the area of the purple rectangle.

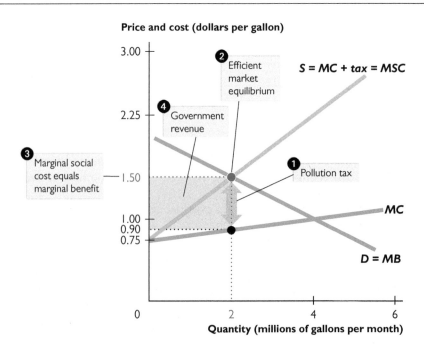

firms (and possibly even households). In an efficient allocation of emissions quotas to firms, each firm has the same marginal social cost of production and emissions abatement. So to allocate the cap efficiently across firms, the government would need to know a lot about each firm's production and abatement costs.

A Pigovian tax achieves an efficient allocation of pollution across firms because each firm chooses how much to produce and pollute by taking the tax into account, and then produces the quantity at which marginal social cost equals price. Because all firms face the same market price, they also incur the same marginal social cost.

The government solves the allocation problem by making an initial distribution of the cap across firms and then allows the firms to trade in a market for emission permits. Firms that have a low marginal abatement cost sell permits and make big cuts in pollution. Firms that have a high marginal abatement cost buy permits and make smaller cuts or perhaps even no cuts in pollution.

The market in permits determines the equilibrium price of emissions and each firm, confronted with that price, maximizes profit by setting its marginal pollution cost or marginal abatement cost, whichever is lower, equal to the market price of a permit. By confronting polluters with a price of pollution, trade in pollution permits can achieve the same efficient outcome as a Pigovian tax.

Cap-and-trade has been used by the EPA to address sulfur dioxide and lead emissions and has been very successful in reducing the levels of concentration of these pollutants in the atmosphere. (See *Eye on the U.S. Economy* below.)

EYE on the U.S. ECONOMY
U.S. Air Pollution Trends

Air quality in the United States has improved. The figure shows the trends for the atmospheric concentrations of five main air pollutants monitored by the Environmental Protection Agency (EPA) since 1980 and a sixth pollutant (suspended particulates) monitored since 1990.

By using a mix of regulation, pollution limits, economic incentives, and permit trading, the EPA has almost eliminated lead and has substantially decreased sulfur dioxide, carbon monoxide, nitrogen dioxide, and suspended particulates.

Ozone is harder to eliminate, but it has nonetheless fallen to 70 percent of its 1980 level.

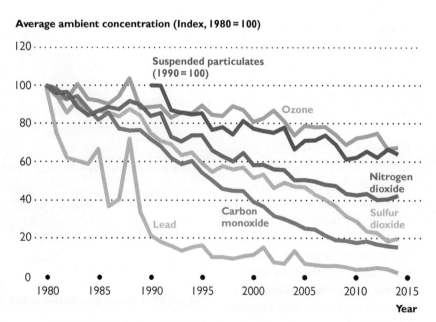

SOURCE OF DATA: Environmental Protection Agency, http://www.epa.gov/airtrends.

EYE on CLIMATE CHANGE
MyEconLab Critical Thinking Exercise

How Can We Limit Carbon Emissions?

The Problem

The Earth's temperature is rising and so is the amount of carbon dioxide, CO_2, in the atmosphere. Figure 1 shows these trends. The scientific consensus is that human economic activity is their major source.

Figure 2 shows that China, the United States, and Europe create 54 percent of carbon emissions and another eight large emitters create a further 25 percent.

On current trends, by 2050, three quarters of carbon emissions will come from developing economies and by 2100, the temperature will have increased by 3°C to a level that brings extreme weather and widespread coastal flooding.

Economist Nicholas Stern, principal author of *The Stern Review on the Economics of Climate Change*, says that carbon emission is "the greatest market failure the world has ever seen," and to avoid the risk of catastrophic climate change, the upward CO_2 trend must be stopped. Most economists agree with Stern and favor action.

Coping with the Problem

A global problem requires global action, and the first steps in this direction were taken at a 2015 United Nations climate change conference in Paris where 197 countries agreed to
1. Limit greenhouse gases emitted by human activity to the same levels that can be absorbed naturally, beginning as early as possible between 2050 and 2100.

Figure 1 Temperature and CO_2

SOURCES OF DATA: Met Office Hadley Centre and Scripps Institution of Oceanography.

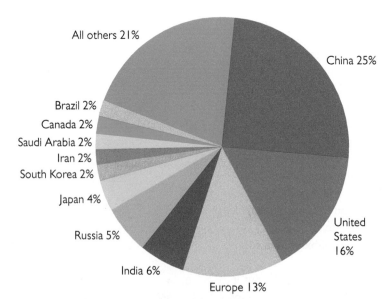

Figure 2 The Global Distribution of CO_2 Emissions

SOURCES OF DATA: Energy Information Administration.

Greenhouse gas emission is "the greatest market failure the world has ever seen."

To avoid the risk of catastrophic climate change, the upward CO_2 trend must be stopped.

Nicholas Stern

2. Keep global temperatures "well below" 2°C above pre-industrial levels and to "endeavor to limit" them to 1.5°C above by 2100.
3. Provide "climate finance" payments by rich countries of at least $100 billion a year starting in 2020 and more by 2025 to help poorer countries leapfrog fossil fuels and move straight to renewables.
4. Review each country's voluntary contribution to cutting emissions every five years.

If carbon emissions are to be cut, incentives must change. The cost of carbon-emitting activities must rise and the cost of alternative clean-energy technologies must fall. Disagreement centers on how to change incentives.

Should countries use carbon taxes or should they cap emissions and introduce carbon trading? Should clean energy and the research to develop new green technologies be subsidized?

Carbon Taxes

The Canadian province of British Columbia, Ireland, and the United Kingdom are among those making their carbon footprints smaller by taxing carbon-emitting activities. British Columbia has a tax of $30 per ton of carbon emitted. Ireland and the United Kingdom have steep taxes on gasoline. Figure 3 shows the large U.K. gas tax and contrasts it with the very low U.S. gas tax.

Cap-and-Trade

Cap-and-trade—capping emissions and issuing tradeable emissions permits—has been used successfully by the EPA to cut local air pollutants, particularly lead. The system is also in use in Europe, but the cap is too large and the price is too low.

Subsidize Green Alternatives

Many countries provide subsidies to power utilities when they install wind farms or arrays of solar panels. The cost of these technologies is falling and they provide an increasing percentage of energy demand.

"For little environmental benefit, we could end up sacrificing growth, jobs, and opportunities for the big majority, especially in the developing world."

Bjørn Lomborg

Why Isn't More Being Done?

Why don't we have more aggressive caps and stronger incentives to encourage a larger reduction in carbon emissions? Four reasons are

1. Developing economies want to develop *and* want low-cost energy. With the currently available technologies, coal is an attractive choice for them.
2. Getting global agreement is hard. Paris 2015 was the first time that every country signed onto a plan.
3. The costs of lowering emissions are certain and are borne now while most of the benefits come in the future. Bjørn Lomborg, author of *The Skeptical Environmentalist*, says that "For little environmental benefit, we could end up sacrificing growth, jobs, and opportunities for the big majority, especially in the developing world."
4. Technology is advancing and the cost of cleaner energy is falling, so there is a temptation to rely on this trend continuing. An example is replacing coal with gas, which halves the carbon emissions from electricity generation and which fracking technology has made a cost-effective option.

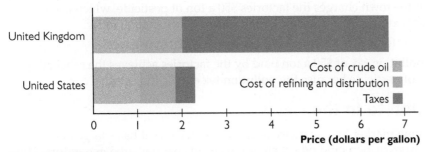

Figure 3 Gasoline Taxes

SOURCES OF DATA: Energy Information Administration, Automobile Association, and authors' assumptions.

MyEconLab Study Plan 10.1
Key Terms Quiz
Solutions Video

CHECKPOINT 10.1

Explain why negative externalities lead to inefficient overproduction and how property rights and pollution taxes can achieve a more efficient outcome.

Practice Problems

Figure 1 illustrates the unregulated market for a pesticide. When factories produce pesticide, they also create waste, which they dump into a lake on the edge of the town. The marginal external cost of the dumped waste is equal to the marginal private cost of producing the pesticide (that is, the marginal social cost of producing the pesticide is double the marginal private cost).

1. What is the quantity of pesticide produced if no one owns the lake and what is the efficient quantity of pesticide? What is the deadweight loss?

2. If the town owns the lake, what is the quantity of pesticide produced and how much does the town charge the factories to dump waste?

3. If the pesticide factories own the lake, how much pesticide is produced?

4. If no one owns the lake and the government levies a pollution tax, what is the tax per ton of pesticide that achieves the efficient outcome?

In the News

Could U.S. pollution regulations help smog-enshrouded China?
Beijing officials issued a "red alert" for air quality, closed schools, limited automobile traffic, and kept people indoors to avoid toxic smog. Most of Beijing's energy comes from carbon-emitting coal. The U.S. EPA is working with China to develop a national cap-and-trade system.
Source: The Christian Science Monitor, December 8, 2015

Explain the inefficiency in Beijing's market for electricity and contrast it with the U.S. market. How can cap-and-trade achieve an efficient outcome?

Solutions to Practice Problems

1. In Figure 2, production is 30 tons a week, the efficient quantity is 20 tons a week, and the deadweight loss is the area of the gray triangle.

2. The quantity of pesticide produced is the efficient quantity, 20 tons a week, and the town charges the factories $50 a ton of pesticide, which is the marginal external cost of the pollution produced by that quantity.

3. The factories produce the efficient quantity: 20 tons a week.

4. A pollution tax of $50 a ton paid by the factories achieves the efficient quantity of pesticide because the pollution tax equals the external cost.

Solution to In the News

The Beijing market for electricity is inefficient because it has a large external cost arising from carbon (and other) emissions from coal powered generators. The marginal social cost of electricity exceeds its marginal benefit by a large amount. The U.S. market for electricity is also inefficient but less so than Beijing's. Cap-and-trade can achieve an efficient outcome by confronting power utilities with the marginal *social* cost of their production.

FIGURE 1

Price (dollars per ton)

FIGURE 2

Price and cost (dollars per ton)

10.2 POSITIVE EXTERNALITIES: EDUCATION

MyEconLab Concept Video

Education benefits the students who receive it, and the many other people with whom a well-educated person interacts. To study the economics of education, we must distinguish between its private benefits and its social benefits.

■ Private Benefits and Social Benefits

A *private benefit* is a benefit that the consumer of a good or service receives. The **marginal private benefit** (*MB*) is the benefit from an additional unit of a good or service that the consumer of that good or service receives.

An *external benefit* is a benefit from a good or service that someone other than the consumer receives. A **marginal external benefit** is the benefit from an additional unit of a good or service that people other than the consumer enjoy.

Marginal social benefit (*MSB*) is the marginal benefit enjoyed by society—by the consumers of a good or service (marginal private benefit) and by everyone else who benefits from it (the marginal external benefit). That is,

$$MSB = MB + \text{Marginal external benefit}$$

Figure 10.5 illustrates these benefit concepts. It uses college education as an example, but the same principles apply to all levels of education. The marginal benefit curve, *MB*, describes the marginal private benefit—such as expanded job opportunities and higher incomes—enjoyed by college graduates. Marginal private benefit decreases as the quantity of education increases.

Marginal private benefit
The benefit from an additional unit of a good or service that the consumer of that good or service receives.

Marginal external benefit
The benefit from an additional unit of a good or service that people other than the consumer of that good or service enjoy.

Marginal social benefit
The marginal benefit enjoyed by society—by the consumer of a good or service and by everyone else who benefits from it. It is the sum of marginal private benefit and marginal external benefit.

■ FIGURE 10.5

An External Benefit

MyEconLab Animation

The *MB* curve shows the marginal private benefit enjoyed by the people who receive a college education. The *MSB* curve shows the sum of marginal private benefit and marginal external benefit.

When 15 million students attend college

❶ Marginal private benefit is $10,000 per year.

❷ Marginal external benefit is $15,000 per year.

❸ Marginal social benefit is $25,000 per year.

But college graduates generate external benefits. On the average, college graduates communicate more effectively with others and tend to be better citizens. Their crime rates are lower, and they are more tolerant of the views of others. A society with a large number of college graduates can support activities such as high-quality music, theater, and other organized social activities.

In the example in Figure 10.5, the marginal external benefit is $15,000 per year when 15 million students enroll in college. Marginal social benefit is the sum of marginal private benefit and marginal external benefit. For example, when 15 million students a year enroll in college, the marginal private benefit is $10,000 per year and the marginal external benefit is $15,000 per year, so the marginal social benefit is $25,000 per year.

The marginal social benefit curve, *MSB,* is the sum of marginal private benefit and marginal external benefit. It is steeper than the *MB* curve because marginal external benefit diminishes for the same reasons that *MB* diminishes.

When people make decisions about how much schooling to undertake, they consider only its private benefits and if education were provided by private schools that charged full-cost tuition, there would be too few college graduates.

Figure 10.6 shows the underproduction that would occur if all college education were left to the private market. The supply curve is the marginal cost curve of the private schools, *S = MC.* The demand curve is the marginal private benefit curve, *D = MB.* Market equilibrium is at a tuition of $15,000 per year and 7.5 million students enroll per year. At this equilibrium, the marginal social benefit is $38,000 per year, which exceeds the marginal cost by $23,000 per year. Too few students enroll in college. The efficient number of students is 15 million per year, with marginal social benefit equal to marginal cost. The gray triangle shows the deadweight loss created by the underproduction.

FIGURE 10.6

Underproduction with an External Benefit   MyEconLab Animation

The market demand curve is the marginal private benefit curve, *D = MB.* The supply curve is the marginal cost curve, *S = MC.*

❶ Market equilibrium is at a tuition of $15,000 per year with 7.5 million students per year enrolled.

The marginal social benefit curve is *MSB,* so the market equilibrium is inefficient because ❷ marginal social benefit exceeds ❸ marginal cost.

❹ The efficient number of students is 15 million a year.

❺ The gray triangle shows the deadweight loss created because too few students enroll in college.

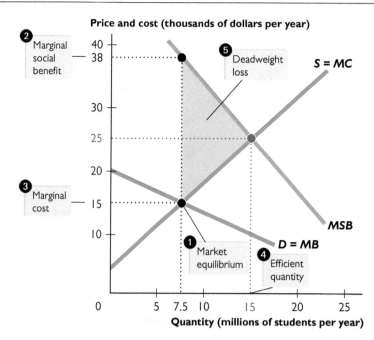

Government Actions in the Face of External Benefits

To get closer to producing the efficient quantity of a good or service that generates an external benefit, we make public choices through governments and modify the market outcome. To achieve a more efficient allocation of resources in the presence of external benefits, such as those that arise from education, governments can use three devices:

- Public provision
- Private subsidies
- Vouchers

Public Provision

Public provision is the production of a good or service by a public authority that receives most of its revenue from the government. Education services produced by public universities, colleges, and schools are examples of public provision.

Figure 10.7 shows how public provision might overcome the underproduction that arises in Figure 10.6. Public provision cannot lower the cost of production, so marginal cost is the same as before. Marginal private benefit, marginal external benefit, and marginal social benefit are also the same as in Figure 10.6.

The efficient quantity occurs where marginal social benefit equals marginal cost. In Figure 10.7, this quantity is 15 million students per year. Tuition is set to ensure that the efficient number of students enroll. That is, tuition is set at the level that equals the marginal private benefit at the efficient quantity. In Figure 10.7, tuition is $10,000 a year. The rest of the cost of the public college is borne by the taxpayers and, in this example, is $15,000 per student per year.

Public provision
The production of a good or service by a public authority that receives most of its revenue from the government.

FIGURE 10.7

Public Provision to Achieve an Efficient Outcome

MyEconLab Animation

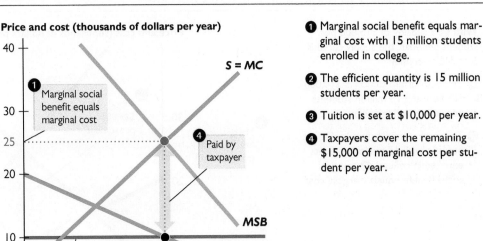

Price and cost (thousands of dollars per year)

Quantity (millions of students per year)

❶ Marginal social benefit equals marginal cost with 15 million students enrolled in college.

❷ The efficient quantity is 15 million students per year.

❸ Tuition is set at $10,000 per year.

❹ Taxpayers cover the remaining $15,000 of marginal cost per student per year.

Subsidy
A payment by the government to a producer to cover part of the costs of production.

Private Subsidies

A **subsidy** is a payment by the government to a producer to cover part of the costs of production. By giving producers a subsidy, the government can induce private decision makers to consider external benefits when they make their choices.

Figure 10.8 shows how a subsidy to private colleges works. In the absence of a subsidy, the marginal cost curve is the market supply curve of private college education, $S = MC$. The marginal benefit is the demand curve, $D = MB$. In this example, the government provides a subsidy to colleges of $15,000 per student per year. We must subtract the subsidy from the marginal cost of education to find the colleges' supply curve. That curve is $S = MC - subsidy$ in the figure. The equilibrium tuition (market price) is $10,000 per year, and the equilibrium number of students is 15 million per year. To educate 15 million students, colleges incur a marginal cost of a student of $25,000 per year. The marginal social benefit of a student is also $25,000 per year. So with marginal cost equal to marginal social benefit, the subsidy achieves an efficient outcome. The tuition and the subsidy just cover the colleges' marginal cost of a student per year.

Public Provision Versus Private Subsidy   In the two methods we've just studied, the number of students who enroll and the tuition are the same. So are these two methods of providing education services equally good? This question is difficult to resolve. The bureaucrats that operate public schools don't have as strong an incentive to minimize costs and maximize *quality* as those who run private schools. But for elementary and secondary education, charter schools might be an efficient compromise between traditional public schools and subsidized private schools.

FIGURE 10.8

Private Subsidy to Achieve an Efficient Outcome   MyEconLab Animation

With ❶ a subsidy of $15,000 per student per year, the supply curve is $S = MC - subsidy$.

❷ The equilibrium tuition is $10,000 per year and 15 million students per year enroll in college.

❸ The market equilibrium is efficient because with 15 million students enrolled in college, ❹ marginal social benefit equals marginal cost.

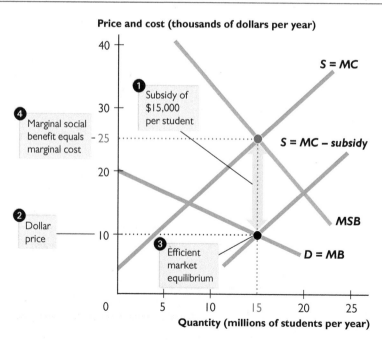

Vouchers

A **voucher** is a token that the government provides to households, which they can use to buy specified goods or services. The SNAP food stamp benefits provided by the U.S. Department of Agriculture to low-income households are an example of a voucher. Vouchers for college education could be provided to students.

Suppose that the government provides each student with a voucher. Students would choose the college to attend and use dollars plus the voucher to pay the tuition. Colleges would exchange the vouchers they receive for dollars from the government. If the government set the value of the voucher equal to the marginal external benefit of a year of college at the efficient number of students, then the outcome would be efficient.

Figure 10.9 illustrates an efficient voucher scheme. The government issues vouchers worth $15,000 per year, equal to the marginal external benefit at the efficient number of students. Each student pays $10,000 per year tuition and the government pays $15,000 per voucher, so the college collects $25,000 per student per year. The voucher scheme results in 15 million students attending college, the marginal cost equals the marginal social benefit, and the outcome is efficient.

Do Vouchers Beat Public Provision and Subsidy? Vouchers provide public financial resources to the consumer rather than the producer. Economists generally believe that vouchers offer a more efficient outcome than public provision and subsidies because they combine the benefits of competition among private colleges with the injection of the public funds needed to achieve an efficient number of students. Also, students and their parents can monitor school performance more effectively than the government can.

Voucher
A token that the government provides to households, which they can use to buy specified goods or services.

▮ **FIGURE 10.9**

Vouchers Achieve an Efficient Outcome

MyEconLab Animation

With vouchers for college, students are willing to pay MB plus the value of the voucher.

❶ The government issues vouchers to each student valued at $15,000, equal to the marginal external benefit of a year of college at the efficient number of students.

❷ The market equilibrium is efficient because with 15 million students enrolled in college, ❸ marginal social benefit equals marginal cost.

❹ Each student pays tuition of $10,000 (the dollar price) and the school collects $15,000 (the value of the voucher) from the government.

CHECKPOINT 10.2

Explain why positive externalities lead to inefficient underproduction and how public provision, subsidies, and vouchers can achieve a more efficient outcome.

Practice Problems

FIGURE 1

Cost and price
(thousands of dollars)

Students (thousands per year)

Figure 1 shows the marginal private benefit from college education. The marginal cost of a college education is a constant $6,000 a year. The marginal external benefit from a college education is a constant $4,000 per student per year.

1. What is the efficient number of students? If colleges are private (no government involvement), how many people enroll, what is the tuition, and what is the deadweight loss?

2. If the government provides public colleges, what is the tuition that will achieve the efficient number of students? How much must taxpayers pay?

3. If the government subsidizes private colleges, what subsidy will achieve the efficient number of college students?

4. If the government offers each student a voucher, what value of the voucher will achieve the efficient number of students?

In the News

Students across America march for tuition-free college
Students at colleges and universities from Los Angeles to New York are demonstrating in support of free education. The website studentmarch.org says: "Education should be free. The United States is the richest country in the world, yet students have to take on crippling debt in order to get a college education."
Sources: *Reuters*, November 12, 2015, and www.studentmarch.org

If college becomes tuition-free, how will the number of students enrolled change and will the outcome be efficient?

Solutions to Practice Problems

FIGURE 2

Cost and price
(thousands of dollars)

1. In Figure 2, the efficient number of students is 50,000 a year. With no government involvement, enrollment is 30,000 students a year and tuition is $6,000 a year. The gray triangle shows the deadweight loss.

2. To enroll the efficient 50,000 students, public colleges would charge $2,000 per student and taxpayers would pay $4,000 per student (Figure 2).

3. A subsidy of $4,000 per student (equal to marginal external benefit).

4. A voucher valued at $4,000 will achieve an efficient enrollment of 50,000. The private college tuition is $6,000. 50,000 students will enroll if the dollar cost is $2,000 per student. So the value of the voucher will have to be $4,000.

Solution to In the News

Setting tuition at zero will increase the number of students enrolled in colleges and universities—a movement downward along the demand curve. College education has an external benefit, so an efficient outcome occurs when tuition is less than marginal cost and marginal social benefit equals marginal cost. It is unlikely that zero tuition is efficient and it is likely that it would bring overproduction.

CHAPTER SUMMARY

Key Points

1. **Explain why negative externalities lead to inefficient overproduction and how property rights and pollution taxes can achieve a more efficient outcome.**

   - External costs are costs of production that fall on people other than the producer of a good or service. Marginal social cost equals marginal private cost plus marginal external cost.

   - Producers take account only of marginal private cost and produce more than the efficient quantity when there is a marginal external cost.

   - Sometimes it is possible to overcome a negative externality by assigning a property right.

   - When property rights cannot be assigned, governments might overcome a negative externality by mandating clean technologies (command-and-control), imposing pollution taxes, or using a cap-and-trade program.

2. **Explain why positive externalities lead to inefficient underproduction and how public provision, subsidies, and vouchers can achieve a more efficient outcome.**

   - External benefits are benefits that are received by people other than the consumer of a good or service. Marginal social benefit equals marginal private benefit plus marginal external benefit.

   - External benefits from education arise because better-educated people are better citizens, commit fewer crimes, and support social activities.

   - Vouchers or subsidies to private colleges or the provision of public education below cost can achieve a more efficient provision of education.

Key Terms

MyEconLab Key Terms Quiz

Abatement technology, 249
Coase theorem, 249
Command-and-control regulation, 251
Externality, 244
Marginal external benefit, 257
Marginal external cost, 246

Marginal private benefit, 257
Marginal private cost, 246
Marginal social benefit, 257
Marginal social cost, 246
Negative externality, 244
Positive externality, 244

Property rights, 249
Public provision, 259
Subsidy, 260
Voucher, 261

CHAPTER CHECKPOINT

Study Plan Problems and Applications

Table 1 shows the demand schedule for electricity from a coal-burning utility. Table 2 shows the utility's cost of producing electricity and the external cost of the pollution created. Use this information to work Problems **1** to **3**.

TABLE 1   DEMAND FOR ELECTRICITY

Price (cents per kilowatt)	Quantity demanded (kilowatts per day)
4	500
8	400
12	300
16	200
20	100
24	0

TABLE 2   PRIVATE AND EXTERNAL COSTS

Quantity (kilowatts per day)	Marginal cost	Marginal external cost
	(cents per kilowatt)	
0	0	0
100	2	2
200	4	4
300	6	6
400	8	8
500	10	10

TABLE 3

Students (millions per year)	Marginal benefit (dollars per student per year)
1	5,000
2	3,000
3	2,000
4	1,500
5	1,200
6	1,000
7	800
8	500

1. With no pollution control, calculate the quantity of electricity produced, the price of electricity, and the marginal external cost of the pollution generated.

2. With no pollution control, calculate the quantity of electricity produced, the marginal social cost of the electricity generated, and the deadweight loss.

3. If the government levies a pollution tax such that the utility generates the efficient quantity of electricity, calculate the quantity of electricity generated, the price of electricity, the size of the pollution tax, and the tax revenue.

Use the following information to work Problems **4** and **5**.

Tom and Larry must spend a day working together. Tom likes to smoke cigars and the price of a cigar is $2. Larry likes a smoke-free environment.

4. If Tom's marginal benefit from a cigar a day is $20 and Larry's marginal benefit from a smoke-free environment is $25 a day, what is the outcome if they meet at Tom's home? What is the outcome if they meet at Larry's home?

5. If Tom's marginal benefit from a cigar a day is $25 and Larry's marginal benefit from a smoke-free environment is $20 a day, what is the outcome if they meet at Tom's home? What is the outcome if they meet at Larry's home?

Use Table 3 and the following information to work Problems **6** to **8**.

The marginal cost of educating a college student is $5,000 a year. Table 3 shows the marginal benefit schedule from a college education. The marginal external benefit from a college education is a constant $2,000 per student per year. There are no public colleges.

6. With no government involvement in college education, how many students enroll, what is the tuition, and what is the deadweight loss created?

7. If the government subsidizes colleges and sets the subsidy so that the efficient number of students enroll, what is the subsidy per student, how many students enroll, and what is the cost to taxpayers?

8. If the government offers vouchers to students, what is the value of the voucher that will encourage the efficient number of students to enroll?

9. **Two Philadelphia highways waste a million hours**
   A study of highway use says that on two short stretches of expressway in Philadelphia, delays of 1 million hours a year cost $22 million in lost time and waste 375,700 gallons of fuel.
   Source: Bob McGovern, *PhillyVoice*, November 23, 2015
   What is the externality described in the news clip? How could road tolls and high parking levies reduce congestion on Philadelpia roads? If road tolls and parking charges cut commute times, would the Philadelphia road system be more efficient? Explain your answers.

 10. Read *Eye on Climate Change* on pp. 254–255 and then describe the government actions that could decrease carbon emissions. Explain why the government is not taking these actions more aggressively.

Instructor Assignable Problems and Applications

MyEconLab Homework, Quiz, or Test if assigned by instructor

1. The price of gasoline in Europe is about three times that in the United States, mainly because the European gas tax is higher than the U.S. gas tax. How would an increase in the gas tax in the United States to the European level change carbon emissions? Would this tax increase bring greater efficiency or would it increase deadweight loss?

2. **The warming Arctic affects us all**
   Arctic temperatures are rising twice as fast as the global average and receding sea ice threatens polar bears, walruses, and seals that exist nowhere else on earth and face an increased risk of extinction.
   Source: *Truthout*, December 4, 2015

   What is the externality described in the news clip? How could property rights influence the amount of damage done to the Arctic Sea and its wildlife?

Use the following information to work Problems **3** and **4**.

City ponders ban on plastic bags
Most plastic shopping bags end up in the landfill or as litter. Tacoma city officials are considering banning them or allowing them for a fee of 5 or 10 cents.
Source: *Tacoma Weekly*, December 8, 2015

3. Explain how a Tacoma charge will change the use of plastic bags and how the deadweight loss created by plastic bags will change.

4. Explain why a Tocoma ban on plastic bags would be inefficient.

Use the following information to work Problems **5** to **7**.

The marginal cost of educating a college student online is $3,000 a year. Table 1 shows the marginal private benefit schedule from a college education. The marginal external benefit is 50 percent of the marginal private benefit.

5. With no government involvement in college education, how many students enroll and what is the tuition? Calculate the deadweight loss created.

6. If the government subsidizes colleges so that the efficient number of students will enroll, what is the cost to taxpayers?

7. If the government offers vouchers to students and values them so that the efficient number of students will enroll, what is the value of the voucher?

8. **Worse than useless**
   Europe's Emissions Trading Scheme (ETS) has too many carbon emission permits trading at too low a price.
   Source: *The Economist*, January 25, 2014

   Explain the conditions under which the ETS, a cap-and-trade system, would reduce the amount of carbon emissions to the efficient quantity. Use a graph of the European market for electricity to illustrate your explanation. On your graph, show the effects of having too many emission permits.

9. **Carbon tax debate heats up in Montpelier, VT**
   Vermonters are debating the pros and cons of a state carbon tax—a new tax on gasoline, heating oil, and other fossil fuels sold in the state. Backers say the tax revenue would be used to cut other taxes and increase energy efficiency.
   Source: Watchdog.org, December 3, 2015

   Draw a graph of the market for gasoline in Vermont to show the effects of a state carbon tax.

TABLE 1

Students (millions per year)	Marginal private benefit (dollars per student per year)
1	6,000
2	5,000
3	4,000
4	3,000
5	2,000
6	1,000

Multiple Choice Quiz

1. Electricity has a negative production externality because _____.
   A. its marginal benefit decreases as more of it is consumed
   B. the marginal private cost of producing it increases as more of it is produced
   C. the marginal social cost of producing it exceeds the marginal private cost of producing it
   D. a marginal external cost lowers the marginal benefit from consuming it

2. A steelmaking plant pollutes the air and water so _____.
   A. the marginal social cost of producing steel exceeds the marginal private cost by the amount of the marginal external cost
   B. the marginal social cost of producing steel is less than the marginal private cost by the amount of the marginal external cost
   C. the marginal private cost of producing steel equals the marginal external cost plus the marginal social cost
   D. the marginal private cost of producing steel minus the marginal social cost equals the marginal external cost

3. An unregulated paint factory that pollutes a river results in _____ and _____.
   A. overproduction; a price that exceeds the marginal benefit from the good
   B. underproduction; a price that equals the marginal benefit from the good
   C. the efficient quantity produced; a marginal benefit equal to the marginal social cost
   D. an inefficient quantity produced; a marginal benefit below the marginal social cost

4. Steel production creates pollution. If a tax is imposed on steel production equal to the marginal external cost of the pollution it creates, _____.
   A. steel producers will cut pollution to zero
   B. the deadweight loss created by steel producers will be cut to zero
   C. the market price of steel will rise by the amount of the tax
   D. steel producers will continue to produce the inefficient quantity of steel

5. A good or service with a positive externality is one which _____.
   A. everyone wants to have access to
   B. is produced in the social interest
   C. the marginal social benefit exceeds the marginal private benefit
   D. the marginal external benefit exceeds the marginal private benefit

6. Because education generates a positive externality, _____.
   A. everyone who wants a college education should get one
   B. graduates' marginal benefit exceeds the society's value of the education
   C. the quantity of education undertaken will achieve the social interest if it is free
   D. subsidies to colleges or vouchers to students are means of achieving the efficient number of graduates

Should America spend more on transportation infrastructure?

Public Goods and Common Resources

11

When you have completed your study of this chapter, you will be able to

1 Distinguish among private goods, public goods, and common resources.

2 Explain the free-rider problem and how public provision might help to overcome it and deliver an efficient quantity of public goods.

3 Explain the tragedy of the commons and review its possible solutions.   MyEconLab Big Picture Video

267

11.1 CLASSIFYING GOODS AND RESOURCES

Why do governments use tax dollars to build highways, bridges, and tunnels? Why don't profit-seeking private firms build and sell the services of the transportation infrastructure? What's the difference between fish in the Pacific Ocean and fish on East Point Seafood Company's Seattle fish farm? What's the difference between a live Taylor Swift concert and a concert on network television? What's the difference between education and fast food? Each pair differs in many ways, but key is the extent to which people can be *excluded* from enjoying the benefits from them and the extent to which their use by one person *rivals* their use by others.

■ Excludable

Excludable
A good, service, or resource is excludable if it is possible to prevent someone from enjoying its benefits.

Nonexcludable
A good, service, or resource is nonexcludable if it is impossible (or extremely costly) to prevent someone from enjoying its benefits.

A good, service, or resource is **excludable** if it is possible to prevent someone from enjoying its benefits. Brink's security services, East Point Seafood's fish, and Taylor Swift concerts are examples. You must pay to benefit from them.

A good, service, or resource is **nonexcludable** if it is impossible (or extremely costly) to prevent someone from benefiting from it. The services of the city police department, fish in the Pacific Ocean, and a concert on network television are examples. When a police cruiser slows the traffic on a highway to the speed limit, it lowers the risk of an accident to all the road users. It can't exclude some road users from the lower risk. Anyone with a boat can try to catch the fish in the ocean. Anyone with a television can watch a network broadcast.

■ Rival

Rival
A good, service, or resource is rival if its use by one person decreases the quantity available for someone else.

Nonrival
A good, service, or resource is nonrival if its use by one person does not decrease the quantity available for someone else.

A good, service, or resource is **rival** if its use by one person decreases the quantity available for someone else. Brink's security might work for two banks, but one truck can't deliver cash to two banks at the same time. A fish, whether in the ocean or on a fish farm, can be consumed only once. One seat at a concert can hold only one person at a time. These items are rival.

A good, service, or resource is **nonrival** if its use by one person does not decrease the quantity available for someone else. The services of the city police department and a concert on network television are nonrival. The arrival of one more person in a neighborhood doesn't lower the level of police protection enjoyed by the community. When one additional person switches on the TV, no other viewer is affected.

■ A Fourfold Classification

Figure 11.1 classifies goods, services, and resources into four types using the two criteria that we've just considered.

Private Goods

Private good
A good or service that can be consumed by only one person at a time and only by the person who has bought it or owns it.

A good or service that is both rival and excludable (top left of Figure 11.1) is a **private good**: It can be consumed by only one person at a time and only by the person who has bought it or owns it. The fish on East Point's farm are an example of a private good. One person's consumption of a fish rivals others', and everyone except the person who bought a fish is excluded from consuming it.

Public Goods

A good or service that is both nonrival and nonexcludable (bottom right of Figure 11.1) is a **public good**: It can be consumed simultaneously by everyone, and no one can be excluded from enjoying its benefits. A flood-control levee is an example of a public good. Everyone who lives in a protected floodplain enjoys the benefits, and no one can be excluded from receiving those benefits. The system of law and order provided by the courts and the body of laws is another example.

Public good
A good or service that can be consumed simultaneously by everyone and from which no one can be excluded.

Common Resources

A resource that is rival and nonexcludable (top right of Figure 11.1) is a **common resource**: A unit of it can be used only once, but no one can be prevented from using what is available. Ocean fish and the Earth's atmosphere are examples of common resources. Ocean fish are rival because a fish taken by one person is not available for anyone else, and they are nonexcludable because it is difficult to prevent people from catching them. The Earth's atmosphere is rival because oxygen used by one person is not available for anyone else, and it is nonexcludable because we can't prevent people from breathing!

Common resource
A resource that can be used only once, but no one can be prevented from using what is available.

Natural Monopoly Goods

A good that is nonrival but excludable (bottom left of Figure 11.1) is a good produced by a *natural monopoly*. We define natural monopoly in Chapter 16 (p. 402). A natural monopoly is a firm that can produce at a lower cost than two or more firms can. Examples are the Internet, cable television, and a bridge or tunnel. One more user doesn't decrease the enjoyment of the other users, and people can be excluded with user codes, scramblers, and tollgates.

■ **FIGURE 11.1**

Fourfold Classification of Goods

MyEconLab Animation

	Private goods	**Common resources**
Rival	Food and drink Car House	Fish in ocean Atmosphere National parks
	Natural monopoly goods	**Public goods**
Nonrival	Internet Cable television Bridge or tunnel	National defense The law Flood-control levees
	Excludable	**Nonexcludable**

Goods that are rival and excludable are private goods (top left).

Goods that are nonrival and nonexcludable are public goods (bottom right).

Goods and resources that are rival but nonexcludable are common resources (top right).

Goods that are nonrival but excludable are goods produced by a natural monopoly (bottom left).

Source of data: Adapted from and inspired by E. S. Savas, *Privatizing the Public Sector,* Chatham House Publishers, Inc., Chatham, NJ, 1982, p. 34.

EYE on the PAST
Is a Lighthouse a Public Good?

A lighthouse looks like a public good: *nonexcludable* and *nonrival*. But in the eighteenth century, lighthouses in England were built and operated by private companies that earned profits by charging tolls on ships docking at nearby ports. A ship that refused to pay the lighthouse toll was excluded from using the port. So even the services of a lighthouse, when it is near a port, are excludable! Such a lighthouse is an example of a natural monopoly good and not a public good.

 CHECKPOINT 11.1

Distinguish among private goods, public goods, and common resources.

Practice Problems

1. Classify the following services for computer owners with an Internet connection as rival or nonrival and as excludable or nonexcludable:
   • eBay
   • A mouse
   • A Twitter page
   • MyEconLab Web site

2. Classify each of the following items as a public good, a private good, a natural monopoly good, or a common resource:
   • Fire protection
   • A seat at the final match of the U.S. Open (tennis)
   • A pay-per-view movie on television
   • The Ohio River

Solutions to Practice Problems

1. eBay is nonrival and nonexcludable. A mouse is rival and excludable. Twitter is nonrival and you can choose to make your feed excludable or nonexcludable. MyEconLab is nonrival and excludable.

2. Fire protection is nonrival and nonexcludable, so it is a public good. A seat at the U.S. Open final match is rival and excludable, so it is a private good. A pay-per-view movie is nonrival and excludable, so it is a natural monopoly good. The Ohio River is rival and nonexcludable, so it is a common resource.

11.2   PUBLIC GOODS AND THE FREE-RIDER PROBLEM

MyEconLab Concept Video

Why does the U.S. government provide our national defense and district court system? Why do the state governments provide flood-control levees? Why do our city governments provide fire and police services? Why don't we buy our national defense from North Pole Protection, Inc., a private firm that competes for our dollars in the marketplace in the same way that McDonald's does? Why don't private engineering firms provide levees? Why don't we buy our policing and fire services from Brink's and other private firms? The answer is that all of these goods are public goods—goods that are nonexcludable and nonrival—and such goods create a free-rider problem.

■ The Free-Rider Problem

A **free rider** is a person who enjoys the benefits from a good or service without paying for it. Because everyone consumes the same quantity of a public good and no one can be excluded from enjoying its benefits, no one has an incentive to pay for it. Everyone has an incentive to free ride. The *free-rider problem* is that the private market, left on its own, would provide too small a quantity of a public good. To produce the efficient quantity, government action is required.

To see how a private market would provide too little of a public good and how government might provide the efficient quantity, we need to consider the marginal benefit from a public good and its marginal cost. The marginal benefit from a public good is a little different from that of a private good, so we'll begin on the benefit side of the calculation.

Free rider
A person who enjoys the benefits of a good or service without paying for it.

EYE on YOUR LIFE

MyEconLab Critical Thinking Exercise

A Student's Free-Rider Problem and a Market Solution

A music file is nonrival because it can be copied at the click of a mouse. A duplicate file can be created at zero marginal cost. A music file is also effectively nonexcludable because it is extremely costly to prevent someone who wants to make an illegal copy from doing so.

Because a music file is nonrival and nonexcludable, it is a public good with a free-rider problem.

If everyone obtained their music by copying the files of their friends, you can see that it would not take long for the provision of songs to dry up. Professional writers and performers would not be able to generate an

income and only amateurs who write, perform, and record for fun would be left in the business.

This free-rider problem might be tackled by using the copyright laws that restrict the legal right to copy music files. What is wrong with this approach is that making something illegal isn't effective if it is difficult to detect and punish the illegal act. With the spread of ownership of smartphones, laptops, and fast Internet connections, free-riding became a big problem.

As almost always eventually happens, a market solution emerged. That solution is streaming.

Spotify, Apple Music, and others have created subscription services that give access to music but not to files. Subscriptions to streaming services have doubled each year, and singles downloads are now declining.

Illegal file sharing creates a free-rider problem, and streaming services solve it.

■ The Marginal Benefit from a Public Good

Lisa and Max (the only people in a society) share a common parking area that has no security lighting, a public good. Both of them would like some lights, but how many? The answer is determined by marginal benefit and marginal cost.

Lisa and Max know their own marginal benefit from different levels of security lighting, and the tables in parts (a) and (b) of Figure 11.2 show these marginal benefits. The curves MB_L and MB_M are Lisa's and Max's marginal benefit curves. As the quantity of the good increases, each person's marginal benefit from the public good diminishes—just as it does for a private good.

The table in part (c) of Figure 11.2 shows the marginal benefit for the entire economy. We obtain this curve by summing the individual marginal benefits at each quantity. For example, with 3 lights, the marginal benefit is $70 ($40 for Lisa plus $30 for Max). The curve MSB is the marginal social benefit curve.

Because we find the marginal benefit from a public good by summing the marginal benefits of all individuals at each quantity, we find the MSB curve for a public good by summing the individual marginal benefit curves *vertically*. In contrast, to obtain the MB curve for a private good—which is also the market demand curve—we sum the quantities demanded by all individuals at each price—we sum the individual demand curves *horizontally* (see Chapter 4, p. 87).

■ The Marginal Cost of a Public Good

The marginal cost of a public good is determined in exactly the same way as that of a private good. The principle of *increasing marginal cost* that you learned in Chapter 6 applies to the marginal cost of a public good. So the marginal cost curve of a public good slopes upward. A public good does not create an externality, so the marginal cost is also the marginal social cost.

We find the marginal social benefit curves of the law courts, flood-control levees, police protection, and firefighting service by summing the individual marginal benefit curves for these public goods.

FIGURE 11.2

Marginal Benefit from a Public Good

Marginal benefit (dollars per light)

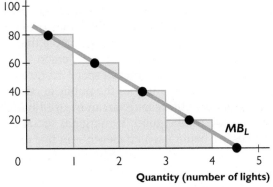

(a) Lisa's marginal benefit

Marginal benefit (dollars per light)

(b) Max's marginal benefit

Marginal social benefit (dollars per light)

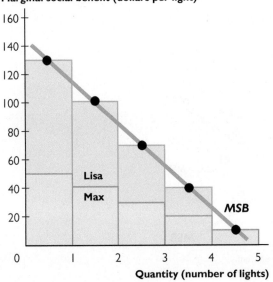

(c) Economy's marginal social benefit

The marginal benefit curves for a public good are MB_L for Lisa and MB_M for Max. The marginal benefit from the public good for the economy is the sum of the marginal benefits of all individuals at each quantity. The marginal social benefit curve for the economy is MSB.

Quantity of lights	0	1	2	3	4	5
Lisa's MB (dollars per light)		80	60	40	20	0

Quantity of lights	0	1	2	3	4	5
Max's MB (dollars per light)		50	40	30	20	10

Quantity of lights	0	1	2	3	4	5
Lisa's MB (dollars per light)		80	60	40	20	0
Max's MB (dollars per light)		50	40	30	20	10
Economy's MSB (dollars per light)		130	100	70	40	10

■ The Efficient Quantity of a Public Good

To determine the efficient quantity of a public good, we use the same principles that you learned in Chapter 10: We find the quantity at which marginal social benefit equals marginal social cost.

Figure 11.3 shows the marginal social benefit curve *MSB* and the marginal social cost curve *MSC* of a public good—surveillance satellites that provide national defense services. The *MSB* curve is based on the same principle that determines the marginal social benefit of the public good in the two-person (Lisa and Max) economy. If marginal social benefit exceeds marginal social cost, resources can be used more efficiently by increasing the quantity of the public good. If marginal social cost exceeds marginal social benefit, resources can be used more efficiently by decreasing the quantity of the public good. If marginal social benefit equals marginal social cost, resources are being used efficiently—in this example, 200 satellites.

■ Private Provision: Underproduction

Could a private firm—say, North Pole Protection, Inc.—deliver the efficient quantity of satellites? Most likely it couldn't, because no one would have an incentive to pay his or her share of the cost of the satellites. Everyone would reason as follows: "The number of satellites provided by North Pole Protection, Inc., is not affected by my decision to pay my share or not. My own private consumption will be greater if I free ride. If I do not pay, I enjoy the same level of security and I can buy more private goods. So I will free ride on the public good." Such reasoning is the free-rider problem. If everyone reasons the same way, North Pole Protection, Inc., has no revenue and so provides no satellites.

■ **FIGURE 11.3**

The Efficient Quantity and Private Underproduction of a Public Good

❶ With fewer than 200 satellites, marginal social benefit *MSB* exceeds marginal social cost *MSC*. An increase in the quantity will make resource use more efficient.

❷ With more than 200 satellites, marginal social cost exceeds marginal social benefit. A decrease in the quantity will make resource use more efficient.

❸ With 200 satellites, marginal social benefit *MSB* equals marginal social cost *MSC*. Resources are used efficiently.

❹ The efficient quantity of the public good is 200 satellites.

❺ Private provision leads to underproduction—in the extreme, to zero production.

■ Public Provision: Efficient Production

The political outcome might be efficient or inefficient. We look first at an efficient outcome. There are two political parties, the Hawks and the Doves, and they agree on all issues except for the quantity of defense satellites. The Hawks prefer 300 satellites, and the Doves prefer 100 satellites. Both parties want to get elected, so they run a voter survey and discover the *MSB* curve of Figure 11.4. They also consult with satellite producers to establish the marginal cost schedule. The parties then do a "what-if" analysis. If the Hawks propose 300 satellites and the Doves propose 100 satellites, the voters will be equally unhappy with both parties. Compared to the efficient quantity of satellites, the Doves propose an under-provision of 100 satellites and the Hawks propose an overprovision of 100 satellites. The deadweight losses are equal, and an election would be too close to call.

Contemplating this outcome, the Hawks realize that they are too hawkish to get elected. They figure that if they scale back to 250 satellites, they will win the election if the Doves propose 100 satellites. The Doves reason in a similar way and figure that if they increase the number of satellites to 150, they can win the election if the Hawks propose 300 satellites. Each party knows how the other is reasoning, so they realize that their party must provide 200 satellites or it will lose the election. So both parties propose 200 satellites. The voters are indifferent between the parties, and each party receives 50 percent of the vote.

FIGURE 11.4

An Efficient Political Outcome

MyEconLab Animation

(a) Parties' preferences

(b) Political outcome

❶ The Doves would like to provide 100 satellites. ❷ The Hawks would like to provide 300 satellites.

❸ The political outcome is 200 satellites: Unless each party proposes 200 satellites, the other party can win an election.

■ Obstacles to Efficient Public Provision

Achieving an efficient political outcome is much harder than describing one. Three obstacles stand in its path:

- Determining benefits and costs
- Bureaucrats' goals and rationally uninformed voters
- Limited funds.

Determining Benefits and Costs

Elections are almost never about a single issue. Satellites compete with MRI scanners, education, and countless other public goods for the taxpayers' dollar. Bureaucrats help politicians to develop detailed proposals for a menu of items.

Benefit-cost analysis
An accounting exercise to determine the total benefit, total cost, and net benefit of a proposed project.

The tool that bureaucrats use in this process is called **benefit-cost analysis**, which is an accounting exercise to determine the total benefit, total cost, and net benefit of a proposed project. By pursuing projects with the highest net benefit, politicians hope to win and keep their seats.

Total benefit and cost are related to marginal benefit and cost and Figure 11.5 shows how. In part (a), at $15 billion each, 200 satellites cost $3 trillion, the area of the red rectangle. In part (b), with the benefit of each satellite shown by the *MSB* curve, the total benefit is $4 trillion, the green area. Net benefit equals total benefit minus total cost and is $1 trillion, the area of the green triangle.

■ FIGURE 11.5

Total Cost, Total Benefit, and Net Benefit   MyEconLab Animation

 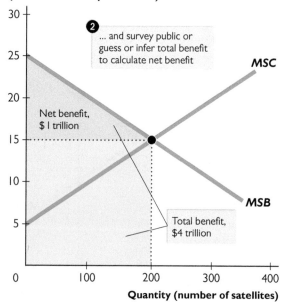

(a) Cost of satellites

❶ Total cost is the cost of each unit multiplied by the quantity bought. The total cost of 200 satellites is $3 trillion.

(b) Benefit of satellites

❷ Total benefit is marginal benefit summed over the 200 satellites bought and net benefit is total benefit minus total cost.

Bureaucrats can get a good estimate of total cost by consulting engineers and others who possess the relevant technical knowledge and by obtaining price quotations from potential suppliers. In the case of surveillance satellites, the price of a Lockheed Martin satellite can be determined and used as input in the benefit-cost analysis.

The benefit is hard to measure. When people buy a private good, they reveal their willingness to pay and their marginal benefit by the choices they make. But votes for packages containing hundreds of projects don't reveal the willingness of voters to pay for any individual project. Public policy planners can sometimes use surveys that ask people to report their valuations of a project. And sometimes they can make inferences. For example, if a transport project will save people time, the value of time might be inferred from wage rates. But sometimes, there is no information and an educated guess must be made.

Because benefits are hard to measure, there will be both underprovision and overprovision of individual public goods.

Bureaucrats' Goals and Rationally Uninformed Voters

Bureau heads have their own goals and one of them is to maximize their budgets to enhance their status and power. For the top Pentagon bureaucrats, the objective is to maximize the national defense budget. They might pursue this goal by trying to persuade politicians that more satellites or more costly satellites are needed.

But won't overpaying for or overproviding satellites cost votes and be opposed by politicians? It would if voters were well informed. But rational voters are not well informed. The reason is that it is rational for a voter to be ignorant about an issue when the cost of information exceeds its benefit.

Rational ignorance is the decision not to acquire information because the marginal cost of doing so exceeds the marginal benefit. Each voter knows that he or she can make no difference to national defense policy and that it would take an enormous amount of time and effort to become even moderately well informed about alternative defense technologies. So voters remain relatively uninformed about the technicalities of defense (and most other) issues, leaving open the opportunity for bureaucrats to overprovide public goods.

Rational ignorance
The decision not to acquire information because the marginal cost of doing so exceeds the marginal benefit.

Limited Funds

The tendency to overprovide public goods is countered by limited funds. Taxes pay for public goods and while voters like public goods, they don't like paying taxes. And overprovision of public goods would mean voters being over-taxed.

Because politicians don't get elected by promising higher taxes, the funds available for providing public goods can be lower than the level needed to provide the efficient quantity.

Eye on the U.S. Infrastructure on p. 278 describes a situation in which there appears to be a clear underprovision arising from limited funds. If there really is underprovision of transportation infrastructure, shouldn't a political party be able to secure more votes by proposing greater provision and higher taxes to pay the bill? If the tax and spend package could be offered with guarantees, that outcome would be feasible. But there is a disconnect in Congress and the state legislatures between higher taxes and improved public goods. Taxes are legislated before the underprovision of public goods is corrected, and politicians can't credibly commit to using the taxes to deliver the promised goods.

EYE on the U.S. INFRASTRUCTURE

Should America Spend More on Transportation Infrastructure?

The Problem

The road transportation infrastructure of the United States consists of 4 million miles of roads, 47,000 miles of interstate highways, and 607,000 bridges.

The gas tax is the main source of funds for maintaining this infrastructure. The federal gas tax has been stuck at 18.4¢ per gallon since 1997 and the last time most states changed the gas tax was before 2000.

Fixed tax rates, declining gas consumption due to more fuel-efficient vehicles, and rising costs of maintaining roads and bridges mean that the funds needed for repairs have outstripped the funds available. Gas tax revenue adjusted for rising prices—the real gas tax—has decreased.

With decreasing real tax revenue, expenditure on maintaining the transportation infrastructure has trended downward. Figure 1 shows the trends in expenditure and taxes, both adjusted for the cost of inflation.

The American Society of Civil Engineers says that 67,500 bridges are structurally deficient and a spending increase of $8 billion annually is needed to bring the nation's bridges to a safe standard by 2028.

Economic Analysis

Figure 2 shows a model of the problem. The x-axis measures the number of bridges repaired per year and the y-axis measures the marginal social benefit and marginal social cost of

repairing a bridge, shown by the *MSB* and *MSC* curves.

In the model economy, it is efficient to repair 6,000 bridges a year at a cost of $3 million per bridge, with a total expenditure of $18 billion per year.

Limited funds block this efficient outcome. The number of bridges repaired is 4,000 per year at a cost of $2.5 million per bridge, with a total expenditure of $10 billion per year.

Because the number of bridges repaired per year is less than the efficient quantity, a deadweight loss is created.

In Figure 2, *MSB* exceeds *MSC*, so voters will support higher taxes and a bigger bridge repair program. In the U.S. economy, politicians have not found that efficient outcome.

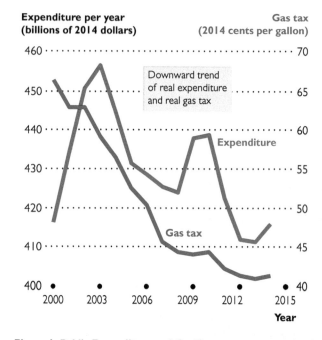

Figure 1 Public Expenditure and Gas Tax

Figure 2 Underprovision of Infrastructure

CHECKPOINT 11.2

MyEconLab Study Plan 11.2
Key Terms Quiz
Solutions Video

Explain the free-rider problem and how public provision might help to overcome it and deliver an efficient quantity of public goods.

Practice Problems

1. For each of the following goods, explain whether there is a free-rider problem. If there is no such problem, how is it avoided?
   - Fire protection
   - A July 4th fireworks display
   - Interstate 80 in rural Wyoming

Use Table 1, which provides data about a mosquito control program, to work Problems **2** and **3**.

2. What quantity of spraying would a private control program provide? What is the efficient quantity of spraying? In a single-issue election on the quantity of spraying, what quantity would the winner of the election provide?

3. Suppose that the government sets up a Department of Mosquito Control and appoints a bureaucrat to run it. Would the department most likely underprovide, overprovide, or provide the efficient quantity of spraying?

TABLE 1

Quantity (square miles sprayed per day)	Marginal social cost	Marginal social benefit
	(dollars per day)	
0	0	6,000
1	1,000	5,000
2	2,000	4,000
3	3,000	3,000
4	4,000	2,000
5	5,000	1,000

In the News

The BBC is a cross between PBS and the IRS
Take a moment to thank the voluntary PBS fundraisers. The British Broadcasting Corporation (BBC) is funded by something called the "license fee," a tax of £145.50 ($245) per year on every household that has a television.
Source: *The Federalist*, August 7, 2014

Do the BBC and PBS produce a public good? Which one has a free-rider problem and how has the other one solved it?

Solutions to Practice Problems

1. Fire protection is a public good; a July 4th fireworks display is a public good. In both cases, the free-rider problem is avoided by public provision and financing through taxes. Interstate 80 in rural Wyoming is a public good. The public good creates a free-rider problem that is avoided because governments collect various taxes via the tax on gas and the vehicle registration fee.

2. A private program would provide zero spraying because the free-rider problem would prevail. The efficient quantity is 3 square miles a day—the quantity at which the marginal social benefit equals the marginal social cost. The winner will provide the efficient quantity: 3 square miles sprayed a day.

3. The Department of Mosquito Control would most likely overprovide because the bureau would try to maximize its budget.

Solution to In the News

Broadcast television is nonrival and nonexcludable, so it is a public good. PBS has a free-rider problem because only viewers who choose to contribute toward the cost of its service actually pay, while others free ride. The BBC has solved a free-rider problem by being funded by a compulsory fee that works like a tax.

MyEconLab Concept Video

11.3   THE TRAGEDY OF THE COMMONS

Tragedy of the commons
The overuse of a common resource that arises because its users have no incentive to conserve it and use it sustainably.

Overgrazing the pastures of a village in Middle Ages England and overfishing North Atlantic cod during recent decades are tragedies of the commons. The **tragedy of the commons** is the overuse of a common resource—a resource that is nonexcludable but rival—that arises because its users have no incentive to conserve it and use it sustainably.

To study the tragedy of the commons, its cause, and its possible remedies, we'll study the overfishing and depletion of the cod stock. You're about to discover that there are two problems that give rise to the tragedy of the commons:

- Unsustainable use of a common resource
- Inefficient use of a common resource

■ Unsustainable Use of a Common Resource

Renewable common resources such as fish and trees replenish themselves by the birth and growth of new members of the population.

Think about cod in the North Atlantic. At any given time, there is a *stock* of cod, a *rate of renewal*, and a rate of use—a *catch rate*. If the rate of renewal exceeds the catch rate, the cod stock grows and cod is being caught sustainably. The cod stock is also being used sustainably if its rate of renewal equals the catch rate and the stock remains constant. But if the catch rate exceeds the rate of renewal, the stock decreases and the cod stock is being used unsustainably.

The sustainable catch depends on the stock. With a small stock, few fish are born, so only a small quantity can be sustainably caught. With a large stock, many

EYE on the PAST
The Commons of England's Middle Ages

The term "the tragedy of the commons" comes from fourteenth century England, where areas of rough grassland surrounded villages. The commons were open to all and were used for grazing cows and sheep owned by the villagers.

Because the commons were open to everyone, no one had an incentive to ensure that the land was not overgrazed. The result was an overgrazing situation similar to that of overfishing in some of today's oceans.

During the sixteenth century, when the price of wool increased, England became a wool exporter to the world. Sheep farming became

profitable and sheep owners needed better control of the land they used, so the commons were gradually

enclosed and privatized. Overgrazing ended, and land use became more efficient.

fish are born but they must compete with each other for food, so only a few survive to reproduce and to grow large enough to be caught. So again, the sustainable catch is small. Between a small and a large stock is a stock at which, given the availability of food, the rate of renewal is at its maximum. At this stock, the sustainable catch rate is also at its maximum.

Figure 11.6 illustrates the relationship between the stock and sustainable catch. The *sustainable catch curve, SCC,* shows the sustainable catch rate at each stock size. As the stock increases, the sustainable catch increases to a maximum and then decreases.

If the catch rate is less than the sustainable catch rate, at a point such as *A*, the cod stock grows. If the quantity caught equals the sustainable catch, at any point on the *SCC*, the fish stock remains constant and is available for future generations of fishers in the same quantity that is available today. But if the quantity caught exceeds the sustainable catch, at a point such as *B*, the fish stock shrinks and, unchecked, eventually falls to zero.

You now understand the sustainable use of a resource, but another problem is its efficient use.

■ Inefficient Use of a Common Resource

Even if the catch is sustainable, it will exceed the efficient catch: overfishing occurs. Why does overfishing occur? The answer is that fishers face only their own *private* cost and don't face the cost they impose on others—the *external* cost. In pursuit of self-interest, the fishers ignore this external cost. Let's explore overfishing in more detail, starting with the marginal social cost of catching fish.

The pursuit of self-interest results in overfishing.

■ **FIGURE 11.6**

Sustainable Catch   MyEconLab Animation

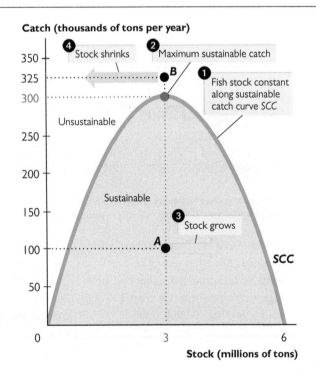

❶ Along the sustainable catch curve, *SCC*, the fish stock is constant.

❷ As the fish stock increases (on the *x*-axis), the sustainable catch (on the *y*-axis) increases to the maximum sustainable catch. As the stock increases further, the fish must compete for food and the sustainable catch falls.

❸ If the catch is less than the sustainable catch, such as at point *A*, the fish stock grows.

❹ If the catch exceeds the sustainable catch, such as at point *B*, the fish stock diminishes.

Marginal Social Cost

The *marginal social cost* of catching fish is the marginal private cost plus the marginal external cost.

The *marginal private cost* of catching fish is the fishers' cost of keeping a boat and crew at sea for long enough to increase the catch by one ton. The principle of increasing marginal cost applies to catching fish just as it applies to other production activities. Crew fatigue, overfull refrigerators, and a lower speed to conserve fuel decrease the catch per hour, so the marginal private cost of catching fish increases as the quantity caught increases.

The *marginal external cost* of catching fish is the cost per additional ton that one fisher's production imposes on all other fishers. This additional cost arises because one fisher's catch decreases the remaining stock, which in turn decreases the renewal rate of the stock and makes it harder for others to find and catch fish. Marginal external cost also increases as the quantity of fish caught increases.

Because both components of marginal social cost increase as the quantity caught increases, marginal social cost increases with the quantity of fish caught.

 EYE on the GLOBAL ECONOMY

The North Atlantic Cod Tragedy of the Commons

Before 1970, Atlantic cod was abundant. It had been fished for many centuries and was a major food source for the first European settlers in North America. In 1812, there were more than 1,600 fishing boats in the waters off New England and Newfoundland, Canada. At that time, cod were huge fish, weighing in at more than 220 pounds and measuring up to 6 feet in length.

Fish were caught using lines and productivity was low. But low productivity limited the catch and enabled cod to be caught sustainably over hundreds of years.

The situation changed dramatically during the 1960s with the introduction of high-efficiency nets (called trawls, seines, and gill nets), sonar technology to find fish concentrations, and large ships with efficient processing and

Fish landings (thousands of tons per year)

SOURCE OF DATA FOR GRAPH: Millennium Ecosystem Assessment.
SOURCE OF INFORMATION: Codfishes —Atlantic cod and its fishery, http://science.jrank.org/

storage facilities. These technological advances brought soaring cod harvests. In less than a decade, cod landings increased from less than 300,000 tons a year to 800,000 tons.

This volume of cod could not be taken without a serious collapse in the stock and in 1992, a total ban on cod fishing in the North Atlantic stabilized the population but at a very low level.

Marginal Social Benefit and Demand

The marginal social benefit from fish is the price that consumers are willing to pay for an additional pound of fish. Marginal social benefit decreases as the quantity of fish consumed increases, so the market demand curve, which is also the marginal social benefit curve, slopes downward.

Overfishing Equilibrium

Figure 11.7 illustrates overfishing and how it arises. The market demand curve for fish is the marginal social benefit curve, *MSB*. The market supply curve is the marginal private cost curve, *MC*. Market equilibrium occurs at the intersection point of these two curves. The equilibrium quantity is 800,000 tons of fish per year and the equilibrium price is $10 per pound. At the market equilibrium quantity, marginal social cost exceeds marginal social benefit.

Efficient Equilibrium

The efficient quantity is where marginal social benefit equals marginal social cost. In Figure 11.7, the efficient quantity of fish is 300,000 tons. At this quantity, the marginal social cost (on the *MSC* curve) and marginal social benefit (on the *MSB* curve) are equal.

Deadweight Loss from Overfishing

Deadweight loss measures the cost of overfishing. The gray triangle in Figure 11.7 illustrates this loss. It is the marginal social cost minus the marginal social benefit from all the fish caught in excess of the efficient quantity.

■ **FIGURE 11.7**

Why Overfishing Occurs   MyEconLab Animation

The market supply curve is the marginal private cost curve, *MC*, and the market demand curve is the marginal social benefit curve, *MSB*.

❶ The market equilibrium occurs at a quantity of 800,000 tons and a price of $10 a pound—an overfishing equilibrium.

❷ The marginal social cost curve is *MSC* and the efficient equilibrium is at a quantity of 300,000 tons a year.

❸ The market equilibrium quantity exceeds the efficient quantity and overfishing brings a deadweight loss.

MyEconLab Concept Video

■ Using the Commons Efficiently

It is easier to define the conditions under which a common resource is used efficiently than to deliver those conditions. To use a common resource efficiently, it is necessary to design an incentive mechanism that confronts the users of the resource with the marginal social consequences of their actions. The same principles apply to common resources as those that you met in Chapter 10 when you studied the external cost of pollution.

The three main methods that might be used to achieve the efficient use of a common resource are

- Property rights
- Production quotas
- Individual transferable quotas (ITQs)

Property Rights

A common resource that no one owns and that anyone is free to use contrasts with *private property*, which is a resource that someone owns and has an incentive to use in the way that maximizes its value. The resource is used efficiently. One way of overcoming the tragedy of the commons is to convert a common resource to private property. With private property rights, the owner of the resource faces the same conditions as society faces. It doesn't matter who owns the resource. The users of the resource that someone owns are confronted with the opportunity cost of using it. If the user is the owner, the opportunity cost of using it is forgone rental income. If the resource is used by someone who leases it from its owner, the opportunity cost of using it is the rent paid to the owner.

Figure 11.8 illustrates the efficient outcome when private property rights over a resource are established and enforced. The marginal private cost curve, *MC*, and the market supply curve, *S*, are the same as the marginal social cost curve, *MSC*: the curve labeled $S = MC = MSC$. The demand curve is the marginal social benefit curve, *MSB*. The market price and equilibrium quantity are determined by supply and demand at $15 per pound and an annual catch of 300,000 tons. At this quantity marginal social benefit equals marginal social cost, so the quantity produced is the efficient quantity.

The private property solution to the tragedy of the commons is available in some cases. It was the solution to the original tragedy of the commons in England's Middle Ages. It is also a solution that has been used to prevent overuse of the airwaves that carry smartphone services. The right to use this space (called the frequency spectrum) has been auctioned by governments to the highest bidders. The owner of each part of the spectrum is the only one permitted to use it (or to license someone else to use it).

But assigning private property rights is not always feasible and it isn't a practical solution to the problem of overfishing. The cost of policing millions of square miles of ocean would be far greater than the benefit arising from it. Also, there would be international disputes about which country had the right to enforce property rights. Further, in some cases and the ocean fish stock is one of them, people have an emotional objection to assigning private property rights. Critics of private property rights say it is immoral for someone to own a resource that they regard as public. In the absence of property rights, some form of government intervention is used, one of which is a production quota.

Wireless communications companies bid in government auctions to be the owners of the frequency spectrum.

FIGURE 11.8

Property Rights Achieve the Efficient Use of a Common Resource   MyEconLab Animation

Price and cost (dollars per pound)

With property rights to the fish stock assigned, fishers pay the owner of the fish stock for permission to fish and face the marginal social cost of their decisions.

1 The marginal cost curve, which is also the market supply curve, includes all the costs of fishing, so it is also the marginal social cost curve, $S = MC = MSC$.

2 The market equilibrium occurs at the intersection of MSC and MSB and the resource use is efficient.

3 The quantity caught, 300,000 tons, is the efficient quantity.

Production Quotas

A *production quota* is an upper limit to the quantity of a good that may be produced in a specified period. The quota is allocated to individual producers, so each producer has its own quota.

Figure 11.9 shows a production quota that achieves an efficient outcome. The quota limits the catch (production) to 300,000 tons, the efficient quantity at which marginal social benefit, *MSB*, equals marginal social cost, *MSC*. If everyone catches their own quota, the outcome is efficient. But implementing a production quota has two problems.

First, it is in every fisher's self-interest to catch more fish than the quantity permitted under the quota. The reason is that the market price exceeds marginal private cost, so by catching more fish, a fisher gets a higher income. If enough fishers break the quota, overfishing occurs and the tragedy of the commons remains.

Second, marginal cost is not, in general, the same for all producers—as we're assuming here. Some producers have a comparative advantage in using the resource. Efficiency requires that the quota be allocated to the producers with the lowest marginal cost. But the government department that allocates quotas does not have information about the marginal cost of individual producers. Even if the government tried to get this information, producers would have an incentive to lie about their costs so as to get a bigger quota.

A production quota can work, but only if the activities of every producer can be monitored and all producers have the same marginal cost. Where producers are difficult or very costly to monitor or where marginal cost varies across producers, a production quota cannot achieve an efficient outcome.

■ **FIGURE 11.9**

A Production Quota to Use a Common Resource Efficiently   MyEconLab Animation

❶ A production quota is set at the efficient quantity and each fisher is assigned a share of the quota.

❷ The market equilibrium is efficient, but the price, $15 a pound, exceeds the fishers' marginal cost, $5 a pound.

❸ Fishers earn a profit on the marginal catch.

❹ With price exceeding marginal cost, fishers have an incentive to break the quota and overfish.

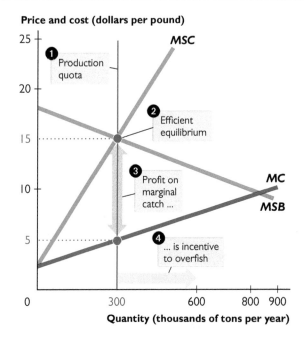

Individual Transferable Quotas

Where producers are difficult to monitor or where marginal cost varies across producers, a more sophisticated quota system, called an individual transferable quota, can be effective. An **individual transferable quota (ITQ)** is a production limit assigned to an individual who is then free to transfer (sell) the quota to someone else. A market in ITQs emerges and ITQs are traded at their market price.

Individual transferable quota (ITQ)
A production limit assigned to an individual who is then free to transfer (sell) the quota to someone else.

The market price of an ITQ is the highest price that someone is willing to pay for one. That price is marginal social benefit minus marginal cost. The price of an ITQ will rise to this level because fishers who don't have a quota would be willing to pay this amount to get one.

A fisher with an ITQ could sell it for the market price, so by not selling the ITQ the fisher incurs an opportunity cost. The marginal cost of fishing, which now includes the opportunity cost of the ITQ, equals the marginal social benefit from the efficient quantity.

Figure 11.10 illustrates how ITQs work. Each fisher receives an allocation of ITQs and the total catch permitted by the ITQs is 300,000 tons per year. Fishers trade ITQs: Those with low marginal cost buy ITQs from those with high marginal cost, and the market price of an ITQ settles at $10 per pound of fish. The marginal private cost of fishing now becomes the original marginal private cost, *MC*, plus the price of the ITQ. The marginal private cost curve shifts upward from *MC* to *MC + price of ITQ* and each fisher is confronted with the marginal social cost of fishing.

Now no one has an incentive to cheat and exceed the quota because to do so would send marginal cost above the market price and result in a loss on the marginal catch. The outcome is efficient.

EYE on the GLOBAL ECONOMY
ITQs Work

Economists agree that ITQs offer an effective tool for achieving an efficient use of the stock of ocean fish.

Iceland, the Netherlands, and Canada were the first countries to adopt ITQs in the late 1970s. New Zealand was the first country to adopt them as a national policy in 1986.

Today, 28 U.S. fisheries and 150 major fisheries and 100 smaller fisheries around the world, representing 10 percent of the world's marine life harvest, is managed by ITQs.

Marine biologists and economists agree that ITQs prevent fish stocks from collapsing and restore fisheries in critical decline.

Studies based on large data sets from more than 10,000 fisheries recorded for more than half a century have shown that without ITQs, there would be a major collapse of the global fish stock, but that with ITQs, a fish crisis has been averted.

One study found that ITQs even reverse a trend decline and turn it around to a trend recovery.

Fisheries that are managed with ITQs are half as likely to collapse as those that are not.

ITQs help maintain fish stocks, but they also reduce the size of the fishing industry. This consequence of adopting ITQs to restore fish stocks pits the use of ITQs against the self-interest of fishers.

In all countries, the fishing industry opposes restrictions on its activities, but in the countries that pioneered ITQs, the opposition was not strong enough to block them.

In the United States the opposition to ITQs was so strong that the fishing industry persuaded Congress to outlaw them. In 1996, Congress passed the Sustainable Fishing Act that put a moratorium on ITQs that lasted until 2004. Since then, many U.S. fisheries have been managed by ITQs and have begun to see their benefits. ITQs are a success story.

FIGURE 11.10

An ITQ to Use a Common Resource Efficiently

MyEconLab Animation

ITQs are issued such that the quantity of fish caught equals the efficient quantity.

❶ The market price of an ITQ equals the marginal external cost of fishing and confronts fishers with the marginal social cost of their decisions.

❷ The market equilibrium is efficient with 300,000 tons a year caught at the marginal social cost and market price of $15 a pound.

MyEconLab Study Plan 11.3
Key Terms Quiz
Solutions Video

CHECKPOINT 11.3

Explain the tragedy of the commons and review its possible solutions.

Practice Problems

Cows graze on common pasture and can produce milk in the amounts shown in Table 1. The marginal private cost of producing milk is zero.

1. What is the quantity of milk produced if use of the common pasture is not regulated? Use a graph to illustrate your answer.
2. What is the efficient quantity of milk to produce? On a graph show the deadweight loss from overproduction.
3. If the common pasture were converted to private land and fenced off, what quantity of milk would be produced?
4. If ITQs were issued for the efficient quantity of milk production, what would be the market price of an ITQ?

In the News

Can ecotourism help save endangered species?
Well-practiced ecotourism is helping to conserve the orangutan, humpback whale, African lion, snow leopard, and many other species and drawing dollars to the cause.

Source: www.thetravelworld.com, May 22, 2012

Explain how ecotourism changes incentives and might avoid the tragedy of the commons for many species, including those mentioned in the news clip.

Solutions to Practice Problems

1. The quantity of milk produced is 100 gallons a day—the quantity at which the marginal private cost equals the marginal social benefit. See Figure 1.
2. The efficient quantity of milk is 60 gallons a day—the quantity at which the marginal social cost equals the marginal social benefit. Marginal social cost equals marginal private cost plus marginal external cost. The gray area in Figure 2 shows the deadweight loss from overproduction.
3. If the common pasture were converted to private land and fenced off, the quantity of milk produced would be the efficient quantity—60 gallons a day.
4. The market price of an ITQ would be $6 a gallon, which equals the marginal external cost at the efficient quantity of milk.

Solution to In the News

There is a tradeoff between hunting and killing animals for their meat, skin, tusks, or other parts and maintaining a healthy population of animals to be viewed by curious and interested tourists. With a thriving ecotourist industry, communities living close to populations of orangutans, humpback whales, African lions, and snow leopards have an incentive to protect the animals, earn an income from ecotourists, and not overuse their natural resources.

TABLE 1

Quantity of milk (gallons per day)	Marginal external cost	Marginal social benefit
	(dollars per gallon)	
0	0	15
20	2	12
40	4	9
60	6	6
80	8	3
100	10	0

FIGURE 1

FIGURE 2

CHAPTER SUMMARY

Key Points

1. Distinguish among private goods, public goods, and common resources.

- A private good is a good or service that is rival and excludable.
- A public good is a good or service that is nonrival and nonexcludable.
- A common resource is a resource that is rival but nonexcludable.

2. Explain the free-rider problem and how public provision might help to overcome it and deliver an efficient quantity of public goods.

- A public good creates a free-rider problem—no one has a private incentive to pay her or his share of the cost of providing a public good.
- The efficient level of provision of a public good is that at which marginal social benefit equals marginal social cost.
- Competition between political parties, each of which tries to appeal to the maximum number of voters, can lead to the efficient scale of provision of a public good and to both parties proposing the same policies.
- Obstacles to efficient political outcomes are the difficulty of estimating social benefit, bureaucrats' goals, and rational ignorance.
- When bureaucrats try to maximize their budgets, and if voters are rationally ignorant, public goods might be overprovided.

3. Explain the tragedy of the commons and review its possible solutions.

- Common resources create the tragedy of the commons—no one has a private incentive to conserve the resource and use it at an efficient rate.
- A common resource is used to the point at which the marginal private cost equals the marginal social benefit.
- The efficient use of a common resource is the point at which marginal social benefit equals marginal social cost.
- A common resource might be used efficiently by creating a private property right, setting a quota, or issuing individual transferable quotas.

Key Terms

MyEconLab Key Terms Quiz

CHAPTER CHECKPOINT

Study Plan Problems and Applications

Use the following list of items to work Problems **1** and **2**.

- New Year's Eve celebrations in Times Square, New York
- A city's sewer system
- New York subway system
- A skateboard
- Cable TV
- Niagara Falls

TABLE 1

Units of public good	Total benefit		
	Wendy	Sara	Tom
0	0	0	0
1	20	10	30
2	40	15	50
3	60	20	60
4	80	25	65
5	100	30	67

1. Classify each of the items in the list as a private good, a public good, a common resource, or a natural monopoly good. Explain each classification.

2. For each public good in the list, is there a free-rider problem? If not, how is the free-rider problem avoided?

3. Table 1 sets out total benefit from a public good for Wendy, Sara, and Tom, who are the only people in the society. If the government provided 3 units of the public good, calculate the marginal social benefit.

Use Figure 1 to work Problems **4** and **5**. It shows the marginal social benefit and marginal social cost of a waste disposal system in a city of 1 million people.

4. What is the efficient capacity of the system and how much would each person have to pay in taxes if the city installed the efficient capacity?

5. If voters are well informed about the costs and benefits of the waste disposal system, what capacity will voters choose? If voters are rationally ignorant, will bureaucrats install the efficient capacity? Explain your answer.

FIGURE 1

Marginal benefit and marginal cost (dollars per million gallons)

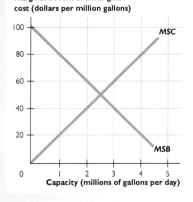

Use Figure 2, which shows the market for North Atlantic tuna, to work Problems **6** to **8**.

6. a. What is the quantity of tuna that fishers catch and the price of tuna? Is there overfishing? Explain why or why not.
b. If the stock of tuna is used efficiently, what would be the price of fish?

7. a. With a quota of 40 tons a month for the tuna fishing industry, what is the equilibrium price of tuna and the quantity of tuna that fishers catch?
b. Is the equilibrium an overfishing equilibrium?

8. If the government issues ITQs to individual fishers that limit the total catch to the efficient quantity, what is the market price of an ITQ?

9. U.S. issues Arctic drilling permit to Royal Dutch Shell
The U.S. government has given Royal Dutch Shell permission to drill for oil and natural gas in the Arctic Ocean. Environmentalists say it is the wrong decision.

Source: *The Wall Street Journal*, August 17, 2015

FIGURE 2

Price and cost (dollars per ton)

Are the oil and gas reserves public goods, private goods, or common resources? When an oil company receives a permit to develop a particular oil reserve, is that oil reserve a public good or a private good? Will the oil company produce an inefficient quantity or the efficient quantity? Explain.

 10. Read *Eye on the U.S. Infrastructure* on p. 278 and then explain why it would be efficient to repair more bridges every year and why we don't do so.

Instructor Assignable Problems and Applications

1. a. What type of good is a highway bridge?
   b. Why might a bridge be provided by government rather than privately?
   c. Why might it be efficient to charge drivers a toll every time they use a bridge?
   d. What information would be needed to determine the efficient number of bridges to repair each year?

Use Table 1, which provides data about a dandelion control program, to work Problems **2** and **3**.

2. What quantity of spraying would a private control program provide? What is the efficient quantity of spraying?

3. Two political parties, the Conservers and the Eradicators, fight an election in which the only issue is the quantity of spraying to undertake. The Conservers want no spraying and the Eradicators want to spray 2.5 square miles a day. The voters are well-informed about the benefits and costs of the program. What is the outcome of the election?

4. If hikers and others were required to pay a fee to use the Appalachian Trail, would the use of this common resource be more efficient? Would it be even more efficient if the most popular spots such as Annapolis Rock had more highly priced access? Why do you think we don't see more market solutions to the tragedy of the commons?

Use the following information to answer Problems **5** to **7**.

A natural spring runs under land owned by ten people. Each person has the right to sink a well and can take water from the spring at a constant marginal cost of $5 a gallon. Table 2 sets out the marginal external cost and the marginal social benefit from the water.

5. Draw a graph to illustrate the market equilibrium. On your graph, show the efficient quantity of water taken.

6. If the government sets a production quota on the total amount of water such that the spring is used efficiently, what would that quota be?

7. If the government issues ITQs to land owners that limit the total amount of water taken to the efficient quantity, what is the market price of an ITQ?

8. **Waukesha deserves a shot at Great Lakes water supply**
   The city of Waukesha, Wis., has applied to borrow water from Lake Michigan under the Great Lakes Compact, an agreement between the states and Canadian provinces that border the Great Lakes designed to meet long-term drinking water needs for communities like Waukesha.
   Source: www.startribune.com, December 11, 2015
   Is water in the Great Lakes a public good, a private good, or a common resource? What are the goals of the Compact? How might they be achieved?

9. **The Great Pacific Tuna Cartel**
   Eight small Pacific islands with control of 5.5 million square miles of prime tuna fishing waters, have tripled the access fee for U.S. tuna fishers from $21 million to $63 million and increased monitoring of these waters.
   Source: *The Wall Street Journal*, March 20, 2013
   Explain how the Pacific islands' action influences the efficiency of the use of tuna resources and illustrate your answer with a graph of the tuna market.

TABLE 1

Quantity (square miles sprayed per day)	Marginal social cost	Marginal social benefit
	(dollars per day)	
0.5	0	600
1.0	100	500
1.5	200	400
2.0	300	300
2.5	400	200
3.0	500	100

TABLE 2

Quantity of water (gallons per day)	Marginal external cost	Marginal social benefit
	(dollars per gallon)	
10	1	10
20	2	9
30	3	8
40	4	7
50	5	6
60	6	5
70	7	4

Multiple Choice Quiz

1. A good is _____ if it is possible to prevent someone from enjoying its benefits and such a good might be a _____ good.

   A. rival; private
   B. excludable; public
   C. excludable; private
   D. nonexcludable; common resource

2. A free-rider problem arises if a good is _____.

   A. nonrival and nonexcludable
   B. nonrival and excludable
   C. rival and nonexcludable
   D. rival and excludable

3. The marginal social benefit from a public good is _____.

   A. the quantity demanded by all the people at a given price
   B. the amount that all the people are willing to pay for a given quantity
   C. the amount that all the people are willing to pay at a given quantity for one more unit
   D. the quantity demanded by all the people at a given marginal social cost

4. The efficient quantity of a public good is most likely to be delivered by _____.

   A. an election contest between two parties that want different quantities
   B. highly trained bureaucrats
   C. efficient private companies
   D. an individual transferable quota

5. A renewable common resource is used sustainably if _____.

   A. private benefits and public benefits are equal
   B. private benefits equal private costs
   C. the rate of renewal of the resource equals its rate of use
   D. the rate of use of the resource equals the social benefit from its use

6. Overfishing occurs if, at the quantity caught, _____.

   A. marginal social cost equals marginal private cost plus marginal external cost
   B. marginal social benefit equals the fishers' marginal private cost
   C. marginal social benefit equals marginal social cost
   D. marginal social benefit equals marginal private cost plus marginal external cost

7. All the following can achieve an efficient use of a common resource *except* _____.

   A. a production quota equal to the marginal external cost
   B. individual transferable quotas that total the efficient quantity
   C. assigning property rights to convert the common resource to private use
   D. individual transferable quotas that trade at marginal external cost

8. When ITQs are assigned, the market price of an ITQ equals the _____.

   A. marginal benefit consumers receive from the fish caught
   B. marginal private cost of fishing
   C. marginal external cost of fishing
   D. marginal social cost of fishing

How do you avoid buying
a lemon?

Private Information and Healthcare Markets

12

When you have completed your study of this chapter, you will be able to

1   Describe the lemons problem and explain how the used-car market solves it.

2   Describe the asymmetric information problems in the insurance market and explain how they are solved.

3   Explain the information problems and other economic problems in healthcare markets.

MyEconLab Big Picture Video

293

12.1   THE LEMONS PROBLEM AND ITS SOLUTION

In all the markets that you've studied so far, buyers and sellers are well informed about the features and the value of the item being traded. Buyers know the benefits they get and sellers know the costs they incur. The buyers' marginal benefit determines demand, the sellers' marginal cost determines supply, and demand and supply together determine the equilibrium price and quantity. If none of the obstacles to efficiency described in Chapter 6 (see p. 158) are present, then the market allocates resources efficiently.

In some markets, either the buyer or the seller has some relevant information to a transaction—**private information**—that the other lacks. One example of these markets is the market for used cars. In this market, each seller has private information about the quality of the vehicle offered for sale. When you buy a used car, you hope it isn't a lemon, but until you have driven it for a month or two, you won't know for sure. But the person who sells you the car knows. When one side of a market has private information, we call the situation one of **asymmetric information**—a situation in which *either* the buyer *or* the seller has *private information*. How does a market with asymmetric information work? What determines the equilibrium price and quantity? Is the market efficient or inefficient?

These are the questions we'll now answer.

Private information
Information relevant to a transaction that is possessed by some market participants but not all.

Asymmetric information
A situation in which either the buyer or the seller has private information.

■ A Market for Used Cars with a Lemons Problem

When a person buys a used car, it might turn out to be a lemon. If the car *is* a lemon, it is worth less to the buyer than if it has no defects. Does the used-car market have different prices reflecting different qualities—a low price for a lemon and a higher price for a car without defects? It turns out that it does. But the market needs some help in overcoming what is called the **lemons problem**—the problem that when it is not possible to distinguish reliable products from lemons, there are too many lemons—perhaps only lemons—and too few reliable products—perhaps none.

To see how the used-car market overcomes the lemons problem, we'll first look at a market that *does* have a lemons problem.

To explain the lemons problem as clearly as possible, we'll assume that there are only two kinds of cars: defective cars—*lemons*—and cars without defects, which we'll call *good cars*. Whether a car is a lemon is private information that is available only to the current owner. The buyer can't tell whether the car for sale is a lemon until after buying it, driving it for a few weeks, and learning as much about it as its current owner knows.

Lemons problem
The problem that when it is not possible to distinguish reliable products from lemons, there are too many lemons and too few reliable products.

George Akerlof of the University of California, Berkeley, and 2001 Nobel Laureate, was the first person to pose the lemons problem and the challenge that it presents for markets to allocate resources efficiently.

Buyers' Decisions and Demand

Even though the buyers of used cars don't know whether they are buying a good car or a lemon, the law of demand applies. The lower the price of a car, the greater is the quantity of cars demanded. But what determines demand and the willingness to pay is a bit different. To see why, let's think about the choice that a car buyer called Greg is about to make.

Greg wants to buy a used car and he would like to avoid buying a lemon. He knows that for him, the value of a good car—his marginal benefit—is $20,000. But Greg has a low income, some spare time, and he knows how to fix a car, so he would be willing to buy a lemon if he could get it for an appropriately low price—a price equal to his marginal benefit from a lemon, which he says is $10,000.

Now think about Greg's dilemma. He has found a car priced at $15,990 (in the photo). He likes the look of the car, but is it a good one or a lemon? If the car is a good one, he gets a marginal benefit of, and would be willing to pay, $20,000. So buying the car for $15,990 gives him a consumer surplus of $4,110. But if the car is a lemon, his marginal benefit is only $10,000, so paying $15,990 for the car leaves him with a negative consumer surplus (a consumer deficit!) of $5,990.

Will Greg pay $15,990? The answer depends on the odds of avoiding a lemon and how Greg regards taking risks. Although he doesn't know the quality of the car, he knows what all his friends have told him about the cars they've bought from the same dealer. If all his friends bought good cars, he will be thinking that this car is most likely a good one too. In this case, he is willing to pay $20,000 and at $15,990, he would buy this car.

But if all Greg's friends bought lemons, he will be thinking that this car is most likely a lemon too. In this case, he is willing to pay only $10,000, so $15,990 is much more than he would be willing to pay.

Other buyers are making decisions like Greg's and figuring out what they are willing to pay for a car of unknown quality. Some buyers are willing to pay more than Greg and some less. At higher prices, there are fewer buyers and at lower prices more buyers. The demand curve for used cars slopes downward.

Figure 12.1 illustrates the demand for used cars. If previous buyers say that they've never seen a lemon, buyers expect no lemons and the demand curve for used cars is D_G. If previous buyers say that they've never seen a good car, buyers expect only lemons and the demand curve is D_L. If previous buyers say that some cars were good ones and some were lemons, buyers expect to see some of each type of car and the demand curve will lie between D_G and D_L.

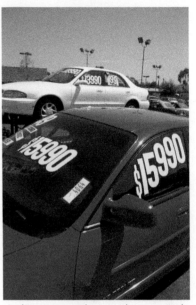

Is this car a good one with a marginal benefit of $20,000 and a consumer surplus of $4,110? Or is it a lemon with a marginal benefit of $10,000 and a consumer "deficit" of $5,990? Will Greg buy it?

■ FIGURE 12.1

The Demand for a Used Car of Unknown Quality   MyEconLab Animation

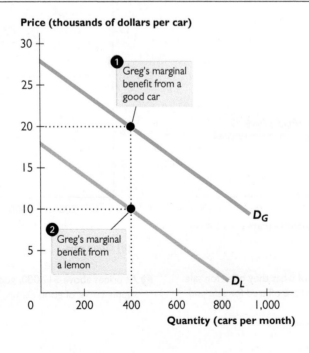

❶ If all Greg's friends bought good used cars, Greg might expect to buy a good one too and be willing to pay $20,000—his marginal benefit from a good car. The demand curve for good cars is D_G.

❷ If all Greg's friends bought lemons, Greg might expect to buy a lemon too and be willing to pay $10,000—his marginal benefit from a lemon. The demand curve for lemons is D_L.

The demand curve for used cars of unknown quality lies between D_L and D_G.

Sellers' Decisions and Supply

Now think about the sellers of used cars, who know the quality of their cars. There is nothing special about this supply: Sellers know their marginal cost, so they know the quantity they are willing to supply at a given price. The marginal cost of a lemon is less than that of a good car and over a range of low prices, only lemons are supplied. At higher prices, the quantity of lemons supplied falls off and good cars start to be supplied.

Figure 12.2 shows an example of what the supply curves might look like. In this example, lemons are offered for sale at prices up to $12,000 and at that price all the lemons available are supplied and good cars start to be offered for sale.

The Market Outcome

Demand and supply determine the price of a used car and the quantity traded, but the market doesn't work well. To explain, we'll focus on an extreme outcome in which only lemons get traded.

Suppose that buyers have learned from their friends that everyone who has bought a used car got a lemon. They assume that they, too, will get a lemon. Consequently, the demand for used cars is based on the willingness to pay for a lemon. The market demand is the demand for lemons, which delivers a low market price. At this low market price, good cars are worth more to their owners than

FIGURE 12.2

The Supply of Used Cars   MyEconLab Animation

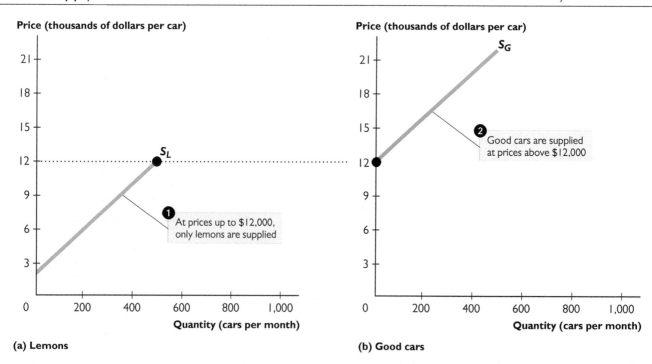

(a) Lemons

(b) Good cars

Suppliers of used cars know the quality of what they offer for sale.
❶ At prices below $12,000, only lemons are offered for sale and the supply curve of lemons is S_L.

❷ At prices above $12,000, good cars are offered for sale and the supply curve of good cars is S_G.

they would get from selling them, so no good cars are offered for sale: only lemons are available. So lemons are the only cars traded.

Figure 12.3 illustrates the used-car market that we've just described. The demand for used cars, D, is equal to the demand for lemons, D_L. The supply of used cars, S, is the supply of lemons up to $12,000 a car (the green segment of the supply curve) and the supply of lemons plus the supply of good cars at prices above $12,000 (the blue segment of the supply curve).

The equilibrium price is $10,000 per car and 400 lemons are traded each month.

Adverse Selection

This market suffers from adverse selection, a general problem that arises in markets with private information. **Adverse selection** is the tendency for people to enter into transactions that bring them benefits from their private information and impose costs on the uninformed party.

For example, Jackie hires salespeople and offers them a fixed wage contract. The only people Jackie attracts are lazy workers. Hardworking salespeople don't work for Jackie because they can earn more by working for someone who pays by results. Jackie's fixed-wage contract adversely selects those with private information—knowledge that they are lazy in this case—who use that knowledge to their own benefit and to impose costs on Jackie.

In the used-car market, the low price adversely selects lemons. The owners of lemons have a greater incentive to offer their cars for sale. In the extreme case (and in the above example), good cars disappear from the market. The owners of good cars have no incentive to offer them for sale. They hold on to their good cars because the market price is less than the owners' minimum supply price.

Adverse selection
The tendency for people to enter into transactions that bring them benefits from their private information and impose costs on the uninformed party.

▮ FIGURE 12.3

The Lemons Problem in a Used-Car Market   MyEconLab Animation

Price (thousands of dollars per car)

① At the equilibrium quantity and price ...

② ... all the cars are lemons

$D = D_L$

Quantity (cars per month)

The demand for used cars is the demand for lemons, so the demand curve is labeled $D = D_L$. The supply curve of used cars is S. The green portion of the curve is the supply of lemons and the blue portion adds the supply of good cars.

❶ The equilibrium price of a used car is $10,000.

❷ 400 used cars a month are traded and they are all lemons. At the equilibrium price, no good cars are offered for sale.

EYE on the MARKET FOR USED CARS

How Do You Avoid Buying a Lemon?

The used-car market in the United States might have a lemons problem, but it definitely works: It is a very active and successful market.

In 2008 (the latest year for which data are available), 50,000 used-car dealers sold 37 million cars at an average price of $8,000 per car.

This scale of operation contrasts with the market for new cars in which around 40 domestic and foreign producers sold 13 million cars at an average price of $26,500 per car.

The stock of cars on U.S. roads is 250 million, so with 37 million being traded, more than one car in seven changes hands each year.

What makes this market work and helps it overcome the lemons problem? The answer is dealers' warranties and third-party inspection services.

By offering warranties, dealers *signal* that the cars they are selling are free from defects and, if a car should turn out to be a lemon, the dealer will bear the cost of fixing it.

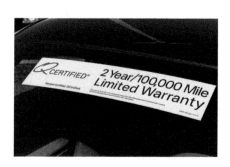

MyEconLab Concept Video

Signaling
When an informed person takes an action that sends information to uninformed people.

■ A Used-Car Market with Dealers' Warranties

How can used-car dealers convince buyers that a car isn't a lemon and that it is worth more than a lemon? The answer is: By giving a guarantee in the form of a warranty, the dealer *signals* which cars are good ones and which cars are lemons.

Signaling occurs when an informed person takes actions that send information to uninformed people. The grades and degrees that a university awards students are signals. They inform potential (uninformed) employers about the abilities of the people they are considering hiring—see *Eye on Your Life* on p. 313.

In the market for used cars, dealers send signals by giving warranties on the used cars they offer for sale. The message in the signal is that the dealer agrees to pay the costs of repairing the car if it turns out to have a defect.

Buyers believe the signal because the cost of sending a false signal is high. A dealer who gives a warranty on a lemon ends up bearing a high cost of repairs—and gains a bad reputation. A dealer who gives a warranty only on good cars has few repair costs and a reputation that gets better and better. It pays dealers to send an accurate signal, and it is rational for buyers to believe the signal.

So a car with a warranty is a good car; a car without a warranty is a lemon. Buyers are now effectively as informed as sellers, so the demand for cars depends on whether the car is a good one or a lemon. Because the willingness to pay for a good car is greater than that for a lemon, the demand for good cars is greater than the demand for lemons. But there is still a demand for lemons from people with a low income and a skill at fixing faulty cars.

So there are now two markets for used cars: one for good cars and one for lemons and in each market there is a price. Warranties solve the lemons problem and enable the used-car market to function efficiently.

Figure 12.4 illustrates this outcome. In part (a), the demand for and supply of lemons determine the price of a lemon. In part (b), the demand for and supply of good cars determine the price of a good car. Both markets are efficient. The marginal

■ **FIGURE 12.4**

Warranties Make a Used-Car Market Efficient   MyEconLab Animation

(a) Lemons

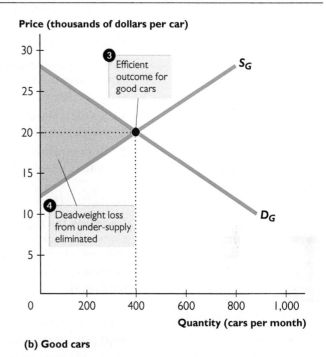

(b) Good cars

❶ The demand for and supply of lemons determine the equilibrium price and quantity of lemons and ❷ the deadweight loss from the oversupply of lemons (gray triangle) is eliminated.

❸ The demand for and supply of good cars determine the equilibrium price and quantity of good cars and ❹ the deadweight loss from the undersupply of good cars (gray triangle) is eliminated.

cost of each quality of car equals its marginal benefit and the deadweight loss that arises with asymmetric information is eliminated.

Pooling Equilibrium and Separating Equilibrium

You've seen two outcomes in the market for used cars. Without warranties, there is only one message visible to the buyer: All cars look the same. So there is one price regardless of whether the car is a good car or a lemon. It is as if all the cars, good ones and lemons, are in one big pool. We call the outcome in a market when only one message is available and an uninformed person cannot determine quality a **pooling equilibrium**. In the example above, only lemons were traded. But in such a market it is possible that a few good cars will be traded, though not enough to make buyers believe they will be lucky enough to get one.

In a used-car market with warranties, there are two messages. Good cars have warranties, and lemons don't. So there are two car prices for the two types of cars. The information created by warranties *separates* good cars and lemons. So the outcome in a market when signaling provides full information to a previously uninformed person is called a **separating equilibrium**.

Notice that no government action is needed to get the used-car market to work well. Dealers' warranties, voluntarily provided, do the job. Nonetheless, consumer protection laws in most states include "lemon laws" and a federal "lemon law" specifies statutory remedies for used-car buyers in the event that a dealer fails to honor its warranty.

Pooling equilibrium
The outcome when only one message is available and an uninformed person cannot determine quality.

Separating equilibrium
The outcome when signaling provides full information to a previously uninformed person.

MyEconLab Study Plan 12.1
Key Terms Quiz
Solutions Video

 # CHECKPOINT 12.1

Describe the lemons problem and explain how the used-car market solves it.

Practice Problems

An earthquake damaged car factories and decreased the production of popular Japanese cars. The demand for good late-model used cars soared and car dealers scrambled to get their hands on used vehicles.

1. Explain the effect of the eathquake on the price of a good used car and the price of a lemon.

2. If you have a late-model car that you know isn't a lemon, will you sell it privately or sell it to a dealer? Explain your answer.

In the News

Choosing the right college

Connie Pollack, a college admissions consultant, says that the challenge for the student is to find the college that pushes the right academic, financial, and social buttons to deliver four happy years without having to make a new choice after the first year.

Source: *Pittsburgh Post-Gazette*, February 12, 2016

Do the applicants or the colleges have private information? Give an example of such private information. Does this market have an adverse selection problem?

Solutions to Practice Problems

1. The increase in demand for good used cars shifts the demand curve rightward. With no change in supply, the price of a good car rises. At the higher price, the *quantity supplied* of good cars increases. The higher price for good cars gives dealers an incentive to fix problems with lemons and offer them for sale with a warranty as good cars, so the supply of lemons decreases (lemons and good cars are substitutes in production—see Chapter 4, pp. 95–96). The decrease in the supply of lemons raises their price.

2. If you sell your used car privately, you offer it without a warranty. Assuming the potential buyer doesn't know you, your car without a warranty would be perceived as a lemon. You would not be able to sell it for the price of the good car that it is. You would sell it to a dealer if he offered you more than the price of a lemon.

Solution to In the News

Colleges and students know the grades and test scores, so these are not private information. Students know how dedicated they are to studying, how they will finance four years at college, and what social activities they want to experience. The student's true "academic, financial, and social buttons" are private information. Colleges try to draw more applicants by looking like comfortable, friendly, safe, and relaxed places with engaged and helpful faculty and staff. The true quality of the college and its faculty is the college's private information. With both colleges and potential students having private information, adverse selection occurs in the market for college places and the best match isn't always achieved.

12.2   INFORMATION PROBLEMS IN INSURANCE MARKETS

MyEconLab Concept Video

Just as buyers and sellers gain from trading goods and services, so they can also gain by trading risk. But risk is a "bad," not a good. The good that is traded is *risk avoidance*. A buyer of risk avoidance can gain because the value of avoiding a risk is greater than the price that must be paid to others to get them to bear shares of the risk. And a seller of risk avoidance faces a lower cost of risk than the price that people are willing to pay to avoid it.

People trade risk in financial markets and insurance markets. Here, we'll focus on insurance markets.

■ Insurance Markets

You can see in *Eye on the U.S. Economy* below that insurance plays a huge role in our economic lives.

Insurance reduces the risk that each person faces by sharing or *pooling* the risks. When you buy insurance against the risk of an unwanted event, you pay an insurance company a *premium*. If the unwanted event occurs, the insurance company pays you the amount of the insured loss.

EYE on the U.S. ECONOMY
Insurance in the United States

We spend 11 percent of our income on insurance. That's more than we spend on cars or food. In addition, we buy Social Security and unemployment insurance through our taxes.

Auto insurance reduces the risk of financial loss in the event of an auto accident or theft. We spent $112 billion on this insurance in 2014 (see the figure).

Property and casualty insurance reduces the risk of financial loss in the event of an accident involving damage to property or persons. It includes workers' compensation and fire insurance. In 2014, we spent $390 billion on this insurance.

Life insurance reduces the risk of financial loss in the event of death. Almost 80 percent of households in the United States have life insurance,

and the amount paid in premiums in 2014 was $487 billion.

Health insurance reduces the risk of financial loss in the event of illness.

It can provide funds to cover both lost earnings and the cost of medical care. We spent $991 billion on this type of insurance in 2014.

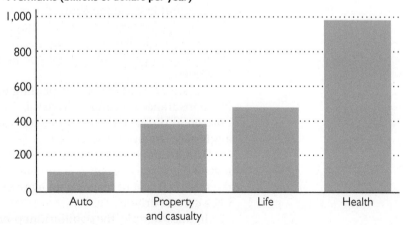

SOURCES OF DATA: Insurance Information Institute (www.iii.org) and Centers for Medicare and Medicaid Services (www.cms.gov).

Think about auto collision insurance. You know that there is a chance that you will be involved in an auto accident. The chance is small but always present. If you do have an accident and your car gets seriously damaged, you face the cost and inconvenience of getting it fixed. Worse, if you suffer serious personal injury, you also face a loss of income and the cost of medical care. For you, the cost of an auto accident is large and if you had to bear such cost, you'd like some help.

Because the chance that you will have a serious and costly auto accident is small, you can get that help by making a deal with an auto insurance company that is beneficial to both you and the insurer: You pay an annual premium to the insurance company and the company pays you a sum of money based on an agreed formula if you have an accident and incur a loss.

Insurance companies can get information from statistics on past accidents and costs that enable them to determine the premiums and payout conditions they can offer and still earn a profit. None of the company's policyholders knows whether they'll have an accident and the insurance company doesn't know *who* will have an accident, but it knows *how many* accidents there will be and what they will cost. An insurance company can *pool* the risks of a large population and enable everyone to share the costs.

People are risk averse—they don't like risk—so they are happy to buy insurance at prices that enable insurance companies to make a profit. By spreading the risk, insurance companies lower the risk for everyone.

But insurance companies do have a problem and it is a general problem that affects all types of insurance: Their customers have private information about their own behavior and its effects on the likelihood that they will make an insurance claim. There is asymmetric information in the insurance market.

■ Asymmetric Information in Insurance

Although asymmetric information is present in all types of insurance, we'll stick with auto collision insurance. Some drivers are careful and some are aggressive. A careful driver is less likely to have an accident than an aggressive driver. Each driver knows which type he or she is, but the insurance company doesn't know. Yet it would benefit the insurance company to know, for it could then charge the higher-risk aggressive driver a higher premium and the lower-risk careful driver a lower premium.

Without knowledge about driver types, all insured drivers get the same deal. There is a *pooling equilibrium* like that in the used-car market without dealer warranties. Careful drivers and aggressive drivers pay the same premium, but the insurance companies incur losses on aggressive drivers and make profits on careful drivers.

Figure 12.5 illustrates this pooling equilibrium outcome. The demand for collision insurance by careful drivers is D_C and the demand by all drivers is D. The horizontal distance between the curves D_C and D is the quantity demanded by aggressive drivers at each price.

The insurance companies don't know the driver type to which they are selling, so the supply curve, S, is the same for all drivers. It is based on an average of the marginal cost of insuring an aggressive driver and the marginal cost of insuring a careful driver.

In this example, the equilibrium premium is $1,000 a year and 60 million careful drivers and 60 million aggressive drivers are insured.

You're now going to see that this outcome is inefficient for two reasons: it creates moral hazard and adverse selection.

■ **FIGURE 12.5**

Inefficient Pooling Equilibrium in an Auto Insurance Market   MyEconLab Animation

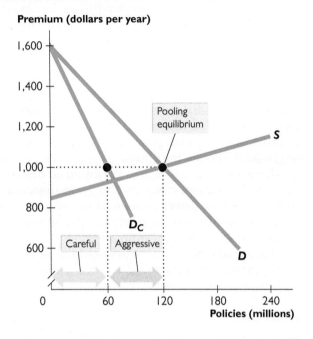

With no information on driver type, insurance companies offer all drivers the same deal. The insurance supply curve is S.

The demand curve D_C is the demand for auto insurance by careful drivers. The demand curve $D = D_C + D_A$ is the demand for auto insurance by all drivers. The horizontal distance between the two demand curves is the quantity demanded by aggressive drivers at each premium level.

A pooling equilibrium occurs at the intersection of S and D at a premium of $1,000 a year with 120 million insured drivers divided equally between careful and aggressive.

In this equilibrium, moral hazard and adverse selection make insurance companies look for ways of separating the two driver types.

Moral Hazard

Moral hazard is the tendency for a person with private information to use it in ways that impose costs on an uninformed party with whom they have made an agreement.

Moral hazard arises in many settings. For example, big banks face moral hazard. They know they are too big for governments to let them fail so they make loans that are too risky. Insurance companies face moral hazard because an insured person is less likely than an uninsured person to behave in ways that avoid the insured loss. For example, fire insurance lessens the incentive to install smoke detectors, fire alarms, and a sprinkler system.

In the case of auto insurance, a driver with full collision coverage has less incentive than a driver with little or no collision coverage to drive carefully. Once a person has bought insurance, her or his incentives change and the change adversely affects the interest of the insurance company.

Adverse Selection

Adverse selection arises because people at greater risk are more likely to buy insurance than those for whom a risk is very small. For example, a person with a family history of serious illness is more likely to buy health insurance than a person with a family history of good health. Similarly, an aggressive driver is more likely than a careful driver to take the fullest possible coverage. So more of the insured risks arise from the activities of the riskiest people.

Insurance companies have an incentive to find ways around the moral hazard and adverse selection problems. By doing so, they can lower premiums for low-risk people and raise premiums for high-risk people.

Moral hazard
The tendency for a person with private information to use it in ways that impose costs on an uninformed party with whom they have made an agreement.

Insurance companies try to make a careless driver or an aggressive driver pay a higher premium…

… than a careful driver.

■ Screening in Insurance Markets

Screening occurs when an uninformed person creates an incentive for an informed person to reveal relevant private information. Insurance companies use the "no-claim" bonus and the deductible as *screens* to separate high-risk aggressive drivers and low-risk careful drivers and set premiums in line with the risk arising from the two types of drivers.

No-Claim Bonus

A *no-claim bonus* is a discount in the insurance premium for drivers who don't make claims. A driver accumulates a no-claim bonus by driving safely and avoiding accidents. The longer the period of no-claim, the greater is the no-claim bonus. And the greater the bonus, the greater is the incentive to drive carefully.

The no-claim bonus enables the informed driver to reveal her or his type to the uninformed insurance company and get insurance at a lower price, in line with the lower risk that the driver presents. A driver who makes claims also reveals her or his type to the insurance company and gets insurance at a higher price, in line with the higher risk that the driver presents.

The no-claim bonus helps to lessen the moral hazard problem. With a bonus at stake for making a claim, a driver has a stronger incentive to be careful and try harder to avoid accidents.

Deductible

Insurance companies also use a deductible. A *deductible* is the amount of a loss that the insured person agrees to bear personally. The larger the deductible, the lower is the premium, and the decrease in the premium is more than proportionate to the increase in the deductible. By offering insurance with full coverage—no deductible—on terms that are attractive only to aggressive high-risk drivers and by offering coverage with a deductible on more favorable terms that are attractive to careful low-risk drivers, insurance companies can do profitable business with everyone. Aggressive high-risk drivers choose policies with a low deductible and a high premium; careful low-risk drivers choose policies with a high deductible and a low premium.

The size of the deductible chosen reveals to the insurance company whether the driver is aggressive or careful.

■ Separating Equilibrium with Screening

With screening that indicates driver types, insurance companies can supply insurance on different terms to the different groups. With only two groups, aggressive and careful, it can offer premiums at two different levels: a higher premium for aggressive drivers and a lower premium for careful drivers. The higher premium is an incentive for aggressive drivers to behave as if they were careful, so the number of aggressive drivers decreases and the number of careful drivers increases. The outcome is a separating equilibrium.

Figure 12.6 illustrates this outcome and contrasts it with the pooling equilibrium that arises without screening.

Figure 12.6(a) shows the situation for careful drivers and 12.6(b) for aggressive drivers. We're assuming that the two groups are of equal size in the sense that they have identical demand curves, D_C and D_A (as before in Figure 12.5). But as you're about to see, the two groups don't end up of equal size when they have responded to the incentives they face.

FIGURE 12.6

Two Outcomes in Auto Insurance Compared

MyEconLab Animation

(a) Careful drivers

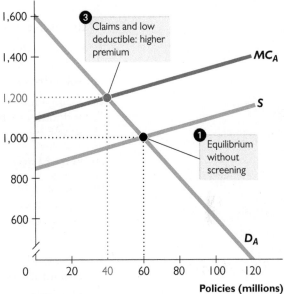

(b) Aggressive and careless drivers

Careful drivers in part (a) have demand curve D_C and aggressive and careless drivers in part (b) have demand curve D_A. With no screening, the supply curve of insurance is S in both parts.

1 Without screening the equilibrium premium is $1,000 and 60 million drivers are careful and 60 million are aggressive and careless.

With screening, the supply of insurance to careful drivers is MC_C in part (a) and to aggressive and careless drivers is MC_A in part (b).

In part (a), **2** equilibrium occurs at a premium of $800 and 80 million drivers reveal that they are careful.

In part (b), **3** equilibrium occurs at a premium of $1,200 and 40 million drivers reveal that they are aggressive and careless.

In a separating equilibrium, 20 million drivers switch from being aggressive to being careful.

Without screening provided by a no-claim bonus and deductible, insurance companies offer the same supply of insurance to all drivers. The equilibrium without screening is the same as in Figure 12.5: Everyone pays $1,000 a year and there are 60 million of each type of driver.

With screening, the insurance companies base their supply to each group on the marginal cost (*MC*) of serving them. For careful drivers in part (a), the supply curve is MC_C. The equilibrium insurance premium is $800 a year and the number of drivers who are, or who behave as if they are, careful increases to 80 million. Without screening, the market *under*provides insurance to this group and is inefficient. With screening, the market is efficient.

For the aggressive drivers in part (b), the marginal cost of serving them is MC_A and this marginal cost determines the supply to this group. The equilibrium insurance premium is $1,200 a year and the number of drivers who remain aggressive decreases to 40 million. Without screening, the market *over*provides insurance to this group and is inefficient. Again, with screening, the market is efficient.

You've now seen two examples of markets with asymmetric information in which creative signaling and screening overcome what would be market failure and achieve an efficient outcome.

MyEconLab Study Plan 12.2
Key Terms Quiz
Solutions Video

 CHECKPOINT 12.2

Describe the asymmetric information problems in the insurance market and explain how they are solved.

Practice Problems

1. Pam is a low-risk careful driver and Fran is a high-risk aggressive driver. What might an auto-insurance company do to get Pam and Fran to reveal their driver type?

2. Using Figure 12.6, show the deadweight losses that arise in an equilibrium without screening that are avoided in a separating equilibrium with screening.

In the News

Insurers aim to track drivers through smartphones
Auto-insurance companies are testing smartphone apps that monitor their customers' driving habits.

Source: *Forbes*, August 5, 2014

1. How could auto-insurance companies use information on driving habits? Is that information private and asymmetric?

2. How might smartphone monitoring of driving habits influence adverse selection and moral hazard?

Solutions to Practice Problems

1. The insurance company will offer policies with deductibles that enable drivers to reveal their private information. Pam reveals that she is a low-risk driver by taking a high deductible and low premium. Fran reveals that she is a high-risk driver by taking a low deductible and high premium.

2. For low-risk careful drivers, by taking a high deductible and low premium, 80 million get insurance for $800 a year compared to 60 million paying $1,000 a year without screening. The gray triangle in Figure 1 shows the deadweight loss from underprovision without screening. This deadweight loss is avoided by screening.
For high-risk aggressive drivers, by taking a low deductible and high premium, 40 million get insurance for $1,200 a year compared to 60 million paying $1,000 a year without screening. The gray triangle in Figure 2 shows the deadweight loss from overprovision without screening. This deadweight loss is avoided by screening.

Solutions to In the News

1. Auto-insurance companies can use information about driving habits obtained from smartphone apps to separate the market by known risk differences and this information makes driving habits neither private nor asymmetric.

2. Adverse selection: With information on driving habits available to auto-insurance companies, adverse selection is reduced. Moral hazard: Knowing that their driving is being monitored, driving carelessly is more costly, so some careless drivers become less careless.

FIGURE 1

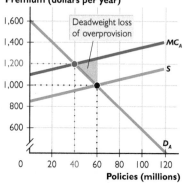

FIGURE 2

Premium (dollars per year)

12.3 THE ECONOMICS OF HEALTHCARE

Governments in the United States spend more on healthcare than on any other item, and by a big margin. The key reason is that if left to the market alone healthcare would be underprovided and unfairly distributed.

You are now going to see how governments influence the provision of healthcare, how healthcare markets in the United States compare with those in some other countries, and how it might be possible to improve on our current healthcare programs.

We begin by seeing why an unregulated market without government intervention would underprovide and unfairly distribute healthcare—why there would be a healthcare market failure.

■ Healthcare Market Failure

Healthcare consists of healthcare services (the services of physicians, specialists, nurses, other professionals, and hospitals) and health insurance. Both of these components of healthcare would be underprovided and unfairly distributed without some government action.

Four features of healthcare make it a special good:

- Asymmetric information
- Underestimation of benefit
- Underestimation of future needs
- Inequality in the ability to pay

Asymmetric Information

Asymmetric information is present in both the market for health insurance and the market for healthcare services. In the insurance market, the buyers—potential patients—have private information and in the care market the sellers—physicians and hospitals—have private information. These information asymmetries lead to adverse selection and moral hazard.

Adverse Selection and Moral Hazard in Health Insurance Some people exercise, eat healthy diets, watch their weight, and rarely get sick. Others are couch potatoes who don't exercise, eat high-fat and high-sugar diets, are overweight, and not only get sick more often but also are at long-term risk for diabetes and heart disease.

Information about whether a person has a healthy or unhealthy lifestyle is private information not available to the insurance companies.

Adverse selection arises because some of the healthiest people choose to not buy insurance. Moral hazard arises because once insured, a person has less incentive to adopt a healthy lifestyle and some will yield to the temptation to drift into unhealthy habits.

Faced with a lack of information about individual lifestyle choices, providers of health insurance (like auto-insurance suppliers) offer lower premiums with high deductibles so that buyers can reveal information about their lifestyle. The fittest and healthiest choose a high deductible and low premium and the least fit and unhealthiest choose a low deductible and high premium. The market tries to find a separating equilibrium. But the other problems that we examine below make an efficient outcome unlikely.

Moral Hazard in Healthcare Services   High-quality providers of healthcare services diagnose and prescribe treatments reliably and at the lowest possible cost. Low-quality providers make diagnosis errors and over-prescribe expensive drugs and other treatments. But the information about the quality and reliability of the healthcare provider is private. The buyers (patients and insurance companies) don't know the quality of the providers. In this regard, the market for healthcare services is like the market for used cars.

Moral hazard arises that increases the cost of healthcare services. Providers have an incentive to play it safe and overtreat a patient. Neither the patient nor the insurance company has information with which to prevent this inefficiency.

Health Maintenance Organizations partly address this moral hazard problem. By working with a limited number of service providers, an insurance company can monitor the quality of the service and control costs. But even with this arrangement, the service provider has more information than the insurer so the problem is lessened but not completely overcome.

Underestimation of Benefit

People don't have enough information to value the benefit of healthcare correctly. Most people lack the medical knowledge to determine their treatment needs. And many (especially healthy and young people) optimistically underestimate the health risks that they face. So they undervalue the insurance policies that can help them pay for healthcare; and they undervalue the healthcare resources that stand ready to help them when needed.

EYE on the U.S. ECONOMY
Healthcare in the United States: A Snapshot

Expenditure on healthcare takes 17.5 percent of U.S. incomes. Forty-one percent of this expenditure is private—spending on health insurance and out-of-pocket payments for healthcare services. The rest is financed by taxes—spending by federal and state governments on Medicare, Medicaid, and other public programs.

Figure 1 shows the distribution of the healthcare dollar across these types of expenditures.

Of the 318 million people in the United States in 2014, 190 million had private health insurance.

More than one half of all employed people—about 70 million—buy health insurance through their employer.

Tax breaks are available on health-insurance payments, the largest being for the self-employed who can deduct the entire payment.

About 75 million people limit their healthcare cost by using a Health Maintenance Organization (HMO).

The federal and state Medicare and Medicaid programs cover almost 119 million people.

An estimated 36 million have no health insurance, and a further 25 million are reckoned to be underinsured—have some insurance but not enough for a big emergency.

Some of the uninsured are healthy and *choose* not to insure. Others can't afford insurance and don't qualify for

Medicare or Medicaid.

Per person covered, government programs are more costly than private insurance because they serve the aged, the disabled, and the chronically sick.

Figure 2 shows expenditure per person. With almost 119 million people covered by Medicare and Medicaid at a total cost of $1,115 billion, governments spend $9,389 per person per year on public programs.

The cost of private insurance per person covered is 56 percent of the cost of the government programs at $5,219 per person per year.

Out-of-pocket expenditure, which includes spending by the uninsured, is $1,037 per person per year.

Underestimation of Future Needs

People take too short a view of the benefits of healthcare. The young and healthy know that they will become old and less healthy and will likely become big consumers of healthcare. But the time horizon over which they plan doesn't stretch that far into the future. The end result is that many people perceive too small a marginal benefit from health insurance, and they are not willing to pay what it is actually worth to them.

Inequality in the Ability to Pay

For many people, the price of health insurance is beyond their ability to pay for it. Two groups of people are unable to afford adequate health insurance: those with a long-term health problem and the aged. But these people are the ones with the greatest need for healthcare.

Most people want to live in a society that treats these less healthy, older, and poorer people with compassion and ensure that they are provided with access to affordable healthcare. So there is an additional social benefit from healthcare for less healthy, older, and poorer people.

Because asymmetric information brings adverse selection and moral hazard, and because the marginal social benefit of healthcare exceeds the marginal benefit perceived by its consumers, a competitive market in healthcare would underprovide it. And the underprovision of the competitive market has two dimensions. It is inefficient, and it is unfair.

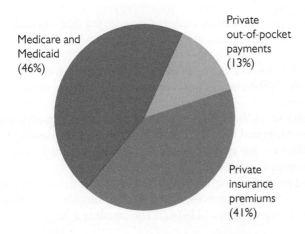

Figure 1 Private and Public Expenditures on Healthcare

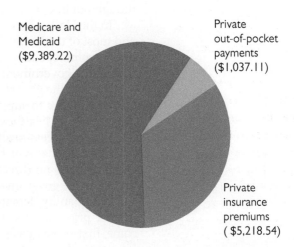

Figure 2 Private and Public Expenditures per Person

SOURCE OF DATA: Centers for Medicare and Medicaid Services, Data Tables 1, 2, and 22.

Because the market would deliver an inefficient and unfair outcome, health-care is provided by the public choices of governments. But with alternative methods and scales of public provision available, governments must consider the effects of the alternatives in making their choices.

■ Alternative Public Choice Solutions

We're now going to examine the public choices that deliver healthcare services. You can see in *Eye on the Global Economy* on p. 311 that there is a wide range of levels of expenditure on healthcare. Public expenditures pay 83 percent of the healthcare bills in the United Kingdom, 70 percent in Canada, and 46 percent in the United States. But among these three countries, public expenditure per person is highest in the United States.

Different political priorities lead to this variety in healthcare expenditures. And the differences have implications for both the efficiency and the cost of healthcare.

We'll look at three approaches to supplementing or replacing the market: one used in Canada and the United Kingdom and two used in the United States. The three approaches are

- Universal coverage, single payer
- Private and government insurance
- Subsidized private insurance: Obamacare

Universal Coverage, Single Payer

In Canada and the United Kingdom, healthcare is provided by a system with two key features: universal coverage and a single payer.

Universal coverage means that everyone is covered by health insurance, with no exceptions and no excluded preconditions.

Single payer means that the government alone pays the healthcare bills. The government pays the doctors, nurses, and hospitals. In the United Kingdom, though not in Canada, the government also pays for prescription drugs.

In the United Kingdom, most of the doctors are employed by the government and most of the hospitals are government owned. In Canada, the doctors and hospitals are independent private agents, but they may not sell their services other than to the government.

Because the government is the sole buyer of healthcare services, it chooses the quantity of care to supply. A public choice, not a market equilibrium, determines the quantity of healthcare service.

Patients access healthcare services at a zero (or low) price, so the quantity demanded is that at which the marginal benefit is zero (or low). But the demand for healthcare has no direct effect on the quantity actually available, which is determined by the government's supply decision.

The quantity demanded exceeds the quantity supplied and in the absence of a market price to allocate the scarce resources, services are allocated on a first-come, first-served basis (see Chapter 6, pp. 141–142). The result is a long wait time for treatment.

Defenders of this system say that inefficiencies are small and worth accepting because the outcome is fair as everyone has equal access to services. But it isn't exactly true that everyone has equal access. Some people are better at playing the system than others and are able to jump the line.

EYE on the GLOBAL ECONOMY
Healthcare Expenditures and Health Outcomes

The best U.S. healthcare is the best in the world, but it is costly. And U.S. healthcare expenditure is projected to rise as the "baby boom" generation ages.

Figure 1 compares U.S. healthcare expenditure with that of seven other rich countries. The data are average dollars spent on healthcare per person in each country. (The data here are measured on a different basis to those on p. 308.) The figure shows that the United States spends twice as much per person as Canada, Germany, France, and Australia; 2.5 times that of the United Kingdom and Japan; and three times that of Italy.

Another feature of U.S. healthcare expenditure that you can see in Figure 1 is its very large public component (the blue bars in the figure).

Government expenditure per person on healthcare in the United States is higher than in any of the other countries in the figure. It exceeds that in Canada, where selling private health insurance is illegal, and in Germany and France, where there is a greater acceptance of high taxes and big government than in the United States.

A further feature of U.S. healthcare is that health outcomes, measured by life expectancy and quality of health, are as good or better in the other rich countries than those in the United States.

The World Health Organization has constructed an index of the efficiency of healthcare based on life expectancy, health quality, and the fairness of financing care. Figure 2 shows the efficiency index for the same countries

as those in Figure 1. Despite its high expenditure, the United States is at the bottom of this efficiency table.

Comparing the data in the two figures makes U.S. healthcare look the costliest and least efficient. But the comparison is not unbiased. It ignores the effects of international trade in healthcare services. Tens of thousands of Canadians as well as people from farther away come to the United States to get high-quality healthcare. Expenditure on these foreigners raises U.S expenditure in Figure 1 and the greater healthiness of these foreigners raises the efficiency indexes of other countries in Figure 2. It also gives a low weight to wait times for treatment, which are greater in other countries than in the United States. Also, these data are pre-Obamacare.

Figure 1 Healthcare Expenditure

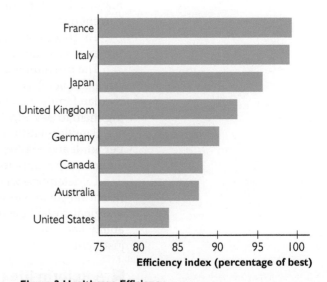

Figure 2 Healthcare Efficiency

Sources of data: World Development Indicators, World Bank, and the World Health Organization.

Private and Government Insurance

In the United States, most healthcare services are provided by private doctors and hospitals that receive their incomes from three sources: private health insurance, governments, and patients. Private health insurance pays 41 percent of the bills; government Medicare, Medicaid, and other programs pay 46 percent; and the remaining 13 percent comes from patients. Patients' out-of-pocket payments arise because some people are uninsured, and those who are insured face deductibles in their private insurance policies or co-payments for services provided under Medicare and Medicaid.

The scale of out-of-pocket costs combined with conditions set out in insurance plans and the demand for healthcare service determine the quantity of healthcare service provided. Measured by visits to a physician's office, that quantity is 1 billion patients per year. (The average number of physician visits is 3 per person per year.)

Inefficient Overproduction? We don't know whether private insurance together with Medicare and Medicaid provides the efficient quantity of healthcare. But the scale of expenditure on these programs relative to what is spent in other rich countries, suggests that they do overprovide.

Uncontrolled Expenditure Government healthcare expenditure is determined by the quantity of care demanded, not by a fixed budget. Without changes in the Medicare and Medicaid programs, this expenditure will grow as the aged population grows.

Obamacare

The *Patient Protection and Affordable Care Act, 2010* (Obamacare) has created a Health Insurance Marketplace to provide subsidized insurance.

On the supply side of the new marketplace are private insurers. On the demand side are the uninsured and those who want to find a better plan than their current one.

To qualify for subsidies, plans offered through the marketplace must cover pre-existing conditions, preventive services, and 10 essential health benefits.

The premium paid for one of these plans depends on family size and income. An example: A couple both aged 31 with two children and earning close to the median family income of $55,000 receive a subsidy (as a tax credit) of $3,636 leaving them to pay $3,984 for a $7,620 policy.

Families with no health insurance are required to pay an annual fee of $695 per adult and $347.50 per child or 2.5 percent of income, whichever is higher, with a maximum family fee of $2,085 a year.

To determine whether the outcome of the Obamacare subsidy achieves an efficient outcome, we would need to have an estimate of the extent to which the marginal social benefit of health insurance for the affected families exceeds their ability and willingness to pay for it. The subsidy might be too large, too small, or just right.

◼ A Reform Idea?

The power of the market leads economists to seek a market solution to all resource allocation problems, and healthcare is no exception.

The Medicare and Medicaid programs are in effect an open-ended commitment of public funds to the healthcare of the aged and those too poor to buy private healthcare. Healthcare in the United States faces two problems: Too many people are uninsured and healthcare costs too much. These problems are going to get worse if nothing major is done to reverse a trend.

The Patient Protection and Affordable Care Act (Obamacare) addresses the first of these problems by requiring everyone to be insured and by creating a new Pre-Existing Condition Insurance Plan, financed partly by the government. But the Act does little to address the problem of overexpenditure, and this problem is extremely serious. It is so serious that without massive change, the present open-ended healthcare programs will bankrupt the United States.

A solution to both the problem of coverage and access and the problem of overexpenditure has been suggested by Laurence Kotlikoff, an economics professor at Boston University.

He proposes a universal private health insurance Basic Plan that creates incentives to improve health and deliver healthcare services efficiently. Each year, each American gets a voucher to buy health insurance from a company of their choice. The voucher's value equals the expected cost of covering the person, which is determined by health indicators. (Example: An 80-year-old diabetic might get a $70,000 voucher while a healthy 14-year-old girl might get a $3,000 voucher.) The total value of vouchers does not exceed 10 percent of total U.S. income. Public expenditure on healthcare grows as income grows, and an Independent Panel adds procedures and technologies covered by the Basic Plan but at a slower pace than in the current system.

Healthcare vouchers would work like the education vouchers that we explain in Chapter 10 (see p. 261). They would provide the cost discipline of the British and Canadian systems with the choice that is so important and valued by Americans.

Professor Laurence J. Kotlikoff of Boston University; author of The Healthcare Fix *and creator of* Medicare Part C for All.

EYE on YOUR LIFE
Signaling Your Ability

MyEconLab Critical Thinking Exercise

You've seen how used-car dealers signal with warranties. You, too, send signals.

You know how smart you are and how hard you're willing to work. But this information is private. It is known to you but not to your potential employers.

How can you signal your ability to potential employers? The answer is by your choice of education.

Michael Spence, an economist at Stanford University and joint winner of the 2001 Nobel Prize with George Akerlof and Joseph Stiglitz, explained how education choices send signals.

Think of people as having just two possible levels of ability: either high or low. Each person knows her or his own ability, but potential employers don't have this information.

People send signals to potential employers by their choice of education. For a person with low ability, the opportunity cost of a university education is high—not just the tuition and cost of books, but the cost in time and effort to get passing grades.

For a person with high ability, the opportunity cost of a college or university education is lower. For these

people, good grades take hard work but they can be attained with reasonable effort. So only people with high ability choose a college or university education.

Employers know each person's education (and grades), so they can offer a high wage for high ability and a low wage for low ability. There is a separating equilibrium in the market for workers of differing ability.

Even if your education contributed nothing to improve your ability, your eductaion choice would still signal your ability.

MyEconLab Study Plan 12.3
Solutions Video

 CHECKPOINT 12.3

Explain the information problems and other economic problems in healthcare markets.

Practice Problems

1. Describe the asymmetric information problem in the market for healthcare services and explain how the problem is dealt with.

2. What are the sources of inefficiency in the U.S. health-insurance market?

In the News

Are out-of-pocket medical costs too high?
Health-insurance premiums have increased and been accompanied by higher deductibles, which means that out-of-pocket costs have increased. Some say higher out-of-pocket costs lower prices and send buyers to efficient healthcare providers. Others say higher out-of-pocket costs puts quality healthcare out of reach for those with lower incomes.

Source: *The Wall Street Journal*, April 10, 2016

1. How do larger deductibles and larger out-of-pocket costs change the incentives that people face in the market for health insurance?

2. How do larger deductibles and larger out-of-pocket costs influence adverse selection and moral hazard in the market for health insurance?

Solutions to Practice Problems

1. In the market for healthcare services, the suppliers are physicians, specialists, other healthcare professionals, and hospitals. The demanders are patients and the insurance companies that pay most of the patients' bills. Asymmetric information arises because medical workers have private information about a patient's condition, the treatments available, and the cost-effectiveness of the treatment they prescribe. Healthcare providers face moral hazard. HMOs, with insurance companies selecting and monitoring service providers, lessen the moral hazard.

2. Two sources of inefficiency in the U.S. market for health insurance are pre-existing conditions and other serious health risks that are uninsurable and the underprovision that arises from 46 million Americans having no health insurance and millions more being underinsured.

Solutions to In the News

1. Larger deductibles and larger out-of-pocket costs strengthen the incentives for: (1) Healthy families to buy healthcare insurance; (2) People not to visit the doctor with minor health problems; (3) People with unhealthy lifestyles to try to reform.

2. Larger deductibles and larger out-of-pocket costs decrease adverse selection as healthier people choose to buy insurance with lower premiums; and decrease moral hazard as insured people, faced with higher deductibles, have a strengthened incentive to adopt a healthy lifestyle.

CHAPTER SUMMARY

Key Points

1. Describe the lemons problem and explain how the used-car market solves it.

- In some markets, one side of a market has private information—asymmetric information.
- In the market for used cars, the seller knows and the buyer doesn't know if a car is a lemon.
- Adverse selection results in a pooling equilibrium with too many lemons and too few good cars being traded.
- Dealers' warranties act as signals and enable the market to achieve a separating equilibrium that is efficient.

2. Describe the asymmetric information problems in the insurance market and explain how they are solved.

- In insurance markets, buyers are better informed than sellers about the risk being insured.
- Without screening, too few low-risk people would be insured.
- Moral hazard arises in insurance: An insured person has less incentive than an uninsured person to avoid the insured loss.
- The no-claim bonus and deductible reveal risk and enable insurance markets to reach an efficient separating equilibrium.

3. Explain the information problems and other economic problems in healthcare markets.

- Governments provide healthcare because asymmetric information, underestimation of its value, failure to look far enough into the future, and the inability of many to pay for it bring healthcare market failure.
- A free market would underprovide healthcare and distribute it unfairly.
- In some countries, governments provide healthcare at a zero or low price and ration with wait times.
- U.S. private insurance, Medicare, and Medicaid possibly overprovide for those covered.
- Obamacare provides subsidized insurance and compels everyone to make a minimum contribution for health coverage.
- Healthcare vouchers could cut cost, increase coverage, and retain choice.

Key Terms

MyEconLab Key Terms Quiz

Adverse selection, 297
Asymmetric information, 294
Lemons problem, 294

Moral hazard, 303
Pooling equilibrium, 299
Private information, 294

Screening, 304
Separating equilibrium, 299
Signaling, 298

CHAPTER CHECKPOINT

Study Plan Problems and Applications

1. Judy knows that her car is a lemon and offers it for sale. If the used-car market is working efficiently, will buyers know whether her car is a lemon? Why or why not?

2. Some car dealers offer used cars for sale with warranties and some offer them without warranties. Describe the equilibrium in the market for used cars. Is the market efficient?

3. **Stalling complaints about fixed GM cars**
   In 2014, GM recalled 2.6 million vehicles to repair a safety defect in their ignition switches. Some of the recalled vehicles stalled and locked up, but a concerned GM said the problem with the recalled part did not appear to be the source of vehicles stalling.

   Source: NBC News, January 17, 2016

   Did GM sell some lemons? If GM did, what was the private information that it had that buyers did not know? If GM didn't sell lemons, explain why not.

Use the following information to work Problems **4** and **5**.

Mary is an 18-year-old student, who recently bought a used car. Mary is looking to buy car insurance. Insurance companies compete for her business.

4. Is there a moral hazard problem in a transaction between Mary and an insurance company? Explain why or why not.

5. Is there an adverse selection problem in a transaction between Mary and an insurance company? Explain why or why not.

6. If you have private information that you are a more aggressive driver than your driving record indicates, would you buy collision insurance? If the insurance company offers you a large deductible or a no-claim bonus are you likely to take the offer? Why or why not?

Use the following information to work Problems **7** to **9**.

President Obama campaigned on a healthcare reform plan that did not include mandatory health insurance. Hillary Clinton wanted mandatory health insurance with no opting out. In 2009, the President said he would support making health insurance mandatory with the cost covered by employers, but those who could not afford to pay and small businesses would be exempt.

7. If health insurance were optional, would healthy people be more likely or less likely to buy insurance?

8. What obstacles to efficiency does optional health insurance create?

9. U.S. healthcare per person costs twice that of other rich countries. Does the United States overprovide? Do other countries underprovide? What economic concepts do you need to answer? What data might be relevant?

10. If U.S. healthcare were delivered like basic education is, how would the healthcare system compare to that in Canada? Would it be efficient?

 11. Read *Eye on the Market For Used Cars* on p. 298 and then explain how a warranty signals that a car isn't a lemon and why it is in a used-car dealer's self-interest to offer a warranty.

Instructor Assignable Problems and Applications

MyEconLab Homework, Quiz, or Test if assigned by instructor

1. Describe the used-car market in the United States. How many used cars get traded per year and at what average price? How does the market enable buyers to avoid lemons? What role, if any, do governments play in the used-car market?

2. Zaneb is a high-school teacher and is well known in her community for her honesty, integrity, and sense of social responsibility. She is shopping for a used car. She plans to buy the car from a local car dealer and auto insurance from a major insurance company. What asymmetric information problems is Zaneb likely to encounter and what arrangements are likely to help cope with those problems? Explain your answers.

3. Suppose that there are two national football leagues: The Time League and The Bonus for Win League. The players have private information about their effort. In The Time League, players receive a fixed wage based on the time they spend practicing and playing matches. In The Bonus for Win League, the players are paid one wage for a loss, a higher wage for a tie, and the highest wage of all for a win. Describe the moral hazard and adverse selection problems in these two leagues. Which league best addresses these problems?

4. **Oilers, Jets top NHLers' no-trade lists**
   ESPN asked 10 player agents to name their top three most frequent no-trade teams. The top three, in order, were the Edmonton Oilers, the Winnipeg Jets, and the New York Islanders.

   Source: *Sportsnet*, March 25, 2016

   Provide an example of private information that a hockey player who wants a no-trade clause possesses. Does a hockey player with a long-term contract that includes a no-trade clause present a moral hazard to his team? Does a hockey player with a long-term contract that includes a no-trade clause present adverse selection problems to his team?

5. What are the key economic problems in providing an efficient quantity and distribution of healthcare insurance and service? Explain how the U.S. healthcare system addresses these problems.

6. What are the three alternative approaches for supplementing or replacing the market in healthcare services and how does each address the sources of healthcare market failure?

7. What are the problems that Medicare and Medicaid address and what problems do they cause?

8. What is the cost of healthcare in the United States compared to that in Canada and the United Kingdom? Do health outcomes correlate with healthcare costs? Can you think of explanations for the facts you've just provided?

9. What is Laurence Kotlikoff's proposal for fixing healthcare in the United States? Draw a graph to illustrate how his proposal would work and show whether it could be efficient.

Multiple Choice Quiz

1. A market with asymmetric information is one in which _____.

   A. sellers offer a product for sale at a low price and buyers are pleased to get a bargain
   B. sellers know how reliable the product is and they share that information with buyers
   C. only the buyers or the sellers have information about the quality of the product
   D. buyers are willing to pay less for the product than the price at which sellers are offering it for sale

2. The lemons problem arises in markets in which _____.

   A. sellers are better informed than buyers about which products are reliable
   B. buyers are better informed than sellers about which products are reliable
   C. there is a shortage of lemons
   D. buyers have private information

3. In the market for used cars with no warranties, _____ lemons are bought and the equilibrium is a _____ equilibrium.

   A. too few; separating
   B. too many; separating
   C. only; pooling
   D. no; pooling

4. In a used-car market in which dealers offer cars with warranties, _____.

   A. there is private information
   B. a separating equilibrium does not occur
   C. a lemons problem does not arise
   D. the market is inefficient

5. Moral hazard arises in the insurance market because _____.

   A. buyers of insurance have private information that they can use
   B. insurance companies can offer a range of premiums to buyers
   C. buyers can opt to take a deductible or a no-claim bonus
   D. insurance companies can match premiums to customer risk

6. The private market delivers *too little* healthcare because _____.

   A. insurance companies cannot avoid the problems of moral hazard and adverse selection
   B. too many young healthy people buy insurance
   C. insurance companies cannot monitor healthcare providers
   D. insurance companies profits are too large

7. The healthcare system in the United States costs per person _____ what it costs in other rich countries and U.S. health outcomes rank _____.

   A. double; lower
   B. half; higher
   C. double; higher
   D. half; lower

How much would you
pay for a song?

Consumer Choice and Demand

When you have completed your study of this chapter, you will be able to

1 Calculate and graph a budget line that shows the limits to a person's consumption possibilities.

2 Explain marginal utility theory and use it to derive a consumer's demand curve.

3 Use marginal utility theory to explain the paradox of value: why water is vital but cheap while diamonds are relatively useless but expensive.

MyEconLab Big Picture Video

13.1 CONSUMPTION POSSIBILITIES

How much you are willing to pay for a song depends on your income and on how much you want the song. We begin our study of consumption choices by looking at how income and prices limit what a person can afford. We describe the limit on buying plans by using a budget line. Let's look at the budget line of Tina—a student like you.

■ The Budget Line

Budget line
A line that describes the limits to consumption possibilities and that depends on a consumer's budget and the prices of goods and services.

A **budget line** describes the limits to consumption possibilities. Tina has already committed most of her income to renting an apartment, buying textbooks, paying her campus meal plan, and saving a few dollars each month. Having made these decisions, Tina has a remaining budget of $4 a day, which she spends on two goods: bottled water and chewing gum. The price of water is $1 a bottle, and the price of gum is 50¢ a pack. If Tina spends all of her available budget, she reaches the limits of her consumption of bottled water and gum.

Figure 13.1 illustrates Tina's budget line. Rows *A* through *E* in the table show five possible ways of spending $4 on these two goods. If Tina spends all of her $4 on gum, she can buy 8 packs a day. In this case, she has nothing available to spend on bottled water. Row *A* shows this possibility. At the other extreme, if Tina spends her entire $4 on bottled water, she can buy 4 bottles a day and no gum. Row *E* shows this possibility. Rows *B*, *C*, and *D* show three other possible combinations that Tina can afford.

FIGURE 13.1

Consumption Possibilities   MyEconLab Animation

Tina's budget line shows the boundary between what she can and cannot afford. The rows of the table list Tina's affordable combinations of bottled water and chewing gum when her budget is $4 a day, the price of water is $1 a bottle, and the price of chewing gum is 50¢ a pack. For example, row *A* tells us that Tina exhausts her $4 budget when she buys 8 packs of gum and no water.

The figure graphs Tina's budget line. Points *A* through *E* on the graph represent the rows of the table.

Possibility	Water (bottles per day)	Chewing gum (packs per day)
A	0	8
B	1	6
C	2	4
D	3	2
E	4	0

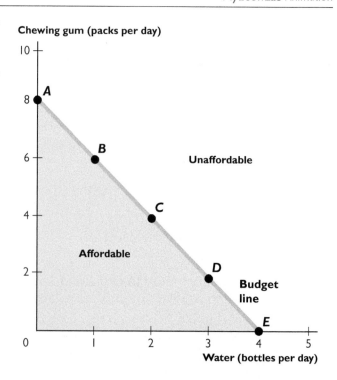

Points *A* through *E* in Figure 13.1 graph the possibilities in the table. The line passing through these points is Tina's budget line, which marks the boundary between what she can and cannot afford. She can afford any combination on the budget line and inside it (in the orange area). She cannot afford any combination outside the budget line (in the white area).

The budget line in Figure 13.1 is similar to the *production possibilities frontier,* or *PPF,* in Chapter 3 (pp. 60–61). Both curves show a limit to what is feasible. The *PPF* is a technological limit, so it changes only when technology changes. The budget line depends on the consumer's budget and on prices, so it changes when the budget or prices change.

■ A Change in the Budget

Figure 13.2 shows the effect of a change in Tina's budget on her consumption possibilities. When Tina's budget increases, her consumption possibilities expand, and her budget line shifts outward. When her budget decreases, her consumption possibilities shrink and her budget line shifts inward.

On the initial budget line (the same as in Figure 13.1), Tina's budget is $4. On a day when Tina loses her wallet with $2 in it, she has only $2 to spend. Her new budget line in Figure 13.2 shows how much she can consume with a budget of $2. She can buy any of the combinations on the $2 budget line.

On a day when Tina sells an old CD for $2, she has $6 available and her budget line shifts rightward. She can now buy any of the combinations on the $6 budget line.

■ **FIGURE 13.2**

Changes in a Consumer's Budget

MyEconLab Animation

A decrease in the budget shifts the budget line leftward, and an increase in the budget shifts the budget line rightward.

Lower prices in a sale expand consumption possibilities.

■ Changes in Prices

If the price of one good rises when the prices of other goods and the budget remain the same, consumption possibilities shrink. If the price of one good falls when the prices of other goods and the budget remain the same, consumption possibilities expand. To see these changes in consumption possibilities, let's see what happens to Tina's budget line when the price of a bottle of water changes.

A Fall in the Price of Water

Figure 13.3 shows the effect on Tina's budget line of a fall in the price of a bottle of water from $1 to 50¢ when the price of gum and her budget remain unchanged. If Tina spends all of her budget on bottled water, she can now afford 8 bottles a day. Her consumption possibilities have expanded. Because the price of gum is unchanged, if she spends all her budget on gum, she can still afford only 8 packs of gum a day. Her budget line has rotated outward.

A Rise in the Price of Water

Figure 13.4 shows the effect on Tina's budget line of a rise in the price of a bottle of water from $1 to $2 when the price of gum and her budget remain unchanged. If Tina spends all of her budget on bottled water, she can now afford only 2 bottles a day. Tina's consumption possibilities have shrunk. Again, because the price of gum is unchanged, if Tina spends all her budget on gum, she can still afford only 8 packs of gum a day. Her budget line has rotated inward.

■ **FIGURE 13.3**

A Fall in the Price of Water

MyEconLab Animation

When the price of water falls from $1 a bottle to 50¢ a bottle, the budget line rotates outward and becomes less steep.

Possibility	Water (bottles per day) $1 a bottle	Water (bottles per day) 50¢ a bottle	Chewing gum (packs per day)
A	0	0	8
B	1	2	6
C	2	4	4
D	3	6	2
E	4	8	0

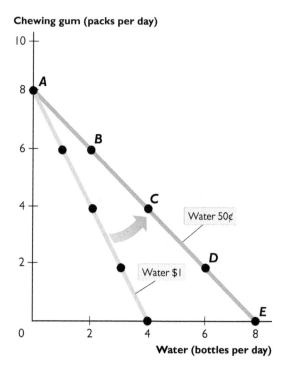

■ Prices and the Slope of the Budget Line

Notice that when the price of bottled water changes and the price of gum remains unchanged, the slope of the budget line changes. In Figure 13.3, when the price of bottled water falls, the budget line becomes less steep. In Figure 13.4, when the price of a bottle of water rises, the budget line becomes steeper.

Recall that "slope equals rise over run." The rise is an *increase* in the quantity of gum, and the run is a *decrease* in the quantity of bottled water. The slope of the budget line is negative, which means that there is a tradeoff between the two goods. Along the budget line, consuming more of one good implies consuming less of the other good. The slope of the budget line is an *opportunity cost*. It tells us what the consumer must give up to get one more unit of a good.

Let's calculate the slopes of the three budget lines in Figures 13.3 and 13.4:

- When the price of water is $1 a bottle, the slope of the budget line is 8 packs of gum divided by 4 bottles of water, which equals 2 packs of gum per bottle.
- When the price of water is 50¢ a bottle, the slope of the budget line is 8 packs of gum divided by 8 bottles of water, which equals 1 pack of gum per bottle.
- When the price of water is $2 a bottle, the slope of the budget line is 8 packs of gum divided by 2 bottles of water, which equals 4 packs of gum per bottle.

FIGURE 13.4

A Rise in the Price of Water

MyEconLab Animation

Possibility	Water (bottles per day)		Chewing gum (packs per day)
	$2 a bottle	$1 a bottle	
A	0	0	8
		1	6
B	1	2	4
		3	2
C	2	4	0

When the price of water rises from $1 a bottle to $2 a bottle, the budget line rotates inward and becomes steeper.

Think about what these slopes mean as opportunity costs. When the price of water is $1 a bottle and the price of gum is 50¢ a pack, it costs 2 packs of gum to buy a bottle of water. When the price of water is 50¢ a bottle and the price of gum is 50¢ a pack, it costs 1 pack of gum to buy a bottle of water. And when the price of water is $2 a bottle and the price of gum is 50¢ a pack, it costs 4 packs of gum to buy a bottle of water.

Another name for an opportunity cost is a relative price. A **relative price** is the price of one good in terms of another good. If the price of gum is 50¢ a pack and the price of water is $1 a bottle, the relative price of water is 2 packs of gum per bottle. It is calculated as the price of water divided by the price of gum ($1 a bottle ÷ 50¢ a pack = 2 packs per bottle).

When the price of the good plotted on the *x*-axis falls, other things remaining the same, the budget line becomes less steep, and the opportunity cost and relative price of the good on the *x*-axis fall.

Relative price
The price of one good in terms of another good—an opportunity cost. It equals the price of one good divided by the price of another good.

EYE on the U.S. ECONOMY
Relative Prices on the Move

Over a number of years, relative prices change a great deal and the figure shows some of these changes between 2005 and 2015 for 15 items that feature in most students' budgets.

These relative prices are measured as the price of the item in terms of a basket of other goods—as the price of the item divided by the average price of all goods and services.

Eggs, textbooks, and beef had the largest relative price increases. Air travel, chicken, apples, electricity, coffee, bread, gasoline, and oranges also had higher relative prices.

The largest relative price decrease is that of a computer, which has fallen by 92 percent. The relative prices of smartphone plans, tomatoes, and bananas have also fallen.

These changes in relative prices change consumption possibilities and change peoples' choices. Lower relative prices provide an incentive to buy greater quantities; higher relative prices provide an incentive to find substitutes and buy smaller quantities.

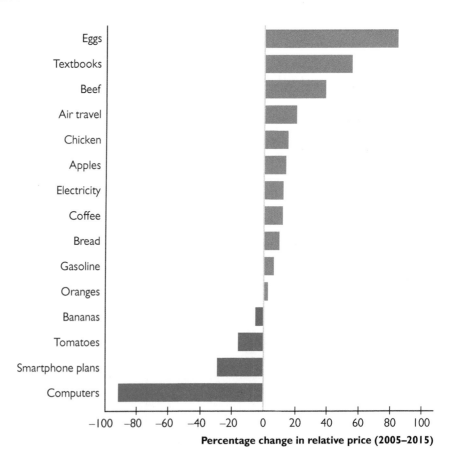

SOURCE OF DATA: Bureau of Labor Statistics.

CHECKPOINT 13.1

MyEconLab Study Plan 13.1
Key Terms Quiz
Solutions Video

Calculate and graph a budget line that shows the limits to a person's consumption possibilities.

Practice Problems

Jerry's burger and magazine budget is $12 a week. The price of a burger is $2, and the price of a magazine is $4.

1. List the combinations of burgers and magazines that Jerry can afford.

2. What is the relative price of a magazine? Explain your answer.

3. Draw a graph of Jerry's budget line with the quantity of magazines plotted on the *x*-axis. Describe how his budget line changes if, other things remaining the same, the following changes occur one at a time:
   • The price of a magazine falls.
   • Jerry's budget for burgers and magazines increases.

In the News

Gas price could fall below $2 a gallon
The price of gasoline keeps falling. It was close to $3.50 a gallon a year ago, is $2.59 a gallon now, and is expected to fall below $2 a gallon by year's end.
Source: CNBC, August 11, 2015

Donna buys only two goods: gasoline and pasta. Explain how the events in the news clip change Donna's consumption possibilities, the relative price of pasta, and her budget in terms of pasta.

Solutions to Practice Problems

1. Jerry can afford 3 magazines and no burgers; 2 magazines and 2 burgers; 1 magazine and 4 burgers; no magazines and 6 burgers.

2. The relative price of a magazine is the number of burgers that Jerry must forgo to get 1 magazine, which equals the price of a magazine divided by the price of a burger, or 2 burgers per magazine.

3. The budget line is a straight line from 6 burgers on the *y*-axis to 3 magazines on the *x*-axis (Figure 1). With a fall in the price of a magazine, Jerry can buy more magazines. His budget line rotates outward (Figure 2). With a bigger budget, Jerry can buy more of both goods. His budget line shifts outward (Figure 3).

Solution to In the News

When the price of gas falls, Donna's consumption possibilities expand—her budget line rotates outward. The relative price of pasta is its price divided by the price of gas. A fall in the price of gas raises the relative price of pasta. Donna's budget in terms of pasta is the maximum quantity of pasta that she can buy. This quantity does not change when the price of gas falls.

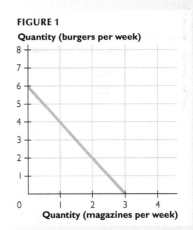

FIGURE 1
Quantity (burgers per week)

FIGURE 2
Quantity (burgers per week)

FIGURE 3
Quantity (burgers per week)

13.2 MARGINAL UTILITY THEORY

Utility
The benefit or satisfaction that a person gets from the consumption of a good or service.

The budget line tells us about consumption *possibilities*, but it doesn't tell us a person's consumption *choice*. Choices depend on *possibilities* and *preferences*. To describe preferences, economists use the concept of utility.* **Utility** is the benefit or satisfaction that a person gets from the consumption of a good or service. To understand how we use utility to explain people's choices, we distinguish between two concepts:

- Total utility
- Marginal utility

■ Total Utility

Total utility
The total benefit that a person gets from the consumption of a good or service. Total utility generally increases as the quantity consumed of a good increases.

Total utility is the total benefit that a person gets from the consumption of a good or service. Total utility depends on the quantity of the good consumed *in a given period*—more consumption generally gives more total utility. Table 13.1 shows Tina's total utility from bottled water and chewing gum. If she consumes no bottled water and no gum, she gets no utility. If she consumes 1 bottle of water a day, she gets 15 units of utility. If she consumes 1 pack of gum a day, it provides her with 32 units of utility. As Tina increases the quantity of bottled water or the packs of gum she consumes, her total utility increases.

■ Marginal Utility

Marginal utility
The change in total utility that results from a one-unit increase in the quantity of a good consumed.

Marginal utility is the change in total utility that results from a one-unit increase in the quantity of a good consumed. Table 13.1 shows the calculation of Tina's marginal utility from bottled water and chewing gum. Let's find Tina's marginal utility from a 3rd bottle of water a day (highlighted in the table). Her total utility from 3 bottles is 36 units, and her total utility from 2 bottles is 27 units. So for Tina, the marginal utility from drinking a 3rd bottle of water each day is

Marginal utility from the 3rd bottle of water = 36 units − 27 units = 9 units.

In the table, marginal utility appears midway between the quantities because the *change* in consumption produces the *marginal* utility. The table displays the marginal utility from each quantity of water and gum consumed.

Notice that Tina's marginal utility decreases as her daily consumption of water and gum increases. For example, her marginal utility from bottled water decreases from 15 units from the first bottle per day to 12 units from the second and 9 units from the third. Similarly, her marginal utility from chewing gum decreases from 32 units from the first pack per day to 16 units from the second and 8 units from the third. This decrease in marginal utility as the quantity of a good consumed increases is called the principle of **diminishing marginal utility**.

Diminishing marginal utility
The general tendency for marginal utility to decrease as the quantity of a good consumed increases.

To see why marginal utility diminishes, think about the following situations: In one, you've been studying all day and have had nothing to drink. Someone offers you a bottle of water. The marginal utility you get from that water is large. In the other, you've been drinking all day and you've drunk 7 bottles. Now someone offers you another bottle of water, and you say thanks very much and sip it slowly. You enjoy the 8th bottle of the day, but the marginal utility from it is tiny.

---

*Economists also use an alternative method of describing preferences called *indifference curves*, which are described in the optional appendix to this chapter.

EYE on the PAST

Jeremy Bentham, William Stanley Jevons, and the Birth of Utility

The concept of utility was revolutionary when Jeremy Bentham (1748–1832) proposed it in the early 1800s. He used the idea to advance his then radical support for free education, free medical care, and social security. It was another fifty years before William Stanley Jevons (1835–1882) developed the concept of *marginal* utility and used it to predict people's consumption choices. For the first time, economists could distinguish between cost and value and a basic theory of demand was born.

Jeremy Bentham

William Stanley Jevons

■ **TABLE 13.1**

Tina's Total Utility and Marginal Utility

Bottled water			Chewing gum		
Quantity (bottles per day)	Total utility	Marginal utility	Quantity (packs per day)	Total utility	Marginal utility
0	0		0	0	
		15			32
1	15		1	32	
		12			16
2	27		2	48	
		9			8
3	36		3	56	
		6			6
4	42		4	62	
		5			4
5	47		5	66	
		4			2
6	51		6	68	
		3			1
7	54		7	69	
		2			0
8	56		8	69	

The table shows Tina's total utility and marginal utility from bottled water and chewing gum.

Marginal utility is the change in total utility when the quantity consumed increases by one unit. When Tina's consumption of bottled water increases from 2 bottles a day to 3 bottles a day, her total utility from bottled water increases from 27 units to 36 units. So Tina's marginal utility from the 3rd bottle of water is 9 units.

Total utility increases and marginal utility diminishes as the quantity of a good consumed increases.

Similarly, suppose you've been out of gum for more than a day. A friend offers you a pack. Relief! You chew and receive a lot of utility. On another day, you've gone through 7 packs and chewed until your jaw aches. You're offered an 8th pack, and this time you say thanks, no thanks! The 8th pack of gum would bring you no marginal utility.

■ Graphing Tina's Utility Schedules

We illustrate a consumer's preferences with a total utility curve and a marginal utility curve like those in Figure 13.5. Part (a) shows that as Tina drinks more bottled water, her total utility from water increases. It also shows that total utility increases at a decreasing rate—diminishing marginal utility. Part (b) graphs Tina's marginal utility from water. The steps in part (a) are placed side by side in part (b). The curve that passes through the midpoints of the bars in part (b) is Tina's marginal utility curve.

The numbers in Table 13.1 and the graphs in Figure 13.5 describe Tina's preferences and, along with her budget line, enable us to predict the choices that she makes. That is our next task.

MyEconLab Concept Video

■ Maximizing Total Utility

The consumer's goal is to allocate the available budget in the way that maximizes total utility. The consumer achieves this goal by choosing the affordable combination of goods at which the *sum* of the utilities obtained from all goods consumed is as large as possible.

We can find a consumer's best budget allocation by using a two-step **utility-maximizing rule**:

Utility-maximizing rule
The rule that leads to the greatest total utility from all the goods and services consumed. The rule is
1. Allocate the entire available budget.
2. Make the marginal utility per dollar equal for all goods.

1. Allocate the entire available budget.
2. Make the marginal utility per dollar equal for all goods.

Allocate the Available Budget

If a consumer can buy more of one good without buying less of another good, then total utility can be increased. When utility is maximized, it isn't possible to buy more of one good without decreasing the quantity of another good. In this situation, the consumer has allocated the entire available budget.

With a budget of $4, the price of water at $1 per bottle, and the price of gum at 50¢ a pack, Tina allocates her budget to bottled water and gum at a point *on* her budget line in Figure 13.1 (p. 320). If she was at a point *inside* her budget line, she could buy more water or more gum without giving up any of the other good and she would not be maximizing utility.

Equalize the Marginal Utility Per Dollar

Marginal utility per dollar
The marginal utility from a good relative to the price paid for the good.

The second step to maximizing utility is to find the affordable combination that makes the marginal utility per dollar from both goods equal. The **marginal utility per dollar** from a good is the marginal utility from the good relative to the price paid for the good.

Calculating the Marginal Utility Per Dollar The marginal utility per dollar from a good equals the marginal utility (MU) from the good divided by the price (P) paid for the good. For example, if Tina buys 2 packs of gum, her marginal utility from gum (MU_G) is 16 units. At a price (P_G) of 50¢ a pack, her marginal utility *per dollar* from gum (MU_G/P_G) is 16 units ÷ 50¢, which equals 32 units per dollar.

Tina's Utility-Maximizing Choice If Tina spends $1 more on water and $1 less on gum, her total utility from water increases, her total utility from gum decreases, and her total utility from both water and gum might increase, decrease, or not

FIGURE 13.5

Total Utility and Marginal Utility

(a) Total utility

(b) Marginal utility

The table shows Tina's total utility from bottled water and calculates her marginal utility.

Part (a) graphs Tina's total utility from bottled water. It also shows the extra total utility she gains from each additional bottle of water—her marginal utility—as the steps along the total utility curve.

Part (b) shows how Tina's marginal utility from bottled water diminishes by placing the bars shown in part (a) side by side as a series of declining steps.

Water (bottles per day)	0	1	2	3	4	5	6	7	8
Total utility	0	15	27	36	42	47	51	54	56
Marginal utility		15	12	9	6	5	4	3	2
	A	B	C	D	E	F	G	H	I

change. What happens to her total utility from both goods depends on the marginal utility per dollar for each good.

- If the marginal utility per dollar from water *exceeds* that from gum, total utility increases.
- If the marginal utility per dollar from water *is less than* that from gum, total utility decreases.
- If the marginal utility per dollar from water *equals* that from gum, total utility remains the same.

By spending $1 more on water and $1 less on gum, Tina's total utility increases only if the marginal utility per dollar from water exceeds the marginal utility per dollar from gum. As she spends more on water and less on gum, the marginal utility from water decreases and the marginal utility from gum increases. When Tina has allocated her dollars so that the marginal utility per dollar is the same for both goods, total utility cannot be increased any further: Utility is maximized.

Table 13.2 shows Tina's utility-maximizing choice. If Tina chooses row *B* (1 bottle of water and 6 packs of gum) her marginal utility per dollar from water (15 units per dollar) *exceeds* her marginal utility per dollar from gum (4 units per dollar). She can increase total utility by spending more on water and less on gum.

If Tina chooses row *D* (3 bottles of water and 2 packs of gum) her marginal utility per dollar from water (9 units per dollar) *is less than* her marginal utility per dollar from gum (32 units per dollar). She can increase total utility by spending more on gum and less on water.

If Tina chooses row *C* (2 bottles of water and 4 packs of gum) her marginal utility per dollar from water (12 units per dollar) *equals* her marginal utility per dollar from gum. This combination maximizes Tina's total utility.

■ Finding an Individual Demand Curve

We can use marginal utility theory to find a person's demand schedule and demand curve. In fact, we've just found one entry in Tina's demand schedule and one point on her demand curve for bottled water: When the price of bottled water is $1 and other things remain the same (the price of gum is 50¢ and her budget is $4 a day), the quantity of water that Tina buys is 2 bottles a day (row *C* in Table 13.2).

Which one has the highest marginal utility per dollar?

■ TABLE 13.2

Tina's Marginal Utilities per Dollar: Water $1 a Bottle and Gum 50¢ a Pack

The rows of the table show Tina's marginal utility per dollar from water and gum for the affordable combinations when the price of water is $1 a bottle, the price of gum is 50¢ a pack, and her budget is $4.

By equalizing the marginal utilities per dollar from water and gum, Tina maximizes her total utility. Her utility-maximizing choice is to buy 2 bottles of water and 4 packs of gum.

	Bottled water			Chewing gum		
	Quantity (bottles per day)	Marginal utility	Marginal utility per dollar	Quantity (packs per day)	Marginal utility	Marginal utility per dollar
A	0			8	0	0
				7	1	2
B	1	15	15	6	2	4
				5	4	8
C	2	12	12	4	6	12
				3	8	16
D	3	9	9	2	16	32
				1	32	64

TABLE 13.3

Tina's Marginal Utilities per Dollar: Water 50¢ a Bottle and Gum 50¢ a Pack

	Bottled water			Chewing gum		
	Quantity (bottles per day)	Marginal utility	Marginal utility per dollar	Quantity (packs per day)	Marginal utility	Marginal utility per dollar
D	3	9	18	5	4	8
E	4	6	12	4	6	12
F	5	5	10	3	8	16

The rows of the table show Tina's marginal utility per dollar from water and gum for the affordable combinations when the price of water is 50¢ a bottle, the price of gum is 50¢ a pack, and her budget is $4. By equalizing the marginal utilities per dollar from water and gum, Tina maximizes her total utility. Her utility-maximizing choice is to buy 4 bottles of water and 4 packs of gum.

To find another point on Tina's demand curve for bottled water, let's see what Tina buys when the price of water falls to 50¢ a bottle. If Tina continued to buy 2 bottles of water and 4 packs of gum, her marginal utility per dollar from water would increase from 12 to 24 and be twice the marginal utility per dollar from gum (row C in Table 13.2). Also, Tina would spend only $3, so she would have another $1 available.

Row E of Table 13.3 shows Tina's new utility-maximizing choice, and this choice is a second point on her demand curve for bottled water: When the price of bottled water is 50¢ (other things remaining the same), Tina buys 4 bottles of water a day. Figure 13.6 shows Tina's demand curve that we've just derived.

FIGURE 13.6

Tina's Demand for Bottled Water   MyEconLab Animation

When the price of water is $1 a bottle (and Tina's budget is $4 and the price of a pack of gum is 50¢), she buys 2 bottles of water and 4 packs of gum a day. Tina is at point C on her demand curve for water.

When the price of water falls to 50¢ a bottle and other things remain the same, Tina buys 4 bottles of water and 4 packs of gum a day and moves to point E on her demand curve for bottled water.

MyEconLab Study Plan 13.2

Key Terms Quiz

Solutions Video

 # CHECKPOINT 13.2

Explain marginal utility theory and use it to derive a consumer's demand curve.

Practice Problems

TABLE 1

Burgers		Magazines	
Quantity per week	Total utility	Quantity per week	Total utility
0	0	0	0
1	14	1	100
2	24	2	120
3	32	3	134
4	38	4	144

Table 1 shows Jerry's total utility from burgers and magazines. The price of a burger is $2, the price of a magazine is $4, and Jerry has $12 a week to spend.

1. Calculate Jerry's marginal utility and marginal utility per dollar from burgers when he buys 4 burgers a week. Calculate Jerry's marginal utility per dollar from magazines when he buys 1 magazine a week.

2. If Jerry buys 4 burgers and 1 magazine a week, does he maximize his total utility? To maximize total utility will he buy more or fewer burgers? Explain.

3. What quantities of burgers and magazines maximize Jerry's utility?

In the News

Bird flu spikes egg prices; some hit $3 a dozen

Egg prices have tripled at some supermarkets as buyers scramble for solutions.

Source: *USAToday*, June 9, 2015

How does the event described in the news clip change the budget line and the quantity of eggs that Americans buy?

Solutions to Practice Problems

1. The marginal utility from the 4th burger equals the total utility from 4 burgers minus the total utility from 3 burgers, which is 6 units. Jerry's marginal utility per dollar from burgers (MU_B/P_B) equals his marginal utility of 6 units divided by the price of a burger, $2, which equals 3 units per dollar. The marginal utility from the first magazine is 100 units. Jerry's marginal utility per dollar from magazines (MU_M/P_M) equals his marginal utility, 100 units, divided by the price of a magazine, $4, which is 25 units per dollar.

2. If Jerry buys 4 burgers for $8 and 1 magazine for $4, he spends his $12 budget. Marginal utility per dollar from burgers (MU_B/P_B) = 3 (Solution 1) is *less* than his marginal utility per dollar from magazines (MU_M/P_M) = 25 (Solution 1), so Jerry does *not* maximize total utility. To do so, he must buy fewer burgers and more magazines.

3. Jerry maximizes utility if he buys 2 burgers and 2 magazines a week. He spends $4 on burgers, $8 on magazines, his $12 budget. His marginal utility from burgers (24 − 14) is 10. Dividing 10 by $2 gives ($MU_B/P_B$) = 5 units per dollar. His marginal utility from magazines (120 − 100) is 20. Dividing 20 by $4 gives ($MU_M/P_M$) = 5 units per dollar. Jerry's marginal utility per dollar from each good is 5 units per dollar, so his utility is maximized.

Solution to In the News

The budget line rotates inward. Consumers allocate their budget between eggs (E) and other items (X) such that (MU_E/P_E) = (MU_X/P_X). As the price of eggs (P_E) rises, (MU_E/P_E) falls. So with (MU_E/P_E) < (MU_X/P_X), consumers will reallocate their income to make (MU_E/P_E) rise and equal (MU_X/P_X). To make (MU_E/P_E) rise, (MU_E) must rise, which will occur as the quantity of eggs bought decreases.

13.3 EFFICIENCY, PRICE, AND VALUE

Marginal utility theory helps us to deepen our understanding of the concept of efficiency and to see more clearly the distinction between *value* and *price*. Let's see how.

■ Consumer Efficiency

When Tina allocates her limited budget to maximize her total utility, she is using her resources efficiently. Any other allocation of her budget would leave her able to attain a higher level of total utility.

But when Tina has allocated her budget to maximize her total utility, she is *on* her demand curve for each good. A demand curve describes the quantity demanded at each price *when total utility is maximized*. When we studied efficiency in Chapter 6, we learned that a demand curve is also a willingness-to-pay curve. It tells us a consumer's *marginal benefit*—the benefit from consuming an additional unit of a good. You can now give the idea of marginal benefit a deeper meaning.

> Marginal benefit is the maximum price a consumer is willing to pay for an extra unit of a good or service when total utility is maximized.

■ The Paradox of Value

For centuries, philosophers were puzzled by the paradox of value. Water is more valuable than a diamond because water is essential to life itself. Yet water is much cheaper than a diamond. Why? Adam Smith tried to solve this paradox, but it was not until marginal utility theory had been developed that anyone could give a satisfactory answer.

You can solve this puzzle by distinguishing between *total* utility and *marginal* utility. Total utility tells us about relative value; marginal utility tells us about relative price. The total utility from water is enormous, but remember, the more we consume of something, the smaller is its marginal utility. We use so much water that its marginal utility—the benefit we get from one more glass of water—diminishes to a small value. Diamonds, on the other hand, have a small total utility relative to water, but because we buy few diamonds, they have a large marginal utility. When a household has maximized its total utility, it has allocated its budget so that the marginal utility per dollar is equal for all goods. Diamonds have a high price and a high marginal utility. Water has a low price and a low marginal utility. When the high marginal utility of diamonds is divided by the high price of a diamond, the result is a marginal utility per dollar that equals the low marginal utility of water divided by the low price of water. The marginal utility per dollar is the same for diamonds as for water.

Consumer Surplus

Consumer surplus measures value in excess of the amount paid. In Figure 13.7, the demand for and supply of water in part (a) determine the price of water P_W and the quantity of water consumed Q_W. The demand for and supply of diamonds in part (b) determine the price of a diamond P_D and the quantity of diamonds Q_D. Water is cheap but provides a large consumer surplus, while diamonds are expensive but provide a small consumer surplus.

FIGURE 13.7

The Paradox of Value   MyEconLab Animation

Part (a) shows the demand for water, *D*, and the supply of water, *S*. Demand and supply determine the price of water at P_W and the quantity at Q_W. The consumer surplus from water is the large green triangle.

Part (b) shows the demand for diamonds, *D*, and the supply of diamonds, *S*. Demand and supply determine the price of a diamond at P_D and the quantity at Q_D. The consumer surplus from diamonds is the small green triangle.

Water is valuable—has a large consumer surplus—but cheap. Diamonds are less valuable than water—have a smaller consumer surplus—but are expensive.

(a) Water

(b) Diamonds

MyEconLab Critical Thinking Exercise

EYE on SONG DOWNLOADS AND STREAMING

How Much Would You Pay for a Song?

We can work out the willingness to pay for a song by finding the demand curve for songs and then finding the consumer surplus. To find the demand curve, we need to look at the expenditures, quantities, and prices in the market for songs.

In 2015, Americans spent $6.3 billion on all forms of recorded music, down from $14 billion in 2000. But the combined quantity bought *increased* from 1 billion in 2000 to 1.5 billion in 2015 and the average price of a unit of recorded music fell from $14 to $4.28.

The average price fell because the mix of formats changed dramatically. In 2000, we bought almost 1 billion CDs, but in 2015 we bought only 98 million. Instead of buying CDs, we downloaded 1.3 billion music files and paid for 16 million streaming subscriptions.

Figure 1 shows the longer history of the changing formats of recorded music.

The music that we buy is several different goods. We'll distinguish singles from albums and focus on the demand for singles.

In 2000, we bought 100 million singles at an average price of $5.00. In 2015, we downloaded 1,200 million singles at an average price of $1.20.

Figure 2 shows the demand curve in the market for singles. One point on the demand curve is the 2000 price and quantity—100 million at $5.00 per single. Another point on the demand curve is that for 2015—1,200 million singles downloaded at $1.20 each.

If the demand curve has not shifted and is linear (assumed here), we can calculate the change in consumer

Units (millions per year)

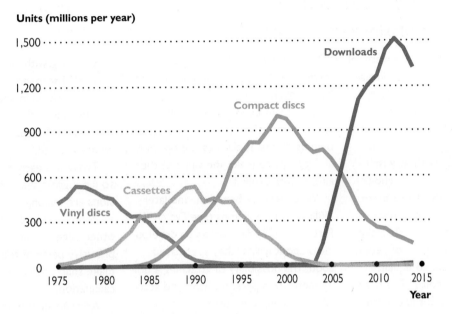

Figure 1 Changing Formats of Recorded Music

SOURCE OF DATA: Recording Industry Association of America.

surplus generated by the fall in the price and the increase in the quantity demanded. In Figure 2, the area shaded green shows this change in consumer surplus. That increase in consumer surplus is 2.47 billion, which is $2.06 per single.

The increase in consumer surplus of $2.06 per song is an estimate of how much more an average buyer would be willing to pay for an average song.

Paid subscriptions for streaming increase consumer surplus even more. A streaming subscription is a fixed cost per month, so the price of a song—an average price—is the monthly subscription divided by the number of different songs played. But the price of the marginal song is zero, and consumer surplus becomes the entire area under the demand curve at a zero price minus the fixed subscription cost.

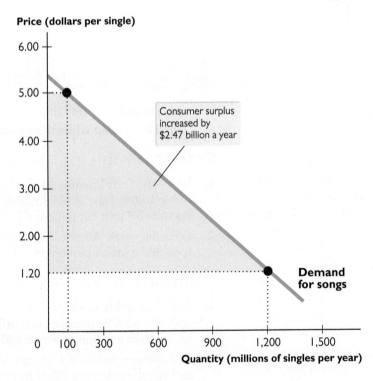

Figure 2 The Market for Singles

EYE on YOUR LIFE
Do You Maximize Your Utility?

You might be thinking that this marginal utility stuff is pretty unreal! You know that you don't go around the shops with a marginal utility calculator in hand. You just buy what you can afford and want, and that's all there is to it.

Well, marginal utility theory isn't about how people make their choices. It's about what choices people make. It's a tool that enables economists to explain the choices that people make.

You see lots of examples of people juggling their purchases to equalize marginal utilities per dollar. The next time you're in a checkout line, note the items that someone had second thoughts about and stuffed into the magazine rack alongside the tabloids.

When the crunch came to pay, the marginal utility per dollar was just not high enough.

You might even find yourself actually using marginal utility to make your own decisions. It clarifies the options, and it helps to make the value of the alternatives explicit.

When Jeremy Bentham, and later William Stanley Jevons (see *Eye on the Past* on p. 327), first began to develop ideas about utility, they speculated about the possibility of attaching a utility meter to a person's head and actually measuring the utility.

Today, a new branch of economics called *neuroeconomics* is moving toward achieving that nineteenth-century dream.

Working with neuroscientists and using MRI scanners, economists are placing subjects in decision-making situations and observing how the brain behaves as choices are made and outcomes learned.

These are early days, but results so far suggest that while some decisions are rational (and can be seen to be computed in the frontal cortex), other decisions are made using primitive parts of the brain that make snap choices without careful calculation.

As neuroeconomics advances, it will illuminate the way choices are made and might improve our ability to predict the choices that people make.

 ## CHECKPOINT 13.3

Use marginal utility theory to explain the paradox of value: why water is vital but cheap while diamonds are relatively useless but expensive.

Practice Problems

1. In a year, Tony streams 50 movies at $3 each and pays $50 for 10,000 gallons of tap water. Tony is maximizing total utility. If Tony's marginal utility from water is 0.5 unit per gallon, what is his marginal utility from a movie?

2. Over the years, Americans have spent a smaller percentage of income on food and a larger percentage on cars. Explain the paradox of value.

Solutions to Practice Problems

1. Marginal utility from a movie ÷ $3 = Marginal utility from a gallon of tap water ÷ 0.5¢. So the marginal utility from a movie is 600 times the marginal utility from a gallon of water: 600 × 0.5 or 300 units.

2. The average person has one car and the marginal utility from driving the car exceeds the marginal utility from food. While food is cheap and cars are expensive, consumers allocate their income to make the marginal utility per dollar from food and cars equal. There is no paradox of value.

CHAPTER SUMMARY

Key Points

1. **Calculate and graph a budget line that shows the limits to a person's consumption possibilities.**

   - Consumption possibilities are constrained by the budget and prices. Some combinations of goods are affordable, and some are not affordable.
   - The budget line is the boundary between what a person can and cannot afford with a given budget and given prices.
   - The slope of the budget line determines the relative price of the good measured on the x-axis in terms of the good measured on the y-axis.
   - A change in one price changes the slope of the budget line. A change in the budget shifts the budget line but does not change its slope.

2. **Explain marginal utility theory and use it to derive a consumer's demand curve.**

   - Consumption possibilities and preferences determine consumption choices.
   - Total utility is maximized when the entire budget is spent and marginal utility per dollar is equal for all goods.
   - If the marginal utility per dollar from good A exceeds that from good B, total utility increases if the quantity purchased of good A increases and the quantity purchased of good B decreases.
   - Marginal utility theory implies the law of demand. That is, other things remaining the same, the higher the price of a good, the smaller is the quantity demanded of that good.

3. **Use marginal utility theory to explain the paradox of value: why water is vital but cheap while diamonds are relatively useless but expensive.**

   - When consumers maximize total utility, they use resources efficiently.
   - Marginal utility theory resolves the paradox of value.
   - When we talk loosely about value, we are thinking of *total* utility or consumer surplus, but price is related to *marginal* utility.
   - Water, which we consume in large amounts, has a high total utility and a large consumer surplus but a low price and low marginal utility.
   - Diamonds, which we consume in small amounts, have a low total utility and a small consumer surplus but a high price and a high marginal utility.

Key Terms

MyEconLab Key Terms Quiz

Budget line, 320
Diminishing marginal utility, 326
Marginal utility, 326

Marginal utility per dollar, 328
Relative price, 324
Total utility, 326

Utility, 326
Utility-maximizing rule, 328

CHAPTER CHECKPOINT

Study Plan Problems and Applications

Amy has $12 a week to spend on coffee and soda. The price of coffee is $2 a cup, and soda is $1 a can. Use this information to work Problems **1** and **2**.

1. Draw a graph of Amy's budget line. Can Amy buy 7 cans of soda and 2 cups of coffee a week? Can she buy 7 cups of coffee and 2 cans of soda a week? What is the relative price of a cup of coffee?

2. Suppose that the price of soda remains at $1 a can but the price of coffee rises to $3 a cup. Draw Amy's new budget line. If she buys 6 cans of soda, what is the maximum number of cups of coffee she can buy in a week? Has the relative price of coffee changed?

Use Table 1, which shows Ben's utility, to work Problems **3** and **4**.

3. Calculate the values of *A*, *B*, *C*, and *D* in the table. Does the principle of diminishing marginal utility apply to Ben's consumption of orange juice? Why or why not?

4. Would Ben ever want to buy more than one carton of orange juice a day or no orange juice? Explain your answer.

5. Every day, Josie buys 2 cups of coffee and 1 sandwich for lunch. The price of coffee is $2 a cup and the price of a sandwich is $5. Josie's choice of lunch maximizes her total utility, and she spends only $9 on lunch. Compare Josie's marginal utility from coffee with her marginal utility from the sandwich.

6. Susie spends $28 a week on sundaes and magazines. The price of a sundae is $4 and the price of a magazine is $4. Table 2 shows Susie's marginal utility from sundaes and magazines. How many sundaes does she buy? If the price of a sundae doubles to $8 and other things remain the same, how many sundaes will she buy? What are two points on her demand curve for sundaes?

7. When Erin has $25 to spend, she sees 2 movies at $10 a movie ticket and buys 1 six-pack of soda. Calculate the price of soda. If her budget for soda and movies increases to $50, what is the change in the relative price of a movie ticket? How does her marginal utility per dollar from movies change?

8. **Watch video without dinging data caps**
   Verizon, the biggest wireless company, will let its customers watch ad-sponsored video free from data caps.
   Source: Associated Press, December 15, 2015
   Explain the effect of exempting video from data caps on a person's budget line and the quantities of video and other data used.

9. **Compared to other liquids, gasoline is cheap**
   In 2008, when gasoline hit $4 a gallon, motorists complained, but they didn't complain about $18 for 16 ml of HP ink ($4,294.58 per gallon).
   Source: *The New York Times*, May 27, 2008
   Explain why the prices of printer ink and gasoline might provide an example of the paradox of value.

10. Read *Eye on Song Downloads and Streaming* on pp. 334–335, then draw a student's budget lines for single songs versus other goods and services in 2000 and 2015. Explain why the budget line changed between 2000 and 2015.

TABLE 1

Orange juice (cartons per day)	Total utility	Marginal utility
0	0	
		7
1	7	
		5
2	A	
		B
3	15	
		2
4	C	
		D
5	18	

TABLE 2

Sundaes		Magazines	
Quantity per week	Marginal utility	Quantity per week	Marginal utility
1	60	1	40
2	56	2	32
3	50	3	28
4	42	4	25
5	32	5	23
6	20	6	22

Instructor Assignable Problems and Applications

MyEconLab Homework, Quiz, or Test if assigned by instructor

1. In 2015, Americans downloaded 1,200 million singles at $1.20 each and 100 million albums at $10 each. They also bought 1 million singles on vinyl at $11 each and 100 million albums on CDs at $12.50 each. What does marginal utility theory tell you about the ratio of the marginal utility from singles on vinyl to the marginal utility from singles downloads? What does it tell you about the ratio of the marginal utility from albums on CDs to the marginal utility from album downloads?

2. Tim buys 2 smoothies and sees 1 movie a week when he has $16 to spend, the price of a movie ticket is $8, and the price of a smoothie is $4. What is the relative price of a movie ticket? If the price of a movie ticket falls to $4, how will Tim's consumption possibilities change? Explain.

3. Jim spends all his income on apartment rent, food, clothing, and vacations. He gets a pay raise from $3,000 a month to $4,000 a month. At the same time, airfares and other vacation-related expenses increase by 50 percent. How has Jim's budget in terms of airfares and other vacation-related expenses changed? Is Jim better off or worse off in his new situation?

Use Table 1, which shows Martha's total utility from burgers and pasta, to work Problems **4** to **6**.

4. When Martha buys 3 burgers and 2 dishes of pasta a week, what is her total utility and her marginal utility from the third burger? If the price of a burger is $4, what is her marginal utility per dollar from burgers?

5. When the price of a burger is $4, the price of pasta is $8 a dish, and Martha has $24 a week to spend, she buys 2 burgers and 2 dishes of pasta. Does she maximize her total utility? Explain your answer.

6. When the price of a burger is $4, Martha has $24 to spend, and the price of pasta falls from $8 to $4 a dish, how many burgers and dishes of pasta does Martha buy? What are two points on Martha's demand curve for pasta?

Use the following information to work Problems **7** and **8**.

Table 2 shows the marginal utility that Ali gets from smoothies and movies. Ali has $30 a week to spend. The price of a movie ticket is $6, and the price of a smoothie is $3.

7. If Ali buys 4 smoothies a week and sees 3 movies, does he spend all $30? What is his utility from smoothies and his utility from movies? Does he maximize his utility? If not, which good must he buy more of?

8. When Ali allocates his budget so as to maximize his utility, what does he buy and what is the marginal utility per dollar?

Use the following information to work Problems **9** and **10**.

Apple Music could match Spotify subscribers by 2016
Apple Music is expected to have 16 million paid subscribers by the end of 2016. Spotify has 20 million paid subscribers.

Source: *Newsweek*, December 18, 2015

9. Compare the budget line for a streaming subscription with that for song downloads at $1 per song.

10. Compare the marginal utility of a downloaded song with that of a streamed song.

TABLE 1

Burgers		Pasta	
Quantity per week	Total utility	Dishes per week	Total utility
0	0	0	0
1	10	1	20
2	18	2	36
3	25	3	48
4	31	4	56
5	36	5	60
6	40	6	62

TABLE 2

Quantity per week	Marginal utility from	
	Smoothies	Movies
1	7	30
2	6	24
3	5	18
4	4	12
5	3	6
6	2	0

Multiple Choice Quiz

1. A consumer's consumption possibilities depend on all of the following items *except* _____.

   A. the prices of the goods that the consumer wants to buy
   B. the consumer's budget
   C. the quantities of the goods that the consumer can afford
   D. the consumer's preferences

2. Jane's budget line _____.

   A. shifts outward with no change in its slope if her budget increases and prices don't change
   B. rotates inward if the prices of both goods double and her budget doesn't change
   C. shifts inward with no change in its slope if the price of one good rises and her budget doesn't change
   D. rotates outward if her budget increases and prices don't change

3. Total utility _____ and marginal utility _____ as more of a good is consumed.

   A. increases; increases
   B. diminishes; diminishes
   C. increases; diminishes
   D. diminishes; increases

4. Tom will maximize his total utility if he buys the quantities of pasta and milk at which _____.

   A. the marginal utility from pasta equals the marginal utility from milk
   B. he spends all of his budget and marginal utility from each good is equal
   C. the marginal utility from the more expensive good is less than the marginal utility from the cheaper good
   D. he spends all his budget and the marginal utility per dollar from pasta and milk are equal

5. Sara buys bread and bananas and is maximizing her total utility. If the price of bananas rises, Sara will maximize her total utility by _____.

   A. increasing her budget so that she can buy the same quantities
   B. buying more bananas and less bread
   C. buying fewer bananas and possibly more bread
   D. buying less bread and possibly more bananas

6. When Joe's budget increases, he will spend the increase in his budget on _____.

   A. normal goods
   B. inferior goods
   C. more of all the goods he usually buys
   D. essential goods

7. The paradox of value arises when people _____.

   A. prefer to buy cheap goods rather than expensive goods
   B. spend more on expensive useless goods than on cheap useful goods
   C. buy so much of a useful good that its price falls
   D. get the same marginal utility per dollar from cheap useful goods and useless expensive goods

APPENDIX: INDIFFERENCE CURVES

You are going to discover a neat idea—that of drawing a map of a person's preferences. A preference map is based on the intuitively appealing assumption that people can sort all the possible combinations of goods into three groups: preferred, not preferred, and indifferent. To make this idea concrete, let's ask Tina to tell us how she ranks combinations of bottled water and chewing gum.

■ An Indifference Curve

Figure A13.1(a) shows part of Tina's answer. She tells us that she currently consumes 2 bottles of water and 4 packs of gum a day at point C. She then lists all the combinations of bottled water and chewing gum that she says are as acceptable to her as her current consumption. When we plot these combinations of water and gum, we get the green curve. This curve is the key element in a map of preferences and is called an indifference curve.

An **indifference curve** is a line that shows combinations of goods among which a consumer is *indifferent*. The indifference curve in Figure A13.1(a) tells us that Tina is just as happy to consume 2 bottles of water and 4 packs of gum a day at point C as to consume the combination of water and gum at any other point along the indifference curve. Tina also says that she prefers all the combinations of bottled water and gum above the indifference curve—the yellow area—to those on the indifference curve. These combinations contain more water, more gum, or

Indifference curve
A line that shows combinations of goods among which a consumer is *indifferent*.

■ **FIGURE A13.1**

A Preference Map

MyEconLab Animation

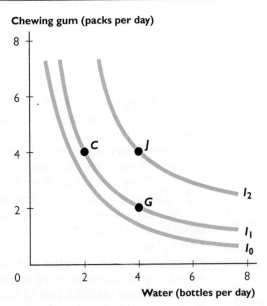

(a) Tina's indifference curve

(b) Tina's preference map

In part (a), Tina consumes 2 bottles of water and 4 packs of chewing gum a day at point C. She is indifferent between all the points on the green indifference curve. She prefers any point above the indifference curve (yellow area) to any point on it, and she prefers any point on the indifference curve to any point below it (gray area).

Part (b) shows three indifference curves of Tina's preference map. She prefers point J to point C or G, so she prefers any point on I_2 to any point on I_1.

more of both. She also prefers any combination on the indifference curve to any combination in the gray area below the indifference curve. These combinations contain less water, less gum, or less of both.

The indifference curve in Figure A13.1(a) is just one of a whole family of such curves. This indifference curve appears again in Figure A13.1(b) labeled I_1. The curves labeled I_0 and I_2 are two other indifference curves. Tina prefers any point on indifference curve I_2, such as point J, to any point on indifference curve I_1, such as points C or G. She prefers any point on I_1 to any point on I_0. We refer to I_2 as being a higher indifference curve than I_1 and to I_1 as being higher than I_0.

A preference map is a series of indifference curves that resemble the contour lines on a map. By looking at the shape of the contour lines on a map, we can draw conclusions about the terrain. Similarly, by looking at the shape of the indifference curves, we can draw conclusions about a person's preferences.

■ Marginal Rate of Substitution

Marginal rate of substitution
The rate at which a person will give up good Y (the good measured on the y-axis) to get more of good X (the good measured on the x-axis) and at the same time remain on the same indifference curve.

The concept of the marginal rate of substitution is the key to "reading" a preference map. The **marginal rate of substitution** (*MRS*) is the rate at which a person will give up good Y (the good measured on the y-axis) to get more of good X (the good measured on the x-axis) and at the same time remain indifferent (remain on the same indifference curve). The marginal rate of substitution is measured by the magnitude of the slope of an indifference curve.

If the indifference curve is *steep*, the marginal rate of substitution is *high*. The person is willing to give up a large quantity of good Y to get a small quantity of good X while remaining indifferent. If the indifference curve is *flat*, the marginal rate of substitution is *low*. The person is willing to give up only a small amount of good Y to get a large amount of good X and remain indifferent.

Figure A13.2 shows you how to calculate the marginal rate of substitution. Suppose that Tina consumes 2 bottles of water and 4 packs of gum at point C on indifference curve I_1. We calculate her marginal rate of substitution by measuring the magnitude of the slope of the indifference curve at point C. To measure this magnitude, place a straight line against, or tangent to, the indifference curve at point C. Along that red line, as gum consumption decreases from 8 packs to zero packs, water consumption increases from zero bottles to 4 bottles. So at point C, Tina is willing to give up 8 packs of gum to get 4 bottles of water, or 2 packs of gum per bottle. Her marginal rate of substitution is 2.

Now suppose that Tina consumes 4 bottles of water and 2 packs of gum at point G. The slope of the indifference curve at point G now measures her marginal rate of substitution. That slope is the same as the slope of the line tangent to the indifference curve at point G. Here, as chewing gum consumption decreases from 4 packs to zero, water consumption increases from zero to 8 bottles. So at point G, Tina is willing to give up 4 packs of chewing gum to get 8 bottles of water, or 1/2 a pack of gum per bottle. Her marginal rate of substitution is 1/2.

Diminishing marginal rate of substitution
The general tendency for the marginal rate of substitution to decrease as the consumer moves down along the indifference curve, increasing consumption of the good measured on the x-axis and decreasing consumption of the good measured on the y-axis.

As Tina moves down along her indifference curve, her marginal rate of substitution diminishes. Diminishing marginal rate of substitution is the key assumption of consumer theory. **Diminishing marginal rate of substitution** is the general tendency for the marginal rate of substitution to diminish as the consumer moves down along an indifference curve, increasing consumption of the good measured on the x-axis and decreasing consumption of the good measured on the y-axis. The shape of a person's indifference curves incorporates the principle of the diminishing marginal rate of substitution because the curves are bowed toward the origin.

FIGURE A13.2

The Marginal Rate of Substitution   MyEconLab Animation

The magnitude of the slope of an indifference curve is called the marginal rate of substitution (*MRS*).

The red line at point *C* tells us that Tina is willing to give up 8 packs of gum to get 4 bottles of water. Her marginal rate of substitution at point *C* is 8 divided by 4, which equals 2.

The red line at point *G* tells us that Tina is willing to give up 4 packs of gum to get 8 bottles of water. Her marginal rate of substitution at point *G* is 4 divided by 8, which equals 1/2.

Consumer Equilibrium

The consumer's goal is to buy the affordable quantities of goods that make her or him as well off as possible. The indifference curves describe the consumer's preferences, and they tell us that the higher the indifference curve, the better off is the consumer. So the consumer's goal can be restated as: to allocate his or her budget in such a way as to get onto the highest attainable indifference curve.

The consumer's budget and the prices of the goods limit the consumer's choices. The budget line illustrated in Figure 13.1 (p. 320) summarizes the limits on the consumer's choice. We combine the indifference curves of Figure A13.1(b) with the budget line of Figure 13.1 to work out the consumer's choice and find the consumer equilibrium.

Figure A13.3 shows Tina's budget line from Figure 13.1 and her indifference curves from Figure A13.1(b). Tina's *best affordable point* is 2 bottles of water and 4 packs of gum—at point C. Here, Tina

- Is on her budget line.
- Is on her highest attainable indifference curve.
- Has a marginal rate of substitution between water and gum equal to the relative price of water in terms of gum.

For every point inside the budget line, such as point *L*, there are points *on* the budget line that Tina prefers. For example, she prefers any point on the budget line between *F* and *H* to point *L*. So she chooses a point on the budget line.

■ **FIGURE A13.3**

Consumer Equilibrium

Tina's best affordable point is *C*. At that point, she is on her budget line and also on the highest attainable indifference curve.

At a point such as *H*, Tina is willing to give up more bottled water in exchange for chewing gum than she has to. She can move to point *L*, which is just as good as point *H*, and have some unspent budget. She can spend that budget and move to *C*, a point that she prefers to point *L*.

Checked out at the best affordable point.

Every point on the budget line lies on an indifference curve. For example, point *F* lies on the indifference curve I_0. At point *F*, Tina's marginal rate of substitution (the magnitude of the slope of the indifference curve I_0) is greater than the relative price (the magnitude of the slope of the budget line). Tina is willing to give up more chewing gum to get an additional bottle of water than the budget line says she must. So she moves along her budget line from *F* toward *C*. As she does so, she passes through a number of indifference curves (not shown in the figure) located between indifference curves I_0 and I_1. All of these indifference curves are higher than I_0 so Tina prefers any point on them to point *F*. When Tina gets to point *C*, she is on the highest attainable indifference curve. If she keeps moving along the budget line, she starts to encounter indifference curves that are lower than I_1. So Tina chooses point *C*—her best affordable point.

At the chosen point, the marginal rate of substitution (the magnitude of the slope of the indifference curve) equals the relative price (the magnitude of the slope of the budget line).

We can now use this model of consumer choice to predict the effect of a change in the price of water on the quantity of water demanded. That is, we can use this model to generate the demand curve for bottled water.

■ **Deriving the Demand Curve**

To derive Tina's demand curve for bottled water, we change the price of water, shift the budget line, and work out the new best affordable point. Figure A13.4(a) shows the change in the budget line and the change in consumer equilibrium when the price of water falls from $1 a bottle to 50¢ a bottle.

Initially, when the price of water is $1 a bottle, Tina consumes at point *C* in part (a). When the price of a bottle of water falls from $1 to 50¢, her budget line rotates outward and she can now get onto a higher indifference curve. Her best affordable point is now point *K*. Tina increases the quantity of water she buys from 2 to 4 bottles a day. She continues to buy 4 packs of gum a day.

Figure A13.4(b) shows Tina's demand curve for bottled water. When the price of water is $1 a bottle, she buys 2 bottles a day, at point *A*. When the price of water falls to 50¢ a bottle, she buys 4 bottles a day, at point *B*. Tina's demand curve traces out her best affordable quantity of water as the price of a bottle of water varies.

▨ **FIGURE A13.4**

Deriving Tina's Demand Curve   MyEconLab Animation

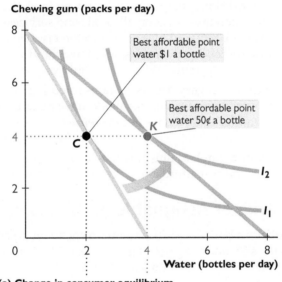

(a) Change in consumer equilibrium

In part (a), when the price of water is $1 a bottle, Tina consumes at point *C*. When the price of water falls from $1 to 50¢ a bottle, she consumes at point *K*.

In part (b), when the price of water is $1 a bottle, Tina is at point *A*. When the price of water falls from $1 to 50¢ a bottle, Tina moves along her demand curve for bottled water from point *A* to point *B*.

(b) Demand curve

APPENDIX CHECKPOINT

Study Plan Problems and Applications

Sara has $12 to spend on popcorn and nuts. Popcorn is $3 a bag, and nuts is $3 a bag. Figure 1 illustrates Sara's preferences. Use Figure 1 to work Problems **1** to **3**.

FIGURE 1
Popcorn (bags)

1. What is the relative price of nuts and what is the opportunity cost of a bag of nuts? Draw a graph of Sara's budget line with nuts on the x-axis.

2. What quantities of popcorn and nuts does Sara buy and what is her marginal rate of substitution of popcorn for nuts at her consumption point?

3. Suppose that the price of nuts falls to $1.50 a bag and the price of popcorn and Sara's budget remain unchanged. What quantities of popcorn and nuts does Sara buy now? What are two points on Sara's demand curve for nuts?

4. In most states, there is no sales tax on food. Some people say that a consumption tax—a tax on all goods and services—would be better. If all sales taxes are replaced by a consumption tax, what would happen to the relative price of food and haircuts and how would you change your purchases of food and haircuts? Which tax would you prefer?

5. **Taxes on sugary drinks work as intended**
   Governments around the world have put a tax on sugary drinks, and the demand for these drinks has decreased.

   Source: *The Economist*, November 28, 2015

   Draw a graph to illustrate how a tax on sugary drinks changes the budget line, the best affordable point, and the demand for sugary drinks.

MyEconLab Homework, Quiz, or Test if assigned by instructor

FIGURE 2
Root beer (bottles per month)

Instructor Assignable Problems and Applications

Marc has a budget of $20 a month to spend on lattes and e-books. The price of a latte is $5, and the price of an e-book is $10. Figure 2 illustrates his preferences. Use Figure 2 to work Problems **1** to **3**.

1. What is the relative price of a latte in terms of e-books and what is the opportunity cost of a latte? Draw a graph of Marc's budget line with e-books on the x-axis.

2. What quantities of lattes and e-books does Marc buy? At his consumption point, calculate his marginal rate of substitution of e-books for lattes.

3. If the price of an e-book falls to $5 but the price of a latte and Marc's budget remain unchanged, what quantities of lattes and e-books does Marc now buy? What are two points on Marc's demand curve for e-books?

4. **The Beatles set to stream on Christmas Eve**
   The Beatles are set to join the streaming revolution as its revenue generation overtakes that from downloads.

   Source: *Billboard*, December 18, 2015

   Draw a graph to illustrate a Beatle fan's preferences, and budget lines for streaming versus other goods and for downloads versus others goods. On your graph, show the best affordable point before and after Christmas 2015.

MyEconLab Key Terms Quiz

Key Terms

Diminishing marginal rate of substitution, 342	Indifference curve, 341	Marginal rate of substitution, 342

Which store has the lower costs: Walmart or 7-Eleven?

Production and Cost

14

When you have completed your study of this chapter, you will be able to

1 Explain and distinguish between the economic and accounting measures of a firm's cost of production and profit.

2 Explain the relationship between a firm's output and labor employed in the short run.

3 Explain the relationship between a firm's output and costs in the short run.

4 Derive and explain a firm's long-run average cost curve.

MyEconLab Big Picture Video

MyEconLab Concept Video

14.1 ECONOMIC COST AND PROFIT

A Walmart store is much larger than a 7-Eleven and clearly costs more to operate. But which store has the lower cost per customer served? Now the answer is not so obvious. You'll find the answer at the end of this chapter.

Like a Walmart store and a 7-Eleven, the 20 million firms in the United States differ in size. They also differ in what they produce. But all firms perform the same basic economic function: They hire factors of production and organize them to produce and sell goods and services. To understand the behavior of a firm, we need to know its goals.

■ The Firm's Goal

If you asked a group of entrepreneurs what they are trying to achieve, you would get many different answers. Some would talk about making a high-quality product, others about business growth, others about market share, and others about job satisfaction of the work force. All of these goals might be pursued, but they are not the fundamental goal. They are a means to a deeper goal.

The firm's goal is to *maximize profit*. A firm that does not seek to maximize profit is either eliminated or bought by firms that *do* seek to achieve that goal. To calculate a firm's profit, we must determine its total revenue and total cost. Economists have a special way of defining and measuring cost and profit, which we'll explain and illustrate by looking at Sam's Smoothies, a firm that is owned and operated by Samantha.

■ Accounting Cost and Profit

In 2016, Sam's Smoothies' total revenue from the sale of smoothies was $150,000. The firm paid $20,000 for fruit, yogurt, and honey; $22,000 in wages for the labor it hired; and $3,000 in interest to the bank. These items totaled $45,000.

Sam's accountant said that the depreciation of the firm's blenders, refrigerators, and shop during 2016 was $10,000. Depreciation is the fall in the value of the firm's capital, and accountants calculate it by using the Internal Revenue Service's rules, which are based on standards set by the Financial Accounting Standards Board. So the accountant reported the firm's total cost for 2016 as $55,000 and the firm's profit as $95,000—$150,000 of total revenue minus $55,000 of total costs.

Sam's accountant measures cost and profit to ensure that the firm pays the correct amount of income tax and to show the bank how Sam's has used its bank loan. Economists have a different purpose: to predict the firm's decisions. These decisions respond to *opportunity cost* and *economic profit*.

■ Opportunity Cost

To produce its output, a firm employs factors of production: land, labor, capital, and entrepreneurship. Another firm could have used these same resources to produce other goods or services. In Chapter 3 (pp. 66–67), resources can be used to produce either smartphones or bikes, so the opportunity cost of producing a smartphone is the number of bikes forgone. Pilots who fly passengers for Southwest Airlines can't at the same time fly freight for FedEx. Construction workers who are building an office high-rise can't simultaneously build apartments. A journalist writing for the *New York Times* can't at the same time create

Web news reports for CNN. And Samantha can't simultaneously run her smoothies business and a flower shop.

The highest-valued alternative forgone is the opportunity cost of a firm's production. From the viewpoint of the firm, this opportunity cost is the amount that the firm must pay the owners of the factors of production it employs to attract them from their best alternative use. So a firm's opportunity cost of production is the cost of the factors of production it employs.

To determine these costs, let's return to Sam's and look at the opportunity cost of producing smoothies.

Explicit Costs and Implicit Costs

The amount that a firm pays to attract resources from their best alternative use is either an explicit cost or an implicit cost. A cost paid in money is an **explicit cost**. Because the amount spent could have been spent on something else, an explicit cost is an opportunity cost. The wages that Samantha pays labor, the interest she pays the bank, and her expenditure on fruit, yogurt, and honey are explicit costs.

A firm incurs an **implicit cost** when it uses a factor of production but does not make a direct money payment for its use. The two categories of implicit cost are economic depreciation and the cost of the resources of the firm's owner.

Economic depreciation is the opportunity cost of the firm using capital that it owns. It is measured as the change in the *market value* of capital—the market price of the capital at the beginning of the period minus its market price at the end of the period. Suppose that Samantha could have sold her blenders, refrigerators, and shop on December 31, 2015, for $250,000. If she can sell the same capital on December 31, 2016, for $246,000, her economic depreciation during 2016 is $4,000. This is the opportunity cost of using her capital during 2016, not the $10,000 depreciation calculated by Sam's accountant.

Interest is another cost of capital. When the firm's owner provides the funds used to buy capital, the opportunity cost of those funds is the interest income forgone by not using them in the best alternative way. If Sam loaned her firm funds that could have earned her $1,000 in interest, this amount is an implicit cost of producing smoothies.

When a firm's owner supplies labor, the opportunity cost of the owner's time spent working for the firm is the wage income forgone by not working in the best alternative job. For example, instead of working at her next best job that pays $34,000 a year, Sam supplies labor to her smoothies business. This implicit cost of $34,000 is part of the opportunity cost of producing smoothies.

Finally, a firm's owner often supplies entrepreneurship, the factor of production that organizes the business and bears the risk of running it. The return to entrepreneurship is **normal profit**. Normal profit is part of a firm's opportunity cost because it is the cost of a forgone alternative—running another firm. Instead of running Sam's Smoothies, Sam could earn $16,000 a year running a flower shop. This amount is an implicit cost of production at Sam's Smoothies.

■ Economic Profit

A firm's **economic profit** equals total revenue minus total cost. Total revenue is the amount received from the sale of the product. It is the price of the output multiplied by the quantity sold. Total cost is the sum of the explicit costs and implicit costs and is the opportunity cost of production.

Explicit cost
A cost paid in money.

Implicit cost
An opportunity cost incurred by a firm when it uses a factor of production for which it does not make a direct money payment.

Economic depreciation
An opportunity cost of a firm using capital that it owns—measured as the change in the *market value* of capital over a given period.

Normal profit
The return to entrepreneurship. Normal profit is part of a firm's opportunity cost because it is the cost of not running another firm.

Economic profit
A firm's total revenue minus total cost.

■ **TABLE 14.1**

Economic Accounting

Item		
Total Revenue		$150,000
Explicit Costs		
Cost of fruit, yogurt, and honey	$20,000	
Wages	$22,000	
Interest	$3,000	
Implicit Costs		
Samantha's forgone wages	$34,000	
Samantha's forgone interest	$1,000	
Economic depreciation	$4,000	
Normal profit	$16,000	
Opportunity Cost		$100,000
Economic Profit		$50,000

Because one of the firm's implicit costs is *normal profit*, the return to the entrepreneur equals normal profit plus economic profit. If a firm incurs an economic loss, the entrepreneur receives less than normal profit.

Table 14.1 summarizes the economic cost concepts, and Figure 14.1 compares the economic view and the accounting view of cost and profit. Sam's total revenue (price multiplied by quantity sold) is $150,000; the opportunity cost of the resources that Sam uses is $100,000; and Sam's economic profit is $50,000.

■ **FIGURE 14.1**

Two Views of Cost and Profit   MyEconLab Animation

Both economists and accountants measure a firm's total revenue the same way. It equals the price multiplied by the quantity sold of each item.

Economists measure economic profit as total revenue minus opportunity cost. Opportunity cost includes explicit costs and implicit costs. Normal profit is an implicit cost.

Accountants measure profit as total revenue minus explicit costs—costs paid in money—and depreciation.

The economic view   The accounting view

CHECKPOINT 14.1

MyEconLab Study Plan 14.1
Key Terms Quiz
Solutions Video

Explain and distinguish between the economic and accounting measures of a firm's cost of production and profit.

Practice Problems

Lee, a programmer, earned $35,000 in 2015, but in 2016, he began to manufacture body boards. After one year, he submitted the following data to his accountant.

- He stopped renting out his cottage for $3,500 a year and used it as his factory. The market value of the cottage increased from $70,000 to $71,000.
- He spent $50,000 on materials, phone, utilities, etc.
- He leased machines for $10,000 a year.
- He paid $15,000 in wages.
- He used $10,000 from his savings account, which pays 5 percent a year interest.
- He borrowed $40,000 at 10 percent a year from the bank.
- He sold $160,000 worth of body boards.
- Normal profit is $25,000 a year.

1. Calculate Lee's explicit costs, implicit costs, and economic profit in 2016.

2. Lee's accountant recorded the depreciation on Lee's cottage during 2016 as $7,000. What did the accountant say Lee's profit or loss was in 2016?

In the News

What does it cost to make 100 pairs of running shoes?
An Asian manufacturer of running shoes pays its workers $275 to make 100 pairs an hour. Workers use company-owned equipment that costs $300 an hour in forgone interest and economic depreciation. Materials cost $900.

Source: washpost.com

Which costs are explicit costs? Which are implicit costs? With total revenue from the sale of 100 pairs of shoes of $1,650, calculate economic profit.

Solutions to Practice Problems

1. Lee's explicit costs are costs paid with money: $50,000 on materials, phone, utilities, etc; $10,000 on leased machines; $15,000 in wages; and $4,000 in bank interest. These items total $79,000.
   Lee's implicit costs are $35,000 in forgone wages; $3,500 in forgone rent; the $1,000 increase in the value of his cottage is economic depreciation of −$1,000; $500 in forgone interest; and $25,000 in normal profit. These items total $63,000.
   Economic profit equals total revenue ($160,000) minus total cost, which equals $79,000 + $63,000, or $142,000. So economic profit in 2016 was $160,000 − $142,000, or $18,000.

2. The accountant measures Lee's profit as total revenue minus explicit costs minus depreciation: $160,000−$79,000−$7,000, or $74,000.

Solution to In the News

Explicit costs are wages ($275) and materials ($900). Implicit costs are the forgone interest and economic depreciation ($300). Economic profit equals total revenue ($1,650) minus total cost ($1,475), which is $175.

MyEconLab Concept Video

SHORT RUN AND LONG RUN

The main goal of this chapter is to explore the influences on a firm's costs. The key influence on cost is the quantity of output that the firm produces per period. The greater the output rate, the higher is the total cost of production. But the effect of a change in production on cost depends on how soon the firm wants to act. A firm that plans to change its output rate tomorrow has fewer options than a firm that plans ahead and intends to change its production six months from now.

To study the relationship between a firm's output decision and its costs, we distinguish between two decision time frames:

- The short run
- The long run

The Short Run: Fixed Plant

Short run
The time frame in which the quantities of some resources are fixed. In the short run, a firm can usually change the quantity of labor it uses but not its technology and quantity of capital.

The **short run** is the time frame in which the quantities of some resources are fixed. For most firms, the fixed resources are the firm's technology and capital—its equipment and buildings. The management organization is also fixed in the short run. The fixed resources that a firm uses are its *fixed factors of production* and the resources that it can vary are its *variable factors of production*. The collection of fixed resources is the firm's *plant*. So in the short run, a firm's plant is fixed.

Sam's Smoothies' plant is its blenders, refrigerators, and shop. Sam's cannot change these inputs in the short run. An electric power utility can't change the number of generators it uses in the short run. An airport can't change the number of runways, terminal buildings, and traffic-control facilities in the short run.

To increase output in the short run, a firm must increase the quantity of variable factors it uses. Labor is usually the variable factor of production. To produce more smoothies, Sam must hire more labor. Similarly, to increase the production of electricity, a utility must hire more engineers and run its generators for longer hours. To increase the volume of traffic it handles, an airport must hire more check-in clerks, cargo handlers, and air-traffic controllers.

Short-run decisions are easily reversed. A firm can increase or decrease output in the short run by increasing or decreasing the number of labor hours it hires.

The Long Run: Variable Plant

Long run
The time frame in which the quantities of *all* resources can be varied.

The **long run** is the time frame in which the quantities of *all* resources can be varied. That is, the long run is a period in which the firm can change its *plant*.

To increase output in the long run, a firm can increase the size of its plant. Sam's Smoothies can install more blenders and refrigerators and increase the size of its shop. An electric power utility can install more generators. And an airport can build more runways, terminals, and traffic-control facilities.

Long-run decisions are not easily reversed. Once a firm buys a new plant, its resale value is usually much less than the amount the firm paid for it. The fall in value is economic depreciation. It is called a *sunk cost* to emphasize that it is irrelevant to the firm's decisions. Only the short-run cost of changing its labor inputs and the long-run cost of changing its plant size are relevant to a firm's decisions.

We're going to study costs in the short run and the long run. We begin with the short run and describe the limits to the firm's production possibilities.

14.2   SHORT-RUN PRODUCTION

MyEconLab Concept Video

To increase the output of a fixed plant, a firm must increase the quantity of labor it employs. We describe the relationship between output and the quantity of labor employed by using three related concepts:

- Total product
- Marginal product
- Average product

■ Total Product

Total product (*TP*) is the total quantity of a good produced in a given period. Total product is an output *rate*—the number of units produced per unit of time (for example, per hour, day, or week). Total product changes as the quantity of labor employed increases and we illustrate this relationship as a total product schedule and total product curve like those in Figure 14.2. The total product schedule (the table below the graph) lists the maximum quantity of smoothies per hour that Sam can produce with her existing plant at each quantity of labor. Points *A* through *H* on the *TP* curve correspond to the columns in the table.

Total product
The total quantity of a good produced in a given period.

■ FIGURE 14.2

Total Product Schedule and Total Product Curve

MyEconLab Animation

The total product schedule shows how the quantity of smoothies that Sam's can produce changes as the quantity of labor employed changes. In column *C*, Sam's employs 2 workers and can produce 3 gallons of smoothies an hour.

The total product curve, *TP*, graphs the data in the table. Points *A* through *H* on the curve correspond to the columns of the table. The total product curve separates attainable outputs from unattainable outputs. Points below the *TP* curve are inefficient. Points on the *TP* curve are efficient.

Quantity of labor (workers)	0	1	2	3	4	5	6	7
Total product (gallons per hour)	0	1	3	6	8	9	9	8
	A	*B*	*C*	*D*	*E*	*F*	*G*	*H*

Like the *production possibilities frontier* (see Chapter 3, p. 62), the total product curve separates attainable outputs from unattainable outputs. All the points that lie above the curve are unattainable. Points that lie below the curve, in the orange area, are attainable, but they are inefficient: They use more labor than is necessary to produce a given output. Only the points *on* the total product curve are efficient.

■ Marginal Product

Marginal product
The change in total product that results from a one-unit increase in the quantity of labor employed.

Marginal product (*MP*) is the change in total product that results from a one-unit increase in the quantity of labor employed. It tells us the contribution to total product of adding one additional worker. When the quantity of labor increases by more than one worker, we calculate marginal product as

Marginal product = Change in total product ÷ Change in quantity of labor.

Figure 14.3 shows Sam's Smoothies' marginal product curve, *MP*, and its relationship with the total product curve. You can see that as the quantity of labor increases from 1 to 3 workers, marginal product increases. But as more than 3 workers are employed, marginal product decreases. When the seventh worker is employed, marginal product is negative.

Notice that the steeper the slope of the total product curve in part (a), the greater is marginal product in part (b). And when the total product curve turns downward in part (a), marginal product is negative in part (b).

The total product curve and marginal product curve in Figure 14.3 incorporate a feature that is shared by all production processes in firms as different as the Ford Motor Company, Jim's Barber Shop, and Sam's Smoothies:

- Increasing marginal returns initially
- Decreasing marginal returns eventually

Increasing Marginal Returns

Increasing marginal returns
When the marginal product of an additional worker exceeds the marginal product of the previous worker.

Increasing marginal returns occur when the marginal product of an additional worker exceeds the marginal product of the previous worker. The source of increasing marginal returns is increased specialization and greater division of labor in the production process.

For example, if Samantha employs just one worker, that person must learn all the aspects of making smoothies: running the blender, cleaning it, fixing breakdowns, buying and checking the fruit, and serving the customers. That one person must perform all these tasks.

If Samantha hires a second person, the two workers can specialize in different parts of the production process. As a result, two workers can produce more than twice as much as one worker. The marginal product of the second worker is greater than the marginal product of the first worker. Marginal returns are increasing. Most production processes experience increasing marginal returns initially.

Decreasing Marginal Returns

Decreasing marginal returns
When the marginal product of an additional worker is less than the marginal product of the previous worker.

All production processes eventually reach a point of *decreasing* marginal returns. **Decreasing marginal returns** occur when the marginal product of an additional worker is less than the marginal product of the previous worker. Decreasing marginal returns arise from the fact that more and more workers use the same equipment and work space. As more workers are employed, there is less and less that is productive for the additional worker to do. For example, if Samantha hires a

■ **FIGURE 14.3**

Total Product and Marginal Product

MyEconLab Animation

(a) Total product curve

The table calculates marginal product, and the orange bars illustrate it. When labor increases from 2 to 3 workers, total product increases from 3 gallons to 6 gallons of smoothies an hour. So marginal product is the orange bar whose height is 3 gallons (in both parts of the figure).

In part (b), marginal product is graphed midway between the labor inputs to emphasize that marginal product is the result of *changing* the labor input. Marginal product increases to a maximum (when 3 workers are employed in this example) and then declines—diminishing marginal product.

(b) Marginal product curve

Quantity of labor (workers)	0	1	2	3	4	5	6	7
Total product (gallons per hour)	0	1	3	6	8	9	9	8
Marginal product (gallons per worker)		1	2	3	2	1	0	−1

fourth worker, output increases but not by as much as it did when she hired the third worker. In this case, three workers exhaust all the possible gains from specialization and the division of labor. By hiring a fourth worker, Sam's produces more smoothies per hour, but the equipment is being operated closer to its limits. Sometimes the fourth worker has nothing to do because the machines are running without the need for further attention.

Hiring yet more workers continues to increase output but by successively smaller amounts until Samantha hires the sixth worker, at which point total product stops rising. Add a seventh worker, and the workplace is so congested that the workers get in each other's way and total product falls.

Decreasing marginal returns are so pervasive that they qualify for the status of a law: the **law of decreasing returns**, which states that

> As a firm uses more of a variable factor of production, with a given quantity of fixed factors of production, the marginal product of the variable factor eventually decreases.

Law of decreasing returns
As a firm uses more of a variable factor of production, with a given quantity of fixed factors, the marginal product of the variable factor eventually decreases.

■ Average Product

Average product (*AP*) is the total product per worker employed. It is calculated as

Average product = Total product ÷ Quantity of labor.

Another name for average product is *productivity*.

Figure 14.4 shows the average product of labor, *AP*, and the relationship between average product and marginal product. Average product increases from 1 to 3 workers (its maximum value) but then decreases as yet more workers are employed. Notice also that average product is largest when average product and marginal product are equal. That is, the marginal product curve cuts the average

Average product
Total product divided by the quantity of a factor of production. The average product of labor is total product divided by the quantity of labor employed.

FIGURE 14.4

Average Product and Marginal Product   MyEconLab Animation

The table calculates average product. For example, when the quantity of labor is 3 workers, total product is 6 gallons an hour, so average product is 6 gallons ÷ 3 workers, which equals 2 gallons per worker.

The average product curve is *AP*.

For the quantity of labor at which marginal product *exceeds* average product, average product is *increasing* and the *AP* curve is upward sloping.

For the quantity of labor at which marginal product is *less than* average product, average product is *decreasing* and the *AP* curve is downward sloping.

Quantity of labor (workers)	0		1		2		3		4		5		6		7
Total product (gallons per hour)	0		1		3		6		8		9		9		8
Marginal product (gallons per worker)		1		2		3		2		1		0		−1	
Average product (gallons per worker)			1.0		1.5		2.0		2.0		1.8		1.5		1.1	
			B		**C**		**D**		**E**		**F**		**G**		**H**

product curve at the point of maximum average product. For employment levels at which marginal product exceeds average product, the average product curve slopes upward and average product increases as more labor is employed. For employment levels at which marginal product is less than average product, the average product curve slopes downward and average product decreases as more labor is employed.

The relationship between average product and marginal product is a general feature of the relationship between the average value and the marginal value of any variable. *Eye on Your Life* looks at a familiar example.

EYE on YOUR LIFE

MyEconLab Critical Thinking Exercise

Your Average and Marginal Grades

Jen, a part-time student, takes one course each semester over five semesters. In the first semester, she takes calculus and her grade is a C (2). This grade is her marginal grade. It is also her average grade—her GPA.

In the next semester, Jen takes French and gets a B (3)—her new marginal grade. When the marginal value exceeds the average value, the average rises. Because Jen's marginal grade exceeds her average grade, the marginal grade pulls her average up. Her GPA rises to 2.5.

In the third semester, Jen takes economics and gets an A (4). Again her marginal grade exceeds her average, so the marginal grade pulls her average up. Jen's GPA is now 3—the average of 2, 3, and 4.

In the fourth semester, she takes history and gets a B (3). Now her marginal grade equals her average. When the marginal value equals the average value, the average doesn't change. So Jen's average remains at 3.

In the fifth semester, Jen takes English and gets a C (2). When the marginal value is below the average

value, the average falls. Because Jen's marginal grade, 2, is below her average of 3, the marginal grade pulls the average down. Her GPA falls.

This relationship between Jen's ❶ marginal grade and ❷ average grade is similar to the relationship between marginal product and average product.

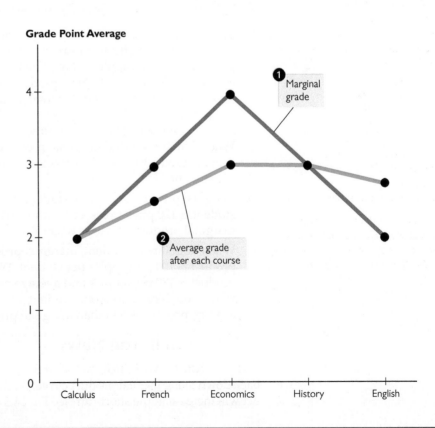

MyEconLab Study Plan 14.2
Key Terms Quiz
Solutions Video

 # CHECKPOINT 14.2

Explain the relationship between a firm's output and labor employed in the short run.

Practice Problems

TABLE 1

Labor (students)	Total product (pineapples per day)
0	0
1	100
2	220
3	300
4	360
5	400
6	420
7	430

Tom leases a farmer's field and grows pineapples. Tom hires students to pick and pack the pineapples. Table 1 sets out Tom's total product schedule.

1. Calculate the marginal product of the third student and the average product of three students.

2. Over what range of numbers of students does marginal product increase?

3. When marginal product increases, is average product greater than, less than, or equal to marginal product?

In the News

Deere, struggling with sales, to lay off 220
Deere & Co. plans to lay off 220 workers and decrease its output of farm equipment.

Source: *The Wall Street Journal*, November 30, 2015

If Deere & Co. is operating at maximum total product before it cuts its workforce, how will the marginal product of a worker change in the short run?

Solutions to Practice Problems

1. The marginal product of the third student is the change in total product that results from hiring the third student. When Tom hires 2 students, total product is 220 pineapples a day. When Tom hires 3 students, total product is 300 pineapples a day. Marginal product of the third student is the total product of 3 students minus the total product of 2 students, which is 300 pineapples − 220 pineapples or 80 pineapples a day.
Average product equals total product divided by the number of students. When Tom hires 3 students, total product is 300 pineapples a day, so average product is 300 pineapples ÷ 3 students, which equals 100 pineapples per student.

2. Marginal product of the first student is 100 pineapples a day, of the second student is 120 pineapples a day, and of the third is 80 pineapples a day. So marginal product increases when Tom hires the first and second students.

3. When Tom hires 1 student, marginal product is 100 pineapples and average product is 100 pineapples per student. When Tom hires 2 students, marginal product is 120 pineapples and average product is 110 pineapples per student. When Tom hires the second student, marginal product is increasing and average product is less than marginal product.

Solution to In the News

As Deere cuts its workforce, output at the plant will decrease as Deere slides back down along its total product curve. At the same time, Deere's marginal product will increase in the short run (see Fig 14.3 on p. 355).

14.3 SHORT-RUN COST

MyEconLab Concept Video

To produce more output (total product) in the short run, a firm must employ more labor, which means that it must increase its costs. We describe the relationship between output and cost using three cost concepts:

- Total cost
- Marginal cost
- Average cost

■ Total Cost

A firm's **total cost** (TC) is the cost of all the factors of production used by the firm. Total cost divides into two parts: total fixed cost and total variable cost. **Total fixed cost** (TFC) is the cost of a firm's fixed factors of production: land, capital, and entrepreneurship. In the short run, the quantities of these inputs don't change as output changes, so total fixed cost doesn't change as output changes. **Total variable cost** (TVC) is the cost of a firm's variable factor of production—labor. To change its output in the short run, a firm must change the quantity of labor it employs, so total variable cost changes as output changes.

Total cost is the sum of total fixed cost and total variable cost. That is,

$$TC = TFC + TVC.$$

Table 14.2 shows Sam's Smoothies' total costs. Sam's fixed costs are $20 an hour regardless of whether it operates or not—TFC is $20 an hour. To produce smoothies, Samantha hires labor, which costs $12 an hour. TVC equals the number of workers multiplied by $12 per hour. For example, to produce 6 gallons an hour, Samantha hires 3 workers, so TVC is $36. TVC increases as output increases. TC is the sum of TFC and TVC. So to produce 6 gallons an hour, TC is $56 an hour. Check the calculation in each row and note that to produce some outputs—2 gallons an hour, for example—Sam hires a worker for only part of an hour.

Total cost
The cost of all the factors of production used by a firm.

Total fixed cost
The cost of the firm's fixed factors of production—the cost of land, capital, and entrepreneurship.

Total variable cost
The cost of the firm's variable factor of production—the cost of labor.

■ TABLE 14.2

Sam's Smoothies' Total Costs

Labor (workers per hour)	Output (gallons per hour)	Total fixed cost	Total variable cost	Total cost
		(dollars per hour)		
0	0	20	0	20.00
1.00	1	20	12.00	32.00
1.60	2	20	19.20	39.20
2.00	3	20	24.00	44.00
2.35	4	20	28.20	48.20
2.65	5	20	31.80	51.80
3.00	6	20	36.00	56.00
3.40	7	20	40.80	60.80
4.00	8	20	48.00	68.00
5.00	9	20	60.00	80.00

Sam's fixed factors of production are land, capital, and entrepreneurship. Total fixed cost is constant regardless of the quantity produced. Sam's variable factor of production is labor. Total variable cost is the cost of labor. Total cost is the sum of total fixed cost and total variable cost.

The highlighted row shows that to produce 6 gallons of smoothies, Sam's hires 3 workers. Total fixed cost is $20 an hour. Total variable cost is the cost of the 3 workers. At $12 an hour, 3 workers cost $36. Sam's total cost of producing 6 gallons an hour is $20 plus $36, which equals $56.

360 Part 5 • A CLOSER LOOK AT DECISION MAKERS

Figure 14.5 illustrates Sam's total cost curves. The green total fixed cost curve (*TFC*) is horizontal because total fixed cost does not change when output changes. It is a constant $20 an hour. The purple total variable cost curve (*TVC*) and the blue total cost curve (*TC*) both slope upward because variable cost increases as output increases. The arrows highlight total fixed cost as the vertical distance between the *TVC* and *TC* curves.

Let's now look at Sam's Smoothies' marginal cost.

■ Marginal Cost

In Figure 14.5, total variable cost and total cost increase at a decreasing rate at small levels of output and then begin to increase at an increasing rate as output increases. To understand these patterns in the changes in total cost, we need to use the concept of *marginal cost*.

Marginal cost
The change in total cost that results from a one-unit increase in output.

A firm's **marginal cost** is the change in total cost that results from a one-unit increase in output. Table 14.3 on p. 361 calculates the marginal cost for Sam's Smoothies. When, for example, output increases from 5 gallons to 6 gallons an hour, total cost increases from $51.80 to $56. So the marginal cost of this gallon of smoothies is ($56 − $51.80), or $4.20. Notice that marginal cost is located midway between the total costs to emphasize that it is the result of *changing* outputs.

Marginal cost tells us how total cost changes as output changes. The final cost concept tells us what it costs, on average, to produce a unit of output. Let's now look at Sam's average costs.

■ **FIGURE 14.5**

Total Cost Curves at Sam's Smoothies

MyEconLab Animation

Total fixed cost (*TFC*) is constant—it graphs as a horizontal line—and total variable cost (*TVC*) increases as output increases. Total cost (*TC*) also increases as output increases.

The vertical distance between the total cost curve and the total variable cost curve is total fixed cost, as illustrated by the two arrows.

■ Average Cost

There are three average cost concepts:

- Average fixed cost
- Average variable cost
- Average total cost

Average fixed cost (*AFC*) is total fixed cost per unit of output. **Average variable cost** (*AVC*) is total variable cost per unit of output. **Average total cost** (*ATC*) is total cost per unit of output. The average cost concepts are calculated from the total cost concepts as follows:

$$TC = TFC + TVC.$$

Divide each total cost term by the quantity produced, Q, to give

$$\frac{TC}{Q} = \frac{TFC}{Q} + \frac{TVC}{Q}.$$

or

$$ATC = AFC + AVC$$

Table 14.3 shows these average costs. For example, when output is 6 gallons an hour, *AFC* is ($20 ÷ 6), which equals $3.33; *AVC* is ($36 ÷ 6), which equals $6.00; and *ATC* is ($56 ÷ 6), which equals $9.33. Note that *ATC* ($9.33) equals *AFC* ($3.33) plus *AVC* ($6.00).

Average fixed cost
Total fixed cost per unit of output.

Average variable cost
Total variable cost per unit of output.

Average total cost
Total cost per unit of output, which equals average fixed cost plus average variable cost.

■ TABLE 14.3

Sam's Smoothies' Marginal Cost and Average Cost

Output (gallons per hour)	Total cost (dollars per hour)	Marginal cost (dollars per gallon)	Average fixed cost	Average variable cost	Average total cost
				(dollars per gallon)	
0	20.00		–	–	–
		12.00			
1	32.00		20.00	12.00	32.00
		7.20			
2	39.20		10.00	9.60	19.60
		4.80			
3	44.00		6.67	8.00	14.67
		4.20			
4	48.20		5.00	7.05	12.05
		3.60			
5	51.80		4.00	6.36	10.36
		4.20			
6	56.00		3.33	6.00	9.33
		4.80			
7	60.80		2.86	5.83	8.69
		7.20			
8	68.00		2.50	6.00	8.50
		12.00			
9	80.00		2.22	6.67	8.89

To produce 6 gallons of smoothies an hour, Sam's total cost is $56. Table 14.2 shows that this total cost is the sum of total fixed cost ($20) and total variable cost ($36).

Marginal cost is the increase in total cost that results from a one-unit increase in output. When Sam's increases output from 5 gallons to 6 gallons an hour, total cost increases from $51.80 to $56.00, an increase of $4.20 a gallon. The marginal cost of the sixth gallon an hour is $4.20. Marginal cost is located midway between the total costs to emphasize that it is the result of *changing* output.

When Sam's produces 6 gallons an hour, average fixed cost ($20 ÷ 6 gallons) is $3.33 a gallon; average variable cost ($36 ÷ 6 gallons) is $6.00 a gallon; average total cost ($56 ÷ 6 gallons) is $9.33 a gallon.

Figure 14.6 graphs the marginal cost and average cost data in Table 14.3. The red marginal cost curve (*MC*) is U-shaped because of the way in which marginal product changes. Recall that when Samantha hires a second or a third worker, marginal product increases and output increases to 6 gallons an hour (Figure 14.3 on p. 355). Over this output range, marginal cost decreases as output increases. When Samantha hires a fourth or a fifth worker, marginal product decreases but output increases up to 9 gallons an hour (Figure 14.3). Over this output range, marginal cost increases as output increases.

The green average fixed cost curve (*AFC*) slopes downward. As output increases, the same constant total fixed cost is spread over a larger output. The blue average total cost curve (*ATC*) and the purple average variable cost curve (*AVC*) are U-shaped. The vertical distance between the average total cost and average variable cost curves is equal to average fixed cost—as indicated by the two arrows. That distance shrinks as output increases because average fixed cost decreases with increasing output.

The marginal cost curve intersects the average variable cost curve and the average total cost curve at their minimum points. That is, when marginal cost is less than average cost, average cost is decreasing; and when marginal cost exceeds average cost, average cost is increasing. This relationship holds for both the *ATC* curve and the *AVC* curve and is another example of the relationship you saw in Figure 14.4 for average product and marginal product.

FIGURE 14.6

Average Cost Curves and Marginal Cost Curve at Sam's Smoothies   MyEconLab Animation

Average fixed cost decreases as output increases. The average fixed cost curve (*AFC*) slopes downward.

The average total cost curve (*ATC*) and average variable cost curve (*AVC*) are U-shaped. The vertical distance between these two curves is equal to average fixed cost, as illustrated by the two arrows.

Marginal cost is the change in total cost when output increases by one unit. The marginal cost curve (*MC*) is U-shaped and intersects the average variable cost curve (*AVC*) and the average total cost curve (*ATC*) at their minimum points.

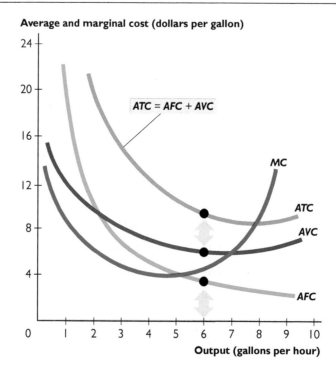

Average and marginal cost (dollars per gallon)

■ Why the Average Total Cost Curve Is U-Shaped

MyEconLab Concept Video

Average total cost, *ATC*, is the sum of average fixed cost, *AFC*, and average variable cost, *AVC*. So the shape of the *ATC* curve combines the shapes of the *AFC* and *AVC* curves. The U shape of the average total cost curve arises from the influence of two opposing forces:

- Spreading total fixed cost over a larger output
- Decreasing marginal returns

When output increases, the firm spreads its total fixed costs over a larger output and its average fixed cost decreases—its average fixed cost curve slopes downward.

Decreasing marginal returns means that as output increases, ever larger amounts of labor are needed to produce an additional unit of output. So average variable cost eventually increases, and the *AVC* curve eventually slopes upward.

The shape of the average total cost curve combines these two effects. Initially, as output increases, both average fixed cost and average variable cost decrease, so average total cost decreases and the *ATC* curve slopes downward. But as output increases further and decreasing marginal returns sets in, average variable cost begins to increase. Eventually, average variable cost increases more quickly than average fixed cost decreases, so average total cost increases and the *ATC* curve slopes upward.

All the short-run cost concepts that you've met are summarized in Table 14.4.

■ TABLE 14.4

A Compact Glossary of Costs

Term	Symbol	Definition	Equation
Fixed cost		The cost of a fixed factor of production that is independent of the quantity produced	
Variable cost		The cost of a variable factor of production that varies with the quantity produced	
Total fixed cost	*TFC*	Cost of the fixed factors of production	
Total variable cost	*TVC*	Cost of the variable factor of production	
Total cost	*TC*	Cost of all factors of production	$TC = TFC + TVC$
Marginal cost	*MC*	Change in total cost resulting from a one-unit increase in output (*Q*)	$MC = \Delta TC \div \Delta Q^*$
Average fixed cost	*AFC*	Total fixed cost per unit of output	$AFC = TFC \div Q$
Average variable cost	*AVC*	Total variable cost per unit of output	$AVC = TVC \div Q$
Average total cost	*ATC*	Total cost per unit of output	$ATC = AFC + AVC$

*In this equation, the Greek letter delta (Δ) stands for "change in."

■ Cost Curves and Product Curves

A firm's cost curves and product curves are linked, and Figure 14.7 shows how. The upper graph shows the average product curve, *AP*, and the marginal product curve, *MP*. The lower graph shows the average variable cost curve, *AVC*, and the marginal cost curve, *MC*.

As labor increases up to 2.5 workers a day (upper graph), output increases to 4 units a day (lower graph). Marginal product and average product rise and marginal cost and average variable cost fall. At the point of maximum marginal product, marginal cost is at a minimum.

As labor increases to 3.5 workers a day (upper graph), output increases to 7 units a day (lower graph). Marginal product falls and marginal cost rises, but average product continues to rise and average variable cost continues to fall. At the point of maximum average product, average variable cost is at a minimum. As labor increases further, output increases. Average product diminishes and average variable cost increases.

■ Shifts in the Cost Curves

The position of a firm's short-run cost curves, in Figures 14.5 and 14.6, depends on two factors:

- Technology
- Prices of factors of production

Technology

A technological change that increases productivity shifts the total product curve upward. It also shifts the marginal product curve and the average product curve upward. With a better technology that increases productivity, the same factors of production can produce more output, so an advance in technology lowers the average and marginal costs and shifts the short-run cost curves downward.

For example, advances in robotic technology have increased productivity in the automobile industry. As a result, the product curves of Chrysler, Ford, and GM have shifted upward, and their average and marginal cost curves have shifted downward. But the relationships between their product curves and cost curves have not changed. The curves are still linked, as in Figure 14.7.

Often a technological advance results in a firm using more capital, a fixed factor of production, and less labor, a variable factor of production. For example, today telephone companies use computers to connect long-distance calls instead of the human operators they used in the 1980s. When a telephone company makes this change, total variable cost decreases and total cost decreases, but total fixed cost increases. This change in the mix of fixed cost and variable cost means that at small output levels, average total cost might increase, but at large output levels, average total cost decreases.

Prices of Factors of Production

An increase in the price of a factor of production increases costs and shifts the cost curves. But how the curves shift depends on which resource price changes. An increase in rent or some other component of *fixed* cost shifts the fixed cost curves (*TFC* and *AFC*) upward and shifts the total cost curve (*TC*) upward but leaves the variable cost curves (*AVC* and *TVC*) and the marginal cost curve (*MC*) unchanged.

FIGURE 14.7

Product Curves and Cost Curves

MyEconLab Animation

Average product and marginal product

Maximum MP

Maximum AP

AP

MP

Rising MP and falling MC, rising AP and falling AVC

Falling MP and rising MC, rising AP and falling AVC

Falling MP and rising MC, falling AP and rising AVC

Labor

Cost (dollars per unit)

Minimum AVC

MC

AVC

Minimum MC

Output

A firm's *MC* curve is linked to its *MP* curve. If, as the firm hires more labor up to 2.5 workers a day, the firm's marginal product rises, its marginal cost falls. If marginal product is at a maximum, marginal cost is at a minimum. If, as the firm hires more labor, its marginal product diminishes, its marginal cost rises.

A firm's *AVC* curve is linked to its *AP* curve. If, as the firm hires more labor up to 3.5 workers a day, its average product rises, its average variable cost falls. If average product is at a maximum, average variable cost is at a minimum. If as the firm hires more labor its average product diminishes, its average variable cost rises.

An increase in wage rates or some other component of *variable* cost shifts the variable cost curves (*TVC* and *AVC*) and the marginal cost curve (*MC*) upward but leaves the fixed cost curves (*AFC* and *TFC*) unchanged. So, for example, if the interest expense paid by a trucking company increases, the fixed cost of transportation services increases, but if the wage rate paid to truck drivers increases, the variable cost and marginal cost of transportation services increase.

MyEconLab Study Plan 14.3
Key Terms Quiz
Solutions Video

CHECKPOINT 14.3

Explain the relationship between a firm's output and costs in the short run.

Practice Problems

Tom leases a farmer's field for $120 a day and grows pineapples. He pays students $100 a day each to pick pineapples and he leases capital at $80 a day. Table 1 shows Tom's daily output.

1. What is Tom's total cost and average total cost of 300 pineapples a day?

2. What is the marginal cost of picking a pineapple when the quantity increases from 360 to 400 pineapples a day?

3. At what output is Tom's average total cost a minimum?

In the News

Colorado companies plan to hire in 2016

Nearly a quarter of Denver-area technology executives plan to increase production and add new positions in 2016.

Source: *Denver Business Journal*, December 21, 2015

Explain how increasing production by adding new positions changes a Denver-area firm's short-run average cost and marginal cost. How will the firm's short-run average cost curve and marginal cost curve change if the wage rate rises?

Solutions to Practice Problems

1. Total cost is the sum of total fixed cost and total variable cost. Tom leases the field for $120 a day and capital for $80 a day, so Tom's total fixed cost is $200 a day. Total variable cost is the wages of the students. To produce 300 pineapples a day, Tom hires 3 students, so total variable cost is $300 a day and total cost is $500 a day. Table 2 shows the total cost (*TC*) schedule. Average total cost is the total cost divided by total product. The total cost of 300 pineapples a day is $500, so average total cost is $1.67 a pineapple. Table 2 shows the average total cost schedule.

2. Marginal cost is the increase in total cost that results from picking one additional pineapple a day. When the quantity picked increases from 360 to 400 pineapples a day, total cost (from Table 2) increases from $600 to $700. The increase in the number of pineapples is 40, and the increase in total cost is $100. Marginal cost is the increase in total cost ($100) divided by the increase in the number of pineapples (40), which is $2.50 per pineapple. So the marginal cost of a pineapple is $2.50.

3. At the minimum of average total cost, average total cost equals marginal cost. Minimum average total cost of a pineapple between 300 and 360 pineapples is $1.67. Table 2 shows that the marginal cost of increasing output from 300 to 360 pineapples a day is $1.67 a pineapple.

Solution to In the News

An increase in output and employment increases the firm's short-run average cost and marginal cost as the firm moves along its *ATC* and *MC* curves. If the wage rate rises, average cost and marginal cost increase at *all* output levels and the *MC*, *AVC*, and *ATC* curves shift upward.

TABLE 1

Labor (students)	Output (pineapples per day)
0	0
1	100
2	220
3	300
4	360
5	400
6	420
7	430

TABLE 2

Labor	TP	TC	MC	ATC
0	0	200		—
			1.00	
1	100	300		3.00
			0.83	
2	220	400		1.82
			1.25	
3	300	500		1.67
			1.67	
4	360	600		1.67
			2.50	
5	400	700		1.75
			5.00	
6	420	800		1.90
			10.00	
7	430	900		2.09

14.4 LONG-RUN COST

MyEconLab Concept Video

In the long run, a firm can vary both the quantity of labor and the quantity of capital. A small firm, such as Sam's Smoothies, can increase its plant size by moving into a larger building and installing more machines. A big firm such as General Motors can decrease its plant size by closing down some production lines.

We are now going to see how costs vary in the long run when a firm varies its plant—the quantity of capital it uses—along with the quantity of labor it uses.

The first thing that happens is that the distinction between fixed cost and variable cost disappears. All costs are variable in the long run.

■ Plant Size and Cost

When a firm changes its plant size, its cost of producing a given output changes. In Table 14.3 on p. 361 and Figure 14.6 on p. 362, the lowest average total cost that Samantha can achieve is $8.50 a gallon, which occurs when she produces 8 gallons of smoothies an hour. Samantha wonders what would happen to her average total cost if she increased the size of her plant by renting a bigger building and installing a larger number of blenders and refrigerators. Will the average total cost of producing a gallon of smoothies fall, rise, or remain the same?

Each of these three outcomes is possible, and they arise because when a firm changes the size of its plant, it might experience

- Economies of scale
- Diseconomies of scale
- Constant returns to scale

Economies of Scale

Economies of scale are features of a firm's technology that make average total cost *fall* as the output rate increases. The main source of economies of scale is greater specialization of both labor and capital.

Specialization of Labor If Ford produced 100 cars a week, each production line worker would have to perform many different tasks. But if Ford produces 10,000 cars a week, each worker can specialize in a small number of tasks and become highly proficient at them. The result is that the average product of labor increases and the average total cost of producing a car falls.

Specialization also occurs off the production line. For example, a small firm usually does not have a specialist sales manager, personnel manager, and production manager. One person covers all these activities. But when a firm is large enough, specialists perform these activities. Average product increases, and the average total cost falls.

Specialization of Capital At a small output rate, firms often must employ general-purpose machines and tools. For example, with an output of a few gallons an hour, Sam's Smoothies uses regular blenders like the one in your kitchen. But if Sam's produces hundreds of gallons an hour, it uses commercial blenders that fill, empty, and clean themselves. The result is that the output rate is larger and the average total cost of producing a gallon of smoothies is lower.

Economies of scale
Features of a firm's technology that make average total cost *fall* as output increases.

Specialization of both labor and capital on an auto-assembly line.

Diseconomies of Scale

Diseconomies of scale
Features of a firm's technology that make average total cost *rise* as output increases.

Diseconomies of scale are features of a firm's technology that make average total cost *rise* as output increases. Diseconomies of scale arise from the difficulty of coordinating and controlling a large enterprise. The larger the firm, the greater is the cost of communicating both up and down the management hierarchy and among managers. Eventually, management complexity brings rising average total cost. Diseconomies of scale occur in all production processes but in some perhaps only at a very large output rate.

Constant Returns to Scale

Constant returns to scale
Features of a firm's technology that keep average total cost constant as output increases.

Constant returns to scale are features of a firm's technology that keep average total cost *constant* as output increases. Constant returns to scale occur when a firm is able to replicate its existing production facility including its management system. For example, Ford might double its production of Fusion cars by doubling its production facility for those cars. It can build an identical production line and hire an identical number of workers. With the two identical production lines, Ford produces exactly twice as many cars. The average total cost of producing a Fusion is identical in the two plants. Ford's average total cost remains constant as it increases production.

■ The Long-Run Average Cost Curve

Long-run average cost curve
A curve that shows the lowest average total cost at which it is possible to produce each output when the firm has had sufficient time to change both its plant size and labor employed.

The **long-run average cost curve** shows the lowest average total cost at which it is possible to produce each output when the firm has had sufficient time to change both its plant size and its labor force.

Figure 14.8 shows Sam's Smoothies' long-run average cost curve *LRAC*. This long-run average cost curve is derived from the short-run average total cost curves for different possible plant sizes.

With its current small plant, Sam's Smoothies operates on the average total cost curve ATC_1 in Figure 14.8. The other three average total cost curves are for

▓ FIGURE 14.8

Long-Run Average Cost Curve   MyEconLab Animation

In the long run, Samantha can vary both the plant size and the quantity of labor she employs. The long-run average cost curve traces the lowest attainable average total cost of producing each output. The dark blue curve is the long-run average cost curve *LRAC*.

Sam's experiences economies of scale as output increases up to 14 gallons an hour, constant returns to scale for outputs between 14 gallons and 19 gallons an hour, and diseconomies of scale for outputs that exceed 19 gallons an hour.

successively bigger plants. In this example, for outputs up to 8 gallons an hour, the existing plant with average total cost curve ATC_1 produces smoothies at the lowest attainable average cost. For outputs between 8 and 16 gallons an hour, average total cost is lowest on ATC_2. For outputs between 16 and 24 gallons an hour, average total cost is lowest on ATC_3. And for outputs in excess of 24 gallons an hour, average total cost is lowest on ATC_4.

The segment of each of the four average total cost curves for which that plant has the lowest average total cost is highlighted in dark blue in Figure 14.8. The scallop-shaped curve made up of these four segments is Sam's Smoothies' long-run average cost curve.

Economies and Diseconomies of Scale

When economies of scale are present, the *LRAC* curve slopes downward. The *LRAC* curve in Figure 14.8 shows that Sam's Smoothies experiences economies of scale for output rates up to 14 gallons an hour. At output rates between 14 and 19 gallons an hour, the firm experiences constant returns to scale. And at output rates that exceed 19 gallons an hour, the firm experiences diseconomies of scale.

EYE on RETAILERS' COSTS

MyEconLab Critical Thinking Exercise

Which Store Has the Lower Costs: Walmart or 7-Eleven?

Walmart's "small" supercenters measure 99,000 square feet and serve an average of 30,000 customers a week. The average 7-Eleven store, most of which today are attached to gas stations, measures 2,000 square feet and serves 5,000 customers a week.

Which retailing technology has the lower operating cost? The answer depends on the scale of operation.

At a small number of customers per week, it costs less per customer to operate a store of 2,000 square feet than one of 99,000 square feet.

In the figure, the average total cost curve of operating a 7-Eleven store of 2,000 square feet is $ATC_{7\text{-}Eleven}$ and the average total cost curve of a store of 99,000 square feet is $ATC_{Walmart}$. The dark blue curve is a retailer's long-run average cost curve *LRAC*.

If the number of customers is Q a week, the average total cost per transaction is the same for both stores.

For a store that serves more than Q customers a week, the least-cost method is the big store.

For fewer than Q customers a week, the least-cost method is the small store. The least-cost store is not always the biggest store.

MyEconLab Study Plan 14.4
Key Terms Quiz
Solutions Video

CHECKPOINT 14.4

Derive and explain a firm's long-run average cost curve.

Practice Problems

To grow pineapples, Tom leases 1 field for $120 a day and capital for $80 a day and hires students at $100 a day each. Suppose that Tom now leases 2 fields for $240 a day and twice as much capital for $160 a day. Table 1 shows his outputs.

1. What is Tom's average total cost of a pinapple when he farms 2 fields and produces 220 pineapples a day?

2. Make a graph of Tom's average total cost curves using 1 field and 2 fields. Show on the graph Tom's long-run average cost curve. Over what output range will Tom use 1 field? 2 fields?

3. Does Tom experience constant returns to scale, economies of scale, or diseconomies of scale?

In the News

Hiring spree at Tesla Motors

Bay Area-based electric car maker Tesla is looking to hire 1,648 workers to expand its model lineup, build a battery factory, and develop self-driving cars.
Source: CBS San Francisco, December 8, 2015

Explain the effects of the expansion plan on Tesla's total fixed cost, total variable cost, short-run *ATC* curve, and *LRAC* curve.

Solutions to Practice Problems

1. Total cost equals fixed cost ($400 a day) plus $100 a day for each student. Tom can produce 220 pineapples with 2 fields and 1 student, so total cost is $500 a day. Average total cost is the total cost divided by output, which at 220 pineapples a day is $500 divided by 220, or $2.27. The "*ATC* (2 fields)" column of Table 2 shows Tom's average total cost schedule for 2 fields.

2. Figure 1 shows Tom's average total cost curve using 1 field as ATC_1. This curve graphs the data on *ATC* (1 field) and *TP* (1 field) in Table 2, which was calculated in Table 2 on p. 366. Using 2 fields, the average total cost curve is ATC_2. Tom's long-run average cost curve is the lower segments of the two *ATC* curves, highlighted in Figure 1. If Tom produces up to 300 pineapples a day, he will use 1 field. If he produces more than 300 pineapples a day, he will use 2 fields.

3. Tom experiences economies of scale up to an output of 740 pineapples a day because as he increases his plant and produces up to 740 pineapples a day, the average total cost of picking a pineapple decreases. (We don't have enough information to know what happens to Tom's average total cost if he uses three fields and three units of capital.)

Solution to In the News

Expanding the model lineup, building a battery factory, and developing a self-driving car will raise Tesla's total fixed cost; hiring 1,648 workers will raise Tesla's total variable cost. As Tesla increases output, it will move along its *ATC* curve. With a larger capacity, Tesla will move rightward along its *LRAC* curve.

TABLE 1

Labor (students per day)	Output 1 field	Output 2 fields
	(pineapples per day)	
0	0	0
1	100	220
2	220	460
3	300	620
4	360	740
5	400	820
6	420	860
7	430	880

TABLE 2

TP (1 field)	ATC (1 field)	TP (2 fields)	ATC (2 fields)
100	3.00	220	2.27
220	1.82	460	1.30
300	1.67	620	1.13
360	1.67	740	1.08
400	1.75	820	1.10
420	1.90	860	1.16
430	2.09	880	1.25

FIGURE 1

Average total cost (dollars per pineapple)

CHAPTER SUMMARY

Key Points

1. **Explain and distinguish between the economic and accounting measures of a firm's cost of production and profit.**

   - Firms seek to maximize economic profit, which is total revenue minus total cost.
   - Total cost equals opportunity cost—the sum of explicit costs and implicit costs, which include normal profit.

2. **Explain the relationship between a firm's output and labor employed in the short run.**

   - In the short run, the firm can change the output it produces by changing only the quantity of labor it employs.
   - A total product curve shows the limits to the output that the firm can produce with a given quantity of capital and different quantities of labor.
   - As the quantity of labor increases, the marginal product of labor increases initially but eventually decreases—the law of decreasing returns.

3. **Explain the relationship between a firm's output and costs in the short run.**

   - As total product increases, total fixed cost is constant, and total variable cost and total cost increase.
   - As total product increases, average fixed cost decreases; average variable cost, average total cost, and marginal cost decrease at small outputs and increase at large outputs so their curves are U-shaped.

4. **Derive and explain a firm's long-run average cost curve.**

   - In the long run, the firm can change the size of its plant.
   - Long-run cost is the cost of production when all inputs have been adjusted to produce at the lowest attainable cost.
   - The long-run average cost curve traces out the lowest attainable average total cost at each output when both the plant size and labor can be varied.
   - The long-run average cost curve slopes downward with economies of scale and upward with diseconomies of scale.

Key Terms

MyEconLab Key Terms Quiz

Average fixed cost, 361
Average product, 356
Average total cost, 361
Average variable cost, 361
Constant returns to scale, 368
Decreasing marginal returns, 354
Diseconomies of scale, 368
Economic depreciation, 349

Economic profit, 349
Economies of scale, 367
Explicit cost, 349
Implicit cost, 349
Increasing marginal returns, 354
Law of decreasing returns, 356
Long run, 352
Long-run average cost curve, 368

Marginal cost, 360
Marginal product, 354
Normal profit, 349
Short run, 352
Total cost, 359
Total fixed cost, 359
Total product, 353
Total variable cost, 359

CHAPTER CHECKPOINT

Study Plan Problems and Applications

1. Joe runs a shoe shine stand at the airport. Joe has no skills, no job experience, and no alternative job. Entrepreneurs in the shoe shine business earn $10,000 a year. Joe pays the rent of $2,000 a year, and his total revenue is $15,000 a year. He borrowed $1,000 at 20 percent a year to buy equipment. At the end of one year, Joe was offered $500 for his business and all its equipment. Calculate Joe's annual explicit costs, implicit costs, and economic profit.

2. Len's body board factory rents equipment for shaping boards and hires students. Table 1 sets out Len's total product schedule. Construct Len's marginal product and average product schedules. Over what range of workers do marginal returns increase?

TABLE 1

Labor (workers per day)	Total product (body boards per day)
0	0
1	20
2	44
3	60
4	72

Use the following information to work Problems **3** to **6**.

Len's body board factory pays $60 a day for equipment and $200 a day to each student it hires. Table 1 sets out Len's total product schedule.

3. Construct Len's total variable cost and total cost schedules. What does the difference between total cost and total variable cost at each output equal?

4. Construct the average fixed cost, average variable cost, and average total cost schedules and the marginal cost schedule.

5. At what output is Len's average total cost at a minimum? At what output is Len's average variable cost at a minimum?

6. Explain why the output at which average variable cost is at a minimum is smaller than the output at which average total cost is at a minimum.

7. Table 2 shows the costs incurred at Pete's peanut farm. Complete the table.

TABLE 2

Labor	TP	TVC	TC	AFC	AVC	ATC	MC
0	0	0	100				
1	10	35					
2	24	70					
3	38	105					
4	44	140					

8. **Gap to close 175 stores in North America**
   Gap announced that it will close 175 (nearly 26 percent) of its North American stores. It will terminate an unknown number of workers and cut 250 headquarters jobs.

   Source: *The Washington Post*, June 15, 2015

   Thinking of a Gap store as a unit of capital, explain why Gap is reducing the number of stores and workers. Is Gap making a long-run decision or a short-run decision? Is Gap taking advantage of economies of scale?

9. Read *Eye on Retailers' Costs* on p. 369 and draw a graph to show how the retailers' cost curves would change if they introduced cost-saving self-checkouts.

Instructor Assignable Problems and Applications

MyEconLab Homework, Quiz, or Test if assigned by instructor

1. If the *ATC* curves of a Walmart store and a 7-Eleven are like those in *Eye on Retailers' Costs* on p. 369, and if each type of store operates at its minimum *ATC*, which store has the lower total cost? How can you be sure? Which has the lower marginal cost? How can you be sure? Sketch each firm's marginal cost curve.

2. Sonya used to earn $25,000 a year selling real estate, but she now sells greeting cards. The return to entrepreneurship in the greeting cards industry is $14,000 a year. Over the year, Sonya bought $10,000 worth of cards from manufacturers and sold them for $58,000. Sonya rents a shop for $5,000 a year and spends $1,000 on utilities and office expenses. Sonya owns a cash register, which she bought for $2,000 with funds from her savings account. Her bank pays 3 percent a year on savings accounts. At the end of the year, Sonya was offered $1,600 for her cash register.
Calculate Sonya's explicit costs, implicit costs, and economic profit for the year.

Use the following information to work Problems **3** to **5**.

Yolanda runs a bullfrog farm. When she employs 1 person, she produces 1,000 bullfrogs a week. When she hires a second worker, her total product doubles. Her total product doubles again when she hires a third worker. When she hires a fourth worker, her total product increases but by only 1,000 bullfrogs. Yolanda pays $1,000 a week for equipment and $500 a week to each worker she hires.

3. Construct Yolanda's marginal product and average product schedules. Over what range of workers does Yolanda's experience increasing marginal returns?

4. Construct Yolanda's total variable cost and total cost schedules. Calculate Yolanda's total fixed cost.

5. At what output is Yolanda's average total cost at a minimum?

6. Table 1 shows some of the costs incurred at Bill's Bakery. Calculate the values of *A, B, C, D,* and *E*. Show your work.

TABLE 1

Labor	TP	TVC	TC	AFC	AVC	ATC	MC
1	100	350	850	**C**	3.50	**D**	2.50
2	240	700	**B**	2.08	2.92	5.00	E
3	380	**A**	1,550	1.32	2.76	4.08	5.83
4	440	1,400	1,900	1.14	3.18	4.32	11.67
5	470	1,750	2,250	1.06	3.72	4.79	

7. **Solar and wind got so cheap, so fast**
Solar panels and wind turbines are more efficient than they used to be and they cost less to produce.
Source: *The Atlantic*, December 2, 2015
Explain how the facts reported in the news clip affect the short-run and long-run average total cost of producing electricity. How do the facts affect the marginal cost of producing electricity?

Multiple Choice Quiz

1. A firm's cost of production equals _____.
   A. all the costs paid with money, called explicit costs
   B. the implicit costs of using all the firm's own resources
   C. all explicit costs and implicit costs, excluding normal profit
   D. the costs of all resources used by the firm whether bought in the market-place or owned by the firm

2. The average product of labor increases as output increases if _____.
   A. marginal product exceeds average product
   B. average product exceeds marginal product
   C. total product increases
   D. marginal product increases

3. Marginal returns start to decrease when more and more workers _____.
   A. have to share the same equipment and workspace
   B. produce less and less total output
   C. require jobs to be too specialized
   D. produce less and less average product

4. Average variable cost is at a minimum when _____.
   A. marginal cost equals average variable cost
   B. average total cost is at a minimum
   C. marginal cost exceeds average fixed cost
   D. average total cost exceeds average variable cost

5. An increase in the rent that a firm pays for its factory does not increase _____.
   A. total cost
   B. fixed cost
   C. marginal cost
   D. average fixed cost

6. An increase in the wage rate _____.
   A. shifts the average total cost curve and the marginal cost curve upward
   B. shifts the average fixed cost and average variable cost curve upward
   C. increases average variable cost but does not change marginal cost
   D. does not change average variable cost but increases average total cost

7. When average variable cost is at its minimum level, marginal product _____.
   A. equals average product
   B. exceeds average product
   C. is less than average product
   D. is at its maximum level

8. In the long run, with an increase in the plant size, _____.
   A. the short-run average total cost curve shifts downward
   B. the long-run average cost curve slopes downward
   C. the short-run average total cost curve shifts downward if economies of scale exist
   D. the average total cost of production rises

Where have all the record stores gone?

Perfect Competition

15

CHAPTER CHECKLIST

When you have completed your study of this chapter, you will be able to

1 Explain a perfectly competitive firm's profit-maximizing choices and derive its supply curve.

2 Explain how output, price, and profit are determined in the short run.

3 Explain how output, price, and profit are determined in the long run and explain why perfect competition is efficient.

 MyEconLab Big Picture Video

MARKET TYPES

The four market types are

- Perfect competition
- Monopoly
- Monopolistic competition
- Oligopoly

■ Perfect Competition

Perfect competition
A market in which there are many firms, each selling an identical product; many buyers; no barriers to the entry of new firms into the industry; no advantage to established firms; and buyers and sellers are well informed about prices.

Perfect competition exists when

- Many firms sell an identical product to many buyers.
- There are no barriers to entry into (or exit from) the market.
- Established firms have no advantage over new firms.
- Sellers and buyers are well informed about prices.

These conditions that define perfect competition arise when the market demand for the product is large relative to the output of a single producer. This situation arises when economies of scale are absent so the efficient scale of each firm is small. But a large market and the absence of economies of scale are not sufficient to create perfect competition. In addition, each firm must produce a good or service that has no characteristics that are unique to that firm so that consumers don't care from which firm they buy. Firms in perfect competition all look the same to the buyer.

Wheat farming, fishing, wood pulping and paper milling, the manufacture of paper cups and plastic shopping bags, lawn service, dry cleaning, and the provision of laundry services are all examples of highly competitive industries.

■ Other Market Types

Monopoly
A market in which one firm sells a good or service that has no close substitutes and a barrier blocks the entry of new firms.

Monopoly arises when one firm sells a good or service that has no close substitutes and a barrier blocks the entry of new firms. In some places, the phone, gas, electricity, and water suppliers are local monopolies—monopolies that are restricted to a given location. For many years, a global firm called DeBeers had a near international monopoly in diamonds. Microsoft has a near monopoly in producing the operating system for a personal computer.

Monopolistic competition
A market in which a large number of firms compete by making similar but slightly different products.

Monopolistic competition arises when a large number of firms compete by making similar but slightly different products. Each firm is the sole producer of the particular version of the good in question. For example, in the market for running shoes, Nike, Reebok, Fila, Asics, New Balance, and many others make their own versions of the perfect shoe. The term "monopolistic competition" reminds us that each firm has a monopoly on a particular brand of shoe but the firms compete with each other.

Oligopoly
A market in which a small number of interdependent firms compete.

Oligopoly arises when a small number of *interdependent* firms compete. Airplane manufacture is an example of oligopoly. Oligopolies might produce almost identical products, such as Duracell and Energizer batteries; or they might produce differentiated products, such as the colas produced by Coke and Pepsi.

We study perfect competition in this chapter, monopoly in Chapter 16, monopolistic competition in Chapter 17, and oligopoly in Chapter 18.

15.1 A FIRM'S PROFIT-MAXIMIZING CHOICES

MyEconLab Concept Video

A firm's objective is to maximize its *economic profit*, which is equal to *total revenue* minus the *total cost* of production. *Normal profit*, the return that the firm's entrepreneur can obtain on average, is part of the firm's cost.

In the short run, a firm achieves its objective by deciding the quantity to produce. This quantity influences the firm's total revenue, total cost, and economic profit. In the long run, a firm achieves its objective by deciding whether to enter or exit a market.

These are the key decisions that a firm in perfect competition makes. Such a firm does *not* choose the price at which to sell its output. The firm in perfect competition is a **price taker**—it cannot influence the price of its product.

■ Price Taker

To see why a firm in perfect competition is a price taker, imagine that you are a wheat farmer in Kansas. You have a thousand acres under cultivation—which sounds like a lot. But then you go on a drive through Colorado, Oklahoma, Texas, and back up to Nebraska and the Dakotas. You find unbroken stretches of wheat covering millions of acres. And you know that there are similar vistas in Canada, Argentina, Australia, and Ukraine. Your thousand acres are a drop in the ocean. Nothing makes your wheat any better than any other farmer's, and all the buyers of wheat know the price they must pay. If the going price of wheat is $4 a bushel, you are stuck with that price. You can't get a higher price than $4, and you have no incentive to offer it for less than $4 because you can sell your entire output at that price.

The producers of most agricultural products are price takers. We'll illustrate perfect competition with another agriculture example: the market for maple syrup. The next time you pour syrup on your pancakes, think about the competitive market that gets this product from the sap of the maple tree to your table!

Dave's Maple Syrup is one of more than 11,000 similar firms in the maple syrup market of North America. Dave is a price taker. Like the Kansas wheat farmer, he can sell any quantity he chooses at the going price but none above that price. Dave faces a *perfectly elastic* demand. The demand for Dave's syrup is perfectly elastic because syrup from Don Harlow, Casper Sugar Shack, and all the other maple farms in North America are *perfect substitutes* for Dave's syrup.

We'll explore Dave's decisions and their implications for the way a competitive market works. We begin by defining some revenue concepts.

■ Revenue Concepts

In perfect competition, market demand and market supply determine the price. A firm's *total revenue* equals this given price multiplied by the quantity sold. A firm's **marginal revenue** is the change in total revenue that results from a one-unit increase in the quantity sold.

> **In perfect competition, marginal revenue equals price.**

The reason is that the firm can sell any quantity it chooses at the going market price. So if the firm sells one more unit, it sells it for the market price and total revenue increases by that amount. This increase in total revenue is marginal revenue.

The table in Figure 15.1 illustrates the equality of marginal revenue and price. The price of syrup is $8 a can. Total revenue is equal to the price multiplied by the

Price taker
A firm that cannot influence the price of the good or service that it produces.

Wheat farmers and maple syrup farmers are price takers.

Marginal revenue
The change in total revenue that results from a one-unit increase in the quantity sold.

quantity sold. So if Dave sells 10 cans, his total revenue is $8 × 10, which equals $80. If the quantity sold increases from 10 cans to 11 cans, total revenue increases from $80 to $88, so marginal revenue is $8 a can, the same as the price.

Figure 15.1 illustrates price determination and revenue in the perfectly competitive market. Market demand and market supply in part (a) determine the market price. Dave is a price taker, so he sells his syrup for the market price. The demand curve for Dave's syrup is the horizontal line at the market price in part (b). Because price equals marginal revenue, the demand curve for Dave's syrup is Dave's marginal revenue curve (*MR*). The total revenue curve (*TR*), in part (c), shows the total revenue at each quantity sold. Because he sells each can for the market price, the total revenue curve is an upward-sloping straight line.

■ Profit-Maximizing Output

As output increases, total revenue increases, but total cost also increases. Because of *decreasing marginal returns* (see Chapter 14, pp. 354–356), total cost eventually increases faster than total revenue. There is one output level that maximizes economic profit, and a perfectly competitive firm chooses this output level.

▨ **FIGURE 15.1**

Demand, Price, and Revenue in Perfect Competition

(a) Maple syrup market

(b) Dave's marginal revenue

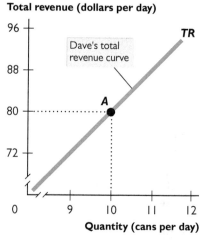

(c) Dave's total revenue

Quantity sold (cans per day)	9	10	11
Price (dollars per can)	8	8	8
Total revenue (dollars per day)	72	80	88
Marginal revenue (dollars per can)	8		8

Part (a) shows the market for maple syrup. The market price is $8 a can. The table calculates total revenue and marginal revenue.

Part (b) shows Dave's marginal revenue curve (*MR*), which is also the demand curve for Dave's syrup.

Part (c) shows Dave's total revenue curve (*TR*). Point *A* corresponds to the second column of the table.

One way to find the profit-maximizing output is to use a firm's total revenue and total cost curves. Profit is maximized at the output level at which total revenue exceeds total cost by the largest amount. Figure 15.2 shows how to do this for Dave's Maple Syrup.

The table lists Dave's total revenue, total cost, and economic profit at different output levels. Figure 15.2(a) shows the total revenue and total cost curves. These curves are graphs of the numbers shown in the first three columns of the table. The total revenue curve (*TR*) is the same as that in Figure 15.1(c). The total cost curve (*TC*) is similar to the one that you met in Chapter 14 (p. 360). Figure 15.2(b) is an economic profit curve.

Dave makes an economic profit on outputs between 4 and 13 cans of syrup a day. At outputs of fewer than 4 cans a day and more than 13 cans a day, he incurs an economic loss. Outputs of 4 cans and 13 cans of syrup a day are *break-even points*—points at which total cost equals total revenue and economic profit is zero.

The profit curve is at its highest when the vertical distance between the *TR* and *TC* curves is greatest. In this example, profit maximization occurs at an output of 10 cans of syrup a day. At this output, Dave's economic profit is $29 a day.

FIGURE 15.2

Total Revenue, Total Cost, and Economic Profit

MyEconLab Animation

(a) Revenue and cost

(b) Economic profit and loss

Quantity (Q) (cans per day)	Total revenue (TR)	Total cost (TC)	Economic profit (TR − TC)
	(dollars per day)		
0	0	15	−15
1	8	22	−14
2	16	27	−11
3	24	30	−6
4	32	32	0
5	40	33	7
6	48	34	14
7	56	36	20
8	64	40	24
9	72	44	28
10	80	51	29
11	88	60	28
12	96	76	20
13	104	104	0
14	112	144	−32

The table calculates Dave's economic profit at each quantity of syrup produced.

In part (a), economic profit (total revenue minus total cost) is the vertical distance between the total revenue (*TR*) and total cost (*TC*) curves.

In part (b), economic profit is the height of the profit curve, *TR* − *TC*.

If Dave produces less than 4 cans of syrup a day, he incurs an economic loss.

If Dave produces between 4 and 13 cans of syrup a day, he makes an economic profit. Dave's maximum economic profit is $29 a day when he produces 10 cans of syrup a day.

■ Marginal Analysis and the Supply Decision

Another way to find the profit-maximizing output is to use *marginal analysis,* which compares marginal revenue, *MR*, with marginal cost, *MC*. As output increases, marginal revenue is constant but marginal cost eventually increases.

If marginal revenue exceeds marginal cost ($MR > MC$), then the revenue from selling one more unit exceeds the cost of producing that unit and an *increase* in output increases economic profit. If marginal revenue is less than marginal cost ($MR < MC$), then the revenue from selling one more unit is less than the cost of producing that unit and a *decrease* in output increases economic profit. If marginal revenue equals marginal cost ($MR = MC$), then the revenue from selling one more unit equals the cost incurred to produce that unit. Economic profit is maximized and either an increase or a decrease in output *decreases* economic profit. The rule ($MR = MC$) is a prime example of marginal analysis.

Figure 15.3 illustrates these propositions. If Dave increases output from 9 to 10 cans of syrup a day, marginal revenue ($8) exceeds marginal cost ($7), so by producing the 10th can economic profit increases. The last column of the table shows that economic profit increases from $28 to $29. The blue area in the figure shows the increase in economic profit when Dave produces the 10th can per day.

If Dave increases production from 10 to 11 cans of syrup a day, marginal revenue ($8) is less than marginal cost ($9), so by producing the 11th can, economic profit decreases. The last column of the table shows that economic profit decreases from $29 to $28. The red area in the figure shows the economic loss that arises when Dave increases production from 10 to 11 cans of syrup per day.

FIGURE 15.3

Profit-Maximizing Output   MyEconLab Animation

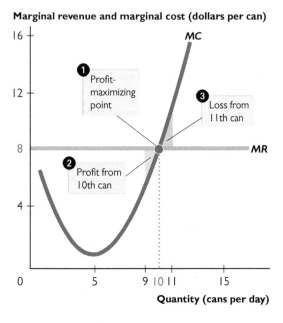

Marginal revenue and marginal cost (dollars per can)

Quantity (Q) (cans per day)	Total revenue (TR) (dollars per day)	Marginal revenue (MR) (dollars per can)	Total cost (TC) (dollars per day)	Marginal cost (MC) (dollars per can)	Economic profit (TR − TC) (dollars per day)
8	64		40		24
		8		4	
9	72		44		28
		8		7	
10	80		51		29
		8		9	
11	88		60		28
		8		16	
12	96		76		20

❶ Profit is maximized when marginal revenue equals marginal cost at 10 cans of syrup a day. **❷** If Dave increases output from 9 to 10 cans of syrup a day, marginal cost is $7, which is less than the marginal revenue of $8, so profit increases. **❸** If Dave increases output from 10 to 11 cans of syrup a day, marginal cost is $9, which exceeds the marginal revenue of $8, so profit decreases.

Dave maximizes economic profit by producing 10 cans of syrup a day, the quantity at which marginal revenue equals marginal cost.

A firm's profit-maximizing output is its *quantity supplied*. Dave's *quantity supplied* at a price of $8 a can is 10 cans a day. If the price were higher than $8 a can, he would increase production. If the price were lower than $8 a can, he would decrease production. These profit-maximizing responses to different prices are the foundation of the law of supply:

> Other things remaining the same, the higher the price of a good, the greater is the quantity supplied of that good.

■ Temporary Shutdown Decision

MyEconLab Concept Video

Sometimes, the price falls so low that a firm cannot cover its costs. What does the firm do in such a situation? The answer depends on whether the firm expects the low price to be permanent or temporary.

If a firm incurs an economic loss that it believes is permanent and sees no prospect of ending, the firm exits the market. We'll study this action later in this chapter when we look at the firm's decisions in the long run (pp. 390–393).

If a firm incurs an economic loss that it believes is temporary, it remains in the market, but it might temporarily shut down. To decide whether to produce or to shut down, the firm compares the loss it would incur in the two situations.

Loss When Shut Down

If the firm shuts down temporarily, it receives no revenue and incurs no variable costs. The firm still incurs fixed costs. So, if a firm shuts down, it incurs an economic loss equal to total fixed cost. This loss is the largest that a firm need incur.

Loss When Producing

A firm that produces an output receives revenue and incurs both fixed costs and variable costs. The firm incurs an economic loss equal to total fixed cost *plus* total variable cost *minus* total revenue. If total revenue exceeds total variable cost, the firm's economic loss is less than total fixed cost. But if total revenue is less than total variable cost, the firm's economic loss will exceed total fixed cost.

The Shutdown Point

If total revenue is less than total variable cost, a firm shuts down temporarily and limits its loss to an amount equal to total fixed cost. If total revenue just equals total variable cost, a firm is indifferent between producing and shutting down. This situation arises when price equals minimum average variable cost and the firm produces the quantity at which average variable cost is a minimum—called the **shutdown point**.

Figure 15.4 illustrates the firm's shutdown decision and the shutdown point that we've just described for Dave's maple syrup farm. Dave's average variable cost curve is *AVC* and his marginal cost curve is *MC*. Average variable cost has a minimum of $3 a can when output is 7 cans of syrup a day. The *MC* curve intersects the *AVC* curve at its minimum. (We explained this relationship between the marginal and average values of a variable in Chapter 14; see pp. 356–357 and pp. 360–362.) The figure shows the marginal revenue curve *MR* when the price is $3 a can, a *price equal to minimum average variable cost.*

Shutdown point
The point at which price equals minimum average variable cost and the quantity produced is that at which average variable cost is at its minimum.

■ **FIGURE 15.4**

The Shutdown Decision   MyEconLab Animation

Price and cost (dollars per can)

Quantity (Q) (cans per day)	Total revenue (TR)	Total variable cost (TVC)	Total fixed cost (TFC)	Total cost (TC)	Economic profit (TR – TC)
		(dollars per day)			
6	18	19	15	34	–16
7	21	21	15	36	–15
8	24	25	15	40	–16

❶ The shutdown point is at minimum average variable cost. At a price below minimum average variable cost, the firm shuts down and produces no output. At a price equal to minimum average variable cost, the firm is indifferent between shutting down and producing no output or producing the output at minimum average variable cost. Either way, **❷** the firm minimizes its economic loss and incurs a loss equal to total fixed cost.

If Dave produces at the shutdown point, he produces 7 cans of syrup a day and sells them for $3 a can. He incurs an economic loss equal to $2.14 a can and a total economic loss of $15 a day. Dave's loss equals total fixed cost. If Dave shuts down, he also incurs an economic loss equal to total fixed cost.

The table lists Dave's total revenue, total variable cost, total fixed cost, total cost, and economic profit at three output levels. The middle output, 7 cans of syrup a day, is that at which Dave's average variable cost is at its minimum—$3 a can. The numbers in the table show that when the price is $3 a can and Dave produces 7 cans of syrup a day, he incurs a loss, and that loss equals total fixed cost.

■ **The Firm's Short-Run Supply Curve**

A perfectly competitive firm's short-run supply curve shows how the firm's profit-maximizing output varies as the price varies, other things remaining the same. This supply curve is based on the marginal analysis and shutdown decision that we've just explored.

Figure 15.5 derives Dave's supply curve. Part (a) shows the marginal cost and average variable cost curves, and part (b) shows the supply curve. There is a direct link between the marginal cost and average variable cost curves and the firm's supply curve. Let's see what that link is.

In Figure 15.5(a), if the price is above minimum average variable cost, Dave maximizes profit by producing the output at which marginal cost equals marginal revenue, which also equals price. We determine the quantity produced at each price from the marginal cost curve. At a price of $8 a can, the marginal revenue curve is MR_1 and Dave maximizes profit by producing 10 cans a day. If the price rises to $12 a can, the marginal revenue curve is MR_2 and Dave increases production to 11 cans a day.

If price equals minimum average variable cost, Dave maximizes profit (minimizes loss) by either producing the quantity at the shutdown point or shutting down and producing no output. But if the price is below minimum average variable cost, Dave shuts down and produces no output.

Figure 15.5(b) shows Dave's short-run supply curve. At prices that exceed minimum average variable cost, the supply curve is the same as the marginal cost curve. At prices below minimum average variable cost, Dave shuts down and produces nothing. His supply curve runs along the vertical axis. At a price of $3 a can, Dave is indifferent between shutting down and producing 7 cans of syrup a day at the shutdown point (T). Either way, he incurs a loss equal to total fixed cost.

So far, we have studied one firm in isolation. We have seen that the firm's profit-maximizing actions depend on the price, which the firm takes as given. In the next section, you'll learn how market supply is determined.

■ **FIGURE 15.5**

A Perfectly Competitive Firm's Supply Curve   MyEconLab Animation

(a) Marginal cost and average variable cost

(b) Firm's supply curve

Part (a) shows Dave's profit-maximizing output at various prices. At $12 a can, Dave produces 11 cans of syrup a day; at $8 a can, he produces 10 cans of syrup a day; and at $3 a can, he produces either 7 cans of syrup a day or nothing.

At any price below $3 a can, Dave produces nothing. The minimum average variable cost is the shutdown point.

Part (b) shows Dave's supply curve. At $3 a can, Dave is indifferent between producing the quantity at the shutdown point T and not producing.

At all prices above $3 a can, Dave's supply curve is made up of the marginal cost curve, in part (a), *above* minimum average variable cost.

At all prices below $3 a can, Dave produces nothing and his supply curve runs along the vertical axis.

CHECKPOINT 15.1

Explain a perfectly competitive firm's profit-maximizing choices and derive its supply curve.

Practice Problems

1. Sarah's Salmon Farm produced 1,000 fish last week. The marginal cost was $30 a fish, average variable cost was $20 a fish, and the market price was $25 a fish. Did Sarah maximize profit? If Sarah did not maximize profit and if nothing has changed will she increase or decrease the number of fish she produces to maximize her profit this week?

Use the following information to work Problems **2** to **4**.

Trout farming is a perfectly competitive industry and all trout farms have the same cost curves. When the market price of a fish is $25, farms maximize profit by producing 200 fish a week. At this output, average total cost is $20 a fish, and average variable cost is $15 a fish. Minimum average variable cost is $12 a fish.

2. If the price of a fish falls to $20, will a farm produce 200 fish a week?
3. If the price of a fish falls to $12, what will the trout farmer do?
4. What are two points on a trout farm's supply curve?

In the News

U.S. Steel lays off 756
With a drop in the demand for steel pipe and tube, U.S. Steel Corporation will idle plants in Ohio and Texas and lay off 756 workers.
Source: The Wall Street Journal, January 6, 2015

As U.S. Steel responded to the fall in demand, how did its marginal cost change? What can you say about minimum AVC in the plants that closed?

Solutions to Practice Problems

1. Profit is maximized when marginal cost equals marginal revenue. In perfect competition, marginal revenue equals the market price, which was $25 a fish last week. Because marginal cost exceeded marginal revenue, Sarah did not maximize profit. To maximize profit, Sarah will decrease her output until marginal cost falls to $25 a fish (Figure 1).

2. The farm will produce fewer than 200 fish a week. The marginal cost curve slopes upward, so to lower marginal cost to $20, the farm cuts production.

3. If the price of a fish falls to $12, farms cut output until marginal cost equals $12. Because $12 a fish is also minimum average variable cost, farms are at the shutdown point—some farms produce the profit-maximizing output and others produce nothing.

4. One point on a farmer's supply curve is 200 fish at $25 a fish. Another point is the shutdown point (Solution 3) or zero at a price below $12 a fish.

Solution to In the News

The fall in demand for steel pipe and tube lowered the price of steel pipe and tube. U.S. Steel cut production. Marginal cost decreased to equal the lower price. At the plants that closed temporarily, the firm's minimum AVC exceeded price.

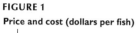

FIGURE 1
Price and cost (dollars per fish)

Quantity (fish per week)

Demand and supply determine the price and quantity in a perfectly competitive market. We first study short-run supply when the number of firms is fixed.

Market Supply in the Short Run

The market supply curve in the short run shows the quantity supplied at each price by a fixed number of firms. The quantity supplied at a given price is the sum of the quantities supplied by all firms at that price.

Figure 15.6 shows the supply curve for the competitive syrup market. In this example, the market consists of 10,000 firms exactly like Dave's Maple Syrup. The table shows how the market supply schedule is constructed. The shutdown point occurs at a price of $3 a can. At prices below $3 a can, every firm in the market shuts down; the quantity supplied is zero. At a price of $3 a can, each firm is indifferent between shutting down (producing nothing) or operating and producing 7 cans of syrup a day. The quantity supplied by each firm is *either* 0 or 7 cans of syrup a day, and the quantity supplied in the market is *between* 0 (all firms shut down) and 70,000 cans (all firms produce 7 cans a day each). At prices above $3 a can, we sum the quantities supplied by the 10,000 firms, so the quantity supplied in the market is 10,000 times the quantity supplied by one firm.

At prices below $3 a can, the market supply curve runs along the vertical axis. Supply is perfectly inelastic. At $3 a can, the market supply curve is horizontal. Supply is perfectly elastic. Above $3 a can, the supply curve is upward sloping.

FIGURE 15.6

The Market Supply Curve

MyEconLab Animation

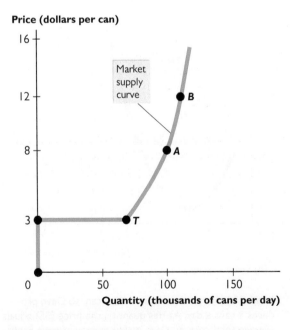

	Price	Dave's quantity supplied	Market quantity supplied
	(dollars per can)	(cans per day)	
B	12	11	110,000
A	8	10	100,000
T	3	0 or 7	0 to 70,000

A market with 10,000 identical firms has a supply schedule like that of an individual firm, but the quantity supplied is 10,000 times greater. Market supply is perfectly elastic at the price at which the shutdown point occurs.

■ Short-Run Equilibrium in Normal Times

Market demand and market supply determine the price and quantity bought and sold. Figure 15.7(a) shows a short-run equilibrium in the syrup market. The market supply curve S is the same as that in Figure 15.6.

If the demand curve D_1 shows market demand, the equilibrium price is $5 a can. Although market demand and market supply determine this price, each firm takes the price as given and produces its profit-maximizing output, which is 9 cans of syrup a day. With 10,000 identical firms, market output is 90,000 cans a day.

Figure 15.7(b) shows the situation that Dave faces. The price is $5 a can, so Dave's marginal revenue is constant at $5 a can. Dave maximizes profit by producing 9 cans of syrup a day.

Figure 15.7(b) also shows Dave's average total cost curve (*ATC*). Recall that average total cost is the cost per unit produced. It equals total cost divided by the quantity of output produced.

Here, when Dave produces 9 cans of syrup a day, his average total cost is $5 a can, exactly the same as the market price. So Dave sells syrup for exactly the same price as his average cost of production and economic profit is zero.

Making zero economic profit means that Dave earns *normal profit* from running his business.

The short-run equilibrium in which a firm makes zero economic profit is just one of three possible situations. A competitive market might also deliver a positive economic profit or an economic loss. Let's look at these other two cases.

FIGURE 15.7

Zero Economic Profit in the Short Run   MyEconLab Animation

(a) Syrup market

(b) Dave's syrup

In part (a), with the market demand curve D_1 and the market supply curve S, the equilibrium market price of syrup is $5 a can.

In part (b), marginal revenue is $5 a can, so Dave produces 9 cans a day. At this quantity, the price ($5) equals average total cost, so Dave makes zero economic profit.

Short-Run Equilibrium in Good Times

Market demand might be greater or less than D_1 in Figure 15.7 and the price might be higher or lower than $5 a can. Figure 15.8(a) shows another short-run equilibrium in the syrup market. The supply curve S is the same as that in Figure 15.6.

If the demand curve D_2 shows market demand, the equilibrium price is $8 a can. Although market demand and market supply determine this price, each firm takes the price as given and produces its profit-maximizing output, which is 10 cans of syrup a day. Because the market has 10,000 identical firms, market output is 100,000 cans of syrup a day.

Figure 15.8(b) shows the situation that Dave faces. The price is $8 a can, so Dave's marginal revenue is constant at $8 a can. Dave maximizes profit by producing 10 cans of syrup a day.

Figure 15.8(b) also shows Dave's average total cost curve (ATC). Recall that average total cost is the cost per unit produced. It equals total cost divided by the quantity of output produced. Here, when Dave produces 10 cans of syrup a day, his average total cost is $5.10 a can. So the price of $8 a can exceeds average total cost by $2.90 a can. This amount is Dave's economic profit per can.

If we multiply the economic profit per can of $2.90 by the quantity of syrup produced, 10 cans a day, we arrive at Dave's economic profit, which is $29 a day. The blue rectangle shows this economic profit. The height of that rectangle is the profit per can, $2.90, and the length is the 10 cans of syrup a day, so the area of the rectangle (height × length) measures Dave's economic profit of $29 a day.

FIGURE 15.8

Positive Economic Profit in the Short Run   MyEconLab Animation

(a) Syrup market

(b) Dave's syrup

In part (a), with the market demand curve D_2 and the market supply curve S, the equilibrium market price of syrup is $8 a can.

In part (b), marginal revenue is $8 a can. Dave produces 10 cans a day. Because price ($8) exceeds average total cost ($5.10), Dave makes a positive economic profit.

■ Short-Run Equilibrium in Bad Times

Figure 15.9 shows the syrup market in a loss-incurring situation. The market demand curve is now D_3. The market still has 10,000 firms and their costs are the same as before, so the market supply curve, S, is also the same as before.

With the demand and supply curves shown in Figure 15.9(a), the equilibrium price of syrup is $3 a can and the equilibrium quantity is 70,000 cans a day.

Figure 15.9(b) shows the situation that Dave faces. The price is $3 a can, so Dave's marginal revenue is constant at $3 a can. Dave maximizes profit by producing 7 cans of syrup a day.

Figure 15.9(b) also shows Dave's average total cost curve (*ATC*), and you can see that when Dave produces 7 cans of syrup a day, his average total cost is $5.14 a can. Now the price of $3 a can is less than average total cost by $2.14 a can. This amount is Dave's economic loss per can. If we multiply the economic loss per can of $2.14 by the quantity of syrup produced, 7 cans a day, we arrive at Dave's economic loss, which is shown by the red rectangle.

Figure 15.9(b) also shows Dave's average variable cost curve (*AVC*). Notice that Dave is operating at the shutdown point. Dave might equally well produce no output. Either way, his economic loss would be equal to his total fixed cost. If the price were a bit higher than $3 a can, Dave would still incur an economic loss, but a smaller one. And if the price were lower than $3 a can, Dave would shut down and incur an economic loss equal to total fixed cost.

FIGURE 15.9

Economic Loss in the Short Run   MyEconLab Animation

(a) Syrup market

In part (a), with the market demand curve D_3 and the market supply curve S, the equilibrium market price of syrup is $3 a can.

(b) Dave's syrup

In part (b), Dave's marginal revenue is $3 a can, so he produces 7 cans of syrup a day. At this quantity, the price ($3) is less than average total cost ($5.14), so Dave incurs an economic loss shown by the red rectangle.

CHECKPOINT 15.2

Explain how output, price, and profit are determined in the short run.

Practice Problems

Tulip growing is perfectly competitive and all growers have the same costs. The market price is $25 a bunch, and each grower maximizes profit by producing 2,000 bunches a week. Average total cost is $20 a bunch, and average variable cost is $15 a bunch. Minimum average variable cost is $12 a bunch.

1. What is the economic profit that each grower is making in the short run?

2. What is the price at the grower's shutdown point?

3. What is each grower's economic profit at the shutdown point?

In the News

Airfares will drop to record lows this fall
With a fall in the price of jet fuel, the price of an average round-trip airline ticket will slip to $244 next month, about 5% lower than the same time last year.
Source: *Fortune*, July 27, 2015

Explain how a fall in the price of jet fuel changes the marginal cost of producing air trips and changes the equilibrium price and quantity of air trips in the short run.

Solutions to Practice Problems

1. The market price ($25) exceeds the average total cost ($20), so growers make an economic profit of $5 a bunch. Each grower produces 2,000 bunches a week, so a grower's economic profit is $10,000 a week.
Figure 1 illustrates the situation. The grower's marginal revenue equals the market price ($25 a bunch). The grower maximizes profit by producing 2,000 bunches, so at 2,000 bunches the marginal cost curve (*MC*) cuts the marginal revenue curve (*MR*). The average total cost of producing 2,000 bunches is $20, so the *ATC* curve passes through this point. Economic profit equals the area of the blue rectangle.

2. The price at which a grower will shut down temporarily is equal to minimum average variable cost—$12 a bunch (Figure 1).

3. At the shutdown point, the grower incurs an economic loss equal to total fixed cost. Figure 2 shows the data to calculate *TFC*. When 2,000 bunches a week are grown, *ATC* is $20 a bunch and *AVC* is $15 a bunch.
ATC = *AFC* + *AVC*, so *AFC* = *ATC* − *AVC*. *AFC* is $5 a bunch. Total fixed cost equals $10,000 a week— *TFC* = *AFC* × *Q*, $5 a bunch × 2,000 bunches a week. At the shutdown point, the grower incurs an economic loss of $10,000 a week.

Solution to In the News

A fall in the price of jet fuel decreases an airline's marginal cost of producing air trips. The airline's marginal cost curve shifts downward. With lower marginal cost of an air trip, the market supply of air trips increases and the market supply curve shifts rightward. The increase in supply lowers the equilibrium price of an air trip and increases the equilibrium quantity of air trips in the short run.

FIGURE 1
Price and cost (dollars per bunch)
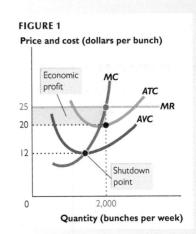
Quantity (bunches per week)

FIGURE 2
Price and cost (dollars per bunch)

Quantity (bunches per week)

15.3   OUTPUT, PRICE, AND PROFIT IN THE LONG RUN

Competitive markets are in a constant state of change. Price, quantity, and economic profit fluctuate as demand and supply change. None of the three situations that we described on the previous pages—normal times, good times, or bad times—last forever in perfect competition. Market forces operate to compete away economic profits and eliminate economic losses to move the price toward the lowest possible price. That price equals minimum average total cost. In the long run, a firm in perfect competition produces at minimum average total cost and makes zero economic profit. (The firm's entrepreneur earns normal profit—part of the firm's total costs.)

Figure 15.10 illustrates a perfectly competitive market in long-run equilibrium and highlights the forces that bring the market to this situation. In Figure 15.10(a), the firm's average total cost curve is *ATC*, and the firm produces at the point of minimum average total cost—9 cans a day at an average total cost of $5 a can. If the price rises above or falls below $5 a can, market forces operate to move the price back toward $5 a can. The arrows pointing toward $5 represent these forces.

In Figure 15.10(b) the market demand curve is *D*. With this market demand, the price equals minimum average total cost only if the market supply curve is *S*. If supply is less than *S* (the supply curve is to the left of *S*), the price is above $5 a can; if supply exceeds *S* (the supply curve is to the right of *S*), the price is below $5 a can. Market forces operate to shift the supply curve back to *S*, and the arrows pointing toward *S* represent these forces.

FIGURE 15.10

Long-Run Equilibrium

(a) Dave's syrup

(b) Syrup market

In part (a), minimum average total cost is $5 a can. In long-run equilibrium, the price and marginal revenue are pulled to this level. The firm makes zero economic profit.

In part (b), if the price is above $5 a can, above minimum *ATC* in part (a), supply increases and the price falls. If the price is below $5, supply decreases and the price rises.

■ Entry and Exit

Entry and exit are the market forces that shift the supply curve and move the price to minimum average total cost in the long run. In the short run, firms might make a positive economic profit (as in Figure 15.8) or incur an economic loss (as in Figure 15.9). But in the long run, firms makes zero economic profit.

In the long run, firms respond to economic profit and economic loss by either entering or exiting a market. New firms enter a market in which the existing firms are making economic profits, and some existing firms exit a market in which firms are incurring economic losses. Temporary economic profit or temporary economic loss, like a win or loss at a casino, does not trigger entry and exit. But the prospect of persistent economic profit or economic loss does.

Entry and exit influence the market price, the quantity produced, and economic profit. The immediate effect of the decision to enter or exit a market is to shift the market supply curve. If more firms enter a market, supply increases and the market supply curve shifts rightward. If some firms exit a market, supply decreases and the market supply curve shifts leftward.

Let's see what happens when new firms enter a market.

The Effects of Entry

Figure 15.11 shows the effects of entry. Initially, the market is in long-run equilibrium. Demand is D_0, supply is S_0, the price is $5 a can, and the quantity is 90,000 cans of syrup a day. A surge in the popularity of syrup increases market demand, and the demand curve shifts to D_1. The price rises to $8 a can, and firms in the syrup market increase output to 100,000 cans a day and make an economic profit.

Times are good for syrup producers like Dave, so other potential syrup producers want some of the action. New firms begin to enter the market. As they enter,

With the prospect of economic profit, a new business opens.

FIGURE 15.11

The Effects of Entry

MyEconLab Animation

Starting in long-run equilibrium,

① Market demand increases and the market demand curve shifts from D_0 to D_1. The price of syrup rises from $5 to $8 a can.

Economic profit brings entry.

② As firms enter the market, the market supply curve shifts rightward, from S_0 to S_1. The equilibrium price falls from $8 to $5 a can, and the quantity produced increases from 100,000 to 140,000 cans of syrup a day.

supply increases and the market supply curve shifts rightward to S_1. With the greater market supply and unchanged market demand, the market price falls from $8 to $5 a can and the equilibrium quantity increases to 140,000 cans a day.

Market output increases, but because the price falls, Dave and the other producers decrease output. As the price falls, each firm's output gradually returns to its original level. Because the number of firms in the market increases, the market as a whole produces more.

As the price falls, each firm's economic profit decreases. When the price falls to $5 a can, economic profit disappears and each firm makes zero economic profit. The entry process stops, and the market is again in long-run equilibrium.

You have just discovered a key proposition:

> Economic profit is an incentive for new firms to enter a market, but as they do so, the price falls and the economic profit of each existing firm decreases.

■ The Effects of Exit

Figure 15.12 shows the effects of exit. Again we begin on demand curve D_0 and supply curve S_0 in long-run equilibrium. A new high-nutrition breakfast food decreases the demand for maple syrup. The market demand curve shifts from D_0 to D_2. Firms' costs are the same as before, so the market supply curve is S_0.

With demand at D_2 and supply at S_0, the price falls to $3 a can and 70,000 cans a day are produced. The firms in the syrup market incur economic losses.

Times are tough for syrup producers, and Dave must seriously think about leaving his dream business and finding some other way of making a living. But other producers are in the same situation as Dave, and some start to exit the market while Dave is still thinking through his options.

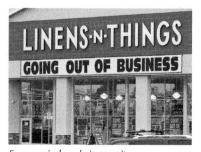

Economic loss brings exit.

■ **FIGURE 15.12**

The Effects of Exit

MyEconLab Animation

Starting in long-run equilibrium,

❶ Market demand decreases and the market demand curve shifts from D_0 to D_2. The price of syrup falls from $5 to $3 a can.

Economic loss brings exit.

❷ As some firms exit the market, the market supply curve shifts leftward, from S_0 to S_2. The equilibrium price rises from $3 to $5 a can, and the quantity produced decreases from 70,000 to 50,000 cans of syrup a day.

As some firms exit, the market supply curve shifts leftward to S_2, output decreases from 70,000 to 50,000 cans of syrup a day and the market price rises from $3 to $5 a can.

As the price rises, Dave and each other firm that remains in the market move up along their supply curves and increase output. That is, for each firm that remains in the market, the profit-maximizing output *increases*. As the price rises and each firm sells more, economic loss decreases. When the price rises to $5 a can, each firm makes zero economic profit. Dave earns normal profit (part of the firm's total cost) and he is happy that he can still make a living producing syrup.

You have just discovered a second key proposition:

Economic loss is an incentive for firms to exit a market, but as they do so, the price rises and the economic loss of each remaining firm decreases.

Change in Demand

Initially, a competitive market is in long-run equilibrium and the firms are making zero economic profit (and entrepreneurs are earning normal profit). Now market demand increases. The market price rises, firms increase production to keep marginal cost equal to price, and firms make an economic profit. The market is now in short-run equilibrium but not in long-run equilibrium.

Economic profit is an incentive for new firms to enter the market. As firms enter, market supply increases and the market price falls. With a lower price, firms decrease output to keep marginal cost equal to price. Notice that as firms enter the market, market output increases, but each firm's output decreases. Eventually, enough firms enter to eliminate economic profit and the market returns to long-run equilibrium.

The key difference between the initial long-run equilibrium and the new long-run equilibrium is the number of firms. A permanent increase in demand increases the number of firms. Each firm produces the same output in the new long-run equilibrium as initially and makes zero economic profit. In the process of moving from the initial equilibrium to the new one, firms make economic profit.

The demand for airline travel in the world economy increased during the 1990s, and the deregulation of the airlines freed up firms to seek profit opportunities. The result was a massive rate of entry of new airlines. The process of competition and change in the airline market were similar to what we have just studied.

A decrease in demand triggers a similar response, except in the opposite direction. The decrease in demand brings a lower price, economic loss, and exit. Exit decreases market supply, raises the price, and eliminates the economic loss.

Technological Change

New technologies lower cost, so as firms adopt a new technology, their cost curves shift downward. With lower costs, market supply increases and the price falls. Firms that use the new technology make an economic profit and firms that stick with the old technology incur economic losses. New-technology firms enter and old-technology firms exit. The price keeps falling until all the firms are using the new technology and economic profit is zero. The lower prices and better products that technological advances bring are permanent gains for consumers. *Eye on Record Stores* (on pp. 394–395) looks at the effects of technological change in the retail market for recorded music.

EYE on RECORD STORES

Where Have All the Record Stores Gone?

Beecker Street Records in New York City (see p. 375) describes its inventory as vintage and out-of-print LPs and CDs. No longer do record stores sell the latest singles and albums.

The world was very different in 1995, when more than 8,000 record stores traded in an almost perfectly competitive market.

Figure 1 illustrates the average total cost curve, ATC, marginal cost curve, MC, and marginal revenue curve, MR_0, for one of these 8,000 stores.

Competition was fierce in the record retail business and economic profit was hard to find. In Figure 1, the record store is earning zero economic

profit and the market is in long-run equilibrium.

Although competition was fierce, it was about to notch up a gear. The dot-com boom had started.

The expansion of the Internet during the 1990s laid the foundation for many new ways of doing business. One of these was a new way of delivering recorded music.

Amazon was one of the first firms to take advantage of the technological advance made possible by the Internet when Amazon.com started trading in 1995.

At first, Amazon was an online bookstore. But entrepreneur Jeff

An Amazon server farm replaces hundreds of traditional record stores.

Figure 1 Small Independent Record Store Before Internet

Figure 2 Amazon Enters CD Retail Market

Bezos quickly saw that the technologies being laid down for selling books could also be used to sell CDs (and just about anything).

This new technology also had much lower costs than traditional "bricks and mortar" retailing.

Figure 2 shows the average total cost curve and marginal cost curve using Amazon's lower-cost technology. The numbers are just examples, but first look carefully at the axes of Figures 1 and 2. Amazon can produce a larger output at a lower cost than the traditional record store can.

Online retailing wasn't profitable at first, but with its superior low-cost technology economic profit eventually rolled in. Figure 2 shows the economic profit available at the prices charged by traditional record stores applied to a store using the new technology.

Positive economic profit attracts new entry. And that's what happened in the online music business. The technology also kept advancing, with MP3 files replacing physical CDs. As Amazon, Apple's iTunes store, and others entered the market for MP3 downloads, the price of recorded music fell and firms' profits were trimmed.

Figure 3 shows where perfect competition among online music download stores drives the price and quantity. Price falls to make marginal revenue MR_1, a level at which economic profit has vanished in a new long-run equilibrium.

This lower price means hard times for small independent record stores. The fall in price is too big for these small stores to cover even their average variable cost, AVC, and with no

prospect of prices rising again, the independent stores avoid the economic losses by exiting.

Figure 4 illustrates the economic loss incurred by a traditional independent record store facing competition from online retailers when marginal revenue has fallen to MR_1.

Faced with this loss, the store exits. That's where the record stores have gone. They've exited to avoid the losses created by online competition.

Sundance, in San Marcos, Texas, is one of 4,000 traditional record stores that exited.

Figure 3 More Large Online Music Stores Enter and Compete   **Figure 4 Small Independent Record Store Exits**

■ Is Perfect Competition Efficient?

An efficient outcome is one in which scarce resources are allocated to their highest-value use. Perfect competition achieves such an outcome. It is efficient.

To see why, first recall the conditions for an efficient allocation of resources. Resources are used efficiently when it is not possible to get more of one good without giving up something that is valued more highly. When this outcome is achieved, marginal benefit equals marginal cost and total surplus (consumer surplus plus producer surplus) is maximized. That is the outcome achieved in perfect competition.

We derive a firm's supply curve in perfect competition from its marginal cost curve. The supply curve is the marginal cost curve at all points above the minimum of average variable cost (the shutdown price). Because the market supply curve is found by summing the quantities supplied by all the firms at each price, the market supply curve is the entire market's marginal cost curve.

The market demand curve is the marginal benefit curve. Because the market supply curve and market demand curve intersect at the equilibrium price, that price equals both marginal cost and marginal benefit.

Figure 15.13 illustrates the efficiency of perfect competition. We've labeled the market demand curve $D = MB$ and the market supply curve $S = MC$ to remind you that these curves are also the marginal benefit (MB) and marginal cost (MC) curves.

These demand and supply curves intersect at the equilibrium price and equilibrium quantity. The price equals marginal benefit and marginal cost, total surplus is maximized, and the equilibrium quantity is efficient. Any departure from this outcome is inferior to it and brings an avoidable deadweight loss.

FIGURE 15.13

The Efficiency of Perfect Competition   MyEconLab Animation

---

❶ Market equilibrium occurs at a price of $5 a can and a quantity of 90,000 cans of syrup a day.

❷ The supply curve is also the marginal cost curve.

❸ The demand curve is also the marginal benefit curve.

At the market equilibrium, marginal benefit equals marginal cost.

❹ The efficient quantity of syrup is produced.

❺ Total surplus, the sum of consumer surplus and producer surplus, is maximized.

■ Is Perfect Competition Fair?

You've seen many situations in which perfect competition brings gains and losses. When the demand for an item decreases, most producers incur at least a temporary loss and some of them go out of business. When a technological change lowers costs, entrepreneurs who are quick to adopt the technology gain and others who respond slowly lose. Is it fair that some entrepreneurs gain and others lose?

When a natural disaster such as extreme weather or an earthquake strikes, the prices of essential items sold in competitive markets shoot upward, bringing gains for sellers and pain for buyers. Is that type of outcome fair?

You studied the fairness of markets in Chapter 6 (pp. 161–163) and saw two views of what is fair: fair rules and a fair result. According to the fair-rules view, an outcome is fair if property rights are enforced and people acquire resources, goods, and services through voluntary exchange. According to the fair-result view, an outcome is fair if the poorest aren't too poor and the richest aren't too rich. Are the competitive market outcomes we've just described fair on these two views of fairness?

The situations we've described appear to be fair on both views. Perfect competition places no restrictions on anyone's actions, all trade is voluntary, consumers pay the lowest possible prices, and entrepreneurs earn only normal profit. But price hikes arising from shortages following a natural disaster might be exceptions. In such situations, large windfall gains for a few and high prices for essential items for many might be regarded as an unfair result. If it is considered unfair, it must be compared with the fairness of an alternative mechanism for allocating scarce resources.

EYE on YOUR LIFE
The Perfect Competition That You Encounter

MyEconLab Critical Thinking Exercise

Many of the markets that you encounter every day are highly competitive and almost perfectly competitive. While you don't run into perfect competition on a daily basis, you do have dealings in some perfectly competitive markets. Two of those markets are the Internet auctions organized by eBay and one of its subsidiaries, StubHub.

If you have a ticket for a game between the Giants and the Braves but can't use it, you can sell it on StubHub for the going market price (minus a commission). And if you're desperate to see the game but missed out on getting a ticket, you can buy

one for the going price (plus a commission) on the same Web site.

StubHub takes a commission and makes a profit. But competition between StubHub, Ticketmaster, and other ticket brokers ensure that profits are competed away in the long run, with entrepreneurs earning normal profit.

Just about every good or service that you buy and take for granted, no matter where you buy it, is available because of the forces of competition. Your home, your food, your clothing, your books, your DVDs, your MP3 files, your computer, your bike, your car,…; the list is endless. No one organizes all the magic that enables

you to buy this vast array of products. Competitive markets and entrepreneurs striving to make the largest possible profit make it happen.

When either demand or technology changes and makes the current allocation of resources the wrong one, the market swiftly and silently acts. It sends signals to entrepreneurs that bring entry and exit and a new and efficient use of scarce resources.

It is no exaggeration or hype to say that your entire life is influenced by and benefits immeasurably from the forces of competition. Adam Smith's invisible hand might be hidden from view, but it is enormously powerful.

MyEconLab Study Plan 15.3

Solutions Video

CHECKPOINT 15.3

Explain how output, price, and profit are determined in the long run and explain why perfect competition is efficient.

Practice Problems

Tulip growing is a perfectly competitive industry, and all tulip growers have the same cost curves. The market price of tulips is $15 a bunch, and each grower maximizes profit by producing 1,500 bunches a week. The average total cost of producing tulips is $21 a bunch. Minimum average variable cost is $12 a bunch, and the minimum average total cost is $18 a bunch.

1. What is a tulip grower's economic profit in the short run and how does the number of tulip growers change in the long run?

2. In the long run, what is the price and the tulip grower's economic profit?

In the News

California's commercial drone industry is taking off
Customers are finding ever more creative ways to use drones, and 3D Robotics Inc., America's largest producer of consumer drones, expects sales to soar.

Source: *Los Angeles Times*, June 13, 2015

Explain what is happening in the market for commercial drones. How would you expect the price of a drone to change in the short run and the long run? How would you expect the economic profit of a drone producer such as 3D Robotics to change in the short run and in the long run?

Solutions to Practice Problems

1. The price is less than average total cost, so the tulip grower is incurring an economic loss in the short run. Because the price exceeds minimum average variable cost, the tulip grower continues to produce. The economic loss equals the loss per bunch ($21 minus $15) multiplied by the number of bunches (1,500 per week), which equals $9,000 per week (Figure 1). Because tulip growers are incurring economic losses, some growers will exit in the long run. The number of tulip growers will decrease.

2. In the long run, the price will be such that economic profit is zero. That is, as growers exit, the price will rise until it equals minimum average total cost. In the long run, the price will be $18 a bunch (Figure 2) and a tulip grower will make zero economic profit because average total cost equals price.

Solution to In the News

With customers finding ever more creative ways to use drones, the demand for drones is increasing. In the short run, an increase in demand brings a rise in the price of a drone and an increase in the quantity of drones supplied. The higher price increases the economic profit of drone producers in the short run. Economic profit is an incentive for new firms to enter the market. In the long run, entry increases supply, which lowers the price and increases the quantity of drones demanded. As the price of a drone falls, economic profit decreases. In the new long-run equilibrium, the price of a drone is lower and drone producers make zero economic profit.

FIGURE 1

Price and cost (dollars per bunch)

Quantity (bunches per week)

FIGURE 2

Price and cost (dollars per bunch)

Quantity (bunches per week)

CHAPTER SUMMARY

Key Points

1. **Explain a perfectly competitive firm's profit-maximizing choices and derive its supply curve.**

   - A perfectly competitive firm is a price taker.
   - Marginal revenue equals price.
   - The firm produces the output at which price equals marginal cost.
   - If price is less than minimum average variable cost, the firm temporarily shuts down.
   - A firm's supply curve is the upward-sloping part of its marginal cost curve at all prices at or above minimum average variable cost (the shutdown point) and the vertical axis at all prices below minimum average variable cost.

2. **Explain how output, price, and profit are determined in the short run.**

   - Market demand and market supply determine price.
   - Firms choose the quantity to produce that maximizes profit, which is the quantity at which marginal cost equals price.
   - In short-run equilibrium, a firm can make a positive economic profit, make zero economic profit, or incur an economic loss.

3. **Explain how output, price, and profit are determined in the long run and explain why perfect competition is efficient.**

   - Economic profit induces entry, which increases market supply and lowers price and profit. Economic loss induces exit, which decreases market supply, raises price, and lowers the losses.
   - In the long run, economic profit is zero and there is no entry or exit.
   - An increase in demand increases the number of firms and increases the equilibrium quantity.
   - An advance in technology that lowers the cost of producing a good increases market supply, lowers the price, and increases the quantity.
   - Perfect competition is efficient because it makes marginal benefit equal marginal cost, and it is fair because trade is voluntary, consumers pay the lowest possible prices, and entrepreneurs earn normal profit.

Key Terms

MyEconLab Key Terms Quiz

Marginal revenue, 377
Monopolistic competition, 376
Monopoly, 376

Oligopoly, 376
Perfect competition, 376

Price taker, 377
Shutdown point, 381

CHAPTER CHECKPOINT

Study Plan Problems and Applications

LIST

- Wheat
- Jeans
- Printer cartridges
- Toothpaste
- Gym membership in a town with one gym

1. Look at the list to the left. In what type of market is each good or service in the list sold? Explain your answers.

2. Explain why in a perfectly competitive market, the firm is a price taker. Why can't the firm choose the price at which it sells its good?

3. Table 1 shows the demand schedule for Lin's Fortune Cookies. Calculate Lin's marginal revenue for each quantity demanded. Compare Lin's marginal revenue and price. In what type of market does Lin's Fortune Cookies operate?

Table 1 shows the demand schedule for Lin's Fortune Cookies. Table 2 shows some cost data for Lin's. Use this information to work Problems 4 to 7. (Hint: Make a sketch of Lin's short-run cost curves.)

4. At a market price of $50 a batch, what quantity does Lin's produce and what is the firm's economic profit in the short run?

5. At a market price of $35.20 a batch, what quantity does Lin's produce and what is the firm's economic profit in the short run?

6. Create Lin's short-run supply schedule and make a graph of Lin's short-run supply curve. Explain why only part of Lin's short-run supply curve is the same as its marginal cost curve.

7. At a market price of $83 a batch, what quantity does Lin's produce and what is the firm's economic profit in the short run? Do firms enter or exit the market and what is Lin's economic profit in the long run?

TABLE 1

Price (dollars per batch)	Quantity demanded (batches per day)
50	0
50	1
50	2
50	3
50	4
50	5
50	6

TABLE 2

Quantity (batches per day)	AFC	AVC	ATC	MC
	(dollars per batch)			
1	84.0	51.0	135	
				37
2	42.0	44.0	86	
				29
3	28.0	39.0	67	
				27
4	21.0	36.0	57	
				32
5	16.8	35.2	52	
				40
6	14.0	36.0	50	
				57
7	12.0	39.0	51	
				83
8	10.5	44.5	55	

Use the following information to work Problems **8** to **10**.

Quebec losing hold over maple syrup industry to U.S. competition

The Federation of Quebec Maple Syrup Producers tries to limit production and stockpiles a "strategic reserve" to keep the price of syrup high. But Quebec producers are feeling increased competition from Vermont, New York, and Maine, where market share has increased and is expected to increase further in 2017 and 2018.

Source: *The Globe and Mail*, April 6, 2015

8. Draw a graph to describe the maple syrup market and the cost and revenue of one maple syrup producer in 2016, assuming that all producers are making a positive economic profit because of the actions of the Federation of Quebec Maple Syrup Producers.

9. Starting with the industry making a positive economic profit, explain how the maple syrup market and the profit of an individual producer will change in the long run.

10. If the demand for maple syrup increases, what will happen to price, quantity, and the economic profit of a producer in the short run and in the long run?

 11. Read *Eye on Record Stores* on pp. 394–395 and explain how Internet retailing of recorded music changed the constraints faced by small traditional record stores. Why did many record stores exit rather than shut down temporarily?

Instructor Assignable Problems and Applications

MyEconLab Homework, Quiz, or Test if assigned by instructor

1. Why did Amazon enter the market for recorded music and why did independent record stores exit?

2. How does competition among online music retailers influence economic profit?

3. Look at the list to the right. In what type of market is each of the goods and services in the list sold? Explain your answers.

4. Suppose that the restaurant industry is perfectly competitive. Joe's Diner is always packed in the evening but rarely has a customer at lunchtime. Why doesn't Joe's Diner close—temporarily shut down—at lunchtime?

LIST

- Breakfast cereals
- Smartphones
- The only restaurant in a small town
- Oranges
- Air travel in a town serviced by one airline

Use the following information to work Problems **5** to **7**.

Figure 1 shows the short-run cost curves of a toy producer. The market has 1,000 identical producers and Table 1 shows the market demand schedule for toys.

5. At a market price of $21 a toy, what quantity does the firm produce in the short run and does the firm make a positive economic profit, a zero economic profit, or an economic loss?

6. At a market price of $12 a toy, how many toys does the firm produce and what is its economic profit in the short run? How will the number of firms in the market change in the long run?

7. At what market prices would the firm shut down temporarily? What is the market price of a toy in long-run equilibrium? How many firms will be in the toy market in the long run? Explain your answer.

FIGURE 1

Use the following information to work Problems **8** and **9**.

California plans to crack down on the use of fumigants by growers of strawberries. The biggest burden will fall on Ventura County's growers, who produce about 90 percent of the nation's crop.

8. Draw graphs of the U.S. strawberry market in long-run equilibrium before the pollution crackdown: one of the U.S. market and one of a California grower. Now show the short-run effects of the pollution crackdown.

9. On the graph, show the long-run effects of the pollution crackdown.

Use the following information to work Problems **10** and **11**.

Grain, soybean prices fall
Grain and soybean prices tumbled on news that production would be greater than previously expected. The bigger-than-expected production forecasts come as grain farmers are wrestling with a decrease in overseas demand for grain.
Source: *The Wall Street Journal*, November 10, 2015

10. Why did soybean prices fall in 2015? Draw graphs to show the soybean market and the cost and revenue curves of a soybean farmer at the start and end of 2015. Show the change in the soybean farmer's economic profit.

11. Why did grain prices fall in 2015? Draw graphs to show the grain market and the cost and revenue curves of an individual grain farmer at the start and end of 2015. Show the change in the grain farmer's economic profit.

TABLE 1

Price (dollars per toy)	Quantity demanded (thousands of toys per week)
24	1,000
21	1,500
18	2,000
15	2,500
12	3,000

Multiple Choice Quiz

1. In perfect competition, all the following situations arise *except* _____.

A. firms produce an identical good or service
B. each firm chooses the price at which to sell the good it produces
C. firms can sell any quantity they choose to produce at the market price
D. buyers know each seller's price

2. A firm that is producing the quantity at which marginal cost exceeds both average total cost and the market price will increase its economic profit by _____.

A. producing a larger quantity
B. raising the price to equal marginal cost
C. producing a smaller quantity
D. producing the quantity that minimizes average total cost

3. A firm will shut down in the short run if at the profit-maximizing quantity, _____.

A. total revenue is less than total cost
B. marginal revenue is less than average fixed cost
C. average total cost exceeds the market price
D. marginal revenue is less than average variable cost

4. At the shutdown point, the firm _____.

A. incurs an economic loss equal to total variable cost
B. makes zero economic profit
C. incurs a loss equal to total fixed cost
D. stops production to decrease its economic loss

5. In the short run, the profit-maximizing firm will _____.

A. break even if marginal revenue equals marginal cost
B. make an economic profit if marginal cost is less than average total cost
C. incur an economic loss if average fixed cost exceeds marginal revenue
D. incur an economic loss if average total cost exceeds marginal revenue

6. A firm's short-run supply curve is the same as _____ if it produces the good.

A. its marginal revenue curve
B. the upward-sloping part of its marginal cost curve
C. its marginal cost curve above minimum average variable cost
D. its marginal cost curve above minimum average total cost

7. A permanent increase in demand _____ economic profit in the short run and some firms will _____ in the long run.

A. does not change; exit the market
B. increases; enter the market
C. increases; raise their price
D. does not change; advertise their good

8. Perfect competition is efficient because all the following conditions hold *except* _____.

A. total product is maximized
B. firms maximize profit and produce on their supply curves
C. consumers get a real bargain and pay a price below the value of the good
D. firms minimize their average total cost of producing the good

Are Microsoft's prices too high?

Monopoly

When you have completed your study of this chapter, you will be able to

1 Explain how monopoly arises and distinguish between single-price monopoly and price-discriminating monopoly.

2 Explain how a single-price monopoly determines its output and price.

3 Compare the performance of a single-price monopoly with that of perfect competition.

4 Explain how price discrimination increases profit.

5 Explain why natural monopoly is regulated and the effects of regulation.

MyEconLab Big Picture Video

403

16.1 MONOPOLY AND HOW IT ARISES

Microsoft faces almost no competition in the market for PC operating systems. Does the absence of competition result in buyers paying too high a price for Windows? You will find the answer in this chapter.

The market for PC operating systems is an example of **monopoly**, a market in which one firm sells a good or service that has no close substitutes and in which a barrier to entry prevents competition from new firms.

Monopoly
A market in which one firm sells a good or service that has no close substitutes and a barrier blocks the entry of new firms.

■ No Close Substitute

If a good has a close substitute, even though only one firm produces it, that firm effectively faces competition from the producers of substitutes. An example of a good that does not have close substitutes is water supplied by a local public utility. While it does have a close substitute for drinking—bottled spring water—it has no substitutes for doing the laundry, taking a shower, or washing a car.

Technological change can create substitutes and weaken a monopoly. For example, Fedex, UPS, and e-mail are close substitutes for the services provided by the U.S. Postal Service and have weakened its monopoly.

The arrival of a new product can also create a monopoly. For example, the technologies of the information age have provided opportunities for Google and Microsoft to become near monopolies in their markets (See *Eye on the U.S. Economy* on p. 406).

■ Barrier to Entry

Any constraint that protects a firm from facing new competitors is a **barrier to entry**. There are three types of barrier to entry:

Barrier to entry
Any constraint that protects a firm from competitors.

- Natural
- Legal
- Ownership

Natural Barrier to Entry

When economies of scale enable a single firm to meet the entire market demand at a lower average total cost than two or more firms could, a natural barrier to entry creates a **natural monopoly**.

Figure 16.1 illustrates a natural monopoly in the distribution of electric power. Here, the demand curve for electric power is *D*, and the long-run average cost curve is *LRAC*. Economies of scale prevail over the entire length of this *LRAC* curve, indicated by the fact that the curve slopes downward. One firm can produce 4 million kilowatt-hours at 5¢ a kilowatt-hour. At this price, the quantity demanded is 4 million kilowatt-hours. So if the price was 5¢ a kilowatt-hour, one firm could supply the entire market. If two or more firms shared the market, average total cost would be higher.

Natural monopoly
A monopoly that arises because one firm can meet the entire market demand at a lower average total cost than two or more firms could.

To see why the situation shown in Figure 16.1 creates a barrier to entry, think about what would happen if a second firm tried to enter the market. Such a firm would find it impossible to make a profit. If it produced less than the original firm, it would have to charge a higher price and it would have no customers. If it produced the same quantity as the original firm, the price would fall below average total cost for both firms and one of them would be forced out of business. There is room for only one firm in this market.

FIGURE 16.1

Natural Monopoly

MyEconLab Animation

The demand curve for electric power is *D*, and the long-run average cost curve is *LRAC*.

❶ Economies of scale exist over the entire *LRAC* curve.

One firm can distribute 4 million kilowatt-hours at a **❷** cost of 5¢ a kilowatt-hour.

Two firms can distribute this same total output at a **❸** cost of 10¢ a kilowatt-hour.

Four firms can distribute this same total output at a **❹** cost of 15¢ a kilowatt-hour.

One firm can meet the market demand at a lower cost than two or more firms can, and the market is a natural monopoly.

Legal Barrier to Entry

A legal barrier to entry creates a legal monopoly. A **legal monopoly** is a market in which competition and entry are restricted by the granting of a public franchise, government license, patent, or copyright.

A *public franchise* is an exclusive right granted to a firm to supply a good or service, an example of which is the U.S. Postal Service's exclusive right to deliver first-class mail. A *government license* controls entry into particular occupations, professions, and industries. An example is Michael's Texaco in Charleston, Rhode Island, which is the only firm in the area licensed to test for vehicle emissions.

A *patent* is an exclusive right granted to the inventor of a product or service. A *copyright* is an exclusive right granted to the author or composer of a literary, musical, dramatic, or artistic work. Patents and copyrights are valid for a limited time period that varies from country to country. In the United States, a patent is valid for 20 years. Patents are designed to encourage the *invention* of new products and production methods. They also stimulate *innovation*—the use of new inventions—by encouraging inventors to publicize their discoveries and offer them for use under license. Patents have stimulated innovations in areas as diverse as soybean seeds, pharmaceuticals, memory chips, and video games.

Ownership Barrier to Entry

A monopoly can arise in a market in which competition and entry are restricted by a concentration of ownership. An example is the global wholesale market in sunglasses, which is controlled by Luxottica, an Italian firm, that almost certainly made your glasses, regardless of the brand and where you bought them.

Legal monopoly
A market in which competition and entry are restricted by the granting of a public franchise, government license, patent, or copyright.

The global wholesale market for designer sunglasses is close to being a monopoly.

EYE on the U.S. ECONOMY
Information-Age Monopolies

Information-age technologies have created three big natural monopolies—firms with large fixed plant costs but almost zero marginal cost that experience economies of scale.

The operating system of 92 percent of personal computers is some version of Microsoft's Windows. Google performs 66 percent of all Internet searches. And Facebook gets 50 percent of all visits to social media sites.

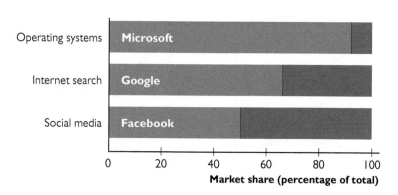

■ Monopoly Price-Setting Strategies

A monopoly faces a tradeoff between price and the quantity sold. To sell a larger quantity, the monopoly must set a lower price. But there are two price-setting possibilities that create different tradeoffs:

- Single price
- Price discrimination

Single Price

Single-price monopoly
A monopoly that must sell each unit of its output for the same price to all its customers.

A **single-price monopoly** is a firm that must sell each unit of its output for the same price to all its customers. Luxottica sells sunglasses (of a given type and quality) for the same price to all its customers. Luxottica is a *single-price* monopoly because if it tried to sell at a higher price to some customers than to others, only the low-price customers would buy from Luxottica. The others would buy from Luxottica's low-price customers.

Price Discrimination

Price-discriminating monopoly
A monopoly that sells different units of a good or service for different prices not related to cost differences.

A **price-discriminating monopoly** is a firm that sells different units for different prices not related to cost differences. Many firms price discriminate. Airlines offer a dizzying array of different prices for the same trip. Pizza producers charge one price for a single pizza and almost give away a second one. Different customers might pay different prices (like airfares), or one customer might pay different prices for different quantities bought (like the bargain price for a second pizza).

When a firm price discriminates, it appears to be doing its customers a favor. In fact, the firm is charging each group of customers the highest price that it can get them to pay and it is increasing its profit.

Not all monopolies can price discriminate. The main obstacle to the practice of price discrimination is resale by the customers who buy for a low price. Because of resale possibilities, price discrimination is limited to monopolies that sell goods and services that cannot be resold.

CHECKPOINT 16.1

MyEconLab Study Plan 16.1
Key Terms Quiz
Solutions Video

Explain how monopoly arises and distinguish between single-price monopoly and price-discriminating monopoly.

Practice Problems

Use the information about the firms listed below to work Problems **1** and **2**.

    a. Coca-Cola cuts its price below that of Pepsi-Cola to increase profit.

    b. A single firm, protected by a barrier to entry, produces a personal service that has no close substitutes.

    c. A barrier to entry exists, but the good has some close substitutes.

    d. A museum offers discounts to students and seniors.

    e. A firm can sell any quantity it chooses at the going price.

    f. A firm experiences economies of scale even when it produces the quantity that meets the entire market demand.

1. Which of the six cases are monopolies or might give rise to monopoly?

2. Which are natural monopolies and which are legal monopolies? Can any of them price discriminate? If so, why?

In the News

Allegiant Air nonstop flights from Tulsa to Washington, D.C./Baltimore
From May 19 to August 16, Allegiant Air will enable Tulsa-area travelers to fly nonstop to Washington, D.C./Baltimore. The airline says the seasonal destination could become year-round if demand is sufficiently large.

                                  Source: *Tulsa World*, January 13, 2016

Allegiant Air is the only airline flying nonstop on this route. What type of monopoly is Allegiant? What would be the barrier to entry?

Solutions to Practice Problems

1. Monopoly arises when a single firm produces a good or service that has no close substitutes and a barrier to entry exists. Monopoly arises in **b** and **f**. In **a**, there is more than one firm. In **c**, the good has close substitutes. In **d**, a monopoly might be able to price discriminate, but other types of firms (for example, pizza producers) price discriminate and they are not monopolies. In **e**, the demand for the firm's output is perfectly elastic and there is no limit to what it can sell. This firm operates in a perfectly competitive market.

2. Natural monopoly exists when one firm can meet the entire market demand at a lower price than two or more firms could: **f** is a natural monopoly, but **b** could be. Legal monopoly exists when the granting of a right creates a barrier to entry: **b** might be a legal monopoly. Because a personal service cannot be resold, **b** could price discriminate.

Solution to In the News

Allegiant Air is a natural monopoly on this nonstop route. Before Allegiant entered the market, demand on this route nonstop was too small for any firm to operate. Allegiant is exploring whether demand is large enough for one firm to be profitable. The barrier to entry is a natural barrier that arises from demand and cost.

16.2 SINGLE-PRICE MONOPOLY

To understand how a single-price monopoly makes its output and price decisions, we must first study the link between price and marginal revenue.

■ Price and Marginal Revenue

Because in a monopoly there is only one firm, the demand for the firm's output is the market demand. Let's look at Bobbie's Barbershop, the sole supplier of haircuts in Cairo, Nebraska. The table in Figure 16.2 shows the demand schedule for Bobbie's haircuts. For example, at $12, consumers demand 4 haircuts an hour (row *E*).

Total revenue is the price multiplied by the quantity sold. For example, in row *D*, Bobbie sells 3 haircuts at $14 each, so total revenue is $42. *Marginal revenue* is the change in total revenue resulting from a one-unit increase in the quantity sold. For example, if the price falls from $16 (row *C*) to $14 (row *D*), the quantity sold increases from 2 to 3 haircuts. Total revenue rises from $32 to $42, so the change in total revenue is $10. Because the quantity sold increases by 1 haircut, marginal revenue equals the change in total revenue and is $10. We place marginal revenue between the two rows to emphasize that marginal revenue relates to the *change* in the quantity sold.

Figure 16.2 shows the market demand curve and Bobbie's marginal revenue curve (*MR*) and also illustrates the calculation that we've just made. At each output, marginal revenue is less than price—the marginal revenue curve lies below the demand curve because a lower price is received on *all* units sold, not just on the marginal unit. For example, at a price of $16, Bobbie sells 2 haircuts (point *C*). If she lowers the price to $14 a haircut, she sells 3 haircuts and has a revenue gain

■ **FIGURE 16.2**

Demand and Marginal Revenue

The table shows the market demand schedule for haircuts and Bobbie's total revenue and marginal revenue schedules.

If the price of a haircut falls from $16 to $14, the quantity sold increases from 2 to 3 haircuts.

❶ Total revenue lost on the first 2 haircuts is $4; ❷ total revenue gained on the third haircut is $14; so ❸ marginal revenue is $10.

	Price (dollars per haircut)	Quantity demanded (haircuts per hour)	Total revenue (dollars per hour)	Marginal revenue (dollars per haircut)
A	20	0	0	
				18
B	18	1	18	
				14
C	16	2	32	
				10
D	14	3	42	
				6
E	12	4	48	
				2
F	10	5	50	

of $14 on the third haircut. But she now receives only $14 a haircut on the first two—$2 a haircut less than before. So she loses $4 of revenue on the first 2 haircuts. To calculate marginal revenue, she must deduct this amount from the revenue gain of $14. So her marginal revenue is $10, which is less than the price $14.

Notice that the marginal revenue curve has *twice the slope* of the demand curve. A fall in price of $10 increases the quantity demanded by 5, but marginal revenue falls by $10 when the quantity increases by 2.5.

◼ Marginal Revenue and Elasticity

In Chapter 5 (pp. 122–123), you learned about the *total revenue test* for the price elasticity of demand. If a *fall* in price *increases* total revenue, demand is elastic; and if a *fall* in price *decreases* total revenue, demand is inelastic.

The total revenue test implies that when demand is elastic, marginal revenue is positive and when demand is inelastic, marginal revenue is negative. Figure 16.3 illustrates this relationship between elasticity and marginal revenue.

In part (a) as the price *falls* from $20 to $10, marginal revenue (shown by the blue bars) is *positive* and total revenue in part (b) *increases*, so demand is elastic. In part (a) as the price *falls* from $10 to zero, marginal revenue (the red bars) is *negative* and total revenue in part (b) *decreases*, so demand is *inelastic*. At a price of $10, total revenue is at a maximum, demand is unit elastic, and marginal revenue is zero.

◼ **FIGURE 16.3**

Marginal Revenue and Elasticity   MyEconLab Animation

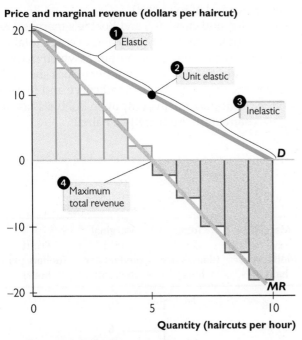

(a) Demand and marginal revenue

(b) Total revenue

As the price falls, if marginal revenue is positive (the blue bars), ❶ demand is elastic; if marginal revenue is zero, ❷ demand is unit elastic; if marginal revenue is negative (the red bars), ❸ demand is inelastic. At zero marginal revenue in part (a), ❹ total revenue is maximized. And at maximum total revenue in part (b), ❺ marginal revenue is zero.

The relationship between marginal revenue and elasticity implies that a monopoly never profitably produces along the inelastic range of its demand curve. If a monopoly did produce along the inelastic range of its demand curve, it could increase total revenue by raising its price and selling a smaller quantity. Also, by producing less, the firm's total cost would fall and the firm's profit would increase. Let's look at a monopoly's output and price decision.

■ Output and Price Decision

To determine the output level and price that maximize a monopoly's profit, we study the behavior of both revenue and costs as output varies.

Table 16.1 summarizes the information we need about Bobbie's revenue, costs, and economic profit. Economic profit, which equals total revenue minus total cost, is maximized at $12 an hour when Bobbie sells 3 haircuts an hour for $14 each. If she sold 2 haircuts for $16 each, her economic profit would be only $9. And if she sold 4 haircuts for $12 each, her economic profit would be only $8.

You can see why 3 haircuts is Bobbie's profit-maximizing output by looking at the marginal revenue and marginal cost. When Bobbie increases output from 2 to 3 haircuts, her marginal revenue is $10 and her marginal cost is $7. Profit increases by the difference, $3 an hour. If Bobbie increases output yet further, from 3 to 4 haircuts, her marginal revenue is $6 and her marginal cost is $10. In this case, marginal cost exceeds marginal revenue by $4, so profit decreases by $4 an hour.

Figure 16.4 illustrates the information contained in Table 16.1. Part (a) shows Bobbie's total revenue curve (*TR*) and her total cost curve (*TC*). It also shows Bobbie's economic profit as the vertical distance between the *TR* and *TC* curves. Bobbie maximizes her profit at 3 haircuts an hour and earns an economic profit of $12 an hour ($42 of total revenue minus $30 of total cost).

Figure 16.4(b) shows the market demand curve (*D*) and Bobbie's marginal revenue curve (*MR*) along with her marginal cost curve (*MC*) and average total cost curve (*ATC*). Bobbie maximizes profit by producing the output at which marginal cost equals marginal revenue—3 haircuts an hour. But what price does she charge for a haircut? To set the price, the monopoly uses the demand curve and finds the highest price at which it can sell the profit-maximizing output. In Bobbie's case, the highest price at which she can sell 3 haircuts an hour is $14 a haircut.

■ **TABLE 16.1**

A Monopoly's Output and Price Decision

	Price (dollars per haircut)	Quantity demanded (haircuts per hour)	Total revenue (dollars per hour)	Marginal revenue (dollars per haircut)	Total cost (dollars per hour)	Marginal cost (dollars per haircut)	Profit (dollars per hour)
A	20	0	0		12		−12
				18		5	
B	18	1	18		17		1
				14		6	
C	16	2	32		23		9
				10		7	
D	14	3	42		30		12
				6		10	
E	12	4	48		40		8
				2		15	
F	10	5	50		55		−5

When Bobbie produces 3 haircuts an hour, her average total cost is $10 (read from the *ATC* curve at the quantity 3 haircuts) and her price is $14 (read from the *D* curve). Her profit per haircut is $4 ($14 minus $10). Bobbie's economic profit is shown by the blue rectangle, which equals the profit per haircut ($4) multiplied by the number of haircuts (3 an hour), for a total of $12 an hour.

A positive economic profit is an incentive for firms to enter a market. But barriers to entry prevent that from happening in a monopoly. So in a monopoly, the firm can make a positive economic profit and continue to do so indefinitely.

A monopoly charges a price that exceeds marginal cost, but does it always make an economic profit? The answer is no. Bobbie makes a positive economic profit in Figure 16.4. But suppose that Bobbie's landlord increases the rent on her barbershop. If Bobbie pays an additional $12 an hour in shop rent, her fixed cost increases by that amount. Her marginal cost and marginal revenue don't change, so her profit-maximizing output remains at 3 haircuts an hour. Her profit decreases by the additional rent of $12 an hour to zero. If Bobbie pays more than an additional $12 an hour for rent, she incurs an economic loss. If this situation were permanent, Bobbie would go out of business. But monopoly entrepreneurs are creative, and Bobbie might find another shop at a lower rent.

FIGURE 16.4

A Monopoly's Profit-Maximizing Output and Price   MyEconLab Animation

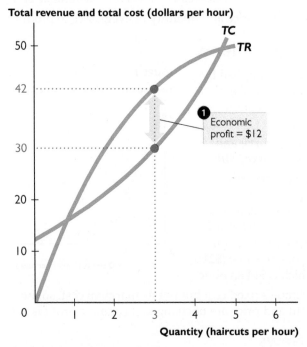

(a) Total revenue and total cost

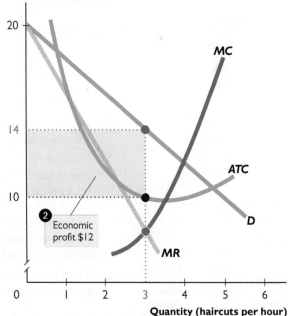

(b) Demand, marginal revenue, and marginal cost

In part (a), economic profit is maximized when total revenue (*TR*) minus total cost (*TC*) is greatest. **1** Economic profit is the vertical distance between the *TR* and *TC* curves. The profit-maximizing output is 3 haircuts an hour and economic profit is $12 an hour.

In part (b), economic profit is maximized when marginal cost (*MC*) equals marginal revenue (*MR*). The price is determined by the demand curve (*D*) and is $14. **2** Economic profit, the blue rectangle, is $12—the profit per haircut ($4) multiplied by 3 haircuts.

MyEconLab Study Plan 16.2
Solutions Video

CHECKPOINT 16.2

Explain how a single-price monopoly determines its output and price.

Practice Problems

Minnie's Mineral Springs is a single-price monopoly. Table 1 shows the demand schedule for Minnie's spring water (columns 1 and 2) and the firm's total cost schedule (columns 2 and 3).

1. Calculate Minnie's total revenue and marginal revenue schedules.
2. Draw the demand curve and Minnie's marginal revenue curve.
3. Calculate Minnie's profit-maximizing output, price, and economic profit.
4. If Minnie's is hit with a conservation tax of $14 an hour, what are Minnie's new profit-maximizing output, price, and economic profit?

TABLE 1

Price (dollars per bottle)	Quantity (bottles per hour)	Total cost (dollars per hour)
10	0	1
9	1	2
8	2	4
7	3	7
6	4	12
5	5	18

In the News

Macy's and Luxottica sign exclusive agreement

Macy's and Luxottica will add 500 LensCrafters locations to their current 670 locations of Sunglass Hut. Together, Macy's and Sunglass Hut have more than tripled the size of the sunglass business at Macy's in the past six years. Luxottica makes most of the eyewear sold in North America.

Source: *Business Wire*, November 11, 2015

How does Luxottica determine the price and quantity of eyeglasses to produce?

Solutions to Practice Problems

TABLE 2

Quantity (bottles per hour)	Total revenue (dollars per hour)	Marginal revenue (dollars per bottle)
0	0	
1	9	9
2	16	7
3	21	5
4	24	3
5	25	1

1. Total revenue equals price multiplied by quantity sold. Marginal revenue equals the change in total revenue when the quantity increases by one unit (Table 2).

2. Figure 1 shows the demand curve and Minnie's marginal revenue curve, *MR*.

3. Marginal cost, *MC*, is the change in total cost when the quantity produced increases by 1 bottle (Table 3). Profit is maximized when $MR = MC$ by producing 3 bottles an hour (Figure 1). The price is $7 a bottle. Economic profit equals total revenue ($21) minus total cost ($7), which is $14 an hour.

FIGURE 1

Price and cost (dollars per bottle)

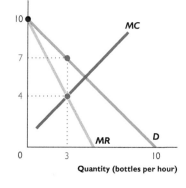

Quantity (bottles per hour)

TABLE 3

Quantity (bottles per hour)	Total cost (dollars per hour)	Marginal cost (dollars per bottle)
0	1	
1	2	1
2	4	2
3	7	3
4	12	5
5	18	6

4. The $14 tax increases Minnie's fixed cost but not its marginal cost, so the profit-maximizing output and price are unchanged. Economic profit is zero.

Solution to In the News

Luxottica is (almost) a monopoly and it sets the price of eyeglasses to maximize economic profit. Luxottica knows its total costs, so it calculates the marginal cost of a pair of glasses. The firm uses its market experience to estimate the demand for glasses and calculates marginal revenue. The firm produces the number of pairs of glasses that makes marginal revenue equal to marginal cost and sets the highest price that its customers are willing to pay for the profit-maximizing quantity.

16.3   MONOPOLY AND COMPETITION COMPARED

MyEconLab Concept Video

Imagine a market in which many small firms operate in perfect competition. Then suppose that a single firm buys out all these small firms and creates a monopoly. What happens in this market to the quantity produced, the price, and efficiency?

■ Output and Price

Figure 16.5 shows the market that we'll study. The market demand curve is D. Initially, with many small firms in the market, the market supply curve is S, which is the sum of the supply curves—and marginal cost curves—of the firms. The equilibrium price is P_C, which makes the quantity demanded equal the quantity supplied. The equilibrium quantity is Q_C. Each firm takes the price P_C and maximizes its profit by producing the output at which its own marginal cost equals the price.

A single firm now buys all the firms in this market. Consumers don't change, so the demand curve doesn't change. But the monopoly recognizes this demand curve as a constraint on its sales and knows that its marginal revenue curve is MR.

The market supply curve in perfect competition is the sum of the marginal cost curves of the firms in the industry. So the monopoly's marginal cost curve is the market supply curve of perfect competition—labeled $S = MC$. The monopoly maximizes profit by producing the quantity at which marginal revenue equals marginal cost, which is Q_M. This output is smaller than the competitive output, Q_C. The monopoly charges the price P_M, which is higher than P_C.

> **Compared to perfect competition, a single-price monopoly produces a smaller output and charges a higher price.**

FIGURE 16.5

Monopoly's Smaller Output and Higher Price

MyEconLab Animation

❶ A competitive industry produces the quantity Q_C at price P_C.

❷ A single-price monopoly produces the quantity Q_M at which marginal revenue equals marginal cost and sells that quantity for the price P_M. Compared to perfect competition, a single-price monopoly produces a smaller output and raises the price.

◼ Is Monopoly Efficient?

You learned in Chapter 6 that resources are used efficiently when marginal benefit equals marginal cost. Figure 16.6(a) shows that perfect competition achieves this efficient use of resources. The demand curve ($D = MB$) shows the marginal benefit to consumers. The supply curve ($S = MC$) shows the marginal cost (opportunity cost) to producers. At the competitive equilibrium, the price is P_C and the quantity is Q_C. Marginal benefit equals marginal cost, and resource use is efficient. Total surplus (Chapter 6, p. 155), the sum of *consumer surplus*, the green triangle, and *producer surplus*, the blue area, is maximized.

Figure 16.6(b) shows that monopoly is inefficient. Monopoly output is Q_M and price is P_M. Price (marginal benefit) exceeds marginal cost and the underproduction creates a *deadweight loss* (Chapter 6, p. 157), which is shown by the gray area. Consumers lose partly by getting less of the good, shown by the gray triangle above P_C, and partly by paying more for the good. Consumer surplus shrinks to the smaller green triangle. Producers lose by selling less of the good, shown by the part of the gray area below P_C, but gain by selling their output for a higher price, shown by the dark blue rectangle. Producer surplus expands and is larger in monopoly than in perfect competition.

◼ **FIGURE 16.6**

The Inefficiency of Monopoly   MyEconLab Animation

(a) Perfect competition

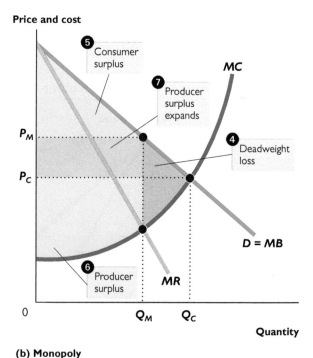

(b) Monopoly

In perfect competition, ❶ the equilibrium quantity is the efficient quantity, Q_C, because at that quantity the price, P_C, equals marginal benefit and marginal cost. The sum of ❷ consumer surplus and ❸ producer surplus is maximized.

In a single-price monopoly, the equilibrium quantity, Q_M, is inefficient because the price, P_M, which equals marginal benefit, exceeds marginal cost. ❹ A deadweight loss arises. ❺ Consumer surplus shrinks, and ❻ producer surplus expands by the area ❼.

■ Is Monopoly Fair?

Monopoly is inefficient because it creates a deadweight loss. But monopoly also *redistributes* consumer surplus. The producer gains, and the consumers lose.

Figure 16.6 shows this redistribution. The monopoly gets the difference between the higher price, P_M, and the competitive price, P_C, on the quantity sold, Q_M. So the dark blue rectangle shows the part of the consumer surplus taken by the monopoly. This portion of the loss of consumer surplus is not a loss to society. It is redistribution from consumers to the monopoly producer.

Are the gain for the monopoly and the loss for consumers fair? You learned about two standards of fairness in Chapter 6: fair *rules* and a fair *result*. Redistribution from the rich to the poor is consistent with the fair-result view. So on this view of fairness, whether monopoly redistribution is fair or unfair depends on who is richer: the monopoly or the consumers of its product. It might be either. Whether the *rules* are fair depends on whether the monopoly has benefited from a protected position that is not available to anyone else. If everyone is free to acquire the monopoly, then the rules are fair. So monopoly is inefficient and it might be, but is not always, unfair.

The pursuit of monopoly profit leads to an additional costly activity that we'll now describe: rent seeking.

■ Rent Seeking

Rent seeking is the lobbying for special treatment from the government to create economic profit or to divert consumer surplus or producer surplus away from others. ("Rent" is a general term in economics that includes all forms of surplus such as consumer surplus, producer surplus, and economic profit.) Rent seeking does not always create a monopoly, but it always restricts competition and often creates a monopoly.

Rent seeking
The lobbying for special treatment from the government to create economic profit or to divert consumer surplus or producer surplus away from others.

Scarce resources can be used to produce the goods and services that people value or they can be used in rent seeking. Rent seeking is potentially profitable for the rent seeker but costly to society because it uses scarce resources purely to transfer wealth from one person or group to another person or group rather than to produce the things that people value.

To see why rent seeking occurs, think about the two ways in which a person might become the owner of a monopoly:

- Buy a monopoly.
- Create a monopoly.

Buy a Monopoly

A person might try to make a monopoly profit by buying a firm (or a right) that is protected by a barrier to entry. Buying a taxicab medallion in New York City is an example. The number of medallions is restricted, so their owners are protected from unlimited entry into the industry. A person who wants to operate a taxi must buy a medallion from someone who already has one.

But anyone is free to enter the bidding for a medallion. So competition among buyers drives the price up to the point at which they make only zero economic profit. For example, competition for the right to operate a taxi in New York City has led to a price of $600,000 for a taxi medallion, which is sufficiently high to eliminate economic profit for taxi operators and leave entrepreneurs with only normal profit.

Create a Monopoly

Because buying a monopoly means paying a price that soaks up the economic profit, creating a monopoly by rent seeking is an attractive alternative to buying one. Rent seeking is a political activity. It takes the form of lobbying and trying to influence the political process to get laws that create legal barriers to entry. Such influence might be sought by making campaign contributions in exchange for legislative support or by indirectly seeking to influence political outcomes through publicity in the media or by direct contact with politicians and bureaucrats. An example of a rent created in this way is the law that restricts the quantities of textiles that can be imported into the United States. Another is a law that limits the quantity of tomatoes that can be imported into the United States. These laws restrict competition, which decreases the quantity for sale and increases prices.

Rent-Seeking Equilibrium

Rent seeking is a competitive activity. If an economic profit is available, a rent seeker will try to get some of it. Competition among rent seekers pushes up the cost of rent seeking until it leaves the monopoly earning only a zero economic profit after paying the rent-seeking costs.

Figure 16.7 shows a rent-seeking equilibrium. The cost of rent seeking is a fixed cost that must be added to a monopoly's other costs. The average total cost curve, which includes the fixed cost of rent seeking, shifts upward until it just touches the demand curve. Consumer surplus is unaffected. But the deadweight loss of monopoly now includes the original deadweight loss plus the economic profit consumed by rent seeking, which the enlarged gray area shows.

FIGURE 16.7

Rent-Seeking Equilibrium

MyEconLab Animation

❶ Rent-seeking costs exhaust economic profit. The firm's rent-seeking costs are fixed costs. They increase total fixed cost and average total cost. The *ATC* curve shifts upward until, at the profit-maximizing price, the firm breaks even.

❷ Monopoly profit-maximization shrinks consumer surplus relative to its maximum level in perfect competition, but rent-seeking doesn't shrink consumer surplus any further.

❸ The deadweight loss increases and now includes the original deadweight loss plus the economic profit consumed by rent seeking.

CHECKPOINT 16.3

MyEconLab Study Plan 16.3
Key Terms Quiz
Solutions Video

Compare the performance of a single-price monopoly with that of perfect competition.

Practice Problems

Township is a small isolated community served by one newspaper that can meet the market demand at a lower cost than two or more newspapers could. The *Township Gazette* is the only source of news. Figure 1 shows the marginal cost of printing the *Township Gazette* and the market demand for it. The *Township Gazette* is a profit-maximizing, single-price monopoly.

1. How many copies of the *Township Gazette* are printed each day and what is the price of the *Township Gazette*?
2. What is the efficient number of copies of the *Township Gazette* and what is the price at which the efficient number of copies could be sold?
3. Is the number of copies printed the efficient quantity? Explain your answer.
4. On the graph, show the consumer surplus that is redistributed from consumers to the *Township Gazette* and the deadweight loss that arises because the *Township Gazette* is a monopoly.

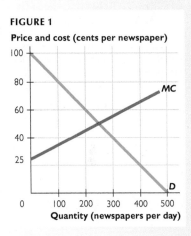

FIGURE 1

Price and cost (cents per newspaper)

In the News

Ticketmaster's near monopoly challenged as technology changes
In the 1990s, to see Michael Jordan or Garth Brooks live you had to buy the ticket through Ticketmaster, or from a scalper. Today, Ticketmaster has merged with concert promoter Live Nation and now controls the sale of tickets to sports and music events. Competitors have entered the market, and event tickets are now sold through Internet auction markets.

How will the increased competition in the sale of tickets affect the service fee component of the price and the efficiency of the market? Will scalpers survive?

Solutions to Practice Problems

1. The profit-maximizing quantity of the *Township Gazette* is 150 a day, where marginal revenue equals marginal cost. The price is 70¢ a copy (Figure 2).
2. The efficient quantity is 250 copies, where quantity demanded (marginal benefit) equals marginal cost and the price would be 50¢ a copy (Figure 2).
3. The number of copies printed is not efficient because the marginal benefit of the 150th copy (70¢) exceeds its marginal cost (40¢) (Figure 2).
4. In Figure 2, the blue rectangle ❶ shows the consumer surplus transferred from the consumers to the *Township Gazette* and the gray triangle ❷ shows the deadweight loss created.

Solution to In the News

The price you pay for an event ticket is the sum of the price of the event plus a service fee. As a monopoly, Ticketmaster charges the profit-maximizing fee. The monopoly has weakened and competition has increased, but sellers still charge the profit-maximizing fee, although a lower fee. The ticket-selling market is more efficient, but scalpers now compete with resale auctions and appear to survive.

FIGURE 2

Price and cost (cents per newspaper)

MyEconLab Concept Video

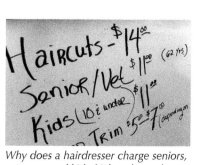

Why does a hairdresser charge seniors, veterans, and kids $3 less than other customers?

16.4   PRICE DISCRIMINATION

Price discrimination—selling a good or service at a number of different prices—is widespread. You encounter it when you travel, go to the movies, get your hair cut, buy pizza, or visit an art museum. At first sight, it appears that price discrimination contradicts the assumption of profit maximization. Why would a movie operator allow children to see movies at half price? Why would a hairdresser charge students and senior citizens less? Aren't these firms losing profit by being nice to their customers?

Deeper investigation shows that far from lowering profit, price discriminators make a bigger profit than they would otherwise. So a monopoly has an incentive to find ways of discriminating and charging each buyer the highest possible price. Some people pay less with price discrimination, but others pay more.

Most price discriminators are *not* monopolies, but monopolies do price discriminate when they can. To be able to price discriminate, a firm must

- Identify and separate different types of buyers.
- Sell a product that cannot be resold.

Price discrimination is charging different prices for a single good or service because the willingness to pay varies across buyers. Not all price *differences* are price *discrimination*. Some goods that are similar but not identical have different prices because they have different production costs. For example, the cost of producing electricity depends on time of day. If an electric power company charges a higher price for consumption between 7:00 and 9:00 in the morning and between 4:00 and 7:00 in the evening than it does at other times of the day, the company is not price discriminating.

■ Price Discrimination and Consumer Surplus

The key idea behind price discrimination is to convert consumer surplus into economic profit. To extract every dollar of consumer surplus from every buyer, the monopoly would have to offer each individual customer a separate price schedule based on that customer's own willingness to pay. Such price discrimination cannot be carried out in practice because a firm does not have enough information about each consumer's demand curve. But firms try to extract as much consumer surplus as possible, and to do so, they discriminate in two broad ways:

- Among groups of buyers
- Among units of a good

Discriminating Among Groups of Buyers

To price discriminate among groups of buyers, the firm offers different prices to different types of buyers, based on things such as age, employment status, or some other easily distinguished characteristic. This type of price discrimination works when each group has a different average willingness to pay for the good or service.

For example, a face-to-face sales meeting with a customer might bring a large and profitable order. For salespeople and other business travelers, the marginal benefit from an airplane trip is large and the price that such a traveler will pay for a trip is high. In contrast, for a vacation traveler, any of several different trips or even no vacation trip are options. So for vacation travelers, the marginal benefit of a trip is small and the price that such a traveler will pay for a trip is low. Because business travelers are willing to pay more than vacation travelers are, it is possible for an airline to profit by price discriminating between these two groups.

Discriminating Among Units of a Good

To price discriminate among units of a good, the firm charges the same prices to all its customers but offers a lower price per unit for a larger number of units bought. When Pizza Hut charges $10 for one home-delivered pizza and $14 for two, it is using this type of price discrimination. In this example, the price of the second pizza is only $4.

Let's see how an airline exploits the differences in demand by business and vacation travelers and increases its profit by price discriminating.

■ Profiting by Price Discriminating

Global Air has a monopoly on an exotic route. Figure 16.8 shows the demand curve (*D*) for travel on this route and Global Air's marginal revenue curve (*MR*). It also shows Global Air's marginal cost (*MC*) and average total cost (*ATC*) curves.

Initially, Global is a single-price monopoly and maximizes its profit by producing 8,000 trips a year (the quantity at which *MR* equals *MC*). The price is $1,200 a trip. The average total cost of a trip is $600, so economic profit is $600 a trip. On 8,000 trips, Global's economic profit is $4.8 million a year, shown by the blue rectangle. Global's customers enjoy a consumer surplus shown by the green triangle.

FIGURE 16.8

A Single-Price Monopoly's Price and Economic Profit

MyEconLab Animation

Global Air has a monopoly on an air route. The demand curve for travel on this route is *D*, and Global's marginal revenue curve is *MR*. Its marginal cost curve is *MC*, and its average total cost curve is *ATC*.

As a single-price monopoly, Global maximizes profit by selling 8,000 trips a year at $1,200 a trip.

❶ Global's customers enjoy a consumer surplus—the green triangle.

❷ Global makes an economic profit of $4.8 million a year—the blue rectangle.

Global is struck by the fact that many of its customers are business travelers, and Global suspects that they are willing to pay more than $1,200 a trip. So Global does some market research, which tells Global that some business travelers are willing to pay as much as $1,800 a trip. Also, these customers almost always make their travel plans at the last moment. Another group of business travelers is willing to pay $1,600. These customers know a week ahead when they will travel, and prefer a flexible ticket. Yet another group is willing to pay up to $1,400. These travelers know two weeks ahead when they will travel, and they are happy to buy a restricted ticket.

So Global announces a new fare schedule: No restrictions, $1,800; 7-day advance purchase, flexible, $1,600; 14-day advance purchase, flexible, $1,400; 14-day advance purchase, must stay at least 7 days, $1,200.

Figure 16.9 shows the outcome with this new fare structure and also shows why Global is pleased with its new fares. It sells 2,000 trips at each of its four prices. Global's economic profit increases by the area of the blue steps in the figure. Its economic profit is now its original $4.8 million a year plus an additional $2.4 million from its new higher fares. Consumer surplus has shrunk to the sum of the smaller green triangles.

■ Perfect Price Discrimination

Perfect price discrimination
Price discrimination that extracts the entire consumer surplus by charging the highest price that consumers are willing to pay for each unit.

But Global thinks that it can do even better. It plans to achieve **perfect price discrimination**, which extracts the entire consumer surplus by charging the highest price that consumers are willing to pay for each unit. To do so, Global must get creative and come up with a host of additional business fares ranging between $2,000 and $1,200, each one of which appeals to a small segment of the business market.

■ **FIGURE 16.9**

Price Discrimination   MyEconLab Animation

Global revises its fare structure. It now offers no restrictions at $1,800; 7-day advance purchase, flexible at $1,600; 14-day advance purchase, flexible at $1,400; and 14-day advance purchase, must stay at least 7 days, at $1,200.

Global sells 2,000 units at each of its four new fares. Its economic profit increases by $2.4 million a year to $7.2 million a year, which is shown by the original profit (light blue rectangle) plus the blue steps. Global's customers' consumer surplus shrinks to the sum of the green areas.

Once Global is discriminating finely between different customers and getting from each customer the maximum he or she is willing to pay, something special happens to marginal revenue. Recall that for the single-price monopoly, marginal revenue is less than price. The reason is that when the price is cut to sell a larger quantity, the price is lower on all units sold. But with perfect price discrimination, Global sells only the marginal seat at the lower price. All the other customers continue to buy the trip at the highest price they are willing to pay. So for the perfect price discriminator, marginal revenue equals price and the demand curve becomes the marginal revenue curve.

With marginal revenue equal to price, Global can obtain yet greater profit by increasing output up to the point at which price (and marginal revenue) is equal to marginal cost.

So Global now seeks additional travelers who will not pay as much as $1,200 a trip but who will pay more than marginal cost. More creative pricing comes up with vacation specials and other fares that have combinations of advance reservation, minimum stay, and other restrictions that make these fares unattractive to Global's existing customers but attractive to a further group of travelers. With all these fares and specials, Global extracts the entire consumer surplus and maximizes economic profit.

Figure 16.10 shows the outcome with perfect price discrimination. The dozens of fares paid by the original travelers who are willing to pay between $1,200 and $2,000 have extracted the entire consumer surplus from this group and converted it into economic profit for Global. The new fares between $900 and $1,200 have attracted 3,000 additional travelers but have taken their entire consumer surplus also. Global is making an economic profit of more than $9 million a year.

FIGURE 16.10

Perfect Price Discrimination

MyEconLab Animation

With perfect price discrimination, the demand curve becomes Global's marginal revenue curve. Economic profit is maximized when the lowest price equals marginal cost.

❶ Global increases output to 11,000 trips a year.

❷ Global's economic profit increases to $9.35 million a year.

EYE on the U.S. ECONOMY
Airline Price Discrimination

United Airlines' normal flexible economy fare from San Francisco to Washington, D.C., is $897, but it has a range of cheaper fares with its lowest-price ticket at $239. On a typical flight, passengers might be paying as many as 20 different fares.

The airlines sort their customers according to their willingness to pay by offering a variety of options that attract price-sensitive leisure travelers but don't get bought by business travelers.

Despite the sophistication of the airlines' pricing schemes, almost 15 percent of seats fly empty. The marginal cost of filling an empty seat is close to zero, so a ticket sold at a few dollars would be profitable.

The airlines compete with online booking sites. Low fares are now feasible, thanks to dozens of online travel agents. Shopping around the airlines with bids from travelers, these travel agents broker thousands of tickets a day and obtain the lowest possible fares for their customers.

Would it bother you to hear how little I paid for this flight?

Credit: William Hamilton

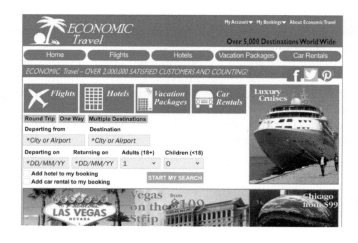

■ Price Discrimination and Efficiency

With perfect price discrimination, the monopoly increases output to the point at which price equals marginal cost. This output is identical to that of perfect competition. Perfect price discrimination pushes consumer surplus to zero but increases producer surplus to equal the sum of consumer surplus and producer surplus in perfect competition. Deadweight loss with perfect price discrimination is zero. So perfect price discrimination produces the efficient quantity.

But there are two differences between perfect competition and perfect price discrimination. First, the distribution of the total surplus is different. It is shared by consumers and producers in perfect competition while the producer gets it all with perfect price discrimination. Second, because the producer grabs all the total surplus, rent seeking becomes profitable.

Rent seekers use resources in pursuit of monopoly, and the bigger the rents, the greater is the incentive to use resources to pursue those rents. With free entry into rent seeking, the long-run equilibrium outcome is that rent seekers use up the entire producer surplus.

CHECKPOINT 16.4

Explain how price discrimination increases profit.

Practice Problems

Village, a small isolated town, has one doctor. For a 30-minute consultation, the doctor charges a rich person twice as much as a poor person.

1. Does the doctor practice price discrimination? Is the doctor using resources efficiently? Does the doctor's pricing scheme redistribute consumer surplus? If so, explain how.

2. If the doctor decided to charge everyone the maximum price that he or she would be willing to pay, what would be the consumer surplus? Would the market for medical service in Village be efficient?

In the News

Where to find the best travel deals

Travel discounts as high as 50 percent are available if you know where to look for them. Examples are companion and two-for-one sales on airlines and Amtrak, and second-, third-, fourth-, or fifth-night-free deals offered by hotels. A Southwest Airlines' senior fare can be up to 40 percent less than other discounted fares.

Source: *USA Today*, December 10, 2015

How do airlines, railroads, and hotels increase profit by price discriminating?

Solutions to Practice Problems

1. The doctor practices price discrimination because rich people and poor people pay a different price for the same service: a 30-minute consultation. The doctor provides the profit-maximizing number of consultations and charges rich people more than poor people. As a monopoly, the total number of consultations is less than that at which marginal benefit equals the marginal cost of providing the medical service. Because marginal benefit does not equal marginal cost, the doctor is not using resources efficiently. With price discrimination, some consumer surplus is redistributed to the doctor as profit.

2. The doctor decides to practice perfect price discrimination. If successful, with perfect price discrimination, marginal revenue equals price. To maximize economic profit, the doctor increases the number of consultations to make the lowest price charged equal to the marginal cost of providing the service. The doctor takes the entire consumer surplus, so consumer surplus is zero.
    Marginal benefit equals price, so resources are being used efficiently.

Solution to In the News

A trip by air or rail or a night in a hotel cannot be resold, so price discrimination is possible. Offering a discount is price discrimination. Price discrimination is profitable because marginal cost is lower than the single-price monopoly's profit-maximizing price. Selling additional units for a discountd price that is greater than marginal cost increases economic profit.

16.5 MONOPOLY REGULATION

Natural monopoly presents a dilemma. With economies of scale, a natural monopoly produces at the lowest possible cost. But with market power, the monopoly has an incentive to raise the price above the competitive price and produce too little—to operate in the self-interest of the monopoly and not in the social interest.

Regulation—rules administered by a government agency to influence prices, quantities, entry, and other aspects of economic activity in a firm or industry—is a possible solution to this dilemma.

To implement regulation, the government establishes agencies to oversee and enforce the rules. For example, the Surface Transportation Board regulates prices on interstate railroads and some trucking and bus lines, and water and oil pipelines. By the 1970s, almost a quarter of the nation's output was produced by regulated industries (far more than just natural monopolies) and a process of deregulation began.

Deregulation is the process of removing regulation of prices, quantities, entry, and other aspects of economic activity in a firm or industry. During the past 30 years, deregulation has occurred in domestic air transportation, telephone service, interstate trucking, and banking and financial services. Cable TV was deregulated in 1984, re-regulated in 1992, and deregulated again in 1996.

Regulation is a *possible* solution to the dilemma presented by monopoly but not a sure-bet solution. There are two theories about how regulation actually works: the *social interest theory* and the *capture theory*.

The **social interest theory** is that the political and regulatory process relentlessly seeks out inefficiency and introduces regulation that eliminates deadweight loss and allocates resources efficiently.

The **capture theory** is that the political and regulatory process gets captured by the regulated firm and ends up serving its self-interest, with maximum economic profit, underproduction, and deadweight loss. The regulator gets captured because the producer's gain is large and visible while each individual consumer's gain is small and invisible. No individual consumer has an incentive to oppose the regulation, but the producer has a big incentive to lobby for it.

Which theory of regulation best explains real-world regulations? Does regulation serve the social interest or the self-interest of monopoly producers?

■ Efficient Regulation of a Natural Monopoly

A cable TV company is a *natural monopoly* (pp. 404–405)—it can supply the entire market at a lower price than two or more competing firms can. Cox Communications, based in Atlanta, supplies cable TV to households in 16 states. It has invested heavily in satellite receiving dishes, cables, and control equipment and so has large fixed costs. These fixed costs are part of the company's average total cost. Its average total cost decreases as the number of households served increases because the fixed cost is spread over a larger number of households. Unregulated, Cox Communications serves the number of households that maximizes profit. Like all single-price monopolies, the profit-maximizing quantity is less than the efficient quantity and underproduction results in a deadweight loss (see Figure 16.6, p. 414).

How can Cox be regulated to produce the efficient quantity of cable TV service? The answer is by being regulated to set its price equal to marginal cost, known as the **marginal cost pricing rule**. The quantity demanded at a price equal

Regulation
Rules administered by a government agency to influence prices, quantities, entry, and other aspects of economic activity in a firm or industry.

Deregulation
The process of removing regulation of prices, quantities, entry, and other aspects of economic activity in a firm or industry.

Social interest theory
The theory that regulation achieves an efficient allocation of resources.

Capture theory
The theory that the regulation serves the self-interest of the producer and results in maximum profit, underproduction, and deadweight loss.

Marginal cost pricing rule
A rule that sets price equal to marginal cost to achieve an efficient output.

to marginal cost is the efficient quantity—the quantity at which marginal benefit equals marginal cost.

Figure 16.11 illustrates the marginal cost pricing rule. The demand curve for cable TV is *D*. Cox's marginal cost curve is *MC*. That marginal cost curve is (assumed to be) horizontal at $10 per household per month—that is, the cost of providing each additional household with a month of cable programming is $10. The efficient outcome occurs if the price is regulated at $10 per household per month with 8 million households served.

But there is a problem: Because average total cost exceeds marginal cost, a firm that follows the marginal cost pricing rule incurs an economic loss. So a cable TV company that is required to use a marginal cost pricing rule will not stay in business for long. How can the firm cover its costs and, at the same time, obey a marginal cost pricing rule?

One possibility is price discrimination (see pp. 418–422). Another possibility is to use a two-part price (called a *two-part tariff*). For example, local telephone companies charge consumers a monthly fee for being connected to the telephone system and then charge a price equal to marginal cost (zero) for each local call. A cable TV operator can charge a one-time connection fee that covers its fixed cost and then charge a monthly fee equal to marginal cost.

■ Second-Best Regulation of a Natural Monopoly

Regulation of a natural monopoly cannot always achieve an efficient outcome. Two possible ways of enabling a regulated monopoly to avoid an economic loss are

- Average cost pricing
- Government subsidy

■ FIGURE 16.11

Natural Monopoly: Marginal Cost Pricing   MyEconLab Animation

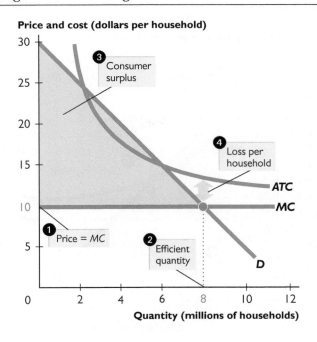

The market demand curve for cable TV is *D*. A cable TV operator's marginal cost *MC* is a constant $10 per household per month. Its fixed cost is large, and the average total cost curve, which includes average fixed cost, is *ATC*.

❶ Price is set equal to marginal cost at $10 a month.

❷ At this price, the efficient quantity (8 million households) is served.

❸ Consumer surplus is maximized as shown by the green triangle.

❹ The firm incurs a loss on each household served, shown by the red arrow.

Average Cost Pricing

Average cost pricing rule
A rule that sets price equal to average total cost to enable a regulated firm to avoid economic loss.

The **average cost pricing rule** sets price equal to average total cost. With this rule the firm produces the quantity at which the average total cost curve cuts the demand curve. This rule results in the firm making zero economic profit—breaking even. But because for a natural monopoly average total cost exceeds marginal cost, the quantity produced is less than the efficient quantity and a deadweight loss arises. Figure 16.12 illustrates the average cost pricing rule. The price is $15 a month and 6 million households buy cable TV. The gray triangle shows the deadweight loss.

Government Subsidy

A government subsidy is a direct payment to the firm equal to its economic loss. But to pay a subsidy, the government must raise the revenue by taxing some other activity. You saw in Chapter 8 that taxes themselves generate deadweight loss.

And the Second-Best Is...

Which is the better option, average cost pricing or marginal cost pricing with a government subsidy? The answer turns on the relative magnitudes of the two deadweight losses. Average cost pricing generates a deadweight loss in the market served by the natural monopoly. A subsidy generates deadweight losses in the markets for the items that are taxed to pay the subsidy. The smaller deadweight loss is the second-best solution to regulating a natural monopoly. Making this calculation in practice is too difficult and average cost pricing is generally preferred to a subsidy.

FIGURE 16.12

Natural Monopoly: Average Cost Pricing

MyEconLab Animation

❶ Price is set equal to average total cost at $15 a month.

At this price, ❷ the quantity of households served (6 million) is less than the efficient quantity (8 million households).

❸ Consumer surplus shrinks to the smaller green triangle.

❹ A producer surplus enables the firm to pay its total fixed cost and break even.

❺ A deadweight loss, shown by the gray triangle, arises.

EYE on MICROSOFT

Are Microsoft's Prices Too High?

MyEconLab Critical Thinking Exercise

Microsoft's prices are too high in the sense that they exceed marginal cost and result in fewer copies sold of the Windows operating system and Office application than the efficient quantities.

Profit Maximization

The figure illustrates how Microsoft prices its products to maximize profit. The demand for copies of the Windows operating system is D. The marginal revenue curve is MR. The marginal cost of an additional copy is very small and we assume it to be zero, with marginal cost curve MC.

Profit is maximized by producing the quantity at which marginal revenue equals marginal cost. In the figure, that quantity is 4 million copies of Windows per month. The price is $300 per copy and Microsoft receives a producer surplus shown by the area of the blue rectangle.

Inefficiency

The efficient quantity is 8 million copies per month, where price and marginal benefit equal marginal cost. Because the actual quantity is smaller than the efficient quantity, a deadweight loss arises and the area of the gray triangle shows its magnitude. The area of the green triangle shows the consumer surplus.

Fixed Cost

The marginal cost of a copy of Windows might be close to zero, but the fixed cost of developing the software is large. Microsoft must earn at least enough revenue to pay these fixed costs.

Earning enough to pay the firm's fixed costs does not inevitably lead to inefficiency. Some firms with zero marginal cost and the market power to charge a high price do choose to provide the efficient quantity of their services at a zero price.

The Google Solution

Google is one such firm. The price of an Internet search on Google is zero. The quantity of searches is that at which the marginal benefit of a search equals the zero marginal cost, so the quantity of searches is the efficient quantity.

Google earns revenue, and a very large revenue, by selling advertising that

more than pays its fixed operating costs.

Efficiency

Advertising on Google is more effective than a TV or poster advertisement because it is targeted at potential buyers of products based on the topics of their searches.

The Google solution delivers the efficient quantity of zero-marginal-cost Internet search activity.

The Google solution might also deliver the efficient quantity of advertising. It will do so if Google is able to achieve perfect price discrimination in the market for advertising.

Implementing average cost pricing presents the regulator with a challenge because it is not possible to be sure of a firm's costs. So regulators use one of two practical rules:

- Rate of return regulation
- Price cap regulation

Rate of Return Regulation

Rate of return regulation
A regulation that sets the price at a level that enables a firm to earn a specified target rate of return on its capital.

Under **rate of return regulation**, the price is set at a level that enables the firm to earn a specified target rate of return on its capital. This type of regulation can end up serving the self-interest of the firm rather than the social interest. The firm's managers have an incentive to inflate costs by spending on items such as private jets, free baseball tickets (disguised as public relations expenses), and lavish entertainment. Managers also have an incentive to use more capital than the efficient amount. The *rate* of return on capital is regulated but not the *total* return on capital, and the greater the amount of capital, the greater is the total return.

EYE on YOUR LIFE
Monopoly in Your Everyday Life

MyEconLab Critical Thinking Exercise

When Bill Gates decided to quit Harvard in 1975, he realized that PCs would need an operating system and applications programs to interact with the computer's hardware. He also knew that whoever owned the copyright on these programs would have a license to print money. And he wanted to be that person.

In less than 30 years, Bill Gates became the world's richest person. Such is the power of the right monopoly.

You, along with millions of other PC users, have willingly paid the monopoly price for Windows and Microsoft Office. Sure, the marginal cost of a copy of these programs is close to zero, so the quantity sold is way too few. There is a big deadweight loss.

Compared with the alternative of no Windows, you're better off. But are you better off than you would be if there were many alternatives to Windows competing for your attention? To answer this question, think about the applications—spreadsheets, word processing, and so on—that you need to make your computer useful. With lots of operating systems, what would happen to the cost of developing applications? Would you have more or less choice?

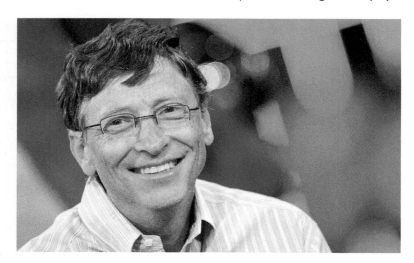

Price Cap Regulation

For the reason that we've just examined, rate of return regulation is increasingly being replaced by price cap regulation. A **price cap regulation** is a price ceiling—a rule that specifies the highest price the firm is permitted to set. This type of regulation lowers the price and gives the firm an incentive to minimize its costs. But what happens to the quantity produced?

Recall that in a competitive market, a price ceiling set below the equilibrium price decreases output and creates a shortage (see Chapter 7, pp. 171–172). In contrast, in natural monopoly a price ceiling increases output. The reason is that at the regulated price, the firm can sell any quantity it chooses up to the quantity demanded. So each additional unit sold brings in the same additional revenue: marginal revenue equals price. The regulated price exceeds marginal cost, so the profit-maximizing quantity becomes the quantity demanded at the price ceiling.

Figure 16.13 illustrates this outcome. Unregulated, a cable TV operator maximizes profit by serving 4 million households at a price of $20 a month. With a price cap set at $15 a month, the firm is permitted to sell any quantity it chooses at that price or at a lower price. The profit-maximizing quantity now increases to 6 million households. Serving fewer than 6 million households, the firm incurs a loss—average total cost exceeds the price cap. Serving more than 6 million households is possible but only by lowering the price along the demand curve. Again, average total cost exceeds price and the firm incurs a loss.

In Figure 16.13, the price cap delivers average cost pricing. In practice, the regulator might set the cap too high. For this reason, price cap regulation is often combined with *earnings sharing regulation*—a regulation that requires firms to make refunds to customers when profits rise above a target level.

Price cap regulation
A rule that specifies the highest price that a firm is permitted to set—a price ceiling.

■ **FIGURE 16.13**

Natural Monopoly: Price Cap Regulation   MyEconLab Animation

❶ With no regulation, a cable TV operator serves 4 million households at a price of $20 a month.

❷ A price cap regulation sets the maximum price at $15 a month.

❸ Only when 6 million households are served can the firm break even. (When fewer than 6 million households are served or more than 6 million households are served, the firm incurs an economic loss.) The firm has an incentive to keep costs as low as possible and to produce the quantity demanded at the price cap.

❹ The price cap regulation lowers the price and increases the number of households served.

MyEconLab Study Plan 16.5

Key Terms Quiz

Solutions Video

CHECKPOINT 16.5

Explain why natural monopoly is regulated and the effects of regulation.

Practice Problems

An unregulated natural monopoly bottles Elixir, a unique health product that has no substitutes. The monopoly's total fixed cost is $150,000, and its marginal cost is 10¢ a bottle. Figure 1 illustrates the demand for Elixir.

1. How many bottles of Elixir does the monopoly sell and what is the price of a bottle of Elixir? Is the monopoly's use of resources efficient?

2. Suppose that the government introduces a marginal cost pricing rule. What is the price of Elixir, the quantity sold, and the monopoly's economic profit?

3. Suppose that the government introduces an average cost pricing rule. What is the price of Elixir, the quantity sold, and the monopoly's economic profit?

In the News

Michigan's oversight of cable TV firms shuts off

Michigan's cable TV subscribers have had to live with soaring monopoly fees, and on January 1, 2016, they became even more vulnerable as funds that regulators had used for cable TV oversight were cut off.

Source: *Detroit Free Press*, December 31, 2015

How could the Michigan regulators have protected cable TV subscribers from rising fees and why, most likely, didn't they?

Solutions to Practice Problems

1. The monopoly will produce 1 million bottles a year—the quantity at which marginal revenue equals marginal cost. The price is 30¢ a bottle—the highest price at which the monopoly can sell the 1 million bottles a year (Figure 2). The monopoly's use of resources is inefficient. If resource use were efficient, the monopoly would produce the quantity at which marginal benefit (price) equals marginal cost: 2 million bottles a year.

2. With a marginal cost pricing rule, the price is 10¢ a bottle and the monopoly produces 2 million bottles a year. The monopoly incurs an economic loss equal to its total fixed costs of $150,000 a year. The monopoly would need a subsidy from the government to keep it in business.

3. With an average cost pricing rule, the firm produces the quantity at which price equals average total cost. Average total cost equals average variable cost plus average fixed cost. Average variable cost equals marginal cost and is 10¢ a bottle. Average fixed cost is $150,000 divided by the quantity produced. For example, at 1 million bottles, average fixed cost is 15¢ and at 1.5 million bottles, average fixed cost is 10¢ a bottle. The average total cost of producing 1.5 million bottles is 20¢ a bottle and they can be sold for 20¢ a bottle. So the monopoly produces 1.5 million bottles a year and breaks even.

Solution to In the News

Rate of return regulation or price cap regulation might have been used to keep cable TV rates close to marginal cost or average total cost. Most likely cable TV prices are not regulated because the cable TV firms have captured the regulator.

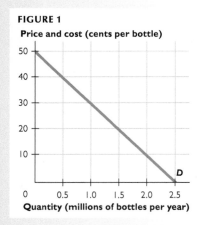

FIGURE 1

Price and cost (cents per bottle)

Quantity (millions of bottles per year)

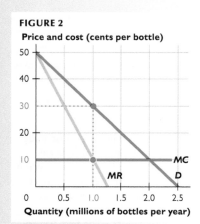

FIGURE 2

Price and cost (cents per bottle)

Quantity (millions of bottles per year)

CHAPTER SUMMARY

Key Points

1. **Explain how monopoly arises and distinguish between single-price monopoly and price-discriminating monopoly.**

   - In monopoly, a single producer of a good or service that has no close substitutes operates behind a natural, legal, or ownership barrier to entry.
   - A monopoly can price discriminate when there is no resale possibility.
   - Where resale is possible, a firm charges a single price.

2. **Explain how a single-price monopoly determines its output and price.**

   - The demand for a monopoly's output is the market demand, and a single-price monopoly's marginal revenue is less than price.
   - A monopoly maximizes profit by producing the quantity at which marginal revenue equals marginal cost and by charging the maximum price that consumers are willing to pay for that quantity.

3. **Compare the performance of a single-price monopoly with that of perfect competition.**

   - A single-price monopoly price is higher and quantity produced is smaller than in a perfectly competitive market and a deadweight loss arises.
   - Monopoly imposes a loss on society that equals its deadweight loss plus the cost of the resources devoted to rent seeking.

4. **Explain how price discrimination increases profit.**

   - Perfect price discrimination captures the entire consumer surplus. Prices are the highest that each consumer is willing to pay for each unit.
   - With perfect price discrimination, the monopoly is efficient but rent seeking uses some or all of the producer surplus.

5. **Explain why natural monopoly is regulated and the effects of regulation.**

   - Regulation might achieve an efficient use of resources or help the monopoly to maximize economic profit.
   - A natural monopoly is efficient if its price equals marginal cost, but a second-best outcome is for price to equal average total cost.
   - A price cap supported by earnings sharing regulation is the most effective practical method of regulating a natural monopoly.

Key Terms

MyEconLab Key Terms Quiz

Average cost pricing rule, 426
Barrier to entry, 404
Capture theory, 424
Deregulation, 424
Legal monopoly, 405
Marginal cost pricing rule, 424

Monopoly, 404
Natural monopoly, 404
Perfect price discrimination, 420
Price cap regulation, 429
Price-discriminating monopoly, 406
Rate of return regulation, 428

Regulation, 424
Rent seeking, 415
Single-price monopoly, 406
Social interest theory, 424

MyEconLab Chapter 16 Study Plan

CHAPTER CHECKPOINT

Study Plan Problems and Applications

Use the following information to work Problems **1** to **3**.

Elixir Spring produces a unique and highly prized mineral water. The firm's total fixed cost is $5,000 a day, and its marginal cost is zero. Table 1 shows the demand schedule for Elixir Spring water.

TABLE 1

Price (dollars per bottle)	Quantity (bottles per day)
10	0
8	2,000
6	4,000
4	6,000
2	8,000
0	10,000

1. On a graph, show the demand curve for Elixir water and Elixir Spring's marginal revenue curve. What are Elixir's profit-maximizing price, output, and economic profit?

2. Compare Elixir's profit-maximizing price with the marginal cost of producing the profit-maximizing output. At the profit-maximizing price, is the demand for Elixir Spring water inelastic or elastic?

3. Suppose that there are 1,000 springs, all able to produce this water at zero marginal cost and with zero fixed costs. Compare the equilibrium price and quantity produced with Elixir Spring's price and quantity produced.

4. Blue Rose Inc. is the only flower grower to have cracked the secret of making a blue rose. Figure 1 shows the demand for blue roses and the marginal cost of producing a blue rose. What is Blue Rose's profit-maximizing output? What price does Blue Rose Inc. charge and is it efficient?

Hawaii Cable Television is a natural monopoly. Sketch a market demand curve and the firm's cost curves. Use your graph to work Problems **5** to **8**.

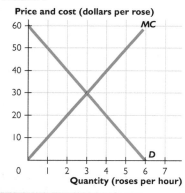

FIGURE 1

Price and cost (dollars per rose)

5. If Hawaii Cable is unregulated and maximizes profit, show in your graph the price, quantity, economic profit, consumer surplus, and deadweight loss.

6. If Hawaii Cable is unregulated and it gives householders a 50 percent discount for second and third connections, describe how its economic profit, consumer surplus, and deadweight loss would change.

7. If Hawaii Cable is regulated in the social interest, show in your graph the price, quantity, economic profit, consumer surplus, and deadweight loss.

8. If Hawaii Cable is subject to a price cap regulation that enables it to break even, show in your graph the price, quantity, economic profit, consumer surplus, and deadweight loss.

Use the following information to work Problems **9** and **10**.

Unfair postal competition

With the rise of e-mail, the volume of snail mail has fallen precipitously, and the U.S. Postal Service has been losing billions of dollars. It is an unjustified legal monopoly that is heavily subsidized and Congress should end it.

Source: The Cato Institute, January 8, 2016

9. Why is the U.S. Postal Service not a natural monopoly? Explain why it could be efficient to keep it in operation with a subsidy.

10. Draw a graph to illustrate the U.S. Postal Service's price, quantity produced, consumer surplus, producer surplus, and deadweight loss.

11. Read *Eye on Microsoft* on p. 427 and explain how Windows' price, quantity bought, consumer surplus, producer surplus, and deadweight loss would change if Microsoft were able to sell ads that appear every time a user opens a program. Illustrate your answer with a graph.

Instructor Assignable Problems and Applications

MyEconLab Homework, Quiz, or Test if assigned by instructor

Use the following information to work Problems **1** and **2**.

Microsoft: We're not gouging Europe on Windows 7 pricing

Regulators in the European Union have charged Microsoft with illegally tying Internet Explorer (IE) to Windows and mandated that a version of Windows be offered stripped of IE. A news report suggested that when Microsoft launches Windows 7, it will charge a higher price for the IE-stripped version than the price for a full version that includes IE. Microsoft denied this report but announced that it would offer the full version of Windows 7 at a lower upgrade price.

Source: computerworld.com

1. How does Microsoft set the price of Windows and would it be in the firm's self-interest to set a different price for a version stripped of IE?

2. Why might Microsoft offer the full version of Windows 7 to European customers at a lower upgrade price?

Use the following information to work Problems **3** and **4**.

Bobbie's Hair Care is a natural monopoly. Table 1 shows the demand schedule (the first two columns) and Bobbie's marginal cost schedule (the middle and third columns). Bobbie has done a survey and discovered that she has four types of customers each hour: one woman who is willing to pay $18, one senior who is willing to pay $16, one student who is willing to pay $14, and one boy who is willing to pay $12. Suppose that Bobbie's fixed costs are $20 an hour and Bobbie's price discriminates.

3. What is the price each type of customer is charged and how many haircuts an hour does Bobbie's sell? What is the increase in Bobbie's economic profit that results from price discrimination?

4. Who benefits from Bobbie's price discrimination? Is the quantity of haircuts efficient?

Use the following information to work Problems **5** to **10**.

Big Top is the only circus in the nation. Table 2 sets out the demand schedule for circus tickets and the cost schedule for producing the circus.

5. Calculate Big Top's profit-maximizing price, output, and economic profit if it charges a single price for all tickets.

6. When Big Top maximizes profit, what is the consumer surplus and producer surplus and is the circus efficient? Explain why or why not.

7. At the market equilibrium price, no children under 10 years old attend the circus. Big Top offers children under 10 a discount of 50 percent. How will this discount change the consumer surplus and producer surplus? Will Big Top be more efficient by offering the discount to children?

8. If Big Top is regulated to produce the efficient output, what is the quantity of tickets sold, what is the price of a ticket, and what would be the consumer surplus?

9. If Big Top is regulated to charge a price equal to average total cost, what is the quantity of tickets sold, the price of a ticket, and economic profit?

10. Draw a graph to illustrate the circus market if regulators set a price cap that enables Big Top to break even. Show the deadweight loss in your graph.

TABLE 1

Price (dollars per haircut)	Quantity (haircuts per hour)	Marginal cost (dollars per hour)
20	0	—
18	1	1
16	2	4
14	3	8
12	4	12
10	5	18

TABLE 2

Price (dollars per ticket)	Quantity (tickets per show)	Total cost (dollars per show)
20	0	1,000
18	100	1,600
16	200	2,200
14	300	2,800
12	400	3,400
10	500	4,000
8	600	4,600
6	700	5,200
4	800	5,800

MyEconLab Chapter 16 Study Plan

Multiple Choice Quiz

1. A firm is a natural monopoly if _____.
   - A. it can produce the good at a price below its competitor's price
   - B. it can produce a larger quantity of the good than other firms
   - C. the government grants it a public franchise or patent
   - D. it can satisfy the market demand at a lower average total cost than other firms

2. A monopoly _____.
   - A. can choose its price and output and always has the option of price discriminating
   - B. is a price taker and by offering a range of discounts can price discriminate
   - C. that produces a good that cannot be resold might choose to price discriminate
   - D. book store that offers a discount on Tuesdays is price discriminating

3. A single-price monopoly maximizes profit by producing the quantity at which _____.
   - A. its total revenue will be as large as possible
   - B. marginal revenue equals marginal cost and setting the price equal to marginal revenue
   - C. marginal revenue equals marginal cost and setting the price equal to marginal cost
   - D. marginal revenue equals marginal cost and setting the price equal to the most people are willing to pay for that quantity

4. A monopoly sets its price such that demand for the good produced is
   _____.
   - A. unit elastic
   - B. inelastic
   - C. elastic
   - D. either elastic or inelastic, but never unit elastic

5. A single-price monopoly is _____.
   - A. inefficient because it converts consumer surplus to producer surplus
   - B. inefficient because it produces too small an output and creates a dead-weight loss
   - C. efficient because buyers are paying a price equal to their willingness to pay
   - D. efficient because it is the only producer of the good

6. A monopoly that price discriminates _____.
   - A. benefits buyers because it offers the good at a variety of prices
   - B. gains because it converts consumer surplus to economic profit
   - C. uses resources more efficiently than would a competitive market
   - D. enables buyers to maximize their consumer surplus

7. Governments regulate natural monopoly by capping the price at _____.
   - A. marginal revenue and allowing the monopoly to maximize profit
   - B. marginal cost so that the monopoly is efficient and makes zero economic profit
   - C. average total cost, which allows the monopoly to be inefficient but make zero economic profit
   - D. the buyers' willingness to pay, which makes the monopoly operate efficiently

Which smartphone?

Monopolistic Competition

17

When you have completed your study of this chapter, you will be able to

1 Describe and identify monopolistic competition.

2 Explain how a firm in monopolistic competition determines its output and price in the short run and the long run.

3 Explain why firms develop new and improved products and incur large advertising costs.

MyEconLab Big Picture Video

MyEconLab Concept Video

17.1   WHAT IS MONOPOLISTIC COMPETITION?

Samsung, HTC, Apple: Which smartphone will you choose? Smartphones are sold in a market that is neither perfect competition nor monopoly. Smartphone producers possess some power to set their prices as monopolies do. But unlike monopoly, they face competition from the entry of new firms as the firms in perfect competition do. We call a market like the one in which smartphone producers operate *monopolistic competition*.

■ Describing Monopolistic Competition

Monopolistic competition is a market structure in which

- A large number of firms compete.
- Each firm produces a differentiated product.
- Firms compete on price, quality, and features.
- Firms advertise.
- Firms are free to enter and exit.

Large Number of Firms

In monopolistic competition, as in perfect competition, the industry consists of a large number of firms. The presence of a large number of firms has three implications for the firms in the industry.

About 20 firms, each with a small market share, produce a wide variety of treadmills.

Small Market Share   Each firm has a small share of the market so, while each firm can influence the price of its own product, it has little power to influence the average market price.

No Market Dominance   Each firm must be sensitive to the average market price of the product, but it does not pay attention to any one individual competitor. Because all the firms are relatively small, no single firm can dictate market conditions, so no one firm's actions directly affect the actions of the other firms.

Collusion Impossible   Firms sometimes try to profit from illegal agreements—collusion—with other firms to fix prices and not undercut each other. Collusion is impossible when the market has a large number of firms, as it does in monopolistic competition.

Product Differentiation

Product differentiation
Making a product that is slightly different from the products of competing firms.

Product differentiation is making a product that is slightly different from the products of competing firms. A differentiated product has close substitutes but it does not have perfect substitutes. Some people will pay more for one variety so when its price rises, the quantity demanded decreases but it does not (necessarily) decrease to zero. For example, Adidas, Asics, Diadora, Etonic, Fila, New Balance, Nike, Puma, Under Armour, and Reebok all make differentiated running shoes. Other things remaining the same, if the price of Adidas running shoes rises and the prices of the other shoes remain constant, Adidas sells fewer shoes.

Competing on Price, Quality, and Features

Product differentiation enables a firm to compete with other firms in three areas: price, quality, and features.

Price Because its product is differentiated, a firm in monopolistic competition faces a downward-sloping demand curve, and like a monopoly, the firm can set both its price and its output.

Quality The quality of a product includes its design and reliability, and its ease of use. Go to the J.D. Power Consumer Center at jdpower.com, and you'll see the many dimensions on which this rating agency rates the quality of autos, boats, financial services, travel and accommodation services, telecommunication services, and new homes—all examples of products that have a large range of quality variety. There is a tradeoff between the product's quality and its price. A higher-quality product usully costs more to produce and sells for a higher price.

Features The features of a product include its physical characteristics, the way it works, and things it can do. Differences in features are a key source of product differentiation. Think about the features of a car that make one brand or model different from another. Aside from the shape of its body, its engine design and size, transmission system, and safety features such as audio sensors and rear-view camera are all examples of features that differentiate cars. Just about every product and service that you can think of has differentiating features. Features and quality are related, and as with quality, there is a tradeoff between features and price. More elaborate features cost more to produce and raise the price.

Advertising

Because of product differentiation, a firm in monopolistic competition must advertise its product. A firm that produces a high-quality product wants to sell it for a suitably high price. To be able to do so, it must advertise its product in a way that convinces buyers that they are getting the higher quality for which they are paying. For example, drug companies advertise their brand-name drugs to persuade buyers that they are superior to the lower-priced generic alternatives. A low-quality producer uses advertising to persuade buyers that although the quality is low, the low price more than compensates for this fact.

Entry and Exit

In monopolistic competition, there are no barriers to entry. Consequently, a firm cannot make an economic profit in the long run. When firms make economic profits, new firms enter the industry. This entry lowers prices and eventually eliminates economic profits. When economic losses are incurred, some firms leave the industry. This exit increases prices and profits of the remaining firms and eventually eliminates the economic losses. In long-run equilibrium, firms neither enter nor leave the industry and the firms in the industry make zero economic profit.

■ Identifying Monopolistic Competition

To identify monopolistic competition and distinguish it from perfect competition on the one side and oligopoly and monopoly on the other side, we must determine whether a market has many competing firms or is dominated by a small number of firms. To measure this feature of markets, economists use two indexes called measures of concentration. These indexes are

- The four-firm concentration ratio
- The Herfindahl-Hirschman Index

The Four-Firm Concentration Ratio

The **four-firm concentration ratio** is the percentage of the total revenue of the industry accounted for by the four largest firms in the industry. The range of the concentration ratio is from almost zero for perfect competition to 100 percent for monopoly. This ratio is the main measure used to assess market structure.

Table 17.1 shows two calculations of the four-firm concentration ratio: one for tire makers and one for printers. In this example, 14 firms produce tires. The four largest firms have 80 percent of the industry's total revenue, so the four-firm concentration ratio is 80 percent. In the printing industry, with 1,004 firms, the four largest firms have only 0.5 percent of the industry's total revenue, so the four-firm concentration ratio is 0.5 percent.

A low concentration ratio indicates a high degree of competition, and a high concentration ratio indicates an absence of competition. A monopoly has a concentration ratio of 100 percent—the largest (and only) firm has 100 percent of the total revenue. A four-firm concentration ratio that exceeds 60 percent is regarded as an indication of a market that is highly concentrated and dominated by a few firms—oligopoly. A ratio of less than 40 percent is regarded as an indication of a competitive market—monopolistic competition.

TABLE 17.1

Concentration Ratio Calculations

(a) Firms' total revenue

Tire makers		Printers	
Firm	(millions of dollars)	Firm	(millions of dollars)
Top, Inc.	200	Fran's	4
ABC, Inc.	250	Ned's	3
Big, Inc.	150	Tom's	2
XYZ, Inc.	100	Jill's	1
4 largest firms	700	4 largest firms	10
Other 10 firms	175	Other 1,000 firms	1,990
Industry	875	Industry	2,000

(b) Four-firm concentration ratios

Tire makers	$ million	Printers	$ million
Total revenue of 4 largest firms	700	Total revenue of 4 largest firms	10
Industry's total revenue	875	Industry's total revenue	2,000

Four-firm concentration ratio

$$\frac{700}{875} \times 100 = 80 \text{ percent}$$

Four-firm concentration ratio

$$\frac{10}{2,000} \times 100 = 0.5 \text{ percent}$$

The Herfindahl-Hirschman Index

The **Herfindahl-Hirschman Index**—also called the HHI—is the square of the percentage market share of each firm summed over the 50 largest firms (or summed over all the firms if there are fewer than 50) in a market. For example, if there are four firms in a market and the market shares of the firms are 50 percent, 25 percent, 15 percent, and 10 percent, the Herfindahl-Hirschman Index is

$$HHI = 50^2 + 25^2 + 15^2 + 10^2 = 3,450$$

In perfect competition, the HHI is small. For example, if each of the 50 largest firms in an industry has a market share of 0.1 percent, the HHI is $(0.1^2 \times 50)$, which equals 0.5. In a monopoly, the HHI is 10,000—the firm has 100 percent of the market: $100^2 = 10,000$.

The HHI is one of the measures of the degree of competition used by the U.S. Department of Justice to classify markets and guide decisions on mergers. A market in which the HHI is less than 1,500 is regarded as being competitive and an example of monopolistic competition. A market in which the HHI lies between 1,500 and 2,500 is regarded as being moderately competitive. It is also an example of monopolistic competition. But a market in which the HHI exceeds 2,500 is regarded as being uncompetitive. The Justice Department scrutinizes any merger of firms in a market in which the HHI exceeds 2,500 that is likely to increase the HHI by more than 100 points.

Concentration measures are a useful indicator of the degree of competition in a market, but they must be supplemented by other information to determine a market's structure. Table 17.2 summarizes the range of other information, along with the measures of concentration that determine which market structure describes a particular real-world market.

Herfindahl-Hirschman Index
The square of the percentage market share of each firm summed over the 50 largest firms (or summed over all the firms if there are fewer than 50) in a market.

TABLE 17.2

Market Structure

Characteristics	Perfect competition	Monopolistic competition	Oligopoly	Monopoly
Number of firms in industry	Many	Many	Few	One
Product	Identical	Differentiated	Identical or differentiated	No close substitutes or regulated
Barriers to entry	None	None	Moderate	High
Firm's control over price	None	Some	Considerable	Considerable
Concentration ratio	0	Low	High	100
HHI	Close to 0	Less than 2,500	More than 2,500	10,000
Examples	Wheat, corn	Food, clothing	Computer chips	Local water supply

EYE on the U.S. ECONOMY
Examples of Monopolistic Competition

These ten industries operate in monopolistic competition. They have a large number of firms, shown in parentheses after the industry's name.

The red bars show the percentage of industry total revenue received by the 4 largest firms. The green bars show the percentage of industry total revenue received by the next 4 largest firms. The entire red, green, and blue bars show the percentage of industry total revenue received by the 20 largest firms.

The Herfindahl-Hirschman Index is shown on the right.

SOURCE OF DATA: U.S. Census Bureau.

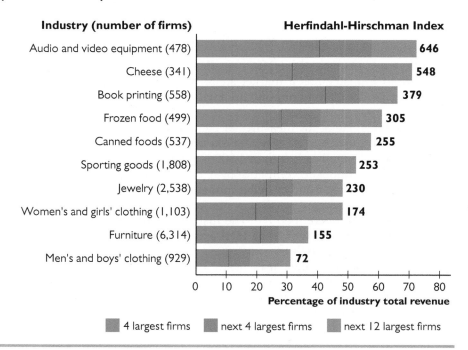

Industry (number of firms) — **Herfindahl-Hirschman Index**

- Audio and video equipment (478) — 646
- Cheese (341) — 548
- Book printing (558) — 379
- Frozen food (499) — 305
- Canned foods (537) — 255
- Sporting goods (1,808) — 253
- Jewelry (2,538) — 230
- Women's and girls' clothing (1,103) — 174
- Furniture (6,314) — 155
- Men's and boys' clothing (929) — 72

Percentage of industry total revenue

■ 4 largest firms ■ next 4 largest firms ■ next 12 largest firms

Limitations of Concentration Measures

The two main limitations of concentration measures alone as determinants of market structure are their failure to take proper account of:

- The geographical scope of the market
- Barriers to entry and firm turnover

Geographical Scope of the Market Concentration measures take a national view of the market, but some goods and services are sold in a *regional* market and some in a *global* one. The ready-mix concrete industry consists of highly concentrated regional markets, but the national concentration numbers suggest a market that is close to perfect competition. The four-firm concentration ratio for automobiles is 87, and the HHI is 2,725. Competition from imports give the market in new automobiles the features of monopolistic competition, but the concentration measures suggest a highly concentrated market.

Barriers to Entry and Firm Turnover A market with a high concentration measure might nonetheless be competitive because low barriers to entry create *potential competition* and a lot of firm turnover. The few firms in a market face competition from many firms that can easily enter the market and will do so if economic profits are available. For example, many small communities have only a small number of restaurants, but there are no restrictions on opening a restaurant and many firms attempt to do so.

CHECKPOINT 17.1

Describe and identify monopolistic competition.

Practice Problems

Table 1 shows the total revenue of the 50 firms in the tattoo industry.

1. Calculate the four-firm concentration ratio and the HHI. What is the market structure of the tattoo industry?

2. What would the market structure of the tattoo industry be if each firm operated in a different city and the cities were spread across the nation?

3. What additional information would you need about the tattoo industry to be sure that it is an example of monopolistic competition?

4. Suppose that a new tattoo technology makes it easier for anyone to enter the tattoo market. How might the market structure change?

TABLE 1

Firm	Total revenue (dollars)
Bright Spots	450
Freckles	325
Love Galore	250
Native Birds	200
Next 16 firms (each)	50
Next 30 firms (each)	20
Industry	**2,625**

In the News

Gloria Jean's hosts "Free Coffee for a Year" sweepstakes
Selling its own-roast light to dark varieties and its signature chillers, mochas, lattes, and hot cocoas, Gloria Jean's Coffees is offering "Free Coffee for a Year" to one sweepstakes winner at each of its 60 locations.
Source: *QSR Magazine*, January 15, 2016

In what type of market does Gloria Jean's compete? Explain your answer.

Solutions to Practice Problems

1. The four-firm concentration ratio is 46.7. Revenue of the four largest firms is $450 + 325 + 250 + 200 = 1,225$, which is 46.7 percent of the total revenue of $2,625. The HHI is 671.14. The market shares from largest to smallest are 17.1, 12.4, 9.5, 7.6, 1.9, and 0.8 percent. Square these numbers to get:
HHI $= 292.41 + 153.76 + 90.25 + 57.76 + (3.61 \times 16) + (0.64 \times 30) = 671.14$.
The four-firm concentration ratio and the HHI suggest that the tattoo industry is an example of monopolistic competition unless there are other reasons that would make the concentration measures unreliable guides.

2. If the 50 firms in the tattoo industry operate in different cities spread across the nation, each firm is effectively without competition. The market might be a series of monopolies.

3. The additional information needed is information about product differentiation; competition on price, quality, and advertising; and evidence of low barriers to the entry of new firms.

4. This new tattoo technology would most likely lead to the entry of more firms, greater product differentiation, and more competition.

Solution to In the News

The market type in which Gloria Jean's Coffees and the other coffee shops compete is monopolistic competition. The number of coffee shops is large, and they offer differentiated coffees and other drinks and food. No single firm completely dominates the market and the firms compete on quality, price, and advertising. New coffee shops are free to enter the market with their own varieties.

17.2 OUTPUT AND PRICE DECISIONS

Think about the decisions that Lucky Brand must make about the jeans it produces. First, Lucky Brand must decide on the design and quality of its jeans and on its advertising program. We'll suppose that the firm has already made these decisions so that we can concentrate on the firm's output and pricing decisions. Then we'll study design, quality, and advertising decisions in the next section.

Because Lucky Brand has chosen the design and quality of its jeans and the amount of advertising, it faces given costs and market demand. How, with these costs and market demand for its jeans, does the firm decide the *quantity* of jeans to produce and the *price* at which to sell them?

■ The Firm's Profit-Maximizing Decision

A firm in monopolistic competition makes its output and price decision just as a monopoly firm does. Lucky Brand maximizes profit by producing the quantity at which marginal revenue equals marginal cost and by charging the highest price that buyers are willing to pay for this quantity.

Figure 17.1 illustrates this decision for Lucky Brand. The demand curve is *D*. The *MR* curve shows the marginal revenue curve associated with this demand curve and the *MR* curve is derived just like the marginal revenue curve of a single-price monopoly in Chapter 16. The *ATC* curve shows the average total cost of producing Lucky jeans, and *MC* is the marginal cost curve. Profit is maximized by producing 125 pairs of jeans a day and selling them at a price of $100 a pair. When the firm produces 125 pairs of jeans a day, average total cost is $50 a pair and economic profit is $6,250 a day ($50 a pair multiplied by 125 pairs a day). The blue rectangle shows Lucky Brand's economic profit.

▇ FIGURE 17.1

Output and Price in Monopolistic Competition

❶ Profit is maximized where marginal revenue equals marginal cost.

❷ Lucky Brand's profit-maximizing quantity is 125 pairs of jeans a day.

❸ The profit-maximizing price is $100 a pair, which exceeds the average total cost of $50 a pair, so Lucky Brand makes an economic profit of $50 a pair.

❹ The blue rectangle illustrates economic profit and its area, which equals $6,250 a day ($50 a pair multiplied by 125 pairs), measures economic profit.

■ Profit Maximizing Might Be Loss Minimizing

Lucky Brand in Figure 17.1 is making a healthy economic profit, but such an outcome is not inevitable. The demand for a firm's product might be too low for it to make an economic profit. Excite@Home was such a firm. Offering high-speed Internet service over the same cable that provides television, Excite@Home hoped to capture a large share of the Internet portal market in competition with AOL, MSN, and a host of other providers.

Figure 17.2 illustrates the situation facing Excite@Home in 2001. The demand curve for its portal service is *D*, the marginal revenue curve is *MR*, the average total cost curve is *ATC*, and the marginal cost curve is *MC*. Excite@Home maximizes profit—equivalently, it minimizes its loss—by producing the output at which marginal revenue equals marginal cost. In Figure 17.2, this output is 40,000 customers connected. Excite@Home charges the highest price that 40,000 buyers are willing to pay for its service, which from the demand curve is $40 a month. With 40,000 customers, Excite@Home's average total cost is $50 a customer, so Excite@Home incurs an economic loss of $400,000 a month ($10 a customer multiplied by 40,000 customers). The red rectangle shows the economic loss.

The largest economic loss that a firm will incur is equal to total fixed cost. The reason is that if the profit-maximizing (loss-minimizing) price is less than average variable cost, the firm will shut down temporarily and produce nothing (just like a firm in perfect competition—see pp. 381–382).

So far, the firm in monopolistic competition looks like a single-price monopoly. It produces the quantity at which marginal revenue equals marginal cost and then charges the highest price that buyers are willing to pay for that quantity. The difference between monopoly and monopolistic competition lies in what happens when firms either make an economic profit or incur an economic loss.

■ FIGURE 17.2

Economic Loss in the Short Run

MyEconLab Animation

❶ Profit is maximized and loss is minimized where marginal revenue equals marginal cost.

❷ The loss-minimizing quantity is 40,000 customers connected.

❸ The price of $40 a month is less than average total cost of $50 a month, so the firm incurs an economic loss of $10 a customer.

❹ The red rectangle illustrates economic loss and its area, which equals $400,000 a month ($10 a customer multiplied by 40,000 customers), measures the economic loss.

■ Long Run: Zero Economic Profit

A firm like Excite@Home is not going to incur an economic loss for long. Eventually, it exits the market. So in the long run, no firm in the market will be incurring an economic loss. Also, there is no restriction on entry in monopolistic competition, so if firms in an industry are making economic profits, other firms have an incentive to enter that industry and each firm's economic profit falls. So in the long run, firms will enter until all firms are making zero economic profit.

Lucky Brand is making an economic profit, which is an incentive for Calvin Klein and other firms to start producing jeans similar to Lucky jeans. As new firms enter the jeans market, the demand for Lucky jeans decreases. At each point in time, the firm maximizes its profit by producing the quantity at which marginal revenue equals marginal cost and by charging the highest price that buyers are willing to pay for this quantity. But as demand decreases, marginal revenue decreases, so the profit-maximizing quantity and price fall.

Figure 17.3 shows Lucky Brand's long-run equilibrium. The demand curve for Lucky jeans and the marginal revenue curve have shifted leftward. The firm produces 75 pairs of jeans a day and sells them for $70 each. At this output level, average total cost is also $70 a pair, so Lucky Brand is making zero economic profit on its jeans. When all the firms in the industry are making zero economic profit, there is no incentive for new firms to enter.

If demand is so low relative to costs that firms incur economic losses, exit will occur. As firms leave an industry, the demand for the products of the remaining firms increases and their demand curves shift rightward. The exit process ends when all the firms in the industry are making zero economic profit.

■ FIGURE 17.3

Output and Price in the Long Run   MyEconLab Animation

Economic profit encourages entry, which decreases the demand for each firm's product. Economic loss encourages exit, which increases the demand for each remaining firm's product.

When the demand curve touches the average total cost curve at the quantity at which marginal revenue equals marginal cost, the market is in long-run equilibrium.

❶ The output that maximizes Lucky Brand's profit is 75 pairs of jeans a day.

❷ The price, $70 a pair, equals average total cost.

❸ Economic profit is zero.

■ Monopolistic Competition and Perfect Competition

MyEconLab Concept Video

Figure 17.4 compares monopolistic competition and perfect competition in the long run and highlights two key differences: excess capacity and markup.

Excess Capacity

A firm's **efficient scale** is the quantity at which average total cost is a minimum—the quantity at the bottom of the U-shaped *ATC* curve. A firm's **excess capacity** is the amount by which its efficient scale exceeds the quantity it produces. Figure 17.4(a) shows that in the long run Lucky Brand has *excess capacity*. Because the demand curve for Lucky jeans is downward sloping, zero economic profit occurs where the *ATC* curve is downward sloping. Figure 17.4(b) shows a firm in perfect competition in the long run. The firm has no excess capacity because its demand curve is horizontal. Zero economic profit occurs at minimum average total cost.

Efficient scale
The quantity at which average total cost is a minimum.

Excess capacity
The amount by which the efficient scale exceeds the quantity that the firm produces.

Markup

A firm's **markup** is the amount by which its price exceeds its marginal cost. Figure 17.4(a) shows Lucky Brand's markup. Figure 17.4(b) shows the zero markup of a firm in perfect competition. Buyers pay a higher price in monopolistic competition than in perfect competition and pay more than marginal cost.

Markup
The amount by which price exceeds marginal cost.

■ **FIGURE 17.4**

Excess Capacity and Markup in the Long Run

MyEconLab Animation

(a) Monopolistic competition

(b) Perfect competition

❶ The efficient scale (at minimum *ATC*) is 100 pairs a day. In the long run in monopolistic competition, the firm produces 75 pairs of jeans a day and has ❷ excess capacity. ❸ Price exceeds ❹ marginal cost by ❺ the markup and ❻ creates a deadweight loss.

In contrast, the firm in perfect competition has no excess capacity and no markup because the demand for the firm's output is perfectly elastic. ❶ The quantity produced equals the efficient scale and ❷ price equals marginal cost.

■ Is Monopolistic Competition Efficient?

You've learned that resources are used efficiently when marginal benefit equals marginal cost. You've also learned that price measures marginal benefit. So if the price of a pair of Lucky jeans exceeds the marginal cost of producing them, then the quantity of Lucky jeans produced is less than the efficient quantity. And you've just seen that in long-run equilibrium in monopolistic competition, that price *does* exceed marginal cost.

Deadweight Loss

Because price exceeds marginal cost, monopolistic competition creates deadweight loss, just like monopoly. Figure 17.4(a) shows this deadweight loss. But is monopolistic competition less efficient than perfect competition?

Making the Relevant Comparison

Two economists meet in the street, and one asks the other, "How is your husband?" "Compared to what?" is the quick reply. This bit of economic wit illustrates a key point: Before we can make an effective comparison, we must check out the available alternatives.

The markup that drives a gap between price and marginal cost in monopolistic competition arises from product differentiation. Lucky Brand jeans are not quite the same as jeans from Banana Republic, CK, Diesel, DKNY, Earl Jeans, Levi, Ralph Lauren, or any of the other dozens of producers of jeans, so the demand for Lucky jeans is not perfectly elastic. The only way in which the demand for jeans from Lucky Brand might be perfectly elastic is if there were only one kind of jeans and Lucky Brand, along with every other firm, made them. In this situation, Lucky jeans would be indistinguishable from all other jeans. They wouldn't even have identifying labels.

If there were only one kind of jeans, the marginal benefit from a pair of jeans would almost certainly be less than it is with variety. People value variety. And people value variety not only because it enables each person to select what he or she likes best but also because it provides an external benefit. Most of us enjoy seeing variety in the choices of others. Contrast a scene from the China of the 1960s when everyone wore a Mao tunic with the China of today, when everyone wears the clothes of their own choosing. Or contrast a scene from the Germany of the 1930s when almost everyone who could afford a car owned a first-generation Volkswagen Beetle with the world of today, with its variety of styles and types of automobiles.

If people value variety, why don't we see infinite variety? The answer is that variety is costly. Each different variety of any product must be designed, and then customers must be informed about it. These initial costs of design and advertising—called setup costs—mean that some varieties that are too close to others already available are just not worth creating.

The Bottom Line

Product variety is both valued and costly. The efficient degree of product variety is the one for which the buyer's willingness to pay equals the marginal cost of product variety. The loss that arises because the willingness to pay for one more unit of a given variety exceeds its marginal cost is offset by the gain that arises from having more product variety. So compared to the alternative—complete product uniformity—monopolistic competition is efficient.

CHECKPOINT 17.2

MyEconLab Study Plan 17.2
Key Terms Quiz
Solutions Video

Explain how a firm in monopolistic competition determines its output and price in the short run and the long run.

Practice Problems

Natti is a dot-com entrepreneur who has established a Web site at which people can design and buy incredible sunglasses. Natti pays $4,000 a month for her Web server and Internet connection. The sunglasses that her customers design are made to order by another firm, and Natti pays this firm $50 a pair. Natti has no other costs. Table 1 shows the demand schedule for Natti's sunglasses.

1. Calculate Natti's profit-maximizing output, price, and economic profit.
2. Do you expect other firms to enter the market and compete with Natti?
3. What happens to the demand for Natti's sunglasses in the long run? What happens to Natti's economic profit in the long run?

TABLE 1

Price (dollars per pair)	Quantity (pairs per month)
250	0
200	50
150	100
100	150
50	200
0	250

In the News

Blockbuster retail stores gone
In 2000, Blockbuster was at the top of the video rental market with solid profits, thousands of retail locations, and millions of customers eager to rent their movies and videogames. Unable to compete with Internet-based services, the last Blockbuster retail store closed in 2014.

Source: *Fortune*, November 9, 2014

Explain why the switch to Internet-based services brought economic loss to Blockbuster and led to its exit.

Solutions to Practice Problems

1. Marginal cost is $50 a pair—the price that Natti pays her supplier of sunglasses. To find marginal revenue, calculate the change in total revenue when the quantity increases by 1 pair of sunglasses. Figure 1 shows the demand curve, marginal revenue curve, and marginal cost curve. Profit is maximized when Natti produces 100 pairs a month at which marginal cost equals marginal revenue and sells them at $150 a pair. Average total cost is $90—the sum of $50 marginal (and average variable) cost and $40 average fixed cost. Economic profit is $60 a pair on 100 pairs a month, or $6,000 a month.

2. Natti is making an economic profit, so firms have an incentive to enter the Web sunglasses market and will do so.

3. As firms enter the market, the demand for Natti's sunglasses decreases. The D and MR curves in Figure 1 shift leftward. The quantity decreases, the price falls, and Natti's economic profit decreases. In the long run, Natti makes zero economic profit.

FIGURE 1

Solution to In the News

As people switched to Internet-based services, the demand for video rental decreased. Blockbuster's marginal revenue decreased and its MR curve shifted leftward. Eventually, with Blockbuster's average total cost exceeding price, the firm was incurring an economic loss. To limit the loss, Blockbuster retail stores were closed, and by 2014 they were all gone.

17.3 INNOVATION AND ADVERTISING

You've seen how a firm makes its output and price decisions for a product that is already designed and advertised. We're now going to study a firm's product design and quality and advertising decisions.

■ Design and Quality Decision

Economic profit attracts entry, and entry erodes profit. To enjoy ongoing economic profit, a firm in monopolistic competition must continually innovate.

The decision to allocate resources to product innovation is made using the same profit-maximizing calculation that you've already studied. At a low level of innovation activity, the marginal revenue it brings in exceeds the marginal cost. At a high level of innovation activity, its marginal cost exceeds marginal revenue. When the marginal cost of innovation activity equals its marginal revenue, the firm is doing the profit-maximizing amount of innovation.

Think about Electronic Arts, which releases a new version of Madden NFL once a year. It could do so twice a year or every two years. Also, the firm could employ more coders and designers to make the game even better than it is, or employ fewer and make an inferior version of the game. For EA, the marginal revenue from a new version equals its marginal cost on a one-year revision cycle.

It is easy to list new designs and new products that transform the quality of life. Kitchen and other household appliances, computers, cars, smartphones, and apps are examples of products that keep getting better. But do we get enough innovation and product improvement? Do consumers get all the features and quality that they are willing to pay for?

The answer is perhaps not. The value to the consumer of a product improvement is its marginal benefit, which equals the amount the consumer is willing to pay. In other words, the value of a product improvement is the increase in price that the consumer is willing to pay. The marginal benefit to the producer is marginal revenue, which, when profit is maximized, equals marginal cost. Because price exceeds marginal cost in monopolistic competition, product improvement is not pushed to its efficient level.

■ Advertising

Firms that differentiate their products need to ensure that their customers and potential customers know the features, quality, and price of their products. Advertising is the means firms use to achieve this end. Advertising is itself a product—a service—that is traded in a monopolistic competition market. That is, the firms that produce advertising services are large in number, differentiate their advertising products, and compete on price, design, and quality.

You already know a lot about the advertising industry. You view its products every day. Some of the biggest producers of advertising services are Google, Facebook, Pinterest, and YouTube, with Snapchat and other specialized social media websites snapping at their heels. In 2016, expenditure on advertising exceeded $200 billion, with a third each spent on Internet advertising, TV commercials, and print (magazines and newspapers). This enormous scale of advertising occurs because it increases advertisers' profits and is profitable for its suppliers.

We'll first look at the demand for advertising and see how it increases the profits of advertisers and at the same time might benefit the buyers of advertised products. Then we'll take a look at the supply side of the advertising market.

A new version of a game is released at an interval and with the features that generate a marginal revenue equal to marginal cost so that profit is maximized.

■ The Demand for Advertising

The demand for advertising arises from its effects on a firm's cost, revenue, and economic profit. We'll look first at its effects on a firm's costs, and then at its effects on demand and revenue.

Advertising and Cost

The cost of advertising is a fixed cost: It does not vary with output. Expenditure on advertising increases a firm's average cost, but it also increases the quantity sold. If advertising increases the quantity sold by a large enough amount, average total cost can fall, profit increase, and the consumer enjoy a lower price.

Figure 17.5 shows how advertising expenditures change a firm's average total cost. The blue curve shows the average total cost of production. The red curve shows the firm's average total cost of production plus the average cost of advertising. The height of the shaded area between the two curves shows the average fixed cost of advertising. The total cost of advertising is fixed. But the average cost of advertising decreases as output increases.

In this example, if the quantity sold increases from 25 pairs of jeans a day with no advertising to 100 pairs of jeans a day with advertising, average total cost falls from $60 a pair to $40 a pair. The reason is that although the total fixed cost has increased, the greater fixed cost is spread over a greater output, so average total cost falls.

To know whether the lower cost and greater quantity increase a firm's profit, we need to see how advertising changes the demand for the firm's product.

■ FIGURE 17.5

Advertising Cost and Total Cost

Advertising costs are fixed costs.

❶ When advertising costs are added to ❷ the average total cost of production, ❸ average total cost increases by more at small outputs than at large outputs.

❹ If advertising enables the quantity sold to increase from 25 pairs of jeans a day to 100 pairs a day, the firm's average total cost *falls* from $60 a pair to $40 a pair.

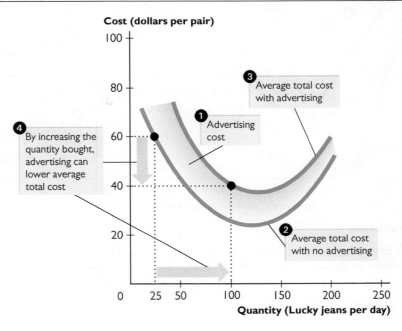

Advertising and Demand

Advertising changes the demand for a firm's product. But how? Does demand increase or does it decrease? The most natural answer is that advertising increases demand. By informing people about the quality of its products or by persuading people to switch from the products of other firms, a firm might expect to increase the demand for its own products.

But all firms in monopolistic competition advertise. And all seek to persuade customers that they have the best deal. If advertising enables a firm to survive, it might increase the number of firms in the market. And to the extent that it increases the number of firms, it decreases the demand for any one firm's product. With all firms advertising, the demand for any one firm's product might become more elastic. So advertising can end up not only lowering average total cost but also lowering the price and decreasing the markup.

Figure 17.6 illustrates this possible effect of advertising. In part (a), with no advertising, the demand for Lucky jeans is not very elastic. Profit is maximized at 75 pairs of jeans a day, and the markup is large. In part (b), advertising, which is a fixed cost, increases average total cost and shifts the average total cost curve upward from ATC_0 to ATC_1, but leaves the marginal cost curve unchanged at MC. The demand for Lucky jeans becomes much more elastic, the profit-maximizing quantity increases, and the firm's markup shrinks.

■ **FIGURE 17.6**

Advertising and the Markup   MyEconLab Animation

(a) No firms advertise

❶ With no firms advertising, the demand for Lucky jeans is low and not very elastic, so ❷ Lucky Brand's markup is large.

(b) All firms advertise

❸ Lucky Brand's advertising shifts its average total cost curve upward from ATC_0 to ATC_1. If, with all firms advertising, the demand for Lucky jeans becomes more elastic, ❹ the price of Lucky jeans falls and Lucky Brand's markup shrinks.

EYE on SMARTPHONES

Which Smartphone?

There is a lot of product differentiation in smartphones: Samsung makes more than 60 varieties; so does HTC; LG makes 26; and Apple makes 13. In the three months from April through June 2016, dozens of new varieties of smartphones were introduced by the top 20 firms in this market. Why is there so much variety in smartphones?

The answer is that preferences are diverse and the cost of matching the diversity of preference is low.

Think about the ways in which smartphones differ: just a few of them are their dimensions, weight, navigation tools, talk time, standby time, screen, camera features, audio features, memory, connectivity, processor speed, storage, and network capability.

Each one of these features comes in dozens of varieties. If we combine only 10 of these features, each having 6 varieties, there are 1 million different possible smartphone designs.

Firms produce variety only when the marginal cost of doing so is less than the marginal benefit. The marginal cost of some smartphone variety is not large. Adding a feature to a camera, making the memory a bit bigger, and using a more economical battery are all relatively low-cost adjustments that phone designers can make.

But a technology exists for adding variety at almost zero cost that increases product differentiation to make each smartphone unique to the preferences of each individual. This technology is the app.

Apple has only 13 versions of the iPhone, but with the growing number of apps, each owner can load their iPhone with all the apps they want.

In long-run equilibrium, entry and innovation will drive economic profit toward zero. Each smartphone maker will offer a degree of product differentiation that equates the marginal cost of variety with its marginal revenue. But the pursuit of economic profit will spur ever more innovation and consumers will be confronted with ever wider choice.

Using Advertising to Signal Quality

In 2014, Budweiser spent $12 million for 90 seconds of Super Bowl TV time to advertise Bud Light. The ad showed a night of partying with Minka Kelly, Arnold Schwarzenegger, Don Cheadle, and a llama in a hotel elevator. No information about Bud Light. So why did Budweiser spend all this money? The answer is to signal a high-quality product.

A **signal** is an action taken by an informed person (or firm) to send a message to less-informed people. Think about two beers: Bud and Dud.

Dud knows that its beer is low quality. So Dud knows that while it could get a lot of people to try Dud by advertising, they would all quickly discover its poor quality and switch back to the beer they bought before. Dud's cost of advertising would exceed the revenue it generated.

Bud, in contrast, knows that its product has a high-quality consistent taste and that once someone has tried it, there is a good chance that they'll never drink anything but Bud. If Bud ran a costly advertising campaign, more people would try Bud and many would stick with it. The revenue earned would exceed the cost of the advertising campaign.

So Bud spends a lot of money to make a big splash. Beer drinkers who see Bud's splashy ads believe that the firm would not spend so much money advertising if its product were not truly good. So the beer drinker reasons that Bud is indeed a really good product. The flashy expensive ad has signaled that Bud is really good without saying anything about Bud.

Signal
An action taken by an informed person (or firm) to send a message to less-informed people.

EYE on YOUR LIFE
Some Selling Costs You Pay

When you buy a new pair of running shoes, you're buying materials that cost $9, paying the producer in Asia and the shipping company for production and transportation costs of $8, paying the U.S. government an import duty of $3, and paying advertisers, retailers, and others who provide sales and distribution services $50.

The table provides a breakdown of the cost of a pair of shoes. Notice the huge gap between the retailer's cost and the price that you pay. The retail markup is about 100 percent.

Running shoes are not unusual. Almost everything that you buy includes a selling cost component that exceeds one half of the total cost. Your clothing, food, electronic items, airline travel, magazines, and even your textbooks cost more to sell than they cost to produce.

| Raw materials $9 | Production costs $8 | Import duty $3 | | Selling costs $50 |

Manufacturer (Asia)		Nike (Beaverton, Oregon)		Retailer (your town)	
Materials	$9.00				
Cost of labor	$2.75	Cost of shoe to Nike	$20.00	Cost of shoe to retailer	$35.50
Cost of capital	$3.00	Sales, distribution, and administration	$5.00	Sales clerk's wages	$9.50
Profit	$1.75	Advertising	$4.00	Shop rent	$9.00
Shipping	$0.50	Research & development	$0.25	Retailer's other costs	$7.00
Import duty	$3.00	Nike's profit	$6.25	Retailer's profit	$9.00
Nike's cost	**$20.00**	**Retailer's cost**	**$35.50**	**Price paid by you**	**$70.00**

Brand Names

Many firms, and Budweiser is one of them, create a brand name and spend a lot of advertising dollars promoting it. Why? What benefit does a brand name bring to justify the sometimes high cost of establishing it? The answer is that a brand name provides consumers with information about the quality of a product and it provides the producer with an incentive to achieve a consistent quality standard.

To see how a brand name helps the consumer, think about how you use one. You're on a road trip, and it is time to find a bed. You see roadside ads for Holiday Inn and for Annie's Driver's Stop. You know about Holiday Inn: You've stayed in one, and you've seen its ads. You know what to expect from it. You have no information at all about Annie's. It might be better than Holiday Inn, but without that knowledge, you're not going to chance it. You use the brand name as information and stay at Holiday Inn.

This same story explains why a brand name provides an incentive to the producer to achieve a consistent quality. Because no one knows whether Annie's is offering a good standard of service, it has no incentive to do so. But equally, because everyone expects a given standard of service from Holiday Inn, a failure to meet a customer's expectation would almost surely lose that customer to a competitor. So Holiday Inn has an incentive to deliver what it promises in the advertising that creates its brand name.

■ The Supply of Advertising

The firms that supply advertising do so jointly with the supply of some other service or good: TV stations with programming, Google with Internet search, Facebook with social media, and *Sports Illustrated* with news and feature articles.

Two-Sided Market

Because firms produce advertising jointly with something else, these firms trade in what has been called a "two-sided market." One side is for advertising and the other side is for the firm's product.

Competition for advertising among TV, social media, and print (magazines and newspapers) is fierce but entry into the market is difficult for TV and social media because startup costs are high and economies of scale reward large players with the lowest average cost. Entry is easier for print producers and a wide variety of niche magazines supply advertising.

When operating in a two-sided market, suppliers of advertising face two interdependent demand curves. The greater the number of users of the firm's product, the greater is the demand for its advertising services. For example, the more people who visit Facebook, the greater is the demand for Facebook advertising.

Profit-Maximizing Decisions

The profit-maximizing decision of Facebook and the other Internet firms is to offer their main product at a zero price to maximize the quantity demanded—maximize the number of users—to make the demand for its advertising services as large as possible. For the same reason, print suppliers of advertising sell the magazines and newspapers for a price close to marginal cost and below average cost. These firms then sell the profit-maximizing quantity of space for advertising. They choose this quantity in the same way as all firms: the quantity that makes marginal revenue equal to marginal cost. They sell the space for the highest price that advertisers are willing to pay determined by the advertisers' demand curve.

■ Equilibrium and Efficiency in the Advertising Market

The quantity and quality of advertising is determined by the interaction of the demand by advertisers and the price and output decisions of the suppliers of advertising. Whether the advertising market does a good job and produces the efficient quantity and quality is not well understood. To the extent that advertising and brand names provide consumers with information about the precise nature of product differences and product quality, they benefit the consumer and enable a better product choice to be made. And to the extent that signalling and brand names provide firms with the incentive to deliver consistent quality, they further benefit the consumer. But the opportunity cost of advertising must be weighed against the gain to the consumer.

The final verdict on the efficiency of monopolistic competition is ambiguous. In some cases, the gains from extra product variety and innovation more than offset the advertising costs and the deadweight loss arising from excess capacity. The smartphone, laptop and tablet computers, streaming video services, games and apps all make our lives easier and more fun. You can book a substitute for your snow-cancelled flight while standing in the checkout line at Target. In a few years from now, you will be able to ride in your driverless vehicle and use travel time for other activities. It seems obvious that gains like these more than offset a bit of deadweight loss from excess capacity and price exceeding marginal cost.

MyEconLab Study Plan 17.3

Key Terms Quiz

Solutions Video

 CHECKPOINT 17.3

Explain why firms develop new and improved products and incur large advertising costs.

Practice Problems

Bianca bakes delicious cookies. Her total fixed cost is $40 a day, and her average variable cost is $1 a bag. Few people know about Bianca's Cookies, and she maximizes her profit by selling 10 bags a day for $5 a bag. Bianca thinks that if she spends $50 a day on advertising, she will sell 25 bags a day for $5 a bag.

1.   If Bianca's belief about the effect of advertising is correct, can she increase her economic profit by advertising?

2.   If Bianca advertises, will her average total cost increase or decrease at the quantity produced?

3.   If Bianca advertises, will she continue to sell her cookies for $5 a bag or will she raise her price or lower her price?

In the News

Snapchat's daily mobile video views said to rival Facebook's
Snapchat is turning into a mobile-video juggernaut that delivers more than 7 billion video clips each day to rival the amount watched on Facebook, which has 15 times as many users. A stronghold in mobile video is good news for Snapchat's advertising dollars.

Source: Bloomberg, January 12, 2016

How does Snapchat help firms in monopolistic competition to maximize profit?

Solutions to Practice Problems

1.   With no advertising, Bianca's total revenue is $50 (10 bags at $5 a bag) and her total cost is $50 ($40 total fixed cost plus $10 total variable cost). Bianca's economic profit is zero. With $50 a day advertising expenditure, total revenue is $125 (25 bags at $5 a bag) and total cost is $115 ($90 total fixed cost plus $25 total variable cost). Bianca's economic profit with no price change is $10 a day, so Bianca can increase her economic profit by advertising.

2.   If Bianca advertises, her average *total* cost will decrease. With no advertising, her average total cost is $5 a bag (total cost of $50 ÷ 10 bags). With advertising, her average total cost is $4.60 a bag (total cost of $115 ÷ 25 bags).

3.   We can't say if Bianca will sell her cookies for $5 a bag. Advertising changes the demand for her cookies. Although it increases fixed cost, marginal cost remains at $1 a bag. Bianca will sell the profit-maximizing quantity at the highest price she can charge for that quantity.

Solution to In the News

In monopolistic competition, entry keeps driving economic profit to zero. Innovation— the development of a new differentiated product—is necessary to boost economic profit. And advertising is necessary to bring new differentiated products to the attention of potential buyers. Snapchat enables advertising to reach a well-defined market of young smartphone users.

CHAPTER SUMMARY

Key Points

1. Describe and identify monopolistic competition.

- Monopolistic competition is a market structure in which a large number of firms compete; each firm produces a product that is slightly different from the products of its competitors; firms compete on price, quality, and advertising; and new firms are free to enter the industry.
- Monopolistic competition is identified by a low degree of concentration measured by either the four-firm concentration ratio or the HHI.

2. Explain how a firm in monopolistic competition determines its output and price in the short run and the long run.

- The firm in monopolistic competition faces a downward-sloping demand curve and produces the quantity at which marginal revenue equals marginal cost and price exceeds marginal cost.
- Entry and exit result in zero economic profit and excess capacity in long-run equilibrium.
- In monopolistic competition, price exceeds marginal cost but buyers benefit from product variety.

3. Explain why firms develop new and improved products and incur large advertising costs.

- Firms in monopolistic competition innovate and develop new products to maintain economic profit.
- Firms create a brand name to signal quality and to provide the incentive to maintain quality.
- Advertising expenditures can lower average total cost and can increase competition and lower price.
- Product development, a brand name, and advertising increase profit but can also benefit buyers.

Key Terms

MyEconLab Key Terms Quiz

Efficient scale, 445
Excess capacity, 445
Four-firm concentration ratio, 438
Herfindahl-Hirschman Index, 439

Markup, 445
Product differentiation, 436
Signal, 451

CHAPTER CHECKPOINT

Study Plan Problems and Applications

1. Think about the markets for cable television service, wheat, athletic shoes, soda, toothbrushes, and ready-mix concrete. Which of these markets are examples of monopolistic competition? Explain your selections.

2. The four-firm concentration ratio for audio equipment makers is 30 and for electric lamp makers is 89. The HHI for audio equipment makers is 464 and for electric lamp makers is 2,850. Which of these markets is an example of monopolistic competition?

FIGURE 1

Price and cost (dollars per pair)

Use Figure 1, which shows the demand curve, marginal revenue curve, and cost curves of Lite and Kool, Inc., a producer of running shoes in monopolistic competition, to work Problems **3** to **5**.

3. In the short run, what quantity does Lite and Kool produce, what price does it charge, and does it make an economic profit?

4. In the short run, does Lite and Kool have excess capacity and what is its markup?

5. Do you expect firms to enter the running shoes market or exit from that market in the long run? Explain your answer.

FIGURE 2

Price and cost (dollars per shirt)

Use Figure 2, which shows the demand curve, marginal revenue curve, and cost curves of Stiff Shirt, Inc., a producer of shirts in monopolistic competition, to work Problems **6** and **7**.

6. In the short run, what is the quantity that Stiff Shirt produces, the price it charges, its economic profit, markup, and excess capacity?

7. In the long run, will new firms enter the shirt market or will firms exit from that market and will the price of a shirt rise or fall? Explain your answer.

8. Mike's, a firm in monopolistic competition, produces bikes. With no advertising, Mike's profit-maximizing output is 500 bikes a day and the price is $100 a bike. Now all firms begin to advertise. With advertising, Mike's maximizes profit by producing 1,000 bikes a day and charging $50 a bike. How does advertising change Mike's markup and excess capacity?

9. **Netflix profits slide**

   Netflix has hit a bump in the road on its quest to reach 60 million to 90 million subscribers in the United States and, by the end of 2016, become fully global. Netflix faces fierce competition from streaming rivals like Amazon, HBO, and Hulu and also competes against cable, satellite, YouTube, and DVDs.

   Source: *The New York Times*, October 14, 2015

   Explain why more firms have entered the streaming-video market and how the economic profit of firms in the market will likely change. What will economic profit be in the long run? Explain your answer.

10. Read *Eye on Smartphones* on p. 451 and explain why smartphone producers offer such a large variety of their products. Draw a graph of a firm's cost and revenue curves if all smartphones are identical. Use your graph to illustrate the effects of the firm introducing a new, differentiated smartphone.

Instructor Assignable Problems and Applications

MyEconLab Homework, Quiz, or Test if assigned by instructor

1. Washtenaw Dairy in Ann Arbor, Michigan, sells 63 flavors of Strohs Mooney's ice cream, and Ben and Jerry's Web site also lists 63 different flavors of ice cream. These numbers are similar to the varieties of smartphones sold by Samsung, Nokia, and Motorola. Toyota makes only 16 varieties of vehicles and Boeing makes 16 varieties of airplanes. Why is there more variety in smartphones and ice cream than in automobiles and airplanes?

2. The HHI for automobiles is 2,350, for sporting goods is 253, for batteries is 2,883, and for jewelry is 230. Which of these markets is an example of monopolistic competition?

Use Figure 1 to work Problems 3 and 4.

Figure 1 shows the demand curve, marginal revenue curve, and cost curves of La Bella Pizza, a firm in monopolistic competition.

3. What is the quantity that La Bella Pizza produces, the price it charges, its markup, and its excess capacity? Is the market in short-run or long-run equilibrium? Explain your answer.

4. If La Bella advertises its pizza online and demand increases, how will the number of pizzas sold change? How will the price of a pizza and La Bella's excess capacity change? Explain your answer.

Use the following information to work Problems 5 and 6.

Sony announces Smart Tennis Sensor

Tennis racket maker Babolat introduced its smart racket Play Pure Drive in 2013. Smash and Shot Stats soon followed. Now Sony is partnering with Wilson to make Smart Tennis Sensor, a device that sits at the bottom of a racket's handle and tracks every metric and statistic that a tennis player or coach could need.

Source: *Gizmag*, August 22, 2014

5. How are Babolat, Sony, and other smart racket producers attempting to maximize economic profit? Draw a graph to illustrate Babolat's short-run economic profit in the market for smart tennis rackets.

6. Explain why the economic profit that Babolat and Sony make in this market is likely to be temporary. Draw a graph to illustrate the outcome in the long run. Show the excess capacity and markup in the long run.

7. Some people happily pay more for Coke or Pepsi than they are willing to pay for a nonbranded cola. And some people happily pay more for Tylenol than they are willing to pay for generic acetaminophen. How do brand names help consumers? How do brand names change the behavior of producers? Why would it not be efficient to make brand names illegal?

Use the following information to work Problems 8 and 9.

Suppose that Tommy Hilfiger's marginal cost of a jacket is a constant $100 and at one of the firm's shops, total fixed cost is $2,000 a day. The profit-maximizing number of jackets sold in this shop is 20 a day. When the shops nearby start to advertise their jackets, this Tommy Hilfiger shop spends $2,000 a day advertising its jackets, and its profit-maximizing output jumps to 50 jackets a day.

8. What is this shop's average total cost of a jacket sold before it starts to advertise? What is its average total cost of a jacket with advertising?

9. What happens to Tommy's markup and its economic profit? Why?

FIGURE 1

Price and cost (dollars per pizza)

Multiple Choice Quiz

1. Monopolistic competition differs from _____.

   A. monopoly because firms cannot set their own price
   B. oligopoly because firms produce differentiated goods or services
   C. perfect competition because the goods or services produced are differentiated
   D. monopoly because the good produced by each firm has no close substitute

2. The four largest firms in a market have the following market shares of total revenue: 20 percent, 15 percent, 10 percent, and 5 percent. The _____ in this industry is _____.

   A. four-firm concentration ratio; 50 percent
   B. four-firm concentration ratio; 750 percent
   C. Herfindahl-Hirschman Index; 50
   D. Herfindahl-Hirschman Index; 2,500

3. A firm in monopolistic competition maximizes its profit by _____.

   A. differentiating its good and producing the quantity at which price equals marginal revenue
   B. producing the quantity at which marginal revenue equals marginal cost and then adding a markup
   C. raising its price and producing so that it always has excess capacity
   D. producing the quantity at which marginal cost equals marginal revenue and charging the highest price at which it can sell that quantity

4. A firm in monopolistic competition that is maximizing profit _____.

   A. always makes a positive economic profit in the short run
   B. never needs to shut down because its price always exceeds minimum average variable cost
   C. might, in the short run, sell at a price that is less than average total cost
   D. shuts down temporarily if it incurs a loss equal to total variable cost

5. In the long run, each firm in monopolistic competition _____.

   A. makes zero economic profit
   B. makes as much economic profit as it would if it were a monopoly
   C. has the same markup and excess capacity as it would if the market were perfectly competitive
   D. creates the same deadweight loss as it would if it were a monopoly

6. If one firm advertises and other firms in the market don't, then _____.

   A. the demand for the advertised good becomes more elastic
   B. the profit-maximizing quantity of the advertised good decreases because total fixed costs increase
   C. the average cost of producing a small quantity of the advertised good rises but the average total cost of producing a large quantity might fall
   D. the economic profit made from the advertised good increases

7. Each firm in monopolistic competition uses a brand name and advertising to achieve all of the following *except* to _____.

   A. differentiate its good from its competitors' goods
   B. signal quality and reliability of its good
   C. signal its market share
   D. influence the demand for its good

Is four too few?

Oligopoly

When you have completed your study of this chapter, you will be able to

1 Describe and identify oligopoly and explain how it arises.

2 Explain the dilemma faced by firms in oligopoly.

3 Use game theory to explain how output and price are determined in oligopoly.

4 Describe the antitrust laws that regulate oligopoly.

MyEconLab Big Picture Video

18.1   WHAT IS OLIGOPOLY?

You have lots of choice when you get a smartphone, but much less choice about your wireless plan provider. Four firms share the U.S. market for wireless service, which is an *oligopoly*. Whether four firms is too few depends on whether they behave like firms in competition or like a monopoly, either of which is possible.

The distinguishing features of oligopoly are that

- A small number of firms compete.
- Natural or legal barriers prevent the entry of new firms.

■ Small Number of Firms

Energizer and Duracell dominate the market for batteries.

In contrast to monopolistic competition and perfect competition, an oligopoly consists of a small number of firms. Each firm has a large share of the market, the firms are interdependent, and they face a temptation to collude.

Interdependence

With a small number of firms in a market, each firm's actions influence the profits of the other firms. To see how, suppose you run one of the three gas stations in a small town. If you cut your price, your market share increases, and your profits might increase too. But the market share and profits of the other two firms fall. In this situation, the other firms will most likely cut their prices too. If they do cut their prices, your market share and profit take a tumble. So before deciding to cut your price, you must predict how the other firms will react and take into account the effects of their reactions on your own profit. Your profit depends on the actions of the other firms, and their profit depends on your actions. You and the other two firms are interdependent.

Temptation to Collude

When a small number of firms share a market, they can increase their profits by forming a cartel and acting like a monopoly. A **cartel** is a group of firms acting together—colluding—to limit output, raise price, and increase economic profit. Cartels are illegal in the United States (and most other countries), although international cartels can operate legally (see *Eye on the Global Economy* on p. 467). But even when there is no formal cartel, firms might try to operate like a cartel.

For reasons that you'll discover in this chapter, cartels tend to be unstable and eventually break down.

Cartel
A group of firms acting together to limit output, raise price, and increase economic profit.

■ Barriers to Entry

Either natural or legal barriers to entry can create oligopoly. You saw in Chapter 16 how economies of scale and market demand form a natural barrier to entry that can create a *natural monopoly*. These same factors can also create a natural oligopoly.

Like natural monopoly, a natural oligopoly arises from the interaction of the market demand for a good or service and the extent of economies of scale in its production. Figure 18.1 illustrates two natural oligopolies.

The demand curve, D (in both parts of the figure), shows the market demand for taxi rides in a town. If the average total cost curve of a taxi company is ATC_1

FIGURE 18.1

Natural Oligopoly   MyEconLab Animation

(a) Natural duopoly

(b) Natural oligopoly with three firms

❶ The lowest possible price is $10 a ride, which equals minimum average total cost. ❷ When a firm produces 30 rides a day, the efficient scale, ❸ two firms can satisfy the market demand. This natural oligopoly has two firms—a natural duopoly.

❹ When the efficient scale of one firm is 20 rides a day, ❺ three firms can satisfy the market demand at the lowest possible price. This natural oligopoly has three firms.

in part (a), the market is a natural **duopoly**—a market with only two firms. You can probably see some examples of duopoly where you live. Some cities have only two suppliers of milk, two local newspapers, two taxi companies, two car rental firms, two copy centers, or two college bookstores.

Duopoly
A market with only two firms.

Notice in part (a) that the efficient scale of one firm is 30 rides a day. The lowest price at which the firm would remain in business is $10 a ride. At that price, the quantity of rides demanded is 60 a day, the quantity that can be provided by just two firms. There is no room in this market for three firms. To sell more than 60 rides a day, the price would have to fall below $10 a ride. But then the firms would incur an economic loss, and one of them would exit. If the market has only one firm, it would make an economic profit and a second firm would enter to take some of the business and economic profit.

If the average total cost curve of a taxi company is ATC_2 in part (b), the efficient scale of one firm is 20 rides a day. This market is large enough for three firms, but it is not large enough for a fourth firm. Economies of scale limit the market to three firms because each firm would incur an economic loss if there were four of them. And this market will not operate with two firms because with only two, economic profit would encourage the entry of a third firm.

EYE on the U.S. ECONOMY
Examples of Oligopoly

You're familiar with a few of the industries shown in the figure. You probably know, for example, that Kellogg's makes most of the breakfast cereals consumed in the United States. It is said that Kellogg's does more business before eight o'clock in the morning than most firms do all day!

You probably also know that Airbus and Boeing make most of the airplanes that fly our skies and that Ford and GM make most of the trucks on America's roads and highways.

Less visible for good health reasons, you might know that Phillip Morris and RJ Reynolds make most of the cigarettes sold in the United States.

Some of the industries in the figure are less familiar, but you use a lot of their products. One of them is the manufacture of glass bottles and jars. When you buy anything that comes in glass, there's a good chance that the container was made in Toledo, Ohio, by Owens-Illinois, the world's largest glass packaging manufacturer.

Three others play a big role in your life. The petrochemical industry makes the plastic in everyday objects from your toothbrush to your computer keyboard. And the computer storage and recording devices industries make the hard drive in your laptop and the microphone in your smartphone.

All of the industries shown in the figure are examples of oligopoly: They are industries dominated by a small number of firms, have a high four-firm concentration ratio, and, with three exceptions, have an HHI that exceeds 2,500. One exception, breakfast cereals, is unquestionably an oligopoly.

In all of these industries, the largest firms pay close attention to each other and think carefully about the impact of their decisions on their competitors and the repercussions they themselves might face from their competitors' reactions. They are industries in which the small number of large firms are interdependent.

A legal oligopoly arises when a legal barrier to entry protects the small number of firms in a market. A city might license two taxi firms or two bus companies, for example, even though the combination of market demand and economies of scale leaves room for more than two firms.

When barriers to entry create an oligopoly, firms can make an economic profit in the long run without fear of triggering the entry of additional firms.

■ Identifying Oligopoly

Identifying oligopoly is the flip side of identifying monopolistic competition. But the borderline between the two market types is hard to pin down. We need to know whether a market is an oligopoly or monopolistic competition for two reasons. First, we want to be able to make predictions about how the market operates and how output and price will respond to such factors as a change in demand or a change in costs. Second, we want to know whether the firms in a market are delivering an efficient outcome that serves the social interest.

The key features of a market that we need to identify are whether the firms are so few that they recognize the interdependencies among them and whether they are acting in a similar way to a monopoly.

As a practical matter, we try to identify oligopoly by looking at the four-firm concentration ratio and the Herfindahl-Hirschman Index, qualified with other information about the geographical scope of the market and barriers to entry.

As we noted in Chapter 17, a market in which the HHI lies between 1,000 and 2,500 is usually an example of monopolistic competition, and a market in which the HHI exceeds 2,500 is usually an example of oligopoly.

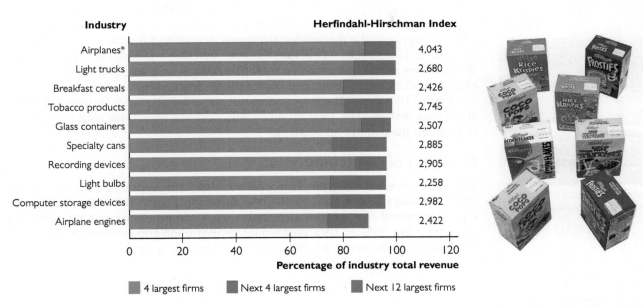

Industry	Herfindahl-Hirschman Index
Airplanes*	4,043
Light trucks	2,680
Breakfast cereals	2,426
Tobacco products	2,745
Glass containers	2,507
Specialty cans	2,885
Recording devices	2,905
Light bulbs	2,258
Computer storage devices	2,982
Airplane engines	2,422

Percentage of industry total revenue

■ 4 largest firms ■ Next 4 largest firms ■ Next 12 largest firms

SOURCES OF DATA: U.S. Census Bureau and item marked * authors calculation from industry report.

 CHECKPOINT 18.1

MyEconLab Study Plan 18.1
Key Terms Quiz
Solutions Video

Describe and identify oligopoly and explain how it arises.

Practice Problems

1. What are the distinguishing features of oligopoly?
2. Why are breakfast cereals made by firms in oligopoly? Why isn't there monopolistic competition in that industry?
3. Duracell's share of revenue in the market for batteries is 45 percent. Energizer's share is 35 percent. A few smaller firms share the rest of the market. In what type of market are batteries sold? Explain your answer.

Solutions to Practice Problems

1. The distinguishing features of oligopoly are a small number of interdependent firms competing behind natural or legal barriers to entry.
2. Breakfast cereals are made by firms in oligopoly because economies of scale and the size of the market limit the number of firms that can make a profit.
3. The market for batteries is an oligopoly, and with two dominant firms it is a duopoly. The number of firms is small, their actions are interdependent, and economies of scale and the market demand create a natural barrier to entry.

Boeing and Airbus share the market for big passenger airplanes.

18.2   THE OLIGOPOLISTS' DILEMMA

Oligopoly might operate like monopoly, like perfect competition, or somewhere between these two extremes. To see these alternative possible outcomes, we'll study duopoly in the market for airplanes. Airbus and Boeing are the only makers of large commercial jet aircraft. Suppose that they have identical costs. To keep the numbers simple, assume that total fixed cost is zero and that regardless of the rate of production, the marginal cost of producing an airplane is $1 million.

Figure 18.2 shows the market demand curve for airplanes. Airbus and Boeing share this market. The total quantity sold and the quantities sold by each firm depend on the price of an airplane.

■ Monopoly Outcome

If this industry had only one firm operating as a single-price monopoly, its marginal revenue curve would be the one shown in Figure 18.2. Marginal revenue equals marginal cost when 6 airplanes a week are produced and the price of an airplane is $13 million. Total cost would be $6 million and total revenue would be $78 million, so economic profit would be $72 million a week.

■ **FIGURE 18.2**

A Market for Airplanes

❶ With market demand curve, *D*, marginal revenue curve, *MR*, and marginal cost curve, *MC*, a monopoly airplane maker maximizes profit by producing 6 airplanes a week and selling them at a price of $13 million an airplane.

❷ With perfect competition among airplane makers, the market equilibrium quantity is 12 airplanes a week and the equilibrium price is $1 million an airplane.

❸ A cartel might achieve the monopoly equilibrium, break down and result in the perfect competition equilibrium, or operate somewhere between these two extreme outcomes.

Cartel to Achieve Monopoly Outcome

Can the two firms achieve the monopoly outcome that we've just found and maximize their joint profit? They can attempt to do so by forming a cartel.

Suppose that Airbus and Boeing agreed to limit the total production of airplanes to 6 a week. The market demand curve tells us that the price of an airplane would be $13 million and economic profit would be $72 million a week. Suppose that the two firms also agree to split the market evenly and each produce 3 airplanes a week. They would each make an economic profit of $36 million a week—see Table 18.1.

Would it be in the self-interest of Airbus and Boeing to stick to their agreement and limit production to 3 airplanes a week each?

To begin answering this question, notice that with the price of an airplane exceeding marginal cost, if one firm increased production, it would increase its profit. But if both firms increased output whenever price exceeded marginal cost, the end of the process would be the same as perfect competition.

■ Perfect Competition Outcome

You can see the perfect competition outcome in Figure 18.2. The equilibrium is where the market supply curve, which is the marginal cost curve, intersects the market demand curve. The quantity is 12 airplanes a week, and the price is the same as marginal cost—$1 million per airplane.

■ Other Possible Cartel Breakdowns

Because price exceeds marginal cost, a cartel is likely to break down. But a cartel might not unravel all the way to perfect competition. In *Eye on the Global Economy* on p. 467, you can see the brief history of a sometimes successful and sometimes unsuccessful cartel in the global market for oil. You can see why a cartel breaks down, but not all the way to perfect competition, by looking at some alternative outcomes in the airplane industry example.

Boeing Increases Output to 4 Airplanes a Week

Suppose that starting from a cartel that achieves the monopoly outcome, Boeing increases output by 1 airplane a week. Table 18.2 keeps track of the data. With Boeing producing 4 airplanes a week and Airbus producing 3 airplanes a week, total output is 7 airplanes a week. To sell 7 airplanes a week, the price must fall. The market demand curve in Figure 18.2 tells us that the quantity demanded is 7 airplanes a week when the price is $11 million an airplane.

The market total revenue would now be $77 million, total cost would be $7 million, and economic profit would fall to $70 million. But the distribution of this economic profit is now unequal. Boeing would gain, and Airbus would lose.

Boeing would now receive $44 million a week in total revenue, have a total cost of $4 million, and make an economic profit of $40 million. Airbus would receive $33 million a week in total revenue, incur a total cost of $3 million, and make an economic profit of $30 million.

So by increasing its output by 1 airplane a week, Boeing can increase its economic profit by $4 million and cause the economic profit of Airbus to fall by $6 million.

Because the two firms in this example are identical, we could rerun the above story with Airbus increasing production by 1 airplane a week and Boeing holding

TABLE 18.1 MONOPOLY OUTCOME

	Boeing	Airbus	Market total
Quantity (airplanes a week)	3	3	6
Price ($ million per airplane)	13	13	13
Total revenue ($ million)	39	39	78
Total cost ($ million)	3	3	6
Economic profit ($ million)	36	36	72

TABLE 18.2 BOEING INCREASES OUTPUT TO 4 AIRPLANES PER WEEK

	Boeing	Airbus	Market total
Quantity (airplanes a week)	4	3	7
Price ($ million per airplane)	11	11	11
Total revenue ($ million)	44	33	77
Total cost ($ million)	4	3	7
Economic profit ($ million)	40	30	70

output at 3 airplanes a week. In this case, Airbus would make $40 million a week and Boeing would make $30 million a week.

Boeing is better off producing 4 airplanes a week if Airbus sticks with 3 a week. But is it in Airbus's interest to hold its output at 3 airplanes a week? To answer this question, we need to compare the economic profit Airbus makes if it maintains its output at 3 airplanes a week with the profit it makes if it produces 4 airplanes a week. What is Airbus' economic profit if it produces 4 airplanes a week with Boeing also producing 4 airplanes a week?

Airbus Increases Output to 4 Airplanes a Week

With both firms producing 4 airplanes a week, total output is 8 airplanes a week. To sell 8 airplanes a week, the price must fall further. The market demand curve in Figure 18.2 tells us that the quantity demanded is 8 airplanes a week when the price is $9 million an airplane.

Table 18.3 keeps track of the data. The market total revenue would now be $72 million, total cost would be $8 million, and economic profit would fall to $64 million. With both firms producing the same output, the distribution of this economic profit is now equal.

Each firm would now receive $36 million a week in total revenue, have a total cost of $4 million, and make an economic profit of $32 million. For Airbus, this outcome is an improvement on the previous one by $2 million a week. For Boeing, this outcome is worse than the previous one by $8 million.

This outcome is better for Airbus, but would Boeing go along with it? You know that Boeing would be worse off if it decreased its output to 3 airplanes a week because it would get the outcome that Airbus has in Table 18.2—an economic profit of only $30 million a week. But would Boeing be better off if it increased output to 5 airplanes a week?

Boeing Increases Output to 5 Airplanes a Week

Suppose now that Airbus maintains its output at 4 airplanes a week and Boeing increases output to 5 a week. Table 18.4 keeps track of the data. Total output is now 9 airplanes a week. To sell this quantity, the price must fall to $7 million an airplane. Market total revenue is $63 million and total cost is $9 million, so economic profit for the two firms is $54 million. The distribution of this economic profit is again unequal. But now both firms would lose.

Boeing would now receive $35 million a week in total revenue, have a total cost of $5 million, and make an economic profit of $30 million—$2 million less than it would make if it maintained its output at 4 airplanes a week. Airbus would receive $28 million a week in total revenue, incur a total cost of $4 million, and make an economic profit of $24 million—$8 million less than before. So neither firm gains by increasing total output beyond 8 airplanes a week.

■ The Oligopoly Cartel Dilemma

With a cartel, both firms make the maximum available economic profit. If both firms increase production, both see their profit fall. If only one firm increases production, that firm makes a larger economic profit while the other makes a lower economic profit. So what will the firms do? We can speculate about what they will do, but to work out the answer, we need some game theory.

TABLE 18.3 AIRBUS INCREASES OUTPUT TO 4 AIRPLANES PER WEEK

	Boeing	Airbus	Market total
Quantity (airplanes a week)	4	4	8
Price ($ million per airplane)	9	9	9
Total revenue ($ million)	36	36	72
Total cost ($ million)	4	4	8
Economic profit ($ million)	32	32	64

TABLE 18.4 BOEING INCREASES OUTPUT TO 5 AIRPLANES PER WEEK

	Boeing	Airbus	Market total
Quantity (airplanes a week)	5	4	9
Price ($ million per airplane)	7	7	7
Total revenue ($ million)	35	28	63
Total cost ($ million)	5	4	9
Economic profit ($ million)	30	24	54

EYE on the GLOBAL ECONOMY
The OPEC Global Oil Cartel

The Organization of the Petroleum Exporting Countries (OPEC) is an international cartel of oil-producing nations that was created in 1960.

OPEC describes its objective as being "to co-ordinate and unify petroleum policies among member countries in order to secure fair and stable prices ..." These words can be interpreted as "restricting the production of oil to keep its price high."

During the 1960s, the cartel quietly built its organization and prepared the ground for its push to dominate the global oil market. OPEC's first opportunity came in 1973 when, with an Arab-Israeli war raging, it organized an embargo on oil shipments to the United States and Europe. The price of oil rose to four times its previous level. OPEC's second opportunity came with the Iranian revolution in 1979 when it more than doubled the price of oil.

The figure shows both these price hikes. The price rose from about $8 a barrel in 1970 to more than $86 a barrel by 1980. (To compare prices over a number of years, we express them in terms of the value of the dollar in 2015.)

During the 1980s, many new sources of oil supply opened up and the OPEC cartel lost control of the global market. The cartel broke down, and the price of oil fell.

The price of oil remained remarkably stable during the 1990s, and the power of OPEC was countered by a large supply of oil from other sources.

From 2003 to 2008, Asian demand for oil grew dramatically and OPEC

OPEC ministers meeting at the organization's headquarters in Vienna

again dominated the global market, restricted its production, and pushed the world price to a new high in 2008.

But OPEC lost power again during the global recession of 2009 and the years that followed. A slowing of growth in China decreased the

demand for oil. And the development of fracking technology in the United States increased the supply of oil and natural gas. In 2015, the United States joined the ranks of oil exporters, which contributed to a steep fall in the oil price.

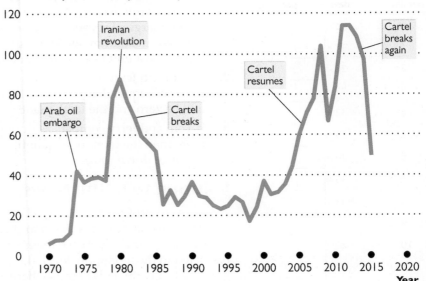

SOURCES OF DATA: OPEC and Bureau of Economic Analysis.

TABLE 1

Price (dollars per unit)	Quantity demanded (units per day)
12	0
11	1
10	2
9	3
8	4
7	5
6	6
5	7
4	8
3	9
2	10
1	11
0	12

TABLE 2

Quantity (units per day)	Total revenue (dollars per day)	Marginal revenue (dollars per unit)
0	0	
		11
1	11	
		9
2	20	
		7
3	27	
		5
4	32	
		3
5	35	
		1
6	36	
		−1
7	35	
		−3
8	32	
		−5
9	27	
		−7
10	20	
		−9
11	11	
		−11
12	0	

CHECKPOINT 18.2

Explain the dilemma faced by firms in oligopoly.

Practice Problems

Isolated Island has two natural gas wells, one owned by Tom and the other owned by Jerry. Each well has a valve that controls the flow of gas. The marginal cost of producing gas is zero. Table 1 gives the demand schedule for the gas.

1. If Tom and Jerry form a cartel and maximize their joint profit, what will be the price of gas and the quantity produced?

2. If Tom and Jerry are forced to sell at the perfectly competitive price, what will be the price of gas and the total quantity produced?

3. If Tom and Jerry compete as duopolists, what will be the price of gas?

In the News

OPEC calls for co-operation to stem price collapse
OPEC has asked the world's largest oil producers to help stop a price collapse. But OPEC member Saudi Arabia, the world's biggest oil exporter, wants to keep output high.

Source: *Financial Times*, January 25, 2016

For information about OPEC, see p. 467. Explain how an effective profit-maximizing oil producers' cartel would influence the global market for oil and the world price of oil. Why does Saudi Arabia want to keep output high?

Solutions to Practice Problems

1. If Tom and Jerry form a cartel and maximize their joint profit, they will charge the monopoly price. This price is the highest price the market will bear when together they produce the quantity at which marginal revenue equals marginal cost. Marginal cost is zero, so we need to find the price at which marginal revenue is zero. Marginal revenue is zero when total revenue is a maximum, which occurs when output is 6 units a day (Table 2) and price is $6 a unit (see the demand schedule in Table 1).

2. If Tom and Jerry are forced to sell at the perfectly competitive price, the price will equal marginal cost. Marginal cost is zero, so in this case, the price will be zero and the total quantity produced will be 12 units a day.

3. If Tom and Jerry compete as duopolists, they will increase production to more than the monopoly quantity. The price will fall, but they will not drive the price down to zero.

Solution to In the News

A successful profit-maximizing oil cartel would operate as a monopoly. It would produce the quantity at which marginal revenue equals marginal cost and agree on production levels for each member of the cartel. With the quantity produced restricted to the monopoly level, the price would be high and would exceed marginal cost. A cartel fails because there is no incentive for each member to stick to its production quota. Because price exceeds marginal cost, each member of the cartel has an incentive to overproduce, like Saudi Arabia in the news clip.

18.3 GAME THEORY

MyEconLab Concept Video

Game theory is the tool that economists use to analyze *strategic behavior*—behavior that recognizes mutual interdependence and takes account of the expected behavior of others. John von Neumann invented game theory in 1937, and today it is a major research field in economics.

Game theory helps us to understand oligopoly and many other forms of economic, political, social, and even biological rivalries. We will begin our study of game theory and its application to the behavior of firms by thinking about familiar games that we play for fun.

■ What Is a Game?

What is a game? At first thought, the question seems silly. After all, there are many different games. There are ball games and parlor games, games of chance and games of skill. But what is it about all these different activities that make them games? What do all these games have in common? All games share three features:

- Rules
- Strategies
- Payoffs

Let's see how these common features of games apply to a game called "the prisoners' dilemma." The **prisoners' dilemma** is a game between two prisoners that shows why it is hard to cooperate even when it would be beneficial to both players to do so. This game captures the essential feature of the duopolists' dilemma that we've just been studying. The prisoners' dilemma also provides a good illustration of how game theory works and how it generates predictions.

■ The Prisoners' Dilemma

Art and Bob have been caught red-handed, stealing a car. During the district attorney's interviews with the prisoners, he begins to suspect that he has stumbled on the two people who committed a multimillion-dollar bank robbery some months earlier. But this is just a suspicion. The district attorney has no evidence on which he can convict them of the greater crime unless he can get them to confess. He makes the prisoners play a game with the following rules.

Rules

Each prisoner (player) is placed in a separate room and cannot communicate with the other player. Each is told that he is suspected of having carried out the bank robbery and that

- If both of them confess to the larger crime, each will receive a reduced sentence of 3 years for both crimes.
- If he alone confesses and his accomplice does not, he will receive an even shorter sentence of 1 year, while his accomplice will receive a 10-year sentence.
- If neither of them confesses to the larger crime, each will receive a 2-year sentence for car theft.

Game theory
The tool that economists use to analyze *strategic behavior*—behavior that recognizes mutual interdependence and takes account of the expected behavior of others.

Prisoners' dilemma
A game between two prisoners that shows why it is hard to cooperate even when it would be beneficial to both players to do so.

Strategies
All the possible actions of each player in a game.

Strategies

In game theory, **strategies** are all the possible actions of each player. Art and Bob each have two possible strategies:

- Confess to the bank robbery.
- Deny having committed the bank robbery.

Payoffs

Because there are two players, each with two strategies, there are four possible outcomes:

- Both confess.
- Both deny.
- Art confesses and Bob denies.
- Bob confesses and Art denies.

Each prisoner can work out exactly what happens to him—his *payoff*—in each of these four situations. We can tabulate the four possible payoffs for each of the prisoners in what is called a payoff matrix for the game. A **payoff matrix** is a table that shows the payoffs for every possible action by each player given every possible action by the other player.

Table 18.5 shows a payoff matrix for Art and Bob. The squares show the payoffs for the two prisoners—the red triangle in each square shows Art's, and the blue triangle shows Bob's. If both prisoners confess (top left), each gets a prison term of 3 years. If Bob confesses but Art denies (top right), Art gets a 10-year sentence and Bob gets a 1-year sentence. If Art confesses and Bob denies (bottom left), Art gets a 1-year sentence and Bob gets a 10-year sentence. Finally, if both of them deny (bottom right), neither can be convicted of the bank robbery charge but both are sentenced for the car theft—a 2-year sentence.

Payoff matrix
A table that shows the payoffs for each player for every possible combination of actions by the players.

TABLE 18.5   PRISONERS' DILEMMA PAYOFF MATRIX

Each square shows the payoffs for the two players, Art and Bob, for each possible pair of actions. In each square, the red triangle shows Art's payoff and the blue triangle shows Bob's. For example, if both confess, the payoffs are in the top left square.

Equilibrium

The equilibrium of a game occurs when each player takes the best possible action given the action of the other player. This equilibrium concept is called **Nash equilibrium**. It is so named because John Nash of Princeton University, who received the Nobel Prize for Economic Science in 1994, proposed it. (The same John Nash was portrayed by Russell Crowe in *A Beautiful Mind*.)

In the case of the prisoners' dilemma, equilibrium occurs when Art makes his best choice given Bob's choice and when Bob makes his best choice given Art's choice. Let's find the equilibrium.

First, look at the situation from Art's point of view. If Bob confesses, it pays Art to confess because in that case, he is sentenced to 3 years rather than 10 years. If Bob does not confess, it still pays Art to confess because in that case, he receives 1 year rather than 2 years. So no matter what Bob does, Art's best action is to confess.

Second, look at the situation from Bob's point of view. If Art confesses, it pays Bob to confess because in that case, he is sentenced to 3 years rather than 10 years. If Art does not confess, it still pays Bob to confess because in that case, he receives 1 year rather than 2 years. So no matter what Art does, Bob's best action is to confess.

Nash equilibrium
An equilibrium in which each player takes the best possible action given the action of the other player.

Because each player's best action is to confess, each does confess and each gets a 3-year prison term. The district attorney has solved the bank robbery. This is the equilibrium of the game.

Not the Best Outcome

The equilibrium of the prisoners' dilemma game is not the best outcome for the prisoners. Isn't there some way in which they can cooperate and get the shorter 2-year prison term? There is not, because the players cannot communicate with each other. Each player can put himself in the other player's place and can figure out what the other will do. The prisoners are in a dilemma. Each knows that he can serve only 2 years if he can trust the other to deny. But each also knows that it is not in the best interest of the other to deny. So each prisoner knows that he must confess, thereby delivering a bad outcome for both.

Let's now see how we can use the ideas we've just developed to understand the behavior of firms in oligopoly. We'll start by returning to the duopolists' dilemma.

■ The Duopolists' Dilemma

The dilemma of Airbus and Boeing is similar to that of Art and Bob. Each firm has two strategies. It can produce airplanes at the rate of

- 3 airplanes a week
- 4 airplanes a week

Because each firm has two strategies, there are four possible combinations of actions for the two firms:

- Both firms produce 3 airplanes a week (monopoly outcome).
- Both firms produce 4 airplanes a week.
- Airbus produces 3 airplanes and Boeing produces 4 airplanes a week.
- Boeing produces 3 airplanes and Airbus produces 4 airplanes a week.

■ The Payoff Matrix

Table 18.6 sets out the payoff matrix for this game. It is constructed in exactly the same way as the payoff matrix for the prisoners' dilemma in Table 18.5. The squares show the payoffs for Airbus and Boeing. In this case, the payoffs are economic profits. (In the case of the prisoners' dilemma, the payoffs were losses.)

The table shows that if both firms produce 4 airplanes a week (top left), each firm makes an economic profit of $32 million. If both firms produce 3 airplanes a week (bottom right), they make the monopoly profit, and each firm makes an economic profit of $36 million. The top right and bottom left squares show what happens if one firm produces 4 airplanes a week while the other produces 3 airplanes a week. The firm that increases production makes an economic profit of $40 million, and the one that keeps production at the monopoly quantity makes an economic profit of $30 million.

Equilibrium of the Duopolists' Dilemma

What do the firms do? To answer this question, we must find the equilibrium of the duopoly game.

TABLE 18.6 DUOPOLISTS' DILEMMA PAYOFF MATRIX

Each square shows the payoffs from a pair of actions. For example, if both firms produce 3 airplanes a week, the payoffs are recorded in the bottom right square. The red triangle shows Airbus's payoff, and the blue triangle shows Boeing's.

TABLE 18.7   THE NASH EQUILIBRIUM

The Nash equilibrium is for each firm to produce 4 airplanes a week.

Using the information in Table 18.7, look at things from Airbus's point of view. Airbus reasons as follows: Suppose that Boeing produces 4 airplanes a week. If I, Airbus, produce 3 a week, I will make an economic profit of $30 million. If I also produce 4 a week, I will make an economic profit of $32 million. So I'm better off producing 4 airplanes a week. Airbus continues to reason: Now suppose Boeing produces 3 a week. If I produce 4 a week, I will make an economic profit of $40 million, and if I produce 3 a week, I will make an economic profit of $36 million. Economic profit of $40 million is better than economic profit of $36 million, so I'm better off if I produce 4 airplanes a week. So regardless of whether Boeing produces 3 a week or 4 a week, it pays Airbus to produce 4 airplanes a week.

Because the two firms face identical situations, Boeing comes to the same conclusion as Airbus, so both firms produce 4 a week. The equilibrium of the duopoly game is that both firms produce 4 airplanes a week.

Collusion Is Profitable but Difficult to Achieve

In the duopolists' dilemma that you've just studied, Airbus and Boeing end up in a situation that is similar to that of the prisoners in the prisoners' dilemma game. They don't achieve the best joint outcome. Because each produces 4 airplanes a week, each makes an economic profit of $32 million a week.

If firms were able to collude, they would agree to limit their production to 3 airplanes a week each and they would each make the monopoly profit of $36 million a week.

The outcome of the duopolists' dilemma shows why it is difficult for firms to collude. Even if collusion were a legal activity, firms in duopoly would find it difficult to implement an agreement to restrict output. Like the players of the prisoners' dilemma game, the duopolists would reach a Nash equilibrium in which they produce more than the joint profit-maximizing quantity.

If two firms have difficulty maintaining a collusive agreement, oligopolies with more than two firms have an even harder time. The operation of OPEC (see *Eye on the Global Economy* on p. 467) illustrates this difficulty. To raise the price of oil, OPEC must limit global oil production. The members of this cartel meet from time to time and set a production limit for each member nation. Almost always, within a few months of a decision to restrict production, some (usually smaller) members of the cartel break their quotas, production increases, and the price sags below the cartel's desired target. The OPEC cartel plays an oligopoly dilemma game similar to the prisoners' dilemma. Only in 1973, 1979–1980, and 2005–2007 did OPEC manage to keep its members' production under control and raise the price of oil.

MyEconLab Concept Video

■ Advertising and Research Games in Oligopoly

Every month, Coke and Pepsi, Nike and Adidas, Procter & Gamble and Kimberly-Clark, Nokia and Motorola, and hundreds of other pairs of big firms locked in fierce competition spend millions of dollars on advertising campaigns and on research and development (R&D). They make decisions about whether to increase or cut the advertising budget or whether to undertake a large R&D effort aimed at lowering production costs or at making the product more reliable. (Usually, the more reliable a product, the more expensive it is to produce, but the more people are willing to pay for it.) These choices can be analyzed as games. Let's look at some examples of these types of games.

Advertising Game

A key to success in the soft drink industry is to run huge advertising campaigns. These campaigns affect market share but are costly to run. Table 18.8 shows some hypothetical numbers for the advertising game that Pepsi and Coke play. Each firm has two strategies: Advertise or don't advertise. If neither firm advertises, they each make $50 million (bottom right of the payoff matrix). If each firm advertises, each firm's profit is lower by the amount spent on advertising (top left square of the payoff matrix). If Pepsi advertises but Coke does not, Pepsi gains and Coke loses (top right square of the payoff matrix). Finally, if Coke advertises and Pepsi does not, Coke gains and Pepsi loses (bottom left square).

Pepsi reasons as follows: Regardless of whether Coke advertises, we're better off advertising. Coke reasons similarly: Regardless of whether Pepsi advertises, we're better off advertising. Because advertising is the best strategy for both players, it is the Nash equilibrium. The outcome of this game is that both firms advertise and make less profit than they would if they could collude to achieve the cooperative outcome of no advertising.

Research and Development Game

A key to success in the facial tissue market is to design a product that people value highly relative to the cost of producing it. The firm that develops the most highly valued product and the least-cost technology for producing it gains a competitive edge. It can undercut the rest of the market, increase its market share, and increase its economic profit. But it is costly to undertake the R&D that can ultimately result in an improved product and increased profit. So the cost of R&D must be deducted from the increased profit. If no firm does R&D, every firm can be better off, but if one firm initiates the R&D activity, all firms must follow.

Table 18.9 illustrates the dilemma (with hypothetical numbers) for the R&D game that Kimberly-Clark (Kleenex) and Procter & Gamble (Puffs) play. Each firm has two strategies: Do R&D or do no R&D. If neither firm does R&D, Kimberly-Clark makes $30 million and Procter & Gamble makes $70 million (bottom right of the payoff matrix). If each firm does R&D, each firm's profit is lower by the amount spent on R&D (top left square of the payoff matrix). If Kimberly-Clark does R&D but Procter & Gamble does not, Kimberly-Clark gains and Procter & Gamble loses (top right square of the payoff matrix). Finally, if Procter & Gamble conducts R&D and Kimberly-Clark does not, Procter & Gamble gains and Kimberly-Clark loses (bottom left square).

Kimberly-Clark reasons as follows: Regardless of whether Procter & Gamble undertakes R&D, we're better off doing R&D. Procter & Gamble reasons similarly: Regardless of whether Kimberly-Clark does R&D, we're better off doing R&D.

Because R&D is the best strategy for both players, it is the Nash equilibrium. The outcome of this game is that both firms conduct R&D. They make less profit than they would if they could collude to achieve the cooperative outcome of no R&D.

The real-world situation has more players than Kimberly-Clark and Procter & Gamble. A large number of other firms, especially producers of store brands, strive to capture market share from Procter & Gamble and Kimberly-Clark. So the R&D effort by these two firms not only serves the purpose of maintaining shares in their own battle but also helps to keep barriers to entry high enough to preserve their joint market share.

TABLE 18.8   THE ADVERTISING GAME PAYOFF MATRIX

For each pair of strategies, the red triangle shows Coke's payoff, and the blue triangle shows Pepsi's. If both firms advertise, they make less than if neither firm advertises. But each firm is better off advertising if the other doesn't advertise. The Nash equilibrium for this prisoners' dilemma advertising game is for both firms to advertise.

TABLE 18.9   THE R&D GAME PAYOFF MATRIX

For each pair of strategies, the red triangle shows Procter & Gamble's payoff, and the blue triangle shows Kimberly-Clark's. If both firms do R&D, they make less than if neither firm undertakes R&D. But each firm is better off doing R&D if the other does no R&D. The Nash equilibrium for this prisoners' dilemma R&D game is for both firms to do R&D.

EYE on YOUR LIFE
A Game You Might Play

The payoff matrix here describes a game that might be familiar to you. But it isn't a prisoners' dilemma. It's a lovers' dilemma.

Jane and Jim have more fun if they do something together than if they do things alone.

But Jane likes the movies more than the ball game, and Jim likes the ball game more than the movies.

The payoff matrix describes how much they like the various outcomes (measured in units of utility).

What do they do?

By comparing the utility numbers for different strategies, you can figure out that Jim never goes to the movies alone and Jane never goes to the ball game alone.

You can also figure out that Jim doesn't go to the ball game alone and Jane doesn't go to the movies alone.

They always go out together. But do they go to the movies or the ball game?

The answer is that we can't tell. This game has no unique equilibrium. The payoffs tell you that Jane and Jim might go to either the game or the movies.

In a repeated game, they'll probably alternate between the two and might even toss a coin to decide which to go to on any given evening.

Payoffs are in units of utility

Repeated Games

The games that we've studied are played just once. In contrast, most real-world games get played repeatedly. This fact suggests that real-world duopolists might find some way of learning to cooperate so that they can enjoy a monopoly profit. If a game is played repeatedly, one player has the opportunity to penalize the other player for previous "bad" behavior. If Airbus produces 4 airplanes this week, perhaps Boeing will produce 4 next week. Before Airbus produces 4 this week, won't it take account of the possibility of Boeing producing 4 next week? What is the equilibrium of this more complicated dilemma game when it is repeated indefinitely?

The monopoly equilibrium might occur if each firm knows that the other will punish overproduction with overproduction, "tit for tat." Let's see why.

Table 18.10 keeps track of the numbers. Suppose that Boeing contemplates producing 4 airplanes in week 1. This move will bring it an economic profit of $40 million and will cut the economic profit of Airbus to $30 million. In week 2, Airbus will punish Boeing and produce 4 airplanes. But Boeing must go back to 3 airplanes to induce Airbus to cooperate again in week 3. So in week 2, Airbus makes an economic profit of $40 million, and Boeing makes an economic profit of $30 million. Adding up the profits over these two weeks of play, Boeing would have made $72 million by cooperating (2 × $36 million) compared with $70 million from producing 4 airplanes in week 1 and generating Airbus's tit-for-tat response.

What is true for Boeing is also true for Airbus. Because each firm makes a larger profit by sticking to the monopoly output, both firms do so and the monopoly price, quantity, and profit prevail.

In reality, whether a duopoly (or more generally an oligopoly) works like a one-play game or a repeated game depends primarily on the number of players and the ease of detecting and punishing overproduction. The larger the number of players, the harder it is to maintain the monopoly outcome.

TABLE 18.10 PAYOFFS WITH PUNISHMENT

	Cooperate		Overproduce	
Period of play	Boeing profit	Airbus profit	Boeing profit	Airbus profit
	(millions of dollars)			
1	36	36	40	30
2	36	36	30	40

EYE on the WIRELESS OLIGOPOLY

Is Four Too Few?

Your smartphone plan is almost certainly with one of four firms: Verizon, AT&T, Sprint, or T-Mobile. The pie chart in Figure 1 shows the four firms' market shares along with that of a token fifth firm, U.S. Cellular.

With a third of the market each, Verizon and AT&T are the dominant players, but sharing almost equally the other third, Sprint and T-Mobile are also significant participants in what is a wireless service oligopoly.

Does this market have enough firms? Is four too few? Would consumers be better served if more firms entered the market?

The number of firms that a market can support depends on the extent of its economies of scale and the market demand. We don't have data on the firms' long-run average cost curves that would tell us about the economies of scale, but we do have information about the firms' profits. We can use

that profit information to get an indirect look at economies of scale.

The pie chart in Figure 2 shows the gross earnings of the four wireless firms. (Gross means before deducting depreciation.)

Because of economies of scale, the two larger firms have much bigger gross profits than the two smaller firms. But the two smaller firms are large enough to earn a profit. With the two smaller firms being profitable, and with each having about a one-sixth market share, it seems likely that demand in the U.S. wireless market is large enough for more than four firms to profitably survive.

If more firms could operate profitably in this market, we should expect to see entry. And that is exactly what is happening. Google, in collaboration with Dish Network, is entering with a virtual wireless service. There might be room for even more firms.

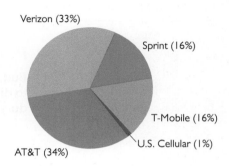

Figure 1 Wireless Subscriber Shares

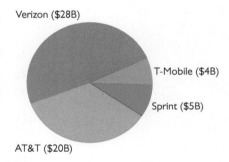

Figure 2 Wireless Gross Profit

SOURCES OF DATA: Statista.com and Forbes.com.

■ Is Oligopoly Efficient?

The quantity produced of any good or service is the efficient quantity if the price (which measures marginal benefit) equals marginal cost. Does oligopoly produce efficient quantities of goods and services?

You've seen that if firms in oligopoly play a repeated prisoners' dilemma game, they can end up restricting output to the monopoly level and making the same economic profit as a monopoly would make. You've also seen that even when the firms don't cooperate, they don't necessarily drive the price down to marginal cost. So generally, oligopoly is not efficient. It suffers from the same source of inefficiency as monopoly.

Also, firms in oligopoly might end up operating at a higher average total cost than the lowest attainable cost because their advertising and research budgets are higher than the socially efficient level.

Because oligopoly creates inefficiency and firms in oligopoly have an incentive to try to behave like a monopoly, the United States has established antitrust laws that seek to reduce market power and move the oligopoly outcome closer to the efficient competitive outcome. In the next section, we study U.S. antitrust law.

CHECKPOINT 18.3

Use game theory to explain how output and price are determined in oligopoly.

Practice Problems

Bud and Wise are the only two producers of New Age beer, which is designed to displace root beer. Bud and Wise are trying to work out the quantity to produce. They know that if

- Both limit production to 10,000 gallons a day, they will make the maximum attainable joint profit of $200,000 a day—$100,000 a day each.
- One produces 20,000 gallons a day while the other produces 10,000 a day, the one that produces 20,000 gallons will make an economic profit of $150,000 and the one that sticks with 10,000 gallons will incur an economic loss of $50,000.
- Both produce 20,000 gallons a day, each will make zero economic profit.

1. Construct a payoff matrix for the game that Bud and Wise must play.
2. Find the Nash equilibrium of the game that Bud and Wise play.
3. What is the equilibrium of the game if Bud and Wise play it repeatedly?

In the News

T-Mobile launches campaign against 'dark duopoly' of AT&T, Verizon
In a social media campaign, T-Mobile CEO John Legere urges wireless users to join him to defeat "the dark force" of AT&T and Verizon. He says they already control too much of the frequency bands used for wireless and that if they get more at the upcoming auction, wireless service will become a duopoly.
Source: *The Dallas Morning News*, June 23, 2015
What is the game that T-Mobile, AT&T, and Verizon are playing?

Solutions to Practice Problems

1. Table 1 shows the payoff matrix for the game that Bud and Wise must play.
2. The Nash equilibrium is for both to produce 20,000 gallons of New Age beer a day. To see why, notice that regardless of the quantity that Bud produces, Wise makes more profit by producing 20,000 gallons of New Age beer a day. The same is true for Bud. So Bud and Wise each produce 20,000 gallons of New Age beer a day.
3. If Bud and Wise play this game repeatedly, each produces 10,000 gallons of New Age beer a day and makes maximum economic profit. They can achieve this outcome by playing a tit-for-tat strategy.

Solution to In the News

T-Mobile, AT&T, and Verizon are playing a prisoners' dilemma game for control of a large share of the frequency bands used by smartphones. Each firm could bid a low price for the share that minimizes its cost, or bid a high price for more than it currently plans to use. The Nash equilibrium is for all three to bid too high a price for too much bandwidth. It is possible that AT&T and Verizon might outbid T-Mobile and become a duopoly.

TABLE 1

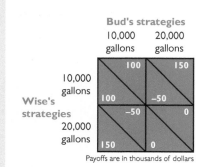

Payoffs are in thousands of dollars

18.4 ANTITRUST LAW

Antitrust law is the body of law that regulates oligopolies and prohibits them from becoming monopolies or behaving like monopolies.

■ The Antitrust Laws

Congress passed the first antitrust law, the Sherman Act, in 1890 in an atmosphere of outrage and disgust at the actions and practices of J. P. Morgan, John D. Rockefeller, and W. H. Vanderbilt—the so-called "robber barons."

A wave of mergers at the turn of the twentieth century produced stronger antitrust laws. The Clayton Act of 1914 supplemented the Sherman Act, and Congress created the Federal Trade Commission to enforce the antitrust laws.

Table 18.11 summarizes the two main provisions of the Sherman Act. Section 1 of the act is precise. Conspiring with others to restrict competition is illegal. But section 2 is general and imprecise. Just what is an "attempt to monopolize"? The Clayton Act and its two amendments, the Robinson-Patman Act of 1936, and the Celler-Kefauver Act of 1950, which outlaw specific practices, answer this question. Table 18.11 describes these practices and summarizes the main provisions of these three acts.

■ Three Antitrust Policy Debates

Price fixing is *always* a violation of the antitrust law. If the Justice Department can prove the existence of price fixing, a defendant can offer no acceptable excuse. But other practices are more controversial and generate debate among antitrust lawyers and economists. We'll examine three of these practices:

- Resale price maintenance
- Predatory pricing
- Tying arrangements

Resale Price Maintenance

Most manufacturers sell their products to the final consumer indirectly through a wholesale and retail distribution system. **Resale price maintenance** occurs when a manufacturer agrees with a distributor on the price at which the product will be resold.

Resale price maintenance (also called vertical price fixing) *agreements* are illegal under the Sherman Act. But it isn't illegal for a manufacturer to refuse to supply a retailer who doesn't accept the manufacturer's guidance on what the price should be.

Attorneys general in 41 states alleged that Universal, Sony, Warner, Bertelsmann, and EMI kept CD prices artificially high between 1995 and 2000 with a practice called "minimum-advertised pricing." The companies denied the allegation but made a large payment to settle the case.

Does resale price maintenance create an inefficient or efficient use of resources? Economists can be found on both sides of this question.

Inefficient Resale Price Maintenance   Resale price maintenance is inefficient if it enables dealers to charge the monopoly price. By setting and enforcing the resale price, the manufacturer might be able to achieve the monopoly price.

Antitrust law
A body of law that regulates oligopolies and prohibits them from becoming monopolies or behaving like monopolies.

Resale price maintenance
An agreement between a manufacturer and a distributor on the price at which a product will be resold.

TABLE 18.11

The Antitrust Laws: A Summary

The Sherman Act, 1890

Section 1:

Every contract, combination in the form of trust or otherwise, or conspiracy, in restraint of trade or commerce among the several States, or with foreign nations, is hereby declared to be illegal.

Section 2:

Every person who shall monopolize, or attempt to monopolize, or combine or conspire with any other person or persons, to monopolize any part of the trade or commerce among the several States, or with foreign nations, shall be deemed guilty of a felony.

Clayton Act, 1914

Robinson-Patman Act, 1936

Celler-Kefauver Act, 1950

These acts prohibit the following practices only if they substantially lessen competition or create monopoly:

1. Price discrimination.
2. Contracts that require other goods to be bought from the same firm (called tying arrangements).
3. Contracts that require a firm to buy all its requirements of a particular item from a single firm (called requirements contracts).
4. Contracts that prevent a firm from selling competing items (called exclusive dealing).
5. Contracts that prevent a buyer from reselling a product outside a specified area (called territorial confinement).
6. Acquiring a competitor's shares or assets.
7. Becoming a director of a competing firm.

Efficient Resale Price Maintenance   Resale price maintenance might be efficient if it enables a manufacturer to induce dealers to provide the efficient standard of service. Suppose that SilkySkin wants shops to demonstrate the use of its new unbelievable moisturizing cream in an inviting space. With resale price maintenance, SilkySkin can offer all the retailers the same incentive and compensation. Without resale price maintenance, a discount drug store might offer SilkySkin products at a low price. Buyers would then have an incentive to visit a high-price shop and get the product demonstrated and then buy from the low-price shop. The low-price shop would be a free rider (like the consumer of a public good in Chapter 11, p. 271), and an inefficient level of service would be provided.

SilkySkin could pay a fee to retailers that provide good service and leave the resale price to be determined by the competitive forces of supply and demand. But it might be too costly for SilkySkin to monitor shops and ensure that they provided the desired level of service.

Predatory Pricing

Predatory pricing is setting a low price to drive competitors out of business with the intention of setting a monopoly price when the competition has gone. John D. Rockefeller's Standard Oil Company was the first to be accused of this practice in the 1890s, and it has been claimed often in antitrust cases since then. Predatory pricing is an attempt to create a monopoly and as such it is illegal under Section 2 of the Sherman Act.

It is easy to see that predatory pricing is an idea, not a reality. Economists are skeptical that predatory pricing occurs. They point out that a firm that cuts its price below the profit-maximizing level forgoes profit during the low-price period. Even if the firm succeeds in driving its competitors out of business, new competitors will enter when the firm raises its price above average total cost and makes an economic profit. So any potential gain from a monopoly position is temporary. A high and certain loss is a poor exchange for a temporary and uncertain gain. No case of predatory pricing has been definitively found.

Tying Arrangements

A **tying arrangement** is an agreement to sell one product only if the buyer agrees to buy another, different product. With tying, the only way the buyer can get the one product is to buy the other product at the same time. Microsoft has been accused of tying Internet Explorer and Windows. Textbook publishers sometimes tie a Web site and a textbook and force students to buy both. (You can't buy the book you're now reading, new, without the Web site. But you can buy the Web site access without the book, so these products are not tied.)

Could publishers of textbooks make more money by tying a book and access to a Web site? The answer is sometimes but not always. Think about what you are willing to pay for a book and access to a Web site. To keep the numbers simple, suppose that you and other students are willing to pay $40 for a book and $10 for access to a Web site. The publisher can sell these items separately for these prices or bundled for $50. There is no gain to the publisher from bundling.

But now suppose that you and only half of the students are willing to pay $40 for a book and $10 for a Web site. And suppose that the other half of the students are willing to pay $40 for a Web site and $10 for a book. Now if the two items are sold separately, the publisher can charge $40 for the book and $40 for the Web site. Half the students buy the book but not the Web site, and the other half buy the Web site but not the book. But if the book and Web site are bundled for $50, everyone buys the bundle and the publisher makes an extra $10 per student. In this case, bundling has enabled the publisher to price discriminate.

There is no simple, clear-cut test of whether a firm is engaging in tying or whether, by doing so, it has increased its market power and profit and created inefficiency.

■ Recent Antitrust Showcase: The United States Versus Microsoft

In 1998, the U.S. Department of Justice, along with a number of states, charged Microsoft, the world's largest producer of software for personal computers, with violations of both sections of the Sherman Act. A 78-day trial followed that pitched two prominent MIT economics professors against each other (Franklin Fisher for the government and Richard Schmalensee for Microsoft).

Predatory pricing
Setting a low price to drive competitors out of business with the intention of setting a monopoly price when the competition has gone.

Tying arrangement
An agreement to sell one product only if the buyer agrees to buy another, different product.

The Case Against Microsoft

The claims against Microsoft were that it

- Possessed monopoly power in the market for PC operating systems.
- Used *predatory pricing* and *tying arrangements* to achieve a monopoly in the market for Web browsers.
- Used other anticompetitive practices to strengthen its monopoly in these two markets.

It was claimed that with 80 percent of the market for PC operating systems, Microsoft had excessive monopoly power. This monopoly power arose from two barriers to entry: economies of scale and network economies. Microsoft's average total cost falls as production increases (economies of scale) because the fixed cost of developing an operating system like Windows is large while the marginal cost of producing one copy of Windows is small. Further, as the number of Windows users increases, the range of Windows applications expands (network economies), so a potential competitor would need to produce not only a competing operating system but also an entire range of supporting applications.

When Microsoft entered the Web browser market with its Internet Explorer (IE), it offered the browser for a zero price. This price was viewed as *predatory pricing*. Microsoft integrated IE with Windows so that anyone who uses this operating system would not need a separate browser such as Netscape Communicator. Microsoft's competitors claimed that this practice was an illegal *tying arrangement*.

Microsoft's Response

Microsoft challenged all these claims. It said that although Windows was the dominant operating system, it was vulnerable to competition from other operating systems such as Linux and Apple's Mac OS and that there was a permanent threat of competition from new entrants.

Microsoft claimed that integrating Internet Explorer with Windows provided a single, unified product of greater consumer value. Instead of tying, Microsoft said, the browser and operating system constituted a single product. It was like a refrigerator with a chilled water dispenser or an automobile with a stereo player.

The Outcome

The court agreed that Microsoft was in violation of the Sherman Act and ordered that it be broken into two firms: an operating systems producer and an applications producer. Microsoft successfully appealed this order. But in the final judgment, Microsoft was ordered to disclose details about how its operating system works to other software developers so that they could compete effectively against Microsoft. In the summer of 2002, Microsoft began to comply with this order.

■ Merger Rules

You've now seen how the antitrust laws can be used to prevent an oligopoly from becoming a monopoly or trying to behave like one. We end by examining another way of trying to gain monopoly power—two or more oligopoly firms merging to increase their ability to control the market price. Mergers are subject to rules that are designed to limit monopoly power from arising and we close our explanation of the antitrust laws by seeing how they are used to review and sometimes to block a merger.

Mergers are often in the headlines. United Airlines and Continental Airlines merged to form United Continental in 2010 and American Airlines and US Airways merged in 2015. Firms can benefit from a merger in two ways: They can lower costs and they can increase market power. Lower costs are not a threat to the social interest but increased market power is. For this reason, the Federal Trade Commission (FTC) challenges proposed mergers that will substantially lessen competition and not bring lower costs.

To determine the effects of a merger on competitiveness, the FTC uses guidelines based on the Herfindahl-Hirschman Index (HHI), which is explained in Chapter 17 (p. 439). *Eye on the U.S. Economy*, below, describes the FTC guidelines and looks at a high-profile merger of smartphone service providers that was blocked by applying the guidelines.

EYE on the U.S. ECONOMY
No Wireless Service Merger

The figure (part a) summarizes the Federal Trade Commission's (FTC) guidelines on mergers. In a market in which the Herfindahl-Hirschman Index (HHI) is less than 1,500, a proposed merger is not challenged. But if the HHI is above 1,500, the FTC considers a challenge. If the HHI is between 1,500 and 2,500, a merger is challenged if it would increase the HHI by more than 100 points. And if the HHI exceeds 2,500, the market is already so concentrated that a merger is challenged if it increases the index by 100 points and normally is blocked if the index rises by more than 200 points.

In 2011, AT&T wanted to buy T-Mobile from the German firm Deutsche Telekom. But the market for wireless service is highly concentrated. Verizon, the largest service provider, had close to 40 percent of the market share. AT&T had a 30 percent share and Sprint and T-Mobile had about 12 percent each. Another 14 small firms shared the remaining market. So the four largest firms in this market

had a 94 percent market share. The HHI was around 2,800.

Part (b) of the figure shows how the HHI would have changed with the merger of AT&T and T-Mobile. It would have increased the HHI by around 700 points.

With an HHI of 2,800 and an increase of 700, there was a presumption that the merger would give AT&T too much market power. The FTC was presented with no evidence to challenge this conclusion, so it decided to block the merger.

(a) The merger guidelines

(b) Merger of wireless service providers

MyEconLab Study Plan 18.4
Key Terms Quiz
Solutions Video

 CHECKPOINT 18.4

Describe the antitrust laws that regulate oligopoly.

Practice Problems

1. Explain each of the following terms:
    - Attempt to monopolize
    - Price fixing
    - Predatory pricing
    - Tying arrangements

2. Since 1987, hundreds of hospital mergers have taken place and rarely has the U.S. Federal Trade Commission challenged a hospital merger. What can you infer about the structure of the market in hospital services?

In the News

Merger of beer giants faces obstacles
Mega-brand beers have lost market share to wine and craft beer. In response, Anheuser-Busch InBev and SABMiller, the two biggest brewers in the world, are discussing a merger that would be scrutinized by antitrust regulators.
Source: *The New York Times*, September 16, 2015

How would a merger benefit the two big brewers? Under what circumstances would the Federal Trade Commission (FTC) challenge the merger?

Solutions to Practice Problems

1. An attempt to monopolize is an attempt by a company to drive out its competitors so that it can operate as a monopoly.

    Price fixing is making an agreement with competitors to set a specified price and not to vary it.

    Predatory pricing is the attempt to drive out competitors by setting a price that is too low for others to make a profit, then setting the monopoly price when the competitors are gone.

    Tying arrangements exist when a company does not offer a buyer the opportunity to buy one item without at the same time buying another item.

2. The U.S. Federal Trade Commission will challenge a hospital merger only if it substantially lessens competition. Such a situation will not arise if (1) the merger will not increase market power either because strong competitors exist or because the merging hospitals are sufficiently differentiated; (2) the merger will allow the hospitals to reduce cost; or (3) the merger will eliminate a hospital that otherwise would have failed and exited the market.

Solution to In the News

A merger of the two big beer producers would make the new giant producer more profitable and more likely to set prices too high. The FTC will look at the beer market HHI. If it is between 1,500 and 2,500, the FTC will challenge the merger if it increases the HHI by more than 100 points. If the HHI exceeds 2,500, the FTC will challenge the merger if it increases the HHI by 100 points and normally will block the merger if it raises the index by more than 200 points.

CHAPTER SUMMARY

Key Points

1. Describe and identify oligopoly and explain how it arises.

- Oligopoly is a market type in which a small number of interdependent firms compete behind a barrier to entry.
- Both natural (economies of scale and market demand) and legal barriers to entry create oligopoly.

2. Explain the dilemma faced by firms in oligopoly.

- If firms in oligopoly act together to restrict output, they make the same economic profit as a monopoly, but each firm can make a larger profit by increasing production.
- The oligopoly dilemma is whether to restrict or expand output.

3. Use game theory to explain how output and price are determined in oligopoly.

- In the prisoners' dilemma game, two players acting in their own interests harm their joint interest. Oligopoly is a prisoners' dilemma game.
- If firms cooperated, they could earn the monopoly profit, but in a one-play game, they overproduce and can drive the price and economic profit to the levels of perfect competition.
- Advertising and research and development create a prisoners' dilemma for firms in oligopoly.
- In a repeated game, a punishment strategy can lead to monopoly output, price, and economic profit.
- Oligopoly is usually inefficient because the price (marginal benefit) exceeds marginal cost and cost might not be the lowest attainable.

4. Describe the antitrust laws that regulate oligopoly.

- The Sherman Act (1890) and the Clayton Act (1914) make price-fixing agreements among firms illegal.
- Resale price maintenance might be efficient if it enables a producer to ensure the efficient level of service by distributors.
- Predatory pricing might bring temporary gains.
- Tying arrangements can facilitate price discrimination.
- The Federal Trade Commission examines and possibly blocks mergers if they would restrict competition too much.

Key Terms

MyEconLab Key Terms Quiz

Antitrust law, 477
Cartel, 460
Duopoly, 461
Game theory, 469

Nash equilibrium, 470
Payoff matrix, 470
Predatory pricing, 479
Prisoners' dilemma, 469

Resale price maintenance, 477
Strategies, 470
Tying arrangement, 479

MyEconLab Chapter 18 Study Plan

CHAPTER CHECKPOINT

Study Plan Problems and Applications

Use the following information to work Problems **1** and **2**.

When the first automobiles were built in 1901, they were made by skilled workers using hand tools. Later, in 1913, Henry Ford introduced the moving assembly line, which lowered costs and speeded production. Over the years, the production line has become ever more mechanized, and today robots replace people in many tasks.

1. Sketch the average total cost curve and the demand curve for automobiles in 1901 and in 2016.

2. Describe the changing barriers to entry in the automobile industry and explain how the combination of market demand and economies of scale has changed the structure of the industry over the past 100 years.

Use the following information to work Problems **3** to **5**.

Isolated Island has two taxi companies, one owned by Ann and the other owned by Zack. Figure 1 shows the market demand curve for taxi rides, *D*, and the average total cost curve of one of the firms, *ATC*.

FIGURE 1

Price and cost (dollars per ride)

3. If Ann and Zack produce the same quantity of rides as would be produced in perfect competition, what are the quantity of rides, the price of a ride, and the economic profit of Ann and Zack? Would Ann and Zack have an incentive to collude and raise their price? Explain why or why not.

4. If Ann and Zack form a cartel and produce the same quantity of rides as would be produced in monopoly, what are the quantity of rides, the price of a ride, and the economic profit of Ann and Zack? Would Ann and Zack have an incentive to break the cartel agreement and cut their price? Explain why or why not.

5. Suppose that Ann and Zack have two strategies: collude, fix the monopoly price, and limit the number of rides or break the collusion, cut the price, and produce more rides. Create a payoff matrix for the game that Ann and Zack play, and find the Nash equilibrium for this game if it is played just once. Do the people of Isolated Island get the efficient quantity of taxi rides?

Use the following information to work Problems **6** and **7**.

Coke, Pepsi and the new front in the cola wars
The cola wars between Coca-Cola and PepsiCo may become even tougher as consumers seek out healthier alternatives to sugary soft drinks. But both Coke and Pepsi are getting higher prices for soda, thanks to new 8-ounce cans replacing the standard 12-ounce size.

Source: CBC News, February 12, 2015

6. Describe the cola wars that Coca-Cola and PepsiCo play as a game. What type of game is it? What are some of the strategies in the game?

7. With two strategies—8-ounce can and 12-ounce can—and with assumed payoffs, create a payoff matrix for the game if the equilibrium outcome is for both firms to choose 8-ounce cans.

8. Read *Eye On the Wireless Oligopoly* on p. 475 and then explain the effects of economies of scale and demand on the market for smartphone plans and illustrate it with a graph based on Figure 18.1.

Instructor Assignable Problems and Applications

MyEconLab Homework, Quiz, or Test if assigned by instructor

1. AT&T and Verizon have two pricing strategies: Set a high (monopoly) price or set a low (competitive) price. Suppose that if they both set a competitive price, economic profit for both is zero. If they both set a monopoly price, AT&T makes an economic profit of $100 million and Verizon makes an economic profit of $200 million. If AT&T sets a low price and Verizon sets a high price, AT&T makes an economic profit of $200 million and Verizon incurs an economic loss of $100 million; if AT&T sets a high price and Verizon sets a low price, AT&T incurs an economic loss of $50 million and Verizon makes an economic profit of $250 million.

    *   Create the payoff matrix for this game.
    *   What is the equilibrium of this game?
    *   Is the equilibrium efficient?
    *   Is this game a prisoners' dilemma?

Use the following information to work Problems **2** and **3**.

The United States claims that Canada subsidizes the production of softwood lumber and that U.S. imports of Canadian lumber damage the interests of U.S. producers. The United States has imposed a tariff on Canadian imports to counter the subsidy. Canada is thinking of retaliating by refusing to export water to California. Table 1 shows a payoff matrix for the game that the United States and Canada are playing.

2. What is the United States' best strategy? What is Canada's best strategy? What is the outcome of this game? Explain.

3. Is this game like a prisoners' dilemma or different in some crucial way? Explain. Which country would benefit more from a free trade agreement?

4. Agile Airlines is making $10 million a year economic profit on a route on which it has a monopoly. Wanabe Airlines is considering entering the market and operating on this route. Agile warns Wanabe to stay out and threatens to cut the price to the point at which Wanabe will make no profit if it enters. Wanabe does some research and determines that the payoff matrix for the game in which it is engaged with Agile is that shown in Table 2. Does Wanabe believe Agile's assertion? Does Wanabe enter or not? Explain.

Use this information to work Problems **5** to **7**.

DOJ investigation prompts lawsuits alleging that airlines are fixing airfares
It is alleged that Southwest Airlines, American Airlines, Delta Air Lines, and United Airlines have been colluding to limit the increases in their capacity with the intent of increasing airfares. The airlines say the allegations are without merit and that the airline industry is highly competitive with more people flying than ever before.

Source: *The Dallas Morning News*, July 8, 2015

5. Explain how limiting the increase in capacity could lead to higher airfares.

6. Explain how limiting the increase in capacity could lead to greater profit for the airlines, smaller consumer surplus, and deadweight loss. Illustrate your explanation with a graph.

7. Describe the fare-fixing scheme as the equilibrium outcome of an oligopoly cartel game played by the airlines. Explain why the cartel survived.

TABLE 1

TABLE 2

MyEconLab Chapter 18 Study Plan

Multiple Choice Quiz

1. Which of the following statements is *incorrect*. In oligopoly, _____.
   A. barriers to entry prevent new firms entering
   B. each firm's profit is influenced by each other firms' advertising
   C. each firm's action is influenced by the actions and reactions of each other firm
   D. each firm is a price taker and the price is the monopoly profit-maximizing price

2. If firms in oligopoly form a cartel, it will likely break down because _____.
   A. firms cannot agree on how to share the economic profit
   B. the price set by the cartel is too low
   C. with price exceeding marginal cost, a firm might expand production to increase its profit
   D. firms realize that their allocation of resources is inefficient

3. The oligopoly dilemma is whether to _____.
   A. act together to restrict output and raise the price
   B. raise the price to the monopoly profit-maximizing price
   C. cheat on others in the cartel to take advantage of profit opportunities
   D. lower the price to the perfectly competitive price

4. In the prisoners' dilemma game, each player _____.
   A. consults the other player to determine his best action
   B. chooses the best outcome for the other player
   C. chooses the best outcome for himself
   D. chooses the best outcome for both players together

5. A Nash equilibrium _____.
   A. is the outcome that delivers maximum economic profit
   B. is the outcome in which each player takes the best action given the other player's action
   C. changes each time the game is played
   D. is the best possible outcome for the two players

6. In an advertising prisoners' dilemma game, _____.
   A. both firms will advertise and end up with lower profits than if neither advertises
   B. only one firm will advertise because the other firm sees the advertising expenditure as a waste
   C. the two firms agree on the total advertising budget and split it equally
   D. neither firm will advertise because both realize that it lowers profit

7. Each of the following practices violates U.S. antitrust law *except* _____.
   A. an agreement to sell one good only if the buyer purchases another good
   B. an agreement between the manufacturer and the seller to charge a given price for the good
   C. starting a price war with other sellers of a similar good
   D. cutting the price to increase market share to 100 percent, then raising the price

Why is a coach worth $7 million?

Markets for Factors of Production

19

When you have completed your study of this chapter, you will be able to

1 Explain how the value of marginal product determines the demand for a factor of production.

2 Explain how wage rates and employment are determined and how labor unions influence labor markets.

3 Explain how capital and land rental rates and natural resource prices are determined.

MyEconLab Big Picture Video

THE ANATOMY OF FACTOR MARKETS

The four factors of production are

- Labor
- Capital
- Land (natural resources)
- Entrepreneurship

Factor markets
The markets in which the services of the factors of production are traded.

Factor prices
The prices of the services of the factors of production.

The *services* of labor, capital, and land are traded in **factor markets**, which determine their **factor prices**. Entrepreneurial services are not traded in markets and entrepreneurs receive the profit or bear the loss that results from their decisions. Let's take a brief look at the anatomy of the factor markets.

Markets for Labor Services

Labor services are the physical and mental work effort that people supply to produce goods and services. A *labor market* is a collection of people and firms who trade *labor services*. Some labor services are traded day by day, called casual labor. People who pick fruit and vegetables often just show up at a farm and take whatever work is available that day. But most labor services, like those of a football coach, are traded on a contract. The price of labor services is a wage rate.

Most labor markets have many buyers and sellers and are competitive. But in some labor markets a labor union organizes labor and introduces an element of monopoly into the market. We'll study both competitive labor markets and labor unions in this chapter.

Markets for Capital Services

Capital consists of the tools, instruments, machines, buildings, and other constructions that have been produced in the past and that businesses now use to produce goods and services. These physical objects are themselves goods—*capital goods*—and are traded in goods markets, just as bottled water and toothpaste are.

A market for *capital services* is a *rental market*—a market in which the services of capital are hired. An example of a market for capital services is the vehicle rental market in which Avis, Budget, Hertz, U-Haul, and many other firms offer automobiles and trucks for hire. The price of capital services is a rental rate.

Most capital services are not traded in a market. Instead, a firm buys capital equipment and uses it itself. But the services of the capital that a firm owns and operates itself have an *implicit* price that arises from depreciation and interest costs (see Chapter 14, p. 349). Think of this price as the *implicit rental rate* of the capital that a firm owns.

Markets for Land Services and Natural Resources

Land consists of all the gifts of nature—natural resources. The market for land as a factor of production is the market for the *services of land*—the *use* of land. The price of the services of land is a rental rate.

Nonrenewable natural resources
Natural resources that can be used only once and cannot be replaced once they have been used.

Most natural resources, such as farm land and rivers, can be used repeatedly. But a few natural resources are nonrenewable. **Nonrenewable natural resources** are resources that can be used only once and cannot be replaced once they have been used. Examples are oil, natural gas, and coal. The prices of natural resources are determined in global *commodity markets* and are called *commodity prices*.

19.1   THE DEMAND FOR A FACTOR OF PRODUCTION

MyEconLab Concept Video

We begin our study of factor markets by learning about the demand for factors of production, and we use labor as the example. The demand for a factor of production is a **derived demand**—it is derived from the demand for the goods and services that it is used to produce. You've seen, in Chapters 15 through 18, how a firm determines its profit-maximizing output. The quantities of factors of production demanded are a direct consequence of firms' output decisions. Firms hire the quantities of factors of production that maximize profit.

To decide the quantity of a factor of production to hire, a firm compares the cost of hiring an additional unit of the factor with its value to the firm. The cost of hiring an additional unit of a factor of production is called the *factor price*. The value to the firm of hiring one more unit of a factor of production is called the factor's **value of marginal product**, which equals the price of a unit of output multiplied by the marginal product of the factor of production. To study the demand for a factor of production, we'll examine the demand for labor.

Derived demand
The demand for a factor of production, which is derived from the demand for the goods and services that it is used to produce.

Value of marginal product
The value to a firm of hiring one more unit of a factor of production, which equals the price of a unit of output multiplied by the marginal product of the factor of production.

■ Value of Marginal Product

Table 19.1 shows you how to calculate the value of marginal product of labor at Max's Wash 'n' Wax car wash service. The first two columns show Max's *total product* schedule—the number of car washes per hour that each quantity of labor can produce. The third column shows the *marginal product* of labor—the change in total product that results from a one-unit increase in the quantity of labor employed. (See Chapter 14, pp. 353–357, for a refresher on product schedules.) Max can sell car washes at the going market price of $6 a wash. Given this information, we can calculate the value of marginal product (fourth column). It equals price multiplied by marginal product. For example, the marginal product of hiring the second worker is 4 car washes an hour. Each wash brings in $6, so the value of marginal product of the second worker is $24 (4 washes at $6 each).

■ TABLE 19.1

Calculating the Value of Marginal Product

	Quantity of labor (workers)	Total product (car washes per hour)	Marginal product (washes per additional worker)	Value of marginal product (dollars per additional worker)
A	0	0		
			5	30
B	1	5		
			4	24
C	2	9		
			3	18
D	3	12		
			2	12
E	4	14		
			1	6
F	5	15		

The value of marginal product of labor equals the price of the product multiplied by the marginal product of labor.

The price of a car wash is $6.

The marginal product of the second worker (in column 3) is 4 washes, so the value of marginal product of the second worker (in column 4) is $6 a wash multiplied by 4 washes, which equals $24.

The Value of Marginal Product Curve

Figure 19.1 graphs the value of marginal product of labor at Max's Wash 'n' Wax as the number of workers that Max hires changes. The blue bars that show the value of marginal product of labor correspond to the numbers in Table 19.1. The curve labeled *VMP* is Max's value of marginal product curve.

◼ A Firm's Demand for Labor

The value of marginal product of labor and the wage rate determine the quantity of labor demanded by a firm. The value of marginal product of labor tells us the additional revenue the firm earns by hiring one more worker. The wage rate tells us the additional cost the firm incurs by hiring one more worker.

Because the value of marginal product decreases as the quantity of labor employed increases, there is a simple rule for maximizing profit: Hire labor up to the point at which the value of marginal product equals the wage rate. If the value of marginal product of labor exceeds the wage rate, a firm can increase its profit by employing one more worker. If the wage rate exceeds the value of marginal product of labor, a firm can increase its profit by employing one less worker. But if the wage rate equals the value of marginal product of labor, the firm cannot increase its profit by changing the number of workers it employs. The firm is making the maximum possible profit.

So the quantity of labor demanded by a firm is the quantity at which the wage rate equals the value of marginal product of labor.

◼ FIGURE 19.1

The Value of Marginal Product at Max's Wash 'n' Wax   MyEconLab Animation

The blue bars show the value of marginal product of the labor that Max hires based on the numbers in Table 19.1.

The orange line labeled *VMP* is the firm's value of marginal product of labor curve.

	Quantity of labor (workers)	Value of marginal product (dollars per additional worker)
A	1	30
B	2	24
C	3	18
D	4	12
E	5	6

■ A Firm's Demand for Labor Curve

A firm's demand for labor curve is also its value of marginal product curve. Figure 19.2 shows Max's value of marginal product curve in part (a) and Max's demand for labor curve in part (b). The *x*-axis measures the number of workers hired in both parts. The *y*-axis measures the value of marginal product in part (a) and the wage rate—dollars per hour—in part (b).

Suppose the wage rate is $15 an hour. You can see in part (a) that if Max hires 1 worker, the value of marginal product of labor is $30 an hour. Because the worker costs only $15 an hour, Max makes a profit of $15 an hour. If Max hires a second worker, the value of marginal product of this worker is $24 an hour, so on the second worker, Max makes a profit of $9 an hour. If Max hires a third worker, the value of marginal product of this worker is $18 an hour, so on this worker, Max makes a profit of $3 an hour. Max's profit on these three workers is $27 an hour—$15 on the first, $9 on the second, and $3 on the third worker.

If Max hired a fourth worker, his profit would fall. The fourth worker generates a value of marginal product of only $12 an hour but costs $15 an hour, so Max does not hire a fourth worker. The quantity of labor demanded by Max when the

■ **FIGURE 19.2**

The Demand for Labor at Max's Wash 'n' Wax   MyEconLab Animation

(a) Value of marginal product

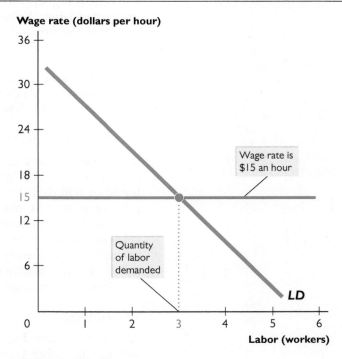

(b) Demand for labor

At a wage rate of $15 an hour, Max makes a profit on the first 3 workers hired but would incur a loss on the fourth worker in part (a), so the quantity of labor demanded is 3 workers in part (b).

Max's demand for labor curve in part (b) is the same as the value of marginal product curve in part (a). The demand for labor curve slopes downward because the value of marginal product of labor diminishes as the quantity of labor employed increases.

wage rate is $15 an hour is 3 workers, which is a point on Max's demand for labor curve, *LD*, in Figure 19.2(b).

If the wage rate rose to $21 an hour, Max would decrease the quantity of labor demanded to 2 workers. If the wage rate fell to $9 an hour, Max would increase the quantity of labor demanded to 4 workers.

A change in the wage rate brings a change in the quantity of labor demanded and a movement along the demand for labor curve. A change in any other influence on the firm's labor-hiring plans changes the demand for labor and shifts the demand for labor curve.

■ Changes in the Demand for Labor

The demand for labor depends on

- The price of the firm's output
- The prices of other factors of production
- Technology

The Price of the Firm's Output

The higher the price of the good or service produced by the firm, the greater is the firm's demand for labor. The price of the firm's good affects the firm's demand for labor through its influence on the value of marginal product of the firm's workers. A higher price of the good or service increases the value of the marginal product of labor. A change in the price of the good or service produced leads to a shift in the firm's demand for labor curve. If the price of the good or service increases, the firm's demand for labor increases and the demand for labor curve shifts rightward.

For example, if the price of a car wash increased to $8, the value of the marginal product of Max's fourth worker would increase from $12 to $16 an hour. At a wage rate of $15 an hour, Max would now hire 4 workers instead of 3.

The Prices of Other Factors of Production

If the price of using capital decreases relative to the wage rate, a firm substitutes capital for labor and increases the quantity of capital it uses. Usually, the demand for labor will decrease when the price of using capital falls. For example, if the price of a car wash machine falls, Max might decide to install an additional machine and lay off a worker. But the demand for labor could increase if the lower price of capital led to a sufficiently large increase in the scale of production. For example, with cheaper capital equipment available, Max might install an additional car wash machine and hire more labor to operate it. These factor substitutions occur in the *long run* when the firm can change the scale of its plant.

Technology

New technologies decrease the demand for some types of labor and increase the demand for other types. For example, if a new automated car wash machine becomes available, Max might install one of these machines and fire most of his workers—a decrease in the demand for car wash workers. But the firms that manufacture and service automatic car wash machines hire more labor—the demand for these types of labor increases. During the 1980s and 1990s, electronic telephone exchanges decreased the demand for telephone operators and increased the demand for computer programmers and electronics engineers.

CHECKPOINT 19.1

MyEconLab Study Plan 19.1
Key Terms Quiz
Solutions Video

Explain how the value of marginal product determines the demand for a factor of production.

Practice Problems

Kaiser's produces smoothies. The market for smoothies is perfectly competitive, and the price of a smoothie is $4. The labor market is competitive, and the wage rate is $40 a day. Table 1 shows Kaiser's total product schedule.

1. Calculate the marginal product and the value of marginal product of the fourth worker.

2. How many workers will Kaiser's hire to maximize its profit? How many smoothies a day will Kaiser's produce?

3. If the price of a smoothie rises to $5, how many workers will Kaiser's hire?

4. Kaiser's installs a machine that increases the marginal product of labor by 50 percent. If the price of a smoothie remains at $4 and the wage rate rises to $48 a day, how many workers does Kaiser's hire?

TABLE 1

Workers	Smoothies per day
1	7
2	21
3	33
4	43
5	51
6	55

In the News

U.S. economy gained jobs in hiring slowdown
The Labor Department reported a slowdown in hiring but not all the news about jobs is gloomy. McDonald's plans to raise wages in a strengthening labor market. And Walmart plans to raise wages to a minimum of $9 an hour.

Source: *The New York Times*, April 4, 2015

Explain why jobs growth is slow in some parts of the economy and strong in others. Why would McDonald's and Walmart raise the wage rates of their workers?

Solutions to Practice Problems

1. The *MP* of the 4th worker equals the *TP* of 4 workers (43 smoothies) minus the *TP* of 3 workers (33 smoothies), which is 10 smoothies. The *VMP* of the 4th worker equals the *MP* of the 4th worker (10 smoothies) multiplied by the price of a smoothie ($4), which is $40 a day.

2. Kaiser's maximizes profit by hiring the number of workers that makes the *VMP* of labor equal to the wage rate ($40 a day). Kaiser's hires 4 workers. The marginal product of the 4th worker is 10 smoothies and the price of a smoothie is $4, so the *VMP* of labor is $40 a day, which equals the wage rate. Kaiser's produces 43 smoothies a day.

3. Kaiser's maximizes profit by hiring 5 workers. The *MP* is 8 smoothies and the price is $5, so the *VMP* of labor is $40 a day—equal to the wage rate.

4. When Kaiser's hires 5 workers, the *MP* is 12 smoothies. The price of a smoothie is $4, so the *VMP* of labor is $48 a day— equal to the wage rate.

Solution to In the News

Firms hire the quantity of labor at which the *VMP* of labor equals the wage rate. Jobs growth is slow if the *VMP* of labor grows slowly and is strong if the *VMP* of labor grows quickly. McDonald's and Walmart would raise the wage rates they pay when the *VMP* of their workers increases and the market wage rate increases.

19.2   LABOR MARKETS

For most of us, a labor market is our only source of income. We work and earn a wage. What determines the amount of labor that we supply?

■ The Supply of Labor

Larry works as a car washer, but he enjoys his leisure time.

People supply labor to earn an income. Many factors influence the quantity of labor that a person plans to provide, but a key factor is the wage rate.

To see how the wage rate influences the quantity of labor supplied, think about Larry's labor supply decision, which Figure 19.3 illustrates. Larry enjoys his leisure time, and he would be pleased if he didn't have to spend his evenings and weekends working at Max's Wash 'n' Wax. But Max pays him $15 an hour, and at that wage rate, Larry chooses to work 30 hours a week. The reason is that he is offered a wage rate that is high enough to make him regard this use of his time as the best available to him. If he were offered a lower wage rate, Larry would not be willing to give up so much leisure. If he were offered a higher wage rate, Larry would want to work even longer hours, but only up to a point. Offer Larry $25 an hour, and he would be willing to work a 40-hour week (and earn $1,000). With the goods and services that Larry can buy for $1,000, his priority would be a bit more leisure time if the wage rate increased further. If the wage rate increased above $25 an hour, Larry would cut back on his work hours and take more leisure. Larry's labor supply curve eventually bends backward.

■ FIGURE 19.3

An Individual's Labor Supply Curve

MyEconLab *Animation*

❶ At a wage rate of $15 an hour,

❷ Larry is willing to supply 30 hours a week of labor.

❸ Larry's quantity of labor supplied ❹ increases as the wage rate increases up to ❺ a maximum, and then further increases in the wage rate ❻ bring a decrease in the quantity of labor supplied.

Larry's labor supply curve is upward sloping but eventually it bends backward.

	Wage rate (dollars per hour)	Quantity of labor (hours per week)
A	40	30
B	35	35
C	30	39
D	25	40
E	20	37
F	15	30
G	10	17
H	5	0

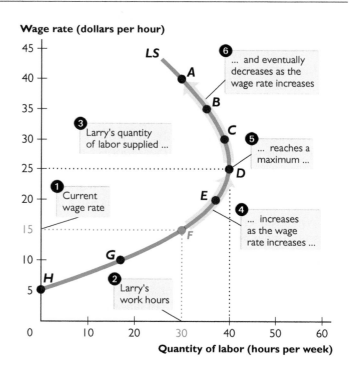

Market Supply Curve

Larry's supply curve shows the quantity of labor supplied by one person as that person's wage rate changes. Most people behave like Larry, but people have different wage rates at which they are willing to work and at which their labor supply curve bends backward. A market supply curve shows the quantity of labor supplied by all households in a particular job. It is found by adding together the quantities supplied by all households at each wage rate. Also, along a market supply curve, the wage rates available in other jobs remain the same. For example, along the supply curve of car wash workers, we hold constant the wage rates of car salespeople, mechanics, and all other types of labor.

Offer Larry more for car washing than for oil changing, and he will supply more of his labor to car washing. The market supply curve in a given job slopes upward like the one in Figure 19.4, which shows the market supply curve of car wash workers in a large city.

◼ Influences on the Supply of Labor

The supply of labor changes when influences other than the wage rate change. The key factors that change the supply of labor are

- Adult population
- Preferences
- Time in school and training

◼ **FIGURE 19.4**

The Supply of Car Wash Workers

MyEconLab Animation

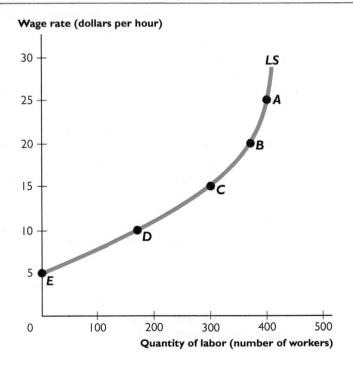

Wage rate (dollars per hour)	Quantity of labor (workers)
A 25	400
B 20	370
C 15	300
D 10	170
E 5	0

The supply curve of car wash workers shows how the quantity of labor supplied changes when the wage rate changes, other things remaining the same.

In a market for a specific type of labor, the quantity supplied increases as the wage rate increases, other things remaining the same.

Adult Population

An increase in the adult population, caused either by a birth rate that exceeds the death rate or by immigration, increases the supply of labor. Historically, the population of the United States has been strongly influenced by immigration.

Preferences

In 2015, 54 percent of women had jobs, up from 36 percent in 1960. In contrast, in 2015, 65 percent of men had jobs, down from 79 percent in 1960. Many factors contributed to these changes, which economists classify as *changes in preferences*. These changes occur slowly but accumulate to make a large difference in the supply of labor. The result has been a large increase in the supply of female labor and a decrease in the supply of male labor.

Time in School and Training

The more people who remain in school for full-time education and training, the smaller is the supply of low-skilled labor. Today in the United States, almost everyone completes high school and more than 50 percent of high-school graduates enroll in college or university. Although many students work part time, the supply of labor by students is less than it would be if they were full-time workers. So when more people pursue higher education, other things remaining the same, the supply of low-skilled labor decreases. But time spent in school and training converts low-skilled labor into high-skilled labor. The greater the proportion of people who receive a higher education, the greater is the supply of high-skilled labor.

When the amount of work that people want to do at a given wage rate changes, the supply of labor changes. An increase in the adult population or an increase in the percentage of women with jobs increases the supply of labor. An increase in college enrollment decreases the supply of low-skilled labor. Later, it increases the supply of high-skilled labor. Changes in the supply of labor shift the supply of labor curve, just like the shifts of the supply curve that you studied in Chapter 4 (p. 95).

■ Competitive Labor Market Equilibrium

Labor market equilibrium determines the wage rate and employment. In Figure 19.5, the market demand curve for car wash workers is *LD*. Here, if the wage rate is $15 an hour, the quantity of labor demanded is 300 workers. If the wage rate rises to $20 an hour, the quantity demanded decreases to 200 workers. And if the wage rate falls to $13 an hour, the quantity demanded increases to 350 workers. The supply curve of car wash workers is *LS*—the same curve as in Figure 19.4.

Figure 19.5 shows the equilibrium in the labor market. The equilibrium wage rate is $15 an hour, and the equilibrium number of car wash workers is 300. If the wage rate exceeded $15 an hour, there would be a surplus of car wash workers. More people would be looking for car wash jobs than firms were willing to hire. In such a situation, the wage rate would fall as firms found it easy to hire people at a lower wage rate. If the wage rate were less than $15 an hour, there would be a shortage of car wash workers. Firms would not be able to fill all the jobs they had available. In this situation, the wage rate would rise as firms found it necessary to offer a higher wage rate to attract workers. Only at a wage rate of $15 an hour are there no market forces operating to change the wage rate.

EYE on the COACH

Why Is a Coach Worth $7 Million?

Nick Saban, head coach of the Alabama Crimson Tide, earns $7 million a year, more than 70 times what the University of Alabama pays an average professor. Why does the University of Alabama pay a football coach the same amount that it pays 70 professors?

Nick Saban is worth 70 professors because his value of marginal product (*VMP*) to the University of Alabama is at least 70 times that of a professor.

Few people have the talent and willingness to work hard and take the stress of being head coach of a top college football program. Mr. Saban is one of these few people and possibly the

best of them. The consequence is that the supply of coaches like Nick Saban is small and inelastic.

To hire a top coach, the University of Alabama must pay the market price and that price is determined by the small supply and a high *VMP*.

The *VMP* of a football coach is high, much higher than that of a professor, because of the revenue that a successful football team generates. Some of that revenue comes directly from the game and includes the football gear and theme clothing licensed by the University. But most of the revenue comes from increased

donations by alumni and wealthy local and national patrons. The better the coach, the better is the team's performance and the greater is the revenue from these sources. Nick Saban brings in at least $7 million a year to the University of Alabama.

In contrast, a professor, even an outstanding one, generates a modest revenue for the University. He or she attracts a few students and obtains some research grant funds from the National Science Foundation or other private foundation. But the *VMP* of a professor is modest—around a 70th of the *VMP* of Nick Saban.

FIGURE 19.5

Labor Market Equilibrium

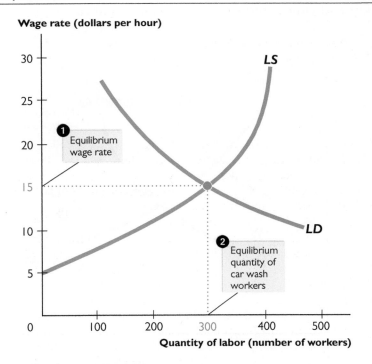

Labor market equilibrium determines the wage rate and employment. The wage rate adjusts to make the quantity of labor demanded equal the quantity of labor supplied.

❶ The equilibrium wage rate is $15 an hour.

❷ The equilibrium quantity of labor is 300 workers.

If the wage rate exceeds $15 an hour, the quantity supplied exceeds the quantity demanded. With a surplus of labor, the wage rate falls.

If the wage rate is below $15 an hour, the quantity demanded exceeds the quantity supplied. With a shortage of labor, the wage rate rises.

Labor union
An organized group of workers that aims to increase the wage rate and influence other job conditions of its members.

■ Labor Unions

A **labor union** is an organized group of workers that aims to increase the wage rate and influence other job conditions of its members. In some labor markets, labor unions have a powerful effect on the wage rate and employment. To see the effects of a labor union, let's see what happens if a union enters a competitive labor market.

A Union Enters a Competitive Labor Market

A labor union that enters a competitive labor market can try to restrict the supply of labor or it can try to increase the demand for labor. If the union restricts the supply of labor below its competitive level, the wage rate rises. If that is all the union is able to do, the wage rate rises, but the number of jobs decreases. There is a trade-off between the wage rate and the number of jobs.

Figure 19.6 illustrates a labor market before and after a union enters it. Before the union enters the market, the demand curve is LD_0, the supply curve is LS_0, the wage rate is $15 an hour, and 300 workers are employed.

When a labor union enters this market, it restricts the supply of labor and the supply of labor curve shifts leftward to LS_1. The wage rate rises to $20 an hour and employment decreases to 200 workers. The union simply picks its preferred position along the demand curve that defines the tradeoff it faces between employment and the wage rate.

Because restricting the supply of labor brings a higher wage rate at the cost of jobs, unions also try to increase the demand for labor.

■ FIGURE 19.6

A Competitive Labor Market and Unionized Labor Market Compared   MyEconLab Animation

❶ In a competitive labor market, the demand for labor is LD_0, the supply of labor is LS_0, the equilibrium wage rate is $15 an hour, and the equilibrium quantity of labor is 300 workers.

❷ A labor union restricts the supply of labor and the supply of labor curve shifts leftward to LS_1.

❸ The wage rate rises to $20 an hour, but employment decreases to 200 workers—jobs are traded off for a higher wage rate.

❹ If the union action increases labor productivity and increases the demand for union labor, the demand for labor curve shifts rightward to LD_1.

❺ With supply at LS_1, the increase in demand raises the wage rate to $25 an hour and employment increases to 250 workers.

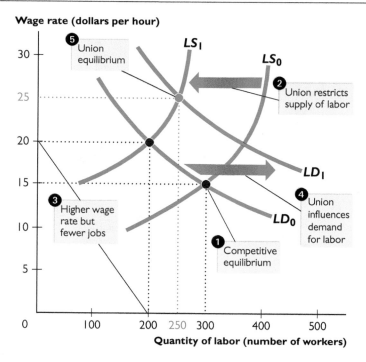

How Labor Unions Try to Increase the Demand for Labor

Labor unions try to increase the demand for union labor by increasing their value of marginal product and by supporting minimum wage laws and import restrictions.

The value of marginal product of union workers might be increased (and the demand for union labor increased) by union-sponsored job training programs, apprenticeship, and other on-the-job training activities.

A minimum wage law might increase the demand for union labor by increasing the cost of employing low-skilled nonunion labor. An increase in the wage rate of low-skilled labor leads to a decrease in the quantity demanded of low-skilled labor and to an increase in the demand for high-skilled union labor, a substitute for low-skilled labor.

By supporting import restrictions, labor unions try to increase the demand for the goods and services produced by union workers.

Figure 19.6 shows the effects of a labor union that is able to increase the demand for the labor of its members. The demand curve shifts rightward to LD_1. With the supply of labor curve LS_1, the wage rate rises to $25 an hour and employment increases from 200 to 250 workers.

How much of a difference to wage rates do unions make? To answer this question, we must look at the wages of unionized and nonunionized workers who do similar work. The evidence suggests that after allowing for skill differences, the union–nonunion wage gap lies between 10 percent and 25 percent. For example, unionized airline pilots earn about 25 percent more than nonunion pilots with the same level of skill.

EYE on YOUR LIFE
Job Choice and Income Prospects

Your job choice will have a big impact on your income. To provide you with some guidance on this impact, the figure shows wage rates for 16 occupations (or groups of occupations) reported by the Bureau of Labor Statistics.

You can see that economists are highly paid but not the highest. John Maynard Keynes, one of the leading economists of the last century, expressed the hope that economists would one day be as useful as dentists. If wage rates measure usefulness, you can see that the average economist isn't as useful as the average dentist. Nor is a university teacher of economics as useful as a dentist!

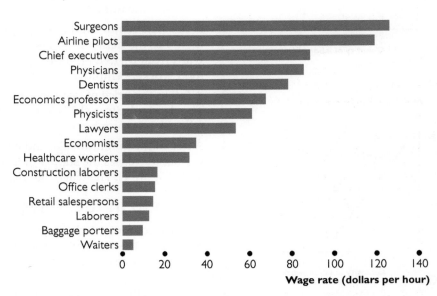

SOURCE OF DATA: National Compensation Survey, Bureau of Labor Statistics.

MyEconLab Study Plan 19.2
Key Terms Quiz
Solutions Video

CHECKPOINT 19.2

Explain how wage rates and employment are determined and how labor unions influence labor markets.

Practice Problems

In Greenville, where fast-food outlets hire teenagers and seniors, the following events occur one at a time and other things remain the same. Explain the influence of each event on the market for fast-food workers.

1. Seniors flock to Greenville and make it their home.
2. Greenville becomes a major tourist center attracting thousands of additional visitors every day.
3. The price of fast food falls.
4. Fast-food workers join a union and it gets a law passed that raises the minimum age and lowers the maximum age of a fast-food worker.

In the News

25 million new jobs coming to America, thanks to technology

Oxford researchers say that half of the jobs in America will be computerized over the next 20 years. Robert Cohen, a senior fellow at the Economic Strategy Institute, says "cloud computing, Big Data, and the Internet of Things will employ millions of people in new types of jobs."

Source: *Fortune*, January 15, 2016

Explain how advances in computer technology destroy and create jobs.

Solutions to Practice Problems

1. An increase in the number of seniors increases the supply of fast-food labor. The supply curve shifts rightward from S_0 to S_2 (Figure 1). The wage rate falls, and the number of fast-food workers employed increases.
2. A boost in visitor numbers increases the demand for fast food, which in turn increases the demand for fast-food workers. The demand curve shifts rightward from D_0 to D_1 (Figure 2). The wage rate rises, and the number of fast-food workers employed increases.
3. A fall in the price of fast food decreases the demand for fast-food workers. The demand curve shifts leftward from D_0 to D_2 (Figure 2). The wage rate falls, and the number of fast-food workers employed decreases.
4. A rise in the minimum age and a fall in the maximum age of a fast-food worker decreases the supply of labor. The supply curve shifts leftward from S_0 to S_1 (Figure 1). The wage rate rises, and the number employed decreases.

Solution to In the News

Advances in computer technology enable computers to replace some types of jobs. An example is self-checkouts replacing grocery store cashiers. Advances in computer technology also enable things to be done that were previously impossible and create new types of jobs. Examples are jobs for salespeople in smartphone stores and jobs for app coders. Advances in computer technology lower the *VMP* of labor in the jobs it destroys and increase the *VMP* of labor in the jobs it creates.

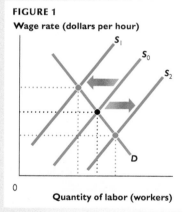

FIGURE 1

Wage rate (dollars per hour)

Quantity of labor (workers)

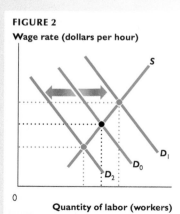

FIGURE 2

Wage rate (dollars per hour)

Quantity of labor (workers)

19.3 CAPITAL AND NATURAL RESOURCE MARKETS

MyEconLab Concept Video

The markets for capital and land can be understood by using the same basic ideas that you've seen when studying markets for labor. But markets for nonrenewable natural resources are different. We'll now examine three groups of factor markets:

- Capital markets
- Land markets
- Nonrenewable natural resource markets

◼ Capital Markets

The demand for capital is based on the *value of marginal product of capital*. Profit-maximizing firms hire the quantity of capital at which the value of marginal product of capital equals the *rental rate of capital*. The *lower* the rental rate, other things remaining the same, the *greater* is the quantity of capital *demanded*. The supply of capital responds in the opposite way to the rental rate. The *higher* the rental rate, other things remaining the same, the *greater* is the quantity of capital *supplied*. The equilibrium rental rate makes the quantity of capital demanded equal to the quantity supplied.

Figure 19.7 illustrates the market for the rental of tower cranes, capital used to construct high-rise buildings. With the demand curve *D* and supply curve *S*, the equilibrium rental rate is $1,000 per day and 100 tower cranes are rented.

◼ **FIGURE 19.7**

A Market for Capital Services

MyEconLab Animation

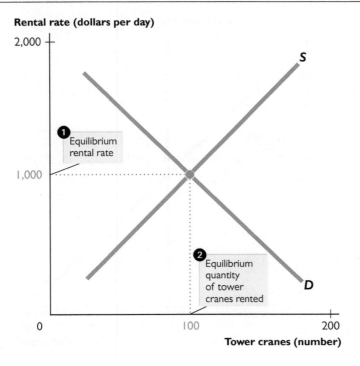

The demand curve for tower crane rentals is *D* and the supply curve is *S*.

❶ The equilibrium rental rate is $1,000 per day.

❷ The equilibrium quantity of cranes rented is 100.

■ Land Markets

The demand for land is a derived demand and is based on the *value of marginal product of land*. The quantity of land demanded for rent is that at which the value of marginal product of land equals the *rental rate of land*. The *lower* the rental rate, other things remaining the same, the *greater* is the quantity of land *demanded*.

But the supply of land is special: The quantity of land is fixed, so the supply of each block of land is *perfectly inelastic*.

The equilibrium rental rate of land makes the quantity of land demanded equal to the quantity available. Figure 19.8 illustrates the market for a 10-acre block in Manhattan. The quantity supplied is 10 acres regardless of the rental rate. The demand curve is *D* and the equilibrium rental rate is $1,000 an acre per day.

The *VMP* of a block of land depends on the prices of the things that the land produces. The *VMP* of farmland in Iowa depends on the price of grain; the *VMP* of land on Fifth Avenue rented by McDonald's depends on the price of a Big Mac.

Notice that the prices of things produced by land influence the rental rate of land and not the reverse. The rental rate of land in Manhattan is high because the high prices of a Big Mac and most other things in Manhattan make the *VMP* of land in Manhattan high. Similarly, relative to Manhattan, the rental rate of land in Des Moines is low because the low prices of a Big Mac and most other things in Des Moines make the *VMP* of land in Des Moines low.

Changes in the prices of the things produced by land change its *VMP*, which changes the rental rate. But for land on a long-term lease, the rental rate equals the *VMP* not in a single year but the *VMP* expected on average over the lease. For this reason, the rental rate of land fluctuates less than the prices of its products.

■ **FIGURE 19.8**

A Market for Land   MyEconLab Animation

The demand curve for a 10-acre block of land is *D*, and the supply curve is *S*.

Market equilibrium occurs at a rental rate of $1,000 an acre per day.

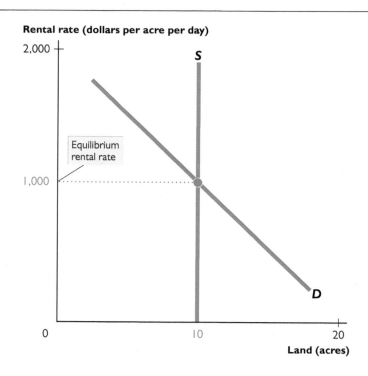

■ Nonrenewable Natural Resource Markets

Nonrenewable natural resources are those that we use to produce energy. Burning one of these fuels converts it to energy and other by-products, and once used the resource cannot be re-used. The natural resources that we use to make metals are also nonrenewable, but they can be used again, at some cost, by recycling them.

The value of marginal product of oil, gas, and coal determine the demand for these nonrenewable natural resources. The demand side of the markets for these resources is just like the demand side of all factor markets.

It is the supply side of a nonrenewable natural resource market that is special.

The Quantity of a Nonrenewable Natural Resource

The *stock* of a nonrenewable natural resource is the quantity in existence at a given time. This quantity is fixed by nature and past use and is independent of the price of the resource. The *proven reserves* of a nonrenewable natural resource is the quantity that has been discovered and that can be accessed at prices close to the current price. This quantity increases over time because advances in technology enable ever less accessible sources to be discovered.

Both of these quantity concepts of a nonrenewable natural resource influence its price, but the influence is indirect. The direct influence on price is the rate at which the resource is supplied for use in production—the *supply of the resource.*

The Supply of a Nonrenewable Natural Resource

The owner of a nonrenewable natural resource is willing to supply any quantity for the right price. But what *is* the right price? It is the price that gives the same expected profit as holding the resource in inventory and selling it next year. This price is lower than the price expected next year by an amount determined by the interest rate.

To see why, think about the choices of Saudi Arabia, a country with a large inventory of oil. Saudi Arabia can sell oil now and use the revenue to buy U.S. government bonds, or it can keep the oil in the ground and sell it next year.

If Saudi Arabia sells the oil and buys bonds, it earns the interest rate on the bonds. If it keeps its oil in the ground this year and sells it next year, it makes a profit equal to the price increase (or incurs a loss equal to the price decrease) between now and next year. If Saudi Arabia expects the percentage rise in the price of oil to exceed the interest rate on bonds, it will hold oil off the market this year. If it expects the percentage rise in the price of oil to be less than the interest rate on bonds, it will want to sell oil today.

Saudi Arabia will be equally happy to sell or hold oil at the price that makes next year's expected price higher than today's price by the same percentage as the interest rate on bonds. For example, if next year's expected price is $84 a barrel and the interest rate is 5 percent (0.05), Saudi Arabia will be willing to sell oil now for $80 a barrel. It will sell none for less than $80 a barrel and will sell as much as possible at more than $80 a barrel.

With the price expected to rise to $84 a barrel next year, Saudi Arabia is indifferent between selling oil now for $80 a barrel and not selling it now but waiting until next year and selling it for $84 a barrel. Saudi Arabia expects to make the same profit either way. So at $80 a barrel, Saudi Arabia will sell whatever quantity is demanded. Saudi Arabia's supply is *perfectly elastic* at $80 a barrel.

Equilibrium in a Nonrenewable Natural Resource Market

In a nonrenewable natural resource market, the equilibrium price is the one that gives suppliers an expected profit equal to the interest rate. The equilibrium quantity is the quantity demanded at that price.

Over time, the equilibrium quantity of natural resources used changes as the demand for them changes. The price also changes over time, for two reasons.

First, expectations change. The forces that influence expectations are not well understood. The expected future price of a natural resource depends on the expected future rate of use and rate of discovery of new sources of supply. But one person's expectation about a future price also depends on guesses about other people's expectations. These guesses can change abruptly and become

EYE on the GLOBAL ECONOMY
Oil and Metal Prices

The price of oil hit a high of $114 a barrel in 2011 and then crashed to less than $30 a barrel in 2016.

Figure 1 shows the history of the real price of oil (measured in terms of the value of money in 2015). It also shows the path that the price would have followed if, starting in 1970, it had risen at a rate equal to the interest rate (the Hotelling Principle). The actual price of oil has fluctuated mostly above the Hotelling price path.

The reason that the price of oil has fluctuated above the level predicted by the Hotelling Principle is that the market has been influenced by the fluctuating strength of a global cartel.

If a nonrenewable natural resource has a small number of producers, it is in the self-interest of these producers to create a cartel, restrict production, and raise the price to the monopoly profit-maximizing level. Established in 1960, the Organization of the Petroleum Exporting Countries (OPEC) had this aim, but it had to wait until 1973 for its first

success. In that year, OPEC had 12 members (Iran, Iraq, Kuwait, Saudi Arabia, Venezuela, Qatar, Indonesia, Libya, United Arab Emirates, Algeria, Nigeria, and Ecuador), and when a group of Arab states led by Egypt and Syria launched an attack against Israel, the predominantly Arab OPEC imposed an oil embargo against the

United States. The price of oil shot up from $10 to $40 a barrel. The Iranian Revolution of 1979 saw a further strenthening of the OPEC cartel, when the price climbed to more than $80 a barrel.

At $80 a barrel, many countries can produce oil at a profit, and advances in production technology made

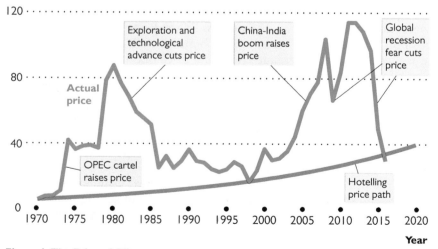

Price (U.S. dollars per barrel: 2015 value of dollar)

Figure 1 The Price of Oil

self-reinforcing. When the expected future price of a natural resource changes for whatever reason, its supply changes to reflect that expectation.

Second, suppliers of a natural resource expect the price to rise by the same percentage as the interest rate. If expectations are correct on average and nothing happens to change expectations, the price *does* rise by the same percentage as the interest rate. The proposition that the price of a nonrenewable natural resource is expected to rise at a rate equal to the interest rate is called the *Hotelling Principle*. It was first realized by Harold Hotelling, an economist at Columbia University.

Eye on the Global Economy below explains why the prices of some natural resources have not followed the path predicted by the Hotelling Principle, and in the case of oil, have mostly been higher than the Hotelling path.

even more new sources of supply profitable. The United States, Canada, Norway, and the United Kingdom ramped up production and delivered a serious blow to OPEC. No longer able to control global production, OPEC lost control of the price, and competitive forces drove it down to $25 a barrel by the late 1990s.

Driven by rapid economic growth in China and India, the demand for oil increased much faster than supply, and during the 10 years from 1998 to 2008 the price rose to $100 a barrel. This price increase was delivered by the working of a competitive market and was only temporary. As China's economic growth slowed and

the world economy grew more slowly, the price of oil fell. By early 2016, oil was under $30 a barrel.

The prices of metal ores in Figure 2 follow similar swings to those in the price of oil during the 2000s. But in earlier years, these prices tell a very different story from that of the price of oil.

Back in 1980, ecologist Paul Ehrlich said that with rapid population growth, the world would run out of natural resources. Arguing that human ingenuity would overcome pressure on resources, economist Julian Simon bet Ehrlich that the prices of five metals would fall during the 1980s.

Figure 2 shows that Simon won the bet, and that metals prices continued to fall through 2002.

But metals prices began to rise in 2003 and they rose more steeply as demand from China and India grew. Then when Asia slowed, metal prices fell again.

SOURCE OF DATA: International Monetary Fund, World Economic Outlook Database, October 2015.

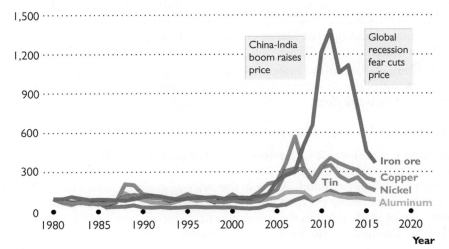

Figure 2 The Price of Metals

■- CHECKPOINT 19.3

Explain how capital and land rental rates and natural resource prices are determined.

Practice Problems

LIST 1

- Beaches in Florida
- Lake Powell
- Empire State Building
- Silver mines in Arizona
- The Great Lakes
- National parks
- Redwood forests
- The Statue of Liberty

1. Which of the items in List 1 are nonrenewable natural resources, which are renewable natural resources, and which are not natural resources? Explain your answers.

2. In the market for a nonrenewable natural resource, explain what determines the equilibrium price and the equilibrium quantity.

In the News

Farmland rents soften with grain prices, but still high
Millions of acres of U.S. farmland that grow corn, soybean, and wheat are rented, and land rent is the biggest cost of growing these crops. With rising crop prices, rents doubled during the past six years. Today, with falling crop prices, rents are falling, but they are still high.

Source: Reuters, December 23, 2014

1. Explain how the price of grain affects the rent in the market for farmland.
2. Why might rents remain high when grain prices fall?

Solutions to Practice Problems

1. Natural resources include all the gifts of nature. A nonrenewable natural resource is one that once used cannot be used again. A renewable natural resource is one that can be used repeatedly.

    Nonrenewable natural resources include silver mines in Arizona.

    Renewable natural resources include beaches in Florida, Lake Powell, the Great Lakes, national parks, and redwood forests.

    The Empire State Building and the Statue of Liberty are national landmarks, but they are not natural resources. Labor and capital were used to build the Empire State Building. The Statue of Liberty was a gift from France and not a gift of nature.

2. In a nonrenewable natural resource market, the equilibrium price is the price that gives suppliers an expected profit equal to the interest rate. The equilibrium quantity is the quantity demanded at that price.

Solutions to In the News

1. Farmland is a renewable resource—a factor of production. The demand for farmland is a derived demand, which is determined by the value of marginal product (*VMP*) of farmland. A rise in the price of grain increases the *VMP* of farmland, increases the demand for farmland, and raises the equilibrium rental rate of land. A fall in the price of grain decreases the *VMP* of farmland, decreases the demand for farmland, and lowers the equilibrium rental rate.

2. Most farmland is rented on a long-term lease. The rental rate equals the *VMP* of farmland not in a single year but on average over the years of a lease. For this reason, the rental rate of farmland fluctuates less than the price of grain.

CHAPTER SUMMARY

Key Points

1. **Explain how the value of marginal product determines the demand for a factor of production.**

   - The demand for a factor of production is a derived demand—it is derived from the demand for the goods and services that the factor of production is used to produce.
   - The quantity of a factor of production that is demanded depends on its price and the value of its marginal product, which equals the price of the product multiplied by marginal product.
   - Changes in technology bring changes in the demand for labor.

2. **Explain how wage rates and employment are determined and how labor unions influence labor markets.**

   - An individual's quantity of labor supplied is influenced by the wage rate: At low wage rates, the quantity of labor supplied increases as the wage rate rises; at high wage rates, the quantity of labor supplied *decreases* as the wage rate rises—the individual's supply of labor curve eventually bends backward.
   - The quantity of labor supplied by all households increases as the wage rate rises—the market supply of labor curve is upward sloping.
   - Wage rates are determined by demand and supply in labor markets.
   - A labor union can raise the wage rate by restricting the supply of labor or by increasing the demand for labor.

3. **Explain how capital and land rental rates and natural resource prices are determined.**

   - Capital and land rental rates are determined by demand and supply in capital and land markets; natural resource prices are determined by demand and supply in commodity markets.
   - The demand for capital, land, and nonrenewable natural resources is determined by the value of their marginal products.
   - The supply of land is perfectly inelastic and the demand for land determines the rental rate.
   - The supply of a nonrenewable natural resource is perfectly elastic at a price that makes its expected price rise at a rate equal to the interest rate. Expectations fluctuate and so do natural resource prices.

Key Terms

MyEconLab Key Terms Quiz

Derived demand, 489
Factor markets, 488
Factor prices, 488

Labor union, 498
Nonrenewable natural resources, 488
Value of marginal product, 489

MyEconLab Chapter 19 Study Plan

 CHAPTER CHECKPOINT

Study Plan Problems and Applications

1. A California asparagus farmer is maximizing profit. The price of asparagus is $2 a bunch, a farm worker's wage rate is $12 an hour, and the asparagus farm employs six workers. What is the marginal product of the sixth farm worker? If, when the price of asparagus rises to $3 a bunch, the farm hires eight workers, what is the marginal product of the eighth worker?

2. Through the 1990s, the percentage of high school students who decided to go to college increased. Draw a demand-supply graph to illustrate the effect of this increase on the market for college graduates. Explain its effect on the market for college professors.

3. If your college switched to online delivery of its courses, what changes do you predict would occur in the factor markets in the town where your college is located?

4. If soccer becomes more popular in the United States and basketball becomes less popular, is it true that professional basketball players will earn more than they earn today? Use the laws of demand and supply in factor markets to explain your answer.

5. Suppose that Palm Island, the world's largest grower of coconuts, plans to build its first airport on 100 acres of productive farm land. Palm Islanders expect the world price of coconuts to rise by 200 percent next year and remain high for the next decade. Explain the influence of these events on Palm Island's labor market and land market.

6. Is it true that the opening of a new diamond mine in the Yukon in Canada will lower the world price of diamonds and lower the wage rate paid to diamond workers in South Africa? Use a graph to illustrate your answer.

Use the following information to work Problems **7** to **9**.

USDA to grant $3 million for robots to roam farmlands
The USDA's National Robotics Initiative (NRI) will give $3 million in grants to farm robotics researchers. Already robots herd sheep, sort grapes, and distinguish good lettuce leaves from bad ones. Research funded by the NRI will develop harvesting systems for orchards; robots that pick, fertilize, and plant apple trees; and new ways to use drones to collect and analyze farm data.

Source: *Modern Farmer*, December 31, 2015

7. Explain the effects of new farm robotic technologies on the value of marginal product of farm capital, farm labor, and farm land.

8. Explain how the widespread use of farm robots will change the rental rate of farm land.

9. Explain how the widespread use of farm robots will create better paying farm jobs.

 10. Read *Eye on the Coach* on p. 497 and then draw demand-supply graphs to illustrate the markets for football coaches and economics professors. Explain the differences in the equilibrium wage rates and the quantities employed.

Instructor Assignable Problems and Applications

MyEconLab Homework, Quiz, or Test if assigned by instructor

1. Is the market for college football coaches competitive? If it is, why don't they all earn the same wage rate? Is the market for Nick Saban competitive? How is his compensation determined?

2. In the years after World War II, the birth rate increased and the so-called baby boom generation was created. That generation is now beginning to retire. Draw a demand-supply graph to illustrate the effects of this increase in the number of seniors on the market for medical services.

Use the following information to work Problems 3 and 4.

A new coffee shop opens and to maximize profit it hires 5 workers at the competitive wage rate. The price of a cup of coffee is $4 and the value of marginal product of workers in the coffee shop is $12 an hour.

3. What is the marginal product of the coffee shop workers? How much does a coffee shop worker earn?

4. If the price of a cup of coffee rises from $4 to $5 and the coffee shop continues to hire workers at the competitive wage rate, explain how the value of marginal product and the number of workers hired will change.

Use the following information to work Problems 5 to 7.

An ex-Google coder makes twice as much freelancing
James Knight quit a well-paid job writing software for Google to go freelance and is now earning about double his Google pay as a freelancer. In a war for talent, companies are paying as much as $1,000 per hour for freelancers with the right skills. The demand for coders soared with the arrival of the iPhone in 2007. More recently, coders started working on software for fridges, watches, and clothing. The Bureau of Labor Statistics says the demand for coders will grow at more than twice the average jobs growth rate.

Source: Bloomberg, January 19, 2016

5. Explain what happened to the value of marginal product of coders after 2007 and explain why it happened.

6. Explain what happened in the market for coders after 2007 to demand, supply, and the quantities demanded and supplied and draw a graph to show the changes that occurred in the market for coders.

7. Explain how the Bureau of Labor Statistics expects the market for coders to change in the future and draw a graph to show the expected changes.

8. Suppose that Bananaland is the world's largest grower of bananas. Bananaland plans to double its population in 3 years by hiring well-educated people from the United States. To increase the number of entrepreneurs, Bananaland encourages anyone with $1 million to immigrate. Explain the influence of these events on Bananaland's labor market and land market.

9. Hong Kong is much more densely populated than is the United States. Compare the rental rate on land in Hong Kong with that in Chicago. Explain why the percentage of commercial buildings that are new is lower in downtown Chicago than in Hong Kong.

Multiple Choice Quiz

1. A firm's demand for labor is determined by _____.

   A. the market wage rate
   B. the price of the good that the firm produces and the wage rate it pays
   C. the marginal product of labor and the market wage rate
   D. the price of the good that the firm produces and the marginal product of labor

2. The value of marginal product of labor increases if _____.

   A. more labor is hired
   B. more of the good is produced
   C. the market price of the good produced rises
   D. using a new technology reduces the demand for labor

3. An individual's supply of labor curve is _____.

   A. horizontal at the market wage rate
   B. upward sloping as the wage rate rises
   C. upward sloping at low wage rates but becomes downward sloping at high wage rates
   D. vertical at the standard number of hours a person works per day

4. In a competitive labor market for bakers, the equilibrium wage rate _____.

   A. rises if bakers become more productive
   B. falls if the supply of bakers decreases
   C. rises if the market price of bakery items falls
   D. rises if new technology makes it easier for anyone to be a baker

5. A union will _____ if it can _____.

   A. raise the wage rate of its members; decrease the marginal product of its union members
   B. raise the wage rate of its members; introduce minimum qualifications, which will restrict membership of the union
   C. increase the number of union jobs; restrict membership of the union
   D. increase the number of union jobs; increase the union wage rate

6. To maximize profit, a firm _____.

   A. uses the quantity of land at which the rental rate equals the value of marginal product of land
   B. balances the rental rate of capital against the wage rate of labor
   C. uses the quantity of capital at which the marginal revenue equals the value of marginal product of capital
   D. uses the quantity of capital at which the suppliers' expected profit equals the value of marginal product of capital

7. Which of the following statements about a nonrenewable natural resource market is *incorrect*?

   A. The demand for the resource is determined by its value of marginal product.
   B. The supply of the resource is perfectly elastic at the market price.
   C. The price of the resource is expected to rise over time at a rate equal to the interest rate.
   D. The supply of the resource is perfectly inelastic.

Who are the rich and the poor?

Economic Inequality

When you have completed your study of this chapter, you will be able to

1 Describe the economic inequality in the United States.

2 Explain how economic inequality arises.

3 Explain how governments redistribute income and describe the effects of redistribution on economic inequality.

 MyEconLab Big Picture Video

20.1 MEASURING ECONOMIC INEQUALITY

Market income
A household's wages, interest, rent, and profit earned in factor markets before paying income taxes.

Money income
Market income plus cash payments to households by the government.

To measure economic inequality, we look at the distributions of income and wealth. A household's *income* is the amount that it *receives in a given period*. A household's **market income** equals the wages, interest, rent, and profit that the household earns in factor markets before paying income taxes. The Census Bureau defines another income concept, **money income**, which equals *market income* plus cash payments to households by the government. We will use the *money income* concept to describe the distribution of income in the United States.

A household's *wealth* is the value of the things it *owns at a point in time*. Wealth is measured as the market value of a household's home, the stocks and bonds that it owns, and the money in its bank accounts minus its debts such as outstanding credit card balances.

To describe the *distribution of income*, imagine the population of the United States lined up from the lowest to the highest income earner. Now divide the line into five equal-sized groups, each with 20 percent of the population. These groups are called *quintiles*.

Next, share out the total money income among these groups so that the shares represent the U.S. income distribution. Table 20.1(a) lists the percentages received by each group.

Share out the pie of total wealth in a similar way. Table 20.1(b) shows the percentages owned by each of *seven* groups. The two poorest quintiles are added together and have negative wealth, while the richest quintile is broken into smaller groups to show the wealth distribution inside that quintile.

▇ TABLE 20.1

The Distributions of Money Income and Wealth in the United States

In part (a), the 20 percent of households with the lowest incomes receive 3.3 percent of total money income, while the 20 percent of households with the highest incomes receive 50 percent of total income.

In part (b), the poorest 40 percent of households have negative wealth, while the richest 1 percent own 36.7 percent.

SOURCES OF DATA: Part (a): Carmen DeNavas-Walt and Bernadette D. Proctor, U.S. Census Bureau, Current Population Reports, P60-252, *Income and Poverty in the United States: 2014*, U.S. Government Printing Office, Washington, DC, 2015.
Part (b): Edward N. Wolff, "Household Wealth Trends in The United States, 1962-2013: What Happened Over the Great Recession?" National Bureau of Economic Research Working Paper 20733, December 2014.

(a) Income distribution in 2014 (median household income $53,657)

		Percentage of		Cumulative percentage of	
		Households	Income	Households	Income
A	Lowest 20	3.3		20	3.3
B	Second 20	9.0		40	12.3
C	Third 20	14.8		60	27.1
D	Fourth 20	22.9		80	50.0
E	Highest 20	50.0		100	100.0

(b) Wealth distribution in 2013 (median household wealth $63,800)

		Percentage of		Cumulative percentage of	
		Households	Wealth	Households	Wealth
A'	Lowest 40	−0.9		40	−0.9
B'	Next 20	2.7		60	1.8
C'	Next 20	9.3		80	11.1
D'	Next 10	11.8		90	22.9
E'	Next 5	12.2		95	35.1
F'	Next 4	28.2		99	63.3
G'	Highest 1	36.7		100	100.0

Lorenz Curves

A **Lorenz curve** graphs the cumulative percentage of income (or wealth) on the *y*-axis against the cumulative percentage of households on the *x*-axis. Figure 20.1 shows the Lorenz curves for income and wealth in the United States. To generate the Lorenz curve for income, we graph the cumulative percentage of income against the cumulative percentage of households. Points *A* to *D* on the graph correspond to the rows identified by those letters in the table. For example, row *B* and point *B* show that the 40 percent of households with the lowest incomes in 2014 received 12.3 percent of total income—3.3 percent plus 9.0 percent from Table 20.1(a).

To generate the Lorenz curve for wealth, we graph the cumulative percentage of wealth against the cumulative percentage of households. Points *A'* to *F'* on the graph correspond to the rows identified by those letters in the table of Figure 20.1. For example, row *C'* and point *C'* show that the poorest 80 percent of households owned 11.1 percent of total wealth—−0.9 percent plus 2.7 percent plus 9.3 percent from Table 20.1(b).

If income (or wealth) were distributed equally, each 20 percent of households would receive 20 percent of total income (or own 20 percent of total wealth), and the Lorenz curve would be the straight line labeled "Line of equality." The Lorenz curves based on the actual distributions of income and wealth are always below the line of equality. The closer the Lorenz curve is to the line of equality, the more equal is the distribution. You can see that the Lorenz curve for wealth is much farther away from the line of equality than is the Lorenz curve for income. The distribution of wealth is much more unequal than the distribution of income.

Lorenz curve
A curve that graphs the cumulative percentage of income (or wealth) against the cumulative percentage of households.

FIGURE 20.1

Lorenz Curves for Income and Wealth in the United States

MyEconLab Animation

Cumulative percentage of		
Households	Income	Wealth
20	A 3.3	
40	B 12.3	A' −0.9
60	C 27.1	B' 1.8
80	D 50.0	C' 11.1
90		D' 22.9
95		E' 35.1
99		F' 63.3

SOURCES OF DATA: See Table 20.1.

❶ If income or wealth were distributed equally, the Lorenz curve would lie along the straight line labeled "Line of equality."

❷ The income Lorenz curve shows the cumulative percentage of income graphed against the cumulative percentage of households. The 20 percent of households with the lowest incomes received 3.3 percent of total income (A), and the 80 percent of households with the lowest incomes received 50 percent of total income (D).

❸ The wealth Lorenz curve shows the cumulative percentage of wealth graphed against the cumulative percentage of households. The poorest 40 percent of households have no wealth (A'), and 99 percent of households own 63.3 percent (F'). The richest 1 percent own 36.7 percent.

■ Inequality over Time

Incomes have been getting more unequal. In 2014, 67 percent of Americans told the Gallup poll that they thought incomes were too unequal. Twenty-three years earlier, in 1991, only 21 percent of Americans thought that the rich were too rich and the poor too poor.

Since the mid-1970s, the highest incomes have increased faster than the lower incomes and the gap between the rich and the poor has widened. Figure 20.2(a) shows this widening gap by looking at the income share of each quintile between 1974 and 2014. The data are based on money income. The share received by the highest quintile increased from 44 percent in 1974 to 51 percent in 2014. All of the other quintiles saw their shares of total income fall.

A key feature of rising inequality is the trend in the incomes of the super rich. Emmanuel Saez of the University of California, Berkeley, used tax returns data to get the numbers graphed in Figure 20.2(b).

After decades of a falling share called the "Great Compression," the share of income received by the richest one percent began to climb in 1975. By 2014 (the latest year in the database), the richest one percent were earning 18 percent of the nation's income. The bottom quintile earns 3.3 percent of total income, so an average household in the top one percent receives 109 times the average income of a household in the lowest quintile. Movie stars, sports stars, and the CEOs of large corporations are among these super rich.

FIGURE 20.2

Trends in the Distribution of Income   MyEconLab Animation

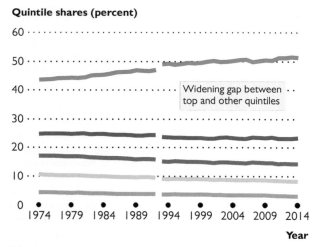

(a) Mean household income quintile shares

(b) The income share of the top 1 percent

SOURCES OF DATA: Part (a): See Table 20.1 Note: The data collection method changed in 1993. Part (b): The World Wealth and Income Database, www.wid.world.

In part (a), from 1974 to 2014 the income share received by the highest quintile rose from 44 percent to 50, percent. The shares received by the other quintiles fell. The lowest quintile share fell from 4 percent to 3.3 percent, the second lowest from 11 percent to 9 percent, and the middle from 17 percent to 14.8 percent.

In part (b), over the 50 years from 1924 to 1974, the income share of the richest 1 percent shrank from 20 percent to 8 percent during the "Great Compression." After 1974, the income share of the top 1 percent increased, and rapidly during the 1980s and 1990s.

■ Poverty

Households with very low incomes are considered to be living in poverty. What is poverty? How do we measure it, how much poverty is there, and is the amount of poverty decreasing or increasing?

Poverty is a state in which a household's income is too low to be able to buy the quantities of food, shelter, and clothing that are deemed necessary. The Census Bureau considers a household to be living in poverty if its income is less than a defined level that varies with household size and that is updated each year to reflect changes in the cost of living. In 2015, the poverty level for a household with 2 adults and 2 children was an income of $24,250.

In 2014, 47 million Americans had incomes below the poverty level. Figure 20.3(a) shows the distribution of poverty by race in 2014. Almost one half (41 percent) of people living in poverty are white.

To measure the *incidence* of poverty, we look at the poverty *rate*—the percentage of families living in poverty. In 2014, the poverty rate was 15 percent. Figure 20.3(b) shows the poverty rates and their trends for white, black, and Hispanic families from 1974 through 2014.

The white poverty rate has fluctuated around 10 percent. For black families, the poverty rate fell from 35 percent in 1983 to 24 percent in 2008, but then increased to 27 percent in 2012. For Hispanic families, the poverty rate increased during the 1980s, then decreased during the 1990s, before increasing again through 2012.

Poverty
A state in which a household's income is too low to be able to buy the quantities of food, shelter, and clothing that are deemed necessary.

■ FIGURE 20.3

Poverty Rates in the United States

MyEconLab Animation

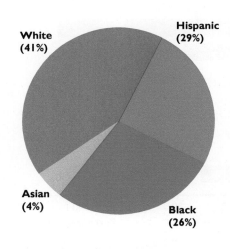

(a) The distribution of poverty in 2014

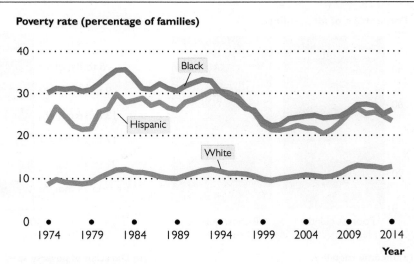

(b) Trends in poverty rates

SOURCE OF DATA: See Table 20.1

Part (a) shows that white families account for 41 percent of the poor. But part (b) shows that the poverty *rates* for blacks and Hispanics are double the rate for whites. The poverty rate of black families fell during the 1980s and the 1990s. The poverty rate of Hispanics also fell during the 1990s, but it had previously increased. The poverty rates of all groups increased in 2009 and 2010.

■ Economic Mobility

Economic mobility is the movement of a family up or down through the income distribution and into and out of poverty. If there were no economic mobility, a family would be stuck at a given point in the income distribution and be persistently rich, middle-class, poor, or in poverty. Also, in such a situation, the data on the *annual* income distribution would be a good indicator of *life-time* inequality. But if there is economic mobility, life-time inequality is not as great as the inequality in a single year. How much economic mobility is there?

Mobility Through the Income Quintiles

One indicator of mobility is the extent to which families move up and down through the income quintiles. Katharine Bradbury, an economist at the Federal Reserve Bank of Boston, has provided information on this mobility. Figure 20.4(a) shows what she found. The figure shows the percentages of families in the poorest and richest quintiles that remained in the same quintile and the percentages of families that moved up or down by one quintile or more than one quintile over a ten-year period.

About 60 percent of families remain in the poorest and richest quintiles, but about 20 percent of families move up or down by more than one quintile. That is, around one in five rich families and one in five poor families become average families over a ten-year period. But because the quintile income shares don't change much, one in five average families become either rich or poor. These data tell us that there is a lot of economic mobility in the United States.

■ FIGURE 20.4

Income Mobility and Poverty Duration   MyEconLab Animation

(a) Income mobility

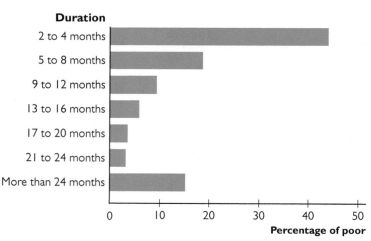

(b) Duration of poverty spell

SOURCES OF DATA: Part (a): Katharine Bradbury, "Trends in U.S. Family Income Mobility, 1969–2006," Federal Reserve Bank of Boston, Working Paper No. 11-10. Part (b): U.S. Census Bureau, Survey of Income and Program Participation.

In part (a), almost 60 percent of families remain in the richest or poorest quintile for a decade or longer and about 20 percent move up or down by more than one quintile during a decade.

In part (b), almost 50 percent of families living in poverty remain in that state for 2 to 4 months. But 15 percent of families living in poverty remain in that state for more than 2 years.

Mobility In and Out of Poverty

Another measure of economic mobility is provided by the duration of poverty. If a household is living in poverty for a few months it faces serious hardship during those months, but it faces a less serious problem than it would if its poverty persisted for several months or, worse yet, for several years, or even generations.

Because the duration of poverty is an additional indicator of the hardship that poverty brings, the Census Bureau provides measures of duration. Figure 20.4(b) shows the data for the period 2009 to 2011, the most recent available.

About 45 percent of poverty lasts for between 2 and 4 months. So for almost a half of poor families, poverty is not persistent. But for 15 percent of poor families, poverty lasts for more than 2 years, so a large number of poor households—about 7 million—experience chronic poverty.

The Sources of Economic Mobility

What are the sources of economic mobility? Some of it arises from fluctuations in job opportunities—from changes in the employment status of families. And some arises from changes over a family's life-cycle. Families experience income growth as their workers become more skilled and experienced. As a family continues to get older and its workers retire, its income falls. So if we look at three households that have identical lifetime incomes—that are economically equal—but one is young, one is middle-aged, and one is old, we will see a great deal of inequality. Inequality of annual incomes overstates the degree of lifetime inequality.

EYE on the GLOBAL ECONOMY
Global Inequality

There is much more income inequality in the global economy than in the United States. The Lorenz curves in this figure provide a comparative picture. You can see that the global Lorenz curve lies much farther from the line of equality than does the U.S. Lorenz curve.

Numbers that highlight the comparison are the percentages of families that get a half (50 percent) of the income. In the United States, the richest 20 percent of families get a half of the income and the remaining 80 percent share the other half. In the global economy the richest 8 percent of families get a half of the income and the remaining 92 percent share the other half.

Global incomes are rising and by some estimates, inequality is decreasing.

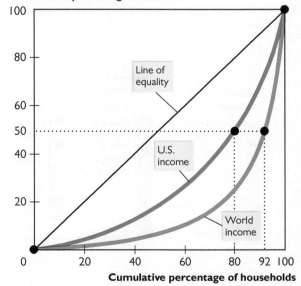

But other estimates suggest that global inequality, like U.S. inequality, is increasing. Better data are needed to settle this issue.

SOURCES OF DATA: U.S. income: See Table 20.1. World income: Branko Milanovic, "Global Income Inequality by the Numbers: in History and Now—An Overview," The World Bank Development Research Group Poverty and Inequality Team, Policy Research Working Paper 6259, November 2012.

EYE on INEQUALITY

Who Are the Rich and the Poor?

In the United States today (excluding the ultra rich sports and entertainment superstars and top corporate executives), the families with the highest incomes are likely to be college-educated Asian married couples between 45 and 54 years of age living together with two children in the Northeast.

At the other extreme, the person with the lowest income is likely to be a black woman over 65 years of age who lives alone somewhere in the South and has fewer than nine years of elementary school education. Another low-income group are young women who have not completed high school,

have a child (or children), and who live without a partner. These snapshot profiles are the extremes in the figure.

The figure illustrates the dominant importance of education in influencing income. People with a post-graduate professional degree (an MBA and a law degree are examples) or a doctorate degree earn, on average, five times the income of someone who has not completed high school.

Household type and size are the next largest influences on income. A married couple with two children have, on average, an income three times that of a single female household.

Race is also a significant factor that influences income. Asian households earn, on average, 75 percent more income than Hispanic origin households.

The age of a householder shows the life-cycle influence on the income distribution. Those aged between 45 and 54 have incomes double those aged 65 and over and aged 15 to 24.

Region of residence has a small influence on income, the Northeast having the highest incomes at almost 20 percent higher than those in the South.

Within these categories, there is enormous individual variation.

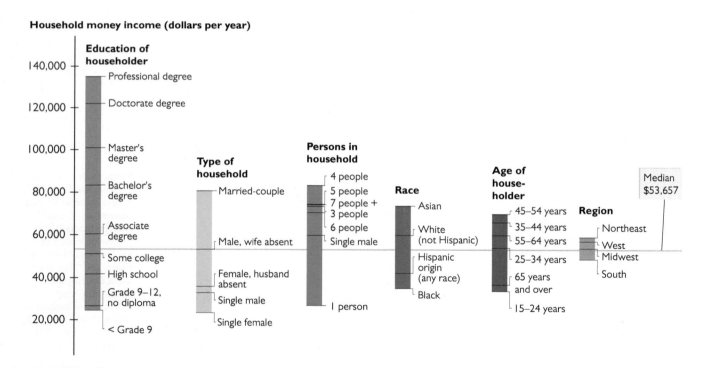

SOURCE OF DATA: Current Population Survey, HINC-01. Selected Characteristics of Households, by Total Money Income in 2014.

CHECKPOINT 20.1

MyEconLab Study Plan 20.1
Key Terms Quiz
Solutions Video

Describe the economic inequality in the United States.

Practice Problems

Table 1 shows the distribution of money income in Canada and Table 20.1(a) on p. 512 shows the distribution of money income in the United States.

1. Create a table that shows the cumulative percentages of households and income in Canada.

2. Draw the Lorenz curves for Canada and the United States. Compare the distribution of income in Canada with that in the United States. Which distribution is more unequal?

In the News

Home prices in 20 U.S. cities climb by most since July 2014

Home prices in 20 U.S. cities increased 5.8 percent from a year earlier, the biggest advance since July 2014. Rising property values are increasing household wealth for homeowners and offsetting some of the fall in wealth resulting from the drop in stock prices.

Source: *Bloomberg*, January 27, 2016

If most of the wealth of the wealthiest households consists of stocks and most of the wealth of other households consists of their homes, explain how the information provided in the news clip changed the distribution of wealth. Which wealth quintile would experience a decrease in its share of wealth?

Solutions to Practice Problems

1. Table 2 shows the cumulative percentages of Canadian households and income: The lowest 20 percent of households receive 4.8 percent of total income and the second lowest 20 percent receive 10.7 percent of total income, so the lowest 40 percent of households receive 15.5 percent of total income. The other rows of the table are calculated in a similar way.

2. A Lorenz curve plots the cumulative percentage of income against the cumulative percentage of households. The blue curve in Figure 1 plots the Canadian data in Table 2. The green curve is the U.S. Lorenz curve. The line of equality shows an equal distribution. The Canadian Lorenz curve lies closer to the line of equality than does the U.S. Lorenz curve, so the distribution of income in the United States is more unequal than that in Canada.

Solution to In the News

A household's wealth is the value of the things it owns at a point in time. Wealth is measured as the market value of a household's home, the stocks and bonds that it owns, and the money in its bank accounts minus its debts. Because most of the wealth of poorer households is made up of their homes, as home prices increased, the percentage of total wealth of the lower quintiles increased and the percentage of total wealth held by the top wealth quintile decreased. The fact that stock prices fell decreased the wealth of the top quintile and lowered its share of wealth further.

TABLE 1   CANADIAN DATA

Households	Money income (percentage)
Lowest 20 percent	4.8
Second 20 percent	10.7
Third 20 percent	16.5
Fourth 20 percent	24.0
Highest 20 percent	44.0

TABLE 2

	Cumulative percentage of
Households	Income
20	4.8
40	15.5
60	32.0
80	56.0
100	100.0

FIGURE 1

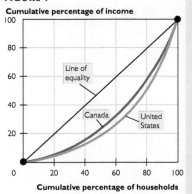

20.2 HOW ECONOMIC INEQUALITY ARISES

Economic inequality arises from a wide variety of factors. The five key ones that we'll examine here are

- Human capital
- Discrimination
- Financial and physical capital
- Entrepreneurial ability
- Personal and family characteristics

■ Human Capital

Human capital is the accumulated skill and knowledge of human beings. To see how human capital differences affect economic inequality, we'll study an economy with two levels of human capital, which we'll call *high-skilled labor* and *low-skilled labor*. Low-skilled labor might be law clerks, hospital orderlies, or bank tellers, and high-skilled labor might be attorneys, surgeons, or bank CEOs.

The Demand for High-Skilled and Low-Skilled Labor

High-skilled workers can perform tasks that low-skilled workers would perform badly or couldn't even perform at all. Imagine an untrained person doing surgery or piloting an airplane. High-skilled workers have a higher value of marginal product (*VMP*) than low-skilled workers do. As we learned in Chapter 19, a firm's demand for labor curve is derived from and is the same as the firm's value of marginal product of labor curve.

   Figure 20.5(a) shows the demand curves for high-skilled and low-skilled labor. At any given employment level, firms are willing to pay a higher wage rate to a high-skilled worker than to a low-skilled worker. The gap between the two wage rates measures the value of marginal product of skill. For example, at an employment level of 2,000 hours, firms are willing to pay a high-skilled worker $25 an hour and a low-skilled worker only $10 an hour, a difference of $15 an hour. Thus the value of marginal product of skill is $15 an hour.

The Supply of High-Skilled and Low-Skilled Labor

A skill is costly to acquire and its opportunity cost includes expenditures, such as tuition, and lower earnings while the skill is being acquired. When a person goes to school full time, that cost is the total earnings forgone. When a person acquires a skill through on-the-job training, he or she earns a lower wage rate than someone who is doing a comparable job but not undergoing training. In this case, the cost of acquiring the skill is equal to the wage paid to a person not being trained minus the wage paid to a person being trained.

   Because skills are costly to acquire, a high-skilled person is not willing to work for the same wage rate that a low-skilled person is willing to accept. The position of the supply curve of high-skilled workers reflects the cost of acquiring the skill. Figure 20.5(b) shows two supply curves: one of high-skilled workers and the other of low-skilled workers. The supply curve of high-skilled workers is S_H, and that of low-skilled workers is S_L.

   The high-skilled worker's supply curve lies above the low-skilled worker's supply curve. The vertical distance between the two supply curves is the

FIGURE 20.5

Skill Differentials

(a) Demand for high-skilled and low-skilled labor

(b) Supply of high-skilled and low-skilled labor

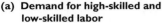

(c) Markets for high-skilled and low-skilled labor

In part (a), D_L is the demand curve for low-skilled labor and D_H is the demand curve for high-skilled labor. ❶ The vertical distance between these two curves is the value of marginal product of skill.

In part (b), S_L is the supply curve of low-skilled workers and S_H is the supply curve of high-skilled workers. ❷ The vertical distance

between these two curves is the required compensation for the cost of acquiring a skill.

In part (c), low-skilled workers earn a wage rate of $10 an hour and high-skilled workers earn a wage rate of $20 an hour. ❸ The $10 equilibrium wage differential is the effect of acquiring skill.

compensation that high-skilled workers require for the cost of acquiring the skill. For example, suppose that the quantity of low-skilled labor supplied is 2,000 hours at a wage rate of $10 an hour. This wage rate compensates the low-skilled workers mainly for their time on the job. Consider next the supply of high-skilled workers. To induce high-skilled labor to supply 2,000 hours, firms must pay a wage rate of $17 an hour. This wage rate for high-skilled labor is higher than that for low-skilled labor because high-skilled labor must be compensated not only for the time on the job but also for the time and other costs of acquiring the skill.

Wage Rates of High-Skilled and Low-Skilled Labor

To work out the wage rates of high-skilled and low-skilled labor, we have to bring together the effects of skill on the demand for and supply of labor.

Figure 20.5(c) shows the demand curves and the supply curves for high-skilled and low-skilled labor. These curves are the same as those plotted in parts (a) and (b). Equilibrium occurs in the market for low-skilled labor where the supply and demand curves for low-skilled labor intersect. The equilibrium wage rate is $10 an hour, and the quantity of low-skilled labor employed is 2,000 hours. Equilibrium in the market for high-skilled workers occurs where the supply and demand curves for high-skilled workers intersect. The equilibrium wage rate is $20 an hour, and the quantity of high-skilled labor employed is 3,000 hours.

As you can see in Figure 20.5(c), the equilibrium wage rate of high-skilled labor is higher than that of low-skilled labor. There are two reasons why this occurs: First, high-skilled labor has a higher value of marginal product than does low-skilled labor, so at a given wage rate, the quantity of high-skilled labor demanded exceeds that of low-skilled labor. Second, skills are costly to acquire, so at a given wage rate, the quantity of high-skilled labor supplied is less than that of low-skilled labor. The wage differential (in this case, $10 an hour) depends on both the value of marginal product of skill and the cost of acquiring it. The higher the value of marginal product of skill, the larger is the vertical distance between the demand curves. The more costly it is to acquire a skill, the larger is the vertical distance between the supply curves. The higher the value of marginal product of skill and the more costly it is to acquire, the larger is the wage differential between high-skilled and low-skilled workers.

Education and on-the-job training enable people to acquire skills and move up through the income distribution. But education is the most important contributor to a higher income, as you can see in *Eye on the U.S. Economy* below.

Discrimination, which we examine next, is another possible source of economic inequality.

EYE on the U.S. ECONOMY
Does Education Pay?

The figure shows that there are large differences in earnings based on the degree of education.

Rates of return on high school and college education have been estimated to be in the range of 5 to 10 percent a year after allowing for inflation, which suggests that a college degree is a better investment than almost any other that a person can undertake.

Based on average income data, the gain from graduating from high school is $17,400 a year. But the gain from going to college or university and getting a bachelor's degree is greater and brings in an additional $50,000 a year.

Remaining at the university to complete a master's degree (usually one more year of study) brings in an extra $15,000 a year, and working for a professional degree increases income by another $62,000 a year.

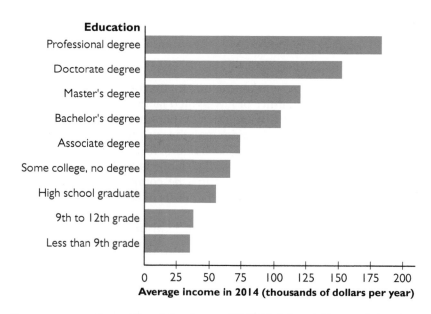

SOURCE OF DATA: Current Population Survey, HINC-01. Selected Characteristics of Households, by Total Money Income in 2014.

■ Discrimination

Persistent earnings differences exist between women and men and among the races. You can see them in *Eye on the U.S. Economy* below. Does discrimination contribute to these differences? It might, but economists can't isolate and measure the effect of discrimination, so we can't say by how much, or even whether, earnings differences arise from this source.

To see the difficulty in isolating the effects of discrimination, consider the market for investment advisors. Suppose that black women and white men are equally good at providing investment advice. If there is no race and sex discrimination, average wage rates are the same for both groups.

But if some people are willing to pay more for investment advice from a white man than they are willing to pay for the same advice from a black woman, the market-determined value of marginal product of black women is lower than that of white men, and the demand for investment advice from black women is lower than that from white men. The result is a lower equilibrium wage rate (and fewer high-paying jobs) for black women than for white men.

For discrimination to work in this way and bring *persistent* wage differences, people must be *persistently* willing to pay more than necessary for investment advice. People will begin to notice that they can get a better deal if they buy investment advice from black women. Substitution away from high-cost white men toward lower-cost black women will shift demand and eventually eliminate the wage difference.

EYE on the U.S. ECONOMY
Sex and Race Earnings Differences

The figure shows the earnings of different race and sex groups expressed as a percentage of the earnings of white men.

In 2015, white women earned, on average, 81 percent of what white men earned. Black men earned 74 percent, and black women earned 67 percent. Men and women of Hispanic origin earned only 69 percent and 62 percent, respectively, of white men's wages.

These earnings differentials have persisted since 2009, and only those of white women have begun to narrow in a significant way.

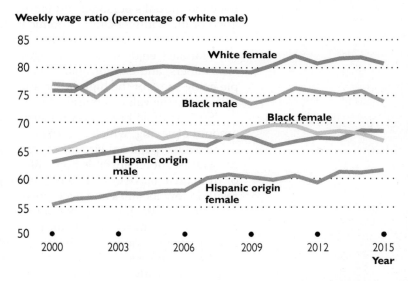

SOURCE OF DATA: Bureau of Labor Statistics.

■ Financial and Physical Capital

The people with the highest incomes are usually those who own large amounts of financial capital and physical capital. These people receive incomes in the form of interest and dividend payments and from capital gains—increases in the stock market value.

Families with a large amount of capital tend to become even more wealthy across generations for two reasons. First, they bequeath wealth to their children and second, rich people marry rich partners (on average).

Saving, and the wealth accumulation that it brings, is not inevitably a source of increased inequality and can even be a source of increased equality. When a household saves to redistribute an uneven income over the life cycle, it enjoys more equal consumption. Also, if a lucky generation that has a high income saves a large amount and makes a bequest to a generation that is unlucky, this act of saving also decreases the degree of inequality.

■ Entrepreneurial Ability

Some of the most spectacularly rich people have benefited from unusual entrepreneurial talent. Household names such as Bill Gates (Microsoft), Sergey Brin and Larry Page (Google), and Mark Zuckerberg (Facebook) are examples of people who began life with modest amounts of wealth and modest incomes and through a combination of hard work, good luck, and outstanding entrepreneurship have become extremely rich.

But some very poor people, and some who fall below the poverty level, have also tried their hands at being entrepreneurs. We don't hear much about these people. They are not in the headlines. But they have put together a business plan, borrowed heavily, and through a combination of hard work, bad luck, and in some cases poor decisions have become extremely poor.

■ Personal and Family Characteristics

Each individual's personal and family characteristics play a crucial role, for either good or ill, in influencing economic well-being.

People who are exceptionally good looking and talented with stable and creative families enjoy huge advantages over the average person. Many movie stars, entertainers, and extraordinarily talented athletes are in this category. These people enjoy some of the highest incomes because their personal or family characteristics make the value of marginal product of their labor very large.

Success often breeds yet further success. A large income can generate a large amount of saving, which in turn generates yet more interest income.

Adverse personal circumstances, such as chronic physical or mental illness, drug abuse, or an unstable home life possibly arising from the absence of a parent or from an abusive or negligent parent, place a huge burden on many people and result in low incomes and even poverty.

A tough life, just like its opposite, can be self-reinforcing. Weak physical or mental health makes it difficult to study and obtain a skill and results in a low labor income or no income because a job is just too hard to hold down. And the children of the poorest people find it hard to get into college and university, and so find it difficult to break the cycle of poverty.

CHECKPOINT 20.2

MyEconLab Study Plan 20.2
Solutions Video

Explain how economic inequality arises.

Practice Problems

In the United States in 2010, 30 million people had full-time managerial jobs that paid an average of $1,200 a week and 10 million people had full-time sales jobs that paid an average of $600 a week.

1. Explain why managers are paid more than salespeople.
2. Explain why, despite the higher weekly wage, more people are employed as managers than as salespeople.
3. As more firms offer their goods and services for sale online, how does the market for salespeople change?

In the News

As Ttech booms, workers turn to coding for career change
Paul Minton, a 26-year-old math major, made $20,000 a year as a waiter. After completing a three-month course at Galvanize, a coding school in San Francisco, his starting salary at a web start-up was more than $100,000 a year. Coding schools can't keep up with the demand for workers like Paul Minton.
Source: *The New York Times*, July 28, 2015

Why are graduates who work as waiters going to coding school?

Solutions to Practice Problems

1. A typical manager has incurred a higher cost of education and on-the-job training than has the typical salesperson. The supply curve of managers, S_H, lies above that of salespeople, S_L (Figure 1). With better education and on-the-job training, managers have more human capital and a higher value of marginal product than do salespeople. The demand curve for managers, D_H, is greater than the demand for salespeople, D_L. Figure 1 illustrates why managers are paid more than salespeople.
2. Figure 1 shows that the demand and supply for each type of labor leads to a greater employment for managers than for salespeople despite the higher wage rate for managers.
3. As more people shop online, firms will hire fewer salespeople. The demand for salespeople will decrease and fewer people will work in sales. How their wage rate and employment will change depends on how the supply of salespeople changes.

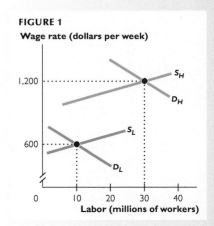

FIGURE 1

Solution to In the News

College graduates have accumulated general human capital but do not have the specific skills that many employers seek and that have a high value of marginal product. Even as a math major, Paul Minton's best-paying job was as a $20,000 a year waiter. By going to coding school, Paul invested in new human capital and obtained skills that are in high demand. The value of marginal product of a skilled coder is greater than that of a waiter, so Paul's wage rate as a coder is higher than as a waiter.

MyEconLab Concept Video

20.3 INCOME REDISTRIBUTION

We've described the distribution of income and wealth in the United States and examined the five main sources of economic inequality. Our task in this final section is to study the *redistribution* of income by government.

How do governments redistribute income? What is the scale of redistribution? Why do we vote for policies that redistribute income? What are the challenges in designing policies that achieve a fair and efficient distribution of income and reduction of poverty?

■ How Governments Redistribute Income

The three main ways in which governments in the United States redistribute income are

- Income taxes
- Income maintenance programs
- Subsidized services

Income Taxes

Income taxes may be progressive, regressive, or proportional (see Chapter 8, p. 207). A *progressive income tax* is one that taxes income at an average rate that increases with the level of income. A *regressive income tax* is one that taxes income at an average rate that decreases with the level of income. A *proportional income tax* (also called a *flat-rate income tax*) is one that taxes income at a constant rate, regardless of the level of income.

The federal government, most state governments, and some city governments impose income taxes. The detailed tax arrangements vary across the individual states, but the income tax system overall is progressive. The poorest working households receive money from the government through an earned income tax credit. The federal income tax rate starts at 10 percent of each additional dollar earned on the lowest taxed incomes and rises through 15 percent, 25 percent, 28 percent, 33 percent, and 35 percent of each additional dollar earned on successively higher incomes.

Income Maintenance Programs

Three main types of programs redistribute income by making direct payments (in cash, services, or vouchers) to people in the lower part of the income distribution. They are

- Social Security programs
- Unemployment compensation
- Welfare programs

Social Security Programs Social Security is a public insurance system paid for by compulsory payroll taxes on employers and employees. Social Security has two main components: Old Age, Survivors, Disability, and Health Insurance (OASDHI), which provides monthly cash payments to retired or disabled workers or their surviving spouses and children; and Medicare, which provides hospital and health insurance for the elderly and disabled. In 2015, Social Security supported 65 million people, who received average monthly checks of $1,340.

Unemployment Compensation   To provide an income to unemployed workers, every state has established an unemployment compensation program. Under these programs, a tax is paid that is based on the income of each covered worker and such a worker receives a benefit when he or she becomes unemployed. The details of the benefits vary from state to state.

Welfare Programs   The purpose of welfare programs is to provide incomes for people who do not qualify for Social Security or unemployment compensation. The programs are

1. Supplementary Security Income (SSI) program, which is designed to help the neediest elderly, disabled, and blind people
2. Temporary Assistance for Needy Families (TANF) program, which is designed to help families that have inadequate financial resources
3. Supplemental Nutrition Assistance Program (SNAP), which is designed to help the poorest households obtain a basic diet
4. Medicaid, which is designed to cover the costs of medical care for households that receive help under the SSI and TANF programs

Subsidized Services

A great deal of redistribution takes place in the United States through the provision of subsidized services—services provided by the government at prices far below the cost of production. The taxpayers who consume these goods and services receive a transfer in kind from the taxpayers who do not consume them. The two most important areas in which this form of redistribution takes place are education—both kindergarten through grade 12 and college and university—and healthcare. But neither necessarily redistributes from the rich to the poor.

In 2015–2016, a student enrolled at the University of California, Berkeley, who is not a resident of California, paid a tuition of $48,240. This amount is probably close to the cost of providing a year's education at Berkeley. But a California resident paid tuition of only $13,432. So California households with a member enrolled at Berkeley received a benefit from the government of $34,808 a year. Many of these households have above-average incomes.

Government provision of healthcare services has grown to equal the scale of private provision. Medicaid provides high-quality and high-cost healthcare to millions of people who earn too little to buy such services themselves. Medicaid redistributes from the rich to the poor. Medicare, which is available to all over 65 years of age, is not targeted at the poor.

■ The Scale of Income Redistribution

A household's income in the absence of government redistribution is its *market income*. We can measure the scale of income redistribution by calculating the percentage of market income paid in taxes minus the percentage received in benefits at each income level. The available data include redistribution through taxes and cash and noncash benefits to welfare recipients. The data do not include the value of subsidized services such as a college education, which might decrease the total scale of redistribution from the rich to the poor.

Figure 20.6 shows how government actions change the distribution of income. Part (a) shows two Lorenz curves and compares them with the line of equality.

Disposable income

Market income plus cash benefits paid by the government minus taxes.

The blue Lorenz curve describes the distribution of *market income*. The red Lorenz curve shows the distribution of **disposable income**, which is income after all taxes and benefits, including Medicaid and Medicare benefits. The Lorenz curve for *disposable income* is closer to the line of equality than that for *market income*, which tells us that the distribution of disposable income is more equal than the distribution of market income.

Figure 20.6(b) shows that redistribution increases the share received by the lowest four quintiles and decreases the share received by the highest quintile.

The sources of income at different income levels provide another measure of the scale of redistribution. The poorest quintile receives 80 percent of its income from the government. The second quintile receives 32 percent of its income from the government. In contrast, the richest quintile receives almost nothing from the government and receives a third of its income from capital—interest, dividends, and capital gains on financial assets.

FIGURE 20.6

The Scale of Income Redistribution   MyEconLab Animation

Taxes and income maintenance programs reduce the degree of inequality that the market generates. In part (a), the Lorenz curve moves closer to the line of equality.

Part (b) shows the redistribution in 2011. The quintile with the lowest incomes received net benefits that increased their share of total income by 2.3 percentage points. The middle two quintiles received bigger shares from redistribution. Even the fourth quintile received more in benefits than it paid in taxes. The quintile with the highest incomes paid taxes that decreased their share of total income by 9.3 percentage points.

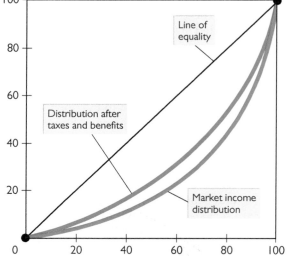

(a) **Before and after redistribution**

(b) **Redistribution**

SOURCE OF DATA: The Distribution of Household Income and Federal Taxes, 2011, Congressional Budget Office, November 2014.

◼ Why We Redistribute Income

Why do we vote for government policies that redistribute income? Why don't we leave everyone to make voluntary contributions to charities that help the poor?

There are two ways of approaching these questions: normative and positive. The normative approach discusses why we *should* compel everyone to help the poor and looks for principles to guide the appropriate scale of redistribution. The positive approach seeks reasons why we *do* compel everyone to help the poor and tries to explain the actual scale of redistribution.

Normative Theories of Income Redistribution

Philosophy and politics, not economics, are the subjects that consider the normative theories of redistribution. Not surprisingly, there are several different points of view on whether income should be redistributed and, if so, on what scale.

Utilitarianism points to the ideal distribution being one of equality. But efficiency is also desirable. And greater equality can be achieved only at the cost of greater inefficiency—the *big tradeoff* (defined in Chapter 6, p. 161). The redistribution of income creates the big tradeoff because it uses scarce resources and weakens incentives, which decreases the total size of the economic pie to be shared.

A dollar collected from a rich person does not translate into a dollar received by a poor person. Some of it gets used up in the process of redistribution. Tax-collecting agencies such as the Internal Revenue Service and welfare-administering agencies (as well as tax accountants and lawyers) use skilled labor, computers, and other scarce resources to do their work. The bigger the scale of redistribution, the greater is the opportunity cost of administering it.

But the cost of collecting taxes and making welfare payments is a small part of the total cost of redistribution. A bigger cost arises from the inefficiency—*excess burden*—of taxes and benefits (see Chapter 8, p. 194). Greater equality can be achieved only by taxing productive activities such as work and saving. Taxing people's income from their work and saving lowers the after-tax income they receive. This lower income makes them work and save less, which in turn results in smaller output and less consumption not only for the rich who pay the taxes but also for the poor who receive the benefits.

Benefit recipients as well as taxpayers face weaker incentives. In fact, under the welfare arrangements that prevailed before the 1996 reforms, the weakest incentives to work were those faced by households that benefited from welfare. When a welfare recipient got a job, benefits were withdrawn and eligibility for programs such as Medicaid ended, so the household in effect paid a tax of more than 100 percent on its earnings. This arrangement locked poor households in a welfare trap.

Recognizing the tension between equality and efficiency, philosopher John Rawls proposed the principle that income should be redistributed to the point at which it maximizes the size of the slice of the economic pie received by the person with the smallest slice.

Libertarian philosophers such as Robert Nozick (see Chapter 6, p. 161) say that any redistribution is wrong because it violates the sanctity of private property and voluntary exchange.

Modern political parties stand in the center of the extremes that we've just described. Some favor a bit more redistribution than others, but the major political parties are broadly happy with the prevailing scale of redistribution.

Positive Theories of Income Redistribution

A good positive theory of income redistribution would explain why some countries have more redistribution than others and why redistribution has increased over the past 200 years. We don't have such a theory, but economists have proposed a promising idea called the median voter theory. The **median voter theory** is that the policies that governments pursue are those that make the median voter as well off as possible. If a proposal can be made that improves the well-being of the median voter, a political party that makes the proposal can improve its standing in an election.

The median voter theory arises from thinking about how a democratic political system such as that of the United States works. In this system, governments must propose policies that appeal to enough voters to get them elected. And in a majority voting system, the voter whose views carry the most weight is the one in the middle—the median voter.

The median voter wants income to be redistributed to the point at which her or his own after-tax income is as large as possible. Taxing the rich by too much would weaken their incentives to create businesses and jobs and lower the median voter's after-tax income. But taxing the rich by too little would leave some money on the table that could be transferred to the median voter.

The median voter might be concerned about the poor and want to reduce poverty. Unselfishly, the median voter might simply be concerned about the plight of the poor and want to help them. Self-interestedly, the median voter might believe that if there is too much poverty, there will be too much crime and some of it will touch her or his life.

If for either reason the median voter wants to help the poor, the political process will deliver a greater scale of redistribution to reflect this voter preference.

■ The Major Welfare Challenge

Among the poorest people in the United States (see p. 518) are young women who have not completed high school, have a child (or children), live without a partner, and are more likely to be black or Hispanic than white. These young women and their children present the major welfare challenge.

There are about 10 million single mothers, and a quarter of them receive no support from their children's fathers. The long-term solution to the problem of these women is education and job training—acquiring human capital. The short-term solution is welfare. But welfare must be designed in ways that strengthen the incentive to pursue the long-term solution. And a change in the U.S. welfare programs introduced during the 1990s pursues this approach.

The Current Approach: TANF

Passed in 1996, the Personal Responsibility and Work Opportunities Reconciliation Act created the Temporary Assistance for Needy Families (TANF) program. TANF is a block grant that is paid to the states, which administer payments to individuals. It is not an open-ended entitlement program. An adult member of a household receiving assistance must either work or perform community service, and there is a five-year limit for assistance.

These measures go a long way toward removing one of the most serious poverty problems while being sensitive to the potential inefficiency of welfare. But some economists want to go further and introduce a negative income tax.

Median voter theory
The theory that governments pursue policies that make the median voter as well off as possible.

Negative Income Tax

The negative income tax is not on the political agenda, but it is popular among economists, and it is the subject of several real-world experiments. A **negative income tax** provides every household with a guaranteed minimum annual income and taxes all earned income at a fixed rate. Suppose the guaranteed minimum annual income is $10,000 and the tax rate is 25 percent. A household with no earned income receives the $10,000 guaranteed minimum income from the government. This household "pays" income tax of *minus* $10,000, hence the name "negative income tax."

A household that earns $40,000 a year pays $10,000—25 percent of its earned income—to the government. But this household also receives from the government the $10,000 guaranteed minimum income, so it pays no net income tax. It has the break-even income. Households that earn between zero and $40,000 a year receive more from the government than they pay to the government. They "pay" a negative income tax.

A household that earns $60,000 a year pays $15,000—25 percent of its earned income—to the government. But this household receives from the government the $10,000 guaranteed minimum income, so it pays a net income tax of $5,000. All households that earn more than $40,000 a year pay more to the government than they receive from it. They pay a positive amount of income tax.

A negative income tax doesn't eliminate the excess burden of taxation, but it does improve the incentives to work and save at all levels of income.

> **Negative income tax**
> A tax and redistribution scheme that provides every household with a guaranteed minimum annual income and taxes all earned income at a fixed rate.

EYE on YOUR LIFE

MyEconLab Critical Thinking Exercise

What You Pay and Gain Through Redistribution

You are on both sides of the redistribution equation, but what's your bottom line? Are you a net receiver or a net payer? Try to work out which one.

Your Tax Payments

You might pay some income tax and you certainly pay sales taxes and taxes on gasoline and other items.

If you have a job, your payslip shows the amount of income tax you're paying.

You can calculate the sales taxes you pay by keeping track for a week every time you buy something.

You can work out how much tax you pay on gas and other items by checking the scale of these taxes in your state at www.taxadmin.org.

Your Benefits

Now for the benefits. If you're receiving any direct cash payments such as unemployment benefits, these are easy to identify. But most likely, you don't receive any money from the government.

You do, though, receive the benefits of services provided by government. The biggest of these is most likely the cost of your education.

It costs much more than the tuition you're paying to provide your education. One estimate of the value of your education is the tuition paid by an out-of-state student minus the tuition paid by a state resident. Work out that number.

Now think about all the other benefits you receive from government. Try to estimate what all the government-provided services are worth to you.

Your Bottom Line

Now work out your bottom line—the benefits you receive minus the taxes you pay. Most likely, you have a net benefit, but that situation will change when you graduate. As your income rises, you will move to the other side of the redistribution equation.

MyEconLab Study Plan 20.3
Key Terms Quiz
Solutions Video

TABLE 1   MARKET INCOME

Households	Income (millions of dollars per year)
Lowest quintile	5
Second quintile	10
Third quintile	18
Fourth quintile	28
Highest quintile	39

TABLE 2   TAXES AND BENEFITS

Households	Income tax rate	Benefits (millions of dollars)
Lowest quintile	0	10
Second quintile	10%	8
Third quintile	18%	3
Fourth quintile	28%	0
Highest quintile	39%	0

CHECKPOINT 20.3

Explain how governments redistribute income and describe the effects of redistribution on economic inequality.

Practice Problems

Table 1 shows the distribution of market income in an economy and Table 2 shows how the government taxes and redistributes income.

1. Calculate the income shares of each quintile after taxes and benefits.
2. Draw this economy's Lorenz curves before and after taxes and benefits.

In the News

Free college and healthcare for all–how would Bernie Sanders pay for it?
Bernie Sanders wants free tuition at public colleges and universities, free healthcare, and a transportation infrastructure program that creates 1 million jobs for disadvantaged youth. Without spelling out the details, he would tax wealthy individuals and corporations and Wall Street stock trades to pay the bill.

Source: *CNN*, January 14, 2016

What features of Bernie's plan make the distribution of income more unequal?

Solutions to Practice Problems

1. Table 3 shows that to obtain the income after taxes and benefits, multiply each quintile's market income by the tax rate, subtract the taxes paid, and add the benefits received. Then calculate each quintile's share of total income.

TABLE 3

Households	Market income (millions of dollars)	Tax paid (millions of dollars)	Benefits received (millions of dollars)	Income after tax and benefits (millions of dollars)	Income after tax and benefits (percentage of total income)
Lowest quintile	5	0.0	10	15.0	16.0
Second quintile	10	1.0	8	17.0	18.1
Third quintile	18	3.2	3	17.8	19.0
Fourth quintile	28	7.8	0	20.2	21.5
Highest quintile	39	15.2	0	23.8	25.4

FIGURE 1

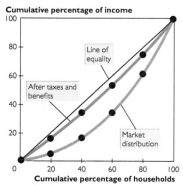

Cumulative percentage of income

Line of equality

After taxes and benefits

Market distribution

Cumulative percentage of households

2. To draw the Lorenz curves, calculate the cumulative shares of total income. For example, before taxes and benefits, the lowest quintile has 5 percent and the two lowest quintiles have 15 percent (5 + 10). After taxes and benefits, the lowest quintile has 16 percent and the two lowest quintiles have 34.1 percent (16.0 + 18.1). Figure 1 plots the Lorenz curves.

Solution to In the News

It is not possible to predict the effects of such a revolutionary economic change on the distribution of income, but two features push against less inequality. First, most of the winners from free tuition would be wealthier families because they have a higher college attendance rate. Second, some of the losers from higher corporate taxes would be older families who rely on income from capital.

CHAPTER SUMMARY

Key Points

1. Describe the economic inequality in the United States.

- The distributions of income and wealth describe economic inequality.
- The 20 percent of households with the lowest incomes receive about 3 percent of total money income and the 1 percent of households with the highest wealth own about one third of total wealth.
- The distribution of income has become more unequal over the past few decades.
- During a decade, almost 20 percent of families move up or down by a quintile or more.
- About 47 million Americans have incomes below the poverty level and for 15 percent of these families, poverty lasts for more than two years.

2. Explain how economic inequality arises.

- Economic inequality arises from inequality of labor market outcomes, ownership of capital, entrepreneurial ability, and personal and family characteristics.
- In labor markets, skill differences result in earnings differences. Discrimination might also contribute to earnings differences.
- Inherited capital, unusual entrepreneurial talent, and personal or family good fortune or misfortune widen the gap between rich and poor.

3. Explain how governments redistribute income and describe the effects of redistribution on economic inequality.

- Governments redistribute income through progressive income taxes, income maintenance programs, and provision of subsidized services.
- Normative theories of redistribution recognize the tension between equality and efficiency—the big tradeoff—and seek principles to guide the political debate.
- The main positive theory of redistribution is the median voter theory.
- The negative income tax is a proposal for addressing the big tradeoff.

Key Terms
MyEconLab Key Terms Quiz

Disposable income, 528
Lorenz curve, 513
Market income, 512
Median voter theory, 530

Money income, 512
Negative income tax, 531
Poverty, 515

CHAPTER CHECKPOINT

Study Plan Problems and Applications

TABLE 1

Households	Money income (percentage)
Lowest quintile	8
Second quintile	13
Third quintile	18
Fourth quintile	23
Highest quintile	38

FIGURE 1

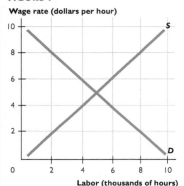

Wage rate (dollars per hour)

Labor (thousands of hours)

TABLE 2

Households	Market income (percentage)
Lowest quintile	5
Second quintile	9
Third quintile	20
Fourth quintile	30
Highest quintile	36

1. Table 1 shows the distribution of money income in Australia. Calculate the cumulative distribution of income for Australia and draw the Lorenz curve for Australian income. In which country is the income distribution more unequal: Australia or the United States?

2. **China inequality among world's worst**
   China has one of the world's highest levels of inequality. A Peking University report says the richest 1 percent own a third of the country's wealth, and the poorest 25 percent own 1 percent of the country's wealth.
                                                     Source: *The Financial Times*, January 14, 2016
   Where is wealth more unequally distributed: China or the United States?

3. Figure 1 shows the market for low-skilled workers. With on-the-job training, low-skilled workers can become high-skilled workers. The value of marginal product of high-skilled workers at each employment level is twice the value of marginal product of low-skilled workers, but the cost of acquiring skill adds $2 an hour to the wage rate that will attract high-skilled labor. What is the equilibrium wage rate of low-skilled labor and the number of low-skilled workers employed? What is the equilibrium wage rate of high-skilled labor and the number of high-skilled workers employed?

4. Why do economists think that discrimination in the labor market is an unlikely explanation for the persistent inequality in earnings between women and men and among the races?

Use Table 2 and the following information to work Problems 5 to 7.

Suppose that the government redistributes income by taxing the 60 percent of households with the highest market incomes 10 percent, then distributing the tax collected as an equal benefit to the 40 percent with the lowest market income.

5. Calculate the distribution of income after taxes and benefits and draw the Lorenz curve (i) before taxes and benefits and (ii) after taxes and benefits.

6. If the cost of administering the redistribution scheme takes 50 percent of the taxes collected, what is the distribution of income after taxes and benefits?

7. If the people whose market incomes are taxed cut their work hours and their market incomes fall by 10 percent, what is the distribution of income after taxes and benefits?

8. **The $1.4 billion trick to make us accept income inequality**
   Lotteries take money from the poor and redistribute it unequally. The poor, the uneducated, and minorities play the lottery the most, and it takes a big chunk of their income.
                                                     Source: *The Huffington Post*, January 12, 2016
   If the news clip is correct, how does a lottery change the distribution of income? Draw two Lorenz curves to illustrate your answer.

9. Read *Eye on Inequality* on p. 518, then rank the influences on the degree of income inequality—education, household type, household size, age of householder, race, and region of residence—in order of importance.

Instructor Assignable Problems and Applications

MyEconLab Homework, Quiz, or Test if assigned by instructor

1. Which influence adds more, on average, to a household's income: getting a professional degree, getting married, getting older, or moving to California? Which of these influences, on average, adds least?

2. Table 1 shows the income share for each household quintile and the cumulative shares. Provide the values for **A, B, C, D**, and **E**.

3. Table 2 shows the distribution of prize money among the top 20 professional golfers. Calculate the cumulative distribution of income of these golfers and draw the prize money Lorenz curve of these golfers. Which distribution is more unequal: the distribution of income of these golfers or that of the United States as a whole?

4. Suppose the cost of acquiring a skill increases and the value of marginal product of skill increases. Draw demand-supply graphs of the labor markets for high-skilled and low-skilled labor to explain what happens to the equilibrium wage rate of low-skilled labor, the equilibrium wage rate of high-skilled labor, and the number of high-skilled workers employed.

TABLE 1

Households	Income	
(quintile)	(%)	(cumulative %)
First	7.4	7.4
Second	13.2	**A**
Third	**B**	38.7
Fourth	25.0	**C**
Fifth	**D**	**E**

TABLE 2

Professional golfers	Income (percentage)
Lowest 20 percent	15
Second 20 percent	16
Third 20 percent	18
Fourth 20 percent	20
Highest 20 percent	31

Use the following information to work Problems **5** and **6**.

In a year, 130,000 aircraft mechanics and service technicians earned an average of $20 an hour whereas 30,000 elevator installers and repairers earned an average of $25 an hour. The skill and training for these two jobs are very similar.

5. Draw the demand and supply curves for these two types of labor. What feature of your graph accounts for the differences in the two wage rates and what feature accounts for the differences in the quantities employed of these two types of labor?

6. Suppose that a government law required both groups of workers to be paid $22.50 an hour. Draw a graph to illustrate what would happen to the quantities employed of the two types of labor.

Use the following information to work Problems **7** to **11**.

California: The nation's most unequal state
In California, researchers found, it really matters where you live. Residents of Silicon Valley live more than four years longer than the average American, earn nearly double the income, and have nearly triple the number of graduate degrees. Residents of Central Valley live nearly a year less than the average American, earn barely more than a poverty-line income, and nearly four in ten failed to graduate from high school.

Source: *CNN*, May 6, 2015

7. Explain why the first sentence of the news clip is not correct.

8. Explain how the news clip confuses cause and effect in its account of economic inequality in California.

9. What is the main source of inequality in California and what are its effects on inequality?

10. Explain how the labor markets of California translate education differences into earnings differences.

11. Illustrate the labor markets for college graduates in Silicon Valley and high school graduates in Central Valley with a graph.

Multiple Choice Quiz

1. A Lorenz curve plots the _____.
   A. trend in the cumulative percentage of income received by each quintile against the trend in the number of households
   B. average income received by each quintile against the number of households in the quintile
   C. percentage of total income received by each quintile against the percentage of households in the quintile
   D. cumulative percentage of income against the cumulative percentage of households

2. Which of the following statements is correct?
   A. The closer the Lorenz curve is to the line of equality, the more unequal is the distribution of income.
   B. The farther the Lorenz curve is from the line of equality, the more unequal is the distribution of income.
   C. If the Lorenz curve crosses the line of equality the distribution of income is more unequal at high income levels than at low income levels.
   D. The Lorenz curve for wealth is closer to the line of equality than the Lorenz curve for income.

3. In recent years, as the gap between the rich and the poor has increased, the Lorenz curve has _____.
   A. shifted away from the line of equality
   B. not changed, but there has been a movement down along it
   C. shifted closer to the line of equality
   D. not changed, but there has been a movement up along it

4. Of all the Americans who live in poverty, most are _____ families, while the highest poverty rate is among _____ families.
   A. black; Hispanic
   B. black; white
   C. white; black and Hispanic
   D. Hispanic; white

5. Economic inequality arises from all of the following *except* _____.
   A. inequality of human capital
   B. inequality of education attainment
   C. a shortage of high-skilled labor
   D. discrimination

6. Income redistribution in the United States results in the income share of the _____ rising and the income share of the _____ falling.
   A. lowest quintile; other four quintiles
   B. two lowest quintiles; other three quintiles
   C. three lowest quintiles; other two quintiles
   D. four lowest quintiles; highest quintile

7. When governments redistribute income, they _____.
   A. give every dollar collected in taxes to poor people
   B. are influenced by how people vote in elections
   C. improve economic efficiency
   D. set the tax and benefit rates that make everyone work and save more

Glossary

Abatement technology A production technology that reduces or prevents pollution. (p. 249)

Ability-to-pay principle The proposition that people should pay taxes according to how easily they can bear the burden. (p. 206)

Absolute advantage When one person (or nation) is more productive than another—needs fewer inputs or takes less time to produce a good or perform a production task. (p. 73)

Adverse selection The tendency for people to enter into transactions that bring them benefits from their private information and impose costs on the uninformed party. (p. 297)

Allocative efficiency A situation in which the quantities of goods and services produced are those that people *value most highly*—it is not possible to produce more of a good or service without giving up some of another good that people *value more highly*. (p. 143)

Antitrust law A body of law that regulates oligopolies and prohibits them from becoming monopolies or behaving like monopolies. (p. 477)

Asymmetric information A situation in which either the buyer or the seller has private information. (p. 294)

Average cost pricing rule A rule that sets price equal to average total cost to enable a regulated firm to avoid economic loss. (p. 426)

Average fixed cost Total fixed cost per unit of output. (p. 361)

Average product Total product divided by the quantity of a factor of production. The average product of labor is total product divided by the quantity of labor employed. (p. 356)

Average tax rate The percentage of income that is paid in tax. (p. 207)

Average total cost Total cost per unit of output, which equals average fixed cost plus average variable cost. (p. 361)

Average variable cost Total variable cost per unit of output. (p. 361)

Barrier to entry Any constraint that protects a firm from competitors. (p. 404)

Benefit The benefit of something is the gain or pleasure that it brings, measured by what you are willing to give up to get it. (p. 9)

Benefit-cost analysis An accounting exercise to determine the total benefit, total cost, and net benefit of a proposed project. (p. 276)

Benefits principle The proposition that people should pay taxes equal to the benefits they receive from public goods and services. (p. 206)

Big tradeoff A tradeoff between efficiency and fairness that recognizes the cost of making income transfers. (p. 161)

Black market An illegal market that operates alongside a government-regulated market. (p. 171)

Budget line A line that describes the limits to consumption possibilities and that depends on a consumer's budget and the prices of goods and services. (p. 320)

Capital Tools, instruments, machines, buildings, and other items that have been produced in the past and that businesses now use to produce goods and services. (p. 37)

Capital goods Goods bought by businesses and governments to increase productive resources to use over future periods to produce other goods. (p. 34)

Capture theory The theory that regulation serves the self-interest of the producer and results in maximum profit, underproduction, and deadweight loss. (p. 424)

Cartel A group of firms acting together to limit output, raise price, and increase economic profit. (p. 460)

Change in demand A change in the quantity that people plan to buy when any influence on buying plans other than the price of the good changes. (p. 88)

Change in the quantity demanded A change in the quantity of a good that people plan to buy that results from a change in the price of the good with all other influences on buying plans remaining the same. (p. 90)

Change in the quantity supplied A change in the quantity of a good that suppliers plan to sell that results from a change in the price of the good with all other influences on selling plans remaining the same. (p. 97)

Change in supply A change in the quantity that suppliers plan to sell when any influence on selling plans other than the price of the good changes. (p. 95)

Circular flow model A model of the economy that shows the circular flow of expenditures and incomes that result from decision makers' choices and the way those choices interact to determine what, how, and for whom goods and services are produced. (p. 48)

Coase theorem The proposition that if property rights exist and the costs of enforcing them are low, then the market outcome is efficient and it doesn't matter who has the property rights. (p. 249)

Command system A system that allocates resources by the order of someone in authority. (p. 141)

Command-and-control regulation The direct regulation of what is and is not permitted. (p. 251)

Common resource A resource that can be used only once, but no one can be prevented from using what is available. (p. 269)

Comparative advantage The ability of a person to perform an activity or produce a good or service at a lower opportunity cost than anyone else. (p. 73)

Complement A good that is consumed with another good. (p. 88)

Complement in production A good that is produced along with another good. (p. 95)

Constant returns to scale Features of a firm's technology that keep average total cost constant as output increases. (p. 368)

Consumer surplus The marginal benefit from a good or service in excess of the price paid for it, summed over the quantity consumed. (p. 149)

Consumption goods and services Goods and services that individuals and governments buy and use in the current period. (p. 34)

Cross elasticity of demand A measure of the responsiveness of the demand for a good to a change in the price of a substitute or complement when other things remain the same. (p. 131)

Cross-section graph A graph that shows the values of an economic variable for different groups in a population at a point in time. (p. 24)

Deadweight loss The decrease in total surplus that results from an inefficient underproduction or overproduction. (p. 157)

Decreasing marginal returns When the marginal product of an additional worker is less than the marginal product of the previous worker. (p. 354)

Demand The relationship between the quantity demanded and the price of a good when all other influences on buying plans remain the same. (p. 85)

Demand curve A graph of the relationship between the quantity demanded of a good and its price when all the other influences on buying plans remain the same. (p. 86)

Demand schedule A list of the quantities demanded at each different price when all the other influences on buying plans remain the same. (p. 86)

Deregulation The process of removing regulation of prices, quantities, entry, and other aspects of economic activity in a firm or an industry. (p. 424)

Derived demand The demand for a factor of production that is derived from the demand for the goods and services that it is used to produce. (p. 489)

Diminishing marginal rate of substitution The general tendency for the marginal rate of substitution to decrease as the consumer moves down along the indifference curve, increasing consumption of the good measured on the x-axis and decreasing consumption of the good measured on the y-axis. (p. 342)

Diminishing marginal utility The general tendency for marginal utility to decrease as the quantity of a good consumed increases. (p. 326)

Direct relationship A relationship between two variables that move in the same direction. (p. 26)

Diseconomies of scale Features of a firm's technology that make average total cost rise as output increases. (p. 368)

Disposable income Market income plus cash benefits paid by the government minus taxes. (p. 528)

Dumping When a foreign firm sells its exports at a lower price than its cost of production. (p. 234)

Duopoly A market with only two firms. (p. 461)

Economic depreciation An opportunity cost of a firm using capital that it owns—measured as the change in the *market value* of capital over a given period. (p. 349)

Economic growth The sustained expansion of production possibilities. (p. 70)

Economic model A description of the economy or part of the economy that includes only those features assumed necessary to explain the observed facts. (p. 15)

Economic profit A firm's total revenue minus total cost. (p. 349)

Economics The social science that studies the choices that individuals, businesses, government, and entire societies make as they cope with *scarcity*, the influences on those choices, and the arrangements that coordinate them. (p. 2)

Economies of scale Features of a firm's technology that make average total cost fall as output increases. (p. 367)

Efficient scale The quantity at which average total cost is a minimum. (p. 445)

Elastic demand When the percentage change in the quantity demanded exceeds the percentage change in price. (p. 116)

Elastic supply When the percentage change in the quantity supplied exceeds the percentage change in price. (p. 126)

Entrepreneurship The human resource that organizes labor, land, and capital to produce goods and services. (p. 38)

Equilibrium price The price at which the quantity demanded equals the quantity supplied. (p. 100)

Equilibrium quantity The quantity bought and sold at the equilibrium price. (p. 100)

Excess burden The amount by which the burden of a tax exceeds the tax revenue received by the government—the deadweight loss from a tax. (p. 194)

Excess capacity The amount by which the efficient scale exceeds the quantity that the firm produces. (p. 445)

Excludable A good, service, or resource is excludable if it is possible to prevent someone from enjoying its benefits. (p. 268)

Explicit cost A cost paid in money. (p. 349)

Export subsidy A payment by the government to a producer to cover part of the cost of production that is exported. (p. 231)

Exports The goods and services that firms in one country sell to people and firms in other countries. (p. 216)

Externality A cost or a benefit that arises from production and that falls on someone other than the producer; or a cost or benefit that arises from consumption and that falls on someone other than the consumer. (p. 244)

Factor markets Markets in which the services of factors of production are bought and sold. (pp. 48, 488)

Factor prices The prices of the services of the factors of production. The wage rate is the price of labor, the interest rate is the price of capital, and rent is the price of land. (p. 488)

Factors of production The productive resources that are used to produce goods and services—

land, labor, capital, and entrepreneurship. (p. 36)

FairTax A proposal to tax the purchase of consumption goods and services above the poverty level, considered by the United States Congress in 1999. (p. 209)

Firms The institutions that organize the production of goods and services. (p. 48)

Flat tax A tax system with a constant average and marginal tax rate: A proportional tax. (p. 208)

Four-firm concentration ratio The percentage of the total revenue in an industry accounted for by the four largest firms in the industry. (p. 438)

Free rider A person who enjoys the benefits of a good or service without paying for it. (p. 271)

Game theory The tool that economists use to analyze *strategic behavior*—behavior that recognizes mutual interdependence and takes account of the expected behavior of others. (p. 469)

Goods and services The objects (goods) and the actions (services) that people value and produce to satisfy human wants. (p. 3)

Goods markets Markets in which goods and services are bought and sold. (p. 48)

Herfindahl-Hirschman Index The square of the percentage market share of each firm summed over the 50 largest firms (or summed over all the firms if there are fewer than 50) in a market. (p. 439)

Horizontal equity The requirement that taxpayers with the same ability to pay should pay the same taxes. (p. 206)

Households Individuals or groups of people living together. (p. 48)

Human capital The knowledge and skill that people obtain from education, on-the-job training, and work experience. (p. 37)

Implicit cost An opportunity cost incurred by a firm when it uses a factor of production for which it does not make a direct money payment. (p. 349)

Import quota A quantitative restriction on the import of a good that limits the maximum quantity of a good that may be imported in a given period. (p. 229)

Imports The goods and services that people and firms in one country buy from firms in other countries. (p. 216)

Incentive A reward or a penalty—a "carrot" or a "stick"—that encourages or discourages an action. (p. 11)

Income elasticity of demand A measure of the responsiveness of the demand for a good to a change in income when other things remain the same. (p. 132)

Increasing marginal returns When the marginal product of an additional worker exceeds the marginal product of the previous worker. (p. 354)

Indifference curve A line that shows combinations of goods among which a consumer is *indifferent*. (p. 341)

Individual transferable quota (ITQ) A production limit that is assigned to an individual, who is free to transfer (sell) the quota to someone else. (p. 286)

Inelastic demand When the percentage change in the quantity demanded is less than the percentage change in price. (p. 116)

Inelastic supply When the percentage change in the quantity supplied is less than the percentage change in price. (p. 126)

Infant-industry argument The argument that it is necessary to protect a new industry to enable it to grow into a mature industry that can compete in world markets. (p. 233)

Inferior good A good for which demand decreases when income increases and demand increases when income decreases. (p. 89)

Interest Income paid for the use of capital. (p. 39)

Inverse relationship A relationship between two variables that move in opposite directions. (p. 27)

Labor The work time and work effort that people devote to producing goods and services. (p. 37)

Labor union An organized group of workers that aims to increase wages and influence other job conditions of its members. (p. 498)

Land The "gifts of nature," or *natural resources*, that we use to produce goods and services. (p. 36)

Law of decreasing returns As a firm uses more of a variable input, with a given quantity of fixed inputs, the marginal product of the variable input eventually decreases. (p. 356)

Law of demand Other things remaining the same, if the price of a good rises, the quantity demanded of that good decreases; and if the price of a good falls, the quantity demanded of that good increases. (p. 85)

Law of market forces When there is a surplus, the price falls; when there is a shortage, the price rises. (p. 100)

Law of supply Other things remaining the same, if the price of a good rises, the quantity supplied of that good increases; and if the price of a good falls, the quantity supplied of that good decreases. (p. 92)

Legal monopoly A market in which competition and entry are restricted by the granting of a public franchise, government license, patent, or copyright. (p. 405)

Lemons problem The problem that when it is not possible to distinguish reliable products from lemons, there are too many lemons and too few reliable products. (p. 294)

Linear relationship A relationship that graphs as a straight line. (p. 26)

Long run The time frame in which the quantities of *all* resources can be varied. (p. 352)

Long-run average cost curve A curve that shows the lowest average total cost at which it is possible to produce each output when the firm has had sufficient time to change both its plant size and labor employed. (p. 368)

Lorenz curve A curve that graphs the cumulative percentage of income (or wealth) against the cumulative percentage of households. (p. 513)

Loss Income earned by an entrepreneur for running a business when that income is negative. (p. 39)

Macroeconomics The study of the aggregate (or total) effects on the national economy and the global economy of the choices that individuals, businesses, and governments make. (p. 3)

Margin A choice on the margin is a choice that is made by comparing *all* the relevant alternatives systematically and incrementally. (p. 10)

Marginal benefit The benefit that arises from a one-unit increase in an activity. The marginal benefit of something is measured by what you *are willing to* give up to get *one additional* unit of it. (p. 10)

Marginal cost The opportunity cost that arises from a one-unit increase in an activity. The marginal cost of something is what you *must* give up to get one additional unit of it. (p. 10) The marginal cost of producing a good is the change in total cost that results from a one-unit increase in output. (p. 360)

Marginal cost pricing rule A rule that sets price equal to marginal cost to achieve an efficient output. (p. 424)

Marginal external benefit The benefit from an additional unit of a good or service that people other than the consumer of the good or service enjoy. (p. 257)

Marginal external cost The cost of producing an additional unit of a good or service that falls on people other than the producer. (p. 246)

Marginal private benefit The benefit from an additional unit of a good or service that the consumer of that good or service receives. (p. 257)

Marginal private cost The cost of producing an additional unit of a good or service that is borne by the producer of that good or service. (p. 246)

Marginal product The change in total product that results from a one-unit increase in the quantity of labor employed. (p. 354)

Marginal rate of substitution The rate at which a person will give up good Y (the good measured on the y-axis) to get more of good X (the good measured on the x-axis) and at the same time remain on the same indifference curve. (p. 342)

Marginal revenue The change in total revenue that results from a one-unit increase in the quantity sold. (p. 377)

Marginal social benefit The marginal benefit enjoyed by society— by the consumer of a good or service and by everyone else who benefits from it. It is the sum of marginal private benefit and marginal external benefit. (p. 257)

Marginal social cost The marginal cost incurred by the entire society—by the producer and by everyone else on whom the cost falls. It is the sum of marginal private cost and marginal external cost. (p. 246)

Marginal tax rate The percentage of an additional dollar of income that is paid in tax. (p. 207)

Marginal utility The change in total utility that results from a one-unit increase in the quantity of a good consumed. (p. 326)

Marginal utility per dollar The marginal utility from a good relative to the price paid for the good. (p. 328)

Market Any arrangement that brings buyers and sellers together and enables them to get information and do business with each other. (p. 48)

Market equilibrium When the quantity demanded equals the quantity supplied—buyers' and sellers' plans are in balance. (p. 100)

Market failure A situation in which the market delivers an inefficient outcome. (p. 157)

Market income A household's wages, interest, rent, and profit earned in factor markets before paying income taxes. (p. 512)

Markup The amount by which price exceeds marginal cost. (p. 445)

Median voter theory The theory that governments pursue policies that make the median voter as well off as possible. (p. 530)

Microeconomics The study of the choices that individuals and businesses make and the way these choices interact and are influenced by governments. (p. 2)

Minimum wage law A government regulation that makes hiring labor services for less than a specified wage illegal. (p. 177)

Money income Market income plus cash payments to households by the government. (p. 512)

Monopolistic competition A market in which a large number of firms compete by making similar but slightly different products. (p. 376)

Monopoly A market in which one firm sells a good or service that has no close substitutes and a barrier blocks the entry of new firms. (pp. 376, 404)

Moral hazard The tendency for a person with private information to use it in ways that impose costs on an uninformed party with whom they have made an agreement. (p. 303)

Nash equilibrium An equilibrium in which each player takes the best possible action given the action of the other player. (p. 470)

Natural monopoly A monopoly that arises because one firm can meet the entire market demand at a lower average total cost than two or more firms could. (p. 404)

Negative externality A production or consumption activity that creates an external cost. (p. 244)

Negative income tax A tax and redistribution scheme that provides every household with a guaranteed minimum annual income and taxes all earned income at a fixed rate. (p. 531)

Negative relationship A relationship between two variables that move in opposite directions. (p. 27)

Nonexcludable A good, service, or resource is nonexcludable if it is impossible (or extremely costly) to prevent someone from enjoying its benefits. (p. 268)

Nonrenewable natural resources Natural resources that can be used only once and that cannot be replaced once they have been used. (p. 488)

Nonrival A good, service, or resource is nonrival if its use by one person does not decrease the quantity available to someone else. (p. 268)

Normal good A good for which demand increases when income increases and demand decreases when income decreases. (p. 89)

Normal profit The return to entrepreneurship. Normal profit is part of a firm's opportunity cost because it is the cost of not running another firm. (p. 349)

Oligopoly A market in which a small number of interdependent firms compete. (p. 376)

Opportunity cost The opportunity cost of something is the best thing you *must* give up to get it. (p. 8)

Payoff matrix A table that shows the payoffs for each player for every possible combination of actions by the players. (p. 470)

Perfect competition A market in which there are many firms, each selling an identical product; many buyers; no barriers to the entry of new firms into the industry; no advantage to established firms; and buyers and sellers are well informed about prices. (p. 376)

Perfect price discrimination Price discrimination that extracts the entire consumer surplus by charging the highest price that consumers are willing to pay for each unit. (p. 420)

Perfectly elastic demand When the quantity demanded changes by a very large percentage in response to an almost zero percentage change in price. (p. 116)

Perfectly elastic supply When the quantity supplied changes by a very large percentage in response to an almost zero percentage change in price. (p. 126)

Perfectly inelastic demand When the percentage change in the quantity demanded is zero for any percentage change in the price. (p. 116)

Perfectly inelastic supply When the percentage change in the quantity supplied is zero for any percentage change in the price. (p. 126)

Pooling equilibrium The outcome when only one message is available and an uninformed person cannot determine quality. (p. 299)

Positive externality A production or consumption activity that creates an external benefit. (p. 244)

Positive relationship A relationship between two variables that move in the same direction. (p. 26)

Poverty A state in which a household's income is too low to be able to buy the quantities of food, shelter, and clothing that are deemed necessary. (p. 515)

Predatory pricing Setting a low price to drive competitors out of business with the intention of setting a monopoly price when the competition has gone. (p. 479)

Price cap A government regulation that places an *upper* limit on the price at which a particular good, service, or factor of production may be traded. (p. 170)

Price cap regulation A rule that specifies the highest price that a firm is permitted to set—a price ceiling. (p. 429)

Price ceiling A government regulation that places an *upper* limit on the price at which a particular good, service, or factor of production may be traded. (p. 170)

Price-discriminating monopoly A monopoly that sells different units of a good or service for different prices not related to cost differences. (p. 406)

Price elasticity of demand A measure of the responsiveness of the quantity demanded of a good to a change in its price when all other influences on buyers' plans remain the same. (p. 114)

Price elasticity of supply A measure of the responsiveness of the quantity supplied of a good to a change in its price when all other influences on sellers' plans remain the same. (p. 126)

Price floor A government regulation that places a *lower* limit on the price at which a particular good, service, or factor of production may be traded. (p. 176)

Price taker A firm that cannot influence the price of the good or service that it produces. (p. 377)

Prisoners' dilemma A game between two prisoners that shows why it is hard to cooperate, even when it would be beneficial to both players to do so. (p. 469)

Private good A good or service that can be consumed by only one person at a time and only by the person who has bought it or owns it. (p. 268)

Private information Information relevant to a transaction that is possessed by some market participants but not all. (p. 294)

Producer surplus The price of a good in excess of the marginal cost of producing it, summed over the quantity produced. (p. 152)

Product differentiation Making a product that is slightly different from the products of competing firms. (p. 436)

Production efficiency A situation in which the economy is getting all that it can from its resources and cannot produce more of one good or service without producing less of something else. (p. 62)

Production possibilities frontier The boundary between the combinations of goods and services that can be produced and the combinations that cannot be produced, given the available factors of production and the state of technology. (p. 60)

Production quota A government regulation in a market that places an upper limit on the quantity that may be supplied. (p. 183)

Profit Income earned by an entrepreneur for running a business. (p. 39)

Progressive tax A tax whose average rate increases as income increases. (p. 207)

Property rights Social arrangements that govern the protection of private property—legally established titles to the ownership, use, and disposal of factors of production and goods and services that are enforceable in the courts. (p. 249)

Proportional tax A tax whose average rate is constant at all income levels. (p. 207)

Public good A good or service that can be consumed simultaneously by everyone and from which no one can be excluded. (p. 269)

Public provision The production of a good or service by a public authority that receives most of its revenue from the government. (p. 259)

Quantity demanded The amount of any good, service, or resource that people are willing and able to buy during a specified period at a specified price. (p. 85)

Quantity supplied The amount of any good, service, or resource that people are willing and able to sell during a specified period at a specified price. (p. 92)

Rate of return regulation A regulation that sets the price at a level that enables a firm to earn a specified target rate of return on its capital. (p. 428)

Rational choice A choice that uses the available resources to best achieve the objective of the person making the choice. (p. 9)

Rational ignorance The decision not to acquire information because the marginal cost of doing so exceeds the marginal benefit. (p. 277)

Regressive tax A tax whose average rate decreases as income increases. (p. 207)

Regulation Rules administered by a government agency to influence prices, quantities, entry, and other aspects of economic activity in a firm or an industry. (p. 424)

Relative price The price of one good in terms of another good—an opportunity cost. It equals the price of one good divided by the price of another good. (p. 324)

Rent Income paid for the use of land (p. 39)

Rent ceiling A regulation that makes it illegal to charge more than a specified rent for housing. (p. 170)

Rent seeking Lobbying and other political activity that aims to capture the gains from trade. The act of obtaining special treatment by the government to create economic profit or divert consumer surplus or producer

surplus away from others.
(pp. 237, 415)

Resale price maintenance An agreement between a manufacturer and a distributor on the price at which a product will be resold. (p. 477)

Rival A good, service, or resource is rival if its use by one person decreases the quantity available to someone else. (p. 268)

Scarcity The condition that arises because wants exceed the ability of resources to satisfy them. (p. 2)

Scatter diagram A graph of the value of one variable against the value of another variable. (p. 24)

Screening When an uninformed person creates an incentive for an informed person to reveal relevant private information. (p. 304)

Search activity The time spent looking for someone with whom to do business. (p. 172)

Self-interest The choices that are best for the individual who makes them. (p. 4)

Separating equilibrium The outcome when signaling provides full information to a previously uninformed person. (p. 299)

Short run The time frame in which the quantities of some resources are fixed. In the short run, a firm can usually change the quantity of labor it uses but not its technology and quantity of capital. (p. 352)

Shutdown point The point at which price equals minimum average variable cost and the quantity produced is that at which average variable cost is at a minimum. (p. 381)

Signal An action taken by an informed person (or firm) to send a message to less-informed people. (p. 451)

Signaling When an informed person takes an action that sends information to uninformed persons. (p. 298)

Single-price monopoly A monopoly that must sell each unit of its output for the same price to all its customers. (p. 406)

Slope The change in the value of the variable measured on the y-axis divided by the change in the value of the variable measured on the x-axis. (p. 29)

Social interest The choices that are best for society as a whole. (p. 4)

Social interest theory The theory that regulation achieves an efficient allocation of resources. (p. 424)

Strategies All the possible actions of each player in a game. (p. 470)

Subsidy A payment by the government to a producer to cover part of the cost of production. (p. 260

Substitute A good that can be consumed in place of another good. (p. 88)

Substitute in production A good that can be produced in place of another good. (p. 95)

Supply The relationship between the quantity supplied and the price of a good when all other influences on selling plans remain the same. (p. 92)

Supply curve A graph of the relationship between the quantity supplied of a good and its price when all the other influences on selling plans remain the same. (p. 93)

Supply schedule A list of the quantities supplied at each different price when all the other influences on selling plans remain the same. (p. 93)

Tariff A tax imposed on a good when it is imported. (p. 225)

Tax incidence The division of the burden of a tax between the buyer and the seller. (p. 192)

Time-series graph A graph that measures time on the x-axis and the variable or variables in which we are interested on the y-axis. (p. 24)

Total cost The cost of all the factors of production used by a firm. (p. 359)

Total fixed cost The cost of the firm's fixed factors of production—the cost of land, capital, and entrepreneurship. (p. 359)

Total product The total quantity of a good produced in a given period. (p. 353)

Total revenue The amount spent on a good and received by the seller and equals the price of the good multiplied by the quantity of the good sold. (p. 122)

Total revenue test A method of estimating the price elasticity of demand by observing the change in total revenue that results from a price change (with all other influences on the quantity sold remaining unchanged). (p. 123)

Total surplus The sum of consumer surplus and producer surplus. (p. 155)

Total utility The total benefit that a person gets from the consumption of a good or service. Total utility generally increases as the quantity consumed of a good increases. (p. 326)

Total variable cost The cost of the firm's variable factor of production—the cost of labor. (p. 359)

Tradeoff An exchange—giving up one thing to get something else. (pp. 8, 63)

Tragedy of the commons The overuse of a common resource that arises when its users have no incentive to conserve it and use it sustainably. (p. 280)

Transactions costs The opportunity costs of making trades in a market or conducting a transaction. (p. 159)

Trend A general tendency for the value of a variable to rise or fall over time. (p. 24)

Tying arrangement An agreement to sell one product only if the buyer agrees to buy another, different product. (p. 479)

Unit elastic demand When the percentage change in the quantity demanded equals the percentage change in price. (p. 116)

Unit elastic supply When the percentage change in the quantity supplied equals the percentage change in price. (p. 126)

Utility The benefit or satisfaction that a person gets from the consumption of a good or service. (p. 326)

Utility-maximizing rule The rule that leads to the greatest total utility from all the goods and services consumed. The rule is: 1. Allocate the entire available budget. 2. Make the marginal utility per dollar equal for all goods. (p. 328)

Value of marginal product The value to a firm of hiring one more unit of a factor of production, which equals the price of a unit of output multiplied by the marginal product of the factor of production. (p. 489)

Vertical equity The requirement that taxpayers with a greater ability to pay bear a greater share of the taxes. (p. 207)

Voucher A token that the government provides to households, which they can use to buy specified goods or services. (p. 261)

Wages Income paid for the services of labor. (p. 39)

Index

Photo Credits

Chapter 12: p. 293: Myrleen Pearson/ Alamy Stock Photo; p. 294: Michael Kleinfeld UPI Photo Service/Newscom; p. 295: Spencer Grant/ PhotoEdit, Inc.; p. 298: Harry Lands/ Alamy Stock Photo; p. 304 top: Don Mason/Blend Images/Getty Images; p. 304 bottom: 1905HKN/E+/Getty Images; p. 313: Courtesy of Laurence Kotlikoff and Boston University.

Chapter 13: p. 319: lzf/Shutterstock; p. 322: Rob Wilkinson/Alamy Stock Photo; p. 327 left: Image Asset Management Ltd./Alamy Stock Photo; p. 327 right: Hulton Archive/Stringer/Getty Images; p. 330: Westend61/Getty Images; p. 344: Alliance/Fotolia.

Chapter 14: p. 347 left: John Gress/ Reuters Pictures; p. 347 right: The Photo Works/Alamy Stock Photo; p. 367: Friedrich Stark/Alamy Stock Photo.

Chapter 15: p. 375: PYMCA/UIG/ Getty Images; p. 377 top: prudkov/ Fotolia; p. 377 bottom: Vicki Beaver/ Alamy Stock Photo; p. 391: Geraint Lewis/Alamy Stock Photo; p. 392: Michael Neelon/Alamy Stock Photo; p. 394: Ryan McVay/DigitalVision/ Getty Images; p. 395: Photo copyright 2016 Ashley Landis, Landis Images.

Chapter 16: p. 403: Ian Dagnall/ Alamy Stock Photo; p. 405: Darren Baker/Fotolia; p. 418: Craig F. Walker/ Denver Post/Getty Images; p. 422 left: William Hamilton; p. 422 right: Richard Parkin; p. 428: Scott Gries/Getty Images Entertainment/Getty Images.

Chapter 17: p. 435: David Paul Morris/Bloomberg/Getty Images; p. 436: Sergey Novikov/Alamy Stock Photo; p. 448: Chris Park/Invision for EA Sports/AP Images; p. 452: Pearson Education.

Chapter 18: p. 459 top left: Roberto Machado Noa/LightRocket/ Getty Images; p. 459 top right: Jamie Squire/Getty Images; p. 459 bottom left: Martin Divisek/Bloomberg/ Getty Images; p. 459 bottom right: Agencja Fotograficzna Caro/Alamy Stock Photo; p. 460: Pearson Education; p. 463: studiomode/Alamy Stock Photo; p. 464: AFP/Getty Images; p. 467: Alexander Klein/ Newscom.

Chapter 19: p. 487: Robert Beck/ Sports Illustrated/Getty Images; p. 494 top: Shariff Che'Lah/Fotolia; p. 494 bottom: Patrick Frischknecht/ AGE Fotostock.

Chapter 20: p. 511: Scott Houston/ Alamy Stock Photo.

Design Elements: Clock icon: tentor/ Shutterstock; Flag icon: Henner Damke/Fotolia.

The Pearson Series in Economics

Abel/Bernanke/Croushore
Macroeconomics*

Bade/Parkin
Foundations of Economics*

Berck/Helfand
The Economics of the Environment

Bierman/Fernandez
Game Theory with Economic Applications

Blanchard
Macroeconomics*

Boyer
Principles of Transportation Economics

Branson
Macroeconomic Theory and Policy

Bruce
Public Finance and the American Economy

Carlton/Perloff
Modern Industrial Organization

Case/Fair/Oster
Principles of Economics*

Chapman
Environmental Economics: Theory, Application, and Policy

Daniels/VanHoose
International Monetary & Financial Economics

Downs
An Economic Theory of Democracy

Farnham
Economics for Managers

Fort
Sports Economics

Froyen
Macroeconomics

Fusfeld
The Age of the Economist

Gerber
International Economics*

Gordon
Macroeconomics*

Greene
Econometric Analysis

Gregory/Stuart
Russian and Soviet Economic Performance and Structure

Hartwick/Olewiler
The Economics of Natural Resource Use

Heilbroner/Milberg
The Making of the Economic Society

Heyne/Boettke/Prychitko
The Economic Way of Thinking

Hubbard/O'Brien
Economics*

InEcon Money, Banking, and the Financial System*

Hubbard/O'Brien/Rafferty
Macroeconomics*

Hughes/Cain
American Economic History

Husted/Melvin
International Economics

Jehle/Reny
Advanced Microeconomic Theory

Keat/Young/Erfle
Managerial Economics

Klein
Mathematical Methods for Economics

Krugman/Obstfeld/Melitz
International Economics: Theory & Policy*

Laidler
The Demand for Money

Lynn
Economic Development: Theory and Practice for a Divided World

Miller
Economics Today*

Understanding Modern Economics

Miller/Benjamin
The Economics of Macro Issues

Miller/Benjamin/North
The Economics of Public Issues

Mishkin
The Economics of Money, Banking, and Financial Markets*

The Economics of Money, Banking, and Financial Markets, Business School Edition*

Macroeconomics: Policy and Practice*

Murray
Econometrics: A Modern Introduction

O'Sullivan/Sheffrin/Perez
Economics: Principles, Applications and Tools*

Parkin
Economics*

Perloff
Microeconomics*

Microeconomics: Theory and Applications with Calculus*

Perloff/Brander
Managerial Economics and Strategy*

Pindyck/Rubinfeld
Microeconomics*

Riddell/Shackelford/Stamos/Schneider
Economics: A Tool for Critically Understanding Society

Roberts
The Choice: A Fable of Free Trade and Protection

Scherer
Industry Structure, Strategy, and Public Policy

Schiller
The Economics of Poverty and Discrimination

Sherman
Market Regulation

Stock/Watson
Introduction to Econometrics

Studenmund
Using Econometrics: A Practical Guide

Todaro/Smith
Economic Development

Walters/Walters/Appel/Callahan/Centanni/Maex/O'Neill
Econversations: Today's Students Discuss Today's Issues

Williamson
Macroeconomics

---

*denotes MyEconLab titles

Visit www.myeconlab.com to learn more.